POLITICS IN THE MIDDLE EAST

The HarperCollins Series in Comparative Politics

Series Editors
Gabriel A. Almond
Lucian W. Pye

Almond/Powell	*Comparative Politics Today: A World View*, Fifth Edition
Almond/Powell/Mundt	*Comparative Politics: A Theoretical Framework*

Country Studies

Barghoorn/Remington	*Politics in the USSR*, Third Edition
Bill/Springborg	*Politics in the Middle East*, Fourth Edition
Dalton	*Politics in Germany*, Second Edition
Ehrmann/Schain	*Politics in France*, Fifth Edition
Pye	*China: An Introduction*, Fourth Edition
Richardson/Flanagan	*Politics in Japan*
Rose	*Politics in England*, Fifth Edition
Wiarda	*Politics in Iberia*

Analytic Studies

Monroe	*The Economic Approach to Politics*
Rustow/Erickson	*Comparative Political Dynamics*
Weiner/Huntington	*Understanding Political Development*

POLITICS IN THE MIDDLE EAST

Fourth Edition

James A. Bill
College of William and Mary

Robert Springborg
MacQuarie University

HarperCollins*CollegePublishers*

Acquisitions Editor: Marcus Boggs
Project Editor: Shuli Traub
Design Supervisor: Mary Archondes
Production Administrator: Hilda Koparanian
Compositor: University Graphics
Printer and Binder:R. R. Donnelley & Sons Company
Cover Printer: The Lehigh Press, Inc.

Politics in the Middle East, Fourth Edition

Copyright © 1994 by HarperCollins College Publishers

Bill, James A.
  Politics in the Middle East / James A. Bill, Robert Springborg. –
4th ed.
    p.   cm. – (The HarperCollins series in comparative politics)
  Includes bibliographical references and index.
  ISBN 0-673-52276–8
  1. Middle East – Politics and government – 1945-   I. Springborg,
Robert. II. Title.   III. Series.
  DS63. 1. B54   1994
  320 . 956–dc20   93-24933
                                                     CIP

93 94 95 96 9 8 7 6 5 4 3 2 1

Contents

Preface

The extraordinary turbulence that defined the Middle East in the 1980s continues unabated in the 1990s. The second Persian Gulf war of 1990–1991 followed in the wake of the 95-month Iran-Iraq conflict that had finally ground to a bloody and inconclusive halt in 1988. The Soviet Union had barely pulled its troops out of Afghanistan when the central communist superpower began itself to disintegrate. This dramatic collapse of the Soviet Union resulted in the unpredictable unleashing of long suppressed social and political forces in the six Muslim republics of Central Asia. This, in turn, injected new complicating factors into the Middle Eastern political equation.

At the same time, Middle Eastern governments struggled to adapt their policies to a new American-dominated world order, an order in which they lost the leverage they had exercised for so long in the bipolar cold war era. The United States, which had sent half a million troops to the Gulf in 1990–1991, found itself still militarily entangled in the area two years later. Like the British and French before them, the Americans were discovering that it is much easier to rush into than to withdraw from the Middle East.

Fundamental unresolved questions of identity, authenticity, and legitimacy continue to plague the region. As the winds of democratization gust unevenly across the world, most Middle Eastern governments still resist transforming their political systems and maintain power through incremental reform, selective coercion, and economic inducement. Genuine political participation remains a distant goal. Nonetheless, there has been movement as defensive political leaders increasingly announce constitutional reform, electoral processes, and the formation of a wide variety of consultative parliamentary bodies. Meanwhile, the powerful force of resurgent populist Islam challenges the contemporary status quo across the region. The dilemmas posed by democratization were seen in Algeria, where the electoral triumph of an Islamic political party in early 1992 led to a coup d'etat by the secularly oriented military.

The thorny Arab-Israeli imbroglio entered a new, more hopeful stage following the desperate Palestinian uprising known as the *intifadah,* the second Gulf war, and the collapse of the USSR. Through the persistent efforts and pressures applied by the U.S. government, the Israelis and Arabs grudgingly began negotiating. This process was lent momentum when Yitzhak Rabin of the Labor Party replaced hardline Likud leader Yitzhak Shamir as prime minister of Israel in July 1992. Still, as humankind rapidly approaches the year 2000, substantial obstacles continue to impede a fundamental Arab–Israeli rapprochement.

Indeed, the profound problems of economic and political development, which intertwine with regional tensions, are also huge and intimidating. In the Middle East, there is sure to be more conflict before cooperation, more war before peace. Despite this, the Middle Eastern peoples, with their ancient history of culture, civility, and humor, are survivors. As we in the West watch them struggle to do so, we must remain aware of the fact that their successes and failures directly affect our own survival and well-being.

Despite the social tumult and political upheaval that prevail in the Middle East, this fourth edition of *Politics in the Middle East* is similar to earlier editions because it analyzes problems, issues, and processes that transcend particular events and that cut across the region chronologically and geographically. This latest edition, nevertheless, contains a number of significant changes.

Chapter 8, which focuses upon the politics of the Persian Gulf, has been completely rewritten. Chapter 1 ("Political Development and the Challenge of Modernization") and Chapter 7 ("The Arab–Israeli Connection") have been substantially revised and updated. All the other chapters have undergone some revision and have been updated. We have paid special attention throughout to important new international developments such as the collapse of the Soviet Union and the continuing political and military conflict in the Persian Gulf. In terms of internal political dynamics, we have revised the book with special sensitivity to the issue of democratization and the deepening and broadening challenge of resurgent populist Islam.

This fourth edition owes much to the numerous suggestions offered by colleagues across the country who have used the book in the classroom. Their reactions and, most important, the comments and recommendations of their students lie behind many of the revisions. We feel that in responding to this valuable input, we have produced a better book.

The system of transliteration in this study generally follows the format used by the *International Journal of Middle East Studies*. We have decided to delete all diacritical marks with the exception of the ayn (') and the hamza (') when they appear in the middle of a word. This decision may upset a number of careful scholars of Middle Eastern history and linguistics. It is done, however, to assist students and nonarea specialists who have expressed their reluctance to plow through numerous dots and dashes, which to them appear randomly sprinkled over the pages of the text. Arabic, Persian, or Turkish words commonly used in English are spelled as they appear in *Webster's Third International Dictionary* or in *Webster's Geographical Dictionary*. Well-known proper names are presented as they generally appear in English or as they have been transliterated by the individuals themselves—for example, Gamal Abdel Nasser, Anwar Sadat, Muhammad Reza Shah Pahlavi, King Farouk, Nuri al-Said, King Hussein, and Kemal Ataturk. This approach, of course, leads to occasional inconsistencies. In response we quote T. E. Lawrence, who, in the preface of his *Seven Pillars of Wisdom,* writes, "Arabic names won't go into English, exactly, for their consonants are not the same as ours and their vowels, like ours, vary from district to district. There are some 'scientific systems' of transliteration, helpful to people who know enough Arabic not to need helping, but a wash-out for the world."

The wisdom and personal support of many individuals have been indispensable to creating this book. Over the years, scholars such as Manfred Halpern, George Lenczowski, and Gabriel Almond have had a great impact on our thinking. More recently, we have benefited from the work of Ervand Abrahamian, Fouad Ajami, Shahrough Akhavi, James Akins, Nazar Al-Hasso, Abbas Amanat, Hooshang Amirahmadi, Lisa Anderson, John Duke Anthony, Ahmad Ashraf, Mohammed Ayoob, George W. Ball, Ali Banuazizi, Peter Bechtold, Joel Beinin, Leonard Binder, Michael Bonine, Ralph Braibanti, Carl Brown, Louis Cantori, William Cleveland, Juan Cole, Richard Cottam, Jill Crystal, Hamid Dabashi, Munther and Mohammed Dajani, Dale Eickelman, Herman Eilts, Kail Ellis, John Esposito, Tawfic Farah, Robert Freedman, Shafeeq Ghabra, Cyrus Ghani, Grace Goodell, Yvonne Haddad, Jo-Ann Hart, Shireen Hunter, J. C. Hurewitz, Farhad Kazemi, Nikki Keddie, Mohammad Koochekzadeh, John Limbert, David Long, William Roger Louis, Ian Lustick, Charles MacDonald, Hafeez Malik, David Menashri, Roy Mottahedeh, Robert G. Neumann, Monte Palmer, John Peterson, James Piscatori, William Quandt, Abdul Karim Rafeq, R. K. Ramazani, Bernard Reich, Alan Richards, Thomas Ricks, William Rugh, Emile Sahliyeh, Mowahed Shah, Oles Smolansky, Robert Snyder, Robert Stookey, Michael Suleiman, Antony Sullivan, Joseph Szyliowicz, Metin Tamkoc, Mark Tessler, Robert Vitalis, John Voll, John Washburn, John Waterbury, Marvin Weinbaum, John Williams, Rita Wright, and Marvin Zonis.

Scholars and teachers such as Bruce Borthwick, John Damis, Manochehr Dorraj, Gene Garthwaite, Arthur Goldschmidt, Jerrold Green, Eric Hooglund, Tareq Ismael, Ersin Kalaycioglu, Yasumassa Kuroda, John Lorentz, Abbass Manafy, Phebe Marr, Robert Noel, Hossein Razi, Gregory Rose, Eliz Sanasarian, and Farzin Sarrabi-Kia have used the book in the classroom or have offered suggestions that have been especially useful. Published reviews of earlier editions by Amir Ferdows, Michael Hudson, Don Peretz, and Frank Tachau were extremely constructive. Specific expertise and assistance have also been provided by Abdul-Reda Assiri, Marguerite Bouraad-Nash, Steven Dorr, Clement Henry, Metin Heper, Jim Hitselberger, Michael Humphrey, Samir Khalaf, Jacob Landau, Ira Lapidus, Fred Lawson, Ann Lesch, William Millward, Emile Nakhleh, Mehdi Noorbaksh, Richard Norton, Jerry Obermyer, Othman Rawwaf, Glenn Robinson, William Royce, Hisham Sharabi, Patricia Springborg, and Andrew Vincent.

We wish to thank the following reviewers of the fourth edition:

Nazli Choucri, Massachusetts Institute of Technology; Bruce Drury, Lamar University; Monte Palmer, Florida State University; and Marvin Weinbaum, University of Illinois. Finally, we thank our editors, Marcus Boggs and Shuli Traub of HarperCollins, for their superb support throughout the production of this latest edition.

James A. Bill
Robert Springborg

EUROPE

ATLANTIC
OCEAN

Istanbul

AEGEAN SEA

MEDITERRANEAN SEA

Tangier
Oran
Algiers
Tunis
TUNISIA

Fez
Casablanca
Marrakech
MOROCCO

Tripoli
Benghazi

ALGERIA
LIBYA

MAURITANIA

MALI
NIGER
CHAD

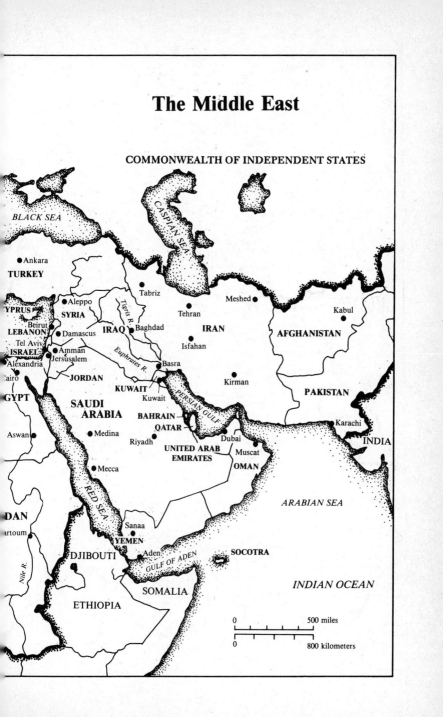

The Middle East

COMMONWEALTH OF INDEPENDENT STATES

BLACK SEA

CASPIAN SEA

●Ankara

TURKEY

Tabriz

Meshed●

●Aleppo

'YPRUS

SYRIA

Tehran●

Kabul●

Beirut

Damascus

IRAQ

Baghdad

IRAN

AFGHANISTAN

LEBANON

Tel Aviv

Isfahan●

ISRAEL

●Amman

Jersusalem

Alexandria

JORDAN

Basra

Kirman●

PAKISTAN

'airo

KUWAIT

GYPT

SAUDI

Kuwait

ARABIA

BAHRAIN

PERSIAN GULF

QATAR

Aswan●

●Medina

UNITED ARAB

EMIRATES

Dubai

Muscat

Karachi●

INDIA

Riyadh●

OMAN

●Mecca

ARABIAN SEA

RED SEA

'DAN

●Sanaa

artoum●

YEMEN

DJIBOUTI

Aden

SOCOTRA

GULF OF ADEN

INDIAN OCEAN

SOMALIA

ETHIOPIA

Tigris R.

Euphrates R.

Nile R.

| 0 | | | | 500 miles |

| 0 | | | | 800 kilometers |

Chapter 1

Political Development and the Challenge of Modernization

*T*he politics of turbulent change and revolutionary upheaval dominate the Middle East in a world caught in the midst of rapid transformation. The dialectical clash between the challenging forces of modernity and the persistent strength of tradition is a fundamental reality in the region. Old human relationships and social structures are crumbling, while new systems remain to be formed. In the midst of such incoherence, many hold a vision of a promising but unknown future; others seek to return to a more familiar past. From Morocco and Algeria on the west to Afghanistan and Pakistan on the east, the peoples of the Middle East find themselves confronted by economic hardship, political crisis, and personal insecurity.

Politically, traditional rulers, revolutionary councils, authoritarian leaders, and religious governing elites live side by side. No form of government seems immune to coups and countercoups. Internal violence sparked by sociopolitical dissatisfaction and interregional warfare dominated by the persisting Arab-Israeli conflict and the fragile situation in the Persian Gulf have become an integral part of the scene. Lavish wealth exists alongside abject poverty, both between and within societies.

The effects of the developmental challenge in the Middle East extend far beyond the confines of the area itself. The international impact of the oil embargo of 1973, the Lebanese civil war of 1975, the Iranian revolution of 1978–1979, the Soviet invasion of Afghanistan in 1979, the Israeli attacks on Lebanon in 1982, and the two Persian Gulf wars in the 1980s and early 1990s are among the cases in point. The continuing impact of the message of revolutionary Iran and the broad appeal of the Islamic revival in the region will have a deep influence in the Third World throughout the 1990s.

At the level of everyday living, change is highly evident, and ancient customs and lifeways are under siege. This is particularly true with respect to the related areas of occupation, transportation, recreation, and education. Stenographers and typists are rapidly replacing calligraphers and scribes; the carpet and metal industries have been transformed by the machine; and factories and assembly lines are taking the place of town workshops and cottage industry. In the realm of transportation, donkeys and camels have already lost their centuries-long domination to automobiles and trucks. Airplanes and airports are omnipresent. Throughout the Middle East, herdsmen and shepherds listen to transistor radios, and television sets now adorn village teahouses. The urban young increasingly flock to movie houses, dance halls, bowling alleys, pool halls, and ski resorts.

Countering this drive to modernity has been a growing trend to recapture important practices of the past. Throughout the region, there is a noticeable return to the veil by significant numbers of young women—women of all social classes. Middle Easterners seem to be increasingly engaged in a search for their roots. The resurgent strength of Islam must be viewed in this light. Social change in the Middle East therefore is marked by a bizarre blend of tradition and modernity. The jagged course of change has left in its wake a number of imbalances, inconsistencies, inequalities, and enigmas: discotheques and mosques, modern luxury hotels and squalid mud huts, nuclear energy programs and the fuel of animal droppings, F-16s and old rifles and daggers, palaces and tents, computerized libraries and omnipresent illiteracy.

Central to the entire problem of change as it is manifested in the Middle East are the related issues of modernization and political development. The revolution of modernization and the politics of development are two of the most critical problems confronting Middle Eastern peoples and cultures. It is here that they are caught in a grim struggle for survival, justice, and happiness. The extraordinary importance of these issues is perhaps matched only by the great difficulty involved in coming to grips intellectually with them. The following section will present some of the definitions and distinctions essential to any serious analysis of the processes of modernization and political development in the Middle East.

THE CHALLENGE OF MODERNIZATION

C. E. Black defines modernization as "the process by which historically evolved institutions are adapted to the rapidly changing functions that reflect the unprecedented increase in man's knowledge, permitting control over his environment, that accompanied the scientific revolution."[1] Dankwart Rustow writes that modernization is a process of "rapidly widening control over nature through closer cooperation among men."[2] And Marion J. Levy, in a major hypothesis in his work, asserts that "the greater the ratio of inanimate to animate sources of power and the greater the multiplication of effort as the effect of applications of tools, the greater is the degree of modernization."[3] Modernization is most concisely defined as the process by which men and women increasingly gain control over their environment.

The process of modernization has, of course, always occurred in society. In the past, the wide variety of responses to environmental challenges produced some very disparate results; this legacy is evident today in much of the developing world, including the Middle East. In the twentieth century, rapid communication not only facilitates the discovery that stages of modernization other than one's own are possible but also enables the experiences of certain cultures to be transmitted to other contexts.

Perhaps the most dramatic dimension of modernization is the technological revolution, which carries with it impressive trends in the areas of industrialization, economic development, and communication. In the Middle East, the constant physical transformations that seem to occur everywhere are outward evidence of technological

---

[1] C. E. Black, *The Dynamics of Modernization* (New York: Harper & Row, 1966), p. 7.

[2] Dankwart A. Rustow, *A World of Nations: Problems of Political Modernization* (Washington, D.C.: The Brookings Institution, 1967), p. 3.

[3] Marion J. Levy, Jr., *Modernization and the Structure of Societies* (Princeton, N.J.: Princeton University Press, 1966), p. 35.

development. Skyscrapers, highway grids, airports, hotels, dams, petrochemical plants, and steel mills continually sprout throughout the area. Spurred by the discovery and exploitation of petroleum and natural gas, these economic and technological factors provide the driving force of modernization.

Closely related to technological advancement are the strides that have been made in education. The grip in which the clerics traditionally have held education in the Middle East has begun to be broken. Literacy programs multiply in the area, while the numbers of school buildings and educational facilities continue to increase at a rapid rate. The result of all this activity has been a heightened consciousness and an expanded scientific and technical knowledge. Acting as a catalyst to all this, of course, are technological forces such as advances in communications and the mass media, which provide the means by which information can be transmitted more quickly, effectively, and universally.

The developments in the Middle East in technology and education have a number of organizational and psychological implications. Organization is becoming more elaborate and specialized, and formal institutions are beginning to replace informal, personal administration. As values and expectations become more secular, important shifts in attitudes are occurring. Traditional emphasis on the spiritual and magical waxes and wanes.

The patterns that constitute the modernization syndrome are mutually reinforcing. This reinforcement accelerates modernization even in societies in which resources are scarce and the population largely continues to follow traditional life-styles. Technological progress promotes educational advancement, which in turn influences attitudes and values that are reflected in organizational settings. Moreover, value systems and organizational styles that are in a state of transformation are highly supportive of continuing and deepening technological and educational change. It is easy to see why modernization is a major obsession of the peoples of the Middle East.

Modernization is inevitable and omnipresent. In the words of Marion Levy, it is a "universal social solvent."[4] Those societies that are relatively more modernized have tended to be located in the West, and hence the process has sometimes been unfortunately referred to

---

[4]Marion J. Levy, Jr., *Modernization: Latecomers and Survivors* (New York and London: Basic Books, 1972).

as Westernization. The inevitability and universality of modernization are products of the increasingly interdependent world in which we live. Although the societies in the Middle East will all struggle in one way or another to modernize, not all will succeed to the same degree. The unevenness of the success of modernization in the various Middle Eastern societies is in itself a source of tension and conflict.

Modernization is an unsettling, disruptive, painful process. The comforts of traditional habits are lost as these habits are uprooted. In modernizing societies, new processes and institutions seem always to be trapped in a state of becoming, and, as a result, the expected uncertainties of the past have given way to the more frightful and unknown insecurities of the present. In the Middle East, where most of the societies have seriously begun to modernize, any slowing or reversal of the process causes great stress. Yet the uneven supply of national resources, the shortage of technical skills, and the weakness of political leadership are all severe impediments to continuing modernization. Modernization is a process in which expectations necessarily race beyond their satisfaction. However, satisfaction must never lag too far behind. In most Middle Eastern societies, the gap between sharpened aspirations and their attainment threatens to become a chasm. The consequent frustrations directly promote social upheaval and political unrest.

The direction and depth of the drive for modernization are determined largely within the political system. The political elites of the various Middle Eastern societies make the basic decisions that shape the strategies of modernization. Modernization in turn affects the capacity of the political system to respond to political challenges. For reasons such as these, the important issue of political development is closely interwoven with the problem of modernization.

THE CONCEPT OF POLITICAL DEVELOPMENT

One survey of the literature on development tallies ten different definitions of political development.[5] There is much confusion about the

---

[5]Lucian W. Pye, *Aspects of Political Development* (Boston: Little, Brown and Co., 1966), pp. 33–45. For a penetrating analysis of the major intellectual attempts to confront the issue of development, see Leonard Binder's chapter, "The Crises of Political Development," in L. Binder et al., *Crises and Sequences in Political Development* (Princeton, N.J.: Princeton University Press, 1971), pp. 3–72.

relationship between the concept of modernization and that of political development. Often the terms are treated as synonymous. In other instances, they are sharply distinguished from each other. In this study, we view the two processes as analytically distinct but actually interrelated. It is in this sense that we will study them in the Middle East.

Alfred Diamant writes that "political development is a process by which a political system acquires an increased capacity to sustain successfully and continuously new type of goals and demands and the creation of new types of organizations."[6] S. N. Eisenstadt provides a similar definition when he discusses a political system's ability to meet changing demands and then "to absorb them in terms of policy-making and to assure its own continuity in the face of continuous new demands and new forms of political organization."[7] Eisenstadt goes on to state that "the ability to deal with continuous changes in political demands is the crucial test of such sustained political development."[8] This concern for the capacity of a political system to meet new challenges is also evident in the Social Science Research Council Committee's work on development. The developmental capacity of politics "is a capacity not only to overcome the divisions and manage the tensions created by increased differentiation, but to respond to or contain the participatory and distributive demands generated by the imperatives of equality. It is also a capacity to innovate and manage continuous change."[9]

The last sentence above introduces a central dimension of our conceptualization of political development. The political system is not only a responsive, reactive mechanism in which demands and challenges are absorbed and digested; it is preeminently a system with a primacy and an autonomy that permits the introduction and generation of change. It is the political system that leads, guides, and directs.

---

[6]Alfred Diamant, "The Nature of Political Development," in *Political Development and Social Change,* ed. Jason L. Finkle and Richard W. Gable (New York: John Wiley and Sons, 1966), p. 92.

[7]S. N. Eisenstadt, "Initial Institutional Patterns of Political Mobilization," *Civilizations* 12 (1962), reprinted in *Political Modernization,* ed. Claude E. Welch, Jr. (Belmont, Calif.: Wadsworth, 1967), p. 252.

[8]*Ibid.*

[9]James S. Coleman's words in Binder et al., *Crises and Sequences,* p. 78.

And it is in this system that the demands and programs of tomorrow often originate. Manfred Halpern therefore defines political development as the "enduring capacity to generate and absorb persistent transformation."[10] Political development as it is discussed in this study involves the capacity of Middle Eastern political systems to initiate, absorb, and sustain continuous transformation.

Among the most important of the demands that the political system must foster and satisfy are the demands for equality of opportunity, political participation, and social justice. These demands are much more difficult to meet than those derived directly from the economic and technological facets of life. The process of political development includes the capacity to provide more and more individuals with the power to improve their own positions in society on the basis of personal merit rather than personal connections. New groups and classes continually appear in society and must be brought effectively into the political process. Finally, the rewards and priorities of the society need to be allocated and reallocated in a way that permits all to expect equal opportunity and to receive just treatment.

By defining political development in terms of a capacity to stimulate demands and to solve problems, one is able to avoid a number of ethnocentric problems that have long haunted developmental studies. The proclivity to define political development in terms of a Western-oriented view of democracy is one example of this ethnocentricity. Many "democratic" systems may not succeed in political development because of their inability to effectively absorb the changes occurring in the contemporary world. In the Middle East, Lebanon is a tragic case in point.

It is also possible that an authoritarian system that is able to overcome its inherent weaknesses concerning the issue of participation may succeed in political development. Using this definition of political development, it is possible to account for the developmental process as it existed in many ancient and traditional systems. Indeed, certain traditional Islamic societies were perhaps more highly developed politically than some contemporary Middle Eastern societies. This need not be surprising, since these traditional systems undoubtedly had much more limited demands placed upon them. To speak of political development as if it were something rare and unique to our mod-

---

[10]Manfred Halpern, "The Rates and Costs of Political Development," *Annals* 358 (March 1965): 22.

ern age hinders our ability to understand the dynamics of change, since it distorts important historical realities.

The contemporary era, however, is fundamentally different from any earlier time because scientific advances and technological revolution have wrought unprecedented change. This change spreads rapidly because of the increasingly interdependent nature of the world. Modernization, or humanity's growing control over the environment, races onward at a breakneck pace. The impact of this modernization on the patterns of political development has been profound. Modernization and political development must be analyzed together.

THE DIALECTICS OF MODERNIZATION AND POLITICAL DEVELOPMENT

Partly to maximize their own power and authority, political elites may seek to generate and accelerate the processes of modernization within their societies. Although such efforts enlarge capacities to meet new challenges, they also help improve the standing of particular societies in the world of nations. The unleashed forces of modernization, meanwhile, influence the behavior and policies of the elites. Leonard Binder writes that in Europe, "the overwhelmingly accepted view was that politics was essentially a response to the historical forces of modernization. Outside of Europe, the prevailing view has been the opposite. Politics is not a response to modernity, it must rather be the cause of modernity if modernity is to be achieved."[11] In this discussion, we view the processes as mutually interactive. Political elites forge modernization policies that strongly affect their future decision-making capacities.

Once modernization has begun, it tends to become a pervasive, persisting process. As a result, the political group that has stimulated and encouraged the modernizing movement often loses its ability to control and regulate the process. Demands increase and outstrip any capacity to cope with them. It is for this reason that political development is a highly problematic process. It cannot be assumed that because "modernization is taking place, political development also must be taking place."[12] It *can* be assumed that there will always be a

---

[11]Binder et al., *Crises and Sequences,* pp. 15–16.

[12]Samuel P. Huntington, "Political Development and Political Decay," *World Politics* 17 (April 1965): 391.

gap between the demands that accompany modernization and the political system's ability to satisfy those demands. In this sense, it is easier to generate change than to absorb it.

Changes occasioned by the forces of modernization usually occur in the physical environment and are most dramatically evident in the areas of technology and economics. Impressive change here, however, does not necessarily signal basic alteration in the sociopolitical system. Traditional patterns of power and authority tend to resist fundamental change. Personal equality, political participation, and social justice are usually the last issues to be confronted. Political elites have vested interests in preserving ongoing political patterns. Yet if political development is to take place, it must involve a capacity for continuous change *especially* with respect to these social and political issues. No matter how much technological and economic growth may occur, there can be no political development without accompanying change in the power and authority structures.

The developmental process is driven by a dialectical dynamic that marks the relationship between demands and capacity. In more conventional terms, the struggle is one for both liberty and security. Figure 1.1 provides a diagrammatic view of this process.

In their important study of comparative politics, Gabriel Almond and G. Bingham Powell identify liberty and security as two basic political goods that societies must provide. They point out that the provision of both of these goods has long been the classic dilemma of politics.

> At the logical extremes, at least, there seem to be negative tradeoffs between liberty and security, and no ready ethical answer dictates the most appropriate balance between them. . . . At some point, liberty for some individuals threatens the security of others. The logical and ethical dilemma does not, however, obviate some very important empirical questions about the relationships between security and liberty. . . . For part of the problem of liberty concerns the use that citizens wish to make of it, and part of the problem of security concerns who shall enforce it.[13]

The increasing demand for liberty and related values such as participation, equality, and justice must be confronted in today's world. There must be either an enhanced capacity to satisfy these demands or a capacity to repress them. The satisfaction of demands is usually

---

[13]Gabriel A. Almond and G. Bingham Powell, Jr., *Comparative Politics: System, Process, and Policy,* 2d ed. (Boston: Little, Brown and Co., 1978), pp. 411–412.

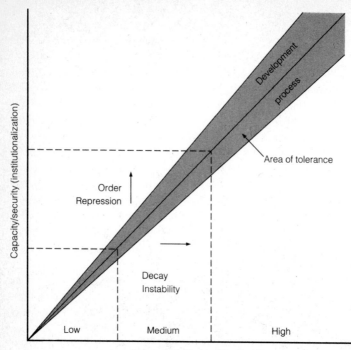

Figure 1.1 The developmental process.

provided by increasing institutionalization and by effective new methods and style of rule. This often means the centralization and concentration of authority as ongoing relations are uprooted and new ones created. The forces of modernization, by providing political elites with more sophisticated techniques of control, can enhance their capacity to meet demands and to provide security. They also, however, can permit elites to stifle demands through repression. Calls for participation, equal opportunity, and justice can be smothered by "security" forces superbly equipped with the most modern technology. When this occurs, demands are confined and bottled up; they not satisfied. Security through repression is often a harbinger of violence and upheaval. At the other extreme is a situation in which anarchy and chaos reign supreme. Here, the society explodes into fragments in the absence of effective institutions and guiding authority.

Almond and Powell investigate some of the conditions for a trade-off between liberty and security by constructing a three-part typology of societies.[14] Society A is one in which the citizens enjoy substantial amounts of both liberty and security. Such a society is usually culturally homogeneous and often lacks deep and divisive ethnic or religious cleavages. Although these societies are characterized by relatively low tension levels, there are short, pendulum-like movements between an emphasis on liberty and an emphasis on security in these societies. In the Middle East, countries that tend to fall into this category include Egypt, Turkey, Israel, Tunisia, and Algeria. With the partial exceptions of Israel and Turkey, the other countries tilt more heavily in the direction of security and central control. This became especially evident in the early 1990s in countries like Tunisia and Algeria (and, to a lesser degree, Egypt) when governing elites tightened control in order to stave off challenges from Islamic populist movements.

Society B is one in which both ethnic and class tensions are so deeply embedded in the social body that the pendulum swings away from security, back through liberty, and ultimately into anarchy. "After a substantial amount of liberty appears, the society collapses at least temporarily into civil war, and security vanishes completely. Moreover, even with very great sacrifices of liberty, it may be impossible to attain high amounts of security."[15] The prototype of Society B is Lebanon, a society torn both vertically and horizontally by religious and class strife. Other Middle Eastern candidates for Society B status include Sudan and Afghanistan.

Society C is one in which coercion and repression are dominant. In its most extreme form, "The massive application of terror tactics—against even high-level officials in the government, not to mention millions of citizens—and a context of constant police and party intervention, complete censorship, and travel control destroys liberty but provides little security. The uncontrolled actions of the regime itself undermine any security for its citizens."[16] Syria, and especially Iraq, are the Middle Eastern societies that most closely approximate the Society C type. Although there are fundamental differences in the political and ideological structures of these two countries, the leader-

---

[14]*Ibid.*, pp. 412–415.

[15]*Ibid.*, p. 413.

[16]*Ibid.*

ship of both has opted to sacrifice liberty for tight control from the center.

The push and pull between the demands of the regime for control and the demands of the populace for freedom and participation exist in a state of constant change. Societies move from one type to another. Algeria, for instance, was an extreme example of Society C when central control was enforced by the French, an outside power. After the revolution, it moved through a short chaotic Society B period, beginning when Ahmad Ben Bella was unable to consolidate control and continuing into the rule of Houari Boumedienne and Chadli Benjedid, whose regimes sought to balance popular demands and central authority. In the late 1980s, Benjedid introduced a process of democratization that led to national elections in December 1991. When the Islamic movement scored a surprisingly strong electoral victory, the Algerian political elite became alarmed. Benjedid resigned and the governing authorities (represented by the High Security Council, backed by the military) declared the December elections null and void and summarily canceled the second round of elections scheduled for January 1992. The system was closed, opened, and is now closed again. The future of democratization in Algeria remains in doubt, and political violence and incoherence seem inevitable.

There is also a continual shifting of emphasis within each type of society. In Egypt, both Nasser and Sadat alternately tightened and relaxed their control. It was shortly after a sudden political crackdown that Sadat was assassinated on October 6, 1981. Although President Husni Mubarak has generally relaxed control from the center, he has also resorted to sporadic political crackdowns that have became more frequent with time.

These examples indicate the delicate dialectic that lies at the core of the process of political development. Its outcome is shaped, however, within the larger field of modernization. It is this latter dynamic that can either retard or promote political development. Dramatic economic and technological growth increases the needs felt by the population. At the same time, such advancement strengthens the capacity of the political elite to exert influence and control. In order to muster the strength necessary to exploit scarce resources and to initiate effective planning programs, Middle Eastern elites have often relied upon authoritarian political methods. When they do this, they risk sliding into repressive and oppressive modes of behavior that fatally weaken their capacities for political development. Centralization and institutionalization may take complete precedence over participation. On the other hand, if the elites govern loosely and decentralization reigns supreme, they may also forfeit their developmental capacities as society breaks down into conflicting ethnic, regional, and class-based cliques. As Figure 1.1 indicates, the developmental process is a wobbly path between repressive rule and anarchical instability. The process is a delicate balance of capacity and demands. Increasing demands require an enhanced capacity to meet them. Development involves a constant push and pull between the two sides of this dialectic. Meanwhile, the fires of modernization continue to crackle. This complicates the developmental process by constantly altering and shifting balances, demands, responses, and capacities.

Any assessment of political development is made difficult by the accompanying processes of modernization that tend initially to suggest fundamental change. In fact, many traditional political systems are able to foster modernization while maintaining ongoing political patterns. In such systems, however, the basic sociopolitical demands usually outstrip the capacity to meet them, ultimately giving rise to revolutionary upheaval. A fundamental difficulty of Middle Eastern politics is the expanding gap between political demands for increased participation and justice and the ability to satisfy such demands. This situation is sometimes partially alleviated by a greater capacity to satisfy material demands, which are also vital to the population. In this arena, modernization plays a temporarily stabilizing role. In the long run, however, there must be an enduring capacity to satisfy continually and effectively the social and political needs of all groups and classes in society.[17]

MODERNIZATION IN THE MIDDLE EAST

Nowhere in the world are the forces of modernization moving more rapidly than in the Middle East. Technological growth, industrial development, and the dramatic expansion of transportation, communication, and housing facilities are evident throughout the area.

---

[17]We note here the extreme difficulty of developing an operational concept of political development. The assessment of capacity to generate and absorb change is obviously more complex than the accumulation and interpretation of modernization data. Nevertheless, we do have some measures of this capacity, although perhaps crude ones. These include the analysis of power structures, authority relations, and political programs and policies.

Another visible sign of the modernizing process is the growth of military activity in the region. Such countries as Israel and Saudi Arabia are now among the world leaders in military expenditures. They are gathering some of the most sophisticated weapons that modern technology can produce. Iran, Turkey, Iraq, Egypt, Syria, and Kuwait are also among the world's largest buyers of arms.

Quantitatively, gigantic advances have also been made in the social fields of health and education. Thousands of new school buildings, clinics, and hospitals have sprouted up throughout the countries of the Middle East. The number of students enrolled in primary, secondary, and higher education in the Middle East has increased more than tenfold since 1950. In recent years, the education explosion has been especially evident at the college and university levels.

The modernization boom has accelerated sharply since 1974, when a fourfold increase in the price of oil suddenly provided a huge pool of the resources essential to modernization. In 1970, the petroleum revenues of the eight major Middle Eastern oil-producing countries were less than $6 billion. By 1974, the figure had ballooned to more than $82 billion. By 1980, Saudi Arabia alone was receiving over $100 billion in petroleum revenues. Although falling oil prices through the 1980s and into the 1990s resulted in a decrease in these revenues, they are still substantial.

It is sometimes not realized that the Middle East is very rich in resources other than petroleum. Iran, for example, has the second largest reserves of natural gas in the world. Only the Soviet Union has more. Algeria and Saudi Arabia also possess huge reserves of this important resource. One of the world's richest deposits of copper has been discovered in Iran. Turkey is the international leader in wolfram production and the third largest producer of chromium. Both Turkey and Iraq have very large deposits of lignite and iron ore. Morocco accounts for more than 90 percent of the exports of phosphates in the world and is the world's fourth largest producer of cobalt. Tunisia, Jordan, and Egypt also have substantial phosphate reserves. Afghanistan has one of the largest iron deposits in the world but is very rich also in copper and chromium. As the oil revenues pour in, they will be used for the exploration and production of other valuable resources. Rapid modernization will be one of the persisting effects of this wealth of resources.

When one examines aggregate data and gross statistical indices, such as annual per capita gross national product (GNP) figures, the conclusions concerning modernization and development are somewhat distorted. The United Arab Emirates, for example, have a per capita GNP that is larger than that of the United Kingdom. The per capita GNP of Kuwait is far larger than that of any of the 36 Latin American countries. In the early 1950s, Libya's per capita GNP was about $40; today, it is over $5,000. Iran's per capita GNP rose from less than $300 in 1960 to nearly $2,000 in 1980. Yet in all these societies the benefits of this wealth are very unevenly distributed. Quantitative measurements, no matter how impressive they may be, indicate very little about the qualitative effects of wealth and resources. In short, they do not address political scientist Harold Lasswell's fundamental question: Who gets what, when, and how? Surely, in any study of the modernization of society and politics, it is necessary to get some sense of how these benefits affect the society at large.

A group of scholars associated with the Overseas Development Council has developed a new index designed to measure more than quantitative growth. Headed by Morris David Morris, a developmental economist with long experience in South Asian studies, this group has taken a significant step away from the emphasis on GNP. In discussing the need for this new measure, Dr. Morris writes:

> The traditional measure of national economic progress—the gross national product (GNP) and its component elements—cannot very satisfactorily measure the extent to which the human needs of individuals are being met, nor should it be expected to do so. There is no automatic policy relationship between any particular level or rate of growth of GNP and improvement in such indicators as life expectancy, death rates, infant mortality, literacy, etc. A nation's economic product at any particular level may be allocated in a variety of ways, both among areas of activities and among social groups; or national policies may emphasize the growth of military power and of sectors of the economy that do not contribute in any obvious way to improving the health and physical well-being of that country's people. Nor does the growth of average per capita GNP or personal disposable income necessarily improve the well-being of large portions of a country's population since that income may flow to social groups in very unequal proportions. The very poorest groups of the society may not benefit much, if at all, from rising incomes and some may even suffer declines in real income. Moreover, even if rising incomes are shared with the poorest groups, there is no guarantee that these increases in income will be spent in ways that improve physical well-being.[18]

---

[18]John W. Sewell et al., *The United States and World Development: Agenda 1977,* published for the Overseas Development Council (New York: Praeger Publishers, 1977), p. 147.

In response to these difficulties, Morris and his colleagues have carefully and conservatively constructed an index known as the Physical Quality of Life Index (PQLI). This measure is a composite of three indicators—life expectancy, infant mortality, and literacy rate. Each indicator is weighted equally, and all the problems of monetary measurement are avoided. The new index is also resistant to charges of ethnocentrism, since its major assumption—that people everywhere desire improvements in life expectancy, infant mortality, and literacy—does not in any way specify how these goals ought to be sought. Finally, the three indicators "do reflect distributional characteristics within countries, for countries cannot achieve high national averages of literacy, life expectancy, and infant mortality unless majorities of their populations are receiving the benefits of progress in each of these areas."[19] The theoretical range of the PQLI is 0 to 100.

Table 1.1 presents the per capita GNP and PQLI for 23 Middle Eastern countries. It also indicates the mid-1990 population figures for each country, as well as the specific statistics that were used in calculating the PQLI: life expectancy at birth, infant mortality per thousand live births, and literacy rate. The data are instructive. The countries with high per capita GNP ranks do not necessarily carry high PQLI rankings as well. The United Arab Emirates (UAE), for example, is the highest-ranking country in the region in per capita GNP ($15,770). Yet the UAE ranks sixth in the PQLI scale. Oman, seventh in per capita GNP, ranks sixteenth in PQLI. Finally, the important country of Saudi Arabia has a surprisingly weak record in the distribution of the fruits of modernization. The kingdom, which is sixth in per capita GNP, is tied for eleventh in PQLI.

---

[19]*Ibid.*, p. 152. The basic statement explaining the construction of the PQLI and its theoretical underpinnings is Morris David Morris, *Measuring the Condition of the World's Poor: The Physical Quality of Life Index,* published for the Overseas Development Council (New York: Pergamon Press, 1979). Professor Neil Richardson of the University of Wisconsin has helped us check the operational soundness of the PQLI by running some dummy data through the outlined procedure. The index appears to be conceptually and operationally sound. It is worth repeating, however, two points made by Morris David Morris. First, the PQLI is a limited measure that does not pretend to address the question of the social or psychological characteristics usually suggested by the pharase "quality of life." Second, the data upon which the index is based are not good. They are, however, the best that are available. This difficulty is surely not unique to these formulations. The quality of data is a problem that plagues all attempts at cross-national analysis.

Table 1.1 MODERNIZATION INDICATORS FOR MIDDLE EASTERN COUNTRIES

Country	Population mid-1990 (millions)	Per capita GNP, 1988 ($)	Physical Quality of Life Index (PQLI)	Life expectancy at birth	Infant mortality per 1,000 live births	Literacy (%)
Afghanistan	15.9	280	30	43	162	29
Algeria	25.6	2,360	71	66	61	57
Bahrain	.5	6,340	87	72	12	77
Egypt	54.7	660	65	62	57	48
Iran	55.6	1,800	73	67	40	54
Iraq	18.8	1,940	72	66	56	60
Israel	4.6	8,650	97	76	10	95
Jordan	4.1	1,500	83	68	36	80
Kuwait	2.1	13,400	87	74	15	73
Lebanon	3.3	700	81	67	40	80
Libya	4.2	5,420	70	63	68	64
Morocco	25.6	830	65	63	68	50
Oman	1.5	5,000	66	68	34	30
Pakistan	114.6	350	54	59	98	35
Qatar	.5	9,930	84	70	26	76
Saudi Arabia	15.0	6,200	73	66	58	62
Sudan	25.2	480	44	52	99	27
Syria	12.6	1,680	76	67	39	65
Tunisia	8.1	1,230	77	68	44	65
Turkey	56.7	1,280	79	66	62	81
United Arab Emirates	1.6	15,770	82	71	22	68
Yemen Arab Republic	7.2	640	48	53	107	39
Yemen, People's Republic	2.6	430	49	53	107	39

Source: Overseas Development Council, *U.S. Foreign Policy and Developing Countries* (Washington, D.C.: Overseas Development Council, 1991), pp. 37–41.

During the 1970s and 1980s, the PQLI figures for nearly all countries in the Middle East increased. Only Lebanon showed little movement in this important indicator. The most dramatic increase occurred in the case of the UAE, where the 1974 figure of 34 had increased to 65 by 1980, to 74 by 1987, and to 82 by 1990. Other countries that show significant PQLI increases include Tunisia (44 to 77), Jordan (48 to 83), and Qatar (32 to 84).[20]

In comparing particular Middle Eastern countries with those of similar population size in other parts of the world on the basis of PQLI, we note the following results. Iraq has a PQLI of 72, while Chile's is 92; despite this, Chile's per capita GNP is less than that of Iraq ($1,510 compared to $1,940). Turkey and Thailand, with per capita GNPs of $1,280 and $1,000 respectively, have PQLIs of 77 and 87. Even more dramatic is the comparison of Morocco with Burma. Morocco's PQLI of 65 is 11 points less than that of Burma; yet the per capita GNP figures are $830 and $220 for Morocco and Burma (Myanmar) respectively.

The Middle Eastern PQLI figures are higher than those of the countries of Black Africa. Ghana, for example, with a population similar to that of Iraq and Chile, has a PQLI of only 61. Ethiopia's PQLI of 40 falls far below that of either Iran or South Korea, countries roughly equivalent to Ethiopia in population. At the same time, however, the per capita GNP figures of these African countries are also very low. For Ghana and Ethiopia, the numbers are $400 and $120 respectively.

The patterns indicated in these comparisons of specific countries are also evident when we analyze per capita GNP and PQLI data for four regions of the Third World. The Middle East, with far and away the largest average per capita GNP, ranks a distant third behind South/Southeast Asia and Latin America in average PQLI. Only Africa has a lower PQLI average than the Middle East. Yet Africa also has a very low average per capita GNP.

The outstanding feature of these regional comparisons is the extraordinary size of the gap between per capita GNP and PQLI in the Middle Eastern countries. The equitable distribution of goods and priorities in the Middle East remains a serious problem.

---

[20]In order to analyze these changes more completely, please compare the figures in Table 1.1 with the figures provided in Table 1.2 on p. 21 of the first and second editions of this book and in Table 1.1 on p. 18 of the third edition.

The gross data that measure modernization are very impressive indeed for the Middle East. This is particularly true of economic modernization. With respect to qualitative progress in such areas of social modernization as health and education, the record is much less imposing. And within this context, quantitative progress far outstrips qualitative change. Education is a case in point. The sharp increases in school enrollment and the dramatic new availability of modern facilities and buildings have not been matched by equivalent progress in educational content. The principal conclusion of Joseph Szyliowicz's major study on education and modernization in the Middle East is precisely that the educational enterprise in Egypt, Turkey, and Iran "has demonstrated a remarkable ability to withstand efforts at reform and to absorb the impact of major external forces without changing."[21]

The bridge between modernization and political development concerns the problems of distribution, which themselves must be solved before quantitative growth can be transformed into qualitative progress. As the analysis of PQLIs has indicated, the countries of the Middle East have not yet successfully met this challenge—a challenge that is above all else political in nature.

POLITICAL DEVELOPMENT IN THE MIDDLE EAST

Processes of modernization run far ahead of advances in political development in the Middle East. The capacity to generate and absorb persistent transformation varies widely from society to society. In all cases, however, the ability to transform fundamentally the basic power configurations has been the rarest form of political change. Even when nations have occasionally sought to do so, they have tended to lack the capacity in the face of a resistant and resilient tradition. Transformations in the economic system have come easiest, followed by alterations in the social system. Political development in the Middle East lags conspicuously.

Spurred by economic modernization and especially by social modernization, the capacity to *generate* change in the political realm has been increasing. By sponsoring advancements in the related fields of education and technology, Middle Eastern elites have been indi-

---

[21]Joseph S. Szyliowicz, *Education and Modernization in the Middle East* (Ithaca, N.Y.: Cornell University Press, 1973), p. 454.

rectly responsible for the burgeoning of indigenous professional middle classes. The members of these middle classes are among those demanding political change and reform. In failing to address these demands, the political elites exhibit their unwillingness to absorb and institutionalize political transformation. This begets a situation in which expanding gaps, like bubbles, burst into one another. The gap between socioeconomic modernization and political development is increased by the capacity to generate transformation and the failure to absorb it.

Change dominates the history of Middle Eastern political systems. Transformation, or radical alteration of the underlying power and authority structure, has been considerably less in evidence. The legitimating authority structure and the fundamental power patterns have consistently weathered changes of rulers, elites, and dynasties. The traditional political patterns of the Islamic Middle East survived by being in a state of constant movement. Continual modification and piecemeal revision effectively deterred system transformation. Political elites in the Middle East carefully implemented policies of both co-optation and coercion. Selective mobility and sporadic repression ensured the preservation of ongoing political patterns by introducing carefully apportioned doses of modifying change. These tactics and techniques still persist to a large degree in the contemporary Middle East.

Perhaps the most critical dimension of political development is participation. The demands of the population for an effective voice in important matters that affect their lives need to be confronted and satisfied. The literature on political development generally argues that participation is furthered by institutionalization and that formal institutions, such as political parties and parliaments, are the most effective instruments for building participation. The Middle Eastern experience provides some differing insights on this issue.

Political institutionalization has never been absent in the Middle East. Masses and elites were bound together by a number of important linkage structures, which included elaborate networks of intermediaries and middlemen composed of messengers, adjutants, clerics, secretaries, advisors, bureaucrats, and secret police. The existence of an informal assembly (the *majlis*) in the traditional Arab world enabled individuals from all walks of life to approach their leaders directly and personally for assistance and aid. This kind of personalized institutionalization resulted in numerous lines of communication through the society. These provided channels through which demands and grievances moved upward to the political elite, while orders and policies poured downward to the middle and lower classes. This was the quality of political participation in traditional Middle Eastern politics. Grievances could often be aired and demands could be heard. The political elite, however, enjoyed the prerogative of action and redress. The petitioners lacked the institutional organization that could guarantee the satisfaction of their demands.

The coming of political parties and parliaments has seldom changed this form of participation. Parties have often existed as loose collections of personal cliques that have penetrated little beyond the upper crust of society. In the upper crust, they have served largely as the instruments of powerful individuals and small elites. This phenomenon has existed even in Tunisia, whose Destourian Socialist (now RCD) Party is the most effective mass party organized at the grass roots level in the Islamic world. Like political parties, Middle Eastern legislatures tend to exist as Western-style institutions grafted to Middle Eastern political systems.

Political participation is a process whereby individuals engage in activity that impinges directly upon the national power and authority structure of society. This activity can be system-challenging or system-supportive. System-supportive participation exists when large numbers of individuals come to support an authority structure to which they have meaningful access and which represents their interests. As the process of participation develops and matures, the masses of people are continually brought into the decision-making process, primarily at the grass roots level of society. Increasing social and political demands emanating from the lower and middle classes accompany this entire movement. The political elite will persistently both encourage and meet these demands for expanding representation.

In the Middle East, the first important break with the past signaling the serious advance of political participation was the overthrow of a number of traditional monarchical regimes. Turkey and Egypt are the two most dramatic early examples of this kind of revolution. The Iranian revolution of 1978–1979 represented a multiclass mass movement that overthrew the Pahlavi ruling elite. The Islamic Republic that replaced the Shah has consistently stressed its commitment to the *mustaza'fin* (the deprived, downtrodden). Yet in all these cases, the issue of participation remains unresolved, as authoritarian rule from the center still predominates. The new regimes may be *for* the people but they are not always *of* the people.

Even revolutionary acts such as the Egyptian revolution of 1952 and the Iranian revolution 25 years later do not guarantee the institutionalization of political participation nor the beginning of political development. Traditional patterns and power resist change and persist. The trauma of political upheaval promotes destruction over construction. Capacity is weakened by an uneven distribution of resources. Often the crucial resources that do exist are drained away in emotion-charged international adventures. The festering Arab-Israeli issue has profoundly stunted the growth of political development both in Egypt and in the region as a whole. The Iran-Iraq war of the 1980s had the same effect on the political systems of these two countries. Saddam Hussein's invasion of Kuwait in 1990 further compromised any chance for effective political development in Iraq. The existence of an attacking outside foe enables regimes to tighten arbitrary and authoritarian rule. Meanwhile, human casualties, physical destruction, shattered morale, national insecurity, and political disillusionment—the inevitable by-products of such conflict—all combine to weaken developmental capacities.

The delicate dialectic between demands and capacity to meet them, between anarchy and repression, between participation and institutionalization, between liberty and security is a particularly important issue in the Middle East. Demands increase dramatically as larger and larger groups of people seek political participation. Harried elites threatened by serious domestic and international problems struggle to maintain their own authority while at the same time striving to modernize their societies. Moderate authoritarianism begins to move in the direction of harsh repression as these elites gradually stifle demands. In the footrace between modernization and political development in the Middle East, modernization always runs out ahead. Manfred Halpern's "authoritarian road to democracy"[22] is in fact a narrow path fraught with peril and false exits.

In the late 1980s and early 1990s, processes of "democratization" were evident throughout much of the Third World. The power of *glasnost* in the Soviet Union and the subsequent collapse of the communist system helped stimulate these processes, which swept most prominently through many countries in Latin America. The Middle East has not been immune from the appeals of democratization, which focus on effective and nationwide political participation. Events in the region such as the Iranian revolution, the Palestinian *intifadah*, the ris-

[22]Manfred Halpern, *The Politics of Social Change in the Middle East and North Africa* (Princeton, N.J.: Princeton University Press, 1963), pp. 223–226.

ing appeal of populist Islam, and the two Gulf wars helped shatter the glass of the political status quo of the region. By 1993, from Morocco and Algeria to Kuwait and Saudi Arabia, entrenched authoritarian-traditional elites grudgingly voiced plans calling for free elections and/or national parliaments. Although they did so primarily for purposes of self-preservation and seldom hesitated from manipulating or interfering in the process whenever they felt the need to do so, the governing elites have begun a march from which ultimately there may be no retreat.

Leading scholars of Middle East politics such as Richard Norton, Muhammad Muslih, Gudrun Krämer, and Ali El-Kenz refer to this developing process as a drive to create civil society, that is, society in which old particularistic clientelism gives way to nationwide political participation institutionalized and legitimized through inclusive organizations such as meaningful political party structures and truly representative parliaments with real decisional power. In their view, only such participatory vehicles can effectively address the central issues of identity, authenticity, and legitimacy. In the words of Norton and Muslih: "In the Middle East, unlike the West, civil society—the clubs, organizations and groups that act as a buffer between state power and the life of the citizen—is often poorly developed."[23] In this situation, the state, directed by entrenched political elites backed by powerful civilian and military bureaucracies, maintains a near monopoly of power. As opposition to this oppression by the state built in the Middle East, "State and civil society found themselves in a brutal confrontation which the implacable logic of balance of forces transformed progressively into an aberrant sociopolitical structure. Anomie became structural."[24] Incoherence became the norm.

Gudrun Krämer writes that it is out of this anomie and incoherence that new demands are persistently beginning to develop. The traditional Middle East profiles of state control are increasingly under siege.

Distinct moves towards liberalization have occurred in the area, with political, social and religious groups ("civil society") demanding the effective protection of human rights and political participation on the one

---

[23]Muhammad Muslih and Augustus Richard Norton, *Political Tides in the Arab World* (New York: Foreign Policy Association, 1991), p. 11.

[24]Ali El-Kenz, *Algerian Reflections on Arab Crises,* trans. R. W. Stookey (Austin: University of Texas Center for Middle Eastern Studies, 1991), p. 46.

hand, and a growing number of Arab governments embarking on cautious and severely circumscribed courses of economic-cum-political liberalization on the other. The demand for human rights, participation and democracy comes from across the political spectrum, from the nationalist and secularist Arab left . . . to the broad Islamist movement that over the last two decades has emerged as a dominant voice in intellectual and political life.[25]

Middle Eastern governments have adopted various and differing strategies for dealing with the challenges of political development. The countries fall into four different categories on the basis of their policies of political development: democratic-populist, traditional-authoritarian, traditional-distributive, and authoritarian-distributive.[26]

The democratic-populist path of development stresses liberal democratic political values and provides relatively open participation through such institutions as parties, parliaments, and elections. Systems in this category are relatively rare throughout the world, and the Middle East is no exception. In recent years, only Israel, Turkey, and Lebanon belonged in this category. Israel's relative success with this form of government stems partly from its ability to import a set of social and political patterns wholesale into the area. Turkey's democratic style survived through extraordinary measures including military intervention and takeovers in 1960, 1971, and 1980. The fragility of the democratic-populist model is best illustrated, however, by the continuing collapse of Lebanon beginning in 1975. Here, a feeble central government stood by helplessly as religious and class tensions erupted into a bitter and bloody civil war and as predatory neighbors such as Syria and Israel invaded and occupied the country.

In the traditional-authoritarian political system, "Emphasis is placed on increasing the order-maintaining and economic-growth-facilitating capacities of the government."[27] Rule is of the most conservative traditional mode, and although economic dynamism is often

---

[25]Gudrun Krämer, "Liberalization and Democracy in the Arab World," *Middle East Report* 22 (January/February 1992):23.

[26]This taxonomy of political systems according to developmental strategies is a variation of that presented in Almond and Powell, *Comparative Politics,* pp. 372–390. The five Almond and Powell developmental strategies are termed democratic-populist, authoritarian-technocratic, authoritarian-technocratic-equalitarian, authoritarian-technocratic-mobilizational, and neo-traditional.

[27]*Ibid.*, p. 376.

present, the benefits tend to coagulate at the top. The monarchies of Jordan, Morocco, Oman, and Saudi Arabia are examples of this kind of system. Security for the ruling house is the overwhelming obsession of the political strategists who direct these governments. Political participation is severely restricted, and all important decision making is monopolized by the central figures in the ruling establishment. Although these governments distribute in varying degrees the goods and services that they control, this is not a high priority on their political agendas. Thus, with the exception of Jordan, which has recently moved impressively in the direction of the democratic-populist model, the traditional-authoritarian countries have relatively low PQLI ratings (see Table 1.1). These systems are increasingly unstable and have been the scenes of numerous challenging incidents, including attempted assassinations, aborted military plots and coup attempts, and religious-inspired upheaval. The fall of Iran's shah in the late 1970s demonstrates the precarious nature of all traditional-authoritarian political systems.

Bahrain, Kuwait, Qatar, and the UAE fall into the traditional-distributive category. Although their systems are governed in much the same way as the major monarchies referred to above, these shaikhdoms are fundamentally different in their greater will and capacity to distribute their wealth through their respective populations. The average PQLI figure for these four shaikhdoms is 85, as opposed to an average of only 72 for the four traditional-authoritarian nation-states. This program of greater distribution is made possible by the enormous hydrocarbon wealth generally present in these small countries. Amid such wealth, the issue of political participation is less urgent.

Most Middle Eastern developmental strategies involve some kind of nonmonarchical authoritarian leadership committed to the mobilization of the masses. This new form of authoritarianism (herein termed authoritarian-distributive) follows on the overthrow of traditional-authoritarian systems and stresses a very specific form of political participation. "Because people are mobilized in the implementation of policies formulated by the party elites, rather than in the making of policies, it is a form of mobilized or structured participation."[28] There are two categories of authoritarian-distributive systems, the radical modernizing model and the extremist Islamic model. Exam-

---

[28]*Ibid.,* p. 381.

ples of the former include countries such as Algeria, Egypt, and Libya. Post-Pahlavi Iran is the major example of the latter type. In all author-itarian-distributive systems, capacity takes precedence over freedom, although the relatively equitable distribution of goods and services is a major priority of this kind of rule. The major difference between tradi-tional-authoritarian and authoritarian-distributive strategies concerns the question of distribution. There is in the latter model greater com-mitment both to political participation and social and economic devel-opment.

In the radical modernizing type of authoritarian-distributive sys-tems, leaders are committed both to rapid modernization and to a broader distribution of the fruits of this modernization to the popula-tion in general. In this situation, the gap between modernization and political development increases as tiny governing elites concentrate political power in their own hands. Examples include Qaddafi's rule in Libya and Husni Mubarak's leadership in Egypt. The Islamic model in Iran also witnesses authoritarian control at the center, although with the end of the Iran-Iraq war and the death of Ayatollah Khomeini in 1989, there has been a liberalization of the system that has included increasingly meaningful elections and vigorous parliamentary politics. The model of revolutionary Iran is especially significant, since it has demonstrated considerable attractiveness and appeal throughout the region, where the revival and resurgence of Islam is everywhere evi-dent.

The developmental struggle is always a grim one. In the Middle East, it has taken on a special urgency because of the accompanying intense and unsettling process of modernization. Gaps, divisions, imbalances, and inequalities are visible everywhere. In one area (Abu Dhabi), the annual per capita GNP approaches $16,000 per year, while in another country (Afghanistan) the figure is less than $300. Such imbalances are as common within countries as between them. In soci-eties like Egypt, Turkey, and Tunisia, 60 percent of the national income has been monopolized by the top 20 percent of the population. In the traditional-authoritarian states, this distribution curve has been even more skewed. Meanwhile, the winds of modernization blow unevenly through the area.

The challenge of development is complicated by four further fac-tors. First, no Middle Eastern society has yet found that it could relax in its quest for development. There are no plateaus and no end points in this journey. Both monarchs and their military-oriented successors have learned this lesson the hard way. Witness the fate of the shah of Iran and of Anwar Sadat of Egypt. The religious leaders who have succeeded the shah and the political descendants of Sadat have all learned that they must face this reality.

Second, there is no particular political or ideological path that ensures success. As our typology of developmental strategies indicates, there are examples of failures in all categories. The democratic-populist model so much admired in the West was dealt a severe blow with the collapse of Lebanon in 1975. The various authoritarian and traditional alternatives have a history of stifling oppression interlaced with continual plotting and coups. Middle Eastern political leaders must write their own prescriptions for development. Thus far, such prescriptions have been singularly unsuccessful.

The third complication concerns the historical and cultural backdrop against which developmental programs must occur. The traditional Islamic system was one of considerable dynamism, social mobility, and personalistic participation. The resurgent strength of Islam and its growing impact on the political process indicate the close relationship that must exist between Islam and the process of political development. The experiments in Pakistan, Saudi Arabia, and Iran demonstrate that the precise dimensions of this relationship have not yet been determined. At this point, Islam is more effective as an ideology of political opposition than as an ideology of political rule.

Finally, the issue of political development in the Middle East is complicated by interregional and international considerations. The Arab-Israeli conflict has already been mentioned. Both the collapse of the Soviet Union and the international energy issue have also had profound effects upon the developmental problem. The massive infusions of military aid into the region have complicated rather than alleviated the problem of political development. This activity has not only deflected attention and resources away from the central issue of development but also tended to strengthen the forces of security at the expense of liberty and participation.

In the Islamic Middle East, Turkey and Egypt have over the years been among the leaders in political development. Although both countries have witnessed many instances of social unrest and political instability, they both have middle-class regimes that have been relatively supportive of political participation. Algeria and Tunisia have also done relatively well in the developmental struggle. Both Algeria and Tunisia, however, face serious political problems. In Algeria, the strong central control is becoming less acceptable as economic problems deepen, and in Tunisia the Destourian Socialist Party (now RCD) is increasingly seen as an instrument of harsh political control. In both countries, the powerful challenge of an Islamic alternative has been met with brutality and repression.

The other authoritarian-distributive regimes (Iraq, Syria, Libya) have been even less successful in political development. Iraq and Syria labor under the severe handicap of deep sectarian, ethnic, and ideological divisions. Although sensitive to the need for popular participation and social equality, the Libyan regime has not yet succeeded in seriously loosening its grip from the center as Mu'ammar Qaddafi clutches all the reins of power in his own hands. In Syria and Iraq, the political situation deteriorated significantly in the early 1980s as the leaders of these countries brutally transformed their regimes into virtual police states.

The families that rule the Persian Gulf shaikhdoms have tended to avoid political development. Because of their extraordinary wealth, however, they have an impressive record of distribution in the social areas of health, education, and housing. This distribution has disguised the absence of political participation and has cushioned popular discontent. Political control remains firmly in the hands of a few members of ruling families, who have shown little inclination to share it. The Iraqi invasion of Kuwait in 1990, however, has forced the leaders of these ministates to rethink their political strategies and to consider seriously broadening political participation.

The most explosive developmental problems in the Islamic Middle East exist in the major monarchies, that is, the traditional-authoritarian governments. With the partial exception of Jordan, traditional power and authority relations persist alongside growing middle classes and deeply religious lower-middle and lower classes whose members remain locked out of the corridors of power. Unlike their tiny counterparts along the Persian Gulf, these monarchies lack the programs necessary to alleviate the tensions arising from the increasing gap between economic modernization and political development. Jordan, Morocco, and Oman lack the resources and revenues. Furthermore, these traditional governments are plagued by visible and especially severe strains of corruption. For these countries, the failure to develop politically can only have violent and costly long-term consequences.

The collapse of Lebanon and the fall of the shah in Iran contain many lessons with respect to the related issues of modernization and political development. Perhaps the most important of these is that an impressive record of modernization does not indicate that political development is also occurring.[29] Rather, modernization may hasten the destruction of the political system by persistently widening the modernization-political development gap. Impressive growth in Lebanon and in Iran in per capita GNP and even in the PQLI had the further effect of lulling both political leaders and political observers into a false sense of complacency. In both countries, the deep group and class divisions were disguised by the deceptively successful environment of modernization. When Lebanon crumbled, it dealt a severe blow to the theory supporting the democratic-populist road to development. The collapse of the Pahlavi dynasty in Iran weakened the argument of those who championed the traditional modernizing monarchical model of government.

All of these case studies indicate the complex delicacy of the related issues of modernization and political development in the Middle East. In a constantly changing situation, there are no obvious success stories and no developmental strategies proven to be successful. Current trends emphasizing democratization, political participation, and the construction of civil society face stiff countervailing forces. Issues of identity, authenticity, and legitimacy remain to be solved. Many of the fundamental problems that now confront the Middle Eastern peoples are directly related to this situation. These problems will be analyzed in depth in the following chapters.

---

[29]This is a theme in Malcolm Kerr's important article, "Rich and Poor in the New Arab Order," *Journal of Arab Affairs* 1 (October 1981): 1–26.

Chapter 2

States, Beliefs, and Ideologies

*P*olitical discourse in the modern Arab world, according to a prominent scholar of the region, "has been awash in ideology."[1] The same could be said of politics in the non-Arab Middle Eastern states of Iran, Turkey, and Israel. Middle Eastern political leaders typically pepper their speeches with ideological terms, nationalist and religious imagery, and attacks on domestic opponents and foreign enemies. By comparison, political discourse in the emerging industrial states of Asia tends to focus more explicitly on economic issues, suggesting that political legitimacy there is measured more in terms of national economic growth than it is in the Middle East. Partly because the pace of industrialization in the Middle East has lagged behind East Asia's and Latin America's, Middle Eastern governments seek to legitimate themselves less through references to financial statements than through manipulating nationalist, religious, and other symbols. In the Middle East the primary purposes of ideology, which consists of beliefs and assertions that rationalize behavior, are not to define concrete objectives or identify strategies through which they might be

---

[1]Michael C. Hudson, *Arab Politics: The Search for Legitimacy* (New Haven: Yale University Press, 1977), p. 20.

achieved. Instead, ideologies are intended "to reassure both articulator and audience, to engender solidarity, and to resolve problems of personal or group identity." They are, in the words of Clement Henry Moore, expressive rather than practical.[2]

Ideologies are both formal dogma and personal guidelines by which individuals define themselves in relation to society. In both of these manifestations Middle Eastern ideologies tend toward instability and fragmentation. They are unstable in that they are prone to rapid change and fragmented because they do not inspire the wholehearted commitment of all those for whom the message is intended. Many countries in the region have ethnic, linguistic, and/or religious minorities that subscribe only partially, if at all, to the ideologies sanctioned by their respective states. Kurds, for example, an ethnolinguistic minority group who are overwhelmingly Sunni Muslim, reside in Iraq, Iran, Turkey, and Syria. In the latter they number a few hundred thousand, constitute less than 2 percent of the population, and are scattered among Muslim and Christian Arabs in Damascus and in the north. Having no hope of achieving independence or even autonomy from the government in Damascus, Syrian Kurds, although strongly aware of their own ethnicity, do not publicly articulate demands. They nevertheless covet the right to use the Kurdish language in schools and in the media and to be permitted other legal forms of ethnic expression. Fellow Kurds across the borders with Turkey and Iraq, however, do constitute large minorities whose powers are enhanced by their geographical concentration. Kurdish demands there, and to a somewhat lesser extent in Iran, have been far more expansive than in Syria, extending to claims for autonomy and even independence. Kurdish insurrections in Turkey and Iraq are paralleled at the ideological level by rejections of Turkish and Iraqi nationalisms and their claims to sovereignty in favor of a well-articulated Kurdish nationalism and its implied claim to the same territories.

Throughout the region, Christians' sense of their own national identities likewise varies in accordance with their possibilities of achieving autonomy or independence. In Lebanon, the collapse of the government in the wake of the 1975–1976 civil war made it possible for the large Christian minority, which constitutes over one-third of the population, to carve out an autonomous region that had many of

---

[2]Clement Henry Moore, "On Theory and Practice Among the Arabs," *World Politics* 19 (October 1971):106–126.

the attributes of a sovereign state until Syria asserted control from late 1989. The ideology of the Lebanese Forces, the most powerful of the Christian militias and political movements, is a strident form of Christian nationalism. It accentuates Lebanon's "distinctive" identity, which it traces to the ancient Phoenicians, thereby devaluing Muslim contributions to Lebanese accomplishments. Christians in the Middle East as a whole, however, constitute only some 3 percent of the total population. Outside Lebanon they have virtually no chance of attaining political autonomy. Accordingly, they typically seek to express themselves politically within a majoritarian rather than minoritarian framework. Christian Palestinian Arabs have played leading roles in formulating Palestinian nationalism and organizing its various political expressions. In the mid-nineteenth century, Syrian Christian intellectuals laid the foundations for Arab nationalism. In Egypt, Coptic Christians played prominent roles in the interwar nationalist movement and continue to occupy cabinet posts and seats in parliament.

As the cases of Kurdish and Christian minorities suggest, political behavior and beliefs are strongly conditioned by immediate demographic and political circumstances and are, therefore, subject to change according to those circumstances. This plasticity at the communal level is mirrored by the multiplicity and flexibility of personal identities. Different components of those complex identities are evoked by varying circumstances. Samir Wahhabi, for example, is a notable from the village of Bait Jann in the Galilee in northern Israel and one-time member of the Knesset (Israeli parliament) for the right-wing Likud Party. He identifies himself as follows: "I belong to the Druze sect, which is part of the Arab minority in Israel. It is part of the Arab nation, and personally my state is the State of Israel. In the past this land was called Palestine, so I could say I belong in that historical sense."[3] To many other Druze from that village, however, Wahhabi's identification with Israel is inappropriate and opportunistic. In their minds the proper Druze identity is Arab and Palestinian, but not Israeli.[4]

Variability of identities of non-Jewish Israelis is not limited to Druze. A sample of Palestinian Arab citizens of Israel were asked in 1966 whether they identified themselves as Israeli, Arab, or Palestin-

[3]Julia Slater, "Palestinians in Israel: Who Are They?" *Middle East International* 329 (July 8, 1988):16.

[4]*Ibid.*, p. 16.

ian. The majority replied that they preferred to call themselves Israelis. A year later, following the June 1967 war, a comparable sample ranked Arab identity first, followed by Palestinian and then Israeli. Seven years later a third survey revealed that only 14 percent of respondents believed the term *Israeli* described them, while 63 percent thought of themselves as Palestinian.[5] This shift in the self-identifications of Palestinian Arabs in Israel reflects the traumatic events of the 1967 war and, more generally, the politicization of that community and its increasing hostility toward Israeli Jews.

Survey research conducted among young citizens from virtually all Arab countries carried out since 1957 for the purpose of gauging preferred identifications of respondents has revealed not only that such identities are multiple but also that they tend to respond to political events and trends. The identities mentioned have included those of family, tribe, ethnic group (Arab, Kurd, Armenian, etc.), religion, citizenship, and political party, movement, and ideology. The percentage of respondents identifying themselves as Arab has declined over the past decade, while preferences for Islamic or specific national identities have increased. These changes parallel what many observers believe to be a declining importance of pan-Arabism and its gradual replacement by state-based nationalisms or political Islam.[6]

Multiplicity and plasticity of identity are a reflection of political reality, not personal capriciousness. In this century, the Middle East has been forced to endure upheavals that have repeatedly altered the structural conditions upon which politically relevant beliefs and identities rest. A Lebanese in his or her late seventies, for example, would have entered the world as a subject of the Ottoman Empire, and would then, for a brief period, have been under the control of the short-lived Damascus-based Arab state of Amir Faisal. Subsequently this person would have become a citizen of French-ruled Lebanon and, after World War II, a citizen of independent Lebanon. For almost a decade and a half after the onset of civil war in 1975, with the almost total collapse of that state, the life of this septuagenarian would

[5]Lewis W. Snider, "Minorities and Political Power in the Middle East," in *The Political Role of Minority Groups in the Middle East,* ed. by R. D. McLaurin (New York: Praeger, 1979), pp. 247–248.

[6]For a review of this survey data, see Tawfic E. Farah, "Introduction," in *Pan-Arabism and Arab Nationalism: The Continuing Debate,* ed. by Tawfic E. Farah (Boulder, Colo.: Westview Press, 1987), pp. 1–18.

have been heavily influenced by one or more of the powerful militias that have all but displaced state authority. Since then, Syria has assumed quasi-sovereign status, rendering Lebanese nationality politically, if not psychologically, marginal.[7]

The Lebanese are not unique in having endured historical odysseys that in a lifetime have taken them through numerous national and subnational administrative arrangements and corresponding demands for political loyalties and identities. Palestinians now in their late seventies, for example, have been subjects of the Ottomans, British, and either the Israelis, Jordanians, or perhaps some other Arab state. These changes in citizenship, combined with the mosaic-like character of religious, ethnic, and linguistic groups in the region, help to account for the failure of any political ideology to be permanently established and thereby utterly transform and homogenize personal political identities.

Ideologies tend to sweep through the area gathering strength like hurricanes, then dissipate without having achieved their objectives. Personal identities modified in response to political victories, charismatic leaders, or ideological slogans can just as easily revert to their original forms when the new ideology and its champion encounter defeats. In the wake of the June 1967 Arab-Israeli war, for example, radical Palestinian nationalism tinged by Maoism swept through the Arab world. The Arab states, having promised to "liberate Palestine"

---

[7]These rapidly changing configurations of sovereign authority, further exacerbated by Lebanon's involvement in the wider Middle East, spawned numerous potential affiliations upon which identities and ideologies can rest. The plethora of choices confronting Lebanese Maronite Christians is instructive:

> If nationalism has rapidly "invaded" the Arab mind, it has not been met with a clear definition of where the nation is. Take the example of a Maronite Lebanese who is told by the historians of his community (and modern warlords) that the Maronite nation has existed for ages. But those Maronites who have rallied round the 1920 French-defined "Grand Liban" tell him that if the Maronites have ever constituted a nation, this nation has now been diluted in the wider Lebanese modern one. Then the proponents of Greater (or Natural) Syria tell him that Lebanon is a purely artificial creation of colonialist France and that his loyalty should go exclusively to a Syrian nation present since Sumer and the Akkadians. Arab nationalists will insist that the Arab nation is the only "true" nation.

Ghassan Salamé, "Introduction," in *The Foundations of the Arab State*, ed. by Ghassan Salamé (London: Croom Helm, 1987), p. 4.

but having in fact worked assiduously to contain Palestinian radical nationalism, were discredited by the crushing defeat. In the postwar climate, guerrilla war, rather than the armies of Egypt, Syria, and Jordan, held out the promise of victory over Israel. But the Arab states regrouped, reestablished their power, and in Jordan in September 1970, which became known as Black September, the Palestine Liberation Organization was crushed. In the wake of that violent confrontation between Palestinian revolutionary mass mobilization and the power of Arab states, infatuation with Palestinian radicalism rapidly faded. Large numbers of Egyptians, Syrians, Iraqis, and other Arabs who had strongly but temporarily identified with the transnationalist revolutionary message disseminated by Palestinians, witnessing the superior power of their own states, reverted to their original national identities and concerns.

In Iran, the 1978–1979 revolution stimulated a wave of enthusiasm for Khomeinism that then swept through the Sunni Muslim Arab world. Impressed by the success of radical Islamic fundamentalism in overthrowing the shah and confronting the United States, Arab Muslims in great numbers became convinced that in radical political Islam they might find solutions to their own problematic confrontations with Israel, the United States, and the authoritarian Arab governments under which they lived. But the Khomeinist image was quickly tarnished by the war with Iraq, by excesses of the new regime, and by the Islamic Republic's inability to put the economy on a sound footing. Enthusiasm for Khomeinism waned, and although Islamic political activism has persisted, in most cases it has distinguished itself from the Iranian version.

That political ideologies are subject to bandwagon effects, rapidly gaining adherents in response to successes and then losing them as a result of setbacks, indicates that those ideologies are not reinforced by being integrated into political structures. Political leaders, unwilling to have their choices constrained, use ideologies not to institutionalize power but as political weapons to gain popular support that can be used to joust with enemies. Ideologies, in short, are seen as useful adjuncts to political power and are nurtured for that purpose. The Safavids, for example, a Turkish-speaking nomadic people who seized power in Iran at the outset of the sixteenth century, cemented ties to their Persian subjects by converting them from Sunni to Shi'i Islam. For this purpose they recruited Shi'i *ulema* (religious scholars) from what are now Bahrain, Lebanon, and Iraq and lavished them with patronage. In return, the ulema propagated a religious doctrine that emphasized subordination to established authority, thereby reinforcing the Safavid claim to rule.

Four and a half centuries later, Gamal Abdel Nasser of Egypt sought to enhance his powers by championing Arab nationalism and Arab socialism. A man of action rather than words, he delegated the important but mundane tasks of formulating ideology and reconciling it with specific political decisions to apparatchiks (party professionals), who previously had perfected their skills when working in radical opposition organizations, such as the Communist Party. In 1962 Saudi Arabia, entering into a military struggle with Egypt in North Yemen and into a broader ideological confrontation with radical Arab nationalism, founded the Muslim League. Its primary purpose was to stimulate Islamic consciousness and, in so doing, to undercut the appeal of radical secularist ideologies, including Nasser's versions of Arab nationalism and socialism. The Muslim League and its successors, the Islamic Pact, formed in 1966, and the Islamic Conference Organization, created in 1972, were staffed with religious functionaries who might be thought of as equivalents to Nasser's secular apparatchiks.[8]

In the wake of the second Gulf war, Galal Amin, an Egyptian academic with a wry sense of humor, identified the qualities that Arab rulers desire in their intellectuals. Shaikh Jabir al-Ahmad al-Sabah of Kuwait requires those who can "evoke Islam, but in moderate dosage and without the least hint of any socialist or Arab nationalist shading." Intellectuals serving King Fahd of Saudi Arabia must be especially knowledgeable about the Quran, particularly "words related to the punishment on the day of atonement . . . while able to skirt any mention of foreign and domestic policy, Israel, or the situation of the mass of Muslims in Saudi Arabia itself." King Hussein of Jordan requires virtually acrobatic skills of those who serve him, so that the delicate balances that sustain his kingdom are not jeopardized. For this advocate "there is nothing wrong with Arab nationalism, socialism and even Israel, provided all this talk is academic in nature and remote from current affairs and any critique of a specific Arab government." In Egypt intellectual hypocrisy in support of the regime "is full of light spirit and good cheer. . . . Both the hypocrite and the subject of

---

[8]On these Islamic organizations see Malcolm H. Kerr, *The Arab Cold War: Gamal'Abdal-Nasir and His Rivals, 1958–1970* (London: Oxford University Press, 1971), pp. 106–114.

hypocrisy are not taken seriously. . . . They function rather like the singer at weddings who celebrates the beauty of the bride while everyone knows that she is very ugly."[9]

The considerable resources expended by the Safavids, Nasser, the Saudis and others to disseminate religious beliefs or political ideologies (and in this context there is no real difference between the two) bespeak the comparative absence of structural legitimacy of their governments. Structural legitimacy, or what Max Weber has termed rational-legal authority, obtains when rules, supported by institutions to enforce them, underpin popular acceptance of government.[10] Such legitimacy is weak in the Middle East. New rulers must somehow solve the problem of how "some men come to be credited with the right to rule over others."[11] Their task is complicated by ethnic, linguistic, and religious diversity. In nine countries in the Middle East, such minorities constitute at least 25 percent of the population. In Syria, Lebanon, Bahrain, and Iraq, religious minorities control the government. In four Arab states bordering the Persian Gulf, resident aliens significantly outnumber citizens.[12]

Nevertheless, the heterogeneity of Middle Eastern populations and its consequences for ideological fragmentation and instability can be overstated. Unifying roles are also played by the predominant language and religion. Arabic, despite local dialects and a sharp distinction between its written and spoken forms, is the mother tongue of the overwhelming majority of residents of Arab countries. In fact, as ranked by linguistic diversity, Arab countries "are among the most homogeneous in the world."[13] Only Iraq, which is about one-quarter Kurdish, is more linguistically fragmented than the majority of the

---

[9]Galal Amin, "The Arab Intellectual and the Crisis in the Gulf," *The Arabs and the Calamity of Kuwait* (Cairo: Madbuli, 1991), pp. 50–57, cited in Raymond Baker, "Imagining Egypt in the New International Order," paper delivered to the annual conference of the Middle East Studies Association of North America (Washington, D.C.: November 23–26, 1991), pp. 26–27.

[10]Max Weber, *The Theory of Social and Economic Organization* (New York: Oxford University Press, 1947), pp. 130–132.

[11]Clifford Geertz, "The Politics of Meaning," *The Interpretation of Cultures* (New York: Basic Books, 1973), p. 317.

[12]R. D. McLaurin, "Minorities and Politics in the Middle East: An Introduction," *The Political Role of Minority Groups*, pp. 1–16.

[13]Hudson, *Arab Politics*, p. 38.

world's nation-states. Islam is another unifying force, being the predominant religion in all states of the region except Israel. So the linguistic and religious bonds that unite most people of the region have often been drawn upon to reinforce political ideologies. Persisting ideological instability and fragmentation must, therefore, be accounted for by causes other than those of ethnic, linguistic, and religious differences.

IDEOLOGY AND STATE FORMATION

The historical development of European ideologies provides a precedent that may be useful in understanding the development of political beliefs in the Middle East. From the time of the French Revolution up to the twentieth century, numerous ideologies contended for supremacy on the European continent. Various nationalisms and versions of democracy, fascism, socialism, and communism emerged as Europe was being carved into its present configuration of nation-states. Indeed, it was the very process of state formation, including the mobilization of citizens, the creation of national economies, and the construction of legitimate political orders that both required and gave birth to those ideologies. These processes were highly conflictual. As Europe was developing its state system and accompanying ideologies, it was wracked with what amounted to almost perpetual civil war from the Napoleonic era until 1945. Since 1989 the state system established by Soviet communism in Eastern Europe has been unraveling and competitive nationalisms reemerging.

The Middle East today is wrestling with the same problems of state formation that have confronted Europe. The states of the Fertile Crescent, which extends from the southeastern Mediterranean coast northward into Syria and down the Tigris and Euphrates rivers into Iraq, were created as a result of the dissolution of the Ottoman Empire and were immediately placed under British or French control. Other countries in the region, including Egypt, Iran, Turkey, and those on the Arabian Peninsula, at the very least had their borders determined through the intervention of imperial powers. In some cases they were entirely the creations of such interventions. All these countries have confronted the interlocking tasks of nation- and state-building. The former is the process whereby a sense of shared national identity, patriotism, and loyalty to homeland develops. State-building refers more specifically to the construction of governmental and political institutions.

The more artificial the country, the more difficult are the challenges of nation- and state-building. Countries of the Fertile Crescent, for example, were carved out of the Ottoman Empire in accordance with British and French desires. National aspirations and identities of residents were not coterminous with state boundaries. To some of these residents, the idea of nation referred to their specific ethnic or religious groups, many of which, as the result of new nation-states having been created, were fragmented, scattered among two or more countries of the region. The Druze were divided among Syria, Lebanon, and Palestine. Kurds, whose nationalist aspirations were frustrated despite their having been supported by President Woodrow Wilson at the Versailles Peace Conference, were left scattered as described above. To many Arabs, the division of their heartland into several small sovereign units, each under the control of Europeans, was a violation of the promise of a united Arab nation made by the British to induce Arab leaders to revolt against the Ottoman Turks during World War I. In their eyes, this fragmentation was also against the natural order of things. To these nationalists, because the region was populated primarily by Arabs it should therefore constitute a single Arab state. Given this array of subnational and transnational identities competing with the new states for the loyalties of their residents, it was inevitable that the Fertile Crescent would become an arena for ideological confrontation. This tendency was further aggravated by Zionist claims on Palestine and, after 1948, by the presence of Israel in the midst of Arab states.

New governments struggled to establish their ideological hegemony over competitive calls for loyalty and identity, a struggle which they have gradually been winning but which is not yet over. Ba'thist ideology, for example, with which the contemporary governments of Syria and Iraq seek to legitimate themselves, originally and unambiguously elevated the principles of Arab nationalism and Arab unity to primacy of place. The concept of *al-qawmiyyat al-Arabiyya*, or loyalty to the generalized Arab nation, was ideally, in Ba'thism, preeminent over *wataniyya*, which is patriotism centered on a specific state. Arab states, in Ba'thist terminology, are still referred to as *aqtar* or *iqlim* (regions.) The term *nation* remains reserved for the Arab world as a whole, but this terminology now has little practical significance. Indeed, since the mid- to late 1970s, the leaders of both Iraq and Syria have increasingly emphasized the indigenous in official historiographies. In Iraq this has meant ascribing an Arab character to all ancient Mesopotamian civilizations, which is a straight-out fabrication, while in Syria it is manifested by references to Greater Syria, a historical-geographical unit centered on today's Syria, Lebanon, Jordan, and Israel. In short, *wataniyya* is displacing *qawmiyya* in Ba'thist ideology.[14] In Lebanon, loyalty to religious sects, or what as a result of European influence came to be called *confessions,* has seriously eroded patriotism focused on the nation-state. In Jordan, the most artificial of the Fertile Crescent states and one whose very existence is challenged by the commitment of its large Palestinian population to Palestinian nationalism, loyalty to King Hussein and the royal family is engendered as the principal element in an otherwise comparatively diffuse and weak nationalism.

For Turkey, Iran, and Egypt, the nation-building process has been easier. Their peoples have stronger national identities based on impressive historical records of accomplishment and traditions of administrative autonomy. For the Turks, the dissolution of the Ottoman Empire provided the opportunity to redefine the remaining geographical core of that entity based on Anatolia as a modern nation-state. Turkish ethnicity was substituted for Islam as the means by which the nation-state was legitimated. Pan-Ottomanism, an unsuccessful nineteenth-century attempt to foster a European-style secular nationalism to integrate the multiethnic, religiously diverse, and disintegrating empire, was abandoned. Iran is centered on a Persian-speaking people who have for millennia inhabited the central plateau area of that country and who constitute a majority of the population. While constructing an identity to serve as the basis for their nation-state, Iranians drew upon both the legacy of a monarchical, imperial tradition that predates Islam and the distinctive Shi'i faith that has for almost five centuries set Iran off from its neighbors. Similarly Egypt, unlike the Arab states in the Fertile Crescent, has a long if intermittent history of governmental autonomy, to say nothing of a remarkable civilization of antiquity whose remains provide visible reminders of what was once achieved.

Yet even for Turkey, Iran, and Egypt, nation-building has not

---

[14]Amatzia Baram, "Territorial Nationalism in the Arab World," *Middle Eastern Studies* 26 (October 1990): 425–448.

been without difficulties and sudden, dramatic changes of course. Turkey has not resolved the contradictions resultant from basing national identity squarely on secularism and Turkish ethnicity. This definition is unacceptable to significant numbers of committed Muslims who want Islam to be enshrined as the state's religion. Similarly, emphasis on Turkish language and ethnicity relegates Kurds to what is at best an ambiguous status. Thus, Islamic revivalism and Kurdish militancy both pose threats to the definition of Turkish national identity.

Reza Shah and his son, Muhammad Reza Shah, like Turkey's Mustafa Kemal (Ataturk), were ardent secularists who sought to construct an Iranian national identity on non-Islamic foundations, which included both European ideas of nationalism and references to ancient Persia. Ayatollah Khomeini and his supporters challenged that conceptualization of Iranian nationalism, legitimating their revolution and the government it established solely on the basis of Shi'i Islam.

Egypt has had persisting problems reconciling national and transnational ideologies. In the first quarter of this century, an Egyptian nationalism centered on that state, and its native Arabic-speaking inhabitants, inspired the anticolonial movement. At the end of the 1930s, the spread of Arab nationalism in the Fertile Crescent, combined with the increasingly violent confrontation between Arabs and Jews in Palestine, stimulated in Egypt the growth of Arabism. It was that sentiment that Nasser, after 1952, enshrined as the central feature of his nationalist, or, more accurately, transnationalist ideology. While Anwar Sadat and, to a much lesser extent, Husni Mubarak have worked to displace Arab nationalism with an Egyptian-centered patriotism, the growing trend of Islamic fundamentalism now offers a new transnationalist ideological challenge to the Egyptian government.

In the Arab states of the Fertile Crescent, nation-building has confronted greater obstacles and suffered more setbacks than it has in Turkey, Iran, and Egypt. Subnational, national, and transnational ideologies continue to compete for the loyalties of Lebanese, Syrians, Iraqis, Palestinians, and Jordanians. Many observers believe, however, that in the struggle to establish ideological hegemony, the Arab states are all gradually eroding minoritarian identities at the subnational level and defeating appeals by secular Arab nationalists and Islamic radicals to forge loyalties at the transnational level. Pan-Arabism, according to Fouad Ajami, "is nearing its end, if it is not already a thing of the past. . . . Now . . . *raison d'état,* once an alien and illegitimate doctrine, is gaining ground. Slowly and grimly with a great deal of anguish, a 'normal' state system is becoming a fact of life."[15] Abdul-Monem al-Mashat argues that the Arab world as a manifestation of the pan-Arab ideal is disintegrating, while William R. Brown describes the Arab nation as dying while, phoenix-like, Arab states are emerging from it.[16]

Others, however, are not so sure. Walid Khalidi contends that in the doctrine of pan-Arabism *"raison d'état* is heresy," for in comparison with the "super-legitimacy" of pan-Arabism the legitimacy of individual Arab states "shrinks into irrelevance."[17] Hassan Nafaa argues that "a workable pan-Arab system of states based on the concept of *raison d'état* is hardly conceivable" because of the various conflicts between those states and because the ideology of pan-Arabism remains vibrant and motivating.[18] In a survey conducted between 1977 and 1979 of 6,000 residents of ten Arab countries, 78.5 percent of respondents said they believed in the existence of an Arab entity and 77.9 percent agreed that this entity constitutes one nation; 53 percent believed that this nation is divided by artificial borders.[19] *Al-Mustaqbal al-Arabi*, a prominent Arabic journal, recently editorialized that

> the failure of the Arab State . . . in achieving true independence [and] . . . in liberating the occupied Arab territories in Palestine . . . will sooner or later strengthen the Arab citizen's conviction that the state has failed to achieve the major objectives it has set for itself. Consequently, this same Arab citizen will be inclined to work at a national [pan-Arab] level and transcend the local state phenomenon.[20]

---

[15]Fouad Ajami, "The End of Pan-Arabism," *Foreign Affairs* 57 (Winter 1978–1979):355–373.

[16]Abdul-Monem Al-Mashat, "Stress and Disintegration in the Arab World," and William R. Brown, "The Dying Arab Nation," in *Pan-Arabism and Arab Nationalism,* pp. 165–176 and 152–164, respectively.

[17]Walid Khalidi, "Thinking the Unthinkable: A Sovereign Palestinian State," *Foreign Affairs* 56 (July 1978):695–696.

[18]Hassan Nafaa, "Arab Nationalism: A Response to Ajami's Thesis on the 'End of Pan-Arabism'," in *Pan-Arabism and Arab Nationalism,* pp. 133–151.

[19]Saad al-Din Ibrahim, *The Trends of Arab Public Opinion Toward the Issue of Unity* (Beirut: Center for Arab Unity Studies, 1980) (in Arabic), cited in Bahgat Korany, "Alien and Besieged Yet Here to Stay: The Contradictions of the Arab Territorial State," in *The Foundations of the Arab State,* pp. 53–54.

[20]K. Hasib, "The Words of *al-Mustaqbal al-Arabi,*" in *al-Mustaqbal al-Arabi* 73 (1985):7, cited in Ghassan Salamé, "'Strong' and 'Weak' States: A Qualified Return to the Muqaddimah," *The Foundations of the Arab State,* p. 226.

There are, then, doubts as to whether the Arab world (and the Middle East more generally) is progressing toward the emergence of a regional political system founded on coherent states legitimated by nationalist ideologies, capable of sustaining productive, nonconflictual interstate relations while rejecting transnational appeals for unification. This should not be surprising. The Middle East, in comparison to Europe, is in relatively early stages of state- and nation-building. That does not mean, however, that those processes will exactly parallel those of Europe. Middle Eastern socioeconomic and political systems prior to the rise of nation-states were fundamentally different from those of Europe. The methods that have been followed in building nation-states also differ. To understand contemporary Middle Eastern ideologies, therefore, one must look in greater detail at the nature of political beliefs prior to the establishment of the modern state system, and then at the process by which those nation-states have been formed.

PREMODERN, PREIDEOLOGICAL PHASE

According to Max Weber, a state is a "compulsory political association with continuous organization [whose] administrative staff successfully uphold a claim to the monopoly of legitimate use of force in the enforcement of its order ... within a given territorial area."[21] Other definitions of the term typically stress powers to implement laws and extract taxes and to command the loyalty and allegiance of citizens.[22] States vary in strength according to their capacity to regulate the behavior of citizens and their ability to remain autonomous from those social forces that seek to capture the state and use it for their own purposes. These social forces can be classes, ethnic and religious groups, tribes, or other units. A state must extract enough revenue in order to pay for armies, bureaucracies, and the other structures that support it. According to Giacomo Luciani, "A state structure will tend to be sta-

---

[21]Weber, *The Theory of Social and Economic Organization*, p. 154.

[22]See, for example, the definition offered by Iliya Harik, "The Origins of the Arab State System," in *The Foundations of the Arab State*, p. 23. For a discussion of definition of the term *state* and the application of that concept to the Middle East, see Bahgat Korany, "Alien and Besieged Yet Here to Stay," pp. 47–74.

ble in history if it commands sufficient resources to guarantee its own survival."[23]

In the Middle East prior to the nineteenth century, the viability of states, as measured by their longevity and degree of control over what was nominally their territory, was highly variable. This was due both to the comparative scarcity of resources and to the segmented, unmobilized nature of society, which impeded the state's access to the resources that did exist. Wealth in the premodern Middle East tended to be generated more from long-distance trade than from agriculture, which itself was extensive rather than intensive except in the Nile Valley and along the eastern Mediterranean coast. By its nature, trade was an activity that governments had difficulty controlling and taxing. Extracting a surplus from agricultural production when farming was widely scattered and mainly at a subsistence level was likely to cost the state more than it would obtain in revenues. The relatively harsh climate, presence of mountains, deserts, and other significant geographical obstacles to transportation and communication, and a general absence of adequate roads further raised the cost to governments for extraction and regulation. *Bedouin* (tribally organized nomads), who in the premodern period constituted about one-fifth of the population of the Middle East, were particularly resistant to governmental control. But even settled urban dwellers were insulated from the weak states that presided over them by a far more dense and complex network of kinship connections than was the case in premodern Europe.

Forced to extract revenues in circumstances of limited and intermittent control over populations and territories, governments developed second-best strategies of indirect taxation. One of them was to hold ethnic, religious, tribal, and other groups responsible for payment of taxes, leaving it to the communities' leaders to collect them. Another method of raising revenue was to rely on *multazims,* or tax farmers. The state would grant *iltizams* (farms) in return for payment of taxes, which the multazims would extract from peasants. These arrangements enabled governments to raise revenues when otherwise none might have been collected. But they were inefficient, for those individuals placed between governments and taxpayers, whether multazims or local notables, retained as high a proportion of revenue as

---

[23]Giacomo Luciani, "Allocation vs. Production States: A Theoretical Framework," in *The Rentier State,* ed. Hazem Beblawi and Giacomo Luciani (London: Croom Helm, 1987), p. 64.

possible for their own use. The pecuniary interests of such middlemen demanded that they seek to weaken government.[24]

Geographical, economic, and social conditions thus limited inter-actions between rulers and ruled to far fewer transactions than occur in a modern nation-state. Prevailing beliefs about the proper relation-ship between ruler and ruled reinforced this loose relationship. That system of belief was founded in Islam.

Islamic Doctrine and Organization

Like other religions, Islam is at the same time theological and socio-logical. It is comprised of both religious doctrine and patterns of social, including political, relationships.[25] The creed of Islam is straightforward and universalistic. The message of the Prophet Muhammad to the residents of Mecca, whose beliefs in the early sev-enth century were shaped by animistic and totemistic religions as well as by Christianity and Judaism, was that God had last revealed himself to humanity by issuing through Muhammad the Quran. That volume, compiled after Muhammad's death, in conjunction with the *hadith*, the teachings and sayings attributed to Muhammad, the compiled form of which is called the *sunna* (traditions), together constitute the sources for the *sharia* (Islamic law). Conversion to Islam, which liter-ally means the surrender of man to God (Allah), requires only the pro-fession of the faith *(shahada)*—"There is no god but God and Muham-mad is the messenger (prophet) of God." The requirements of the faith, its "five pillars," are the shahada, *salat* (prayer), *sawm* (fasting)

---

[24]As late as the mid-nineteenth century the Ottoman annual land tax *(miri)* was collect-ed primarily through middlemen. The consequences of this indirect method are described by Samir Khalaf as follows:

> Officially, the *miri* was supposed to be levied upon all sown land . . . yet neither in its assessment nor collection was the system consistent or regular. Indeed, the tribute was arbitrarily set and varied considerably with changing circumstances. Rather than being proportional to wealth, the *miri* was often a reflection of the amir's power or special standing vis-à-vis the Ottoman Pasha.

Samir Khalaf, *Lebanon's Predicament* (New York: Columbia University Press, 1987), p. 26.

[25]Suad Joseph, "Muslim-Christian Conflicts: A Theoretical Perspective," in *Muslim-Christian Conflicts: Economic, Political, and Social Origins,* ed. by Suad Joseph and Barbara L. K. Pillsbury (Boulder, Colo.: Westview Press, 1979), pp. 1–45.

during the month of Ramadan, *zakat* (almsgiving), and making the *hajj* (pilgrimage) to Mecca at least once during a lifetime.

The simplicity of Islamic doctrine and the ease of conversion to the religion are essential to its universalism. It is intended not as the religion of a specific tribe, group, or nation of peoples or as a faith delineated by specific territory but as a religion appropriate anywhere to which anyone may convert. The period prior to the revelation of God's message to Muhammad in the early seventh century is known to Muslims as the *jahiliyya* (age of ignorance), in which tribal and other particularistic loyalties divided humanity. Islam is thus meant not only to rescue individuals from personal ignorance but also to serve as an antidote to sociopolitical incoherence and conflict.

This universalism in Islam has for politics been a two-edged sword. It facilitated Islam's expansion from the Arabian Peninsula to Indonesia in the east and the Iberian Peninsula in the west, from being a religion of the Arabs to being a faith that now encompasses members of virtually all of the world's major ethnolinguistic groupings and claims 1 billion adherents. On the other hand, unlike some other religions that are associated with a specific tribe or ethnic group, such as Judaism, or that are nonproseltyzing, such as the heterodox Druze faith, Islam, once it had spread beyond the confines of Arabia, no longer benefited from reinforcing tribal, ethnic, or other solidarities. The socioreligious identity that characterizes Muslims is that they are members of the *umma al-Islamiyya,* the community of believers. Unlike adherents to the "political religions" of secular European nationalisms, who identify themselves with reference to a specific territory and state, members of the Islamic *umma* do not constitute a state, nor is their faith associated with any specific land. Islamic doctrine therefore is, strictly speaking, incompatible with nationalism, which refers to a specific people in a particular place.[26] Nationalism to Muslims, according to P. J. Vatikiotis, "implies a pre-Islamic kind of tribal particularism, jahiliyya."[27]

The political cost of Islamic universalism has been high. "The most closely integrated states are those with a *raison d'[ê]tre* ... a 'state idea.' " Such an idea "convinces all the people in all the regions

---

[26]Hamid Enayat, *Modern Islamic Political Thought* (Austin: University of Texas Press, 1982), pp. 111–159.

[27]P. J. Vatikiotis, *Islam and the State* (London: Croom Helm, 1987), p. 10.

(of the state) that they belong together."[28] Zionism, which is the nationalist ideology of Jews, has clear advantages over Islam because it is focused on territory. This is hardly surprising, for Zionism was heavily influenced by European nationalisms, which are themselves powerful state ideas defining common national identities with reference to place of residence. But in the Islamic Middle East, "The nation is considered in religious terms to encompass those beyond and across the territorial boundaries of the individual states. There is a constant clash between the exigencies of the modern territorial state, and the wider nation, or community of believers."[29] While James Piscatori's argument is correct that Muslim political authorities have throughout history accommodated themselves to the reality of statehood, he underemphasizes the fact that the idealized myth of the Islamic umma remains potent.[30] The unresolved paradox of Islamic universalism and a world composed of nation-states periodically assumes political importance, as exemplified by the transnational appeals of the Islamic Republic of Iran and by indictments of sovereignty and nationalism as heretical in Islam by such Islamic activists as Ayatollah Khomeini and the Egyptian Muslim Brother, Sayyid Qutb.[31] There remains, in short, a continuing disjunction between the theory of Islam and the practice of the nation-state.

The universalism of Islam complicated the task of forging a compelling state idea from its doctrine. So too has its political theory caused problems for those who seek to draw upon Islamic doctrine in creating nation-states. The implementation of God's will, which is the principal obligation of Muslims, is not exclusively an individual act. It requires the creation of a social order that operates by Islamic precepts. Accordingly, there is ideally no separation between religion and politics—Islam is both *din wa dawla* (religion and state). In historical reality, however, Christian and Islamic doctrine did not lead to sharply

---

[28]Alasdair Drysdale and Gerald H. Blake, *The Middle East and North Africa: A Political Geography* (New York: Oxford University Press, 1985), p. 178.

[29]Vatikiotis, *Islam and the State,* p. 13.

[30]James A. Piscatori, *Islam in a World of Nation-States* (Cambridge: Cambridge University Press, 1986).

[31]Qutb denounces *al-hakmiyya* (sovereignty) in his most famous work, *Ma'alim Fi al-Tariq (Signs Along the Path)* (Cairo: Wahba Books, 1964) (in Arabic). For an analysis of Qutb's writings, see Gilles Kepel, *Muslim Extremism in Egypt: The Prophet and the Pharaoh* (Berkeley and Los Angeles: University of California Press, 1986), pp. 43–52.

different forms of government. Caliphs (successors to the prophet) had, by the tenth century, become subordinate to sultans, secular leaders whose authority rested primarily on their political power and only secondarily on their religious legitimacy. Since that time and even before, theocratic government in the Middle East has been notable by its absence. Nevertheless, Islam's insistence on the unity of individuals' personal, social, and political life has meant that although outright secular government that explicitly denies Islam's relevance to politics began to take shape in the Middle East from the early nineteenth century, its reconciliation with Islamic doctrine, hence its legitimacy, has never been completely accomplished.

A second aspect of Islamic political theory that has proven difficult to accommodate to the idea of the nation-state is its treatment of the relationship between rulers and ruled. Elegantly simple and well suited to the requirements of the *umma al-mu'minin* (community of believers) when it consisted of Muhammad and his followers, Islam enjoins believers to "Obey God, obey his Prophet, and obey those in authority over you." This fifty-ninth verse from the fourth *sura* (chapter) of the Quran points to a fundamental difference between the conception of legitimate government in Islam and that in the contemporary Western world. In Western systems, sovereignty in theory resides with the people who are, therefore, the ultimate authority to which government is responsible. In Islam, sovereignty rests with God, to whom both rulers and ruled alike are responsible. While rulers, like their subjects, are bound by the provisions of the sharia, in the historical absence of institutions to constrain arbitrary rulers their nominal subordination to religious law was often meaningless.

In the early days of Islam, the issue of mutual obligations between rulers and ruled was a subject of lively controversy and debate. By the twelfth century, however, the sultanate was so ascendant over the barely surviving caliphate that Islamic scholars, including the renowned al-Ghazali (d. 1111), devised justifications for that reality. The community of the faithful was enjoined to obey its ruler simply because the alternative was chaos. This particular resolution of the dilemma besetting relationships between ruler and ruled was not, however, quite the end of the story. Precisely because it so tilted the balance in favor of the sultan, there subsequently arose extreme statements of the rights of the ruled. In the early fourteenth century Ahmad Ibn Taymiyya, a "religious firebrand" in Cairo and Damascus, to whom the political philosophies of numerous contemporary Islamic activists have been traced, preached that Islam justified the right to rebel against unjust rulers.[32] He was executed in 1328 by the Mamlukes then ruling Egypt. Since that time, there have been attempts to resuscitate doctrines similar to those propounded by Ibn Taymiyya, but the major thrust of Islamic political theory and practice has continued in the direction charted by al-Ghazali, who emphasized the obligation of obedience to authority. While that underpinning for government sufficed in the premodern period, appeals for obedience are inadequate bases for legitimacy for nation-states seeking to penetrate their societies to a much greater degree. Increasingly that legitimacy depends on the perceived effectiveness of political participation by citizens.

Even in religiously conservative Saudi Arabia, the issue of whether sovereignty derives from Allah or the people has become of paramount political importance. In the wake of the second Gulf war, King Fahd, seeking to reduce discontent caused by the war and his authoritarian rule, declared that a 60-member *majlis al-shura* (consultative council) would be created. He reserved the right to appoint all members to that council to himself, however, claiming that "The democratic system prevailing in the world does not suit us in this region. . . . The system of free elections is not part of Islamic ideology." Secularized, liberal Saudis contested the king's assertion on the grounds that Islam has long recognized democratic practices and noted that even the Islamic Republic of Iran has a 270-seat elected parliament. For their part, ultrareligious Saudis argued against Fahd on the grounds that proper Islamic government requires true *shura* (consultation), which can only be ensured through elections. Muhammad Hudaibi, leader of the Egyptian Muslim Brotherhood, when asked if Saudi Arabia was a true Islamic society replied, "Of course not, because it does not have an elected government."[33]

Radical Islamic activists are divided among themselves over the issue of whether Islam does or does not require democracy of a Western sort. A spokesperson for Rashid Ghannouchi, head of *al-Nahda*

---

[32]On the influence of Ibn Taymiyya on contemporary Islamic activists, see, for example, Emmanuel Sivan, *Radical Islam: Medieval Theology and Modern Politics* (New Haven: Yale University Press, 1985), pp. 94–107. The term *religious firebrand* is his.

[33]Caryle Murphy, "Saudi Arabia: A True Islamic Society?" *Washington Post* (April 28, 1992), p. 2.

(The Renaissance), the leading Tunisian Islamicist party, argues that "in Islam and in the Koran, the idea of liberty is fundamental. . . . [T]he closest political system to Islam is the democratic system of the West—especially the American Constitution." Ali Benhadj, on the other hand, a prominent figure in an equivalent Islamicist political party in Algeria, has stated that "Democracy is apostasy."[34]

The relative absence of a lexicon of democratic terminology in the major Middle Eastern languages associated with Islam, which are Arabic, Persian, and Turkish, reflects Islam's different conceptualizations of sovereignty and relations between government and the governed. These languages in their classical forms did not have a term for *citizen*. The neologism *muwatan* was coined in the nineteenth century.[35] When confronted with the task of finding a term to convey the meaning of freedom, the Arabic translators of Napoleon's famous declaration to the Egyptian people upon his arrival there in 1798 used the word *hurriyya*, which previously was a term used to distinguish free men from slaves.[36] In Turkish and Arabic, the word now used for independence, *istiqlal*, prior to the latter half of the nineteenth century was principally an Ottoman administrative term which meant "to act alone," and referred to the discretionary powers of high officials.[37]

In addition to coining terms to apply to concepts of government that were introduced in the eighteenth and nineteenth centuries, Muslim proponents of democracy began to "scour religious literature in search of prescriptions for the rights of the individual and checks on state power."[38] Rifa‘a Tahtawi (1801–1873), for example, after a traditional education in Egypt, went to Paris as part of a mission sent by Muhammad Ali. He returned to Cairo and spent much of the remainder of his life reconciling Islam with Western notions of democracy. Tahtawi contended, for example, that the French idea of freedom had its equivalent in the Islamic concept of *adl* (justice, right, equality).[39] This exercise and others like it, however, tended to treat Quranic

---

[34]Cited in James Walsh, "The Sword of Islam," *Time* (June 15, 1992), pp. 30, 34.

[35]Enayat, *Modern Islamic Political Thought*, p. 126.

[36]Bernard Lewis, *The Political Language of Islam* (Chicago: University of Chicago Press, 1988), pp. 109–111.

[37]*Ibid.*, p. 112.

[38]Enayat, *Modern Islamic Political Thought*, p. 131.

[39]*Ibid.*, p. 131.

verses out of context and to stretch analogies, suggesting in the process that classical Islamic political doctrine and European democratic theory were quite different.

The organization of Islam, like its political doctrine, has also not made the tasks of state- and nation-building any easier. There is, for example, no organizational equivalent in Sunni Islam to the Christian church. The ulema, not having an organization autonomous of government, seldom imposed their will on political authorities. "Unwilling to admit the de facto dualism of religious and political affairs to which they had accommodated themselves," the ulema had to adopt a discourse that "tended to be expressive, defending the status quo, rather than practical, instigating fundamental change."[40] While they occasionally mobilized portions of the population, as they did against the Napoleonic invasion of Egypt at the end of the eighteenth century and as they did more frequently in Shi'i Iran, the ulema generally lacked the organizational structure necessary to institutionalize their leadership and power, and so to constrain government. Moreover, while the church served as a model for secular political organization in the West, the absence of an equivalent organization in Sunni Islam meant that secular groupings had no archetype to emulate.

Islamic doctrine and the comparative weakness of the religion's formal organizational structure do not alone account for the absence in the premodern Middle East of a "prolific network of institutions . . . between the state and the individual . . . which simultaneously connects the individual to authority and protects the individual from total political control," thereby creating what has been termed "civil society."[41] Indeed, in the Middle East prior to the rise of modern nation-states, subjects were in any case protected from "total political control" by a rich array of family, tribal, communal, and other groupings. The power of government over individuals was checked by these cohesive social units as well as by the physical barriers mentioned earlier. It is true, however, that there were comparatively few linkages between those traditional organizations and government. Their role was not so much to participate in government to affect decisions, but rather to avoid its reach. When governments, as a result of technological mod-

---

[40]Moore, "On Theory and Practice," p. 114.

[41]Bryan S. Turner, "Orientalism and the Problem of Civil Society in Islam," in *Orientalism, Islam, and Islamicists,* ed. by Asaf Hussain et al. (Brattleboro, Vt.: Aman Books, 1984), p. 27.

ernization, eventually did obtain the resources required to subdue far-flung populations, the traditional organizations of these peoples were simultaneously being undermined through the broader processes of modernization; thus were societies deprived of at least some of the network of institutions which comprise civil society and which both protect individuals and link them to government.

The degree to which Islam contributed to the weakness of civic organization is a highly contentious issue. Some scholars believe that intermediate groups situated between individuals and rulers confronted an impossibly difficult task in limiting arbitrary authority precisely because of Islamic theory and practice. Charles E. Butterworth argues, for example, that there is an absence of democracy in the Arab world because

> there is nothing within the history of Arabic political thought comparable to the radical break with the past effected by Machiavelli and Hobbes in the sixteenth and seventeenth centuries and then refined into a doctrine of liberal democracy. . . . In sum, then, the absence of an unquestioned, perhaps unquestionable, belief in the fundamental need for popular sovereignty is what primarily explains why political life in the Arab world differs so markedly from political life in the west."[42]

Other scholars deny that differences in religious doctrine and organization account for the presence of an established tradition of legitimate opposition to arbitrary governments in the West and the absence of such a tradition in Islam. Civil society in the West is said to have developed because of the prior existence of legal rights for vassals in feudalism, and because a strong, independent middle class emerged comparatively early in Europe.[43] Their equivalents were lacking in the Middle East. Also, prior to the nineteenth century in the Middle East, government was limited and remote, hardly affecting the lives of a great number of its nominal subjects. "It is a recurring historical

---

[42]Charles E. Butterworth, "State and Authority in Arabic Political Thought" in *The Foundations of the Arab State,* pp. 91–92, 111.

[43]See, for example, Turner, "Orientalism," p. 35, and Enayat, *Modern Islamic Political Thought,* pp. 131–135. According to Ira Lapidus, under feudalism vassals had "rights to be consulted, rights to be judged by peers and guarantees as to their incomes and properties. All of these are the basis of our parliamentary notions of democracy and ideas about 'no taxation without representation.' So here is a cultural, conceptual fact which reinforces the institutional differences between the two societies and has favored the formation of European democracies." Personal communication to the authors, September 20, 1988.

truth," according to Hazem Beblawi and Giacomo Luciani, "that demands for democratic participation become louder, sometimes unrestrainable, whenever the state must ask for sacrifices, be they under the form of increased revenue or reduced expenditure."[44] In the West, such demands for participation arose much earlier than in the Middle East because from the end of the feudal era in the fourteenth century the state began to acquire significant fiscal powers. But it was not until the nineteenth and even twentieth centuries that the unquestioned supremacy of government over financial and other matters made it the central focus for its subjects in the Middle East.

Even though Islam regulates the daily lives of most Middle Easterners and profoundly influences their beliefs and attitudes, politics is too complex a phenomenon to be determined entirely by religion, even such an all-embracing one as Islam. Socioeconomic factors have constituted a major contribution to the development of political authority structures and attitudes toward them, but precisely how and to what degree is difficult to determine. What can be said with certainty is that in the premodern Middle East, prior to the emergence of nation-states that regulate comparatively closely the affairs of their citizens, there was a functioning system of government that worked remarkably well and in which Islam played an important role. According to Ira Lapidus, this system was "composed at base of small-scale, local communities unified by an embracing religious affiliation—Islam . . . and organized and identified in lineage, tribal, and ethnic terms."[45] In the words of Albert Hourani, premodern Islamic societies comprised "not so much a single community as a group of communities each of which claimed the immediate loyalty of its members. These communities were regional, religious, or functional, or, to some extent, a mixture of all three."[46] The political regimes that prevailed over these local communities but only loosely regulated their affairs were comprised of royal courts and bureaucratic as well as quasi-feudal institutions, all of which were at least partially legitimated by Islam.

Before the rise of the nation-state in the Middle East, Islam did

---

[44]"Introduction," in *The Rentier State* (London: Croom Helm, 1987), p. 19.

[45]Ira Lapidus, *Contemporary Islamic Movements in Historical Perspective* (Berkeley: Institute of International Studies of the University of California, 1983), p. 50.

[46]Albert Hourani, *Arabic Thought in the Liberal Age, 1798–1939* (London: Oxford University Press, 1962), p. 29.

provide the essential ingredients for functioning political systems. It defined sociopsychological identities and presented an explicit code for the conduct of relations between Muslims and non-Muslims. A comprehensive legal system was supplied by the sharia and those ulema, including *qadis* (Muslim judges), skilled in legal interpretation and adjudication. Finally, Islam legitimated the ruler and, to a lesser extent, the system of governance by virtue of the Islamic injunction on subjects to obey established authority. That this system worked well is attested to by the accomplishments of the great Islamic empires, the first of which came into being over 1,300 years ago and the last of which, the Ottoman, was only finally extinguished in this century. Yet, it is also fair to say that from at least the eighteenth century, the states of the West, increasingly legitimated by nationalist ideologies and capable of mobilizing the energies of their citizens, were far more powerful than Muslim governments of the Middle East. The latter were unable to harness the energies and resources of the remarkably diverse and inward-looking groups of which Middle Eastern societies were composed. The most important of these groups were the various religious communities.

Religious Diversity

Sunni and Shiʻi Islam   There are two major branches of Islam—Sunni and Shiʻi, the former constituting almost 90 percent of the world's Muslims. This division originated in the seventh century as a political dispute between the Shiʻa (party or faction) of Ali, the cousin and son-in-law of the prophet Muhammad, and those who opposed his ascension to the caliphate in 656. The latter became known as Sunnis because of their identification with the Sunna (precedents set by the prophet) and their veneration of the "Golden Age" of Islam under the *Rashidun,* the first four successors (caliphs) to Muhammad (Abu Bakr, Umar, Uthman, and Ali). The Sunnis rose in revolt against the succession of Ali after the murder of the third caliph, Uthman. Muʻawiya, the governor of the Syrian province of the new Arab empire, cousin of Uthman and member of the aristocratic Umayyad family, led the uprising that culminated in 661 with the defeat of Ali's forces.

Muʻawiya created the Umayyad dynasty (661–750), and his son and successor, Yazid, finally ended the possibility that Ali's descendants might ultimately regain the caliphate by having Ali's second son,

Hussain, and his followers massacred at Karbala (in today's Iraq) in 680. From that time, differences between Sunnis and Shi'is, which had been confined until then to the issue of the succession to the caliphate, broadened to include ritual, legal, and theological matters. The schism ultimately took on ethnic and geographic dimensions, for over 50 percent of the world's Shi'is now reside in Iran. The other principal concentrations of them in the Middle East are in the Arab littoral countries of the Persian Gulf, including Iraq, Bahrain, Kuwait, the United Arab Emirates, and the Eastern Province of Saudi Arabia, although there are also significant Shi'i communities in Lebanon, North Yemen, and Syria.

Division of the *Dar al-Islam* (House of Islam) into Sunni and Shi'i has through history exacerbated the problems of state building for Sunnis. With the major exceptions of Fatimid Egypt (968–1171) and post-fifteenth-century Iran, as well as short periods in North Yemen prior to 1962 and Syria since the mid-1960s, the Sunnis have led every government in the area. The Ottomans, beset with the difficulties of ruling a far-flung, heterogeneous empire and having constantly to engage in warfare against the West, had also to contend with a condition of more or less permanent hostility with the Shi'i dynasties in Iran—first the powerful Safavids, subsequently the weaker Qajars. Ottoman-Persian relations, in the absence of religious division, may have taken a different course and one less enervating for both sides.

Of greater and more enduring importance to the issue of state formation in Sunni political systems has been the presence within them of groupings of Shi'is. The writ of government has run up to, but until recently not usually beyond, the boundaries of these communities. Their refractory nature resulted from their minority religious status and accompanying anxieties, and from the inherent weakness of premodern Islamic governments in comparison with the strength of Shi'i informal organizations.

The majority of Shi'is are known as Imamis, or Twelvers, because they trace the line of rightful descent from Ali, who is the first Imam, through twelve successors. The last, Muhammad al-Muntazar (Muhammad the Expected), vanished in about 873 and is expected to return as the *Mahdi* (savior) of humanity at a propitious time. The Twelver sect has adherents in Iran, Lebanon, Iraq, and many Arab countries of the Persian Gulf. In Iran, Twelver Shi'ism is the state religion and the faith of the great majority of the population. Another group of Shi'is, the Isma'ilis, is known as Seveners because they regard

Isma'il as the rightful seventh and last Imam. They are to be found principally in Pakistan, India, and Iran, while a few descendants of the Assassins—radical Isma'ilis who opposed Mamluke rule in the twelfth and thirteenth centuries in the Fertile Crescent—are still resident in the coastal mountains of central Syria. Still another sect, the Fivers, who trace a separate line of succession from the fifth Imam, are also known as Zaydis after the founder of the sect, Zayd, a grandson of the martyred Hussain, son of Ali. The Zaydis are to be found principally in Yemen.

The Kharajites are a non-Shi'i sect who broke with Ali and his supporters because of their disapproval of his willingness to compromise with his Umayyad opponents and his desire for the caliphate to be hereditary. Kharajite survivors, known as Ibadi Muslims, established themselves both in Oman, from whence in the eighteenth century they established a sizable empire, and in southern Algeria. The Druze, who currently reside principally in Lebanon, Syria, and Israel, are an offshot of the Fatimids, who controlled Egypt from the tenth to the twelfth centuries. The Alawis, so named by virtue of their veneration of Ali, who over the past two decades have dominated the Syrian government, are a heterodox sect whose claim to be Shi'i is disputed by some Muslims who consider their profound attachment to Ali, veneration of Jesus, and other of their beliefs to be heretical.

The proliferation of Shi'i sects, each with its own esoteric doctrine to which its supporters frequently adhere with extreme commitment, has rendered governmental control difficult and in some cases impossible. The Assassins are but an extreme case of Shi'i resistance to outside control. Holed up in their mountain redoubts, they fought off Mamluke rule for decades. Such geographical isolation has long characterized Shi'is living in Sunni-ruled lands. The mountains of South Lebanon and coastal Syria, the marshes of southern Iraq, the Jabal Akhdar (Green Mountain) of Oman, the rugged south central area of Anatolia in Turkey, and the oases of southern Algeria are among the traditional bastions of Shi'i and Ibadi preponderance.

In recent years Shi'is have poured out of these peripheral enclaves into the major cities of the Middle East in search of educational, vocational, and other opportunities. Even here, though, they have maintained cohesive communities, which in many instances are within sprawling slums. Like Shi'i societies in the remote areas they left, these new, urban ones are remarkably resistant to governmental control. The poor suburb of al-Thawra in Baghdad, for example, has since the 1960s been a center of Shi'i political activism, providing a constant test of the Iraqi government's control. What have become known in Beirut simply as "the suburbs," by which is meant the southern periphery of that once cosmopolitan Mediterranean city, are, along with the Beqa Valley and the South, the centers of Shi'i strength in Lebanon. The inability of government troops to enter those suburbs since 1975 and the only partial deployment of the much stronger Syrian forces in those suburbs as late as 1992 provide graphic examples of how Shi'i communities have through history succeeded in thwarting governmental control. In Bahrain, Kuwait, and the United Arab Emirates, ministates too small for geography to provide a buffer between community and government, Shi'is have erected a dense network of social institutions centered on clubs, homes, mosques, *diwaniyyas* (assemblies), and *hussainiyyas* (centers for mourning). This network performs the function of sharply defining the community's identity and reinforcing its separateness from Sunnis and their government.

Doctrinal elements of Shi'ism have facilitated challenges to Sunni hegemony and frustrated state-building efforts. *Taqiyya,* the practice of disguising one's true beliefs to hide them from a potential oppressor, is a quietist Shi'i response to perceived threats. Activist political behavior is also condoned by Shi'i doctrine, which emphasizes usurpation of power by the Sunnis, the martyrdoms of Imams Ali and Hussain, and the sufferings of Shi'is everywhere. The themes of usurpation and martyrdom, for example, are portrayed vividly in annual Ashura rites, which commemorate the martyrdom of Hussain in the form of a passion play conducted in the streets. Prior to the Islamic revolution in Iran, *ta'ziyyas,* as passion plays are called there, were used as a vehicle of political protest and mobilization. The evil Yazid, the Umayyad caliph who had Hussain killed, was portrayed as being analogous to the shah.[47]

Further reinforcing the solidarity of Shi'is and delineating the border that separates them from Sunnis is the Shi'i theory and practice of *ijtihad* (interpretation). From the beginning of the tenth century, Sunnis tended to restrict further interpretation, so the "door of ijti-

---

[47]Peter J. Chelkowski, ed., *Ta'ziyeh: Ritual and Drama in Iran* (New York: New York University Press, 1979).

had," if not altogether closed, was nearly so. The possibility that the-
ologians and jurists could apply independent, novel reasoning when
interpreting the Quran and the Sunna was substantially reduced.
Shi'is, on the other hand, never concurred in this conservative step.
Their doctrinal tradition emphasized independence. That predisposition was structurally reinforced by the existence of *mujtahids*, which is
the term given to Shi'i ulema, or mullahs as they are known in Iran,
and means "those who interpret." The practice of *ijtihad* thus under-
scored the importance to Shi'is of their ulema, providing the need and
justification for an independent clergy which Sunni Islam has always
lacked. The Shi'i ulema have thus provided an organizational backbone to their religious community and in so doing further enhanced its
distinctive and separate nature. This independence has clearly hampered the integrative tasks of state-building of those Sunni-dominated
governments that have presided over Shi'is.[48]

But doctrinal differences between Shi'is and Sunnis can be
overemphasized. Both are Muslims and as such believe in the same
pillars of the faith. There are few sharp divergences in their legal systems. As Bernard Lewis observes, divisions between them are "not as
rigid as the differences between Protestants and Catholics, or between
the different Protestant churches in Christendom."[49] In communities
with but one mosque, for example, Sunnis and Shi'is both pray in it.
Among Sunnis there is widespread respect and reverence for Ali and
Hussain. So there are enough similarities to facilitate amicable communal relations. Conversely, there are sufficient differences to stimulate antagonisms and conflicts. Which condition prevails is determined
more by the larger environment within which Sunni–Shi'i relations are
conducted than by factors inherent to the faiths themselves.

Al-Islam al-rasmi Versus al-Islam al-sha'bi   (Establishment
versus Populist Islam.) Most religions, and especially scripturalist ones
that are founded on a corpus of written doctrine, such as the Quran,
the Torah, or the Bible, have both established, official versions and
populist, unofficial variants. Establishment religion is that which
adheres closely to the ideal as described in texts and interpreted by

---

[48]For a recent example of Shi'i resistance, see Augustus Richard Norton, *Amal and the Shia: Struggle for the Soul of Lebanon* (Austin, Tex.: University of Texas Press, 1987).

[49]Bernard Lewis, "The Shi'a in Islamic History," in *Shi'ism, Resistance, and Revolution*, ed. by Martin Kramer (Boulder, Colo.: Westview Press, 1987), p. 22.

religious scholars. In many instances it is a state religion and as such is formally bound up in the legitimacy of government.[50] Populist religion, on the other hand, comprises those religious beliefs and practices which prevail among the people; it emanates from the underside, the periphery of society. Residence in outlying provinces or sprawling slums, illiteracy, and other factors that impede access to religious scholars and written texts, distance populations from established religions and make possible the existence of lively populist movements.

Virtually throughout Islamic history, there have been official and populist Islams, and both have political relevance. Muslim rulers have typically sought to cloak themselves in the legitimacy provided by al-Islam al-rasmi. In return for material favors and recognition of their status, the ulema have generally facilitated that legitimation process by using their prerogatives accordingly. Preaching Friday sermons that underscore obedience to authority, issuing *fatwas* (Islamic legal opinions) supportive of governmental policies, and in general by emphasizing the inseparability of Islam and government, the establishment ulema have contributed to the close identification of al-Islam al-rasmi with the government in control.

Relations between governmental power and populist Islam have been more ambivalent. Recognizing the mobilizational capacities of an Islam that is not under the direct control of the ulema and that frequently contains highly emotive beliefs and practices, rulers have been wary of al-Islam al-sha'bi. One approach has been to outlaw various manifestations of it. In the latter half of the nineteenth and early part of the twentieth centuries in Egypt, for example, the government, under pressure from European powers, sought to suppress what it termed the "excesses of popular religion."

Many of these efforts were directed at Sufi *tariqas* (orders), which are brotherhoods of Islamic mystics. Sufism, a search for divine knowledge through the emotions rather than purely through the intellect, emerged in the ninth century as an antidote to the austere, scripturalist, rational nature of Islam. It has always met with an ambivalent response from the ulema, some of whom have opposed Sufism and

---

[50]The prominent Egyptian writer Fu'ad Zakariyya dubs establishment Islam "Petro-Islam," for it is underpinned by financial subsidies from the conservative, oil-rich Arab states. For a discussion of Zakariyya's indictment of this type of Islam, see Issa J. Boullata, *Trends and Issues in Contemporary Arab Thought* (Albany: State University of New York Press, 1990), pp. 154–157.

others of whom have themselves joined *tariqas.* Large orders, such as the Naqshbandiyya, have swept through the Muslim world at various times in history, carrying with them the potential of widespread political mobilization and disruption. It is not surprising, therefore, that Egyptian governments, like many others, sought at early stages in their consolidation of power to bring Sufi orders under control. Initial efforts focused on ridding orders of distinctive practices that reinforced their identities and elicited strong loyalties and sacrifices from their members. Thus the practice of the *shaikh* (leader) of the order riding on horseback over the backs of prostrate members, as well as self-infliction of wounds, was outlawed in the late nineteenth century. The eventual subordination of Sufi orders to the state, however, was accomplished only years later, when a Supreme Council of Sufi Shaikhs was created, over which was appointed a Shaikh of Shaikhs, who in fact is a civil servant responsible to the government in Egypt.

Governments have also enlisted the support of the ulema in condemning various popular beliefs and practices as non- or anti-Islamic. The *zar,* for example, is a public ceremony in which women, led by an exorcist and accompanied by song and dance, seek to counter the influence of *jinns* (evil spirits) and, according to some interpretations, carve out a sphere of female autonomy in a male-dominated society.[51] Zars have long been officially discouraged in Egypt, yet they still occur. Saint worship, which in strict interpretations of Islam is considered irreligious, is nevertheless widespread. One manifestation of it is pilgrimages to tombs of those venerated as saints and whose *baraka* (heavenly blessing, grace, or power) is sought to assist in resolving personal and social problems. Living persons can also be attributed with baraka, which can reinforce claims to political leadership. Muhammad Ahmad, known as the Mahdi, cultivated a popular belief in his baraka to reinforce his leadership of the anti-British uprising in the Sudan in the 1880s. Mu'ammar Qaddafi is an example of someone having more or less failed in the attempt to appear as one possessed of baraka, while King Hassan of Morocco has enjoyed somewhat greater success in a similar effort.

Fitting loosely within the category of populist Islam are those

---

[51]On zars, see Cynthia Nelson, "Self, Spirit, Possession and World View—Illustration from Egypt," *International Journal of Social Psychiatry* 17:3 (1971):194. On popular religious festivals, see Joseph Williams McPherson, *The Moulids of Egypt* (Cairo: N.M. Press, 1941).

members of the ulema who have in recent years directed their messages to the masses disaffected from the state and from official Islam. Egypt has had the greatest number of such ulema, many of whose reputations have spread throughout the Arab world. Some, like Shaikhs Abd al-Hamid Kishk and Omar Abd al-Rahman, have been accused of being associated with violent underground *jama'at* (groups) of Islamic activists, while others, like Shaikh Mitwalli Sha'rawi, have with the aid of television succeeded in developing a style that appeals to Muslim masses but does not directly challenge established authority. The government of Egypt, like those of other Arab states, monitors very closely the activities of such preachers and occasionally restricts their movements, imprisons them, or closes the mosques in which they preach.

Mosques, in fact, are frequently sites of confrontation between official and organized variants of populist Islam—between government and Islamic activist opposition. Islamic activism, the roots of which are to be found partially in Islamic populism, has in recent years increasingly been centered both in some of the most venerable mosques in major Middle Eastern cities and in the newer, much more humble ones that have sprung up, especially in poorer urban areas. Frequently these new mosques are constructed or dedicated by private individuals and are nothing more than basements of apartment buildings, garages, or other empty spaces. In Egypt, between 1970 and 1981, the number of such *ahli* (private, independent) mosques increased from 20,000 to 40,000.[52] Governments have sought to control such religious spontaneity and underscore their own religiosity. They have attempted to control more closely the activities of imams who preach in mosques and to prevent the proliferation of private mosques. Religious faculties for the training of imams have been expanded out of the calculation that providing officially recognized training for imams and placing them on the public payroll will reinforce their political loyalties and commitment to al-Islam al-rasmi. Governments have also over the past two decades indulged in a frenzy of mosque building and restoration. The erection of new structures and the cleaning and repair of old ones is meant to attest to governmental devoutness and to attract worshipers away from mosques less closely supervised by the representatives of official Islam. The struggle

---

[52]Hamied Ansari, "The Islamic Militants in Egyptian Politics," *International Journal of Middle East Studies* 16 (March 1984):123–144.

to control mosques, which can serve as symbols of either al-Islam al-rasmi or al-Islam al-sha'bi, attests to the contemporary intensity of the conflict between these two Islams.

Non-Muslims About 3 percent of Middle Easterners, mainly in the southern Sudan, believe in non-Muslim tribal religions. Another 3 percent or so are Christian, less than 2 percent are Jewish, and small numbers of Baha'is, Zoroastrians, and believers in other religions are scattered throughout the area. The greatest concentration of Christians is in Egypt, where the some 5 to 8 million Coptic Orthodox and Coptic Catholics constitute more than 6 percent of the population. While Lebanese Christians, including Maronites (a Latin-rite church), Greek Orthodox, Greek Catholics, Armenian Orthodox, and various smaller sects, make up somewhat less than half of the Lebanese population, they number only around 2 million.[53] Jews, of whom there are fewer than 5 million, are now overwhelmingly concentrated in Israel, whereas prior to the creation of that state in 1948, significant communities of Sephardim, who are also termed Oriental Jews, were found in most Arab states. In Morocco, for example, 1 of every 25 citizens in 1948 was Jewish, whereas now the ratio is 1 of every 1,400, even though the 16,000 Jews still in Morocco constitute the largest community of Middle Eastern Jews outside Israel.[54] Despite the comparatively limited numbers of non-Muslims, they, in combination with Shi'is, have complicated state- and nation-building in the region.

From its inception, Islam accorded a subordinate but protected status to Christians and Jews, who as "people of the book" (Bible and Torah, respectively) were respected by Islam. They were obliged to pay a special tribute known as the *jizya,* but otherwise, like other *dhimmis* (tolerated peoples), their individual and collective rights, including those of worship, property, security, and legal autonomy, were recognized and protected. This arrangement was ultimately regularized by the Ottomans who, having captured Istanbul in 1453,

---

[53]Demographic statistics on the Middle East are notoriously unreliable, in part because governments are reluctant to release census figures that pertain to such sensitive questions as numbers of religious minorities. Lebanon, in fact, has not had a census since 1932 because the Christian-dominated government did not want it officially established that their confession is a minority.

[54]Dale F. Eickelman, "Changing Perceptions of State Authority: Morocco, Egypt and Oman," in *The Foundations of the Arab State*, p. 182.

appointed patriarchs of the Greek and Armenian Orthodox and Jewish communities. These minority groups were termed *millets,* a term that by the mid-nineteenth century had been broadened to include ethnic as well as religious communities. According to Suad Joseph, "The dhimmi and millet systems further deterred the development of state institutions," for they segmented the empire, the unity of which was limited to transitory conditions of factional balance.[55] The millets were themselves only loose collectivities, serving more as tax categories than cohesive, self-aware, and self-governing communities. Segmentation of the Ottoman political community and economy was further increased by the fact that religious and ethnic minorities tended to concentrate in various crafts and occupations.

Millets provided channels through which Western influence, both economic and intellectual, began to flow as the Ottoman Empire weakened. Through the Capitulations, which had originally been granted in the sixteenth century to resident foreign communities by Ottoman rulers to facilitate trade but which were subsequently utilized by the West to extract further concessions and were broadened to include local Christians and Jews, significant economic and legal advantages were provided to those minorities. As the "sick man of Europe" decayed further, the European powers, in their scramble to secure concessions, cultivated religious minorities. They legitimated their imperial ambitions by claiming to protect the persecuted. The French cemented ties to Maronite Christians in the Levant, a move the British countered by "protecting" the chief opponents of the Maronites, the Druze.[56] The Russians sought to expand their influence, particularly in Jerusalem, through the Russian Orthodox faith. For the European nations, missionaries performed not just religious but also political roles, mobilizing Eastern Christians in support of Western ideas and specific political claims.

By the beginning of this century, the Ottoman millet system had

---

[55]Joseph, "Muslim-Christian Conflicts," p. 2

[56]The relationship between the French and the Maronites was so intense and wide ranging that in the wake of the Druze-Maronite conflict of 1840–1841 Viconte Onffroy, a French colonial official, saw fit to try to alleviate the situation by encouraging Maronites to migrate to Algeria where they could participate with the French in the colonization of that country. On his plan, see Daad Bou Malhab Atallah, *Le Liban, Guerre Civile ou Conflict International? A Partir du Milieu du XIXe Siecle* (Beirut: Dar al-Hurriyat, 1980), pp. 247–248.

all but broken down under pressures resultant from increasing Western influence and the expanding power of the Ottoman state. Spreading ideas of secular nationalism inspired hope among minorities who sought to escape their subordinate status. In the pre–nation-state period when political control had been weak and intermittent, religious identities had not been sources of major political conflict and had been a sufficient basis upon which to organize communal affairs and relations with higher authority. But the European secular model held out the promise to minorities in the Middle East that religion could be effectively separated from politics. In this way, the political community could be redefined so that Muslims and non-Muslims would be equal citizens. As Middle Eastern governments began to demand more of their subjects, so did those subjects, Muslims and non-Muslims alike, increasingly insist on new relationships with that expanding authority. Political ideologies thus developed in tandem with the process of state formation.

THE EMERGENCE OF MODERN STATES AND IDEOLOGIES

Comparison with Europe

The emergence of European nation-states, accompanied as it was by a protracted civil war, nevertheless occurred in more favorable circumstances than those surrounding the state-building process in the Middle East. The principle of secularism had in much of Western Europe been established by the late eighteenth century.[57] From the seventeenth century, the European economy had been expanding rapidly. The bourgeoisie, that class to which secular nationalism most appealed, gained the upper hand against the aristocracy in the nine-

---

[57]Secularization in Europe, which began with peasant revolts and the Reformation initiated by Martin Luther in the sixteenth century and which was then facilitated by the great religious wars of the seventeenth century, finally came to fruition in conjunction with and possibly only because of the development of modern industrial society. On the travail that accompanied European secularization and its implications for the Middle East, see Bassam Tibi, *The Crisis of Modern Islam: A Preindustrial Culture in the Scientific-Technological Age* (Salt Lake City, Utah: University of Utah Press, 1988), pp. 127–148; and Tamara Sonn, *Between Qur'an and Crown: The Challenge of Political Legitimacy in the Arab World* (Boulder, Colo.: Westview Press, 1990), pp. 1–30.

teenth century. Moreover, Europe was not at the mercy of stronger imperial powers constantly meddling in its internal affairs.

In the Middle East, none of these favorable conditions obtained. In the nineteenth century, as the Iranians and Ottomans began to modernize their societies in order to defend themselves against Western domination, they encountered difficulties in assimilating, organizing, and mobilizing their populations. They drew upon two sources in constructing ideologies to facilitate those tasks: religion and secular nationalism. While the latter came to assume greater importance, it nevertheless never succeeded in supplanting religion as a major source of politically relevant personal identity. This is because "the relationship between nationalism and religion in the Middle East is complex and curvilinear. Both value structures are to varying extents held by an overwhelming majority of the population and generate at times mutually reinforcing, and at other times conflicting, patterns of behavior."[58] Thus political ideologies in the Middle East resemble a museum of intellectual history, for they range from Marxist-Leninism, to classical liberalism, to versions of Islamic fundamentalism that look to the Golden Age of the seventh century for their inspirations.

Whereas European economies were expanding rapidly during the state-formation period, Middle Eastern economies grew unevenly and at a much slower pace. Imperialism did stimulate production of some commodities in the Middle East, especially agricultural raw materials such as cotton and silk, but it undermined production of many others, particularly manufactured goods. The net result was that economies did not expand with sufficient speed or across a broad enough front to provide states with the additional revenues required to finance the necessary institutions. This failure, in turn, reduced the speed and extent to which segments of the population were integrated into the new nation-states. Because states and economies could not demonstrate an ability effectively to provide the resources necessary to ensure the livelihoods of ever-expanding numbers of citizens, the population clung to kinship, sect, and client loyalties that had traditionally provided sources of employment and security.

In Lebanon, where rapid economic growth did occur, the state, hobbled at the outset by the unwillingness of the leaders of the coun-

---

[58]G. Hossein Razi, "Legitimacy, Religion and Nationalism in the Middle East," *American Political Science Review* 84 (March 1990): p. 82.

try's major religious sects to surrender their powers to the new government, never achieved sufficient control over the economy to wean citizens away from their dependence on confessions and kinship groups. Those primordial ties provided jobs, licenses, and other resources which the state could not deliver impartially or directly, a fact of which the Lebanese were all too aware. The Lebanese state, according to Samir Khalaf, "compared to other forms of primordial loyalties and communal allegiences, has always been an enfeebled and residual institution."[59]

In those countries where the state did achieve greater leverage over primordial groupings, faltering economies have subsequently eroded state power, thereby clearing the way for primordialism to reemerge or other challenges to the state to arise. In Egypt, for example, the Egyptian government expanded very rapidly after Nasser consolidated his power in the mid-1950s. The necessary resources were provided by the confiscated assets of foreigners and wealthy Egyptians, while foreign aid made available further revenues to underwrite Nasser's Arab socialism. A fairly comprehensive social welfare system was created, education was made free at all levels, graduates were guaranteed jobs in the civil service, and government employment mushroomed. The state's domination of the economy and its ability to provide resources to citizens underpinned the appeal of Nasserism, an ideology that combined Arab nationalism with socialist ideas and practices while being careful not to appear as anti-Islamic. By the mid-1960s, however, it was apparent that the regime had overextended, there being insufficient economic resources to support such a large state. Erosion of the appeal of Nasserism to Egyptians closely paralleled deterioration in the government's ability to provide adequate jobs, welfare payments, health and educational facilities, and the like. Under Sadat and Mubarak, as economic growth has failed to keep pace with population expansion and the government's share of national wealth has also declined, so have a network of populist Islamic *jam'iyyat* (societies) moved to fill the breach. They provide unemployment insurance, textbooks and free tutors to poor students, clinics and hospitals, and other important services. Not surprisingly, the appeal of Islam as a political doctrine has grown accordingly. To many of those provided services by such societies, "Islam (and not the semi-secular state) is the solution"—the slogan of Egypt's Muslim Brother-

---

[59]Khalaf, *Lebanon's Predicament*, p. 234.

hood. That Islamic societies are becoming "a state within a state" attests to the continued deterioration of the government's ability to influence the lives of citizens.

Role of the Bourgeoisie   The comparatively slow expansion of Middle Eastern economies and, in cases like Lebanon, the state's limited control over resources, have set the Middle Eastern process of state-building apart from that of Europe. The role of independent merchants, manufacturers, and professionals (the *bourgeoisie*) was also vastly greater in Europe than it has been in the Middle East. The reasons for the relative weakness of the bourgeoisie in the Middle East are contentious. One view is that Islam is incompatible with the rise and existence of an independent entrepreneurial class. Ernest Gellner, for example, has argued that because Islam propagates the belief that "the duty of the state is to proscribe evil and enforce good," it habituates Muslims to the idea that resources "should be distributed according to moral and political requirements, and not be left to the vagaries of the market."[60] Gellner implies that the hostility toward a market-based economy creates an inhospitable environment for entrepreneurialism. On the other hand, Maxime Rodinson, a noted French scholar of the Middle East, has written a lengthy book to dispel the belief that Islamic doctrine is hostile to entrepreneurialism.[61] Fawzy Mansour attributes the weakness of the Middle Eastern bourgeoisie to the fact that judicial authority was insufficiently independent and absolute to guarantee impartial, binding adjudication of contractual disputes.[62] Alternatively, Peter Mansfield contends that "a self-confident and enterprising Islamic bourgeoisie did exist in the Middle Ages but it never succeeded in achieving political power as a class because from around the eleventh century this was in the hands of the Mamlukes and other Turkish and Caucasian military."[63] Since these rulers frequently were of tribal origin and more interested in waging war and in agriculture, "They tended to leave trade and commerce to European traders and to non-Muslim ethnic minorities (such

---

[60]Ernest Gellner, "Foreword," in *From Nationalism to Revolutionary Islam,* ed. by Said Amir Arjomand (London: Macmillan, 1984), p. x.

[61]Maxime Rodinson, *Islam and Capitalism* (London: Allen Lane, 1974).

[62]Fawzy Mansour, *The Arab World: Nation, State and Democracy* (London: Zed Books, 1992), p. 72.

[63]Peter Mansfield, *The Arabs* (London: Penguin Books, 1985), pp. 84–85.

as Greeks, Armenians, and Jews) who were, however, completely at the mercy of the despotic power of the Ottoman state."[64] The Middle Eastern bourgeoisie, lacking independence from government, could, in this view, be neither the economic nor the political equivalent of the bourgeoisie in the West that played such an important role in creating capitalism and strong nation-states.

After reasonably strong states did emerge in the Middle East in the 1950s and 1960s, elites in control of them then used those states "to inhibit the development of an independent bourgeoisie . . . which might have threatened political stability" by demanding democratization of those polities and liberalization of their economies.[65] Moreover, Middle Eastern economies have been insufficiently independent and developed to provide adequate foundations upon which indigenous merchants, financiers, and manufacturers might construct internationally competitive enterprises. Hanna Batatu summarizes the comparative role of the bourgeoisie in Europe and the Arab world as follows:

> It is not an accident that the "third estate" played an important role in the emergence of such European nation-states as France or England in the dawn of the modern age, or that the process of German unification was impelled in the 1860s in part by the manufacturing classes of the Rhine region, or that the shipping, manufacturing, and commercial interests in America's thirteen colonies were an important motive force in the 1780s behind the trend toward a strong federal government. In the Arab countries the counterparts of these classes have never been strong in the modern era. International economic relationships have been so structured, the financial, organizational, and technical powers of the multinational corporations have been so overwhelming, and Arab conditions so underdeveloped that, with some exceptions, Arab private entrepreneurs have not been able to grow autonomously, or have been able to thrive only as appendages of either the multinational corporate system or of their own governments.[66]

[64]Bassam Tibi, *Arab Nationalism: A Critical Enquiry* (New York: St. Martin's Press, 1981), p. 51.

[65]Lisa Anderson, "The State in the Middle East and North Africa," *Comparative Politics* 20 (October 1987):11.

[66]Hanna Baṭatu, "The Pan-Arab Experience of Syria's Ba'th Party," in *Arab Nationalism and the Future of the Arab World*, ed. by Hani A. Faris (Belmont, Mass.: Association of Arab-American University Graduates, 1986), p. 63.

Classes Created Through State Formation

Whereas in Europe the state and its ideological underpinning, which was provided by secular nationalism, were fashioned by the bourgeoisie, in the Middle East the state emerged independently of that or any other class. Created as a result of the efforts by ruling elites to defend their territories against the West, and subsequently by colonial administrators, the state in the Middle East was not the product of the bourgeoisie nor of secular nationalism. Instead, the state itself fostered the growth of certain classes and specific ideologies.[67] Seeking to expand and centralize their personal control, rulers "were logically moved to weaken the classes most identified with Islam, especially the ulema, and to establish what is often called secularism, although state control over religion would be a more accurate designation."[68]

Muhammad Ali, who ruled Egypt for most of the first half of the nineteenth century, was the first major Middle Eastern ruler to adopt this strategy. Having been assisted by the ulema in his rise to power amid the chaotic conditions that prevailed after the withdrawal of the French expeditionary force in 1801, once he received Istanbul's formal confirmation of his status as ruler he quickly subordinated the ulema to his will. He and his successors progressively divorced religion from education by sending Egyptians to Europe for advanced training and by creating a state-sponsored educational system. Dar al-Ulum, the famous teacher's training college, along with other state educational institutions and private, European-sponsored ones, gradually marginalized al-Azhar, the thousand-year-old premier Egyptian institution of Islamic learning. Graduates of the state educational system and private European schools played a prominent role in fashioning the secular version of Egyptian nationalism that contributed to the Ahmad al-Arabi and 1919 revolutions, the first of which, in 1882, caused the British to invade Egypt and the second of which resulted in their granting Egypt nominal independence.

Subsequent state-builders elsewhere in the region similarly fostered changes that simultaneously undermined traditional Islam and

---

[67]For an analysis of Tunisia and Libya from this perspective, see Lisa Anderson, *The State and Social Transformation in Tunisia and Libya, 1830–1980* (Princeton, N.J.: Princeton University Press, 1986).

[68]Nikki R. Keddie, "Ideology, Society and the State in Post-Colonial Muslim Societies," in *State and Ideology in the Middle East and Pakistan*, ed. by Fred Halliday and Hamza Alavi (New York: Monthly Review Press, 1988), p. 11.

its leaders, created new social groups and classes, and contributed to the growth of bureaucracies, armies, and other modern state institutions. Ataturk and Reza Shah (whose careers will be examined in greater detail in Chapter 5), for example, both encouraged women to enter the work force so that their labor power would be available to the state and the hold of traditional Islam over them would be reduced. Ataturk's assault on Islam and the Turkish ulema was relentless, including such measures as the abolition of the caliphate, banning of the *fez* (hat with Islamic connotations) and *tekkes* (Dervish groups), and substituting the roman for the Arabic alphabet. Reza Shah, confronting ulema whose independent power was reinforced by Shi'i doctrine and by the financial autonomy resulting from their access to *zakat* and *khums* (Islamic taxes) and from control over income from *waqf* (religious endowments), had to tread more warily. That neither Reza Shah nor his son, Muhammad Reza Shah, ever fully succeeded in subordinating Iranian ulema to the state was made abundantly clear by the revolution of 1978–1979. The growing influence of Islam over Turkish society and politics suggests that Ataturk's steamroller approach suppressed Islam but did not eradicate it as a root source for social and political thought and behavior.

Muhammad Ali, Ataturk, Reza Shah, and other Middle Eastern modernizing rulers greatly enhanced the size and power of the bureaucratic middle class as a by-product of their expansion of public bureaucracies, civilian and military alike. That class, whose interests were coincidental with an expanding state, became the primary bearers of nationalism, whether in the Turkish, Iranian, Egyptian, or Arab variants. Before seizing power in their own right in Turkey, in Egypt, and elsewhere in the Arab world (and briefly in Iran during the Musaddiq interlude from 1951 to 1953), this class had to overcome not only traditional rulers but also another class that had likewise risen to preeminence as a result of the state-formation process. That class comprised rural elites, usually landowners, whose support was required by modernizing governments in order to control the countryside, extract revenues from it, and provide political support against various opponents.

The importance of the landowning class varied in proportion to the strength of the central government. In Turkey, where Ottoman reforms in the nineteenth century paved the way for Ataturk's unrelenting centralization of power, the government did not have to rely heavily on rural notables to control the peasantry or extract revenues.

Thus Ataturk's Turkish nationalism has always been much more closely associated with the bureaucratic middle class than with any other
social force. In Iraq, by contrast, the precarious hold of the regime in
Baghdad forced King Faisal's government to rely heavily on large
landowners and tribal shaikhs. As David Pool has argued, government
in Iraq was comprised of a tripartite coalition consisting of landown-
ers-shaikhs, bureaucrats, and the king with his entourage.[69]

Similarly, in Egypt governments have since the Muhammad Ali
period relied on landowners for purposes of rural control and extraction. As a result, landowners, despite having been subjected to three
agrarian reforms during the Nasser period, have been amazingly successful in maintaining their presence within the political elite.[70] In
Iran, large landowners comprised a key element of support for the
regime of Reza Shah. His son, who wanted greater political autonomy,
sought to undermine some of their power through the land reforms
that he promulgated in 1963. While he did succeed in reducing their
political influence, the loss of the political support of landowners
helped contribute to the shah's overthrow in 1979.

The landlord class brought into existence by state-building contributed some famous leaders to national movements, such as Sa'd
Zaghlul in Egypt. In general, however, this class was not as stridently
nationalist, nor did it exhibit as much ideological homogeneity as the
bureaucratic middle class. Both Islamic reformism and secularism
attracted the landowning class, further exacerbating fissiparous tendencies characteristic of most political organizations based on rural
notables. Landowners tended to be classic liberals, favoring a restricted rather than an interventionist role for government, which put them
at odds with forces seeking to build stronger states. The period of
landowner ascendancy, which was the first half of the twentieth century, has been referred to as the liberal era.

Conflict between the two major classes that had been fostered by
state-building processes came to a head after World War II. In most
instances, the bureaucratic middle class was able to shoulder aside
landowners and other elements of the ancien régime. The success of

---

[69]David Pool, "From Elite to Class: The Transformation of Iraqi Political Leadership,"
in *The Integration of Modern Iraq*, ed. by Abbas Kelidar (New York: St. Martin's Press,
1979), pp. 63–87.

[70]See Leonard Binder, *In a Moment of Enthusiasm: Political Power and the Second
Stratum in Egypt* (Chicago: University of Chicago Press, 1978).

the bureaucratic middle class was due to its close association with the military, to the discrediting of landowners and their allies as defenders of privilege and collaborators with imperialism, and to the superior organization characteristic of middle-class politics. Members of the bureaucratic middle class were strong proponents of secular nationalist ideologies, despite the fact that the large majority of these countries' populations remained religious traditionalists. The existence of this gap, and the failure to bridge it, accounts in large measure for "the return of Islam" in the 1970s and 1980s.

THE CONTENDING IDEOLOGIES

Arab Nationalism

While the state-based nationalisms of Turkey, Iran, and Egypt were from the outset propagated by modernizing rulers, the history of Arab nationalism was different. The earliest manifestations of the Arab Awakening, as George Antonius called it, were the writings of Syrian and Lebanese intellectuals, both Muslim and Christian.[71] In the second half of the nineteenth century, these writers began to articulate thoughts of Arab distinctiveness and identity. Theirs was a response to the increasing emphasis on Turkish ethnicity and, for the Christians at least, Islam, the two chief alternative beliefs/identities through which their proponents sought to legitimate and perpetuate the Ottoman Empire.

Another factor that stimulated the Christians' search for a new political ideology was the breakdown in Muslim–Christian relations that ensued after the withdrawal of Egyptian forces from Syria in 1839. Ibrahim Pasha, Muhammad Ali's son, had sought the support of religious minorities after occupying Syria in 1831. "In every town he occupied," observes Kamal Salibi, "Ibrahim removed the traditional restrictions imposed on Christians and Jews and placed these communities on an equal footing with Moslems."[72] Christians were even granted exemptions from impositions levied on Muslims and Druze.

---

[71]George Antonius, *The Arab Awakening: The Story of the Arab National Movement* (Beirut: Khayyat's, 1955).

[72]Kamal S. Salibi, *The Modern History of Lebanon* (New York: Fredrik A. Praeger Publishers, 1965), p. 28.

When Egyptian protection was withdrawn less than a decade later, Christians, in particular, came under threat from Syrian Muslims who resented their favorable treatment and collaboration, real or imagined.

Christian ideas of Arabism and modes of expressing it were also influenced by educational experiences in Western-supported institutions, most important of which was the Syrian Protestant College, which subsequently became the American University of Beirut. The Arabist literary *nahda* (Renaissance) was led by such Christian scholars as Nasif al-Yaziji (1800–1871), Faris al-Shidyaq (1805–1887), and Butrus al-Bustani (1819–1883). Subsequently, organizations of intellectuals began to spring up, and in 1875 the first "secret society" with a specifically political intent was organized at the Syrian Protestant College.

Christian Arabs, who shared ethnic and linguistic but not religious identities with fellow Arabs, sought to emphasize Arab history and the Arabic language while deemphasizing or altogether eliminating religion as a source of personal and national political identity. In one variant of Christian-propagated Arab nationalism, Antun Sa'ada identified common geographical origins in Greater Syria as the tie that should bind together Syrians, Iraqis, Jordanians, and Palestinians. Sa'ada founded the Syrian Social Nationalist Party in 1932. It was a major force in Lebanese and Syrian politics until the early 1960s and was still operating in the early 1990s.[73]

Ba'thism, the most successful of the intellectual trends within Arab nationalism in that it actually came to power in two states, is most heavily indebted for its principal ideas to the Greek Orthodox thinker and activist Michel Aflaq. His way of dealing with the issue of Islam was to relegate it to the status of having been a historically formative force but one with no specific contemporary ideological or political role. By saying that Islam *was* Arab nationalism, Aflaq could then go on to spell out a romantic, vague, but essentially secular interpretation of that nationalism. Similarly, versions of Arab nationalism that have drawn most heavily on Marxist theories are also typically the products of Christians. George Habash, for example, is a Greek Orthodox doctor trained at the American University of Beirut. Prior to founding the

---

[73]On the Syrian Social Nationalist Party, also known as the PPS, see Labib Zuwiyya Yamak, *The Syrian Social Nationalist Party: An Ideological Analysis* (Cambridge, Mass.: Harvard Middle Eastern Monograph Series, vol. 16, 1966).

Marxist-oriented Popular Front for the Liberation of Palestine, Habash organized the radical Arab Nationalist Movement, which established branches in numerous Arab countries.

Although Christians contributed disproportionately to the Arabist literary revival of the late nineteenth century, the emergence of the Arabist protonationalist movement shortly before and during World War I, and then its conversion into full-fledged Arab nationalism after that time, was due principally to the efforts of Muslim political activists.[74] Like Christians, they had increasingly been alienated by the Ottoman elite's growing emphasis on Turkish ethnicity and language, which, among other things, prejudiced their chances for recruitment and promotion in the Ottoman bureaucracy. Muslim Arab nationalists of this era were also influenced by Islamic modernism or reformism, which held that a revitalization of the true Islam—the Islam of their ancestors—would necessarily restore those to whom Islam was first revealed, the Arabs, to preeminence in the Muslim world. Following the collapse of the Ottoman Empire, Arab nationalism spread rapidly in the newly created Arab states, especially those in the Arab heartland stretching from the Mediterranean coast to the Iran-Iraq border. The relative paucity of wataniyya, combined with the occupation of Syria, Iraq, Palestine, and Lebanon by the British and French, underlay the attraction of al-qawmiyyat al-Arabiyya. The rapid expansion of state structures under colonial control stimulated the growth of the bureaucratic middle class, to whom Arab nationalism had a particularly strong appeal.

Sati al-Husri (1882–1968), a prominent Muslim Arab nationalist whose writings served as textbooks for Arab students of post–World War II generations, personified many of these broader trends. His father, a Syrian, was the Ottoman Qadi in Yemen. Sati al-Husri received a traditional Islamic education. Subsequently he studied in Europe before being assigned by the Ottoman government to a number of teaching and administrative posts. During the twilight of the Ottoman Empire, he made contact with the Arab nationalist underground in Syria. When an Arab state under Amir Faisal was created in Damascus in 1920, Sati al-Husri was named minister of education.

---

[74]For an analysis of the changing historiography of the Arab nationalist movement, see Rashid Khalidi et al., *The Origins of Arab Nationalism* (New York: Columbia University Press, 1991).

After the French thwarted that attempt at statehood some four months later, he accompanied Faisal to Iraq, where the latter was proclaimed king and al-Husri was appointed dean of the Baghdad University Law School. In 1941 he was deported to Syria, following a British-backed coup to overthrow the anti-British government of Rashid Ali al-Gailani. He later went on to Cairo, where for 20 years he worked for the Arab League, which had been founded in 1945.

Sati al-Husri's career reveals much about Arab nationalism. An Ottoman official, he rejected Ottomanism for Arabism. Educated in Islamic schools, he modified Islamic formulations to accommodate European conceptualizations of nationalism. His writings inspired innumerable students and political activists, including Michel Aflaq. His very presence in Cairo from 1947 to 1966 not only served to spread Arab nationalist ideas among Egyptians but also, from the mid-1950s, provided tangible evidence of Nasser's claim that Egypt (and by implication Nasser himself) should be leader of the Arabs.[75] Sati al-Husri, like other prominent intellectual Arab nationalists such as Aflaq, was not just a political thinker but also a symbol exploited in inter-Arab struggles for power and by governments seeking to legitimate themselves.

By the 1960s Arab nationalism appeared to have triumphed. Leading Arab states vied with one another in the claim to be the purest embodiment of that ideology. But their very audacity and grandiose claims, their inability to develop adequately their economies and, ultimately, their defeat by Israel in 1967 not only undermined those governments but eroded the appeal of Arab nationalism itself. That process was further hastened by the new balance of power in inter-Arab politics. Conservative Arab states, especially those in the Gulf, had always been skeptical of Arab nationalism, both because of its radicalism and because it had been used as a foreign policy tool against them by Egypt, Syria, Iraq, and other Arab states. These conservative states, therefore, seized the opportunity to undercut radical Arab nationalism. Their new oil wealth, especially after 1973, made it possible to offer incentives to Arab rulers to establish amicable state-to-state relations, while at the mass level those funds were used to

---

[75]On Sati al-Husri, see William L. Cleveland, *The Making of an Arab Nationalist: Ottomanism and Arabism in the Life and Thought of Sati al-Husri* (Princeton, N.J.: Princeton University Press, 1971); and Tibi, *Arab Nationalism.*

encourage the growth of Islamic ideas, or "Petro-Islam," at the expense of secular versions of Arab nationalism.

The speed with which Arab nationalism was displaced, however, cannot be explained entirely by the defeat in 1967, by the lure of petrodollars, or by the vagaries of inter-Arab politics. Arab nationalism had never been fully secularized or firmly established as the undisputed state idea of countries such as Egypt, Iraq, and Syria. Arab nationalists had seized power through the military and their ideology remained "confined to learned elites."[76] The states over which they presided were never strong enough to relate secular nationalism systematically to political institutions and hence to instruct citizens in precisely what being an Arab nationalist meant. Under these conditions, the political elite gave way to the inevitable by blurring the distinction between Arabism and Islam, for the latter is much more readily understood and accepted at the mass level. This left nationalist elites and their states vulnerable to political appeals couched in straightforward Islamic terminology.

Islamic Reformism

Two strains of Islamic political thought and action have attracted the support of Muslims for more than a century. That which appealed initially to the wealthy, partly Westernized elite, of whom landowners were the most important element, was a modernist, reformist Islam that took shape from the mid-nineteenth century as a result of interaction with European thought. Rifa'a Tahtawi, one of the earliest and most influential Islamic reformers, instructed his fellow Egyptians that Islam was compatible with European conceptions of state, nation, and patriotism. Jamal al-Din al-Afghani (1839–1897), a colorful Iranian thinker and political militant, advocated a "defensive modernization" of Islam, whereby it would be strengthened through a rediscovery of its heritage and by unification of Muslims under a single government. Afghani's ideas served as a point of departure for his Egyptian disciple Muhammad Abduh (1849–1905), whose Salafiyya movement emphasized that Islam could be revitalized only

---

[76]Saad Eddin Ibrahim, "The Concerns and the Challenges," in *Pan-Arabism and Arab Nationalism,* p. 62.

through Western-style rational inquiry and, unlike Afghani's message, by "cultural rather than political activity."[77] While Afghani's and Abduh's thoughts both contributed to the development of Arab nationalism through such thinkers as the Syrian Abd al-Rahman al-Kawakibi and also influenced Islamic revivalism through Abduh's disciple Rashid Rida, the main thrust of the Salafiyya movement was essentially apolitical, hence conservative. Abduh was himself a figure of the religious and social establishments, rising to the post of Qadi with the encouragement of Britain's Lord Cromer, the virtual ruler of Egypt.

Reformist Islam did not become a powerful political movement in its own right for several reasons. Its moderation and stress on accommodation cut it off from a mass base. It was appropriate for the conservative upper class, but that class itself was being challenged by the more radical bureaucratic middle class. When reformist Islam shaded in the direction of anti-imperialist political activism, it immediately encountered the opposition of the occupying power and the local government under its control. Afghani, one of whose followers assassinated Nasir al-Din Shah of Iran in 1896, elicited the fear and scorn of the British. He was eventually banished from Egypt. The more moderate Abduh, on the other hand, was patronized by Lord Cromer out of the calculation that he posed no serious political threat.

Another factor that prevented a reformist Pan-Islam from emerging as the dominant ideology to challenge colonialism was that its legitimacy was tarnished by the last ruling Ottoman sultan, Abd al-Hamid. He terminated the Young Ottomans' experiment with liberalism in 1876, hoping to substitute Pan-Islam for the appeal of political liberty. In so doing he further discredited Islam among those bent on reform, especially the members of the rising middle classes. Finally, moderate, reformist Islam was eclipsed during the colonial and immediate postcolonial periods by Arab nationalism and by Islamic revivalism because both of those alternatives embodied more activist responses to the threat posed by Western intervention and therefore had greater popular appeal.

Contemporary Islamic reformers, like their forerunners, are in

---

[77]Tibi, *Arab Nationalism*, p. 66. *Salaf* means "ancestors," referring to the leaders of Islam in the Golden Age.

conflict with more radical Islamicists. Fu'ad Zakariyya, for example, cautions Egyptian Islamic activists against religious dogmatism and the supposition that contemporary government can be based on Islamic ideals embodied in the Quran or sharia. According to him, "Islam is what Muslims have made of it in history; it is not some ahistorical system beyond human experience."[78] To him, revivalists stress the form rather than the content of Islam, placing undue emphasis on such matters as dress codes at the expense of substantive issues such as welfare and justice. Fu'ad Zakariyya's colleague, Faraj Fuda, an even more trenchant critic of revivalists and a staunch defender of secularism, was gunned down in the streets of Cairo in June 1992 by members of the Islamic Jihad organization.

Islamic Revivalism

Islamic revivalism, also referred to as fundamentalism, Islamic activism or populism, or simply as Islamism or Islamicism, can be traced back to rural tribesmen, such as those associated with the Mahdi in the Sudan or with Abd al-Qadir (1807–1883) in Algeria, who, like the Sudanese Mahdi, resisted foreign control with the aid of radical Islam. Gradually, Abd al-Qadir's movement and other rural uprisings were suppressed as remote areas and their populations were brought under state control. Accompanying that process was the emergence of a new social force to whom Islamic revivalism appealed. This group comprised those individuals who had been profoundly, and generally negatively, affected by the expansion of state power. Even though many had had modern educations, they remained excluded from the benefits and privileges enjoyed by those with better training and preferential access to the state.

Hassan al-Banna, for example, who founded the Muslim Brotherhood in Egypt in 1928, was a poorly paid schoolteacher in the provincial city of Isma'iliyya. Those he recruited to his cause were predominantly of similar lower-middle-class backgrounds. They saw in revivalist Islam a means of overcoming the social injustice they believed to be perpetrated by the secularists in control of the state.

---

[78]Fu'ad Zakariyya, *al-Haqiqa wa-l-Wahm fi al-Haraka al-Islamiyya al-Mu'asira (Reality and Delusion in the Contemporary Islamic Movement)*, cited in Boullata, *Trends and Issues*, p. 155.

Since the 1920s, Islamic revivalism in Egypt and elsewhere in the region has recruited heavily from such marginal elements, including those in traditional occupations threatened by modernization as well as recently urbanized, moderately well-educated individuals who have not been able to find employment commensurate with their educations and expectations.[79]

In recent years revivalism has also been attracting even those who are comparatively well situated in their social orders and political economies. This is due to a general erosion of the quality of life in the poorer countries and the widespread belief there that incumbent governments, seen as being subservient to the West, are responsible for the deterioration of services, rising unemployment, skyrocketing inflation, and corruption. In the rich Arab oil-exporting countries of the Gulf, revivalism attracts Shi'i as well as Sunni Muslims who chafe under the control of the family-based regimes that dominate those states and which are also seen to serve the interests of the West rather than their own populations.

The ideological worldview of revivalism, according to John Esposito, includes the following beliefs: Islam encompasses all aspects of life; shortcomings in Muslim societies result from deviations from the "straight path of Islam" in the direction of Western secularism and materialism; the renewal of society depends upon a return to Islam and the emulation of its earliest practices; Islamic law must replace Western-inspired legal codes; science and technology are acceptable but must be subordinated to Islam; and re-Islamization requires organizational activity. More radical Islamic revivalists believe that violent revolution is required to achieve these objectives because Muslims confront the power of the West and Zionism. They also contend that God has commanded Muslims to live under Islamic government; that governments not based exclusively on the sharia are illegitimate, as is "establishment" Islam; and that jihad against unbelievers, including Christians and Jews, is a religious duty.[80]

While in its extreme forms Islamic revivalism may well be incom-

---

[79]On recruitment of the former type, see Hanna Batatu, "Syria's Muslim Brethren," *Merip Reports* 110 (November–December 1982):12–20. On recruitment of newly urbanized lower-middle-class elements, see Hamied Ansari, *Egypt: The Stalled Society* (Albany: State University of New York Press, 1986), pp. 211–230.

[80]John L. Esposito, *Islam: The Straight Path* (New York: Oxford University Press, 1991), pp. 163–164.

patible with democracy, Islamic activists and their organizations throughout the Middle East have both called for and participated in *ta'addudiyya,* the process of political pluralization.[81] In Algeria, Egypt, Jordan, Kuwait, Sudan, Tunisia, and Yemen, Islamic movements have contested parliamentary elections. Throughout the region, Islamic activists are debating the relationship between Islam and democracy. One school of thought contends that the Quranic concepts of *shura* (consultation), *ijtihad* (interpretation, independent reasoning), and *ijma* (consensus) constrain autocracy or even underpin popular sovereignty. Another view, whose most articulate spokesperson was Egypt's Sayyid Qutb, is that democratization necessarily usurps God's sovereignty and therefore is a form of *jahiliyya,* or ignorance.

The question arises among those fearful of Islamic revivalism as to whether representatives of that movement would continue to be democrats when and if they rose to power. As demands for ta'addudiyya spread in the region, and as governments permit more political participation, this becomes an ever more central question. In Algeria in January 1992, the military provided its own answer. When it appeared inevitable that the Islamic Salvation Front (FIS) would come to power through the ballot box, the army staged a putsch, justifying its actions on the ground that the FIS would usurp all power and abolish democratic practices. The Algerian military thus averted the first vital test of Islamic revivalists' real commitment to democracy. The issue thus remains unresolved, hanging over governments and oppositions alike.

STATE-BUILDING AND THE CHALLENGE OF IDEOLOGY

Arab governments, most of which have rested their claim to legitimate rule on versions of Arab nationalism, have grimly persisted in the face of a growing challenge from those who would seek to mobilize the masses with an Islamicist message. Governments have sought to counter Islamic revivalism by emphasizing their commitments to Islam and by using the powers of the state to stem its growth. But the

---

[81]On this process, see Michael Hudson, "After the Gulf War: Prospects for Democratization in the Arab World," *Middle East Journal* 45 (Summer 1991):407–426.

powers of the state are nowhere so firmly established that its preeminence is guaranteed. In the poorer Arab countries, rapid population growth, stagnating economies, and a decreasing governmental share of national income are eroding the quality of government services. As public infrastructure (roads, hospitals, schools, sanitation services, provision of utilities, and so on) deteriorates, so do questions arise, not only about the competence of political elites but also about the appropriateness of the political ideologies they have propagated. Religious organizations, both Muslim and Christian, some with strong political commitments, are pouring into these administrative and ideological vacuums.

In the wealthy Arab oil-exporting countries, which have been referred to as *rentier* states because they live off "rents"—income from oil—there are other problems.[82] These states have sought to buy the loyalties of their populations by distributing a vast array of goods and services. They too have been unwilling to permit widespread political participation. Dirk Vandewalle observes:

> The rentier nature of state revenue thus militates against the creation of a strong state or the involvement of its corresponding society. In this light the massive revenues accruing to the government in a rentier state are a double-edged sword, allowing the local governments to dole out revenues with minimum attention for representation, on the basis of the reverse principle of no representation without taxation.[83]

Rentier states have sought to depoliticize their populations and to prevent the spread of political ideologies, which they perceive as potential challenges to their power and legitimacy. As substitutes for ideology they have provided "bread and circuses." Kuwait, for example, prior to its invasion by Iraq in 1990, had the world's most comprehensive welfare system, and "circuses" in the form of such diversions as ice rinks and other entertainment complexes. As a result of these policies, "Politics fades away, not merely as a subject for serious discussion, but even as a favorite topic of gossip."[84] What typically passes as semiofficial ideology in these rentier states is a mix of Islam

---

[82]On rentier states, see Beblawi and Luciani, *The Rentier State*.

[83]Dirk Vandewalle, "Political Aspects of State Building in Rentier Economies: Algeria and Libya Compared," in *The Rentier State,* p. 160.

[84]Afsaneh Najmabadi, "Depoliticization of a Rentier State: The Case of Pahlavi Iran," *ibid.,* p. 213.

and loyalty to the ruling family, with a thin veneer of Arab nationalism, which governments are seeking to replace with state-based nationalisms. In sum, neither the poor nor the rich Arab countries have succeeded in creating nation-states based on widespread institutionalized political participation. These governments will, therefore, continue to confront challenges to their legitimacy as the process of state formation proceeds.

In addition to organized opposition movements the largest and most effective of which are Islamicist, there is in many countries a sprawling, unorganized, alienated, and potentially volatile mass public. Often only recently and insecurely urbanized, living in poor quarters, and generally young, those who fall into this category are not yet mobilized by organizations or ideologies. They are, however, ready participants in quasi-organized street violence, such as the bread riots that have affected various countries since the 1970s. This potential opposition force may be the most dangerous of all. It is in some countries comparatively large and strategically located in capital cities. Because its members have so little to lose they are willing to engage in truly desperate acts. The secret police are unable to track down and arrest leadership elements precisely because of the comparative lack of organization. Finally, this sprawling urban lower class provides a vast recruitment pool for radical organizations, especially those of revivalist Islam.

In the face of the challenge mounted by these real and potential opposition forces, governments have responded with placatory policies, such as maintenance of subsidies for basic foodstuffs, and by seeking to divide and rule the opposition, balancing one against the other. They have sought to drive home to reformist and revivalist Muslims the differences that separate their two movements, and to secularists the gap between themselves and Islamicists. They have alternated policies of repression with concessions. In short, they have played for time, hoping that the current phase of oppositional strength and governmental weakness will not be a lasting one. Ultimately they could be successful in this strategy, in part because they may be forced to expand political participation in order to contain the threat to their existence. State formation, in this scenario, would be facilitated by the process of political competition. The government, in creating arenas in which contending forces struggle for power, would serve as midwife to the birth of a participatory political order.

Alternatively, one or more of the organized opposition forces could seize power, or the unorganized opposition could simply swamp political systems by bringing about a protracted breakdown of order. That such scenarios are even possible attests to the magnitude of the problems currently confronting Middle Eastern governments and to the progressive deterioration of ideological consensus. In the absence of such consensus, governmental legitimacy is limited. Secularism is unacceptable to vast numbers of the religiously committed in Arab countries, Turkey, Iran, and Israel, while theocracy is anathema to secularists in those countries. Whether governmental weakness will facilitate a compromise between these and other conflicting forces, or whether it presages the establishment of a new order dominated by one of them, will be the major political question in this region of the world in the 1990s.

Chapter 3

The Genes of Politics: Groups, Classes, and Families

In the Middle East, individuals express their social and political demands through membership in various groups. These collectivities range from family units to class aggregations, from recreational groupings to religious affiliations, from personal cliques to political associations.[1] Middle Eastern societies contain a kaleidoscopic array of overlapping and interlocking groups in constant flux. Individuals maintain membership in a large number of groups. In so doing, they build webs of personal connections that constitute the basic sinews of the social system.

Group formations dominate the vertical dimension of stratification as family, friendship, ethnic, religious, professional, recreational, and political groups and cliques exist in a state of continual interaction. The social and political systems resemble mosaics composed of a "limitless crisscross of groups."[2] Yet this web of fluctuating groups is

---

[1]For purposes of our analysis, a *group* is defined as a collectivity of individuals who interact in varying degrees in pursuance of a common interest or goal. This definition is broad enough to include aggregations exhibiting a wide variety of organizational styles yet narrow enough to exclude collectivities of individuals who neither interact nor share similar goals.

[2]This is Arthur F. Bentley's phrase. See Bentley, *The Process of Government* (Cambridge, Mass.: Harvard University Press, Belknap Press, 1967), p. 204.

not a seamless one. Differing levels of power, wealth, and prestige indicate a system of stratification. The lines etched into this system cut horizontally across other group configurations. In this sense, family, tribal, and religious groups, for example, are embedded within a structure of interrelated classes.

The key political dimensions of power and authority are shaped in the Middle East largely by the prevailing group and class structure. A complex prism of group formations filters political demands and helps determine public policy. Although a changing political system tends to alter the social structure, political changes are often the result of a shifting social structure. The politics of development and modernization are profoundly influenced by the patterns and processes that mark group and class relationships.

In all societies, social structure strongly influences the political process. The patterns of group interaction, however, vary considerably from one area of the world to another. Distinctive characteristics mark the styles of group and class interaction in Islamic cultures and Middle Eastern societies. Some of these patterns are congruent with patterns in other societies; some of them are not. The Middle Eastern patterns are the subject of our analysis.

GROUP STRUCTURE: VERTICAL STRATIFICATION

In the East persons were more trusted than institutions.

T. E. Lawrence
Seven Pillars of Wisdom

The Middle Easterner belongs to a number of groups that vary greatly in their membership, goals, and modes of organization. These groups also differ considerably in their capacity to further the interests of their membership. On the basis of organizational style, groups in the Middle East can be divided into two major categories, formal and informal.[3]

---

[3]The terms *formal* and *informal* risk exposing us to the criticism of ethnocentricity. For the viewpoint of many non-Westerners, even informal groups have form and can therefore be considered formal. We use the term *informal,* however, to refer to an unofficial, fluid, personalistic, and relatively covert type of group structure.

Formal groups are corporate collectivities that are officially organized and visibly operating. Membership is always clearly defined, and the members have specific and sharply differentiated roles. In our group taxonomy, formal groups include both associational and institutional structures.[4] Associational groups are highly organized structures that are formed for the articulation of a specific interest. Examples include trade unions, business organizations, civic clubs, and ethnic, religious, professional, and political associations. Institutional groups exist primarily to perform a certain function but also act to promote their own interests. Although officially organized, like associational groups, they generally operate somewhat more loosely. Institutional groups are usually governmental bodies and include legislatures, bureaucracies, armies, and political parties. Formal groups always maintain a corporate apparatus that includes officials and functionaries with clearly defined responsibilities.

Informal groups are noncorporate, unofficially organized collectivities that articulate their interests in a relatively diffuse manner. This category includes kinship, status, and regional groups as well as anomic aggregations that tend to form spontaneously, such as rioting crowds and demonstrations. Most often, however, informal groups are cliques, factions, or coteries. They are highly personalistic in character and take shape on the basis of constantly fluctuating ties and relations among individuals. The personalistic and amorphous nature of informal groups enables them to maintain a degree of fluidity and flexibility that is absent in the more rigid formal groups.

Patterns of Group Interaction

Formal political associations have been conspicuously absent in the social history of the Islamic Middle East. Even economic association-

---

[4]Associational and institutional interest groups are part of an important typology of groups developed by Gabriel Almond in his comparative study of political systems. For the original presentation of this schema, see Gabriel A. Almond and James S. Coleman, eds., *The Politics of the Developing Areas* (Princeton, N.J.: Princeton University Press, 1960), pp. 33–38; Gabriel A. Almond and G. Bingham Powell, Jr., *Comparative Politics: A Developmental Approach* (Boston: Little, Brown and Co., 1966), pp. 74–78; and Gabriel A. Almond and G. Bingham Powell, Jr., *Comparative Politics: System, Process, and Policy,* 2d ed. (Boston: Little, Brown and Co., 1978), pp. 169–176. The 1978 study places a noticeably stronger emphasis upon nonassociational, informal groups.

al groups have been of limited significance, despite the sporadic appearance of trade union organizations during this century. Nor does the mere existence of associational groups necessarily indicate that they play an active role in the sociopolitical life of the area. Often they exist only as empty organizational shells while their functions are performed by other structures. This generalization is, of course, more applicable to certain Middle Eastern countries than to others. In Morocco, Algeria, Turkey, and Bahrain, labor unions not only exist but also occasionally have had an appreciable impact upon political processes. In Iran and Iraq, on the other hand, the existence of modest union organization has been more a facade than a force. In still other countries, such as Saudi Arabia and Oman, there are no trade union organizations.

Institutional groups have played more important roles in Middle Eastern political history than have associational groups. Although parliaments and political parties are recently established institutional groups, bureaucracies and armies are of more ancient vintage. Thus, while associations are generally twentieth-century phenomena in the Middle East, certain institutional groups have roots that extend back to pre-Islamic days. These groups, however, have tended to be large, sprawling conglomerations composed of personal cliques, familial networks, and regional factions. Middle Eastern military systems today are often analyzed in terms of various officer cliques, while bureaucracies are best understood as systems of administrative factions.

Associational and institutional groups that have played a critical role in Western political systems have been considerably less significant in the Middle Eastern context. The dominant group structure in the Islamic world has been the informal group.[5] Group organization hardens around particular individuals and kinship structures. Small, shifting clusters of individuals form cliques that resemble one another only in their personalistic, informal, fragmented mode of organization. Key political decisions are made in the context of this kind of group. Formal groups exist either as extraneous facades or as general structures within which small, informal groups carry out their important activities. Informal groups penetrate and many times suffuse the more formal aggregations. Decisions attributable to the formal organization may in fact be the product of a parasitical informal group within it.

---

[5]As we will see in Chapter 4, informality is one of the major characteristics of patrimonial social and political systems.

In local Moroccan politics, for example, political parties are perceived by the people "as amalgamations of individuals bound together by a multiplicity of different personal ties rather than by any all-pervasive organizational structure or ideological commitment. . . ."[6] In Lebanon, "loyalty to patrons, relatives or nonrelatives, takes precedence over loyalty to labor unions."[7] In national Iranian politics, the *majlis*, or parliament, "masks a fluctuating and fractionating network of personal cliques, and it is here where decisions are made and business is transacted."[8] The army in such countries as Iraq and Syria has been described as a "collection of factions."[9] The situation is excellently summarized by Clifford Geertz: "Structure after structure—family, village, clan, class, sect, army, party, elite, state—turns out when more narrowly looked at to be an ad hoc constellation of miniature systems of power, a cloud of unstable micropolitics, which compete, ally, gather strength, and very soon overextended, fragment again."[10]

The growth of effective formal groups in the Middle East has been stunted by a number of interrelated factors. These are the technical, social, economic, and political conditions of organization. The formation of a viable formal group structure requires a certain level of organizational skill, a minimal degree of trust and cooperation, a reservoir of funds for equipment and staffing, and a willingness on the part of political elites to tolerate the existence of such groups. In Middle Eastern societies, these conditions of organization are seldom all present at once. Social and political demands, therefore, are formulated and presented in a much different organizational environment.

---

[6]Lawrence Rosen, "Rural Political Process and National Political Structure in Morocco," in *Rural Politics and Social Change in the Middle East,* ed. by Richard Antoun and Iliya Harik (Bloomington: Indiana University Press, 1972), p. 299.

[7]Fuad I. Khuri, "The Changing Class Structure in Lebanon," *Middle East Journal* 23 (Winter 1969):40.

[8]James A. Bill, "The Politics of Legislative Monarchy: The Iranian Majlis," in *Comparative Legislative Systems,* ed. by Herbert Hirsch and M. Donald Hancock (New York: The Free Press, 1971), p. 365.

[9]See P. J. Vatikiotis, *Conflict in the Middle East* (London: George Allen and Unwin, 1971), p. 108.

[10]Clifford Geertz, "In Search of North Africa," *New York Review of Books* 16 (April 22, 1971), p. 20, as quoted in Dale F. Eickelman, "Is There an Islamic City? The Making of a Quarter in a Moroccan Town," *International Journal of Middle East Studies* 5 (June 1974):280.

Groups in the Middle East are necessarily more limited in size in order to maximize trust and cooperative endeavor. Group members protect the private and secret nature of their proceedings in order to strengthen their position against both rival groups and the national political regime. Individuals attempt to retain the greatest possible personal freedom, so that they may move in and out of groups depending upon their perception of their own best interests. This, in turn, promotes considerable fluidity and fragmentation, since group memberships continually change in a manner that defies any rigidity, officiality, or formal routinization.

Besides these negative reasons for the lack of effective formal groups in the Middle East, there are a number of positive explanations. Small, informal groups are able to attain their common goals readily enough to preclude the need for larger groups. Over the centuries in the Islamic world, these small groups have simply proven to be more efficient and effective structures than larger groups. Recent research by economists and political scientists who work with "collective good" theory casts serious doubt on the assumption that it is rational for individual members of a large group to work to achieve the collective good of that group.[11] Instead, it is argued that the individual who fails to contribute to the large group will still stand to share in the reward once the group's goal is attained. In large groups, it may well be that an individual's effort will make no perceptible difference in the attainment of the group's goal. In this situation, the rational individual will not contribute his efforts. Such is the case in most associational and institutional groups.

In a smaller group, each individual's efforts are more likely to make a difference in attaining the group's goal. And in such a group the individual will be more susceptible to the pressures of other group members, who can further cooperation through mutual personal persuasion. In Middle Eastern social history, where action groups have been not only small but also highly personalistic, this has been especially true. In such societies, there is much doubt about the efficacy of membership in, or attachment to, large or mass institutional groups. Personal ties based upon kinship, friendship, and religious and region-

---

[11]For the basic presentation of this theoretical approach, see Mancur Olson, Jr., *The Logic of Collective Action: Public Goods and the Theory of Groups* (New York: Schocken Books, 1968).

al affiliation have been among the best means of ensuring effective individual effort.[12]

One further reason for the emphasis on personal ties in the Islamic Middle East has been a belief in the nobility and generosity of manner. Individuals in Islamic culture who believed in these virtues joined various brotherhoods and guilds that incorporated characteristics of both formal and informal organization. These guilds and brotherhoods have been important political aggregations throughout the history of the Islamic world. The Islamic guild, for example, has generally represented the interests of the lower- and lower-middle-class members of society. It "was a spontaneous development from below, created, not in response to a State need, but to the social requirements of the labouring masses themselves. Save for one brief period, the Islamic guilds have maintained either an open hostility to the State, or an attitude of sullen mistrust, which the public authorities, political and ecclesiastical, have always returned."[13]

The early craft guilds closely resembled Byzantine structures and were organized on the basis of a common craft or skill. With the passage of time, and particularly following the rise of the Qarmatian (Car-

---

[12]Ibn Khaldun's theory of social solidarity (*asabiyya*) proposes that *asabiyya* is critical to successful group activity and ultimately to civilization. *Asabiyya* is the cement of human relations and is based first upon common ancestry and eventually upon common interest and life experience. *Asabiyya* was most easily developed in small, informal, and highly personalistic groups. As Muhsin Mahdi writes: "Solidarity comes into being as a result of common ancestry, but it is usually sustained by external factors: the feeling of relatedness is dictated by the necessity of cooperation and self-defense." (Muhsin Mahdi, *Ibn Khaldūn's Philosophy of History* [London: George Allen and Unwin, 1957], p. 197.) See Ibn Khaldun's own writings about group formation in the Islamic world in *The Muqaddimah: An Introduction to History,* trans. by Franz Rosenthal (Princeton, N.J.: Princeton University Press, 1967).

[13]Bernard Lewis, "The Islamic Guilds," *Economic History Review* 8 (1937):35–36. The research of Gabriel Baer indicates that the craft guilds were both more formally organized and more closely linked to the government than is commonly thought. Baer's arguments, however, are most applicable to guild structures after the eighteenth century. And the brotherhoods were always better examples than the guilds of the type of informal group that existed in opposition to governmental power. The state was better able to infiltrate and control guild structures than brotherhood organizations. For Baer's conclusions concerning Turkish guilds, see "The Administrative, Economic, and Social Functions of Turkish Guilds," *International Journal of Middle East Studies* 1 (January 1970):28–50.

mathian) movement during the ninth to the twelfth centuries,[14] the guilds became deeply infused with a moral and often mystical spirit. This contributed greatly to organizational cohesion and inspired the members to dedicate themselves to furthering group goals. Although the various guilds and brotherhoods had differing organizational emphases, they generally blended formal and informal characteristics. On the one hand, they exhibited such formal accoutrements of organization as elaborate ceremonial activity and a rigid internal hierarchy. On the other hand, they were intensely personalistic and highly secretive. The term *tariqa* ("brotherhood" or "order") literally means a "way" or "path" and refers to a mode of conduct, not to a formal association.[15] Thus, in the Middle Eastern context, even structures as corporate as guilds have an element of informality that renders them a highly diversified composite of organizational types. Like the familial group, which we will discuss below, the guild manages to span the formal-informal dichotomy.

Since activity of informal groups is herein considered the most dominant form of group politics in the Middle East, the following discussion will emphasize this type of group rather than associational and institutional groups. This does not mean that we choose to ignore the latter but rather that we will accord them an emphasis somewhat more commensurate with the political influence they wield in the area of our investigation. To state it quite baldly, a Middle Eastern legislature, for example, is much less important as a decision-making apparatus than are the informal groups that penetrate it, control it, and most important, survive it.

The Politics of Informal Groups

Informal groups, usually referred to as cliques or factions, are a fundamental unit of political action in many societies. In contrast to

---

[14]This was a great liberal movement that swept through the Muslim world, advocating social reform in general and justice and equality in particular. The movement appealed to all classes, sects, and religions but found special acceptance among the artisans, skilled, and semiskilled workers. See L. Massignon, "Karmatians," *The Encyclopaedia of Islam*, 4 vols. (Leiden, The Netherlands: E. J. Brill, 1927), vol. 2:767–772.

[15]This point is made in Fazlur Rahman, *Islam* (Garden City, N.Y.: Anchor Books, 1968), pp. 189–190, and in Morroe Berger, *Islam in Egypt Today* (Cambridge: Cambridge University Press, 1970), p. 67.

northern European and North American societies, where formal groups play a prominent role, the informal group is dominant in southern European, North African, Middle Eastern, and Latin American cultures.

It is true that wherever human beings are gathered, they will develop informal groups. Thus, in American society there are many obvious manifestations of informal-group politics. But even within the United States, the tendency to organize informal rather than formal groups differs in strength from one area of the country to another. In the South and the Southwest, nonassociational groups are prevalent. This once led an observer to characterize the state of Louisiana as "the westernmost of the Arab states."[16] Generally, however, the American political process places relatively less emphasis upon informal groups and relatively more upon such aggregates as trade unions, legislatures, and political parties. This is not the case in much of the world. Studies of Brazil, India, Burma, Taiwan, Japan, and Italy, for example, impressively demonstrate that informal and nonassociational-group politics are dominant in these societies.[17]

The gradual recognition of the critical role that informal groups play in the less industrialized world has been recently accompanied by preliminary analysis, by a small number of scholars of contemporary Middle Eastern political systems, emphasizing this phenomenon. Amal Vinogradov and John Waterbury, for example, introduce the term *security group* to refer to a factional group that "is the maximal unit in which there is some predictability in the exercise of power and authority."[18] Clement H. Moore discusses what he terms *contingent*

---

[16]For reference to this memorable quote, see T. Harry Williams, *Huey Long* (New York: Bantam Books, 1970), p. 194.

[17]A growing number of political scientists, heavily influenced by the patron-client analysis of anthropologists, now stress the important connection between personalistic group structures and politics in the developing world. These studies contain much that is relevant to the Middle East. See, for example, René Lemarchand and Keith Legg, "Political Clientelism and Development," *Comparative Politics* 4 (January 1972):148–178; James C. Scott, "Patron-Client Politics and Political Change in Southeast Asia," *American Political Science Review* 67 (March 1973):103–127; and Arthur J. Lerman, "National Elite and Local Politician in Taiwan," *American Political Science Review* 71 (December 1977):1406–1422.

[18]Amal Vinogradov and John Waterbury, "Situations of Contested Legitimacy in Morocco: An Alternative Framework," *Comparative Studies in Society and History* 13 (January 1971):34.

interest groups that cut across associational interest groups and serve as "gatekeepers" for North African political systems. According to Moore, "Examples of contingent interest groups range from sets of Algerian cousins and fellow maquisards or a Moroccan family of notables to professional veto groups or a handful of individuals out to convince Bourguiba that Ben Salah's Plan is a menace."[19]

The most crucial units of interest aggregation in the Middle East remain informal groups. In Iraq this kind of collectivity is referred to as a *shilla* or *jama'at,* and in Saudi Arabia the term most often used is *bashka.* The Egyptians also use the word *shilla* to refer to a group of approximately two to twelve members who socialize together and who work to help one another advance politically and economically. A slightly more diffuse Egyptian informal group is the *duf'a,* or old-boy network. The *duf'a* (literally "pushing out") is often the general structure from which the more tightly knit *shillas* are formed. In Kuwait, the *diwaniyya* is an informal gathering where men meet to discuss and determine important political questions. Other words in the Arab world that carry the idea of cliques and factions but that sometimes also indicate a higher level of formality, include *kutal* and *fi'at.* In Iran, the sociopolitical system is backed by a gigantic network of informal, personalistic cliques referred to as *dawrahs* ("circles"). Afghan group dynamics are dominated by loose factional aggregates referred to as either *dastahs* ("handfuls of individuals") or *girdabs* ("little whirlpools"). One of the most important of the informal groups in Turkey is the personal collectivity based on *hemseri* ("from the same region") relations. The hemserilik is a group that forms and re-forms as fellow villagers and "hometowners" aggregate to assist one another with social, economic, occupational, and political aims. In Egypt, the same kind of group formation prevails in the *baladiyya,* which is in fact a kind of informal, extended family group.

The juxtaposition of informal groups with formal political associations is seen in the case of Bahrain, an archipelago off the coast of Saudi Arabia, just west of the Qatar peninsula. An early modernizer, Bahrain is the oldest petroleum-producing state in the Persian Gulf and had already established a girls' school in 1928. Strikes and labor unrest have occurred in this small shaikhdom ever since the mid-

---

[19]Clement Henry Moore, *Politics in North Africa: Algeria, Morocco, and Tunisia* (Boston: Little, Brown and Co., 1970), pp. 201–202.

1950s. Ruled absolutely by the al-Khalifa family, this country has nonetheless had notable experience with municipal and national consultative bodies. But the actual politics of Bahrain have taken place within an extensive network of clubs (*nawadi*) and societies (*jam'iyyat*). Numbering approximately one hundred, these informal groups, "whose memberships include a majority of Bahrain's elite public, have played the essential functions performed by political parties in other political systems."[20] Ostensibly organized for social, professional, and recreational purposes, these clubs are often intensely political. The 250-member al-Arabi Club, for example, is composed of educated Bahrainis who push for nationalistic and democratic goals. The University Graduates' Club, on the other hand, is oriented more toward the elite and consists of college-educated intellectuals from both the middle and upper classes. It is the establishment's liberal conscience. These kinds of informal groups in Bahrain coexist both with formal organizations and with the ruling family, whose tentacles reach deep down into the club network.

Informal-group activity in the Middle East has manifested itself in a myriad of ways. Ranging from tiny dyads that plug in and out of one another to enormously complex coalitions based on kinship, these groups have little in common besides their personal, informal nature. Personal homes have served as locations for the meetings of the more exclusive of the groups, while mosques, coffeehouses, teahouses, common rooms, and bazaar shops have served as meeting places for the more inclusive of the groups. Informal groups operating in these kinds of settings constantly relay information through the various societies. It is largely on the basis of this information that personal and political decisions are made. And, it may be added, it is in precisely such groups and such settings that middle-grade army officers sometimes decide to intervene in the political affairs of their countries. The same is even more true of religious opposition organization, as is evidenced by the shah's Iran and Sadat and Mubarak's Egypt.

One of the important characteristics of informal-group politics is an intense and pervasive spirit of personalism. The fundamental social

---

[20]Emile Nakhleh, *Bahrain: Political Development in a Modernizing Society* (Lexington, Mass.: Lexington Books, 1976), p. 41. Most of the information in this paragraph is drawn from the Nakhleh book. For an excellent recent study of Bahraini society and politics, see Fred H. Lawson, *Bahrain: The Modernization of Autocracy* (Boulder, Colo.: Westview Press, 1989).

and political ties tend to be personal in nature.[21] In moving into a wide variety of informal groups, the individual strives to broaden personal contacts in order to gain representation on as many fronts as possible. What determines the Middle Easterner's power and influence "is not the fact that he holds a certain office or even that that office affords certain opportunities for personal aggrandizement but the extent and success with which he as an individual is able to cumulate a wide range of personal ties, to display to others a number of highly valued personal characteristics, and . . . to merge them into a larger framework of political importance reaching up to the very highest government levels."[22] In this kind of environment, individuals develop great skill at personal persuasion as they seek their political goals. Decision making is determined by personal push and pull, as is interestingly indicated by the Turkish expression *torpil* and the Iranian term *parti*. While the formal group tends to deemphasize the personal element, the informal group preserves and promotes personalism.

The personal nature of group politics in the Middle East is exemplified well by the Lebanese *zu'ama* system (singular: *za'im*). In the Lebanese context, the za'im is an informal group leader whose followers support him on the basis of personal loyalty and personal rewards. The personal power of the za'im is rooted in local and regional communities and is buttressed by the fact that the leader and his followers share a common religion or sect. Among the important zu'ama families are the Frangiehs (Maronites), the Jumblatts (Druze), the Shihabs (Sunnites), and the al-As'ads (Shi'is). Leaders with names such as these have been present for years in the national political institutions of Lebanon. When the Maronite leader and Lebanese president-elect Bashir Gemayel was assassinated in 1982, he was replaced in his presidential position by his brother, Amin Gemayel. The strength of the family ties of the zu'ama system is very great indeed. This helps explain the bitterness and depth of the blood feuds that have marked Lebanese politics in recent years.

At the level of the informal group, the argument that Middle Eastern politics is basically nonideological is quite convincing. Commitments are more often to individuals and family units than to ideas.

---

[21]See Chapter 4 for a detailed discussion of personalism in the Middle Eastern variant of patrimonial politics.

[22]Rosen, "Rural Political Process," p. 216.

The precedence of personal ties over ideology is seen in the striking examples of family units that contain within themselves all shades of political and professional commitment. Such families are able to transcend regime changes and even revolution. The Marei family in Egypt is a case in point.

The father, Ahmad Marei, was a well-to-do supporter of the old regime, a member of the Wafd Party, and a parliamentary deputy. During the Nasserite revolution, the influence of the family remained intact. One brother (and the patriarch of the family today), Hassan Marei, was appointed minister of commerce and industry in 1954. Another brother, Sayyid Marei, the most powerful member of the family over the years, had served as a member of Parliament for six years during King Farouk's rule. Under Nasser, Sayyid was minister of agriculture for many years and an important official in the Arab Socialist Union. A third brother, Marei Marei, served as director of the chemical organization during the Nasser period. During these years, the Marei family had the added connection of their more radical cousin, Ali Sabry, a former member of the Free Officers, secretary-general of the Arab Socialist Union, and one of Nasser's five premiers. Despite Sabry's removal from power by President Anwar Sadat in May 1971 and his subsequent imprisonment, the Marei brothers survived well.

During the Sadat period, Hassan Marei remained influential in the industrial community while Marei Marei held a directorship in a state holding company. In 1974, Marei Marei took charge of the very lucrative economic relationships between Egypt and Iran. In September 1971, Sadat appointed the ubiquitous Sayyid Marei deputy premier and minister of agriculture. In October 1974, Sayyid became speaker of the assembly and four years later he settled in as presidential advisor to President Sadat himself. The Marei-Sadat relationship was cemented by the 1975 marriage of Sayyid Marei's son Hassan to Sadat's daughter Noha. Because Sayyid and his son Hassan were so closely associated with the Sadat era, from which Mubarak has tried to distance himself, the new president has not allowed them to reemerge in public life. Hassan has, with his brother Nasr, become a highly successful businessman. Sayyid's brother Marei, who was not a high-profile member of the Sadat entourage, has become the family's active politician. He is the chairman of the foreign relations committee of the Consultative Assembly. The first loyalty of "the Mareis and most other

Egyptians is to the family itself, and political ideology is not sufficiently compelling to undermine primordial family ties."[23]

This pattern of family tenacity and ideological malleability has also prevailed in such countries as Iran, Iraq, Lebanon, and Morocco. Even the leading families of the very conservative shaikhdoms of the Persian Gulf have had members who have espoused radical causes. Shaikh Saqr bin Sultan, who ruled Sharjah between 1951 and 1965, is a notable example. Saqr, a strong Arab nationalist with Nasserist sympathies and a dislike for the British, was deposed in 1965, primarily for these reasons. In 1972, he returned from exile in Cairo and failed in an attempt to regain the throne.

An informal group "is like a cluster of bees round a queen bee. If the queen is damaged they quickly find another to cluster around."[24] The exigencies of politics require an individual to shift positions periodically in order to maintain as much manipulative leeway as possible. The informal group itself will often switch goals and alter the ideas that brought its membership together. Such changes, of course, always mean that a certain percentage of the membership will be lost, but this is one important by-product of the fluidity of this type of group. Individuals retain the capacity to circulate among a host of collectivities, depending on what they consider to be in their own interests. Coalitions are fragile and alliances fleeting in such social and political systems. Even the strongest social cement, personal ties, can be cracked. Yet the adhesive quality remains, so that the relationship can be reestablished whenever the winds of fortune dictate that it be reestablished. This plasticity of informal-group politics promotes an underlying systemic stability in the Middle East.

Informal groups in the Middle East are characterized by alternating fission and fusion. "It is always possible to divide them, to prevent powerful coalitions from forming, for their solidarity, of course, is inversely proportional to their breadth. Hence political showdowns

---

[23]Robert Springborg, *Family, Power, and Politics in Egypt* (Philadelphia: University of Pennsylvania Press, 1982), p. 75.

[24]This statement was made concerning informal-group politics in India. See B. D. Graham, "The Succession of Factional Systems in the Uttar Pradesh Congress Party, 1937–1966," in *Local-Level Politics: Social and Cultural Perspectives*, Marc J. Swartz, ed. (Chicago: Aldine, 1968), p. 355.

rarely occur."[25] Although tension, conflict, and competition infuse this network of "many-stranded coalitions,"[26] the overall group system persists and prevails. The tension promotes balance. "Equilibrium in conflict is not achieved by both or all sides desisting from conflict but rather in both or all sides persisting in conflict. . . . The best defense of a security group lies in keeping up steady pressure against its rivals short of attack."[27] This principle of counterbalancing in group politics is prevalent throughout the Islamic Middle East, although it manifests itself somewhat differently from one society to another. In the traditional countries of the Gulf and Morocco, it helps foster systemic fluidity and flexibility. In Lebanon, on the other hand, it froze into a more rigid pattern, in which groups directly confronted one another; there, the more common pattern of many sides balanced against one another gave way to confrontations between two sides. The fragility of this situation became all too clear in April 1975, when the society exploded into bloody civil war.

This network of floating factions could not persist without a sturdier group backing to help anchor it in the social structure. Individuals require a more reliable vehicle than factions and cliques to defend their interests and to achieve their goals. In the Middle East, this mechanism is the kinship group in general and the family in particular.

The Primordial Group Nexus: The Family

Kinship units are a very special kind of informal group. The family, which is the basic unit and building block of groups in the Middle East, retains characteristics that render it more rigid than most factional and nonassociational groups. Although the lines of association that mark personal cliques and political factions appear and disappear with amazing rapidity, true kinship relations are much more difficult to create and destroy. Ties of kinship remain in existence whether or not political actors choose to recognize them. Since family networks are virtually impossible to destroy, they provide the element of per-

---

[25]Moore, *Politics in North Africa,* p. 202

[26]This phrase is borrowed from Eric Wolf, *Peasants* (Englewood Cliffs, N.J.: Prentice-Hall, 1966), and is quoted in Khuri, "Changing Class Structure," p. 35.

[27]Vinogradov and Waterbury, "Situations of Contested Legitimacy," p. 35.

manence needed to offset the impermanence of other informal groups. Family groupings are the linchpins of the system of group interaction in the Middle East. Indeed, lineage patterns are "the invisible skeleton of the community."[28] Yet this skeleton contains the moving force of the community. In the words of Dale Eickelman; "Kinship relationships should be treated as something which people make and with which they accomplish things."[29]

The traditional Middle Eastern family unit is an extended family, usually consisting of a man, his wife (or wives), his unmarried sons and daughters, and his married sons and their wives and children. In the contemporary urban Middle East, the institution of the extended family is increasingly giving way to the nuclear family, which includes only the husband, wife, and children. Family groups, whether extended or nuclear, are consciously and carefully shaped. Marriage patterns are critical, since they determine the direction in which the family group will move. The most distinctive traditional trait of Middle Eastern marriage is the preferred marriage of a man and his father's brother's daughter (*bint'amm*). This paternal first cousin marriage was designed to strengthen important blood ties and to solidify a constantly expanding family unit. Such an endogamous marriage pattern has significant political implications. In the Middle East, it enabled family heads to enlist the critical support of their brothers and their brothers' sons. In societies deeply divided, this minimal unit of coalition was a relatively effective action group. Few family clusters could afford the internecine conflict that might otherwise have occurred among brothers, nephews, and cousins.[30]

Every individual in the Middle East thus begins with membership in one important informal group, the family. This group seeks to magnify its kinship ties in at least three different ways. First, contacts are strengthened and regular communication is maintained with as many

---

[28]This phrase is John Gulick's. See Gulick, *Social Structure and Culture Change in a Lebanese Village* (New York: Wenner-Gren Foundation, 1955), p. 104.

[29]Dale F. Eickelman, *The Middle East: An Anthropological Approach* (Englewood Cliffs, N.J.: Prentice-Hall, 1981), p. 134.

[30]For excellent discussions of the marriage patterns of Middle Eastern families, see Raphael Patai, *Golden River to Golden Road: Society, Culture, and Change in the Middle East*, 3d ed. (Philadelphia: University of Pennsylvania Press, 1969), pp. 135–176, and Eickelman, *The Middle East: An Anthropological Approach*, 2d ed. (Englewood Cliffs, N.J.: Prentice-Hall, 1989), pp. 151–178.

blood relatives as is practically possible. Even when there is great geo-graphical and genealogical distance separating kinfolk, family members seldom hesitate to approach one another for needed economic and political assistance. In Egypt, for example, "While members of the descent group may not socialize regularly with one another, and may indeed be quite distant genealogically speaking, they have no compunction about asking their kin and affines for economic and political favors."[31]

The second way in which family ties are expanded in the Middle East is by a very broad and flexible definition of kinship. The Afghan concept of *qawm,* for example, defines actual kinship on the basis of deep social and political cooperation among those who live in the same area. Somewhat the same applies in Morocco, where the term *qaraba* or "closeness" is expressed as a blood tie "even when no demonstrable ties exist, because however such ties are valued in practice, they are considered permanent and cannot be broken."[32] Also, kinship ties are often fictitiously manufactured in an attempt to enhance the influence of a particular individual or group. The most common examples of fictive kinship are elaborate arguments that purport to document one's direct descent from the family of the Prophet Muhammad.

Finally, family contacts are broadened by the incorporation into the kinship group of new individuals and other families through marriage. This is why in the Middle East, "Arranging marriages is a highly serious matter, like waging war or making big business deals."[33] The process by which two families are brought together through intermarriage can be described as "family nesting." "Family nesting occurs when two families, tied together through marriage, reinforce that connection through a series of social, economic, and political exchanges."[34] The branches of the family trees in the forests of Middle Eastern society and politics are filled with family nests. In Egypt, the Marei family discussed above nests with other powerful kinship units such as the Muhy al-din, Sabri, Shamsi, Abaza, Mashur, and Elwan

---

[31]Springborg, *Family, Power, and Politics,* p. 54.

[32]Eickelman, *The Middle East,* 2d ed., p. 156.

[33]Hildred Geertz, "The Meanings in Family Ties," in *Meaning and Order in Moroccan Society,* ed. by C. Geertz, H. Geertz, and L. Rosen (New York: Cambridge University Press, 1979), p. 363 as quoted in Eickelman, *The Middle East,* 2d ed., p. 170.

[34]Springborg, *Family, Power, and Politics,* p. 73.

families. The Mareis have even nested with the Sadat family. ". . . It is by nesting with other families that the descent group of the Mareis performs the greatest services for its members. The sheer number of family members involved in these nests, and the scope of their various economic and political activities, provides a complex of opportunities for the exchange of economic and political favors."[35] From the era of Farouk to that of Mubarak, families with whom the Mareis nested were among the most influential in the country.

For the family group to remain strong, its members must maintain a continually updated knowledge of the intricate kinship structure to which they belong. In the Ottoman system, for example, "Every member of the clan kept a genealogical map in his head to orient him in his relations with others."[36] In Turkey, the situation is one "of everyone having to know very precisely to what extended family, to what kin village, to what lineage, to what clan, to what clan federation and to what principality or khanate he belongs."[37] This awareness of precisely where one stands with regard to other group members contributes greatly to group solidarity, and ultimately to the capacity to attain group objectives. Strands of kinship serve, at the very least, as relatively permanent lines of access among group members. It is in the individual's self-interest to be familiar with as many of these connections as possible.

Like all other group formations in the Middle East, the kinship group (whether family, tribe, or clan) is internally divided and fragmented. Intrafamilial tensions, quarrels, and feuds are common in Islamic cultures. Yet within the nuclear family, the divisions are not as deep or the tensions as intense as they are outside the family. More important, the kinship group presents a united front against outside competitors. Fragmented collectivities gain solidarity and cohesion through the pressure exerted by external rival forces. In this system of balancing opposition, the family unit always fares best. This is because the kinship group is the most cohesive and tenacious of the Middle Eastern group formations.

---

[35]*Ibid.*, p. 88.

[36]Serif Mardin, "Historical Determinants of Stratification: Social Class and Class Consciousness in Turkey" (Paper prepared for the Comparative Bureaucracy Seminar, Massachusetts Institute of Technology, Spring 1966), p. 19.

[37]*Ibid.*

In addition to being both a biological and an economic unit, the family is very much a political aggregation. Family members support one another in their drives to improve their respective power and authority positions in the particular community or society. Besides providing support for its members in their efforts to attain political goals, the kinship group is politically relevant in many other ways. It serves, for example, as the staging ground from which individuals can move on to membership in other groups, both formal and informal. The family, in fact, determines much of its members' participation in other collectivities. Such informal groups as personal cliques and political factions have fathers, sons, brothers, nephews, cousins, and in-laws strategically sprinkled throughout them in patterns that tend to benefit the particular family unit. As often as not, a single family is represented in rival political factions, parties, or movements. Thus, although informal-group membership cuts across kinship lines, it is also true that the filaments of kinship cut across the boundaries of cliques and factions. A major function of distributing family members among various other groups is the construction and maintenance of channels of communication among these groups, whether they be rivals or allies.

The ligaments of kinship bind the system of groups into a working whole. They run through rival collectivities, thus softening tensions. And, through membership in both formal and informal groups, blood relatives and in-laws help bind these two major organizational types together. Family members in such institutions as bureaucracies and parliaments are in close touch with relatives who are members of cliques and factions. Decisions made in one context are directly influenced by what occurs in another context.

Morocco has sometimes been referred to as the kingdom of cousins, and monarchical Iran was frequently called the country of one thousand families. Observers have labeled Farouk's Egypt as the land of two thousand families and contemporary Pakistan as the country of sixty families. The intricacies of family relationships explain a great deal about the orientations, formation, and behavior of political elites in the Middle East. The more traditional the society, the more useful kinship analysis will be in understanding it. In all the Middle Eastern countries, however, patterns of kinship and marriage are valuable in understanding the structure of power and authority. Those societies that are developing politically and modernizing rapidly may have a relatively large number of ruling families, as well as a high rate of familial mobility. A study of such family structures can explain much about national elites and the political processes of the societies under investigation. Selected examples follow.

In the three decades prior to 1958, the Iraqi political elite represented a tight cluster of families. The core of the elite included such families as the al-Saids, the al-Askaris, the Kannas, and the Kamals. The famous Nuri al-Said held the post of prime minister 14 times and that of minister 29 times! Ja'far al-Askari, who was assassinated in 1936, was prime minister twice and minister eight times. Nuri al-Said and Ja'far al-Askari married each other's sisters. Tahsin al-Askari followed in the footsteps of his assassinated brother, Ja'far, when in 1942 he assumed two ministerial positions. He was the brother-in-law of Ibrahim Kamal, who was himself a cabinet minister twice. Another al-Askari brother, Abd al-Hadi, married his daughter to Khalil Kanna, who held ministerial posts six different times. Two of Khalil Kanna's brothers were members of the Iraqi parliament.[38]

The Iraqi revolution of 1958 did not destroy the political power of the families. The Ba'thist regime of strongman Saddam Hussein al-Takriti is dominated by Saddam and his relatives from the town of Takrit. In the early 1980s, Saddam's two leading intelligence and security chiefs were his half-brothers Barzan Ibrahim al-Takriti and Watban Ibrahim al-Takriti. Saddam himself was the foster son, nephew, and son-in-law of Khayrallah al-Tulfah, the longtime governor of Baghdad. In the words of a leading scholar of Iraqi politics, the Takritis' power is so great that "it would not be going too far to say that the Takrītīs' rule through the Ba'th party, rather than the Ba'th party through the Takrītīs."[39]

In the shah's Iran, national politics were dominated by family considerations, since the political elite that clustered around the ruling Pahlavi family came from a small number of families. Among the most influential of the elite families in Pahlavi Iran were the following: Alam, Diba, Qaragozlu, Esfandiari, Ardalan, Bayat, Sami'i, Farman-

[38]This information is drawn from Nazar T. Al-Hasso's excellent Ph.D. dissertation. See Al-Hasso, "Administrative Politics in the Middle East: The Case of Monarchical Iraq. 1920–1958" (Ph.D. diss., The University of Texas, Austin, Texas, 1976).

[39]Hanna Batatu, *The Old Social Classes and the Revolutionary Movements of Iraq* (Princeton, N.J.: Princeton University Press, 1978), p. 1088.

farmaian, Bushehri, Jahanbani, and Emami. The ties among key members of these families were easily as close as the ties among the families in Iraq. Long-time minister of culture Mehrdad Pahlbod was the husband of Princess Shams, a sister of Muhammad Reza Shah. Former major general Minbashian was the brother of Pahlbod (formerly Ezzatullah Minbashian). The influential Senator Bushehri was the father of the husband of powerful Princess Ashraf, the twin sister of the shah. Former air force commander Muhammad Khatami was married to the shah's sister Fatima. Ardeshir Zahedi, Iranian ambassador to the United States, was once married to the shah's daughter Shahnaz. During the last years of the shah's rule, there were 40 national elite families that dominated the economic and political systems in Iran.

Despite the shattering nature of the Iranian revolution of 1978–1979, political influence in the Islamic Republic has tended to follow the primordial lines of kinship and family. The strands of kinship about which power coagulates extended outward from the person of Ayatollah Ruhollah Khomeini himself. One of Khomeini's daughters, for example, was married to the influential (now deceased) Ayatollah Eshraqi. More important, Khomeini's son, Ahmad, has been a central figure and middleman ever since his return to Tehran with his father in 1979. Since Khomeini's death in 1989, Ahmad has continued to play an important, if somewhat subdued, role in Iranian politics. Ahmad Khomeini, in turn, is married to the sister of Sadiq Tabataba'i, a quiet force and Khomeini confidant who played a critical role in the formulation of Iranian foreign policy in the years immediately following the revolution.[40]

Family connections loom even larger in the shaikhdoms of the Persian Gulf, where the core of the political elite always consists of members of the ruling family. The remaining members of the elite are drawn from other wealthy, aristocratic families. Political decision making in Saudi Arabia, Kuwait, Qatar, Oman, the United Arab Emirates, and Bahrain is monopolized by the ruling families in these countries. In Bahrain, where political and economic decision making is dominated by Shaikh Isa bin Salman Al-Khalifa and his brother, Shaikh Khali-

---

[40]Detailed information on the web of kinship ties that binds the leaders of the Islamic Republic is found in an article that appeared in *Iran Times,* February 6, 1981, p. 9 (in Persian).

fa bin Salman Al-Khalifa, the names of the leading families such as Kanu, Fakhru, Shirawi, and Mu'ayyid are well known. The following anecdote illustrates that in Bahrain, family is more important than any formal governing body. While in the marketplace in 1973, an elderly Bahraini was told to go vote in the elections for the Constitutional Assembly. The old man looked around and asked, "Who owns that building?" "A Kanu," he was told. "And who owns this one?" "A Mu'ayyid," was the response. "And this third one?" "Shaykh Khalifa." The old man then asked, "Will the elections change any of this?"[41] The right family connections remain an important passport to the elite in much of the Middle East.

Political revolution and economic modernization have hardly lessened the role of the family group in government. It is true that the form of family organization has changed considerably and that kinship relations now crystallize in new ways. The most evident change of this sort is the transfer from the extended to the nuclear family style of household. This change, however, has not fundamentally altered the important role that kinship relations play in the political process. Fuad Khuri writes that "the change from the extended family subculture to that of the nuclear family does not imply the loss of family ties and duties. Family ties and duties, no doubt, continue, but in new forms."[42] The physical living arrangements of the family may be changing, but its sociopolitical demands and supports remain essentially the same.

The Power of Women: A Case Study of Informal Politics

When one examines the informal nature of group politics in the Middle East, a number of previously overlooked and underemphasized dimensions of the political game suddenly come into sharper focus. Persons who were formerly considered peripheral to political decision making take on more central significance. This is precisely the case in cultures where there is no sharp distinction between the private and

---

[41]This story is presented in Nakhleh, *Bahrain*, p. 129 n.

[42]Khuri, "Changing Class Structure," p. 38.

the public spheres or where key community and national decisions are made in informal settings by individuals often considered peripheral to politics. An important case in point is the Middle Eastern woman. Studying the woman's role in society can provoke new insights into the kinds of actors and actresses who play out the political drama and can indicate both the importance of informal politics and the special place that family relationships have in Middle Eastern politics.

For years, Middle Eastern women have been stereotyped as an oppressed and passive group who have been hidden by veils and whose lives have been dominated by men. Western writers in particular have presented the Muslim woman as someone held captive in the kitchen or harem while her husband frolics personally and protects politically a system of polygamy that rationalizes female servitude. Quotations from the Quran and the relative absence of female actresses on the public political stage have often led outsiders to conclude that the woman in Islamic society has been little more than a personal and political cipher. This perspective has been reinforced by Middle Eastern historians and chroniclers who have traditionally downplayed the role of women in their writings. And essayists, both male and female, have distorted the historical position of women in the Middle East as one means of attempting to improve their position today.

In stressing the formal, public, and institutional aspects of political behavior at the expense of the private and informal dimensions, Western analysts have overlooked precisely those individuals who dominate the private and informal aspects. In the Middle East, women are important political forces because of their critical position in the webs of informal relationships that make up the private realm. In the crucial world of informal, private groups, they have been more than the homemakers. They have also been "the matchmakers and the peacemakers."[43] As anthropologist Emrys Peters puts it,

> The pivotal points in any field of power in this, a superficially dominant patrilineal, patrilocal and patriarchal society where the male ethos is vulgar in its brash prominence, are the women. What holds men together, what knots the cords of alliances are not men themselves, but the women who depart from their natal household to take up residence elsewhere

---

[43]We are indebted to Gerald J. Obermeyer for this phrase.

with a man, and who, in this critical position, communicate one group to another.[44]

This quotation refers to only one of the ways in which Middle Eastern women shape political events at all levels of the societies in which they live.

In both the traditional and the modern Middle East, women have exerted political influence through the wide variety of roles that they have played. Perhaps the most important of these have been natal and marital kinship roles. Such natal roles as daughter, sister, cousin, aunt, mother, and grandmother and such marital roles as wife and mother-in-law have been politically strategic throughout Islamic history. The special relationship between mother and son is particularly relevant to our understanding of Middle Eastern political events. As we shall see in the examples discussed below, only the role of wife has been more important in the female repertoire of political roles. One knowledgeable observer writes that "it is hardly surprising that the relationship to the mother is preferred to the paternal one, and that every patriarchal society is condemned to be matriarchal on the edges. On the edges? Not at all! It is a question here of the depths of existence."[45]

Other roles in which Muslim women have exerted influence in the political arena include such diverse traditional callings as prostitute, concubine, entertainer, servant, religious leader, soothsayer, and advisor. More modern roles, such as career woman and politician-

---

[44]Emrys Peters, "Consequences of the Segregation of the Sexes Among the Arabs" (Paper delivered at the Mediterranean Social Science Council Conference, Athens, 1966), p. 15. This important observation has been quoted by such scholars as Cynthia Nelson and Carla Makhlouf, whose works are among the few that stress the political power of women in the Middle East. Anthropologically inclined analysts have been much more sensitive to this power than have political scientists. Two further examples are Elizabeth Warnock Fernea, who has done field work in Iraq, Egypt, and Morocco, and Lois Grant Beck, who has worked in Iran. Cynthia Nelson's field observations come from Egypt, and Carla Makhlouf's from Yemen.

[45]A. Bouhdiba, "The Child and the Mother in Arab-Muslim Society," in *Psychological Dimensions of Near Eastern Studies,* ed. by L. Carl Brown and Norman Itzkowitz (Princeton, N.J.: Darwin Press, 1977), p. 133. For another fine discussion of the power of the mother and mother-in-law in Muslim society, see Fatima Mernissi, *Beyond the Veil: Male-Female Dynamics in a Modern Muslim Society* (Cambridge, Mass.: Schenkman Publishing Co., 1975), pp. 69–79.

stateswoman, are becoming increasingly important with time. Female
revolutionaries and guerrillas are also increasingly active.

Among the tools that Middle Eastern women have used to exert
influence are such resources as wealth, beauty, intelligence, and information, as well as both psychological and physical coercion. They have
often converted the very signs of their oppression into formidable
offensive weapons that have enabled them to secure their interests.
Excellent examples of such weapons are the harem and the veil that
segregate the sexes. The conventional wisdom is that it is the women
who are excluded from the male world, but, as one scholar has recently written: "One can venture to assert that it is in fact the men who are
excluded from the female world, as much, if not more, than females
are excluded from that of man."[46] This researcher goes on to give a
number of examples of how much easier it is for women to penetrate
men's gatherings than for males to participate in those of women.

A survey of Middle Eastern history indicates the important contributions that women have made to the political process. From the
very beginnings of Islam, women have been critical political forces.
Indeed, as we shall see in Chapter 4, there is little doubt that the
Prophet Muhammad could not have succeeded in his mission without
the indispensable support of his first wife, Khadija. Other women who
helped shape the early social system of Islam were Muhammad's wife
A'isha and his daughter Fatima. Fatima's sister-in-law Zaynab was also
a powerful force in early Islamic history, as were the wives of the various imams who were the direct descendants of Fatima and her husband Ali.

The political role of women in the famous Umayyad and Abbasid
caliphates is little known. In both instances, it was critical. This was

---

[46]Carla Makhlouf, *Changing Veils: Women and Modernisation in North Yemen* (Austin,
Tex.: University of Texas Press, 1979). This study contains fascinating material showing
how the veil has traditionally provided Middle Eastern women with a mobile form of
security and anonymity, and has even facilitated the expression of aggressiveness. More
than religious fervor is involved in the return to the veil in the early 1980s by numerous
liberated young women in countries such as Egypt. For a fine study of a Muslim culture
(Tuareg), in which the males are the veiled ones, see Robert F. Murphy, "Social Distance and the Veil," in *Peoples and Cultures of the Middle East,* ed. Louise E. Sweet
(Garden City, N.Y.: Natural History Press, 1970), vol. 1, pp. 290–314. On the informal
power of women among the Tuareg, see R. V. C. Bodley, *The Soundless Sahara* (London: Robert Hale Limited, 1968), p. 82.

especially true during the golden age of the cosmopolitan Abbasid dynasty in the late eighth and early ninth centuries. At a time when Europe was plunged into its Dark Ages and when Charlemagne and his lords "were reportedly dabbling with the art of writing their names,"[47] the powerful Abbasids, ruling from Baghdad, were debating philosophic texts and making gigantic intellectual strides in medicine, astronomy, mathematics, and the arts. The glory and grandeur of this period are captured in romantically imaginative terms in *The Thousand Nights and a Night,* and such rulers of the period as Harun al-Rashid (786–809) and his brilliant son the caliph al-Ma'mun (813–833) are among the most renowned of Eastern rulers. Names such as Umm Salama, Khayzuran, and Zubayda, however, are considerably less known, even among scholars of the area. Umm Salama was the wife of Abu al-Abbas and thus served as a critical link between the two dynasties. A strong personality, she directed her husband's affairs and he "took no decisive measure without Umm Salamah's advice and approval."[48]

Khayzuran was the favorite wife of the third Abbasid caliph, Muhammad al-Mahdi; she was also the mother of the fourth and fifth caliphs, Musa al-Hadi and Harun al-Rashid. A slave girl born in Yemen, she received an excellent education and caught the eye of the caliph al-Mansur, who brought her to the court, where his son al-Mahdi married her. For 30 years, during the reigns of three caliphs, her political power was enormous. Her agents and secretaries were spread throughout the empire; she intervened directly in the administration of justice; she influenced the rise and fall of the caliph's closest advisors; she financed the construction of public works; and she directed the succession of kings. It was Khayzuran who held the system together and ensured the smooth transition of kings both upon the death of her husband and then again when her eldest son, al-Hadi, passed away. Khayzuran was an owner of extensive property, and, next to her illustrious son Harun al-Rashid, she was the wealthiest person in the Muslim world of her day. In describing Khayzuran's role during

---

[47]Philip K. Hitti, *The Near East in History* (Princeton, N.J.: D. Van Nostrand Co., 1961), p. 244.

[48]Nabia Abbott, *Two Queens of Baghdad* (Chicago: University of Chicago Press, 1946), p. 11.

the caliphates of her two sons, one writer succinctly summarizes her position: "The ambitious mother travels in state on the imperial highway of power."[49]

Better known in the annals of Islamic history than Khayzuran is her niece Zubayda, the wife of Harun al-Rashid. One of the greatest builders of public works in Islamic history, Zubayda is remembered particularly for sponsoring the construction of over 10 miles of complex aqueducts leading into Mecca. She spent over 75 million dinars in digging the Mushshash Spring in that holy city—a spectacular feat in any age. Like Khayzuran, Zubayda was intimately involved in all the important political issues of the time. She had influence over judges, police officials, and military generals, not to mention her husband. The observation that "Zubaidah had (complete) control over Hārūn's mind and did with him as she pleased"[50] is perhaps only a slight exaggeration. In the succession battle between her son Muhammad Amin and al-Ma'mun, she played a critical role in Amin's victory. Zubayda was a major force also in turning Harun against the powerful Persian Barmecids, who had directed the political fortunes of the Abbasid dynasty more than any other family. Indirectly, but very effectively, she helped bring about their destruction. Zubayda left her imprint deeply in the sands of Abbasid social and political history.

Moving chronologically onward and geographically southward, we come to the Sulayhid dynasty, which ruled in South Arabia from 1037 to 1138. This Shi'i dynasty made its capital in Sanaa and later in the Dhu Jibla of today's Yemen. The Sulayhi "educated their daughters to the same standards as their menfolk, instilled in them the same moral and political principles, and made them their equals in astuteness, ability, and judgement."[51] The greatest of the Sulayhid queens was Urwa bint Ahmad al-Sulayhi, who upon her husband al-Mukarram's death in 1084 took complete command and ruled for 53 years. A woman of great political acumen, Queen Urwa ruled the Sulayhid state by judiciously emphasizing tactics of compromise, personal maneuver, and the wise appointment of assistants and advisors. Urwa's

---

[49]*Ibid.*, p. 132.

[50]F. Wustenfeld, *Die Chroniken der Stadt Mekka*, vol. 3, p. 15, as quoted in Abbott, *Two Queens*, p. 256.

[51]Robert W. Stookey, *Yemen: The Politics of the Yemen Arab Republic* (Boulder, Colo.: Westview Press, 1978), p. 67.

political success is perhaps largely attributable to the training she received under the direction of another woman, Queen Asma, the wife of the founder of the Sulayhid dynasty.

The Ottoman Empire, which boasts a political history that extended from the thirteenth to the twentieth centuries, is a much more significant example of an Islamic system in which women wielded political power. The Ottoman style, however, is more similar to the Abbasid style of indirect kinship control than to the Sulayhid style of direct rule by a queen. Although one can select any particular sultan and discover in association with him a number of women active in the central decision-making process, we will cut into Ottoman history at perhaps its best-known period of grandeur, the reign of Suleyman I the Lawgiver (1520–1566). Suleyman was known for his legal promulgations and his empire for its architectural creations, naval strength and military expansion deep into Europe. Surrounding Suleyman were three women of particular note—his mother, Hafsa Hatun, and his wives, Hurrem Sultan and Gulbahar Hatun. Their political influence was great, especially in controlling the sultan and the grand vazir, the most important administrative official in the Ottoman system. Of these three women, the most powerful was Hurrem Sultan, a former Russian slave girl known in the West as Roxelana. It was she who convinced Suleyman to let her live with him in the seraglio, "where she obtained complete ascendancy over the Sultan and ruled supreme in the harēm until her death in 1558."[52]

Hafsa Hatun and Hurrem Sultan formed an alliance of convenience to expel one grand vazir and appoint another early in the reign of Suleyman. The new vazir, Ibrahim Pasha, felt indebted to Hafsa Hatun for his position and was careful to do her bidding. Meanwhile, he was independently linked to Suleyman himself, who permitted the vazir to run the empire. Ibrahim Pasha in the process became one of the most powerful of the grand vazirs in Ottoman history. An extraordinarily ambitious person politically, Hurrem Sultan came to regard the vazir as a major competitor and sought to destroy him. When her mother-in-law died in 1534, she moved quickly against the vazir. The now exposed Ibrahim Pasha found an ally in Suleyman's first wife,

---

[52]N. M. Penzer, *The Harēm* (Philadelphia: J. B. Lippincott, 1937), p. 186. There are many sources that describe this period of Ottoman history. For an excellent example, see Stanford Shaw, *History of the Ottoman Empire and Modern Turkey,* vol. 1 (Cambridge: Cambridge University Press, 1976), pp. 87–111.

Gulbahar Hatun, who was anxious that her son Mustafa become the heir apparent. Hurrem Sultan, with her own sons' interests at heart, gathered other supporters (including the French ambassador) and was able to prevail in the struggle. In 1536, Ibrahim Pasha lost not only his job but also his life.

Hurrem Sultan then succeeded in getting her eldest son, Mehmet, named as heir to the throne. With his untimely death, however, Gulbahar Hatun, with the assistance of the new vazir, Hadim Suleyman Pasha, finally placed her son Mustafa in the coveted position. But Hurrem Sultan's power was not to be denied, and she forced this vazir into exile. And she now saw that someone more reliable got the post. Her own son-in-law, Rustem Pasha, became vazir. This new alliance resulted in the execution of Gulbahar Hatun's son Mustafa. When there was a revolt in 1555, partially against this execution, Hurrem Sultan's son Bayizat successfully put it down. When Hurrem Sultan died in 1558, she had determined that one of her sons would become the next sultan. Her son Selim succeeded Suleyman to the throne in 1566 and ruled for eight years as Sultan Selim II. Selim's wife Nurbanu Sultan in fact ruled the empire during his reign. During the rule of her own son, Sultan Murad III, she shared political power with her daughter-in-law Safriyah Sultan. And so it continued. It is small wonder that the Ottoman empire during the sixteenth and seventeenth centuries has come to be historically known as the Sultanate of Woman (*Kadinlar Sultanati*). (For a diagrammatic representation of the women of Suleyman the Lawgiver's reign, see Figure 3.1.)

Early in this century, women played an important part in the various constitutional and revolutionary movements that swept across the

Figure 3.1   The women of Suleyman the Lawgiver's reign. The names of the women in the system appear in boxes.

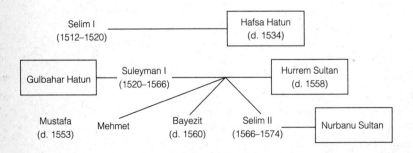

Middle East. An excellent case in point is Halide Edib Adivar, a leading Turkish intellectual, nationalist, and supporter of Mustafa Kemal's movement for independence. Born in 1883, she was educated at the American College for Girls and then began writing and speaking for liberal causes. Her inspired public speeches in support of the nationalist revolution earned her national and even international fame. Her statement that "governments are our enemies, peoples are our friends, and the just revolt of our hearts our strength" became the rallying cry of Turkish nationalists.[53] Halide Edib Adivar actually served in Kemal's army as a corporal, a sergeant, and a sergeant major.

Women also played a critical role in the Iranian constitutional movement from 1905 to 1911. They organized themselves into informal meeting groups (*anjumans*) and did not hesitate to take to the streets in support of their political ideals. When the newly established parliament (*majlis*) faced extinction in 1911, a large group of women marched on the building:

> Three hundred women surrounded the entrance to the *Majlis*, or Parliament, recently formed, and demanded admission. A few only were admitted. They walked in closely veiled, but when they found themselves in the assembly they tore their veils aside, and said that their intention was to kill their husbands, their sons and themselves if the liberty and dignity of Persia were not firmly upheld. They offered their money and jewels, saying: "We are women and cannot fight, but we can give to our country." They had their own places of assembly where they discussed these matters, and they used the Press, and personal influence was largely exerted.[54]

As time has passed, Muslim women have assumed a more direct and dramatic role in Middle Eastern politics. In the Algerian war of independence, women were an important part of the resistance and did everything from hiding fugitives to throwing bombs. National heroine Jamilah Buhrayd, for example, rather than becoming a seamstress, became a revolutionary and was eventually shot, after having been imprisoned and tortured by the French. Young women have been very conspicuous in the Palestine guerrilla movement. Laila

---

[53]Elizabeth Warnock Fernea and Basima Qattan Bezirgan, eds., *Middle Eastern Muslim Women Speak* (Austin, Tex.: The University of Texas Press, 1977), p. 189.

[54]C. Colliver Rice, *Persian Women in Their Ways* (London: Seeley, Service and Co., 1923), p. 270. For an even more dramatic description of this event, see W. Morgan Shuster, *The Strangling of Persia* (New York: Century Co., 1912), p. 198.

Khaled, for example, gained international notoriety when she was captured as part of a four-plane hijacking operation in September 1970.
In May 1972, two young Arab women, former nursing students, participated in the hijacking of a Sabena Boeing 707 to Lod Airport in
Israel. There are many other examples. One observer writes: "Mostly
young and often educated in the West—France, England, the United
States—the Palestinian girl fedayeen have a better political understanding than their male counterparts. Indeed, they are more the
material from which real revolutionaries are made. Proportionate to
their numbers they have caused the Israelis more trouble than have
their male comrades."[55]

This revolutionary role of Muslim women in influencing Middle
Eastern politics is only one of many more direct and formal ways that
they now exert power. As their legal rights expand and as they gain
greater stature in the formal governmental arena, they are conspicuously acquiring political authority. Women's movements are present
in the Middle East, and women are slowly taking their places in government bureaucracies. In so doing, however, they have not relinquished their traditional influence in the informal sphere of power. It
is as part of the informal group or family that women continue to operate most effectively.

In Pahlavi Iran, Empress Farah Diba did not confine herself to
social work and charitable causes. Although she headed nearly 40 different social organizations, she was also involved in political issues. In
the latter half of the 1970s, the empress was the shah's last important
line to reality and was the only person left among his advisors who
could take issue with his decisions. Toward the end, the shah refused
to take the advice of his wife seriously. If he had, the political outcome
in Iran might possibly have been different.

In Tunisia, Wassila bin Amar, the wife of former President Bourguiba, was long embroiled in national politics. Her advice and opinions
often shaped the course of events in that country. In November 1977,
she visited President Sadat in Cairo to indicate her country's support
for his direct approach to peace in the Middle East. Jihan Sadat, the
wife of the assassinated Egyptian president, was an important force in

[55]John Laffin, *Fedayeen: The Arab-Israeli Dilemma* (New York: Free Press, 1973), p. 138.

Egyptian society and politics. She had a significant power base in the presidency, the government more broadly, and within the wealthy bourgeoisie. It took President Mubarak almost five years to dismantle the foundations of her power.

With the resurgence of Islamic movements across the region, women continue to wield influence from behind the veil. The indomitable, independent women of Egypt, for example, have in many cases gone back to traditional garb while at the same time maintaining their integrity and even increasing their power. In Iran, women played a major role in the revolution, donating their jewelry and organizing demonstrations in support of the movement. Since the revolution, veiled women quietly hold influential positions in governmental organizations such as the Ministry of Foreign Affairs and in the major universities in the country. In the division of physical sciences at Beheshti University in 1990, women held three department headships.

Muslim women in the Middle East have never enjoyed legal equality with men and have suffered discrimination in many areas of existence. Any study of the formal scaffolding of the social and political systems clearly demonstrates their lack of authority. Such inequity, however, is not the same as the lack of power. Middle Eastern women have never been powerless. Indeed, they have played a pervasive and persistent part in shaping political decisions and determining political events ever since the time when the widow Khadija married and then materially and psychologically supported the young man Muhammad. Only by analyzing politics at the informal level does one begin to understand and appreciate the significance of women to the entire political process.

Our brief survey of Middle Eastern women in politics yields several general observations. First, women throughout Muslim history have had a more profound impact upon political events than is generally thought. Second, this political power has usually been wielded indirectly and informally through men. Natal and marital relationships have been particularly crucial here. Third, there has been a movement over the past several decades among Middle Eastern women for legal equality and social and political rights. Although this movement has been slowed in recent years by the reassertion of Islam, it is still very much alive, even in the most traditional of countries, such as Saudi Arabia.

In the Middle East, women's liberation is a drive not so much to acquire power as to add authority to power: Why must women's political influence be indirect and confined to the informal arena? Fourth, this drive for authority has not, however, displaced the power and position of women in the traditional realm of informal groups. Middle Eastern women after all are quite sensitive to the fact that this is the main decision-making arena. That is why Algerian heroine Jamilah Buhrayd states: "It's true we don't find as many women in politics as men, but women have always imposed their views in a quieter way without public fuss."[56]

CLASS STRUCTURE: HORIZONTAL STRATIFICATION

It is He who has made us the inheritors of the earth, who has elevated us one above the other by degrees in order to help us experience His gifts.

Quran, Chapter 6, Verse 165

Although informal groups and networks must be taken into account in any study of Middle Eastern politics, the political process is not played out in a seamless web of interacting groups. The above case studies, for example, indicate that it is usually only women of the upper class who in fact influence the national polity. The masses of women (like the masses of men) have little if anything to say about major political decisions. By emphasizing only the group dimension, we suggest that group pluralism promotes equality. What is left out of the equation is the issue of horizontal stratification. Slashing across the web of groups are lines of stratification that profoundly affect not only the group dynamics discussed above but also the entire political process of the Middle East. Serif Mardin cogently summarizes this point when he writes that although membership in a kinship group "raised the expectations of a less prestigious member of the group that he could rise in society, the fact that he belonged to a well-recognized stratum led to frustrations as regards the actual capacity to rise in society."[57]

G. E. von Grunebaum once wrote that "the Muslim's personal equality with his fellows in the faith which is guaranteed, so to speak,

---

[56]Fernea and Bezirgan, *Middle Eastern Women Speak*, p. 261.

[57]Mardin, "Historical Determinants," p. 4.

by his right to a direct relationship with his Lord does in no way preclude elaborate social stratification within the community of Islam."[58] The group network and communalism discussed above cloak a system of horizontal stratification in which Middle Eastern societies break down into a relatively small number of interrelated classes.[59] A class structure always involves entities in superior and subordinate positions. The overall hierarchy of classes is founded upon the unequal possession of one of the fundamental values of social and political life. In the sociological literature, class is most often defined according to one of three different emphases: wealth, status, and power. An individual's place in a social class is determined by his or her position with respect to one of these characteristics. Although all three determinants are interrelated in the sense that the possession of one may strongly affect the acquisition of another, the question of which is the basic criterion remains open. In this volume on the Middle East, we define class in terms of power and employment position.[60]

Class and Power in the Middle East

For our purposes, *power* refers to one's ability to shape and control the behavior of others.[61] This ability may rest as much upon indirect

---

[58]Gustave E. von Grunebaum, *Medieval Islam: A Study in Cultural Orientation*, 2nd ed. (Chicago: University of Chicago Press, 1961), p. 170.

[59]For an important recent study in which "class" is the basic tool of analysis, see Ervand Abrahamian, *Iran Between Two Revolutions* (Princeton, N.J.: Princeton University Press, 1982).

[60]For two explicit attempts to discuss class analysis as it applies to Middle Eastern society and politics, see Jacques Berque, "L'Idée des Classes dans L'Histoire Contemporaine des Arabes," *Cahiers Internationaux de Sociologie* 38 (1965):169–184; and James A. Bill, "Class Analysis and the Dialectics of Modernization in the Middle East," *International Journal of Middle East Studies* 3 (October 1972):417–434. The latter article provides the conceptual and theoretical underpinnings for the linkage of class and power. For a recent formulation, see Alan Richards and John Waterbury, *A Political Economy of the Middle East* (Boulder, Colo.: Westview Press, 1990).

[61]This definition of power is slightly broader than those provided by scholars who have chosen to reword Max Weber's original definition. In our view, a power relation can involve more than getting someone to do what he or she would not otherwise do. It can be a reinforcing pattern whereby one individual encourages another to continue behaving in a certain way, or it may simply be a case of one person's causing another to translate a predisposition into action.

personal maneuvering and verbal persuasion as upon direct threat, coercive demand, or economic inducement. The basis of power may be located in the political, economic, social, educational, religious, or psychological systems. Because Islam is a way of life that involves all of these dimensions, power relations in Islamic societies usually involve a subtly integrated complex of factors. One Islamic scholar writes, for example, that "political influence, military power, administrative rank, wealth, birth, and schooling, in every possible combination, strengthened or counteracted one another in assigning a given individual his place in society."[62] Wealth is but one of a number of important variables that determine one's position in the class structure. Material resources have seldom been enough to enable individuals consistently to attain their goals. Personal contacts, social manipulation, saintly ancestry, mystical strength, familial solidarity, higher education, political maneuvering, and an innate sense of timing are all crucial ingredients that help determine one's class standing.

Among the more common if seldom recognized dimensions of power that have been instrumental in shaping the formation of Middle Eastern class structure are:

1. Exchange transactions in which one person convinces others to accede to his or her wishes by rewarding them for so doing;
2. Informational exchanges that involve dispensing and withholding information of varying degrees of value;
3. Decisional situations in which one person controls the decision-making environment and thus the decisions made therein;
4. Debt-inflicting relationships in which one does favors for others with the confident expectation that they will someday be returned;
5. Overt deference behavior by which one person gains the trust of another and thus makes the temporarily more powerful person vulnerable;
6. Bargaining interactions that occur in environments of doubt, and rest upon such techniques as the bluff and the compromise;
7. Kinship patterns in which family members strive to assist one another to improve their relative positions in the class structure;
8. Modes of misrepresentation that distort reality in a manner designed to shift the balance of interpersonal influence.

---

[62]Von Grunebaum, *Medieval Islam*, p. 212.

The exchange transaction is the simplest and most direct means of exerting power; it is a major pattern in all societies. It is most often expressed as financial dealings, which range all the way from salary transactions to bribery payments. In the Middle East, a disproportionately high percentage of exchange transactions occur in noneconomic terms, since the objects of exchange include personal loyalty, political service, religious approval, and reliable information. Informational exchanges are critical in societies where informality cloaks the exercise of power and where decisions are made within personalistic networks. Indeed, information is a valuable commodity in the Middle East, since it can be used both offensively and defensively. Political elites constantly seek information concerning the actual and potential opposition forces in their societies. Individuals and groups in the middle and lower classes both hoard and barter information in order to improve their own positions in the social structure.

Another dimension of the power syndrome is the phenomenon of "nondecision making," whereby superordinately situated individuals control the behavior of subordinates through the manipulation and control of the environment in which the latter must operate.[63] An example of this phenomenon in the Middle East is the executive control of parliaments and political parties. Decisions tend to be made in the parliaments and parties according to what the deputies believe the will of the ruler or military junta would be. It is not necessary that there be any communication between the leadership and the representative. If deputies do not correctly anticipate what the ruler wants and do not act accordingly, they may find themselves politically unemployed; or, as happened in the mid-1970s in Bahrain and Kuwait, the rulers simply dissolve the parliamentary bodies themselves. Control is thus built into the structure of the system in a less than obvious manner. Learning how to interact in this kind of system is essential to the determination of one's class standing.

One of the most distinctive facets of power relations in Middle Eastern society is debt infliction. In the Muslim community of North Africa, "Every act requires some form of reciprocation as an inherent aspect of its very nature: Every act creates an obligation or expresses a

---

[63]See Peter Bachrach and Morton S. Baratz's classic discussion of the "non-decision-making process" in "Two Faces of Power," *American Political Science Review* 56 (December 1962):947–952.

right held."[64] Those upon whom debts are inflicted are put into a disadvantageous position of dependence. It is in this sense that Fredrik Barth describes the mechanism as it manifests itself in the Swat Valley in Pakistan. The relationship to political power is unmistakable here, since even "gift-giving and hospitality are potent means of controlling others. . . ."[65] As one Lebanese citizen puts it, gifts are "the lubricants of social interaction."[66]

Deference, which is part of the somewhat extravagant patterns of courtesy and politeness that obtain in the Middle East, can be used effectively to balance highly uneven personal relationships. When properly displayed, deference can loosen the control of the more powerful actor over the less powerful individual. Deferential behavior can stimulate a false sense of security in the superior person in any relationship, thus heightening his or her vulnerability. It was in this spirit that the Ziyarid prince Kai Ka'us Ibn Iskandar wrote his son that "if you are being fattened by someone, you may expect very quickly to be slaughtered by him. . . ."[67]

Another context in which power exchange occurs in the Middle East is bargaining, in which the actors in fact agree to disagree. Each side in the encounter uses a wide variety of persuasive techniques in order to further his or her interests. The outcome of the confrontation remains in doubt until the very end of the process, when one side indicates a willingness to accept the terms of the other. An individual who is able to use an effective blend of candor and the bluff, as in bargaining, can greatly enhance his or her position in the social and political hierarchy.

The final two tactics of control and influence have to do with kinship ties and modes of misrepresentation. As we noted earlier, the family is the most cohesive unit in Middle Eastern society. As such, it is least susceptible to radical change and most reliable as a unit of per-

---

[64]Lawrence Rosen, "Muslim-Jewish Relations in a Moroccan City," *International Journal of Middle East Studies* 3 (October 1972):438.

[65]Fredrik Barth, *Political Leadership among Swat Pathans* (London: Athlone Press, 1959), p. 79.

[66]This is reported in Fuad I. Khuri, *From Village to Suburb: Order and Change in Greater Beirut* (Chicago: University of Chicago Press, 1975), p. 86.

[67]Kai Ka'us Ibn Iskandar, *A Mirror for Princes* (The Qābūs-nāma), trans. Reuben Levy (London: Cresset Press, 1951), p. 191.

sonal and group support. The mobility of one family member affects the potential mobility of the whole family. Entire families often move up in the class structure. They are also downwardly mobile. Because of the centrality of the family in determining one's position in the power structure, individuals constantly seek to attach themselves to rising or already prominent families. This is usually accomplished through marriage, but it is also often done through fictive kinship ties. This is only one of the forms of misrepresentation designed to help improve one's class position. To exaggerate and falsely embroider reality at propitious times is a technique more frowned upon in the West than in the Middle East, where such behavior often deflects conflict and prevents violent confrontation. It also is a dimension of influence that must be considered when explaining class membership and class conflict.

The Middle Eastern Class System

There is one further consideration in analyzing power relations in the Middle East. Throughout Islamic history, a person's power position has been closely intertwined with his or her occupational skill. Mode of employment to a large degree determined an individual's capacity to utilize the techniques and to operate effectively in the environment discussed above. An individual was best able to wield power using skills and talents he already possessed. The military, cleric, and bureaucratic occupations provided their practitioners with unusual opportunities to strengthen and improve their positions in the class structure through informed use of the coercive, religious, and political dimensions of power. The intimate connection between power and employment was a direct result of the development of Islamic social history and the Prophet Muhammad's early strictures concerning the occupational bases of the community of Islam. One of the earliest foundations for stratification was the assignment of the believers "to a more or less definite hierarchy of professions."[68] For purposes of the following empirical analysis of horizontal stratification in the Middle East, we define classes as the largest aggregates of individuals united by similar modes of employment and maintaining similar power positions in society.

Classical Islamic thinkers have presented views of horizontal

---

[68]Von Grunebaum, *Medieval Islam*, p. 177.

stratification that range from two-class to eight-class hierarchies. According to the criteria developed above, the traditional Middle Eastern Islamic social structure consisted of seven interrelated classes: the upper (ruling) class, the bureaucratic middle class, the bourgeois middle class, the cleric middle class, the traditional working class, the peasant class, and the nomadic class. This schema includes one upper, three middle, and three lower classes. This designation of upper, middle, and lower refers to the general power categories, while the more specific labels are assigned on the basis of both power and employment. The nomenclature of each class indicates its employment function.

The upper class in the traditional Islamic social structure represented a tiny percentage of the population, usually less than 2 percent. The upper class was a ruling class, since it possessed a monopoly of the instruments of both power and authority in society. This class was composed of the elites that rested at the very apex of the governmental, landholding, religious, tribal, military, and business pyramids of influence. The rulers and the networks of ruling families were at the core of the upper class. Also included were the military leaders, the large native landlords, the highest-level bureaucrats (the vazirs, for example), the leadership of the ulema who supported the system, the tribal chieftains and khans, and the wealthiest merchants and business entrepreneurs. This ruling class exhibited exclusive and inclusive characteristics that tended to balance one another out, ultimately stabilizing membership size. In most cases, a single member of this class had a number of power-laden functions. For example, a member of the ruling family was often at the same time a military leader and a large landlord. The tribal nobility maintained large landholdings and were often among the highest-ranking military officials. In this way, wealth, influence, and coercive power reinforced one another and strengthened one's class position. This helped to narrow upper-class membership. On the other hand, the kinship mechanism tended to expand the size of the upper class while at the same time linking this class to the various middle classes. The extended family ties of a ruler, vazir, or landlord brought new waves of individuals into ruling-class ranks. Indeed, one of the best ways even today to understand ruling classes in Middle Eastern societies is to analyze the structures of leading families.

Ruling classes in the contemporary Islamic Middle East are shaped by the lines of kinship along which power flows. Family ties and intermarriage patterns help solidify an inherently fragmented and fissured upper class. The lack of any strong class consciousness, at least among the ruling class, is partially compensated for by a kind of interfamilial and intrafamilial consciousness. Although studies show that family membership in Middle Eastern upper classes is relatively unstable, there are indications that a small number of families remain in upper-class ranks over time. The informality of family structure in many ways mirrors the character of the upper class, which is also relatively fluid. In an impressive study of the upper class ("patriciate") of Muslim Nishapur from the tenth to the twelfth century, Richard Bulliet writes that "the reality of the patriciate consisted in individuals and families who knew each other and recognized each other as being above the ordinary run of people. There was no formal membership in the patriciate."[69] In sum, the upper class in Islamic history has been a complex of leading clerics, generals, vazirs, khans, and merchant kings familially and informally bound together a round the person of the ruler and his family. By virtue of its advantageous power position, this ruling class directs the political system of society.

The bureaucratic middle class has been the most powerful of the three traditional middle classes. Its membership is composed of the mass of governmental employees who staff the administrative system. Possessing a minimum of traditional education, these individuals are the scribes, accountants, recorders, and bureaucratic functionaries of traditional Middle Eastern society. Like the ruling class, this middle class is rather loosely and informally organized. Although in many Islamic societies there were families that came to be known as bureaucratic families, kinship ties are not as important as class indicators here as they are in the upper class.

In our concentric circles of class and power, the bureaucratic middle class most closely rings the ruling class. It is an important intermediary class that translates the directives of the ruling class into action. This administering class appears to be almost an appendage to the upper class because of its many points of contact with the upper class. Owing to this proximity, the bureaucratic middle class has more often served the interests of the ruling class than those of the other middle and lower classes. While maintaining an important power of its own, this class traditionally viewed its interests as intertwined with those of

---

[69]Richard W. Bulliet, *The Patricians of Nishapur: A Study in Medieval Islamic Social History* (Cambridge, Mass.: Harvard University Press, 1972), p. 86.

the upper class. The proximity to power always held out to the bureaucratic middle class the possibility of movement into upper-class ranks.

Located approximately between the bureaucratic and cleric middle classes is the bourgeois middle class, which is a class of businessmen, merchants, and traders. The symbol and center of activity of this class is the bazaar, or *suq*. As an individual, the merchant or trader has relatively little economic power and virtually no political influence. As a class, however, this bourgeoisie has considerable political power. When ruling-class policies have seriously endangered the interests of commerce and the life-styles of the merchant, the bazaar has often become the heart of opposition to the regime in power. It was out of the ranks of the bourgeoisie that Islam itself developed as a community and civilization. And throughout the history of Islam, a number of social and religious movements have sprung up from this class in opposition to the prevailing political order.

There are three reasons why the merchants and tradesmen have been able to give birth to opposition movements. In the first place, the members of this class managed to institutionalize their traditional informal patterns of interaction in a system of guilds and brotherhoods. Second, their organizational apparatus had a semblance of ideology, which helped provide a rationalization for their activities. This ideology was composed of various folk and mystic Islamic beliefs. Finally, this kind of organizational and ideological framework linked the business middle class with important elements in both the cleric middle class and the traditional working class. The suqs and bazaars were the meeting place for merchant, cleric, and artisan.

The cleric middle class, which is composed of the lower and intermediate ranks of the ulema, is the third traditional middle class. The members of this class enjoy neither the political influence of the bureaucrats nor the wealth of the businessmen. They have, however, possessed important religio-psychological influence over those members of society who have been practicing Muslims. They also have controlled the educational system through their role as teachers and directors of the traditional educational institutions (*maktabs* and *madrasas*). The constituency of the clerics has been largely concentrated within the lower classes, and because of this, the interests of the cleric middle class have been closely entwined with those below them in the social structure.

The three traditional middle classes were closely related to one another in a number of ways. The members of all these classes were the products of the same educational system—a system that was directed by the ulema and that stressed reading, writing, religious law, rhetoric, and the Quran. The educational method used was rote memorization. One result of this was that all traditional middle-class individuals had a similar value system, largely conservative. This meant that these classes rebelled only under very special circumstances, consisting of either a severe and adverse disruption of business conditions or a series of policies by the ruling class that abrogated and contradicted the tenets of Islam. Usually both these conditions had to come about simultaneously in order for these middle classes to move to active opposition. And even then, the bureaucratic middle class seldom participated.

The bulk of the population of all Middle Eastern societies falls into the three lower classes, consisting of workers, peasants, and nomads. Ideally, Islam commands that the community treat the poor and least powerful with compassion. The giving of alms is one of the acts that all the faithful are expected to practice. In describing the class structure of Islamic communities, Imam Ali, son-in-law of the Prophet, said of the lower classes: "Lowest of all are the afflicted and the poor who are the unfortunate and the suffering. They are always the broken-hearted and the weary."[70] In fact, however, the situation of the lower classes has been little improved by such words of sympathy and ideals of charitable assistance. The harsher realities of class structure are reflected in another scheme of classification presented by the Abbasid courtier Yahya al-Fazl. He divides society into four classes and then writes that "the remainder are filthy refuse, a torrent of scum, base cattle, none of whom thinks of anything but his food and sleep."[71]

Most of the members of the lower class belong to the peasant class. In preponderantly agricultural societies, these are the individuals who work the land under a variety of arrangements that only alter the degree of their poverty, dependence, disease, and ignorance. The peasant class, located at the very bottom of the social structure, has very little power and is thus exposed to exploitation by all the other

---

[70]Imam Ali, Farman to Malik Ashtar, governor of Egypt, *Sukhanan-i Ali* [The words of Ali], trans. by Javad Fazil (Tehran, 1966), p. 242 (in Persian).

[71]Ibn al-Faqih, *Kitab al-Buldan,* as quoted in Reuben Levy, *The Social Structure of Islam* (Cambridge: Cambridge University Press, 1957), p. 67.

classes in society. For the individual peasant, this usually means abuse at the hands of landlord, merchant, and government official. Peasants have also often suffered from manipulation by the clerics and from the raids of tribesmen. The situation of the nomadic lower class is not much better than that of the peasants. The tribal masses have existed in a state of subjection to a hierarchy of khans and have had to struggle to make a living from an often inhospitable land. Because of a modicum of natural freedom and their occasional importance as military forces, the tribesmen have been a cut above the peasant in the power structure.

The traditional working class includes such groups as servants, manual laborers, craftsmen, and artisans. In the Middle East, this class has been as much a rural as an urban phenomenon. Like the members of the other lower classes, these workers have earned their livelihood through the use of their physical skills. Working with their hands, they have been scorned by the middle and upper classes. The members of this class have often joined guilds and brotherhoods; accordingly, they have enjoyed some organizational protection. This has placed the traditional working class in the best power position among the lower classes.

The traditional class structure in the Islamic Middle East remains in place to a large extent in contemporary Middle Eastern society. There have been, however, a number of obvious changes that have largely resulted from the forces of modernization discussed in Chapter 1. Land reform programs, coupled with the increasing emphasis upon industrialization, have caused a shifting of the bases of power of the ruling class. Land ownership, which was an important upper-class power credential for centuries, has given way to industrial investment in the form of contracting, banking, export-import trade, and business concessions of all kinds. The traditional middle classes have grown in size relative to the upper and lower classes, with the bourgeois middle class expanding at an especially rapid rate. Nomadic tribes are slowly being forced to settle, and as a result are grudgingly blending into the peasantry. Strong rural-to-urban migration patterns have resulted in the mushrooming growth of shantytowns and the appearance of an unemployed proletariat that continues to expand along the edges of the major cities. This last change is a dramatic one, since it represents the appearance of an important modern addition to the centuries-old class structure.

The relatively recent appearance of two new classes is a significant

THE GENES OF POLITICS: GROUPS, CLASSES, AND FAMILIES **127**

break with the past patterns of horizontal stratification in the area. Both an industrial working class and a professional middle class have emerged as definite formations in the second half of this century. Both classes are the products of the accelerating process of modernization, and their roots trace back to the growth of large industry and the development of modern systems of education in the Afro-Asian world.

Industrialization and urbanization have been the major catalysts for the appearance of the new urban industrial working class. Census data indicate that this class still represents a very small proportion in the various Middle Eastern countries, but that it is growing at a rapid pace. The growing masses of unemployed migrants referred to above are a ready pool of unskilled and semiskilled labor for new industry. This new lower class is more powerful than the traditional lower classes because of its strategic and visible location in the large cities as well as its growing social awareness. The industrial working class, however, has barely begun to realize its potential as a social and political force. This is not the case with the second and more recent class formation.

The Professional Middle Class

The forces of modernization and the acceleration of accompanying social change have given rise to the formation of a new middle class in the Middle East.[72] This class, which we here term the professional middle class, is one whose members derive their power from skills obtained through a modern higher education. Many members of the new class seek to advance themselves through their professional skills and talents rather than through the use of wealth and personal connections, two resources that most of them lack in any case. The professional middle class is not a bourgeois middle class, since its members earn their livelihoods less through ownership of property or entrepreneurship in business than through salaries, technical fees, scholarships, and professional activities. This class is composed of white-collar workers engaged in technical, professional, cultural, and

---

[72]For the pioneering study of this class, see Manfred Halpern, *The Politics of Social Change in the Middle East and North Africa* (Princeton, N.J.: Princeton University Press, 1963). For an analysis of this class as it challenged the shah's regime in Iran, see James Alban Bill, *The Politics of Iran: Groups, Classes and Modernization* (Columbus, Ohio: Charles E. Merrill, 1972).

administrative occupations. Its membership is drawn largely from such groups as teachers, bureaucrats, professors, students, technocrats, engineers, physicians, writers, artists, journalists, and middle-ranking army officers. Among the army officers, we must include political leaders such as Gamal Abdel Nasser, Anwar Sadat, and H'usni Mubarak of Egypt, Houari Boumedienne of Algeria, Mu'ammar Qaddafi of Libya, Hafez al-Assad of Syria, and Ja'far Numairi of Sudan. All rose to power on the wave of the aspirations of the new middle class.

Although the professional middle class is not a class of intellectuals, it may be properly termed an intelligentsia, since it composes the intellectual elite in society. Unlike the educated members of the ruling class, who enjoy the twin privileges of great wealth and political authority, the members of the professional middle class have little other than their education to fall back on. Whereas the members of the traditional middle classes rested their power on the older educational system, dominated by religion, the individuals in the new middle class draw their influence from the modern educational system. And this is what makes them an increasingly indispensable segment of society. Modernization results in constantly accelerated demands for qualified physicians, engineers, technocrats, teachers, and soldiers. Economic and industrial development guarantees the growth of the new middle class.

In Turkey, Egypt, Libya, and Tunisia, members of the professional middle class have come to hold political power and have begun to implement developmental programs with varying degrees of success. In Iraq, Syria, Algeria, and Sudan, individuals from the new middle class have taken political control but have failed to solve the problem of division and discord among groups and classes. This failure has severely retarded political development and modernization. In Morocco, Saudi Arabia, Jordan, and the various Gulf shaikhdoms, the professional intelligentsia remains largely locked out of the political arena. In Morocco and Jordan, where this class is a relatively large one, a number of its members have moved into the political elite as the result of a calculated policy of co-optation on the part of the ruling class. All in all, membership in the professional middle class throughout the Islamic Middle East is rapidly approaching 10 to 12 percent of the population.

The professional middle class is a threat to the traditional sociopolitical system in the Middle East. Many of its members decry the old network of personalism, favoritism, nepotism, and influence wielding that continues in many cases to suffocate their own opportunities to move forward on the basis of technical skills and professional merit. What makes this class such a serious threat to the traditional social structure is not so much that all its members are agents of modernization but that some of its members demand political development. The latter refuse to relate to the ruling class in terms of subservience and deference. Instead, they demand a share of political authority and promise to uproot the power relations upon which the authority structure rests.

The professional middle class is composed of many individuals whose goals include a transformation of power relations and the authority structure. Many of them prefer professionalism to personalism, justice to wealth, intellectual freedom to imposed stability, and effective political participation to political co-optation. Even in Saudi Arabia, a growing professional middle class chafes at the monopolizing power of one family and the social control and economic corruption that prevail in the country. In Lebanon, the new middle class is very weak economically. "But in no sense should this detract from its vital role as carrier of new skills, ideologies, and styles of life. And this is certainly more relevant to its role as an agent of modernization."[73] It was shortly after the Egyptian coup in 1952 that Ahmad Baha'eddine wrote that this new middle class was "the greatest hope we have for progress."[74]

The professional middle class has seldom borne out such hope, however, as it has not been as much a force for development as might have been expected. Besides the extraordinary strength of the traditional political system, there are other reasons why the new middle class has failed to implement much deep-seated change.

---

[73]Samir Khalaf, "Urbanization and Urbanism in Beirut: Some Preliminary Results" (Paper prepared for delivery at the Twenty-first Annual Near East Conference, Princeton, N.J., April 9–10, 1970), p. 37. This paper documents the important appearance of a new professional middle class in the Hamra district of Beirut. See also Samir Khalaf and Per Kongstad, *Hamra of Beirut: A Case of Rapid Urbanization* (Leiden, The Netherlands: E. J. Brill, 1973).

[74]Ahmad Baha'eddine, "Al-iqta'iyyun wal-ra'smaliyyun wal-muthaqqafun"; [Feudalists, capitalists, and intellectuals], in *Rose Al-Yussif*, no. 1353 (May 17, 1954), as quoted in Anouar Abdel-Malek, *Egypt: Military Society*, trans. Charles Lam Markmann (New York: Vintage Books, 1968), p. 178.

Like every other social unit in the Middle East, this class is torn by internal cleavages and tensions. These divisions are along the lines of kinship, ethnicity, religion, occupation, social origins, geography (urban and rural), and university background. All of these divisions in turn affect the individual's orientations toward modernization and political development. The influence of those who would uproot the traditional patterns of power and authority tends to be nullified by those who seek to preserve the traditional processes in order to improve their own positions in the system. This group usually supports modernization at the expense of political development. These are the maneuverers in the new middle class who survive by manipulation while lacking the civility and courteous charm that was the hallmark of the aristocrats of the older generation. It is this segment of the professional middle class that is readily corruptible. In a stirring indictment of this group within the intelligentsia, one novelist writes: "Every country east of the Mediterranean is torn to bits by ever-competing jealous politicos coming to power by some kind of inheritance. . . . But I can envisage the day when these countries will be even worse, torn by degree-holders more self-interested and sycophantic than their predecessors, and far, far less charitable. If you think the sheikh grinds the faces of his tribesmen you should wait and see the Ph.D. grind the faces of all and sundry, without even a touch of the magnanimity we pride ourselves on."[75]

The professional middle class remains crippled in its challenge to traditional sociopolitical relations in the Middle East. The deep fissures throughout the class are intentionally deepened by the ruling class in order to weaken the cohesiveness of this challenging unit. The political elite encourages those elements in the new class that are most susceptible to the blandishments of bribery and personal aggrandizement.

The new middle class carries another major weakness. It is separated from the lower class masses by an enormous social and cultural gap. Engineers or physicians with modern higher educations have separated themselves from the illiterate citizens that make up the majority of their own people. Often educated in universities of the West, multilingual in speech, fashionably chic in dress, secular in thought

---

[75]Jabra I. Jabra, *Hunters in a Narrow Street* (London, 1960), as quoted in *A Middle East Reader,* ed. by Irene L. Gendzier (New York: Pegasus, 1969), p. 114.

and belief, the professional represents the antithesis of the illiterate, suspicious, destitute, and deeply religious peasant. This division became most apparent in the Middle East in Iran after the revolution, when the masses turned to the religious leaders and tradition and away from the secular intelligentsia.

Today, the members of the professional middle class find themselves increasingly swimming against the tides of Islamic fundamentalism. Although they are still dedicated to the transformation of traditional patrimonial rule, there is no longer any guarantee that they are destined to become the leaders of the new political systems. The fact that the religious leaders, with their mass constituency, have hijacked the Iranian revolution is an indication that the professional middle class may no longer be the political force of the future in the Middle East. Increasingly, members of this class are returning to Islam as part of a general search for their dignity, roots, and personal heritage.

Despite all this, the professional middle class continues to grow. A few voices within the class continue to clamor for radical social and political change. And because the ruling class desperately needs the skills and talents of these individuals in order to implement their programs of modernization, these uprooters are slowly improving their power positions. On the basic issues of power and authority relations, the ruling class grudgingly gives ground while working to preserve the ongoing class structure from the challenges presented by the new class. Regardless of who ultimately takes control of future revolutions in the region, the professionals, technicians, and scientists will remain an indispensable part of society. Even the revolutionary regime in Iran has required skilled technicians in the oil fields, talented physicians in the hospitals, competent planners and managers in the bureaucracy, and capable pilots and officers in the military.

The Dynamics of Group–Class Interaction

The dynamics of Middle Eastern social structure develop out of an integrated system of both vertical and horizontal stratification. The overall social structure might best be viewed as an intricate web of groups that is partially partitioned along class lines. Group and class structures relate to each other reciprocally, and it is this reciprocity that builds coherence into the sociopolitical system. The multistranded sinews of group relations bind the class structure together by crisscrossing class cleavages. Ethnic, tribal, religious, and military groups, for example, often draw their membership from several different classes. Here class distinctions are somewhat softened by common group affiliation. At the same time, group formations are molded and shaped to a considerable degree by class. Groups are often structured along class lines, and their memberships remain confined within the boundaries of a single class. Family units, for example, tend to belong to a single class. Certainly, class divisions serve to retard individual and group mobility.

Class conflict in the Middle East is a muted phenomenon. There are three major reasons for this, and all of them relate to the impact of vertical stratification. First, the existence of a wide variety of important intraclass groups in the Middle East renders class units relatively diffuse. Fissures within classes are numerous and deep enough to weaken class cohesion and to retard class consciousness. Loyalty to primordial groups such as the family takes precedence over loyalty to class. Second, the plethora of groups with multiclass membership promotes interclass communication and draws together individuals from differing classes on the basis of shared group goals. As we have pointed out above, this helps to integrate the class structure and therefore to mellow class conflict. Third, the group structure provides a system of mobility channels through which individuals can rise and fall in the class hierarchy. This constant individual movement across class lines lessens the harsh impact of class confrontation.

The pages of Middle Eastern history are dotted with dramatic examples of individual and group mobility. As one writer puts it, in the Middle East "one can be a liar in the morning, a vizir in the evening, and perhaps hanged on the following day."[76] Stretching vertically through the class structure are a number of shifting ladders of group configurations that, although unsteady and unpredictable, nonetheless can be negotiated by enterprising individuals. Many of the rungs of such ladders are difficult to discern because of the informal and concealed nature of their formation. Informal groups are, in general, the most reliable of the groups that span class divisions. Examples of groups that connect the middle and upper classes include military officer cliques, mystic orders, high administrative caucuses, and interfa-

---

[76]Vincent Monteil, *Morocco* (New York: Viking Press, 1964), p. 141, as quoted in Rosen, "Rural Political Process," p. 223.

milial marriage clusters. Let us examine the last example in more depth.

Nuclear families more often tend to be intraclass groups than do extended families, since the latter include a larger number of individuals, each striving to improve his own position in the social system. But once one member of either a nuclear or an extended family is able to improve his class standing, he subsequently acts as a force that helps to propel other family members forward in the power structure. At the very minimum, the individual in the higher class will be able to protect and defend his family's interests. Always, however, when familial membership is spread among classes, it acts as a brake upon class tension and conflict. A more significant aspect of family-group structure in relation to class interaction is the mechanism of interfamilial marriage. In the Middle East, the marriage of two individuals is better described as the union of two families. When the marriage partners are of different social classes, entire family clusters develop relatively tight interclass relationships. Indeed, it is very common and increasingly possible for individuals of middle-class background to search consciously for a mate who comes from a powerful upper-class family.

Many members of the middle-class intelligentsia attempt to improve their power positions by marrying into the ruling class. Some pursue this strategy in a very calculating manner. Others are torn between their commitment to merit and achievement and their desire to gain enough political leverage to enable them to implement their social and political ideas. Practically all of them are forced to rely upon familial connections at many junctures in their professional and political lives. To the more professionally competent and politically radical among them, this is unpalatable business, and many are visibly embarrassed by the fact that they either belong to the ruling class or have married into it. Middle-class professionals thus find themselves in the unenviable position of denigrating their familial ties while at the same time being forced to use these ties in order to survive and advance in society. This kind of pressured compromise is another factor reducing the effectiveness of their class as a revolutionizing force. In terms of this discussion, it represents a method whereby the challenging middle class is bound to the ruling class. Family clusters cut across class lines and then serve as bridges for the upwardly mobile members of the kinship group.

Groups, then, are much more fluid collectivities than classes in the Middle East because they have much greater ranges of mobility. A class can improve its position only by rather limited incremental movements. The ruling class will always be the upper class, and so it is down the line. By definition, classes must always remain in a power hierarchy. Individuals and groups, on the other hand, can rise dramatically or fall meteorically within the social structure. The great movement of individuals and groups increases flexibility in a class structure that would otherwise be fragile and much more susceptible to upheaval and radical change.

The social structure described above is a formidable obstacle to the processes of modernization and political development that are under way in the Middle East. The traditional social system refuses to be torn, and the basic power and authority relations that make up this system are extraordinarily difficult to uproot. Since class conflict, often the agent of transformation, is neutralized, change involves chipping away at pieces of the mosaic. This modifying change seldom disturbs the underlying network of power relations that is the basis for the group and class structure of Middle Eastern societies.

The situation analyzed above varies considerably from one Middle Eastern society to another. Some societies, for example, are relatively congenial to modernization and political development. In these societies, the lines of horizontal stratification are only weakly intersected by communal cleavages. As a result, the traditional social structure is more easily torn, because class configurations are more cohesive internally and more bared to conflict externally. In Turkey, Tunisia, and Egypt, for example, the natural lines of class conflict and power confrontation are relatively infrequently intersected by ethnic, religious, and tribal divisions. In such countries as Syria and Iraq, on the other hand, communalism and the many vertical strands of stratification soften class confrontation and invest the traditional system with a stability nourished by a vast interlocking network of competing groups.

Much can be explained about the outbreak of the Lebanese civil war when it is recognized that the lines separating ethnic and religious groups had come to coincide more and more closely with class lines. The groups lost their cross-cutting character and gradually reinforced the explosive class divisions. In other words, the vertical structure of stratification gradually collapsed until it became a reinforcing part of the system of conflicting classes. The Lebanese upper class was dominated by Christian Arabs, while the lower class was overwhelmingly Muslim. Although there was some noticeable overlap, this had become less the case with time. When the explosion came, therefore, it was fueled by both group and class conflict. The presence of the Palestinians, a highly politicized appendage to the Lebanese lower class, only exacerbated the struggle. When group and class lines begin to coincide in the Middle East, the system begins to lose its balanced stability. Violent conflict is often the result, and the consequent changes can either accelerate or retard development. In Chapters 4 and 5, we will examine those individuals who do most to determine the directions that these changes will take.

Chapter 4

The Politics of Patrimonial Leadership

An important component of the politics of power and change in the Middle East is the issue of political leadership. Although societies are composed of an interrelated network of groups and classes, there is always one group of individuals that has a disproportionate amount of power and political influence. Sometimes referred to as the political elite, this group of leaders shapes the political style and molds the political system of a society. In this chapter, we shall analyze the social characteristics and political methodology of Muslim leadership. In the process, it is also important for us to understand how individuals are recruited into leadership positions.

Middle Eastern political leaders vary considerably from country to country. As the last stronghold of absolute monarchy in the world, the Middle East is the home of four major kingdoms and ten mini-monarchies located along the Persian Gulf. In order of ruling experience, the major monarchs include the following: King Hussein of Jordan, King Hassan of Morocco, Sultan Qabus of Oman, and King Fahd of Saudi Arabia. The other countries are almost all governed by modern authoritarian leaders, most of whom came to power as the result of a military coup or national war of independence. In Iran, a form of Islamic authoritarianism modified by participatory parliamentary politics was born in 1979 and remains alive today. Besides these types of authoritarian control, more representative structures exist imperfectly in Israel and Turkey.

Despite all the differences that separate Middle Eastern leaders and elites, there are in the Muslim world a number of deep-seated and persisting similarities in rule. These similarities, which are the subject of this chapter, have existed throughout Islamic history and can be traced to the days of the Prophet Muhammad, himself the model par excellence of political leadership.

The processes of leadership in the Islamic Middle East have been both represented and shaped by the life of Muhammad. Through the establishment of a new world community in the seventh century, the Prophet combined the roles of messenger of God and leader of men and women. Today, throughout the Islamic world, millions of Muslims continue to pattern their lives after his. It is not surprising, therefore, that twentieth-century Muslim political leaders often imitate the leadership style promoted by the Prophet Muhammad in Arabia some 1,400 years ago.

The very success of Muhammad as a political leader is one of the reasons that he remains a shadowy, distorted, and even frightening figure to many Westerners. In the pantheon of truly great world leaders, the Prophet has been the one most maligned by Western writers, who have for centuries found him a difficult figure to interpret sympathetically. He has been presented in Western literature as a thug, sorcerer, sex fiend, murderer, and epileptic, and even as a defrocked Roman Catholic priest. The ridiculous extreme of this perspective is seen in Guibert de Nogent's statement that Muhammad died "through excessive drunkenness and that his corpse was eaten by pigs on a dung-hill, explaining why the flesh of this animal and wine are prohibited."[1]

Dante's and Voltaire's views on the subject were only slightly more enlightened than those of de Nogent, and Diderot stated that Muhammad was "the greatest friend of woman and the greatest enemy of sober reason who ever lived."[2] Even Edward Gibbon and Washington Irving, whose writings about Muhammad were more

---

[1] Emile Dermenghem, *The Life of Mahomet* (London: George Routledge and Sons, 1930), p. 119.

[2] Tor Andrae, *Mohammed: The Man and His Faith* (New York: Barnes and Noble, 1936), p. 175.

objective, viewed him negatively. In concluding *Mahomet and His Successors,* Irving says that Muhammad had "mental hallucinations," which "continued more or less to bewilder him with a species of monomania to the end of his career, and that he died in the delusive belief of his mission as a prophet."[3]

These views of Muhammad undoubtedly result from ignorance and from insecurity because of the threat that his mission carried for the Western world. After all, Islam has been the only major non-Western, non-Christian movement that both posed a genuine political threat and provided an attractive alternative civilization while challenging Christendom on its own soil. Today, our understanding of the genius of Muhammad's leadership as well as of the patterns of rule of the contemporary leaders of Islamic countries remains sketchy and superficial. The fact that partisan Muslim scholars have tended to view Muhammad idealistically, defensively, and uncritically has not helped to improve this situation. In this chapter, we will attempt to avoid both extremes by analyzing Muhammad primarily and objectively as a political leader. By beginning our analysis with the general patterns of rule that Muhammad generated, we hope to be better able to understand the more contemporary political leaders to be discussed in Chapter 5.

MUHAMMAD: THE POLITICS OF A PROPHET

The Prophet Muhammad was born in Mecca in 570. Social and political life was then dominated by the interaction between clans and tribes, and desert nomads were gradually moving into a more settled world of commerce and trade. This was a time of transition marked by continual feuds among clans and by intense commercial rivalry. The Prophet's personal environment was also unstable; by the time he was 6, he had lost both of his parents. Muhammad was raised first by his grandfather and then by his uncle Abu Talib, who was the head of the clan of Hashim. Although little is actually known about his early life, it is safe to assume that he worked in menial positions related to commerce and caravans. During his first 25 years, Muhammad gained firsthand experience and knowledge of the business, religion, and politics of the day. We know that he traveled to Syria and was in constant touch with peoples throughout that part of the world.

---

[3]Irving, *Mahomet and His Successors,* vol. 1 (New York: G. P. Putnam's Sons, 1893), p. 491.

As an orphan and a member of one of the declining clans of the Quraysh tribe, Muhammad lacked many of the resources necessary to develop any important influence of his own. The first turning point in his life was, therefore, his marriage to the wealthy and twice-widowed Khadija. For the next two decades, Muhammad lived in the community as a prosperous businessman. During this time, he acquired contacts and influence that were to be of fundamental importance to him in his role as prophet and preacher.

In about 610, Muhammad began receiving revelations, and shortly thereafter he began preaching in Mecca and presenting himself as a prophet. Although there were Christians and Jews in Arabia at that time, most of the peoples were pagans and worshipped many gods. Muhammad preached the greatness and goodness of one God and emphasized the Judeo-Christian prophetic tradition. Few Meccans, however, chose to follow him. His earliest converts included his wife, Khadija, his cousin Ali, his adopted son Zayd Ibn Haritha, and Abu Bakr, a respected and prominent Meccan.

As Muhammad continued his preaching and teaching, opposition to him grew. The reasons were many. He threatened the established economic and political order of the day, including the handsome income of the Meccans as custodians of the pagan shrines in their city. In a climate of escalating commerce and preoccupation with profit, his teachings emphasized the illusory nature of material wealth while encouraging such virtues as generosity, charity, and compassion. His criticism of the obsession for material gain was especially provoking, since he had made his own fortune in commerce. By striking at the idea of accumulating wealth, the Prophet was delivering a frontal attack on the Meccan life-style. Besides presenting an economic challenge, Muhammad posed a serious political threat to the leaders of Mecca. By questioning the economic basis of society and attacking the established order, the Prophet could only weaken the existing system. By attracting followers and building a community of his own, he offered the possibility of an alternative order. It is small wonder that the political leaders and influentials in Meccan society became his dogged enemies. Muhammad's following was dominated by the young, the poor, and the dispossessed.

Despite this strong opposition, the Prophet was able to build the core of his Muslim movement while in Mecca. He received most of his revelations and gathered his original followers there during a decade of intense missionary activity. There are two basic reasons why this was possible. First, Muhammad was relatively discreet and diplomatic about his activities. His first efforts were directed toward those in whom he had most trust, such as close relatives, fellow clansmen, and intimate friends.[4] At times, important converts were brought into the community through marriage. This was the case with Uthman, a wealthy merchant who married one of Muhammad's daughters. Outside of this intimate circle of family and friends, attention was directed to those individuals who were most prone to conversion. D. S. Margoliouth writes, for example, that "Abu Bakr probably was aware that women are more amenable to conversion than men, resident foreigners than natives, slaves than freemen, persons in distress than persons in prosperity and affluence."[5] A number of slaves were among the first to embrace the teachings of Muhammad. Finally, the meetings and activities of the first Muslims were carried out very quietly and unostentatiously. They took place in informal settings and personal homes, where they would not invite direct confrontation and public condemnation. The most famous site of this kind was the home of al-Arqam, where Muhammad could usually be found during the day and where his followers came and went at their convenience. From the very earliest days of its development, therefore, Islam has been what has been described as a "secret society."[6]

The second explanation for the Prophet's ability to survive in Mecca concerns the clan politics of the time. Each clan had learned that, in the interests of self-preservation, individual clan members had to be protected from all threats emanating from outside the clan. An individual could rely deeply on the support and protection of his fellow clansmen. Muhammad's clan, headed by his uncle Abu Talib, stood by him and provided him with a protective umbrella against his powerful opponents. Unable to penetrate this cloak of clan unity, the opposition attempted to institute a policy of isolating and boycotting Muhammad's entire clan. But in this system of seventh-century politics, even the boycott failed and was abandoned after two years.

---

[4]Abu Bakr, one of the Prophet's very first converts, was an influential Meccan cloth merchant. He was an extremely valuable ally and possessed a "readiness to follow the fortunes of some one else with complete and blind devotion, never questioning nor looking back; to have believed much was with him a reason for believing more. Mohammad, a shrewd judge of man, perceived this quality and used it." D. S. Margoliouth, *Mohammed and the Rise of Islam,* 3d ed. (New York: G. P. Putnam's Sons, 1905), pp. 83–84.

[5]*Ibid.,* p. 97.

[6]See *ibid.,* pp. 83–117.

The Prophet was able to continue his activities in Mecca as long as his own clan shielded him. With the death of Abu Talib in 619 and the accession of Abu Lahab as head of the Hashim clan, Muhammad lost his clan's protective support. In the same year, his wife Khadija died and he was gradually forced out of Mecca. After numerous hardships, he fled to Medina in 622 in what is known in history as the *hijra* ("Hegira"). He was welcomed in Medina, a city deeply torn by inter-clan strife. It is generally argued that the Medinans saw in Muhammad a leader who could serve as an effective mediator between the constantly warring factions in their city. At the same time, they felt that the enemy of Mecca would serve them as a friend, and that Meccan hegemony in the area would in this way be weakened.

The significance of the hijra to Islamic political development cannot be overemphasized. It marked the beginning of the end of parochial clan politics and the origination of the *umma,* or "community." Clan divisions were to lose their meaning as clans were absorbed into a new religion and a new way of life. The community now had a "religious base" and could be described as a kind of "supertribe."[7] It was during his residence in Medina that Muhammad came to practice the style of leadership that formed the great Islamic community. During these last ten years of his life, he consolidated his position in Medina, defeated and took control of Mecca, converted numerous Arabian tribes to his cause, and began a campaign of expansion that was to continue and spread long after his death.

Crucial to the success of Muhammad in Medina were his military campaigns, which escalated through time. Initially, they were confined to small *razzias,* or "raids," against Meccan commercial caravans. Although these campaigns had very limited success in terms of capture and booty, they served the important purpose of binding together individuals of different clans in a common cause. It was nearly two years before a Meccan caravan was actually captured. Through the constant camaraderie in the relatively safe enterprise of caravan raiding, the followers of Muhammad gradually developed an esprit de corps that enabled them to defeat the Meccans in the critical battles that were to follow. In this regard, it is instructive to note that the extraordinarily significant battle of Badr in 624 developed out of an intended caravan raid. In this battle, the Prophet's forces decisively defeated the Meccans and killed more than a dozen of their leaders.

---

[7]W. Montgomery Watt, *Muhammad: Prophet and Statesman* (London: Oxford University Press, 1961), pp. 94–95.

One year later, Muhammad's forces fought a large attacking Meccan expedition to a standstill in the battle of Uhud. In this encounter, the Prophet himself played an important part in the fighting. Finally, in 627 Muhammad and his community withstood a two-week siege of Medina. This was the last great effort by the Meccans to defeat the new community.

At Medina, the Prophet built solidarity into the community in a variety of ways. Besides the numerous military campaigns directed against a common enemy, there were other catalysts to unity. Those clans in Medina that adamantly opposed Muhammad were either expelled or destroyed. Preeminent among these opposition groups were the three Jewish clans of Qaynuqa, Nadir, and Qurayza. Scattered cases of political assassination also indicate that Muhammad condoned the use of this kind of force against particularly disruptive and resistant personalities.[8] This kind of civil violence was, however, engaged in only as a last resort. The emphasis was upon conversion and reconciliation. A primary means of accomplishing reconciliation was the web of intermarriage that not only bound the Emigrants (original Muslims from Mecca) closer together but also helped bind the Emigrants to the Helpers (Medinan Muslims).

The most outstanding example of the Prophet's flair for consolidation by compromise is the Treaty of Hudaybiya, which was negotiated in 628. Muhammad decided to make a pilgrimage to Mecca and was accompanied by some 1,500 men. The Meccans, who doubted his intentions and suspected a military invasion, prepared to fight. Muhammad camped at al-Hudaybiya on the outskirts of Mecca and from there entered into negotiations with the Meccans. In the end, an agreement was reached whereby the Prophet and his men were to return to Medina. They had permission, however, to return in the following year and to carry out their pilgrimage. Another point in the treaty provided for a ten-year nonaggression pact between the Muslims and the Meccans. Despite strong pressures from numerous individuals in his entourage who considered the expedition a failure, Muhammad returned to Medina. In so doing, he was implementing a brilliant policy of diplomatic tact that insured the peaceful conquest of Mecca two years later. The treaty convinced the Meccans that the

---

[8]An example was the poet Ka'b Ibn al-Ashraf, who continually and bitingly attacked Muhammad and the Muslims. He went so far as to travel from Medina to Mecca, where he attacked the Muslim community in his poetry. He was assassinated in A.D. 624.

Prophet was a reasonable man who did not plan to destroy Mecca. The journey to Hudaybiya was a political foray, not a religious pilgrimage.

When the Prophet Muhammad died in 632, he left behind a community of peoples that was to expand into one of the great civilizations of history. Tribes and clans, cities and empires were drawn together and unified under the ideology of Islam. The political acumen and astute leadership of Muhammad were instrumental in making this possible. These and other qualities of the Prophet have been noted and imitated by Muslims for centuries; Muhammad is the ideal model for all Believers. The reasons are not only that he was the Seal of the Prophets, the Mirror of the Almighty, and the Founder of Islam, but also that he was intensely human. Unlike Christ, Muhammad was not considered divine. One leading Islamic scholar writes that the Prophet "married, had a household, was a father and moreover he was ruler and judge and had also to fight many wars in which he had to undergo painful ordeals."[9] In the words of another analyst: "It is a likeable characteristic of Muhammad that he never claimed perfection or infallibility, but always admitted frankly that he was guilty of shortcomings and mistakes like other men."[10] He lived, in short, as a convincing and believable model after whom all Muslims could pattern their lives.

The Course of Compromise

Muhammad was born into a world of interpersonal feuding, factional strife, and tribal conflict. The political system was an atomistic one in which families and clans survived by remaining in a constant state of embattlement against other families and clans. The lines of confrontation that crisscrossed the system were drawn so rigidly that there was little room for flexible policies of retreat and advance. This was an era of the blood feud, punitive reprisal, and the *lex talionis* ("law of retaliation"). It was into this climate of division and distrust that the Prophet carried the strategy and spirit of compromise. This was, of course, essential if social integration and political unity were to be achieved at all. The need to unite was a fundamental issue in the Middle East then, and it remains a basic issue in the Middle East today. A leader's

---

[9]Seyyed Hossein Nasr, *Ideals and Realities of Islam* (London: George Allen and Unwin, 1966), p. 69.

[10]Andrae, *Mohammed*, p. 179.

political success rests to a great extent upon his ability to integrate and unite the divided and fragmented groups that compose society. An indispensable tool to the implementation of this kind of program is a strategy of political flexibility and compromise.

Muhammad's willingness to compromise is particularly noteworthy because of the climate of feuding in which it occurred. One of the most dramatic demonstrations of this talent is, of course, the Treaty of Hudaybiya referred to above. This is one demonstration of the manner in which age-old hatreds and animosities were overcome. After 20 years of struggle with the Meccans, the Prophet returned victorious to Mecca in the year 630. "There, at a moment when the very people who had caused untold hardships and trials for the Prophet, were completely subdued by him, instead of thinking of vengeance, which was certainly his due, he forgave them."[11] Although many Islamic scholars tend to explain this forbearance in terms of the great nobility, generosity, and compassion of the Prophet, it can also be analyzed as one in a long series of wise political policies. It is significant, however, that the moral virtue of compassion and the political strategy of compromise were inseparably linked in the career of Muhammad.

Throughout his political career, Muhammad tried to soften confrontation and to gain strength and unity by bargaining. Thus, he and his followers entered numerous marriage pacts with both actual and potential opposition forces. Many tribes joined the Muslim community as a result of the Prophet's long and peaceful march to Tabuk on the Gulf of Aqaba in 630. When Muhammad dispatched two missions to Yemen, he told the leaders of both missions: "Make it easy and do not make it too difficult. Be the carriers of good tidings, and do not cause disaffection."[12] Resort to violence and warfare occurred only after other avenues to agreement had been closed.

The success of tribal societies in developing a relatively respected and influential place in the world community is almost directly proportional to their ability to overcome internal dissension and to resist external encroachment. The clans or tribes in Middle Eastern history that have formed the basis for national communities or international empires have been precisely those that have been able to overlook past conflicts and to weld themselves into political units seeking common goals. The will and capacity to compromise at critical junctures is an

---

[11]Nasr, *Ideals and Realities,* pp. 71–72.

[12]Hasan al-Karmi, "The Prophet Muhammad and the Spirit of Compromise," *Islamic Quarterly* 8 (July and December 1964):90.

essential element in this process of integration. The Prophet's style of political leadership included this ingredient.

The Character of Charisma

The Prophet Muhammad viewed himself "as a man who had been given a special commission by God."[13] Although he was thoroughly human, he was not an ordinary human. He was the messenger and prophet of God, and his spiritual teachings were bound up in his social and political life. According to German sociologist Max Weber, a charismatic individual is one who "is set apart from ordinary men and treated as endowed with supernatural, superhuman, or at least specifically exceptional powers or qualities."[14] A charismatic leader is one who possesses a special grace and whose followers are irresistibly drawn to him because of this grace. There is a sensed otherworldly quality that engenders in others trust, commitment, and a willingness to follow. In Islam, there is an important concept that is remarkably similar to the idea of charisma. This is the concept *baraka,* which is a special blessing of divine origin. "God can implant an emanation of *baraka* in the person of his prophets and saints: Muhammad and his descendants are especially endowed therewith. These sacred personages, in their turn, may communicate the effluvia of their supernatural potential to ordinary men. . . ."[15] In contemporary political analysis, the term *charismatic* has come to be applied so loosely and indiscriminately that it has lost the force of its original meaning. If one stands by the Weberian definition, however, genuinely charismatic leaders have been rare in world history. Despite the exclusiveness of this definition, the Prophet Muhammad remains an outstanding case of the charismatic leader and may in fact be the prototype of this rare kind of personality.

All of Muhammad's personal, social, and political activities carried a deep spiritual significance. As a prophet and receptacle of revelation, he held an extraordinary position in the eyes of his followers. The teachings and tenets of Islam became the ideology of his rule, and all

---

[13]Watt, *Muhammad,* p. 15.

[14]Max Weber, *The Theory of Social and Economic Organization* (New York: Oxford University Press, 1947), p. 358.

[15]G. S. Colin, "Baraka," *The Encyclopedia of Islam,* new ed. (London: Luzac and Co., 1960), vol. 1, p. 1032.

aspects of community life were regulated by this ideology. Muhammad's charisma was derived from his role as prophet of God and publicizer of the word of God. As a result, his position as political leader had an extremely solid ideological foundation. Members of the Islamic community, because they were Muslims, considered Muhammad to be the temporal, social, political, and religious leader of society. Muhammad "had been marked out from his early youth, even from his birth, by supernatural signs and qualities."[16] He was a charismatic personality in the full sense of that term.

One of the basic principles of political leadership is that a leader be able to justify his special position by developing a supporting system of ideas and ideals. This kind of ideology may bear little relation to the hard realities of politics and society, but it can play a crucial role in enabling a leader to maintain his rule and to institute effective policies. Muhammad emerges as a model of success in this regard, since the divine and the human, and the spiritual and the material, are inextricably entwined in his message. Muslims did not think of questioning his authority in the community. Thus, he stands in great contrast to numerous contemporary Muslim leaders, who assiduously attempt to build supportive ideologies only on the basis of flimsy and fabricated relationships to Islam or to the Prophet himself.

Much of the appeal of Muhammad's ideological message undoubtedly derived from the social and political content of that message. Islam called for equality, compassion, and unity in a world dominated by inequality, self-aggrandizement, and disunity. In its stress upon equality and simplicity, it appealed to the downtrodden masses. And Muhammad himself lived what he preached. Thus, even Edward Gibbon could write: "The good sense of Mohammed despised the pomp of royalty; the apostle of God submitted to the menial offices of the family; he kindled the fire, swept the floor, milked the ewes, and mended with his own hands his shoes and his woollen garment."[17] In its emphasis upon unity and integration, on the other hand, Islam offered much to the middle and upper strata in society. As the prophet

---

[16]Watt, *Muhammad*, p. 2.

[17]Gibbon, *Decline and Fall of the Roman Empire* (New York: The Modern Library, 1932), vol. 3, p. 116. No matter what their ultimate judgment concerning Muhammad might be, well-known Western interpreters of world history are united in their recognition of the simple and spartan life that he led. Besides Gibbon, Toynbee and Durant also comment specifically about this facet of Muhammad's life.

who announced this message and as a leader who lived by it, Muhammad charismatically built the foundation of a civilization.

The Politics of Personalism

Another pattern of politics that enabled the Prophet Muhammad to gain and consolidate a strong leadership position in the nascent Islamic community was the pervasive pattern of personalism. In societies where clans and kinship groups were the key social and political realities of life, personal ties were the basic channels of power and influence. By analyzing and exploiting the intricate web of personal relations that existed in seventh-century Arabia, Muhammad and his associates were better able to form their new community. Abu Bakr's expertise as a genealogist, which is emphasized in many sources, is highly significant when viewed in this light. As Muhammad's chief advisor, Abu Bakr continually used his deep knowledge of the complex relations of kinship, as well as of the factions and feuding, that marked the society of the day.

One of the major means of consolidation and integration for the Prophet was the manipulation of this personal web through marriage. For Muhammad, "Many of his marriages were political ones which, in the prevalent social structure of Arabia, guaranteed the *consolidation* of the newly founded Muslim community. Multiple marriage, for him, as is true of Islam in general, was not so much enjoyment as responsibility and a means of *integration* of the newly founded society."[18] Muhammad married at least nine times, and one could argue that all of his marriages, even the union with Khadija, were political in nature. W. Montgomery Watt writes that for a "poor orphan" to make his way, "The one possibility was to find a rich woman to marry him, so that he could, as it were, enter into a business partnership with her."[19] It was

---

[18]Nasr, *Ideals and Realities,* p. 70. Italics ours.

[19]Watt, *Muhammad,* p. 10. Watt emphatically emphasizes the importance of the political motive in the Prophet's various marriages. In this study alone, he makes the argument in eight separate places. See pp. 10–12, 79, 102–103, 131, 155–157, 195, 206, 233. In another study Watt writes that "all Muhammad's own marriages can be seen to have a tendency to promote friendly relations in the political sphere." See Watt, *Muhammad at Medina* (Oxford: Clarendon Press, 1956), p. 287. Although, like Watt, we have stressed the political dimensions of Muhammad's marriages, we do not mean to deny the human and personal motives that were also obviously involved.

through marriage that the Prophet hardened the nucleus of his community while softening the resistance of those outside the community.

The central leadership of the Islamic community was tightly bound together through marriage, since the Prophet developed family ties with those among his closest followers who were later to become the first four caliphs (see Figure 4.1). Muhammad himself married A'isha and Hafsa, who were the daughters of Abu Bakr and Umar, respectively. At the same time, he married three of his own daughters to Uthman and Ali. Ali married Fatima, and Uthman first wedded Ruqayya and then upon her death renewed this important tie by marrying her sister Umm Kulthum.[20] The concern for holding the community together can also be seen in the tendency for leading Muslims to marry the widows of those members of the community who died or were killed in battle. Four of the Prophet's wives, for example, were widows of prominent early Muslims. Three of these Muslims had been killed in the important conflicts at Badr and Uhud.

The second category of marriages involved those that were contracted with members of potential or actual opposition forces. Many personal ties were developed with tribal groups throughout Arabia by means of this mechanism. Muhammad himself married three women who were the daughters of non-Muslim tribal notables. In each case, the marriage neutralized much political tension. The most important personal ties established through wedlock, however, were those involving the opposition in Mecca. By marrying the daughter of the influential Meccan leader Abu Sufyan and then one year later wedding the sister-in-law of the new head of the Meccan clan of Hashim, al-Abbas, Muhammad managed to establish intimate personal ties that were crucial to his tranquil conquest of Mecca. This two-pronged policy of developing personal relations both to strengthen an ongoing alliance and to absorb opposition forces is reflected in a split that occurred among Muhammad's wives. The wives divided into two factions—those who had come from within the Muslim community itself and those whose original roots had been in the opposition clans in Mecca.[21]

---

[20]Ali also married a granddaughter of Muhammad's while Umar married both a granddaugher of Muhammad's and a daughter of Ali's.

[21]W. Montgomery Watt, "Ā'ishā Bint Abī Bakr," *The Encyclopedia of Islam*, new ed. (London: Luzac and Co., 1960), vol. 1, p. 308.

Figure 4.1   Consolidation by marriage: The core of the community.

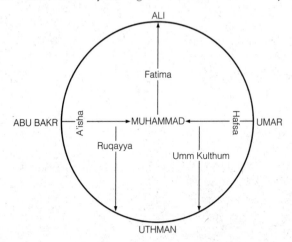

The original Muslim community functioned politically solely on the basis of personalities and personalism. In this sense, it differed very little from the pre-Islamic style of tribal and clan politics. Ruling institutions such as formal administrative organizations were unknown. The Prophet appointed specific individuals to lead military campaigns, diplomatic expeditions, and economic missions, depending upon the exigencies of the moment. As we have seen in the case of the marriage mechanism, personalism had distinct political advantages. Not the least of these was the introduction of a degree of social and political flexibility, which is crucial in the construction of a new social and political system.

The Unity of the Community

Through the interrelated patterns of compromise, charisma, and personalism, the Prophet Muhammad was able to build integrative patterns into a system otherwise prone to disintegration. Through a universal message delivered by a charismatic leader, peoples of widely differing background were attracted to a single community. This process of integration and consolidation is the main principle of

Muhammad's message, for, as Seyyed Hossein Nasr has written, "Unity is the alpha and omega of Islam."[22] Muhammad's charisma was an integrating force that intertwined the spiritual with the material and combined the social, the religious, and the political. The leader himself exhibited an internal unity by combining such virtues as compassion and strength, and this in turn strengthened his charismatic appeal.[23] The ideology professed by a charismatic personality was a key ingredient in sealing the fissures in the social structure. The more practical political policies of compromise and personalism as adopted by Muhammad then enabled him to confront on a daily basis the centrifugal social tendencies. The capacity to compromise dulled old antagonisms and hatreds in a way that allowed policies of personalism to acquire new meaning. Personal ties could now signal a kind of cooperation and conciliation that often led to conversion and consolidation. These three qualities of compromise, charisma, and personalism, were the key elements in the Prophet Muhammad's style of leadership.

PATTERNS OF PATRIMONIALISM IN THE MIDDLE EAST

> *My good Pasha, the will of the people emanates from my will!*
>
> King Farouk of Egypt[24]

In his important analysis and typology of traditional political systems, Max Weber includes two types that he labels patriarchal and patrimonial systems.[25] The patriarchal system is the core of all traditional sys-

---

[22]Nsar, *Ideals and Realities,* p. 29.

[23]For an interesting discussion of this point, see Frithjof Schuon, *Understanding Islam* (London: George Allen and Unwin, 1963), pp. 87–105.

[24]As quoted in P. J. Vatikiotis, *The Egyptian Army in Politics: Pattern for New Nations?* (Bloomington, Ind.: Indiana University Press, 1961), p. 39.

[25]A third type is the feudal system, which was the dominant traditional system in Western societies. For the presentation of Weber's analysis of patriarchal and patrimonial politics, see Weber, *The Theory of Social and Economic Organization,* pp. 341–358; and Reinhard Bendix, *Max Weber: An Intellectual Portrait* (Garden City, N.Y.: Doubleday and Co., 1962), pp. 330–360.

tems and is generally confined to household kinship groups. In patriarchy, the authority relation is one that binds master and family. The head of the household "has no administrative staff and no machinery to enforce his will. . . . The members of the household stand in an entirely personal relation to him. They obey him and he commands them in the belief that his right and their duty are part of an inviolable order that has the sanctity of immemorial tradition. Originally the efficacy of this belief depended on the fear of magical evils that would befall the innovator and the community that condoned a breach of custom."[26]

The patrimonial system, on the other hand, is one in which an identifiable administrative structure develops and spreads throughout the particular society or empire. The tasks of government become more specialized, complex, and elaborate. As a result, the ruler's relation with the ruled tends to be filtered through a huge network of bureaucrats. Owing to the introduction of a more complex and differentiated administrative apparatus, the emphasis on the mysterious and the magical is softened.

The literature that has attempted to analyze this Weberian typology has greatly overemphasized the differences between the patriarchal and patrimonial forms of rule. This has resulted in a misplaced preoccupation with such issues as specialization of roles and differentiation of structures. The key to understanding the traditional processes of leadership rests in the fundamental human relations that bind ruler and ruled. These were shaped in the patriarchal environment and were hardened and routinized in the patrimonial system. In essence, the patrimonial form of rule represents an extension and expansion of the patriarchal system. The relations that bind ruler and ruled, leader and led, master and servant, and king and subject are fundamentally the same in both Weberian categories. Reinhard Bendix defines patrimonial rule, therefore, as "an extension of the ruler's household in which the relation between the ruler and his officials remains on the basis of paternal authority and filial dependence."[27]

In most Islamic societies, patrimonial patterns of leadership have been dominant. The particular manifestation of patrimonial rule that

---

[26]Bendix, *Max Weber*, pp. 330–331.

[27]*Ibid.*, p. 360.

has marked these societies is referred to by Manfred Halpern as a "relationship of emanation." The politics of emanation involves an "encounter in which one treats the other solely as an extension of one's self. The other accepts the denial of his own separate identity because of the mysterious and overwhelming power of the source of this emanation—a yielding which is rewarded with total security."[28] When the Spanish Ummayad caliph Abd al-Rahman al-Nasir died at the turn of the tenth century after 50 years of rule, he was publicly eulogized in terms that capture the basic meaning of rule by emanation: "The souls of the people were absorbed in his soul: when he died they died also."[29] There is little doubt that this caliph possessed baraka in abundance.

In the Islamic world, where religion and politics have always been inseparable, shahs, sultans, and shaikhs have tended to rule in a paternal, patriarchal, and patrimonial manner. Government has been personal, and both civil and military bureaucracies have been little more than extensions of the leader. In the cases of the Ottoman, Safavid, and Moghul empires, the royal household developed into a huge administrative octopus, with the leader as head and the leader's gigantic retinue of personal servants and confidants as tentacles. In patrimonial politics, "bureaucratic recruitment and advances are based on personal confidence and not on objective qualifications; they reflect the more or less precarious balance reached by the prince in his effort to create and maintain a bureaucracy completely dependent upon his power. In each case, the position of the patrimonial bureaucrat must remain what it originally was—an emanation of his relation of purely personal submission to the Lord. . . ."[30]

---

[28]Halpern, "Four Contrasting Repertories of Human Relations in Islam," *Psychological Dimensions of Near Eastern Studies,* ed. by L. Carl Brown and Norman Itzkowitz (Princeton, N.J.: Darwin Press, 1977), p. 64. In this article, Halpern sensitively explores the significance of the politics of emanation to the Middle Eastern peoples and political systems. We have chosen to emphasize his conceptualization of emanation as the central pattern in patrimonialism.

[29]Lisan al-Din Ibn Khatib, [Book of works by leading authors concerning those accepted as kings of Islam] (Rabat, Morocco: New Press, 1934), p. 44 (in Arabic).

[30]Magali Sarfatti, *Spanish Bureaucratic-Patrimonialism in America,* Politics of Modernization Series, no. 1 (Berkeley, Calif.: University of California Institute of International Studies, 1966), p. 8.

In the patrimonial Middle East, the sovereign is located at the center of the political system. He is surrounded by advisors, ministers, military leaders, personal secretaries, and confidants. The one thing that all members of this inner circle share is unquestioned personal loyalty to the leader. This is best indicated by their continual reflection of the will and personality of that leader. These individuals may relate submissively and passively to the leader, but they do not relate in this way to their own peers and followers. Here, they are caught up in the most intense manipulations and machinations possible. The reason for this, of course, is that a minister who relates passively to a monarch on one level is the central source of leadership on another level. Therefore, within his own ministry, he may be the emanating influence, and his subordinates (deputy ministers, director generals, and so on) survive by remaining passive before him. Although the vertical relations tend to be one-sided, the horizontal patterns are characterized by balanced rivalry. Those of relatively equal power and authority are locked in constant conflict and struggle. This conflict can occur only below the level of the sovereign, since the sovereign has no equal in a patrimonial context. This kind of division and rivalry is constantly being sharpened by the competition among the rivals to demonstrate the greatest loyalty to the leader. The leader, in turn, encourages and manipulates this competition. The traditional politics of patrimonial leadership in the Middle East, therefore, tends to consist of chains of vertical emanation and horizontal competition that cut through the sociopolitical fabric (see Figure 4.2).

In the patrimonial style of Middle Eastern leadership, the leader becomes the fount of all important ideas and strategies. Policies and programs emanate from him. New ideas and suggestions that others might have must somehow be submitted to the leader, who may propose them as his own. Historically, the Middle Eastern political landscape is littered with individuals who attempted and failed to project themselves into the political limelight through their own ideas and ambitions. Often, they were the very closest confidants of the leader himself; by staking claim to their own political ground, they challenged the very relation of emanation and hastened their own inevitable political demise. This is precisely what happened when Abbasid caliph Harun al-Rashid in 803 disposed of his powerful Barmecid friend and advisor Ja'far ibn Yahya and imprisoned the other members of Ja'far's family. Numerous similar examples exist in both Ottoman and Persian history.

Figure 4.2   Patrimonial leadership.

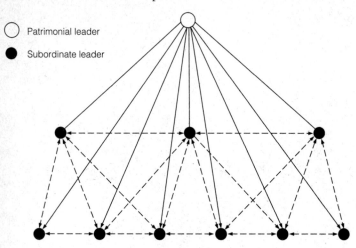

The most famous example of a leader turning against an indepen-dent-minded subordinate in Persian history occurred in the mid-nine-teenth century during the rule of the Qajar dynasty (1779–1925). Nasir al-Din Shah, who ruled Iran for half a century, gave the orders that led to the dismissal and death of his strong-willed and illustrious minister Mirza Taqi Khan Amir Kabir. Mirza Taqi Khan has gone down in Persian history as that country's greatest reformer and most beloved prime minister. Because of this man's brilliance and dramatic administrative programs, the young shah's light only flickered until Mirza Taqi Khan was assassinated in 1851, after having served only three years in the post. As we shall see in Chapter 5, there are many contemporary examples of this pattern.

The nearer individuals are to the patrimonial leader, the more likely they are to have their ideas accepted and implemented by the leader. In such a personal system of politics, physical nearness to the leader is an especially significant variable in explaining the distribution of power and influence. It would be wrong to assume that, in a patri-monial system, those who surround the leader have no influence at all. They always exert a subtle and passive influence, largely by having their ideas absorbed into those of the leader. In such a system, "advi-sors" never demand, seldom suggest, and only advise when advice is actively sought. They more often applaud than appraise. Although their influence on the leader may be sporadic, their influence on everyone else will usually be very intense. The closer an advisor is to the leader, the more influential he will be both with the ruler and with the people.[31]

Middle Eastern societies have been governed by authoritarian patrimonial systems throughout most of history. Islam fostered patrimonial patterns both through its ideals and in reality. The entire philosophical framework that evolved with Islam stressed relations of emanation. The term *Islam* itself means submission, and Islam demands that all believers perfect their acceptance of the Almighty. The Prophet Muhammad is the prototype of the leader linked in the chain of emanation, since he is the one who relates the material to the spiritual. Muhammad represents perfect passivity before God and perfect activity before man. He was the mirror who reflected the word of God, and "he saw nothing except in God and through God."[32] In his relations with man, however, the Prophet lived a vigorous social, political, and religious life, since he traded, fought, judged, and ruled. He was "that warrior on horseback who halts before the mountain of Truth, passive towards the Divine Will, active towards the world. . . ."[33] As Muhammad modeled his life after the Divine, millions of Muslims labor to model their lives after his. The Prophet's community in Medina was a patrimony infused with the charisma of a special leader.

The intermeshing of religion and politics in Islam has meant that political leaders have often had the opportunity to present themselves as linked directly to God. This has helped invest them with a mysterious and otherworldly aura that has allowed them to be exalted as models to be imitated by the people. This is one reason why political leaders in Islamic societies have historically attempted to trace their ances-

---

[31]Because of the continual competition and wielding of influence that occur at all levels of Islamic society, the intricate but effective manner in which subordinates can have their ideas incorporated into those of the ruler, and the constant challenging of particular relations of emanation by those who wish to assert their own power, we cannot characterize Islamic leadership as either "Oriental despotism," to use Wittfogel's term, or "sultanism," to use Max Weber's term. As we shall see, the informal, bargaining, and balancing nature of Middle Eastern politics contradicts such an emphasis on absolute authority, total power, and hardened hierarchy.

[32]Nasr, *Ideals and Realities*, p. 84.

[33]*Ibid.*, p. 9.

try back to the family of the Prophet. The only innate aristocracy in Islamic civilization consists of those individuals in the community who are related to the family of the Prophet Muhammad.

The personal rivalry that has always been central to patrimonial society has led to numerous schisms and divisions within the Islamic community. What has marked all of these splinter movements, however, has been their tendency to reform themselves by placing extreme emphasis upon leadership by emanation. Part of the reason for this is the need for any political movement playing the role of challenger to legitimate its existence and its claims. This must be done as convincingly and dramatically as possible. All Shi'i societies have exhibited the patrimonial rule by emanation in its most pronounced form.[34] This is seen in the significant figure of the Imam, who is the leader par excellence in the Shi'i community.

Ali was the first Imam, and he has been succeeded by other imams, their number varying with the different sects. The imam is not selected by the community, but succeeds by virtue of divine appointment, or *nass*. The imam is the vicegerent of God, and the line of imams consists of a divinely fashioned chain of emanation that is unquestioned in the minds of the believers. Whereas the Sunni caliph is an ordinary mortal, the Shi'i imams exist in a state of permanent grace that renders them infallible, impeccable, and immaculate. The imam is the one who rules by the will of God and in the name of God. In the Iranian version of Shi'i Islam, the twelfth and last Imam has gone into hiding and is meanwhile represented by the important cleric leaders known as *mujtahids*. According to strict Shi'i doctrine, as representatives of the Hidden Imam, these mujtahids are the major sources of interpretation for all social, political, and religious affairs. The shahs, however, traditionally attempted to lock themselves into the legitimizing tradition of the imams. Historically, much of Iranian politics revolved about the relationship between the mujtahids and shahs as they competed for legitimacy by emanation. In the Iranian revolution of 1978–1979, the mujtahids finally triumphed and took direct control of the political system of the country.

Muhammad's early community was organized according to patrimonial principles. The Prophet stood at the head of the sociopolitical

---

[34]For a fine analysis of the Fatimid caliphate, which emphasizes the theoretical aspects of patrimonial patterns of emanation, see P. J. Vatikiotis, *The Fatimid Theory of State* (Lahore, Pakistan: Orientalia Publishers, 1957).

household, and personal ties and relations knit the entire community together. These relations were made particularly binding by the fact that most of the main leaders and followers were brought into the Prophet's own household. The dynamics of Muhammad's leadership that have been briefly sketched above highlight these patterns. Muhammad's charismatic personality and his relation to the Divine enabled individuals such as Abu Bakr to become absorbed in his affairs and to accept his leadership completely. The special charismatic nature of the Prophet's rule by emanation overcame much of the intracommunity dissension and conflict endemic to systems of patrimonial politics. It was when Muhammad died that all of these submerged dissensions broke to the surface and schisms became common.

The patrimonial leaders who succeeded the Prophet found relations of emanation less persuasive and effective. This became more and more the case as dynastic heads became further removed from the days of Muhammad's rule. Islamic history, therefore, is replete with examples of leaders at all levels and in all communities who made dramatic efforts to strengthen the patrimonial patterns by infusing new life into increasingly unbelievable relations of emanation. This was done in two complementary ways: (1) the original charismatic leaders to which the new leaders were attached were accorded supernatural status; and (2) a proclaimed leader attempted to build a special relation between himself and the earlier prototype.

In the first case, the leaders in early Islam are glorified and purified until in some instances they appear to have possessed godly qualities. This has been particularly true in the case of Ali, the fourth caliph and son-in-law of the Prophet. In the second instance, communities develop around individuals who claim to be special representatives or messengers either of these early patrimonial heroes or even of God himself. Saints and holy personages play an important role in Middle Eastern politics and society. One scholar writes, for example, that "the most characteristic social institution of North African religious life is the saint, the holy personage. As Islam does not enjoin celibacy, saints proliferate and form lineages and dynasties."[35] Mahdis, marabouts, and imams have formed political movements of great influence in the

---

[35]Ernest Gellner, "Sanctity, Puritanism, Secularisation and Nationalism in North Africa: A Case Study," mimeographed (n.p., n.d.), p. 1. See also Gellner's fine study, *Saints of the Atlas* (Chicago: University of Chicago Press, 1969).

Middle East. The Moroccan marabouts were the major force shaping the social and political systems in large areas of North Africa until the end of the nineteenth century.[36] In a patrimonial political system, the basic patterns, which often shatter and disintegrate, have traditionally been reknitted through the appearance of a new leader claiming either special supernatural power or a special relation with those who are believed to have had such power.

Patterns of leadership in the Middle East have been highly congruent from institution to institution and from community to community. In the family, school, guild, and government, patrimonialism prevails. Much of the reason for this is the influence of Islam, which penetrates all aspects of a believer's life. In patriarchal or patrimonial societies, the patriarch is the main social and political reality. He is the model, the guide, the innovator, the planner, the mediator, the chastiser, and the protector. The community wraps itself around the leader, who governs through a constantly expanding web of personal relations. Within the family, which is the basic social unit in the Middle East, the father is the unrivaled leader. The situation is best summarized as follows: "The Muslim family has remained patriarchal, and the head of it maintains his authority . . . down to the last day of his life."[37] Traditionally, wives and children have been little more than extensions of the will of the father, whose authority is in his own opinion "natural and divine."[38] One Middle Eastern writer refers to a "blind reverence" that the father receives from his children, who relate to him "as if fearing a mysterious superhuman force."[39] The personal tension that is built into patrimonial systems is dramatically evident in the family, where sibling rivalry takes a particularly intense form. Brother competes against brother, and various shifting alliances are formed as mothers, children, cousins, grandparents, aunts, and

---

[36]Dale Eickelman tells this story well. He defines marabouts as persons "to whom is attributed a special relation toward God which makes them particularly well placed to serve as intermediaries with the supernatural and to communicate God's grace (*baraka*) to their clients." See Eickelman, *Moroccan Islam* (Austin, Tex.: The University of Texas Press, 1976), p. 6.

[37]Maurice Gaudefroy-Demombynes, *Muslim Institutions* (London: George Allen and Unwin, 1961), p. 128.

[38]Cyrus Parham, "Divine Authority of a Persian Father," mimeographed (n.p., n.d.), p. 1.

[39]*Ibid.*, p. 2.

uncles are pulled into the continual competition and conflict. The father or leader tends to promote rather than to alleviate this kind of rivalry.

In educational and occupational settings, the roles and styles of leadership are essentially the same as those that mark the family and the government. The master-apprentice, teacher-student, and shaikh-*murid* ("brotherhood disciple") relations are patterns of superordination and subordination in which the follower's existence is an extension of the leader's being. The teacher-student relation is, in fact, somewhat closer to the father-son relation than to the patterns found in guild and brotherhood organizations. The latter have preserved much more of the otherworldly quality that serves to strengthen the bonds of emanation. This quality has been gradually lost in the educational system as the religious direction of education has given way to secular control. The basic pattern, however, can still be seen in almost any Middle Eastern classroom, where the teacher's person is deferred to and the teacher's word is memorized. In the environment of guilds and brotherhoods, deference becomes devotion, and shaikhs, who are the leaders, command a charismatic control that is generally absent in familial, governmental, and formal educational institutions. In the case of Sufi orders or brotherhoods, "all authority and allocation of authority positions in the hierarchy lie within the purview of the Sheikh, and the subordinates derive their statuses from him."[40] Those who are closest to the shaikh's person have the greatest influence in the order. Therefore, the personal secretaries and attendants of the shaikh are extremely important figures in these organizations. They are, of course, entirely devoted to and dependent upon the leader. In describing this kind of relation between a private secretary and the shaikh in a contemporary Egyptian brotherhood, one member explained that the secretary does not even go to sleep "until the Sheikh tells him to."[41]

Patrimonialism has been the dominant pattern of leadership in Middle Eastern politics for centuries. The strength of this pattern has fluctuated greatly, depending upon the leader, dynasty, society, and era. Patrimonialism was most evident in the heyday of the shahs and

---

[40]Michael Gilsenan, "The Sufi Orders and the Modern World," mimeographed (n.p., September 29, 1967), pp. 7–8.

[41]*Ibid.*, p. 45.

sultans. The politics of patrimonial leadership as manifested in the Middle East reflects six major characteristics: personalism, proximity, informality, balanced conflict, military prowess, and religious rationalization.

Personalism

Patrimonial society rests upon personal relationships. The community or society is essentially an enlarged household, and the personal ties that dominate in the household are the model for the ties in any other patrimonial unit. Middle Eastern societies and political systems grew out of tribal constellations, and the personalism that prevailed in the family and the clan has had a pervasive and protracted influence. The Middle Eastern leader has led by virtue of his personal relations with his followers. Formal organizations and institutions have seldom effectively intervened. Even when institutions such as formal bureaucracies have developed, the real business of ruling and political decision making has resided in personal networks. These networks tend to hold together groups of people, and it is through these networks that the leader has attempted to establish as wide a range of contacts as possible.

In order to rule in this kind of setting, it is essential that the leader gather and retain as much personal information about others in the network as possible. One famous eleventh-century manual on the conduct of kingship advises the prince, "never omit to inform yourself of the doings of others. . . ,"[42] and tells the king that "it is your duty not to be ignorant of conditions in your realm, of the circumstances of your people or those of your soldiers. More particularly you must be vigilant concerning the doings of your vizier. He should not be able to swallow a drink of water without your knowing it. . . ."[43] In this setting, the art of genealogy and the knowledge of friendship relations are serious political pursuits.

The prevalence of personalism is best seen in the great Islamic dynastic systems, where the rulers built gigantic households around their own persons. A more formal bureaucratic state organization also

---

[42]Kai Ka'us Ibn Iskandar, *A Mirror for Princes (The Quabus-nama)*, trans. by Reuben Levy (London: Cresset Press, 1951), p. 194.

[43]*Ibid.*, p. 235.

evolved in these systems in answer to the pressure to administer the large political empires. A distinguished Islamic scholar summarizes this situation as follows: "Throughout the whole system of the Eastern Muslim political organization there runs like a red thread the division of all the organs of administration into two main categories, the dargah (palace) and diwan (chancery)."[44] In the Iranian Safavid system, the royal household was referred to as the *khassah* and the state bureaucracy was known as the *divan*. In the Turkish Ottoman system, the division was between the "imperial household" and the "central administration." In traditional Islamic polities, the royal household has been the crucial arena of politics, since it has consistently dominated the state bureaucracy proper. This has occurred not only because of the superior concentration of power within the royal household, but also because the personalities of the palace have infiltrated the state bureaucracy. Hence, the royal household, which is organized around the person of the king, has in turn wrapped around itself the formal bureaucracy, which expands with the growth of the political unit itself.

The actual transition from a completely personal pattern of leadership to one with bureaucratic and institutional appendages occurred mainly during the rule of the Abbasids (749–1258). This represented, in Weber's terms, a movement from a patriarchal to a patrimonial stage. The Abbasid leaders built an elaborate administrative system that included the office of *vazir* ("prime minister") and more than a dozen large organizational boards that were in turn composed of numerous departments.[45] Despite this bureaucracy, personal relations dominated the system, and the court staff remained the critical force. This dependence of the more formal state bureaucracy upon the person of the king is seen in the role of the vazir himself. Although the vazir usually headed the state bureaucracy in these political systems, he did so as the personal servant of the king and as a leading member of the royal household. It was the *person* of the vazir, not the *office* of vazir, that was the important political consideration.

This traditional style of political rule has carried over into contemporary Middle Eastern politics to a surprisingly large degree. Per-

---

[44]V. V. Barthold, *Turkestan Down to the Mongol Invasion*, 2d ed. (London: Oxford University Press, 1928), p. 227.

[45]Vazir is most closely translated as prime minister. It is sometimes transliterated as vizir or vizier.

sonalism predominates in such societies as Morocco, Jordan, Saudi
Arabia, and the shaikhdoms that still have traditional authoritarian
leaders. In other Middle Eastern countries, the personal dimension of
leadership prevails more at the subnational level, in such institutions
as the family, the school, and the guild. In all of these societies, however, patrimonial personalism continues to shape leadership processes, although it is more and more submerged beneath the growing
facade of formal institutions and bureaucratic machinery. Contemporary Middle Eastern political monarchs constantly describe their societies as large families and emphasize their own special positions as
heads or fathers of these families. It is in this spirit that King Hassan of
Morocco speaks about "the innate nature of Our family, characterized
by its profound wisdom, its great nobility, and the solid communion
which unites us ultimately to our people."[46]

Proximity

Patrimonial leadership attaches particular significance to physical
proximity. Regardless of occupational designation or formal title,
those who live closest to the leader regularly hold major political positions in the traditional Middle Eastern system. Zayd Ibn Haritha, who
was a black slave adopted by Muhammad and Khadija, illustrates the
power of proximity. Because he was the Prophet's adopted son, and
despite his status as slave, Zayd became one of the leading figures in
early Muslim history. Throughout Islamic history, slaves have risen to
great influence. One of the most powerful Islamic political systems
was built by a dynasty whose kings were once slaves. These were the
Mamluks; the word *mamluk* itself means "owned" or "possessed."
They were originally slaves who had served as bodyguards to the Ayyu-
bid dynastic leaders. Proximity to leadership has meant that slaves,
cooks, musicians, and stable keepers have often been able to exert
great political power in traditional Muslim societies.

Although proximity is a consideration relevant to any political system, it assumes special importance in those societies where leadership
is built on a far-flung network of personal relations. Here, those closest to the *person* of the leader tend always to be the most influential.

[46]John Waterbury, *The Commander of the Faithful: The Moroccan Political Elite—A
Study in Segmented Politics* (New York: Columbia University Press, 1970), p. 150.

In patrimonial politics these are often, in the first instance, such family members as brothers, wives, mothers, and uncles. Those who marry into the leader's family and become in-laws also become potential centers of influence. The special personal ties and ideal position of proximity of relatives often mean that when the pattern of emanation is broken, it is broken within this familial core. If anyone makes direct suggestions to the patrimonial leader, or questions or criticizes him, it is almost always a member of the ruling family. Certainly, it is from this source that new ideas are most likely to be entertained and absorbed. In an extended household administration, or patrimonial system, those in the core household or nuclear family will play major roles in political decision making. Western discussions and condemnations of nepotism, ascription, and favoritism must be reevaluated in light of the general structure of patrimonial politics.

Proximity counts most in systems where decision making is highly centralized, highly personal, and highly informal. In nonpatrimonial systems, decision making tends to be more equally distributed throughout the society. Such systems also have formal and associational channels that carry the influence and ideas of those distant from the centers of political decision making to the leader. In the patrimonial Middle East, the most effective way to submit a request or present a petition is to get as close as possible to the leader. The closer an individual is to the center of the personal web of politics, the more likely he is to share in decision making and to have his interests served. It is for this reason that there is constant and unrelenting pressure toward the center of power in traditional patrimonial politics. The leader is always being pressed in upon by individuals who attempt to be in his presence as often and as long as possible. At the same time, those closest to him, such as his advisors, ministers, and confidants, attempt to resist and control the flow of others to this precious territory. In *A Mirror for Princes,* Muslim vazirs are warned, "Wherever the king goes, accompany him; do not leave him alone. . . ."[47]

It is proximity rather than professional merit or occupational position that explains why gardeners, cobblers, barbers, and physicians have moved into positions of great influence in Islamic politics. The patrimonial leader has more often sought the counsel of these individuals than of any others, and at times such service personnel have even-

---

[47]Iskandar, *A Mirror for Princes,* p. 214.

tually replaced their masters and become political leaders in their own right. It is not surprising, therefore, that even in the contemporary Middle East, political leaders rely heavily upon their personal attendants for advice and information. The late Shah of Iran, for example, said that he relied upon his valet and gardener when he needed information. Ayatollah Khomeini listened closely to the advice of his son Ahmad, who was one of the few who had direct access to the Ayatollah.

Those nearest to the person of the leader serve to filter demands and requests, act as information bearers and receptacles of advice, and stand as influential intermediaries between the leader and his masses of followers. Where power is personal and politics are patrimonial, the issue of proximity is critical. The concept of the "inner circle" is particularly relevant to Middle Eastern politics.

Informality

Personal politics tend to be informal politics in the sense that the most important leaders are often those who are not bound by formal contracts or limited by institutional constraints. Even those leaders who visibly combine power and authority have consistently operated in highly personal settings rather than in well-defined formal organizations.

In today's bedouin society, the great importance of the informal leadership structure is still in the person of the *rajal khayr,* or "good man." In the Ayshaybat tribe in western Egypt, this person is more influential than the *aqila,* in whom resides the contractual authority of the tribe. The aqila is, in other words, the formal leader. The rajal khayr is a cultural and political broker who has the loyalty and friendship of the people as well as the attention of high regional government officials, who prefer to work through him. As G. J. Obermeyer writes in an excellent case study of bedouin leadership: "The power of the ʿāqila is limited by the very structure of the role. The role of the rajal khair, being less institutionalized and structured, is less confined with respect to the kind and amount of influence the role-player might exert."[48]

----

[48]Obermeyer, "Leadership and Transition in Bedouin Society: A Case Study," *The Desert and the Sown,* ed. by Cynthia Nelson (Berkeley, Calif.: University of California Institute of International Studies, 1973), p. 164.

Political decision making in the Middle East has been marked by behind-the-scenes planning and negotiation. Leaders have seldom emphasized the establishment of formal political institutions such as parliaments and parties. Where such formal institutions have been constructed, they have often been rationalizing gestures more than seriously conceived political organizations. Once in existence, formal bodies have had relatively little impact upon a leader's political activities.

Informal patterns of control and authority have been responsible for a great deal of uncertainty in the decision-making environment. Middle Eastern political processes reflect a high level of intrigue and counterintrigue as leaders at various levels maneuver in secret and semisecret settings. It is partially because of this emphasis on secrecy and organizational informality that rumors have always been an important political phenomenon in the Middle East. Secrecy and uncertainty breed speculation, and the ability to uncover decisions and deals is an important political resource.

The propensity for informal organization that has marked Middle Eastern social life is most evident in the numerous secret and informal groups. These include secret orders and societies, religious brotherhoods, underground minority organizations, political cliques and *anjumans*, informal coffeehouse groups, Sufi meetings, ritualistic religious gatherings, regular meetings of extended families, royal social circles and *khalvats*, and bureaucratic and parliamentary factions.[49]

Middle Eastern leaders have tended to operate as the centers of webs of personal relationships in which the lines of power and authority are indistinct and constantly changing. Spheres of political authority overlap. Hence, there is always doubt concerning who is closest to the leader and who influenced what decision. With the possible exception of the national political leader, there is even a question about *who* the leader really is. Often the most influential political actors remain in the background, where they are members of the family, the harem, or friendship circles. In Middle Eastern politics, an informal personal organization has tended to rest behind the formal institutional organization. Oftentimes, observers are confused because of the presence of the identifiable leader at the center of both organizations and the presence of certain advisors and confidants in both.

---

[49] *Anjumans* are usually translated as "societies." *Khalvat* was a term used in Iran to refer to a regular social gathering of the shah and his closest male advisors.

This environment of informality has carried several political advantages for the patrimonial leader. It has provided him with an unusually flexible system, since lines of authority and responsibility tend to be fluid and blurred. In such a system, it is difficult for opposition forces to concentrate because targets are neither stable nor well defined. At the same time, the leader enjoys a broad capacity to intervene in governmental affairs and to move subordinates around with ease. Since there are no clearly defined responsibilities, and since hard and fast assignments are nonexistent, the patrimonial leader can interpret spheres of authority in almost any way he chooses. Those individuals who are most apt to challenge the leader find themselves severely crippled in this informal environment. They lack institutional foundations and formal supports that they can cling to, and therefore find themselves highly dependent upon the personal whim and will of the leader. Informal politics tend to conceal the merit of aspiring statesmen, and as a result these statesmen are seldom able to build the popularity necessary for the crystallization of opposition to the leader. Finally, informality builds distrust among those who are relatively influential in the system. Individuals report confidentially and personally to the leader, and this often involves statements about the activities and ambitions of other political figures. Such a semisecret pattern of politics enables the leader to engender a great deal of division and distrust among his subordinates. This division has been institutionalized as overlapping lines of authority by which officials exert control in one another's area of expertise.

In patrimonial leadership, visibility and formality have been subordinated to personalism and covert organization. This characteristic has provided Middle Eastern leaders with a maximum amount of maneuverability and a minimum degree of accountability. Even in the contemporary Middle East of complex and sophisticated organization charts, the business of politics is negotiated outside of and in spite of these instruments. Political blueprints such as constitutions and fundamental laws heavily mask the actual patterns and processes by which political leaders make decisions and protect their interests.

Balanced Conflict

The patrimonial leader in the Middle East has ruled on the foundation of pervasive division and personal rivalry. In the Middle Eastern context, the dictum "divide and rule" takes on special meaning. Cutting through all levels in the Islamic system is a built-in rivalry that marks interpersonal, intergroup, and interclass relations. The leader who seeks to divide and rule, therefore, has an ideal social system within which to operate. Rivalry is institutionalized in the system, and the traditional ruler had only to encourage processes that were already at work. This is why unity is the most sought-after and least achieved goal in Islamic history.

Personal rivalry has so permeated the Middle Eastern social structure that it manifests itself in institutions all the way from the family to the national bureaucracy. In Egyptian village society, for example, intense sibling rivalry is considered essential to a child's growth. Parents continually sharpen and intensify rivalry among their children. This is done in numerous dramatic ways, including labeling the children with names that invite conflict. In one Egyptian family, for example, the elder brother was called "the stupid one," while the younger brother was nicknamed "the clever one."[50] In a study of Lebanese village life, it was found that fewer than half of the children sampled could name three persons they considered friends. The reasons for this reported scarcity of friendship relations were explained in terms of grudges, feuds, and rivalries.[51] The oft-quoted Arab proverb "I against my brother, my brother and I against my cousin, my cousin and I against the stranger" describes this general pattern very well.

At the national political level, the same pattern is evident in the way that leaders and rulers play their advisors and subordinates off against one another. The contemporary rulers of Morocco, Jordan, and Saudi Arabia have become especially adept in this skill and largely owe their continued existence as powerful monarchs to it. In Iran after the revolution, Ayatollah Khomeini shrewdly remained above conflicting factions. From here he played political groups off against one another, for example, the radical leftists against the extremists on the right. By splintering the potential opposition forces and at the same time standing above them as supreme arbiter, several Middle Eastern leaders have managed to maintain firm control in the political arena. Any concentration of skill, energy, or power is immediately shattered through

---

[50]Hammed Ammar, *Growing Up in an Egyptian Village* (New York: Octagon Books, 1966), p. 110.

[51]Judith R. Williams, *The Youth of Haouch El Harimi: A Lebanese Village*, Harvard Middle East Monograph Series, vol. 20 (Cambridge, Mass.: Harvard University Press, 1968), pp. 91–92.

leadership tactics of division and redivision. In the traditional Abbasid, Ottoman, Safavid, and Moghul administrative systems, the most important and influential political functions were constantly divided and redistributed among larger and larger numbers of officials. When a political figure became particularly influential, his title and function were given to a second and rival administrator, and influence was thus divided and shared. Tension was thereby instilled into the particular political sphere, and the personal power of the individual in control of this sphere was substantially lessened, if not halved.

The politics of rivalry and conflict not only served to buttress leadership positions but also reinforced systemic stability. The tension was balanced in such a way that overwhelming concentrations of power seldom developed outside the sphere of the national political ruler. Manfred Halpern analyzes the Islamic system in terms of its "ability to convert tensions into balances" and its capacity to bind society together "through conflict no less than through collaboration."[52] In contemporary Morocco, "All seek to maintain in the midst of the group that tension which is life, that variety that is solidarity."[53] The Moroccan monarch operates a system in which "no group may be permitted to become too strong, and to counter hegemonic tendencies life is breathed into rival groups."[54] In Iran, the late shah created a stable balance of tension in which ministers, courtiers, security agents, military leaders, industrialists, and clerics were systematically divided against one another at all levels. The last four kings of Saudi Arabia have promoted the distrust and animosity that mark the relationships between many of their half-brothers, while at another level the national guard stands in direct rivalry with the regular army. The Nassers, Bourguibas, Saddam Husseins, Qaddafis, and al-Assads have also promoted rivalry. In the Middle East, political leaders have traditionally expended much of their energies in manipulating personal networks of stabilizing tensions. A premium has been placed upon a leader's ability to sense the location of threatening power concentrations and then to splinter those concentrations either by deepening existing divisions or by fostering new personal rivalries.

---

[52]Manfred Halpern, *The Politics of Social Change in the Middle East and North Africa* (Princeton, N.J.: Princeton University Press, 1963), pp. 10, 18.

[53]Jacques Berque, *Structures Sociales du Haut-Atlas* (Paris, 1955), p. 449, as quoted in Waterbury, *The Commander of the Faithful*, p. 61.

[54]Waterbury, *The Commander of the Faithful*, p. 148.

Military Prowess

Max Weber writes that "with the development of a purely personal administrative staff, *especially a military force* under the control of the chief, traditional authority tends to develop into 'patrimonialism.'"[55] The key to patrimonial politics is the existence of a military force that is at the personal disposal of the leader. Within the Islamic world, this consideration has been a central one. Here, among the most highly respected qualities of leadership are personal bravery and physical courage. Islamic scholars present "combativeness" as one of the three great characteristics of the Prophet Muhammad.[56] The famous Islamic leaders are known and remembered for their bravery in battle and their victory in military campaigns. The warrior hero is a deeply admired figure in Middle Eastern history. Leaders who have been able to conduct themselves well on the field of battle have always had a marked advantage in the arena of domestic politics.[57]

This emphasis on physical courage and military prowess is to be expected in a culture that developed out of a tribal context, and in which tribes continue to play a prominent social and political role. Throughout the Middle East today groups still exist that follow the Shi'i path or worship Ali primarily because of his personal courage and valor, which are summed up in his titles Lion of God and Sword of Islam. This inspiration was key to the fighting commitment of the young Iranian soldiers who died in large numbers in the war with Iraq in the 1980s.

The emphasis on personal courage and valor runs deep throughout Middle Eastern society. Bravery is so highly esteemed that it carries favorable moral connotations. The Arabic word *shaja'a,* which is also commonly used in Persian, implies a personal bravery that is especially infused with virtue and uprightness. It implies a kind of chivalrous courage. Throughout Middle Eastern history, the personally brave and physically courageous have had about them an aura of knightliness. Combativeness and chivalry could not be separated.

---

[55]Weber, *The Theory of Social and Economic Organization,* p. 347. Emphasis ours.

[56]See, for example, Nasr, *Ideals and Realities,* p. 73; and Schuon, *Understanding Islam,* p. 88.

[57]The reverse is also true, since failure in combat is as much a moral as a physical blow to Islamic leaders and societies. The impact of the Arab-Israeli conflict, for example, must be interpreted in this light.

Local champions such as *pahlavans* not only had tremendous physical strength but also were exceptionally kind, generous, and noble. Islamic guilds and brotherhoods traditionally supported and promoted ideals of physical and moral courage. Military valor and success, therefore, have invested Islamic leaders with additional strength and appeal in the eyes of their followers.

Military force was a major factor in the rise to power of Middle Eastern political leaders. A strong and effective military has also been an important tool enabling a ruler to continue to rule. A leader who has had several successful foreign military campaigns to his credit has been more effective in preserving his domestic rule. The deep patterns of division and discord described above persistently threaten to shatter the system and to destroy the ruler in the process. One scholar stresses the fact that "a patrimonial system is characterized by constant tension between centripetal and centrifugal forces."[58] The patrimonial leader's key instrument in encouraging and buttressing the centripetal forces is his military organization. While promoting tension and discord in particular areas throughout the system, the patrimonial leader must at the same time guard against having balances become imbalances and rivals unite in a common front against him. It is only his military that can enable him to salvage his position and his life in such circumstances.

Despite its importance, the military organization is subject to the same patterns and pressures that characterize other institutions in patrimonial settings. The leader or ruler attempts to control the military as an emanation of his own will and personality and usually assumes the title Commander-in-Chief or Commander of the Faithful. The military forces are his "personal instrument."[59] The centrality of the leader in military matters can be seen diagrammatically in the Middle Eastern "battle order" described by Ibn Khaldun.[60] Surrounded by his closest confidants, the ruler stands at the center of his forces. The latter consist of four armies, situated at the front and rear and on the right and left flanks of the leader.

[58]Robert H. Jackson, "Social Structure and Political Change in Ethiopia and Liberia," *Comparative Political Studies* 3 (April 1960):38.

[59]Bendix, *Max Weber,* p. 344.

[60]Ibn Khaldun, *The Muqaddimah,* trans. by Franz Rosenthal (Princeton, N.J.: Princeton University Press, 1967), p. 225.

Throughout the history of the Middle East, the characteristics of personalism, proximity, informality, and balanced rivalry also pervaded the military organization. Only the most trusted relatives and confidants were appointed military leaders. Those closest to the ruler, such as bodyguards and armed retainers, were recruited among slaves, orphans, and prisoners, and as a result maintained no entangling alliances or loyalties outside of their relation to the leader. It was essential that they be completely subsumed in the shadow of the ruler, to whom they owed everything. To ensure this kind of absolute loyalty and submission, the mechanism of balanced rivalry is seen in perhaps its most critical manifestation in the arena of the armed forces. Different military leaders and different military bodies have existed in constant tension with one another and have served as watchdogs of one another. Sometimes these intramilitary divisions reflected tribal cleavages; sometimes entirely new tribes were created both to strengthen loyalty and to serve as armed checks against other military units.

The modern Middle East has its authentic military heroes. For the Turks, Ataturk was the great hero of the First World War. Abdul Aziz Ibn Saud was the illustrious warrior king in Saudi Arabia. King Hussein of Jordan has demonstrated physical courage on numerous occasions. Both Gamal Abdel Nasser and General Naguib, the titular leader of the 1952 Egyptian coup, had distinguished records in the fighting in Palestine.

There is bound to be a close connection between military upheaval and the turnover of political leaders. The proliferation of military coups that continues to mark Middle Eastern politics represents the failure of leaders and rulers to establish viable patrimonial patterns with respect to the military. The challenge to leadership has come not so much from the society at large as from within the military itself. When leadership rests so heavily upon the military reed, then it must be prepared to collapse whenever that reed breaks.

Religious Rationalization

Islam provided the patrimonial leader with an ideology that buttressed the political patterns by which he ruled. Chains of emanation are more firmly fashioned when they lead to the Almighty, and Islamic leaders have traditionally endeavored to demonstrate their own linkages with God and his Prophet Muhammad. Although actual effective theocratic leadership died with the Prophet in 632, Islamic leaders ever since have sought to be theocratic leaders. As time passed, this tendency became more and more pronounced, while theocratic leadership became less and less credible. The political meaning of the word *caliph* was gradually transformed from "deputy of the emissary of God" to "God's representative on earth."[61] The Islamic political leaders, who had at one time been considered the Prophet's deputies, later became known as God's deputies. Even the concept of *sultan,* which developed a connotation of secular as opposed to religious authority, soon made the linkage with the Divine. This occurred when the actual sultan began referring to himself as the Shadow of God.[62] The concept of *imam* has been the best example of leadership related directly to the Divine, for unlike the caliph and the sultan, the imam has always been considered the infallible vicegerent of God. Despite the various titles and personalities involved, however, the Middle Eastern style of patrimonial leadership has usually meant the conscious establishment of some form of linkage between the leader and the Divine.

This pattern has provided political leaders with a rationalization and justification for their positions. It has been argued that "stiff religious cement" has been the strength of the patrimonial system of rule.[63] In one of the classic studies of politics, Gaetano Mosca analyzes the traditional strength of the Turkish nation in the following terms: "The Turkish peasants in Rumelia and Anatolia believed sincerely and deeply in Islam, in the Prophet, in the sultan as the Prophet's vicar, and the beliefs for which they were asked to make the utmost sacrifices were the beliefs that ordinarily filled their lives and made up their moral and intellectual worlds."[64] In a smoothly functioning system of leadership by emanation, to challenge the leader often meant nothing less than to challenge the rule of God. It is for this reason that political rebellion took the form of religious schisms and that the chal-

---

[61]V. V. Barthold, "Caliph and Sultan," *The Islamic Quarterly* 7 (July and December, 1963):124–125.

[62]*Ibid.,* p. 130.

[63]Gaetano Mosca, *The Ruling Class,* trans. Hannah D. Kahn (New York: McGraw-Hill Book Co., 1939), p. 345.

[64]*Ibid.,* p. 108.

lenging political figures stressed their own special relation to the Almighty.

The Politics of Patrimonial Recruitment: General Observations

Contrary to what is often thought, the ranks of Middle Eastern political leadership are relatively permeable. Within certain patrimonial limits, vertical mobility is possible, and outsiders are often able to penetrate elite circles. In such systems, the personalistic networks of leadership can be penetrated, especially on the basis of family, kinship, and friendship relations. As Almond and Powell point out: "Perhaps the oldest and most traditional means of access to political elites is personal connection. By personal connection channels we mean the use of family, school, local, and social ties as instruments for contacting political elites."[65] In the Middle East, the determination of who is to move in or out of the elite is often still determined by these factors.

Built into and stretching throughout these webs of personal connections are three broader channels of mobility. These are the military, bureaucratic, and religious channels, and it is through them that most individuals have made their entrance into the political elite. Although the personalistic-patrimonial factors discussed above decidedly influence who moves through these channels, the very existence of the channels has helped to institutionalize mobility.

The Middle Eastern patrimonial system of leadership remains largely intact today. There are, however, a number of strong recruitment considerations that increasingly influence leadership composition. The most important of them are professional skill, talent, and merit. Political elites have been driven, because of the forces of modernization, to recruit individuals who have technical and professional competence. Ministries of health are increasingly headed by medical doctors and health administrators; national petroleum companies are directed by better and better qualified petroleum engineers, geologists, and economists; national educational systems are guided by Mid-

---

[65]Gabriel A. Almond and G. Bingham Powell, Jr., *Comparative Politics: System, Process, and Policy,* 2d ed. (Boston: Little, Brown and Co., 1978), p. 178.

dle Eastern specialists in the field of education. A look through the curriculum vitae of the representatives of various countries in the Organization of Petroleum Exporting Countries (OPEC) is one good way of documenting this trend. Even in the most traditional of patrimonial systems, such as Saudi Arabia, Kuwait, and Abu Dhabi, the educated technocrats have moved into decision-making positions.

Despite the changes in some of the qualifications necessary for entry into the elites, there are impressive indications that patrimonialism prevails.

First, recruitment processes are personally and firmly controlled from the center of the system. This is as true in more radical systems such as those in Syria and Iraq as it is in such traditional countries as Jordan and Morocco. In all of these systems the considerations of political loyalty, personal connections, and complete central control remain at least as important in determining entry into the elite as those of professional expertise, personal merit, and institutional position.

The second sign of patrimonial persistence in the Middle East concerns the directional flow of the recruitment patterns. In an analysis of the politics of elite recruitment, Almond and Powell stress that the political party is the most common contemporary channel of recruitment.[66] This has not been the case in Middle Eastern patrimonial politics. Although political parties exist in most of the societies, political leaders are not generally recruited from the parties. Instead, the parties (as well as the legislatures) are headed by individuals who are already national political leaders. The patrimonial head selects the party leadership from among proven confidants, advisors, or ministers. In several Middle Eastern systems, party positions (whether leadership or rank-and-file) more often reflect a move out of than a move into the national political elite. Parties and legislatures many times serve as the political dumping grounds for former members of the elite who have fallen from favor in the patrimonial establishment.

The continued strength of patrimonialism in the Middle East has meant that the personalistic networks that are directed from the center have a profound effect on both the shape of the political system and that system's capacity to confront the problems of modernization and political development. The patrimonial leaders and the political

---

[66]*Ibid.*, pp. 123–126.

elites that surround them play a disproportionate role in determining the future of their societies. Although their policies at one level may be very similar from society to society, at another level there are striking differences. In some societies, the traditional webs of patrimonialism operate today just as they have for centuries; in other societies, these webs have begun to be torn and are unraveling in differing ways. In Chapter 5 we will examine a number of case studies of Middle Eastern patrimonial leaders with special focus on the differing ways that they have coped with the challenge of change.

Chapter 5

The Politics of Leaders and Change

*T*he policies whereby Middle Eastern societies have confronted the challenge of change have been determined to a large extent by political leaders. As we have seen in Chapter 4, the political processes of patrimonial systems are shaped around the patrimonial leader, who plays a disproportionate role in the decision-making process. The centrality of the national political leader assures him a critical position in confronting the important related issues of modernization and political development. The leader's tactics and strategies in this regard have far-reaching consequences for the political system and for the peoples of the society concerned.

Throughout Middle Eastern history, leaders have held a wide variety of attitudes toward change. In many cases, the political leadership has chosen to resist the forces of change. In other cases, Middle Eastern leaders have taken a more flexible stance and have attempted to meet the challenge through programs of reform and revision. Their strategy has been to forestall major transformations by encouraging incremental adjustments. In still other instances, leaders have pursued revolutionary goals that involve radical social and political change. In all these cases, however, the leader has maintained a special position: He has controlled the instruments of persuasion and coercion that are essential to the implementation of any of these policies.

In this chapter, our analysis will emphasize Middle Eastern political leaders who have in this century chosen to promote various programs of change. Modernization has been a goal shared by all of these leaders. Political development, however, has not always been favored. We will analyze three pairs of leaders from three major Middle Eastern countries. These are Mustafa Kemal Ataturk and Ismet Inonu of Turkey, Reza Shah and Muhammad Reza Shah Pahlavi of Iran, and Gamal Abdel Nasser and Anwar Sadat of Egypt.

Before discussing these leaders, we shall devote a few paragraphs to the more traditional Middle Eastern leader. It is against this backdrop of traditional leadership that the more modern and often more progressive leaders have òperated. In all of these case studies, traditional patrimonial styles and tactics have still been very much in evidence.

TWENTIETH-CENTURY TRADITIONAL LEADERS

Twentieth-century Middle Eastern political history has been largely dominated by a number of colorful traditional leaders who did much to shape the destinies of their nations. In most cases, they resisted change and as a result became its victims. Some were hopelessly corrupt and venal in their personal and political lives; others were models of integrity, whose life-styles were simple and ascetic. All failed in one way or another to understand a changing world. Among the least impressive of these leaders are King Farouk of Egypt, Regent Abd al-Ilah of Iraq, Sultan Mehmet V and Sultan Mehmet VI of Turkey, Shaikh Shakhbut of Abu Dhabi, and Sultan Said bin Taymur of Oman. Traditional leaders of considerably more talent and integrity include King Idris of Libya, Zahir Shah of Afghanistan, King Abdullah of Jordan, King Muhammad V of Morocco, and especially, King Abdul Aziz Ibn Saud of Saudi Arabia.

Sultan Said bin Taimur ruled Oman for 38 years (1932–1970). Although he was educated at a British school in India, the Sultan spent nearly four decades walling his country in against the forces of change. Even after oil was discovered in Oman, he stubbornly refused to expend his resources on development programs. During his rule, no tractors were allowed in the sultanate; the occasional importation of an automobile had to be personally approved by the Sultan himself; religious taxes were collected in the provinces in Maria Theresa dollars as late as the 1960s; houses could be rebuilt only from the actual material with which they were originally constructed; women were forbidden to accompany their husbands abroad; and Omanis educated overseas were not allowed to return to work in their own country.

Sultan Said was opposed to education, financial expenditure, and modernization in his country. He felt that the British lost India because they had educated the people, and he therefore decided to close the only three primary schools in Oman, just before he was deposed in 1970. He considered the schools to be hotbeds of communism. The Sultan ruled supreme and kept his people in fear and subjection. The channels of access and personal contact that were such an essential part of Islamic patrimonial politics were destroyed by this traditional leader. After 1958, he kept himself in isolation in the coastal city of Salala. His officials, working in an atmosphere "made even more oppressive by his absence, one might describe it as disembodiment, in Salala,"[1] made no decisions. Sultan Said even locked up his son Qabus (the present ruler of Oman) when Qabus returned to Oman in 1966 after receiving a British education at Sandhurst.

British disappointment with the old Sultan led to his overthrow in July 1970. His demise was inevitable; his long period of reactionary rule had resulted in a guerrilla war that broke out in the province of Dhufar. By 1970, the opposition forces had taken most of Dhufar and were even shelling Sultan Said's palace. He had been consistent in his determined opposition to any kind of change or innovation. Because of British support and his geographic position in what were then the backwaters of the Middle East, he made this policy stick for a surprisingly long time. But in the end he failed. As Ian Skeet presciently wrote before the Sultan's fall, his kind of policy "is just plugging the holes in the barbed wire round the country's borders; one day the barbed wire will be rolled aside, and none of the Sultan's restrictions will help him one iota."[2]

If Sultan Said is one of the least successful traditional leaders in the Middle East of this century, King Abdul Aziz Ibn Saud is one of the most successful. Ibn Saud's style of leadership very closely approx-

[1]Ian Skeet, *Muscat and Oman: The End of an Era* (London: Faber and Faber, 1974), p. 168. Most of the material in this section has been drawn from Skeet's informed and entertaining book or from Fred Halliday, *Arabia Without Sultans* (New York: Vintage Books, 1974), pp. 277–315.

[2]Skeet, *Muscat and Oman,* p. 196.

imated that of the classical model analyzed in Chapter 4. Born in 1880 in Central Arabia, Ibn Saud grew up in an environment of vigorous conflict among clans. In 1901, he was a banished youth whose clan was ruled by its enemies and whose immediate family was in exile in Kuwait. By 1934, he had conquered the territories of Najd, Hasa, Hijaz, and Asir and had welded them together into one political unit known as the Kingdom of Saudi Arabia. In so doing, he had healed the rifts within his own family, defeated or co-opted the other clans, taken Hasa from the Turks, and conquered Mecca and Hijaz at the expense of the Hashemite King Hussein (the great-grandfather of the present King Hussein of Jordan).

Abdul Aziz Ibn Saud ruled personally, informally, and patriarchally. He ran his kingdom as a gigantic personal household, which it in fact very nearly was. Ibn Saud had an estimated three hundred wives in his lifetime, as well as large numbers of concubines and slave girls. In 1955, it was estimated that there was one prince for every 5,000 persons in Saudi Arabia.[3] Like the Prophet Muhammad, after whom he patterned his life, Ibn Saud used marriage as an important political tool. Through the years, he married into all the leading tribal families in Najd. His links with the Sudairi family, from which four of his wives came, were especially strong; these wives bore fifteen of his sons. Today, King Fahd is the most influential of seven full brothers who are the sons of Ibn Saud and Hussa bint Ahmad al-Sudairi.

In this setting, Ibn Saud balanced rivalries and directed the personal and political fortunes of all of the other main actors in the system. He made it his business to stay informed. "He had a deep knowledge of his people, their friendships and intermarriages, their blood feuds and causes of quarrel, so that he could play the one against the other."[4] He never allowed power to concentrate at any point in the system other than at his own feet. He once stated; "Two things I will not stomach: firstly a rebel (*marij*); and secondly the feigned loyalty of two persons inwardly leagued against me."[5] Ibn Saud was also famous for his accessibility and approachability. Quite unlike Sultan Said, he spent several hours each day listening to the complaints and problems of his people.

---

[3]H. St. John Philby, *Sa'udi Arabia* (London: Ernest Benn, 1955), p. 298.

[4]H. C. Armstrong, *Lord of Arabia* (Beirut: Khayyat's, 1944), p. 111.

[5]H. St. John Philby, *Arabian Jubilee* (London: Robert Hale, 1954), p. 106.

Finally, Ibn Saud was a great warrior. The first 30 years of his leadership were a time of constant warfare. It was during this period that he became a legend as he personally developed military strategy and led his soldiers into battle. At the end of these three decades of military struggle and political consolidation, Ibn Saud carried the marks of a dozen wounds, all attesting to the central role he played in the business of physical combat.

Although he founded a country and forged a following of disparate peoples into a nation, he stumbled when confronted with the challenges of modernization and political development. Between the time when oil was discovered at Jebel Dhahran in 1938 and when he died in 1953, Ibn Saud clung desperately to tradition. As a result, he was unable to cope effectively with the new forces and demands that burst upon him and his society. He did not think to concern himself with widening the base of political participation; he watched social and economic gaps widen among his people; he failed to stem the tide of peculation, corruption, and waste that washed through his kingdom; he did little to build health and educational facilities. These tasks were only taken up later by his successors.

Still, Abdul Aziz Ibn Saud was the greatest Middle Eastern traditional leader of this century. He combined wit and physical courage with personal charisma and deep religious beliefs to consolidate a people and build a nation.[6]

The political leaders discussed in the following sections attempted to move out ahead in their societies and to confront the forces of modernization. The one who did this earliest and most dramatically was a Turk born only a year before the great Ibn Saud. He came to be known as Ataturk.

ATATURK: THE REVOLUTIONARY FATHER OF TURKEY

The modern Turkish state owes its political form and indeed its very existence to one remarkable military and political leader—Ataturk. First called Mustafa, he was given the additional name of Kemal ("per-

[6]For more detailed analysis of the patrimonial politics of Abdul Aziz Ibn Saud, see J. A. Bill and C. Leiden, *The Middle East: Politics and Power* (Boston: Allyn and Bacon, 1974), pp. 125–133.

fection") by an instructor in secondary school. After his victory over the Greeks at Sakarya in 1921, the Grand National Assembly at Ankara gave him the title of Ghazi ("victor"). In 1934, the Assembly bestowed on him the surname Ataturk, or Father of the Turks. In this book, we will refer to him both as Kemal and as Ataturk.

Kemal was born in Salonika in Macedonia in 1881. His family was of the very lowest echelons of the middle class. His father, a onetime low-ranking civil servant, was a failure in both the timber business and the salt trade and died when Kemal was only 11. An extremely independent personality, Kemal was thrown out of one school before he settled into a military education that included military prep school in Salonika military academy at Monastir, and the War College and the Staff College at Constantinople. In 1905, he graduated from the Staff College as a captain in the sultan's army. On his final examination and in his personnel file, the following assessment was reportedly written: "A brilliant student officer, difficult in temperament, precise and technically a perfectionist, politically unstable."[7] Shortly after graduation, Kemal was arrested and imprisoned for plotting against the ruling authorities.

Kemal was born into a world of transition in which ancient social and political institutions were crumbling. The once powerful Ottoman Empire was on its last legs. On all its borders, the empire was besieged by various ethnic minority groups who fought to separate themselves from the system. Meanwhile, liberal ideas from the West were breeding dissatisfaction among the empire's educated middle-class population. It is thus not accidental that the Young Turk movement was born and nurtured in the westernmost sector of the empire. Macedonians were conspicuous among the revolutionaries.

The sultanate in Constantinople was corrupt and venal, and its policies were increasingly unpopular. When pushed, Sultan Abdul Hamid had declared some reforms, only to repeal them when pressures were relaxed. In 1876, he agreed to a constitution providing for the establishment of a consultative assembly; in 1877, he dissolved the assembly; in 1896, a major coup attempt failed. Meanwhile, political opposition had spread everywhere and had become deeply rooted

---

[7]Ray Brock, *Ghost on Horseback: The Incredible Atatürk* (Boston: Little, Brown and Co., 1954), p. 21. Although this book tends towards the sensational and owes too much to the fertile imagination of the author, it makes interesting reading and succeeds in capturing the colorfully human nature of Kemal.

even within the sultan's own armed forces. Kemal was one of the most disenchanted of the young officers who saw their decrepit system crumbling around them. A fierce nationalist, he determined from the beginning that the Turkish nation had to be reformed, strengthened, and regenerated.

After a few months in jail, Kemal was posted to the Fifth Army in Damascus, where he immediately began to establish political opposition societies among his military colleagues on the Syrian front. His Vatan ("Fatherland") Society was soon swallowed up by the Young Turks' Committee of Union and Progress, which on July 23, 1908, forced the sultan to restore the constitution and to recall his consultative assembly. Between 1908 and the outbreak of World War I in 1914, Kemal floated on the fringes of the Young Turks in a relationship marked by mutual distrust. Although his military skills were used by Enver Pasha and the other leaders during this time, he was carefully locked out of the corridors of power. "He was a realist, who thought in terms not of gestures but of action, thoughtfully conceived, scientifically planned and systematically executed. Too many of those whom he saw around him, and who were pretending to govern the country, were men of words, of undigested feelings and vague ideas."[8]

Although Kemal personally opposed the Turkish alliance with Germany in World War I, he earned his place in military history for his brilliant defense in 1915 at Gallipoli, where the Turks repelled a major Allied offensive spearheaded by the finest soldiers of the British Empire. Poorly armed and outnumbered, the Turkish troops under Kemal successfully held off the seasoned Australian, New Zealand, and British troops who desperately fought to break through to the Dardanelles and to clear the way to Constantinople. During this nine-month siege and bitter fighting, Kemal proved himself to be not only a brilliant military tactician but also an inspiration to his soldiers. He moved constantly among his men in the front trenches and miraculously survived a direct hit in his chest when shrapnel shattered the watch in his breast pocket. As he told his outgunned Fifty-Seventh Regiment: "I don't order you to attack, I order you to die; others troops and commanders can come and take our places."[9] The men of

---

[8]Lord Kinross, *Atatürk: The Rebirth of a Nation* (London: Weidenfeld and Nicolson, 1964), p. 44. This remains the best biography of Ataturk. For a fine article-length study, see Dankwart A. Rustow's own analysis in his edited volume *Philosophers and Kings: Studies in Leadership* (New York: George Braziller, 1970), pp. 208–247.

[9]Kinross, *Atatürk,* p. 76.

the Fifty-Seventh did die for their leader and for their country. Kemal somehow survived; he had taken the first major step toward becoming the Father of the Turks.

The Allies' victory in 1918 ended the Young Turks' ascendancy and forced their leaders into exile. The British appearance in Constantinople and a subsequent Greek movement into Smyrna were shocking and unacceptable events for Turkish patriots. Kemal left for Anatolia, where he began an opposition independence movement. In 1919, he organized congresses at Erzerum and Sivas, where delegates drafted and ratified a national pact legitimizing their movement. Turkey was in upheaval. During the next four years, Kemal put the pieces of the country back together. The task was a formidable one, since in the process he had to organize a political and military force that would not only hang together but also be strong enough to defeat the tribes and brigands in Anatolia; repulse and drive a major invading Greek force from the heart of Turkey; maneuver the British and Russians out of the area; and replace the Sultan's government, still claiming legitimacy in Constantinople, with a new nationalist government, resident in Ankara.

In 3½ years of brutal but brilliant military campaigns and pressure-packed political infighting, Kemal accomplished all these goals. In November 1922, he proclaimed the abolition of the sultanate; in October 1923, Turkey was declared a republic and Kemal became its first president; and in March 1924, the caliphate was abolished. Kemal was president of Turkey until his death in 1938.

During his 15 years as president, Ataturk did not choose to rest on his military laurels. Instead, he began a program of social, cultural, and political modernization that shook the country to its roots. His program struck at the foundation of the conservative religious culture of the day and stressed national, secular, and modern goals. In a characteristic style, he directly and publicly attacked the very symbols of the old system by outlawing the fez, condemning the veil, and reforming the alphabet.

These shattering changes in important symbols were accompanied by major reforms in the fields of administration, education, and law. One of Ataturk's most important contributions was the successful establishment of an independent and effective judiciary. The programs of reform were backed by an international policy that was astutely conceived and implemented. This foreign policy was based on a premise stressing the consolidation of national power, not the expansion of national boundaries. It also emphasized the necessity of avoiding international entanglements such as the one that contributed to the disaster of World War I. It was Ataturk who established the policy that enabled Ismet Inonu to keep Turkey out of World War II. Despite tremendous pressures, Turkey did not take a formal position until February 1945, when it declared war on the Axis powers.[10]

Ataturk was not a liberal democrat. He was an authoritarian ruler who exercised power bluntly and forcefully. In his own words, "I don't act for public opinion. I act for the nation and for my own satisfaction."[11] He had climbed the ladder of power by himself and had survived everything from several serious illnesses[12] and difficult military campaigns to political plots and assassination attempts. When he finally reached a position of national political power, he did not hesitate to take severe measures against those whom he considered threats to himself or to his programs. The major example of this occurred when, in 1926, Kemal used an abortive plot against his life as a rationale for imprisoning, exiling, or executing those he considered members of a serious political opposition. Among them were several of his oldest comrades and friends who had stood behind him in the difficult years in Anatolia. Many of these individuals were liberal thinkers who had begun to resist his personal, arbitrary rule. As Kazim Karabekir, a trusted military leader whose assistance was crucial to Kemal's success in Anatolia, put it, "I am in favour of the Republic, but I am against personal rule."[13]

Yet there is another side to the story. Kemal was always scrupulously careful to seek legitimation for his actions and to base them upon legal principles emanating from the people. Even as a rebel, he insisted on congresses and constitutional pacts that would provide political legitimacy for his movement. He also campaigned hard

---

[10]For Ataturk and his successors as makers of foreign policy, see Metin Tamkoç's excellent book *The Warrior Diplomats* (Salt Lake City: University of Utah Press, 1976).

[11]Kinross, *Atatürk,* p. xvii.

[12]Physical ailments plagued Kemal throughout his life, yet he conquered these problems just as he overcame the social and political problems that confronted him. Besides sustaining a minor battle wound and some broken ribs, he survived two major attacks of malaria, three severe cases of influenza, a debilitating ear infection, and kidney problems that tormented him for 25 years. As a young man, he contracted gonorrhea, the effects of which were lasting. He died of cirrhosis of the liver and complications thereof.

[13]Kinross, *Atatürk,* p. 382.

Table 5.1 LIFE OF ATATURK: MAJOR EVENTS

1881	Born in Salonika
1893	Enters military secondary school in Salonika; given added name Kemal
1899	Enters War College in Constantinople
1905	Graduates from Staff College with rank of captain
1908	Young Turk revolution
1914	Beginning of World War I; Turkey signs secret alliance with Germany; Russia, Britain, and France declare war on Turkey
1915	Kemal distinguishes himself at Gallipoli
1919	Leaves for Anatolia; issues declaration of independence; calls nationalist congresses at Sivas and Erzerum
1921	Defeats the invading Greeks at Battle of Sakarya
1922	Proclaims abolition of the sultanate
1923	Founds the Republican Peoples' Party; becomes president of the Turkish Republic
1924	Abolishes the caliphate
1926	Trials and suppression of opposition at Izmir and Ankara
1934	Takes name of Ataturk; women given the right to vote in parliamentary elections and to become members of parliament
1938	Dies in Istanbul

among the people and created a major and lasting political party, the Republican People's Party. He twice experimented with a two-party system but gave it up when it proved unworkable. Ataturk once admitted that he was a dictator yet went on to point out: "But I have not had pyramids built in my honour like the Pharaohs of Egypt. I did not make people work for my sake, threatening them with whips when I wanted an idea to be accepted by the country. I first called a congress, I debated the situation with the people, I carried out my plans only after taking authority from the people."[14] His may not have always been a government by the people, but it was in many ways a government for the people.[15]

---

[14]*Ibid.*, p. 438.

[15]This terminology is Kemal Karpat's, as presented in his study *Turkey's Politics: The Transition to Multi-Party Politics* (Princeton, N.J.: Princeton University Press, 1959), pp. 50–51. It is quoted in the writings of Metin Heper.

Patterns of Rule

Ataturk was one of the most colorful political leaders of this century. He was a man of imposing appearance, with peculiarly striking eyes. "Wide-set beneath the broad brow and the eyebrows that curled upwards like whiskers, they gleamed with a cold steady challenging light, for ever fixing, observing, reflecting, appraising, moreover uncannily capable of swivelling two ways at once so that they seemed to see both upwards and downwards, before and behind."[16]

Kemal's personal life was almost completely uninhibited. He drank and gambled incessantly; and he enjoyed the company and entertainment provided by women and spent a good part of his life in cafes, hotels, and brothels. During the critical early years of his political opposition both to the sultan and to the young Turks, these personal activities led the establishment forces to underestimate the danger that he posed to them. At the same time, Kemal used these informal gatherings to discuss social and political issues and to gather information that passed through these grapevines. Just as Ismet Inonu was able to convert his physical liability of near-deafness into a political asset, Kemal's personal habits were not complete liabilities to him. A French writer wrote at the time that Turkey was governed by one drunkard, one deaf man, and three hundred deaf-mutes (the assembly deputies). When he heard this, Kemal responded, "The man is mistaken. Turkey is governed by one drunkard."[17]

Ataturk's political style in many ways sharply broke with traditional Middle Eastern patterns. Although he would on occasion use the *hocas* (clerics) to legitimize a particular political move, he refused to use Islam as any kind of overarching ideology. Quite to the contrary, he had a strong personal aversion to religion and sought to smash its influence. Much is written about his charismatic personality, and he indeed had many of the extraordinary attributes of a charismatic leader. This can be seen even today in Turkey, where the anniversaries of his death are national mourning days, and where thousands upon thousands of Turkish citizens continue to file past his mausoleum in Ankara. But Ataturk was little impressed by his own charisma. He was often annoyed, for example, when other dignitaries would fawn over

---

[16]Kinross, *Atatürk,* p. 163.

[17]*Ibid.,* p. 261.

him. He once became so irritated when the mayor of a city he was visiting insisted on waiting on him in person at the dinner table that he snapped, "For God's sake, sit down! Are you a waiter, or the mayor of this city?"[18] Ataturk institutionalized and routinized his charisma by building organizations, such as the Republican People's Party, that would transcend the existence of one man. In the words of one leading authority on Turkish politics, Ataturk was "an organization man thrown into a charismatic situation."[19]

Although Kemal learned to play his subordinates one against the other and on occasion to maneuver clandestinely, he was essentially very direct. In the context of Turkish politics of the day, this directness often seemed crude, brutal, and even stupid. As his major biographer writes, "He detested the shifts and evasions of the oblique approach to Oriental politics, the circumlocutions and imprecisions of its thought and speech. He liked to speak his mind directly, to call spades spades. His outspokenness indeed not only infuriated his enemies but, on occasion, embarrassed his friends."[20] Nor did Kemal play favorites with friends and relatives. One of the major reasons he divorced his wife, Latife, was that she continually interfered in matters of national politics. Finally, Ataturk was not interested in amassing a fortune for himself and his family. Although he lived comfortably, he was by no means financially corrupt. His life-style was in fact quite modest.

Ataturk was above all a realist. He understood power and people and had an unusual ability to bridge the gap between ideal and reality. He used idealists and dreamers, but he never trusted them. He considered them much more dangerous than the small-time politicians who lacked vision. Ataturk himself was both a visionary and a hard, experienced political realist.

Champion of Change or Camouflaged Conservative?

A number of excellent analyses of the Ataturk period make compelling arguments that Kemal's programs and policies were in essence conservative and nonrevolutionary. Although this school admits that dramatic changes were initiated in the cultural and religious systems of

---

[18]*Ibid.*, p. 368.

[19]Rustow, *Philosophers and Kings,* p. 212.

[20]Kinross, *Atatürk,* p. 45.

Turkey, the question at issue is that of social structure. Ataturk's programs were initiated without basically altering the traditional class structure. Special care was taken to avoid upsetting the local landlords and aristocracy who controlled power throughout the country. Those at the bottom of the power structure witnessed very little change in their standard of living. If anything, the peasants' standard of living became worse during Kemalist rule. Land reform, for example, was almost completely ignored during Kemal's lifetime. In the words of Arnold Leder:

> From its earliest days in the Turkish War of Independence when it sought the cooperation of the local notables in the countryside, the Kemalist movement became a collaborative movement. The nationalist struggle led by the Kemalists was fought against foreign enemies and not against a particular social class. The Kemalists did not undertake radical change in Turkey's social structure. In fact, they established a tacit alliance with the traditional elites in the countryside. This alliance was reflected in Kemalist political organization where local notables dominated the lower levels of the Republican People's party. The Kemalists made no effort to broaden the party's popular base and to enlist the support of the peasants. Similarly, Kemalist ideology emphasized not the drastic restratification of society but rather harmony, national solidarity, and the prosperity of all segments of society.[21]

Another study by a leading Turkish political scientist concludes in this regard that "the Atatürk Revolution exploited the basic bifurcation between the educated elite and the uneducated masses, rather than deploring it or immediately attacking it."[22]

This failure to transform the national class structure has been one factor in the political problems that have plagued Turkey since Ataturk's death. Indeed, the creation of the Democrat Party in 1946 and its stunning victory over the Republican People's Party in the general election of 1950 may have been major symptoms of the depth of the social and political problems inherited from the days of Ataturk. Since Ataturk's time, there has been a broadening diffusion of power into the Turkish countryside, although the real inclusion of the provin-

[21]Leder, "Collaboration Politics and the Turkish Revolution" (Paper delivered at the 1976 Annual Meeting of the Middle East Studies Association, Los Angeles, 11–13 November 1976), p. 29.

[22]Ergun Özbudun, *Social Change and Political Participation in Turkey* (Princeton, N.J.: Princeton University Press, 1976), p. 43.

cial lower classes within the national decision-making structure remains to be seen.[23]

Questions concerning the depth of Ataturk's reforms are legitimate ones. His revolution did not transform the social, political, or economic conditions of the masses of Turkish peasants. Still, this failure should not be allowed to obscure the immensity of the social and political changes that Ataturk did implement successfully. At bottom, his revolution was a middle-class movement that destroyed a number of traditional symbols and built a new political system. In this sense, it was more radical than the American Revolution and in some respects paralleled the French Revolution, also a middle-class affair. In the context of the time, it stands as a revolution of modernization and a movement of substantial political development.

Politically, a 600-year-old national ruling institution and its attendant ruling class were destroyed and replaced by a middle-class elite that introduced new political ideas and institutions, including a political party of genuine consequence. These were structural transformations of lasting impact, which set the stage for subsequent political development, such as the birth of a political opposition (the Democrat Party) that was permitted to win in elections. In this rare political event, in which an authoritarian regime voluntarily relinquished power, it was Ataturk's old lieutenant, the dedicated Kemalist Ismet Inonu, who made the decision to permit the opposition to win.[24]

In the section above, we have seen how Ataturk broke many of the traditional interpersonal patterns that had dominated Ottoman patri-

---

[23]See Frank Tachau, "Turkish Provincial Party Politics," in *Social Change and Politics in Turkey*, Kemal H. Karpat et al. (Leiden, The Netherlands: E. J. Brill, 1973), pp. 282–314; and Karpat's own article "Political Development in Turkey, 1950–1970," *Middle Eastern Studies* 8 (October 1972):349–375.

[24]Inonu's decision was based on a number of personal, political, and ideological factors. First, he hoped at the time to demonstrate to the West the democratic nature of his regime. See Dankwart A. Rustow, "The Development of Parties in Turkey," in *Political Parties and Political Development*, ed. by J. La Palombara and M. Weiner (Princeton, N.J.: Princeton University Press, 1966), p. 122. Second, Inonu felt that the establishment of an opposition political party would help lower the level of discontent in the country. See Leslie L. Roos, Jr., and Noraloo P. Roos, *Managers of Modernization* (Cambridge, Mass.: Harvard University Press, 1971), p. 40. Third, Inonu and his advisors believed that the Republican People's Party was strong enough in the Turkish countryside to guarantee victory in any election. See Kemal Karpat, "Society, Economics, and Politics in Contemporary Turkey," *World Politics* 17 (October 1964):58. These positions are all drawn together and analyzed in the writings of Arnold Leder.

monial rule. These and the broader political changes discussed above were successfully implemented despite the serious opposition of at least four groups. Of these groups, two were obvious forces of the ancien régime—the sultanate's political establishment and the omnipresent religious hierarchy. The two others, however, were groups of former liberal allies who were, ironically, more conservative than Kemal. These were the Young Turks on the one hand and the group of his earliest supporters and comrades on the other hand. In the case of the former, ". . . theirs was essentially a conservative revolution. . . . Imperialists in essence, blind to the new nationalist forces now at work in the modern world, the Young Turks aspired merely to conserve, if in a more liberal form, the Ottoman Empire of their forebears."[25] At the same time, old comrades such as Hussain Rauf, Ali Fuad, and Kazim Karabekir were more liberal idealists and preferred democracy over revolutionary change. "Kemal was embarking on a social revolution. Rauf and his friends, at this stage, preferred social evolution."[26] Despite this encircling and committed opposition, Ataturk rammed through as much radical political change as was possible at the time.

A comparison of Ataturk and Ismet Inonu, his long-time friend and trusted lieutenant, also helps demonstrate the nature of Ataturk's revolution. Inonu had served Kemal loyally and was the one lieutenant who survived his leader's inner-circle purges.[27] The two men comple-

---

[25]Kinross, *Atatürk*, p. 30.

[26]*Ibid.*, p. 392. These associates were generally of well-to-do upper-class and upper-middle-class background and were therefore more closely tied to the old system than Kemal, who was obviously their social inferior. In 1924, this group resigned from the Republican People's Party and formed their own organization, called the Progressive Republican Party. Kemal used a Kurdish rebellion as the major excuse for disbanding the Progressive Party. For an analysis of the character of Ataturk's political elite, see Joseph S. Szyliowicz's study of leadership in modern Turkey in Frank Tachau, ed., *Political Elites and Political Development in the Middle East* (Cambridge, Mass.: Schenkman Publishing Co., 1975), pp. 23–68. Another good source is Frederick Frey's article in *Political Elites in the Middle East,* ed. by George Lenczowski (Washington, D.C.: American Enterprise Institute, 1975), pp. 41–82

[27]Toward the end, personal tensions that had been building up for many years between Ataturk and Inonu began to break into the open. Kinross reports one such exchange that took place in 1937. The pressured and normally unflappable Inonu lost his temper and blurted to Ataturk, "How much longer is this country going to be governed from a drunkard's table?" To this Ataturk coldly responded, "You seem to forget that it was a drunkard who appointed you to your post." Kinross, *Atatürk*, p. 486.

mented each other perfectly. Ataturk was direct, forceful, and mercurial while Inonu was conservative, retiring, and unspectacular. When Ataturk died in 1938, Inonu was the natural choice to replace him as president. For the next 35 years, he played a prominent role in directing Turkey's political destiny. Inonu's most famous political decision was his call in 1945 for the formation of an opposition party (referred to above). This remarkable move transformed Turkey into a multiparty state. In taking this action, Inonu not only broadened participatory politics in Turkey but also carved out a place for himself, independent of Ataturk, in the pantheon of Turkish political leaders.

Although many observers interpret Inonu's programs as moving far beyond the policies of Ataturk in the field of political development, there is another position that needs to be presented. The argument has been made that in promoting liberalization and introducing pluralist politics into Turkey, Inonu hampered the system's capacity for development. By stepping aside and opening the arena to all comers, he introduced a period of tense and competitive factional politics that has ever since slowed the Turkish drive to develop. From the days of Menderes's prime ministry, beginning in 1950, to the debilitating political struggles in 1977 and 1978 between Suleyman Demirel of the Justice Party and Bulent Ecevit of the Republican People's Party, the political process in Turkey has been weakening. The severity of the crisis is seen in the direct intervention of the military into the political arena in 1960, 1971, and 1980.

This position is supported strongly in an excellent and provocative study by a young Turkish social scientist and diplomat, who wrote that with Inonu's "democratization of political life, the principle of revolutionism was effectively shelved. . . . The capacity of Turkish leaders to introduce orderly change from above, a capacity that was in evidence during Ataturk's time, was lost for the sake and as a result of democracy. Ataturk had started a revolution; Inonu arrested it."[28]

There is certainly truth in both sides of this debate, which focuses

---

[28]Osman Faruk Logoglu, "Ismet Inonu and the Political Modernization of Turkey, 1945–1965," Ph.D. diss. (Princeton University, 1970), p. 255. With regard to Ataturk's strategy of change, Logoglu writes: "There has been no rigorous exposition of the meaning of the well-established proposition that Ataturk tried to convert only the elite or the intelligentsia and did not really try to reach the peasant masses. The meaning of the corollary proposition that Ataturk had the insight to realize he could not change the masses without first transforming the elite needs to be restated as well." See pp. 255–256.

directly on the developmental dialectic discussed in Chapter 1. Authoritarianism at the center endangers participation in the periphery (Ataturk's case). Liberalization, however, tends to create fragmentation, which in turn weakens capacity for development (Inonu's case). The parallel processes of modernization and political development must be continuing ones. Ataturk started a revolution. It was up to his successors to continue it, widen it, and deepen it.

MUHAMMAD REZA SHAH PAHLAVI: THE TRADITIONALISM OF A MODERNIZING MONARCH

In June of 1934, President Kemal Ataturk welcomed an important neighboring head of state to Turkey for a three-week official state visit. The visitor was Reza Shah, the founder of the Pahlavi dynasty of Iran. Like Ataturk, Reza Shah was a man of imposing presence. Standing well over 6 feet in height, he had the flashing eyes of an eagle and a personality that scorched friend and foe alike. The two leaders had much in common. Both were military men and avid nationalists who consolidated their nations and built strong central political control over their peoples. Both leaders also sought to modernize and reform their countries. Reza Shah, who was three years older than Ataturk, was greatly impressed by the latter's reform programs as well as by the level of modernity he witnessed in Turkey. Partly as a result of this visit, he lashed out at such symbols of tradition as the ulema, while at the same time sporadically modernizing the economic, educational, and military systems in his country. Yet Reza Shah's programs of reform never approached the depth or breadth of those instituted by his contemporary in Turkey.[29]

After participating in the military coup of 1921, Reza Khan crowned himself shah of Iran in 1926. In so doing, he chose to continue patrimonial monarchy, a system of leadership that Ataturk had vigorously dismantled in Turkey. Patrimonial monarchism dominated Iranian politics until 1979, when Reza Shah's eldest son, Muhammad Reza, was overthrown by a massive revolutionary movement.

Although an impressive nation builder and leader who rose to power from a lowly and illiterate background, Reza Shah in the end

---

[29]The major comparison of Ataturk and Reza Shah as modernizers is Richard H. Pfaff, "Disengagement from Traditionalism in Turkey and Iran," *Western Political Quarterly* 16 (March 1963):79–98.

only shuffled the old power relations in Iran. The major political change was the existence of a new royal family at the center of the system. By the time he abdicated in 1941, Reza Shah had acquired in his own name the largest landholdings in Iran and was drawing an annual income of well over $3 million a year.[30] Although he maintained parliamentary forms and procedures, he completely controlled the political process. His rule was absolute and oppressive; he disposed of whomever he considered to be a threat to himself or to his son.

It was within this repressive political climate that Reza Shah built a railway, founded a modern educational system, developed a national army, and supported such strong symbolic measures as the unveiling of women and the condemnation of the clerics. The old social structure and the traditional patrimonialism were strongly protected, however, by the new ruling Pahlavi family. One Persian source describes the patrimonial role of Reza Shah as follows: "The Shah expected that all government employees consider themselves completely subservient to his desires and that they not show any personality of their own. . . . Those favored by the Shah did their best to carry out his desires while at the same time trying to insure that these efforts did not become too well known and thus draw fame upon themselves."[31] The last shah of Iran, Muhammad Reza, once wrote that "all over the world, the father helps shape the character of the son. In my case, my father influenced me more by far than has anyone else."[32]

Muhammad Reza Shah Pahlavi was born on October 26, 1919. At the age of 13, he began his studies at Le Rosey School in Rolle, Switzerland. He returned to Iran four years later, and between 1936 and 1941 he received a military and political education that was directed primarily by his father. With the Allied invasion of Iran in 1941 and his father's humiliating abdication, Muhammad Reza became shah of Iran. The next dozen years were very painful and insecure for the young shah, as is well symbolized by the attempt on his life in 1949, which, face-to-face with an armed assassin, the shah survived by "shadow-dancing and feinting."[33]

---

[30]Great Britain, Public Record Office, F. O. 371/18992, from Mallet (Tehran), November 28, 1935.

[31]*Sharq-i Tarik* [The Dark East] (Tehran: Taban Press, 1942), pp. 69–71. In Persian.

[32]Mohammad Reza Shah Pahlavi, *Mission for My Country* (New York: McGraw-Hill, 1961), p. 45.

[33]*Ibid.*, p. 57.

The shah managed to dodge and weave his way through the 1940s, during which time he was the target of challenges emanating from many different directions. On the left, the Communist Tudeh Party threatened to capture the entire political system, while on the right, both knowledgeable statesmen and conservative clerics sought to control the shah and to take power themselves. Foreign interference was intense, and the young ruler found himself sandwiched between nationalist fervor and imperialist power. It was during these early years that the shah learned the art of political maneuver and perfected the traditional techniques of divide and rule. When such basic rationalizations of rule as charisma and religion are absent, the patrimonial leader is forced to rely entirely upon personal manipulative techniques. This was exactly the situation for the shah of Iran in the 1940s; besieged and surrounded by opponents and critics, he managed to survive by constantly refining those methods of patrimonial rule that were at his disposal.

In the early 1950s, the shah and the monarchy of Iran were faced with a challenge of the most serious proportions. A charismatic personality rose within Iran and, rallying the masses behind him, confronted the shah and threatened to transform social and political patterns. Muhammad Musaddiq rose to influence primarily on the basis of his attack against foreign interests in Iran and his direct drive to nationalize the Anglo-Iranian Oil Company. Although the apologetic (as opposed to analytic) literature concerning Pahlavi politics has attempted to portray Musaddiq as somehow being in league with the British, the British had already, in their diplomatic reports in the 1930s, tagged him as "a demagogue and a windbag."[34]

Musaddiq was known in Iran as an impeccably honest personality who refused to accede to foreign interests. The dramatic proof of this was his successful campaign to nationalize the oil company. Musaddiq was prime minister from April 1951 to August 1953. During this time, he became internationally famous as he nationalized the oil company and slowly undermined the power of the shah. He fell from office during the chaotic events of August 1953, which included the shah's returning to Iran and the throne a few days after a hurried flight out of

---

[34]Great Britain, Public Record Office, F.O. 371/20837, Seymour to Eden, April 12, 1937. For the convoluted reasoning that implies Musaddiq's proximity to the British, see Ramesh Sanghvi, *Aryamehr: The Shah of Iran* (New York: Stein and Day, 1968), pp. 142–245, 213.

the country. Street fighting and military activity that month involved the Tudeh forces, proshah elements, Musaddiqists, and Americans who directly intervened on behalf of the shah.[35]

Much of Musaddiq's support came from the rising professional middle class, whose members tended to be highly nationalistic and critical of the corruption that pervaded the Iranian socioadministrative system. Musaddiq, who retained in his behavior vestiges of the old aristocracy from which he had come, nonetheless entertained middle-class values and was able to gain strength and support across class lines. Although he may have been a poor politician in the Iranian context, Musaddiq was a charismatic leader who challenged the very roots of Pahlavi patrimonialism.

The Musaddiq challenge represented an intolerable situation for the shah, since it directly struck at the very foundation upon which all patrimonial leaders must base their power—their indisputable and central right to rule. The threat from Musaddiq was particularly serious because he donned a patrimonial mantle of his own that was heavily embroidered with charisma.[36]

Following the fall of Musaddiq, the shah began a concerted program to solidify his position as leader of all Iranians. Between 1954 and 1961, he pursued a policy of consolidation through coercion and thus adopted political tactics reminiscent of those used by his father in the 1930s. Besides building up military resources such as the army and the gendarmerie, the shah organized an extensive secret-police system (SAVAK) in 1957. SAVAK became a key element in Pahlavi politics from then on.

Beginning in 1963, the shah's style of leadership shifted to an emphasis upon the introduction of reform programs. Policies of coercion were balanced with programs of co-optation as the shah initiated a campaign to foster reform from above. In the mid-1960s, he spoke often about the need for revolutionary programs in Iran. By the end of the 1960s, he was quoting Lenin in his speeches, and many of his supporters were referring to opponents of the regime as reactionary, feu-

---

[35]For recent detailed analyses of these events and of the Musaddiq period in general, see James A. Bill and William Roger Louis, eds., *Musaddiq, Iranian Nationalism and Oil* (Austin: University of Texas Press, 1988).

[36]E. A. Bayne writes that "the Shah's historic image was dimmed by the burning fire of Mossadegh's charisma." Bayne, *Persian Kingship in Transition* (New York: American Universities Field Staff, 1968), p. 160.

dal, and right wing. The shah outlined the core of the reform program in January 1963, when he announced the six principles of the White Revolution. This "Revolution of the Shah and the People," as it was referred to in Persian, was expanded until it included 19 different points. The most important were the first 12: (1) land reform, (2) nationalization of forests and pastures, (3) public sale of state-owned factories to finance land reform, (4) profit sharing in industry, (5) reform of electoral law to include women, (6) literacy corps, (7) health corps, (8) reconstruction and development corps, (9) rural courts of justice, (10) nationalization of the waterways, (11) national reconstruction, and (12) educational and administrative revolution.

Despite these reforms, which were never completely and effectively implemented, political opposition, unrest, instability, and violence all increased in Iran during the last 15 years of the shah's rule. By the mid-1970s, urban guerrillas dedicated to the overthrow of the shah clashed constantly with security forces. Between 1970 and 1976, the shah's longtime policy of blending programs of repression with those of reform was abandoned, and a period of stifling police rule was ushered in. People were arrested and harassed arbitrarily and often; censorship became unusually heavy-handed and indiscriminate; and for the first time during the shah's rule, torture was systematically utilized in the prisons. A 1976 study prepared by the International Commission of Jurists reported that "there can be no doubt that torture has been systematically practiced over a number of years against recalcitrant suspects under interrogation by the SAVAK."[37] When questioned about torture, the shah said: "I am not bloodthirsty. I am working for my country and the coming generations. I can't waste my time on a few young idiots. I don't believe the tortures attributed to the SAVAK are as common as people say, but I can't run everything."[38]

This sharp shift in the direction of repressive rule sacrificed the more subtle dimensions of patrimonial rule to harsh police control.

---

[37]William J. Butler and Georges Levasseur, *Human Rights and the Legal System in Iran* (Geneva: International Commission of Jurists, 1976), p. 22. For various sources discussing the severity of secret police tactics in Iran, see Amnesty International, *Annual Report, 1974–75* (London, 1975); U.S. Congress, House Committee on International Relations, Subcommittee on International Organizations, *Human Rights in Iran* (Washington, D.C.: Government Printing Office, 1977).

[38]Gérard de Villiers, *The Imperial Shah: An Informal Biography* (Boston: Little, Brown and Co., 1976), p. 259.

Table 5.2   LIFE OF MUHAMMAD REZA SHAH PAHLAVI: MAJOR EVENTS

1919	Born in Tehran
1926	Reza Khan crowned shah of Iran; Muhammad Reza declared Crown Prince
1932	Enters Le Rosey School in Switzerland
1936	Returns to Tehran; enrolls in military academy
1941	Reza Shah abdicates; Muhammad Reza takes oath as shah of Iran; Tudeh Party established in Tehran
1946	Russian army withdraws from Azerbaijan
1950	Shah announces intention to divide lands among peasants
1951	Muhammad Musaddiq becomes prime minister; nationalization of Anglo-Iranian Oil Company
1953	Fall of Musaddiq; shah reassumes power
1957	Establishment of Security Organization (SAVAK)
1959	Shah marries Farah Diba
1960	Birth of Crown Prince Reza
1963	Announces White Revolution; countrywide riots and demonstrations put down with force
1967	Formal coronation of Muhammad Reza Shah and Empress Farah
1971	Celebration of 2,500 years of Iranian monarchy
1975	Establishes one-party system—the National Resurgence Party
1978	Masses of Iranian citizens riot and demonstrate against the shah's rule; shah institutes government by martial law
1979	Shah goes into exile; Ayatollah Ruhollah Khomeini returns to Iran after 15 years in exile
1980	Muhammad Reza Shah dies in Egypt

One result was a marked rise in opposition activity, which took the form of urban violence promoted by expanding guerrilla groups. Thousands of incidents occurred throughout Iran; new, superbly organized opposition groups even managed to infiltrate the shah's highly touted security forces. The tighter the police turned the screws, the more fanatic the opposition became. Dozens of young women, along with the men, joined the guerrillas as a vicious circle of repression and reaction set in. Meanwhile, in the mosques throughout the country, religious leaders increased sharply their critical social and political commentary.

Then, at the end of 1976 and in early 1977 and coinciding partly with the appearance of the Carter administration in Washington, the shah began to cut back on the repression and tried to return to more flexible patrimonial tactics. A period of liberalization began and was accompanied by a marked decrease in guerrilla-sponsored violence. Letters, petitions, and communications of all kinds flooded the offices of the shah and his political elite. When a leading Iranian newspaper raised a question in one of its columns concerning "what is wrong in Iran," it received over 40,000 letters. This kind of overwhelming response frightened the regime which reverted to heavy-handed police tactics resulting in a wave of violence that shook the country to its roots in 1978.

Drawing its inspiration from the charismatic, uncompromising leadership of Ayatollah Ruhollah Khomeini in exile in Iraq and then France, the popular opposition gathered momentum and strength as the year progressed. Rallying around the Shi'i religious leaders, individuals drawn from all social classes demonstrated violently against the shah's rule in the city of Qom in January, in Tabriz in February, and in Tehran and other cities in March, April, and May. Then in August, September, and December of 1978, the opposition to the shah exploded into mass marches and demonstrations involving hundreds of thousands of dissatisfied citizens.

Shaken and stunned in the face of massive national rebellion, the shah tried a number of desperate measures of both concession and repression. Concessions were half-measures that only whetted the appetite of the popular opposition; repression gave the revolution over 10,000 martyrs and strengthened the resolve and commitment of the challenging forces. When the traditional twin tactics of alternating coercion and cooptation failed to stem the revolutionary tide, the shah was left baffled and bewildered. Already somewhat weakened by a five-year struggle with cancer and psychologically unwilling to relinquish the mantle of absolute monarchy, he watched in disbelief as his people, always chanting "Marg bar shah" ("Death to the Shah"), rose to overthrow him.

On January 3, 1979, the Iranian Majlis approved the shah's reluctant appointment of Shahpour Bakhtiar, a liberal and former National Front member, as prime minister of Iran. On January 16, Muhammad Reza Shah left Iran for a "vacation" abroad—a vacation from which he was never to return. On January 31, Ayatollah Khomeini, the implacable foe of the shah, returned to Iran in triumph after 15 years of exile abroad. The shah spent the last 18 months of his life seeking a permanent residence in exile. After shuffling from Egypt to Morocco to the Bahamas to Mexico to the United States to Panama, the shah returned to Egypt, where he died of cancer on July 27, 1980.

Patterns of Rule

Muhammad Reza Shah Pahlavi was a political leader who practiced to perfection the techniques and tactics of patrimonial rule for nearly four decades in Iran. He was presented to his people as the source of all ideas and the fount of all good. Each of the points in the White Revolution, therefore, was attributed to the shah, and much has been written about how these ideas suddenly came to his mind.[39]

Individuals competed relentlessly with one another to have their ideas presented to the shah, who, they hoped, would include them in his personal program for national development. In his book published in 1978, the shah patrimonially discussed his role as national mentor, teacher, and creator of revolutionary ideas: "I accept most willingly this mission for teaching and advice because of the knowledge I command on the most extensive scale of my country's national and international problems and because I am, myself, the architect and founder of the social revolution of which all Iranian developments of the day are the reflection."[40] The strength of this pattern is also seen in the words of former prime minister, minister of court, tribal aristocrat, and lifelong friend and confidant of the shah, Asadollah Alam: "I cannot say that he is faultless. Everyone, as you say, has faults. . . . [H]is fault to my mind is that he is really too great for his people—his ideas are too great for we people to realize it."[41] This kind of subservience, displayed even by the most important officials, is a central ingredient in patrimonial rule.

A special effort was made in Iran to portray the Shah to his people as an unquestioned patrimonial leader. Because he had to bargain for survival during the first 12 years of his rule and because he lacked

---

[39]See, for example, "Brilliant Idea Was Born on a Murky Day," *Kayhan International* (Tehran), November 22, 1966, p. 4. This article explains how the idea of a literacy corps suddenly popped into the shah's mind.

[40]Mohammed Reza Shah Pahlavi, *Towards the Great Civilization* (Tehran: n. p., 1978).

[41]Margaret Laing, *The Shah* (London: Sidgwick and Jackson, 1977), p. 231.

charisma, the years following the fall of Musaddiq were years in which
"a sophisticated apparatus would work assiduously to create the
supreme patriarchal image, and a secret police would guard it."[42]

The source of power must be visible to everyone everywhere. Pictures of the shah and his immediate family adorned government
offices and public places throughout the country. Statues of the shah
stood in the middle of village squares, city parks, and even on the tops
of mountain peaks. Shrubbery in public gardens was cut in the form of
Persian script spelling out the shah's name. His likeness was woven
into Persian carpets, and over 75 different sets of Iranian postage
stamps carried the royal portrait. Millions of colored lights were lit
throughout the country on the shah's birthday, and a huge party was
held annually in his presence at Amjadieh Stadium in Tehran.

The shah attempted to legitimize his rule in a number of other
ways. He sought to develop systems of thought, for example, that
stressed monarchical, religious, and reform considerations. The ideology of reform was developed to buttress the traditional rationalizations
of monarchy and religion. The elite constantly argued that the Iranians
had an inherent need for monarchy. This was manifested in the continuous national celebrations that were organized for almost a decade
to commemorate Iran's 2,500 years of monarchy. Nevertheless, it
became increasingly difficult to reconcile philosophies of reform with
philosophies of monarchy, since "the dialectic of king and modernizing polity has not been fully resolved."[43]

The use of religion as a legitimating device was also difficult for
the shah, who had to compete in this regard with the mujtahids, who
were the representatives of the Hidden Imam in society. The shah
attempted in various ways, therefore, to reveal his special relation with
the divine. He argued that the peasants often referred to him as the
Shadow of God, and he apparently believed that he was guided and
guarded by some superhuman force. In his autobiography, the shah
credited his numerous escapes from personal and political disaster to
"some unseen hand" and claimed that from childhood he "felt that
perhaps there is a supreme being who is guiding me."[44] He stated that
"my reign has saved the country, and it has done so because God was

---

[42]Bayne, *Persian Kingship,* p. 167.

[43]*Ibid.,* p. 97

[44]Pahlavi, *Mission for My Country,* pp. 55, 58.

on my side," and that "God is my only friend."[45] In the end, however, the shah decided to strengthen the rationalization of his rule by stressing an ideology of reform, since this appeared more believable to growing forces within his society as well as to the twentieth-century world at large.

The traditional characteristics of personalism, proximity, informality, and balanced conflict also permeated the rule of Muhammad Reza Shah. His was an "individual approach to kingship,"[46] and he ruled at the center of a complex web of personal relations. It was especially in the early and middle years of his rule that the shah had contact with as many officials and personalities as possible. In this kind of political setting, the issue of physical proximity assumed reciprocal significance. Individuals held influence commensurate to their nearness to the patrimonial leader, while the leader felt it important to be in personal contact with advisors, friends, officials, and confidants. Just as the family patriarch deems it essential to his position as patriarch to maintain personal communication with all of his children, so also did the patrimonial leader consider it important to his position to be in touch with as many members of his society as possible. In Pahlavi Iran, there was tremendous pressure constantly exerted by individuals everywhere to move towards the shah, who was the locus of power. At the same time, the shah stated that "one of the principal problems of government is to know the right people and in necessary numbers. Either these people must be presented to you—and you need time to become acquainted and to know them—or you must search for them."[47]

In this highly personal system of patrimonial rule, informality prevailed, and individuals were balanced against individuals. The shah operated through informal meetings, personal cliques, and trusted groups of friends and family. Rivalry and tension were omnipresent; over the years, the shah proved himself a master at playing key subordinates off against one another. As a result, for years no one became overly powerful and the leader remained far above any potential challenger. In the shah's Iran, the network of balanced rivalry encom-

---

[45]See "An Oriana Fallaci Interview: The Shah of Iran," *The New Republic* (December 1, 1973): 17; and de Villiers, *Imperial Shah,* p. 273.

[46]Bayne, *Persian Kingship,* p. 239.

[47]*Ibid.,* p. 193.

passed the royal family, courtiers, personal adjutants, ministers, military officers, and all economic and political figures of any important standing. This pattern was reflected most dramatically in the case of 12 different military and security organizations, all of which stood in rivalry with one another. This organizational tension was the direct result of the intense personal competition that marked the relations among the leaders of these agencies. It was the patrimonial leader who kept these lines of tension finely adjusted.

Finally, the shah of Iran always sought to maintain a special and direct control over the military. As shah and commander in chief, he handpicked the military leaders, primarily on the basis of their loyalty to him. The downfall of several important politicians of the past occurred after they challenged the shah for control of the military. The shah prided himself on his knowledge of military science and claimed that he understood the necessity of military power because of "my father's examples, *and* because I am a soldier."[48] His special emphasis on the military is seen in the huge expenditures that were funneled into military and security establishments. By the late 1970s, they absorbed approximately 40 percent of the Iranian budget. Between 1972 and 1977, U.S. military sales to Iran totalled $16.2 billion, while the Pahlavi defense budget increased by nearly 700 percent over this six-year period.[49] The shah of Iran once summarized his own view of his relation to the military in the peculiarly patrimonial phrase, "I am the army."[50]

The Patrimonial Path to Revolution

As long as Muhammad Reza Shah pursued proven programs of patrimonialism seasoned with the flavor of serious reform, he was able to buy time and to maintain control. His land reform and literacy programs co-opted the ideas of the challenging professional middle class while proposing to improve the living standards of the masses of Iranian people. The Pahlavi game plan called for massive economic growth

---

[48]Bayne, *Persian Kingship*, p. 139.

[49]U.S. Congress, Senate Committee on Foreign Relations, Subcommittee on Foreign Assistance, Staff Report, *U.S. Military Sales to Iran* (Washington, D.C.: Government Printing Office, 1976); and *The Christian Science Monitor*, January 20, 1978, p. 5.

[50]Bayne, *Persian Kingship*, p. 186.

blended with moderate and controlled social reform all in the service of the preservation and perpetuation of the traditional patrimonial political status quo.[51]

The fact that the shah's reform program was designed to protect rather than to transform traditional political patterns can be documented by analyzing the direction and the methodology of the reforms. The core of the "White Revolution" consisted of programs that could only buttress the patrimonial position of the ruler. Viewed from this perspective, the land reform program served to weaken precisely those forces that traditionally threatened the patrimonial leader, that is, the old aristocratic, landed families and the Shi'i religious establishment. By cutting back on the economic power of the ulema, the shah hoped to improve his position relative to theirs. By replacing aristocratic officials at the national political level with workers and bureaucrats with no independent power base, the shah sought to strengthen his own position.

The actual administration of the reform program was implemented according to traditional patterns. Personalism, rivalry, insecurity, distrust, and uncoordinated ad hoc decision making prevailed. Political opportunists entered the arena and tainted and impeded the programs. The built-in rivalry that debilitated reform efforts was seen in the important task of land reform. At first, the ministries of agriculture, interior, and economy competed for control of the program. Later, a separate ministry of land reform and rural cooperatives was established, as well as a ministry of agricultural products and consumer goods and a ministry of natural resources. There was also an agricultural bank and an agricultural development fund. All of these organizations, and others (e.g., the plan organization) were bound together in an interlocking network of competition that prevented any individual or any ministry from becoming too powerful—or too effective. It also prevented successful land reform from occurring.[52]

---

[51]For a detailed study of the shah's strategy of patrimonialism and system preservation, see James A. Bill, *The Politics of Iran: Groups, Classes and Modernization* (Columbus, Ohio: Charles E. Merrill, 1972). For a fascinating inside view, see Asadollah Alam, *The Shah and I: The Confidential Diary of Iran's Royal Court, 1969–1977* (New York: St. Martin's Press, 1992). For a valuable scholarly account, see Marvin Zonis, *Majestic Failure: The Fall of the Shah* (Chicago: University of Chicago Press, 1991).

[52]For documentation, see Eric J. Hooglund's excellent *Land and Revolution in Iran, 1960–1980* (Austin, Tex.: The University of Texas Press, 1982).

The shah's reform programs suffered from other serious maladies. Patrimonial politics are susceptible to the abuses of corruption, favoritism, cronyism, and nepotism. In the shah's Iran, these abuses bubbled outward from the very center of the system and became both more pronounced and more visible through the decade of the 1970s. When oil revenues increased from slightly more than $2 billion in 1972 to over $20 billion in 1974, the opportunities for graft, bribery, and general corruption also increased tenfold. In the process, the gap in income distribution increased significantly and the masses of Iranian people found themselves relatively worse off after the reform program than they were prior to 1963. By using and then abusing patrimonialism, the shah in the end only alienated the very constituency whose support he was seeking to gain.

In 1970, the shah of Iran began a dramatic shift in his tactics of patrimonial rule. Coercion and repression took precedence over cooptation and reform. A major target of this new, hard-line policy was the ulema. In a system of patrimonial rule, it is extremely difficult for the leader to tolerate competing centers of leadership. It is especially difficult when these individuals carry charismatic qualities derived from the ideology of Islam. Yet over the years, the Iranian shahs had managed to live in a state of uneasy coexistence with the Shi'i clerics and had allowed them to maintain their own sphere of influence. Between 1970 and 1976, however, the shah's security apparatus attacked the religious leaders frontally; many were arrested and imprisoned, and some were executed. In the process, the Iranian government closed down religious publishing houses, disbanded religious student groups, and infiltrated mosque and endowment (*awqaf*) organizations. This policy alienated the entire religious establishment, and the clerics rallied to the leadership of Ayatollah Ruhollah Khomeini, a leading mujtahid with unassailable opposition credentials.

The ineffectiveness of many of the reform programs and the generally sad state of the lower-class masses provided a ready constituency for the harried religious leaders. Meanwhile, the shah himself had lost his patrimonial touch and had committed the grave error of isolating himself from his people. The patrimonial leader at the center of the familial polity had cut himself off from his advisors and his people. With the deaths of shrewd old patrimonial cronies and advisors, such as Asadollah Alam and Manuchehr Eghbal, and with his own increasing megalomania, the shah lost touch. Toward the end, he even refused to listen to the advice along his last line to reality, that of Empress Farah.[53] Instead, the shah consulted seriously only with the American and British ambassadors, two outside diplomats whose own understanding of Iran was flawed.

The very fact that the Pahlavi government was so deeply involved with the West (especially the United States) also only exacerbated the situation. Not only had the patrimonial leader lost touch with his own constituency, he had shifted his attention more and more to political, economic, and military alliance with outsiders. In the view of many of his former constituents, therefore, the shah had forsaken the country, culture, and Shi'i Islam for external, alien friends. In the eyes of the Iranian people, the patrimonial leader had deserted his family.

Ayatollah Ruhollah Khomeini, the immediate successor to the shah and the hero of the revolution, also led Iran according to patrimonial principles. This is symbolized by the fact that when the shah fell, Iranians immediately replaced his pictures with those of Khomeini. Revolutionary Iran was marked by mobs and masses of Iranian citizens behaving as the very embodiment of the Ayatollah. All the characteristics of patrimonial politics have prevailed during the post-Pahlavi period: personalism, proximity, informality, balanced conflict, and military activity. There has also been considerable violence and insecurity. Yet the Khomeini style of patrimonialism differed significantly from that of the last shah; it carried several important advantages.

First, Khomeini was a genuinely charismatic personality. In this sense, he was much more similar to Musaddiq than to the shah, who always had to labor under the disadvantage of an unimpressive and ordinary personality. The shah's person was deferred to largely because of the power that inhered in the office. Second, Khomeini held legitimate religious credentials. The shah always had to stretch fact and imagination to portray a special Islamic legitimacy. Third, the Ayatollah was never accused of personal corruption but rather led a simple, spartan life. This appealed to his popular constituency, which viewed him as a leader of, for, and from the people. It was also in

---

[53]As the Pahlavi monarchy collapsed, the empress stated that the shah refused even to listen to her advice and counsel. Among other things, she said, "The husband does not always listen to the wife." Personal interview (Bill) with Empress Farah Diba, November 29, 1978, Niavaran Palace, Tehran.

direct contrast to the shah, whose world included the splendor and opulence of palaces, banks, American movie stars, aircraft, modern art, and the Rockefellers. Fourth, the slogan "Neither East nor West" indicates the Khomeinian preoccupation with the destruction of all outside influence in Iran's social and political system. Since the West in general and the United States in particular were most closely associated with the former regime, they were the major targets of attacks by the revolutionary regime. The Soviet Union and communism, however, were also criticized and condemned by the Ayatollah. This strain of patrimonial independence was much more appealing than the policy practiced by the shah, who was widely viewed as a puppet and client of the United States.

These factors all combined to give Khomeini's revolutionary mode of patrimonialism its fifth and major strength: As patrimonial leader, Khomeini managed to build a mass base of support. Although he turned viciously on the old upper and middle classes, Khomeini sought to improve the life of the masses of Iranian people. By stressing the needs of those he called the *mustaza'fin* ("downtrodden," "dispossessed"), he managed to build a large and committed constituency. His government took from the haves and gave to the have-nots. In this way, the Ayatollah was able to remain a patrimonial leader with a mass constituency, unlike the shah, whose patrimonialism rested on only the tiniest and flimsiest of support bases.[54]

Despite these considerations, the patrimonialism of Khomeini and that practiced by his more pragmatic successor, President Ali Akbar Hashemi-Rafsanjani, must somehow come to grips with the related challenges of modernization and political development. Although there is considerable personalism, tense rivalry, and corruption in Rafsanjani's Iran, there is also an attempt to institutionalize the political process and to provide a serious degree of popular participation. Iran's leaders understand that the support of the masses of people will continue only so long as those who govern are able to meet the material and political needs of the population. In the face of severe economic problems, it remains to be seen if the new political elite in the Islamic Republic will succeed in its mission.

---

[54]For more detailed analysis of Khomeini's Iran, see Chapter 8.

GAMAL ABDEL NASSER: PATRIMONIALISM AND TRANSFORMATION

> The man is at once feline and massive. His square build speaks of a peas-
> ant ancestry, the long remembrance of stubborn, fleshy gestures, the rec-
> ompense of a heavy, miserable diet over many generations. But this son
> of the Middle Valley also carries Arab descent in his blood: a Bedouin
> strain had pursued for several centuries in Bani Murr District the syn-
> thesis of Ishmael and Pharaoh. Perhaps this gives his physique that delib-
> erate alertness, his face that sharp breadth, his eyes that brooding nostal-
> gia behind their hard, almost green, gaze. The Arab has risen ponderous-
> ly, one might say, from his long submergence in the soil of Egypt.[55]

Recent Middle Eastern political history is marked by the existence of a handful of leaders who have attempted to uproot many of
the traditional social and political patterns that have prevailed in their
societies. Besides Kemal Ataturk, discussed above, the other major
case in point is Gamal Abdel Nasser of Egypt. Like Ataturk, Nasser
adopted tactics of transformation that left some areas largely
untouched, while in other areas fundamental efforts at change were
made. The life and leadership of Gamal Abdel Nasser in particular
deserves to be analyzed in this light, since Nasser introduced many
revolutionary programs in a society that contains nearly one-third of
the world's Arab population.

Gamal Abdel Nasser was born on January 15, 1918, in Alexandria.
He was raised in the village of Beni Morr in Upper Egypt, the ances-
tral home of his family. Nasser's father was a postal clerk; his mother
died when Gamal was 8 years old. Since his father had remarried and
was constantly being moved about in his work, Gamal spent long periods living with various relatives. As a secondary-school student, he
developed a deep social and political consciousness. He harbored an
early concern about the British presence in Egypt; at the same time,
he grew to dislike the debility and dependence that marked the status
of his country.

Nasser graduated from secondary school in Cairo in 1936 and
afterwards entered the Egyptian Military Academy. Upon graduating
from the academy in 1938 with the rank of second lieutenant, he was

---

[55]Jacques Berque, *Cultural Expression in Arab Society Today*, trans. Robert W. Stookey
(Austin, Tex.: The University of Texas Press, 1978), pp. 15–16.

sent to serve with an infantry company in Upper Egypt. In 1943, Nasser was promoted to the rank of captain and was appointed an instructor at the military academy. In 1948, he distinguished himself in a losing cause in the Palestine campaign. As a patriotic officer, he was disgusted at the inefficiency and decrepitude of the Egyptian political regime. During the 1940s, moreover, Nasser began to blame imperialism and feudalism for the constantly deteriorating state of his country. He read widely and, as a history instructor, refined his social and political ideas. It was during this period that he helped form the Free Officers movement and came into contact with the group of fellow officers who were to play the vital role in changing the course of Egyptian history over the next two decades.

On July 23, 1952, the Free Officers movement carried out a coup that overthrew King Farouk and his traditional regime. A Revolutionary Command Council of 12 officers, including Gen. Muhammad Naguib, took control of the government. At first Naguib was the titular political leader, but by the end of 1954 Gamal Abdel Nasser had ousted him and taken control. Nasser remained the internationally famous leader of Egypt until his heart attack and death on September 28, 1970. During these years, both Nasser and Egypt survived numerous vicissitudes, including crises ranging from an assassination attempt to an invasion by the combined forces of three foreign powers. During his 18 years of leadership in Egypt, Nasser's political activities were divided into three general and overlapping categories: (1) consolidation and maintenance of political power; (2) introduction and continuation of policies of social, economic, and political change within Egypt; and (3) development of an independent foreign policy.

During the first few years of his leadership, Nasser was preoccupied with the task of protecting the ascendant position he had acquired. This meant maintaining the cohesion of the military in general and the Free Officers group in particular, while at the same time repelling opposition forces mobilized by the Communists on the left and the Wafd Party and Muslim Brotherhood on the right. Nasser had strongly suppressed the Brotherhood by 1955; in the late 1950s and early 1960s, he moved sharply and successfully against Communism within Egypt; and by 1965, he had largely managed to destroy the influence of the wealthy bourgeoisie that had formed the backbone of the Wafd Party.

Although these were the most serious organized threats to his power, Nasser's government was faced with political challenges throughout its existence because his revolutionary programs were continually threatening vested interests. As his authoritarianism hardened in order to withstand these kinds of challenges, Nasser came to alienate substantial segments of supporters within the intelligentsia, who chafed under a cloak of repression that suffocated criticism and innovation from below. Democratization was deliberately sacrificed, since the consolidation and maintenance of power were considered essential to successful modernization.

Because Nasser was able to consolidate his forces, he was in turn able to institute change from above. Although individual freedoms were often ruthlessly sacrificed, Nasser nonetheless instituted enough fundamental change to lay a new social, economic, and political foundation for Egyptian society.

Gamal Abdel Nasser once stated that he was a revolutionary and not a politician. He wrote, "Every people on earth goes through two revolutions: a political revolution by which it wrests the right to govern itself from the hand of tyranny, or from the army stationed upon its soil against its will; and a social revolution, involving the conflict of classes which settles down when justice is secured for the citizens of the united nation."[56] In analyzing the political history of post-1952 Egypt, Maxime Rodinson concludes that the two main goals of Nasserism were national independence and modernization.[57] Among the important sociopolitical achievements of Nasser's revolution are (1) the agrarian reform program, (2) the transformation and partial leveling of the class structure, (3) the elimination of conspicuous corruption in the personal household of the national leader, (4) the continuing rise of achievement at the expense of ascription in the administrative system, (5) the expulsion of foreign influence, and (6) the strengthening of the pride and dignity of the Egyptian people. In his attempt to transform the traditional power structure, Nasser came to the conclusion that the process must be a continuing one. Land reform alone could not bring about this transformation, since it was

---

[56]Gamal Abdel Nasser, *Egypt's Liberation: The Philosophy of the Revolution* (Washington, D.C.: Public Affairs Press, 1955), pp. 39–40.

[57]See Maxime Rodinson, "The Political System," in *Egypt Since the Revolution,* ed. by P. J. Vatikiotis (New York: Frederick A. Praeger, 1968), pp. 87–113.

neither deep enough nor fast enough to undercut the power of the traditional ruling class. It was in this context that Nasser instituted the extensive nationalization laws of the 1960–1963 period.

The successes and failures of Nasser's domestic programs rested to a great degree degree upon his ability to guide Egypt through the stormy seas of international politics. It was in this broader area that the Egyptian president expended most of his political energy, and it was here that he witnessed his greatest triumphs and his greatest defeats. His tenure as leader of Egypt was clouded by deep problems directly associated with the Arab-Israeli confrontation, the American-Soviet cold war, the general drive for Arab unity, and the differing Arab stances concerning the entire issue of social and political change. In 1955, President Nasser attended the Bandung Conference, where he rubbed shoulders with Nehru, Sukarno, and Chou En-lai and where he was considered a new leader of the Afro-Asian world. He returned home a hero for his role in a conference that condemned "neocolonialism" and supported "non-alignment." A few months later, Nasser accepted a Soviet arms offer and concluded a deal with Czechoslovakia that electrified the Arab world, since it indicated that Egypt was no longer dependent on the West and would pursue a course of positive neutralism.[58] That same year, Nasser refused to align Egypt with the Anglo-American-sponsored Baghdad Pact, and in 1956, John Foster Dulles withdrew the American offer to help Egypt finance the critically important Aswan High Dam. One week later, Nasser announced the nationalization of the Suez Canal Company, which in turn brought about the abortive invasion of Egypt by Great Britain, France, and Israel. The Soviet Union then took charge of the financing and construction of the High Dam. These events brought together the masses of Egyptians behind Nasser, who had proved to them that Egypt was an independent nation whose dignity could no longer be trampled upon. The significance of the Suez crisis "reached far beyond the event itself, causing a revolutionary transformation of the technocratic, reformist

---

[58]The arms deal took a great deal of personal and political courage on Nasser's part, since it was signed in the face of deep United States opposition. This was a time when American intelligence forces had helped rearrange political regimes in Iran (1953) and Guatemala (1954). When Egypt's panicky ambassador to the United States urged Nasser not to defy Washington in this way, he kept repeating the phrase: "Remember Guatemala, remember Guatemala." Nasser finally said, "To hell with Guatemala" and went ahead with the arms agreement. See Leonard Mosley, *Dulles* (New York: Dial Press, James Wade, 1978), p. 388.

Table 5.3   LIFE OF GAMAL ABDEL NASSER: MAJOR EVENTS

1918	Born in Alexandria
1936	Graduates from Al-Nahda Secondary School in Cairo
1938	Graduates from Egyptian Military Academy
1948	Participates in Palestine campaign; distinguishes himself at Faluja
1952	Free Officers carry out coup against the government of King Farouk
1954	Becomes prime minister and then president of Egypt
1955	Attends Bandung Conference; concludes Soviet arms deal
1956	Nationalization of the Suez Canal Company and invasion of Egypt by Israel, France, and Great Britain
1958	Formation of the United Arab Republic; Nasser elected president
1961	Passage of wide-ranging nationalization laws; United Arab Republic dissolved
1962	Arab Socialist Union organization formed
1967	Arab-Israeli June War; Nasser resigns, but returns to power with massive popular support
1970	Dies in Cairo

government."[59] It was a "charismatic situation"[60] that helped invest Nasser with extraordinary powers as a political leader.

These early successes were of sufficient magnitude to enable both Nasser and Egypt to ride out later disasters. The most serious of these was the June War of 1967, in which Israel (in an impressive and efficient military campaign) left Egypt battered and demoralized. Nasser, who must bear part of the blame for occasioning the conflict, resigned his position, to be called back only hours later by the Egyptian people, who genuinely wanted and demanded his leadership. The existence of Israel haunted Nasser's rule, and he was never able to confront this situation with the same style and success with which he addressed other thorny problems.

In the area of intra-Arab politics, the Egyptian president was only slightly more successful. The United Arab Republic, which was a political and economic union with Syria formed in 1958, was dissolved in 1961 when, among other things, the wealthy Syrian bourgeois families feared the impact of Nasser's revolutionary programs. Nasser success-

[59]Jean Lacouture, *The Demigods: Charismatic Leadership in the Third World,* trans. by Patricia Wolf (New York: Alfred A. Knopf, 1970), p. 110.

[60]*Ibid.*

fully supported the Algerian rebels in Algeria, although in Yemen direct Egyptian military support failed to enable the revolutionaries to take control of the country. The latter adventure cost Egypt dearly in terms of domestic resources and international prestige. Despite this, however, President Nasser's revolutionary programs and ideas spread through the Middle East and acted as catalysts for change in the Arab world. If they did not lead to revolution from below, they inspired the traditional leaders to try to dissipate discontent by initiating reform from above. The land reform programs in Syria, Iraq, Tunisia, Iran, and Turkey, for example, all followed the Egyptian experiment in agrarian reform begun in 1952.

Patterns of Rule

Gamal Abdel Nasser's leadership broke with many of the patterns of traditional patrimonial rule. Although strongly authoritarian, Nasser's techniques did not include the promotion of self-deification. It is true that his image was protected and polished by his governmental and security forces, but he resisted pressures to invest huge resources in the glorification of his person. There were no statues of Nasser, for example, dotting the Egyptian landscape. Nor did his face adorn postage stamps and currency. The Egyptian president consciously sought to transcend the temptation to permit and promote personal exaltation and hero worship. One keen Western observer of Egyptian affairs wrote that "nothing irritates Nasser more than being treated like a modern pharaoh."[61]

A truly charismatic personality need not build monuments to himself and myths for his people; his charisma is based on his extraordinary actions. In Nasser's case, the leader also eschewed any special connection with the divine, whether it be in terms of common ancestry or private visions. Although he never attacked the Islamic clerics in Egypt the way Ataturk did in Turkey, at the same time he did not attempt to build any particularly close political relations with them.[62] The fact that Nasser's charisma is traceable neither to manufactured

[61]*Ibid.*, p. 119.

[62]For the finest investigation of Nasser's relationship to Islam, see Josef Muzikar, "Arab Nationalism and Islam," *Archiv Orientalni* 43 (1975):193–323.

mythology nor to religious connections indicates how divorced his leadership was from the traditional mold. It is precisely this kind of charisma that invested Nasser with the special strength necessary to maintain power and to promote deep change in the face of formidable problems, both internal and external.

The role of the military was crucial to Nasser's leadership. It was through a military coup that he first came to power, and it was through the support of the military that he maintained his position. In the absence of an efficient civil bureaucracy, the Egyptian president was able to call upon personnel from within the military organization to implement administrative and economic programs. As in traditional patrimonial systems, the military was an important prop in Nasser's political structure. There is, however, one important quality that separates the Nassers and the Ataturks from the more traditional leaders. The latter continue to present themselves in military guise and garb in order constantly to display their special and intimate relation with the military. They often explicitly state that they are an embodiment of the military. Nasser, on the contrary, retired from the army in 1955 and deliberately refrained from maintaining any military rank or title.

Personalism and informality are two related characteristics of patrimonial rule that persisted in the leadership of Gamal Abdel Nasser.[63] Nasser never succeeded in moving from rule by personalism to political institutionalization, and as a result there was a lack of political participation and a surplus of political insecurity in Nasser's Egypt. In the latter days of his presidency, heavy-handed maneuverers, such as presidential advisor Sami Sharaf and interior minister Sha'rawi Gom'a, were directing an increasingly disreputable intelligence system that reached into all corners of Egyptian society.

There is evidence that Nasser was not insensitive to the need for wider political participation. He tried three times to construct a mass political party in order to insure a measure of popular participation. His last attempt, which was also his most successful, involved the formation of the Arab Socialist Union in 1962. Such structures were largely ineffectual in Egypt, since they existed as rather sterile appendages to Nasser's personal rule, which Nasser felt bound to

---

[63]For a source that emphasizes and analyzes the informal, personalistic politics of patrimonialism in Egypt, see Robert Springborg, *Family, Power, and Politics in Egypt* (Philadelphia: University of Pennsylvania Press, 1982).

strengthen in order to carry on the revolution. Despite the presence of personalism and informality, Nasser was able to break a number of the patterns that follow in the wake of patrimonialism.

The nepotism that stems from personalism and the corruption that often thrives in the net of informal politics were relatively absent in Nasser's style of leadership. Nasser himself was above reproach in this regard, and he led an austere life much in the style of Chou En-lai and Fidel Castro. Throughout the Middle East, Nasser was known for his personal honesty and integrity. He spoke out constantly against opportunism, corruption, and favoritism. When he died in 1970, he was still living in the modest house that he had purchased as a young officer prior to the 1952 coup. He refused to use his power to further the causes of his family and relatives. Two of his uncles remained fellahin (peasants) in the village of Bani Morr, and his own daughters were unable to attend Cairo University because their entrance examination scores were not high enough.

Mohamed Heikal writes that Nasser "was never interested in women or money or elaborate food. After he had come to power the cynical old politicians tried to corrupt him but they failed miserably. His family life was impeccable."[64] Heikal goes on to point out that although Nasser received millions of pounds in donations, he died with only 610 Egyptian pounds in his personal account. The programmatic manifestations of this new style fostered by Nasser are evident in the Egyptian land reform policy, for, as one expert writes: "The evenhandedness with which the distribution was carried out deserves commendation; no suggestion of favoritism in either the taking of land from large owners or the distribution of it to recipients has arisen—a remarkable accomplishment in view of the inherent temptations to corruption."[65]

Although Gamal Abdel Nasser resorted to the traditional tactic of divide and rule, his colleagues and confidants generally operated as a

---

[64]Mohamed Heikal, *The Cairo Documents* (Garden City, N.Y.: Doubleday and Co., 1973), p. 20. Some of Nasser's leading officials, including what Edward Sheehan calls "the Sharaf-Goma cabal," whose members "were nearly all corrupt," were less principled. Edward R. F. Sheehan, "The Real Sadat and the Demythologized Nasser," *New York Times Magazine,* July 18, 1971, pp. 6–7, 33, 35, 38, 42.

[65]Kenneth B. Platt, *Land Reform in the United Arab Republic,* A.I.D. Spring Review of Land Reform, 2nd ed., vol. 8 (Washington, D.C.: Agency for International Development, 1970), p. 61.

team in leading society. Admittedly, the team was a small and exclusive one. Lenczowski has pointed out that, with only three exceptions, Nasser managed to keep his group of young officers together through more than 12 years of the revolution.[66] While he undoubtedly made the final decisions, the Egyptian president did consult seriously with his close advisors.

The patterns of patrimonial politics were partially uprooted by President Nasser as he endeavored to revolutionize his society. Although personalism continued to prevail, many of the other traditional traits were destroyed. This represents a fundamental step in moving forward with the social and political dimensions of change.

Transforming Leadership

Despite some oil discoveries, Egypt remains one of the poorest and most densely populated societies in the world. Just before the 1952 military coup, a Rockefeller Foundation team reported that the situation of the peasants in Egypt was worse than that of the peasants in any other country in which they had carried out investigations—and this included China and India. According to this report, on a scale of 106.5 for perfect health, India rated 54 and Egypt 15. In one of the villages surveyed north of Cairo, nearly 100 percent of the population had bilarzia, a debilitating parasitical disease that attacks the kidneys and liver; 89 percent had trachoma; over 20 percent were typhoid or paratyphoid carriers. In a village with a population of 4,172, there was not one healthy person. Most of the villagers had from one to four major diseases.[67]

At the time of the report, the political system was a patrimonial monarchy in which all the negative characteristics of that kind of system were magnified. King Farouk often made national political decisions on the advice of his infamous "kitchen cabinet," composed of his valet, mechanic, butler, pilot, and doctor, among others. An Italian

---

[66]George Lenczowski, "The Objects and Methods of Nasserism," in *Modernization of the Arab World*, ed. by J. H. Thompson and R. D. Reischauer (Princeton, N.J.: D. Van Nostrand Co., 1966), p. 207.

[67]For a summary of the findings of the Rockefeller Foundation study from which these figures have been drawn, see Austin L. Moore, *Farewell Farouk* (Chicago: Scholars' Press, 1954), pp. 59–60.

barber became Farouk's closest advisor, and Farouk named his brother-in-law (an honorary "colonel") minister of war. Nepotism prevailed in a demoralizing environment of political vice and personal corruption. Against this background, the changes wrought under Nasser's leadership were dramatic. Measured against the demands of the day and the progress of other non-Western societies, such as Israel, Japan, and China, Egyptian social and political change is less impressive.

Gamal Abdel Nasser was a transforming leader for three basic reasons: He consciously and determinedly sought to ensure that his revolution be radical, political, and continuing in nature. In the 1962 Charter he wrote, "The needs of our country were such that it was not enough to patch up the old and decaying building, try to keep it from falling by means of supports and give the exterior a fresh coat of paint. What was needed was a new and strong building resting on firm foundations and towering high in the sky. . . ."[68] By distinguishing between reforming and transforming change in these kinds of terms, Nasser often indicated his sensitivity to the need to support fundamental social and political transformation. Because of this radical philosophy, Nasser "refused to endorse programs which were primarily political palliatives."[69]

Whereas the reforming leader tends to support economic and material development without altering the political system, the revolutionary leader begins with and emphasizes the political dimension of change. Anouar Abdel-Malek writes that, in Nasser's case, "the principal blow was struck on the sociopolitical level"; Majid Khadduri asserts that "the Revolution's fundamental achievements were essentially political"; and Maxime Rodinson concludes that under Nasser the political structure was "completely reshaped."[70] The political change can be seen at two levels. The first level concerns the patterns of relations through which the political leader personally wields power. As is documented above, Nasser transformed these relations at several key points. The second level involves the more general and collective distribution of power, reflected primarily in the class structure. During

---

[68]Nasser, The Charter, as quoted in J. C. Hurewitz, *Middle East Politics: The Military Dimension* (New York: Frederick A. Praeger, 1969), p. 133.

[69]Keith Wheelock, *Nasser's New Egypt* (London: Atlantic Books, 1960), p. 38.

[70]For these quotations, see Anouar Abel-Malek, *Egypt: Military Society,* trans. by Charles Lam Markmann (New York: Vintage Books, 1968), p. 157; Majid Khadduri, *Political Trends in the Arab World* (Baltimore, Md.: Johns Hopkins University Press, 1970), p. 162; and Rodinson, "The Political System," p. 111.

Nasser's rule, the Egyptian class structure underwent radical change as the influence of the former ruling class, which was composed of both the landed and the industrial aristocracy, was destroyed. The gaps between the various classes were consequently greatly narrowed as a professional middle class composed of technocrats, managers, and professionals took control. It is on this basis that one observer has referred to the Egyptian revolution as "the first true revolution in the Middle East."[71]

Nasser carefully referred to the Egyptian revolution as *thawra* ("a persisting and lasting event") rather than as *inqilab* ("an overthrow"), since he recognized the need for the movement to press forward continually.[72] This forward movement, of course, was essential in order to prevent the old power structure from slowly seeping back into prominence. The modernizing head of government is especially exposed to this danger since "the bourgeoisie attempts to minimize its losses by puffing up the leader. It cuts off some of its own flesh and feeds it to the hero to fatten him up, blow him up, lull him to sleep. Soon enough the deified leader will proclaim the revolution fulfilled in him and the class struggle resolved in him."[73]

In Nasser's Egypt, the old forces of patrimonialism made gallant efforts to infiltrate back into power, and in the late 1950s they were backed and provisioned by the wealthy bourgeoisie. Nasser confronted this challenge and overcame it with his nationalization programs of 1960–1963. This effectively tore the web of families who were the proponents of traditionalism. They had managed to survive the land reform program, since their control spanned industry and trade as well as land.

Although he successfully uprooted the traditional power structure in Egypt, Nasser never managed to establish a new sociopolitical system. Because of the resilience of the old system and the limited resources at hand, the Egyptian president felt it necessary to maintain an authoritarian technocracy, which alienated the intelligentsia and stifled creativity in the society. He was unable to broaden political participation, and therefore the revolutionary patterns he introduced at the center did not take root in the countryside. The resources and energies fruitlessly expended in activities against Israel and in Yemen

---

[71]Harry Hopkins, *Egypt: The Crucible* (Boston: Houghton Mifflin Co., 1969), p. 181.

[72]Lacouture, *The Demigods,* p. 94.

[73]*Ibid.,* p. 293.

seriously injured his capacity to carry out social change in Egypt. Despite all of this, Nasser survived and, although badly scarred, continued to fight for the transformation of his country. His achievements in this regard, though sporadic, were nonetheless impressive enough to distinguish him sharply from most Middle Eastern leaders, both past and present. By the time he died in September 1970, Gamal Abdel Nasser was personally convinced that, with or without him, the revolution he had begun in Egypt would continue. In 1971, Nasser's longtime friend and colleague, Anwar Sadat, emerged as the new president of Egypt. Sadat proved to be an important leader in his own right, but his political programs contrasted significantly with those of his predecessor.

ANWAR SADAT: THE RETURN OF TRADITIONAL PATRIMONIALISM

Born in 1918, the same year as Nasser, Anwar Sadat spent much of his youth hating the British and contemplating political questions. Like Nasser, he came from the lower echelons of the professional middle class. His father, a hospital clerk, was a great admirer of Ataturk, and a picture of the Turkish hero hung in the Sadat house. Sadat entered the Egyptian Military Academy with Nasser in 1936 and graduated with him in 1938. From this time until the successful coup in 1952, he dedicated himself to secret political opposition. During these years, he plotted constantly against both the British and King Farouk and intrigued his way into and out of prison. At one point, he even sought Nasser's permission to blow up the British Embassy. When released from his second imprisonment in 1948, Sadat eked out an existence as a journalist, truck driver, porter, and used-tire salesman. With his military commission restored, Sadat was the one who announced the news of the successful coup of July 1952 to the Egyptian people.

During the 18 years of Nasser's presidency, Anwar Sadat hovered constantly in the shadow of his leader. Although the hotheadedness of his youth occasionally broke to the surface, Sadat did a remarkable job of cloaking his explosive ambition and peasant shrewdness beneath a patient and plodding subservience to Nasser. He refused to join political cliques and power circles, preferring instead to live a life of material pleasure and leisure. Few took him seriously. Meanwhile, he watched and waited, learning all the time. When Nasser died in 1970, Sadat was one of the few members of the original Revolutionary Command Council still around. In 1969, Nasser had shopped around for a new vice-president; he chose Anwar Sadat.

When Sadat succeeded Nasser as president, everyone looked past him to the political heavyweights—menacing figures such as Minister of Presidential Affairs Sami Sharaf, Minister of Interior Sha'rawi Gom'a, and powerful leftist and Arab Socialist Union figure Ali Sabri. Meanwhile, the patient and poker-faced Sadat went about his business quietly, easily, and disarmingly. He made appearances throughout the country, building popularity as he went along; he silently sprinkled a few loyal spies here and there; and, most important, he came to an agreement with the key army officers.

Then, in May 1971, when he had carefully gathered evidence that Sabri and the others had been plotting a coup, Sadat suddenly struck. He forced Ali Sabri to resign on May 2. Ten days later, in another lightning move, he fired secret police head Gom'a and happily accepted the resignations of five other ministers, including that of Sami Sharaf. That autumn, over 90 persons were tried. Sabri, Sharaf, and Gom'a, among others, were jailed.[74] Anwar Sadat had succeeded in consolidating his power.

Once he became president of Egypt, Sadat found himself under great domestic and international pressure. Despite this, he managed to maintain himself in power for over a decade. One of the most important tactics that he used throughout his career was to deny repeatedly that he ever sought political power. In his autobiography he strongly denied that he ever had any interest in political office. Yet the reader of his book cannot help observing that Sadat never refused a political post offered him. Nor, deep down, was he ever pleased that he was an outsider to the Revolutionary Command Council. In his own words; "Why did they attack and ridicule me, as though I was an outsider who wanted to usurp their rights or a stranger who spoke a different language? I was sad. . . ."[75]

---

[74]Sha'rawi Gom'a and several less prominent members of the Sabry group were released from prison when President Sadat granted them amnesty in January 1977. Former minister of war Lt. Gen. Muhammad Fawzi had already been pardoned by Sadat in January 1974.

[75]Anwar el-Sadat, *In Search of Identity: An Autobiography* (New York: Harper & Row, 1978), p. 122. For examples of Sadat's insistent denials that he was ever interested in power, see pp. 83–84, 90, 126, 136, 138, 150, 196, 204, and 314. This autobiography, although fascinating and important reading, is flagrantly self-serving. This is particularly true of Sadat's personal evaluation of Nasser.

Sadat was able to make up for his lack of Nasser-like charisma through a brilliant ability to make the right political moves at precisely the right times. While floating somewhere above political factions and ideological positions, he often darted down to center stage to announce and personally implement dramatic political decisions—decisions that left the world gasping. The most noteworthy of these moves included the expulsion of Soviet advisors from Egyptian soil in July 1972, the initiation of the fourth Arab-Israeli war in October 1973, the historic trip to Israel in November 1977, and the announcement of a framework for peace with Israel at Camp David in September 1978. Whenever domestic political discontent threatened his government, President Sadat responded by announcing a major new policy with special flair and flamboyance.

Anwar Sadat's dramatic sense of timing was developed within the patrimonial context. He was a traditional patrimonial leader par excellence. As we have seen, President Nasser retained much of the patrimonial style in his rule, while at the same time instituting revolutionary changes at many points in the Egyptian system. Sadat spent much of his presidency busily repairing these tears in the body politic. The traditional power structure so severely disrupted during the two decades of Nasserist rule was reinstated by President Sadat. In this sense, he sought to roll back Nasser's revolution.

Upon taking the reins of power in Egypt, Anwar Sadat immediately began to liberalize and democratize Egyptian society. Economically, this meant an opening (*infitah*) of the system to foreign investment and capital. Politically, the liberalization expressed itself in terms of a cautiously guarded return to more political participation. Sadat permitted a wider network of individuals to participate in political decision making, in contrast to Nasser, who had relied upon a smaller core of trusted assistants. One result of this was that although Nasser had had to involve himself directly in many matters, Sadat adopted a more Olympian approach to matters that were not only time-consuming but also political briar patches.

Nor was the Egyptian president always consistent in this regard. "He has invoked democracy and the rule of law, then—without too delicate a regard for either—swept all his suspected rivals off to jail. He has promised real power to the people, and gathered most of the Government into his own hands."[76] Sadat was interested not in con-

---

[76]Sheehan, "The Real Sadat," p. 42.

verting Egypt into a liberal democracy but rather in lengthening and strengthening the patrimonial strands in a way that would recapture the traditional power structure of Egypt, with him as unquestioned leader. The evidence for this tendency is impressive.

In his first book, published in 1957, Anwar Sadat penned a line that could serve as a classic lead sentence in any manual on patrimonial rule: "In Egypt, personalities have always been more important than political programs."[77] Sadat acted accordingly by drawing his family and friends into the center of the political system. Mahmud Abu Wafia, his brother-in-law, was for a time secretary-general of the most important forum within the Arab Socialist Union. Two of his daughters married members of the most important and wealthy aristocratic families in the country, the families of Sayyid Marei and Osman Ahmad Osman. The former (already discussed in Chapter 3) was Sadat's speaker of the People's Assembly and a personal advisor to the president, while the latter was the most powerful contractor in the country.

Sadat was visibly susceptible to the pomp and circumstance so important to traditional patrimonial leaders. Although he did not adopt quite the life-style of the shah of Iran, he was easily more self-indulgent than Nasser. He had a dozen presidential villas and wore field marshal's uniforms designed by Pierre Cardin. He spent more time perhaps with the international jet set than with his own people. The enormous gap here was clearly visible in September 1979, when Frank Sinatra performed a concert before the Sphinx and the pyramids for one of Jihan Sadat's favorite charities. The spectacle was attended by "over 400 partygoers from the United States and Europe who enjoyed what was probably the most extravagant social affair Egypt had seen since before the 1952 revolution that overthrew King Farouk." Before dedicating a song to Mrs. Sadat, Sinatra ventured an opinion about President Sadat: "He really is a great cat. I just adore him." In addition to the concert, there was an international fashion show in which Pierre Balmain introduced his seasonal collection from Paris. His mannequins marched around "in white overcoats and matching jackboots, then in soft dresses and pajamas, and finally in gold fig-leaf bikinis. The models, who had been flown in from Paris, wore Pharaonic jewelry designed by Bulgari, with a total value put at $10 million." Before the show, the wealthy international guests dined

---

[77]Anwar el-Sadat, *Revolt on the Nile* (New York: John Day Co., 1957), p. 27.

on cold lobster, veal, and crepes. "Outside the enclosure's flapping cloth walls, a cordon of white-uniformed policemen, some with automatic rifles, shoved away curious Egyptians from a nearby village."[78]

The major difference between Nasser's and Sadat's styles of rule was the service to which Sadat's patrimonialism was put. Class lines deepened and class divisions became wider in Egypt during the period of Sadat's presidency. This was seen in the political unrest that broke periodically to the surface in Egypt between 1971 and 1981.

In 1972 and 1973, student demonstrations rocked Egypt, and in 1974 an insurrection at the military academy in Cairo was put down with force. Riots in Cairo on New Year's Day 1975 and in April of that year at the major textile center at Mahalla al-Kubra were sparked by social protest and class disaffection. Then, in January 1977, thousands of Egyptians drawn from several social classes demonstrated in violent protest against the government's decision to cut back its subsidies on food costs. The army was called in to suppress the rioters in the worst civil upheaval in Egypt in 25 years. These demonstrations (especially those in 1975 and 1977) carried heavy overtones of outright class conflict. In 1975, the cry was "We do not need a Pasha but we need a President," and in 1977, one of the slogans was "Where is our breakfast you dweller of palaces?"[79] In the 1977 incidents, the patrimonial leader's wife, Jihan, was herself one of the targets of criticism and was given such labels as "the uncrowned queen" and "tomorrow's Cleopatra."[80]

Then, in June 1981, serious riots between Muslims and Copts flared again in the working-class districts of Cairo. By the fall of that year, Sadat was hard-pressed at home as signs of widespread disaffection and alienation bubbled ominously to the surface. Muslim associations and organizations multiplied in number and size and an estimated 40,000 private mosques served as centers for critical discussion of the deep social and political problems that plagued Egypt. In August 1981, over 200,000 people gathered at Abdin Square in Cairo for a prayer rally.

In the first week of September, President Sadat suddenly

---

[78]The quotations in this paragraph are taken from *The New York Times*, September 28, 1979.

[79]See R. Michael Burrell and Abbas R. Kelidar, *Egypt: The Dilemmas of a Nation, 1970–1977*, The Washington Papers, no. 48 (Beverly Hills, Calif.: Sage Publications, 1977), p. 72.

[80]*Events*, March 11, 1977, p. 18.

responded by orchestrating a major crackdown on all sources of potential opposition. His police arrested more than 1,500 people, closed down seven publications, transferred over 100 writers, journalists, and teachers from their jobs, deposed the Coptic patriarch from his position, and moved to place the 40,000 "free" mosques under direct governmental control. Sadat angrily justified this uncharacteristically severe crackdown by stating that it represented an attack against "indiscipline" that had come to dominate Egyptian society. This was the very word that the shah of Iran had often used to justify the repressive policies of his regime in the years just prior to the Iranian revolution.

On October 6, 1981, one month after he had carried out his political crackdown, President Anwar Sadat was reviewing a military parade held to commemorate Egyptian successes in the October 1973 war. At approximately 12:40 P.M., four Egyptian soldiers leaped from a truck in an artillery unit and charged the presidential reviewing stand in a grenade and automatic weapon attack. In this surprise attack, the soldiers assassinated Anwar Sadat as he stood to greet them on a public stage before the eyes of the world in Cairo. The consummate actor and colorful, courageous political leader died at a time when he had clearly lost touch with reality in his own country. "Even after the show was over, he had gotten the role and he went on playing. It was catastrophic."[81]

In the end, Anwar Sadat was a patrimonial leader who became a pseudomonarch and who governed Egypt according to his interpretation of modern, Western pomp and circumstance. According to one informed Egyptian scholar, "Sadat lost control of the internal situation and was, in response perhaps, turning into a neurotic despot slashing right and left."[82] He shifted from being "the paternalistic pious head of the Egyptian family to the single-minded, threatened, vindictive dictator who eliminates any criticism of him and any opposition to his programs. . . . Two processes were at work in the meantime: a Sadatization of Egypt on the one hand, and a deification of Sadat on the other—the rebirth of the Egyptian pharaoh."[83]

---

[81]The words of Mohamed Hassanein Heikal as reported in *The Christian Science Monitor,* December 2, 1981.

[82]Fadwa El Guindi, "The Killing of Sadat and After," *Middle East Insight* 2 (January/February 1983):23.

[83]*Ibid.*

Anwar Sadat's patrimonial rule in the service of tradition brought back class animosity to Egypt. His open-door policy only served to widen the gap between the very rich and the teeming masses of the poor. According to Burrell and Kelidar, "Perhaps the most dangerous aspect of this is that the average Egyptian has been becoming more impoverished at a time when the affluence of a small number of Egyptians has been made ever more apparent. The availability of Western imports—imports widely regarded as nonessential luxuries under Nasser's rule—[has] heightened the sense of impoverishment and deprivation."[84] The fact that rich Arab oil magnates from the Gulf shaikhdoms vacationed in Egyptian resorts and mansions in Alexandria while thousands of Egyptians worked as skilled laborers in the shaikhdoms was an irony not lost on the Egyptian public.

After the 1977 riots, President Sadat emphasized his patrimonial prerogative of control by coercion. Students and other university dwellers were assured from then on that participation in demonstrations and illegal political party membership were punishable by life imprisonment. Sadat redefined his views on liberalization when he told Egyptian students that "politics have no place in our universities" and that "democracy too can have teeth and fangs."[85] After the September 1981 crackdown, he explained to the Egyptian people that they had "to understand that democracy has its own teeth. The next time it is going to be ten times as ruthless."[86]

Anwar Sadat was in some ways a more accomplished patrimonial leader than was his predecessor, Gamal Abdel Nasser. He had more experience, greater flair, the political support of the United States, and considerable economic assistance from the oil-rich conservative Arab countries. Yet Sadat's personal and patrimonial style was enlisted in the defense of the status quo, thereby defying inexorable social forces in Egypt, which grew more explosive with time. As we have seen, Nasser himself was not averse to patrimonial tactics. But he was at the same time dedicated to a continuing program of social change and to the transformation of the class structure of Egypt. He tried to gener-

[84]Burrell and Kelidar, *Egypt,* p. 32. This excellent little book convincingly demonstrates that widening class divisions in Sadat's Egypt led to great political discontent and discord.

[85]*Ibid.,* pp. 41–42.

[86]*The New York Times,* September 27, 1981.

ate and absorb change. As a result, he ruled Egypt for nearly two decades, despite accepting full responsibility for political and national catastrophes such as the June War of 1967.

Sadat became entangled in his own rhetoric and tried to convert international fame into domestic credibility and support. He slowed political development at home while accelerating modernization through a policy of *infitah*. This mode of patrimonial rule ran in the face of the needs and aspirations of the masses of Egyptian citizens who were turning increasingly to Islamic movements for support and sustenance. Sadat's assassins were members of an Islamic fundamentalist group, and although they were tried and executed, they represented only one tiny part of the overall movement in the country.

Sadat's successor, Husni Mubarak, faces a difficult political task. Egypt's social, economic, and political problems remain as intractible as ever. An air force officer for 25 years and the loyal vice-president of Sadat for 6 years, Mubarak was closely associated with Sadat and his policies. Once he took over the presidency of Egypt on October 14, 1981, however, Mubarak immediately tried to distance himself from Sadat's method of rule. He had no intention of repeating the mistakes of his predecessor. Unostentatious and low-key, Mubarak has consciously avoided the opulent and visible patrimonial style of President Sadat. He has attempted to attack corruption, to compromise with the opposition, and to seek to come to grips with Egypt's domestic problems immediately and directly.

In his speech to the Egyptian parliament shortly after he became president, Mubarak described the new course of national action as one of "seriousness, purification, no hypocrisy, no corruption, no playing around with the minds of the people, and no discrimination between the ruler and the ruled."[87] Despite his good intentions, President Mubarak has yet to deliver politically and economically. And pressure continues to build in the Egyptian polity. As Muslim opposition forces challenged the Egyptian government in the early 1990s, Mubarak resorted to increasing repression to maintain control. By 1993, the harshness of this response had created a mode of confrontational politics that cast a dark cloud over the future of the Mubarak regime. Meanwhile, the Egyptian government must somehow meet the basic needs of its rapidly growing population. Pressure cannot be

---

[87]*The Middle East*, December 1981, p. 19.

bottled up indefinitely. On one level, President Mubarak seems to understand this. He has pointed out that "what counts is achievements, not statements."[88] But in the face of a deep Islamic political challenge, he must do more than defend and repress; he must produce economic and political achievements or risk going the way of Anwar Sadat.

LEADERS AND CHANGE: A CONCLUDING PERSPECTIVE

Our case studies of selected Middle Eastern leaders indicate the extraordinary persistence of patrimonial politics in the area. Even revolutionary and charismatic leaders such as Ataturk and Nasser retained characteristics of the patrimonial style. This is one reason why it is supremely difficult to transform national power structures and to introduce political development in Middle Eastern countries: Can one build new political systems using old tools?

Kemal Ataturk and Gamal Abdel Nasser did indeed introduce significant change at various points in their social and political systems. Although it has become common to question the depths of the changes they wrought, there can be little doubt that they were in many ways revolutionaries. But they had unusual advantages. Both gathered great personal and political momentum because of their impeccable credentials as nationalists. They had successfully defied and defeated great European colonialist powers. And both men had an impressive charisma that is seldom seen in the Middle East.

In succeeding their illustrious predecessors, Ismet Inonu and Anwar Sadat were faced with the need to continue and deepen ongoing programs of revolutionary change. Both men chose initially to liberalize and to expand political participation in their societies. Lacking the charisma of Ataturk and Nasser, they sought to build a broader platform of legitimacy and support. Ironically, in the process of doing so they oversaw the gradual decline of revolutionary programs in their societies. The traditional power groups and classes that had been defeated and dismantled by Ataturk and Nasser regrouped and returned to influence. In the case of Egypt especially, the negative

---

[88]*Ibid.*, p. 18.

dimensions of patrimonial politics seeped back into the nooks and crannies of the system.

The challenges of the day are such that patrimonial modes of rule alone will not enable Middle Eastern leaders to satisfy the demands of new social groups and classes. Although this style of rule is so strong that it will perhaps be always present in the Middle East in one form or another, it must be exercised in the context of a strengthened capacity to generate and absorb transforming change. Traditional patrimonial monarchs (such as the last shah of Iran), who promote limited change, provide only a limited answer to the challenge. Modern patrimonial moderates (such as the late Anwar Sadat of Egypt), who stifle political development while promoting a certain level of modernization, are also unable to confront the mounting social problems of their societies successfully. In this context, it is not accidental that both the shah and Sadat met grim personal and political fates. Even newer and bigger versions of the Ataturks and Nassers would have a difficult time in the contemporary world of the Middle East. The problems are many; strong but sensitive leaders are few.

Chapter 6

Institutions of Government: Militaries, Bureaucracies, and Legislatures

*T*hird World political systems are characterized by the dominance of policy-implementing institutions, including the military and the bureaucracy, over policy-making structures such as legislatures, political parties, and formal interest groups. According to a leading scholar of development administration, "The relative weakness of political organs means that the political function tends to be appropriated, in considerable measure, by bureaucrats."[1] Military officers have, if anything, exceeded bureaucrats in their zeal to appropriate political functions. But the balance between governmental institutions of administration and coercion, on the one hand, and political structures, on the other, varies from one region of the Third World to another. In Africa and the Middle East, governmental institutions are especially predominant, or, in the words of an Arab intellectual, "The State means everything and it monopolizes almost all facilities, while the society means very little."[2] In Latin America and East Asia, political institu-

---

[1]Fred W. Riggs, "Bureaucrats and Political Development: A Paradoxical View," in *Bureaucracy and Political Development*, ed. by Joseph La Palombara (Princeton, N.J.: Princeton University Press, 1963), p. 120.

[2] Bassam Tibi, "Political Freedom in Arab Societies," *Arab Studies Quarterly* 6: 3 (Summer 1984): 225.

tions have had greater success in expanding their authority. A simple measure of the balance between state administrative institutions and structures which facilitate political participation is the presence of legislative bodies. In the mid-1970s an observer of comparative legislative development noted that "the overwhelming number of countries without legislatures are in Africa and the Middle East."[3] Constitutional government, which requires the differentiation of separate structures of government and politics in order to perform a wide range of functions, clearly lags in the Middle East.

Effective institutions of political participation that could vigorously defend personal political freedoms have yet to take root in many countries of the region. This is due in part to factors beyond the control of the countries themselves. In much of the Third World in the nineteenth and twentieth centuries, the twin phenomena of defensive modernization, by which local rulers such as Muhammad Ali of Egypt and Ahmad Bey of Tunisia sought to develop their armies and administrative apparati to defend their territories from European encroachments, and then colonialism itself, militated against the institutionalized expression of political demands by the population.

Defensive modernizers did not seek to expand political participation. They were instead intent on rapid military and bureaucratic development to counter foreign threats. Also, the societies they sought to modernize were dominated by traditional elements who, if permitted to engage in politics, would have challenged the authority of the defensive modernizers themselves. Similarly, colonial rulers had scant desire for expanding the political awareness of subject peoples. As Charles Issawi has observed, "No real democracy could develop in Egypt, Iraq, Jordan, Lebanon, and Syria as long as British or French armies of occupation were the determining factor in all political matters. . . . Nor was the situation of unoccupied countries, such as Iran and Turkey, very much better, for both have lived under the shadow of two powerful neighbors."[4]

Examples of colonialist intervention to contain the expansion of political participation in Middle Eastern countries are legion. The

---

[3] Joseph La Palombara, *Politics Within Nations* (Englewood Cliffs, N.J.: Prentice-Hall, 1974), p. 113.

[4] Charles Issawi, "Economic and Social Foundations of Democracy in the Middle East," *International Affairs* 32 (1956), reprinted in *The Arab World's Legacy* (Princeton: The Darwin Press, 1981), pp. 243–244.

British and French stood behind the autocratic Egyptian ruler Khedive Isma'il when in 1878 he was challenged by the Assembly of Notables which sought to restrict monarchical absolutism. In 1942 British tanks surrounded King Farouk's palace in Cairo to force the dismissal of an elected, pro-Axis government. The British even refused the conservative traditionalist, Amir Abdullah of Transjordan, permission in 1924 to hold elections for a parliament. Instead, the British resident supported the creation of an appointed legislative council to serve as a rubber stamp for the executive. "At this particular moment in Jordan's history," according to one of the country's leading political scientists, "the British intended to retard, as they indeed continued to do later, rather than advance the cause of parliamentary government."[5] On the creation of Iraq in the wake of World War I, the British rejected demands for participatory government by nationalist leaders and instead installed Amir Abdullah's brother Faisal on the throne. Shortly thereafter they employed the Royal Air Force to bomb concentrations of tribesmen in the Middle Euphrates region in what was one of the first examples in history of an imperial power using an air force against guerrilla insurgents.

The French record of hostility toward democratic practices in its Middle Eastern mandated territories is also notable. They deposed the popularly endorsed King Faisal in Damascus in 1920 and replaced him with a puppet government. Like the British in Iraq, the French in Syria were then forced in 1925 to intervene militarily to put down a revolt against the government they had imposed. In both Syria and Lebanon, the French employed divide-and-rule tactics to exacerbate religious and ethnic tensions in order to frustrate the emergence of unified, mass-based nationalist movements. The last gasp of British and French imperialism in the Middle East was their invasion, along with Israel, of Egypt in 1956, a military action intended to topple the overwhelmingly popular government of Gamal Abdel Nasser. While the Middle East is by no means unique by virtue of its having had to endure foreign interventions, many of which have been intended to frustrate collective national political action, the degree of intervention is singular. "Because of its focal geographic position at the juncture of

---

[5] Kamel S. Abu Jaber, "The Legislature of the Hashemite Kingdom of Jordan: A Study in Political Development," *The Muslim World*, LIX 3–4 (July–October 1969): 220–250, reprinted in Jacob M. Landau, ed., *Man, State, and Society in the Middle East* (New York: Praeger Publications, 1972), p. 93.

three continents and two oceans, the Middle East has been, through-out recorded history, the most frequently invaded region of the globe."[6]

The end of colonialism in the region was not accompanied by a termination of interventionism. Instead, the United States and the Soviet Union, who in the 1940s and 1950s supplanted British and French domination, perpetuated the practice, albeit in modified form. The CIA and KGB have had significant and sustained covert involve-ments in the domestic affairs of the region's states. The overthrow of the popular nationalist government of Muhammad Musaddiq in Iran in 1953 has been pointed to by CIA operatives as one of their greatest triumphs.[7] Less trumpeted by those same CIA agents were their bun-gled attempts to subvert the Syrian government in the mid-1950s and their failed efforts to topple Nasser in Egypt.[8] The Middle East remains the most active theater of operations in the Third World for American intelligence activities. Direct military interventions by the United States against Lebanon, Syria, Iran, and Libya occurred during the Reagan administration. Operation Desert Storm, launched against Iraqi-occupied Kuwait and Iraq itself on January 17, 1991, involved the greatest concentration of U.S. military force since World War II.

The Soviet Union, prior to its collapse, also actively and directly intervened in the area. The most dramatic case of its coercive inter-vention occurred in Afghanistan during the decade beginning in December 1979 and in South Yemen in January 1986. Along with East German and Cuban forces, the Soviets sided with the pro-Moscow faction of the ruling Yemeni Socialist Party in a civil war that erupted in South Yemen after a failed assassination attempt on President Ali Nasir Muhammad.

Military and covert interventions by outside powers into the poli-tics of Middle Eastern states are inimical to the emergence of consti-

---

[6] Dankart A. Rustow, "The Military in Middle Eastern Society and Politics," in *The Mil-itary in the Middle East: Problems in Society and Government,* ed. by Sydney Nettleton Fisher (Columbus: Ohio State University Press, 1963), p. 5.

[7] Kermit Roosevelt, *Countercoup: The Struggle for the Control of Iran* (New York: McGraw-Hill, 1979).

[8] See Miles Copeland, *Game of Nations* (New York: Simon & Schuster, 1969); William Eveland, *Ropes of Sand: America's Failure in the Middle East* (New York: Norton and Co., 1980); and Douglas Little, "Cold War and Covert Action: The United States and Syria, 1945–1958," *The Middle East Journal* 44 (Winter 1990): 51–75.

tutional, participatory government and frequently have been intended for this purpose. Economic assistance programs, despite their intent, can also militate against the institutionalization of political participation. "In the contemporary era of large-scale technical assistance under international and bi-national programs, we see a continued infusion of external pressure and assistance in the expansion and proliferation of bureaucratic organs, with relatively little attention to the growth of strictly political institutions."[9] It could hardly be otherwise, because foreign assistance is conceived as a technical matter requiring interaction with the host country's bureaucracy or private sector but scarcely if ever with the political system. Indeed, were "political" aid programs designed, they would be construed as interference in host countries' domestic affairs.

American aid to Egypt, which between 1975 and 1992 totaled almost $30 billion, an amount second only to that provided Israel, illustrates both the political sensitivity of foreign aid and the unequal impact it has on administrative as opposed to political institutions. Egyptian intellectuals and opposition politicians have continually alleged that the United States Agency for International Development (USAID) gathers information for the purpose of manipulating Egyptian politics, engages directly in Egyptian domestic economic policy-making, serves as the lever by which Egypt is forced against its will to "normalize" its relations with Israel, and, occasionally, provides cover for intelligence agents.[10] Paradoxically, USAID officials lament their lack of influence over policy-making and fear that the overall impact of their program is to entrench the power of the bureaucracy, which is opposed to further liberalization of the economy or polity. Certainly the resources made available through American assistance to Egypt have gone overwhelmingly to the military and the civil administration and in so doing have provided bases for patronage that reinforce the powers of those institutions.

The threat of violence hanging over Middle Eastern governments is due not only to the actions of outside powers. Indeed, the region has been consumed by warfare between and within states almost without

---

[9] Riggs, "Bureaucrats and Political Development," p. 125.

[10] The most thorough analysis of the U.S. assistance program in Egypt is that by Marvin G. Weinbaum, *Egypt and the Politics of U.S. Aid* (Boulder, Colo.: Westview Press, 1986).

stop since World War II. In the 1980s and early 1990s, civil wars or violent insurgencies have occurred in Lebanon, Sudan, Iraq, Iran, Morocco, Syria, Turkey, Yemen, and territories occupied by Israel. One of the world's most intense and costly wars in the twentieth century in terms of casualties, destruction, expense, and duration was fought between Iran and Iraq from 1980 to 1988. Two and a half years after that war ended, Iraq was devastated by Operation Desert Storm. In the decade of the 1980s, Israel bombed targets in Iraq, Tunisia, and Lebanon, invaded the latter, and engaged the Syrian military on several occasions. By deportations, mass imprisonment, and killings, Israel has sought unsuccessfully since December 1987 to quell the Palestinian uprising in the occupied territories. In the seven years following the signing of the Egyptian-Israeli peace treaty in 1979, armed conflicts in the Middle East resulted in at least a half-million people being killed and more than three million wounded. In late 1986, Egypt's minister of defense said that "one out of every two states is involved in conflicts or violence."[11]

Middle Eastern governments can reasonably expect to employ their militaries against neighboring states or their own populations; they therefore prepare for such eventualities. In Israel, over half the industrial labor force is employed in defense industries.[12] The military is by far the largest employer in the region. One out of every fifty people is a soldier. "If irregular forces (like the Revolutionary Guards in Iran) and militias (like those in Lebanon) are included with regular soldiers, there may be as many as 10 million people in military service in the Middle East."[13] Military spending has increased 1,600 percent in real terms in the Middle East since the mid-1960s. In the 1980s three-quarters of all Third World arms agreements involved a country in the Middle East. During that decade, the region spent $600 billion on the military. Saudi Arabia and Iraq alone accounted for 30 percent of the world's arms purchases.[14] Between 1972 and 1988, Middle

---

[11] "Living by the Sword—A Primer," *Merip Middle East Report* 144 (January–February 1987): 23.

[12] Yoram Peri, *Between Battles and Ballots: Israeli Military in Politics* (Cambridge: Cambridge University Press, 1983), p. 22.

[13] "Living by the Sword," p. 23.

[14] Robert Bailey, "Defence," *Middle East Economic Digest Special Report* (October 31, 1987); and Alasdair Drysdale and Raymond A. Hinnebusch, *Syria and the Middle East Peace Process* (New York: Council on Foreign Relations Press, 1991), pp. 163, 218.

Eastern countries spent more than 11 percent of their gross national product (GNP) on arms—compared with the 2.3 percent spent in Latin America and the 6.3 percent in Asian developing countries. By comparison, the Pentagon's budget for weapons acquisition in 1992 was 1.6 percent of the U.S. GNP.[15] The preponderance of militaries in labor forces and in economies more generally, coupled with the effects of the generalized perception that political violence is inevitable, have perpetuated the imbalance between political institutions and the military.

According to Leon Carl Brown, for over two centuries the Middle East has been plagued not only by military confrontations but also by what he calls "the penetration of its political systems."[16] The protracted decline of the Ottoman Empire invited the European powers to become involved in its politics. Since independence, interference by states of the region in their neighbors' politics has become commonplace. Unassimilated ethnic and religious minority groups and underground political oppositions provide fifth columns through which such influence is wielded. Governments typically try to counter penetration of their political orders by restricting political freedoms. In reviewing the Emergency Decrees which enable the government to rule without reference to the constitution, and which were first declared in 1981, President Mubarak in 1988 cited the threat of foreign subversion and the need to counter it. Similarly, one of King Hussein's advisors told an American author that restrictions on political freedoms were necessary in Jordan because there were too many foreign "lines" running through Jordan.[17] In 1986, the Kuwaiti parliament was prorogued, partly because of Saudi pressure and fear of Iranian subversion. Accompanying the dissolution of parliament was a crackdown on the comparatively freewheeling Kuwaiti press. Forty-nine journalists were arrested—all of them resident aliens. Throughout the Middle East, rulers cite the example of Lebanon as what will happen if too much political freedom is allowed, the implication being that citizens will

---

[15] Norman Kempster, "Hopes for Stopping Mideast Arms Race," *Los Angeles Times* (May 12, 1992), p. 2.

[16] Leon Carl Brown, *International Politics and the Middle East: Old Rules, Dangerous Game* (Princeton, N.J.: Princeton University Press, 1984).

[17] Arthur R. Day, *East Bank/West Bank: Jordan and the Prospects for Peace* (New York: Council on Foreign Relations, 1986), pp. 44–45.

seek foreign allies against their domestic enemies and by so doing bring about a descent into anarchy. Thus the intensity of cross-border interactions in the Middle East results in a widely held belief that political freedoms are bound to be abused by foreign enemies working with fifth-column elements. The most common solution to this problem is for regimes not to permit independent political organization or expression.

The dominance of state structures over institutions of political participation can also be accounted for in the Middle East, as elsewhere in the Third World, by the absence of social and economic prerequisites. Charles Issawi's list of such requirements includes reasonable levels of economic development, industrialization, the egalitarian distribution of wealth, homogeneity of language and religion, educational attainments, and a "habit of co-operative association." Writing in the 1950s, he concluded that by these measures "in the Middle East the economic and social soil is still not deep enough to enable political democracy to strike root and flourish."[18]

Other observers emphasize development deficiencies that take the form of vacuums into which state structures have expanded, thereby stunting the growth of political institutions. For some, the vacuum is the absence of a middle class, or bourgeoisie, that spearheaded the drive for democracy in the West. In Turkey, for example, "the state or the Kemalist cadre who controlled the state apparatus was the driving force behind this scheme of modernisation. In the absence of a modernising bourgeoisie, the bureaucracy had shouldered the task of nation-building."[19] The destabilization of Turkish politics since the mid-1950s is partially the consequence of the political challenge launched by the entrepreneurial middle class against the supremacy of the bureaucracy and the military.

Absence of political institutions at the early stages of political development perpetuates administrative and military supremacy. Once they begin to perform the functions typically associated with parties, legislatures, and interest groups, bureaucracies and militaries render those political institutions irrelevant. Participatory impulses

---

[18] Issawi, "Economic and Social Foundations of Democracy," pp. 244, 258.

[19] Dofu Ergil, "Turkey" in *Electoral Politics in the Middle East: Issues, Voters and Elites,* ed. by Jacob M. Landau, Ergun Özbudun, and Frank Tachau (London: Croom Helm, 1980), p. 13.

are diverted into administrative bodies, "which not only makes independent political parties functionally redundant but 'politicizes' the bureaucracy."[20] According to Manfred Halpern: "Bureaucracies in the Middle East not only administer laws, but, in the absence of parliamentary institutions, usually fashion them."[21] In Sudan, for example, "The bureaucratic sector is dominant and all powerful. There is a grave developmental imbalance between it on the one hand, and parliaments and political parties . . . on the other."[22]

State hegemony over political institutions may also result from factors specific to Middle Eastern political culture. There are doctrinal underpinnings and historical antecedents for an emphasis on military action and intervention by the military into politics. Islamic theology accords legitimacy to warfare. The doctrine of *jihad,* or holy struggle, sanctions military action to expand the *Dar al-Islam* (Abode of Islam) at the expense of the *Dar al-Harb* (Abode of War). Eliezer Be'eri sees a link between the historical existence of slave soldiers (mamlukes or janissaries) and the contemporary role of the military in the Middle East:

> Although one should not overestimate the influence on contemporary political life of an historical phenomenon, which ceased to exist more than a hundred years ago, neither should one disregard the influence on recent developments of relationships which prevailed uninterruptedly for 2 thousand years. . . . In Middle-Eastern society, where there is ample and long precedence of an officer corps separate from the rest of the populace, the corporateness of the officer corps is to a great extent conditioned by its history.[23]

Other scholars dispute the claim that the slave-soldier tradition of rule has contemporary relevance and that contemporary Middle Eastern officer corps are corporate entities. Fuad Khuri, for example, emphasizes that contemporary military institutions can be traced to

[20] Lisa Anderson, "The State in the Middle East and North Africa," *Comparative Politics* 20: 1 (October 1987): 8.

[21] Manfred Halpern, *The Politics of Social Change in the Middle East and North Africa* (Princeton, N.J.: Princeton University Press, 1963), p. 340.

[22] Mukhtar al-Assam, "Bureaucracy and Development in the Sudan," *Journal of Asian and African Studies* 24 (1989): 47.

[23] Eliezer Be'eri, *Army Officers in Arab Politics and Society* (Jerusalem: Israel Universities Press, 1969), p. 298.

Western penetration and resultant state building rather than to earlier antecedents in the classical Islamic empires. "Except for Egypt, Morocco, Turkey and Iran, which had a longer history of professional militarism (dating to the nineteenth century), armed forces, as specialized institutions, came up only after World War I when many of the countries of the Middle East were made separate states under colonial tutelage or protection. Establishing an army or a police force then was part of an effort to build state institutions."[24] Alasdair Drysdale has demonstrated that assumptions about the legacy of military traditions even over much shorter periods may be misleading. Under the French mandate, minorities, particularly Alawis, were overrepresented in the Syrian officer corps as part of a strategy to suppress the nationalist movement. After the mid-1960s, Alawi officers again came to dominate not only the military but all other key structures of the state and the Ba'th party itself. But, Drysdale observes, there is not an unbroken connection between the colonial and contemporary periods. In the first five postindependence classes of officer training school, some 80 percent of all graduates were Sunni Arabs, compared with less than one-half prior to independence. In the 1950s and early 1960s, the Syrian military was "genuinely an agent of national integration in an otherwise fragmented society, a national symbol in a precarious republic."[25] Subsequent deterioration of the Syrian military into a vehicle of minoritarian domination came about as a result of political conflict in the mid-1960s. The contemporary Syrian officer corps should not, therefore, according to Drysdale, be interpreted as a legacy of colonial divide-and-rule policies. It is instead the product of contemporary politics.

Evidence from other Middle Eastern countries supports the contention that the military has intervened in politics not because of its corporate, separate nature, but precisely because it is insufficiently differentiated from society. Recruits into the Egyptian officer corps after nominal independence in 1936, such as Nasser and Sadat, joined not because their families had a tradition of military service but

---

[24] Fuad I. Khuri, "The Study of Civil-Military Relations in Modernizing Societies in the Middle East: A Critical Assessment," in *Soldiers, Peasants, and Bureaucrats: Civil-Military Relations in Communist and Modernizing Societies,* ed. by Roman Kolkowicz and Andrezej Korbonski (London: George Allen and Unwin, 1982), p. 10.

[25] Alasdair Drysdale, "The Syrian Armed Forces in National Politics: The Role of the Geographic and Ethnic Periphery," in *ibid.,* p. 58.

because the corps provided a channel of upward mobility. The army in Egypt, and elsewhere in the region, has until very recently not been so much a distinctive, separate institution as just another part of the state bureaucratic structure. Attitudes of Arab military officers as measured by a content analysis of their journals suggests that "the value orientations of the military do not seem to differ from the adult male behavior expectations."[26] The Prussian officer corps, which emerged in the nineteenth century as the first European force to be professional both in self-conception and by virtue of being above politics, provides a prototype yet to be adopted in its entirety in the Middle East.

Military institutions created in the nineteenth and twentieth centuries as part of the formation of modern states in the Middle East were departures from previous practices, but they may nevertheless have been affected by indigenous traditions. Contemporary political institutions, essentially Western in origin, have probably also been influenced by local traditions that govern relations between rulers and ruled. In the Arab polities of the Gulf, for example, explanations given by rulers when creating consultative assemblies have been couched in Islamic and tribal terms. The Quran enjoins rulers to consult prominent persons on issues of public concern, while "Arab tribal tradition also requires the chief (shaykh) of each tribe to consult notables and senior members of the tribe about their affairs . . . Without consultation, no allegiance is owed to a chief who does not 'sit in majlis' with the notables and senior members of the tribe to exchange views on all matters of public concern."[27]

But the Islamic and tribal injunctions to consult have not, through history, served to buttress institutions of effective widespread political participation, nor are they presently doing so. The tradition of consultation restricted that privilege to prominent personages; it did not make provision for an organized, loyal opposition nor did it provide for representation as opposed to consultation. According to Michael Hudson, "Tribal democracy may be as remote from contemporary forms of government in the Arab world as the New England town meeting is to modern government in America."[28]

The comparative lack of vigor of participatory political organiza-

---

[26] Khuri, "The Study of Civil-Military Relations," p. 13.

[27] Majid Khadduri, "Foreword," in J. E. Peterson, *The Arab Gulf States: Steps Toward Political Participation* (New York: Praeger, 1988), pp. ix–x.

[28] Michael Hudson, *Arab Politics: The Search for Legitimacy* (New Haven, Conn.: Yale University Press, 1977), p. 91.

tions may reflect not only the continuing impact of the tradition of consultation rather than representation, but also the influence of non-democratic authority structures that obtain in a wide variety of social settings, including families, religious organizations, professional associations, voluntary political organizations, neighborhood groups, and so on. "Social scientists," according to the Egyptian sociologist Saad Eddin Ibrahim, "have increasingly come to the realization that other societal institutions must provide a 'democratic infrastructure' for the political system if democracy is to succeed. The family, in particular, is cited as pivotal in this regard. Individuals socialized in an authoritarian type of family are not expected to enhance democratic practices in the political sphere of society at large."[29] Andrea Rugh argues that "the character of social institutions like the family in Egypt tends to promote an authoritarian rather than a democratic style of leadership, with a policy that acquiesces to rather than challenges that leadership. The leaders as father-figures in any case tend to take it as a personal offense when their 'children' become unruly and unwilling to submit to the authority of their elders."[30] While it would be incorrect to assume that behavioral patterns characteristic of small social units are reproduced unchanged in much larger ones, President Sadat's behavior suggests that some connection may exist. He referred to himself as "Father of the Egyptian Family" and chastised his critics as errant children. When that admonition failed of its objective, he dissolved parliament, banned opposition parties, and then, just prior to his assassination, threw some 1,600 opposition political activists in jail.

Throughout the Middle East, autonomous, formally organized political activity is rare. Voluntary associations are closely monitored by governments that require "individuals desiring to form an association [to] submit a formal request to the government, usually the Ministry of the Interior." But, Kevin Dwyer adds, "Either with the authorization or without it, the association is likely to be under constant observation . . . and control or harassment from above become more onerous the more controversial are the group's aims."[31] Local govern-

[29] Saad Eddin Ibrahim, "The Socio-Economic Requisites of Democracy," in *Democracy in Egypt. Cairo Papers in Social Science* 1, 2, ed. by Ali Dessouki (1978), p. 59.

[30] Andrea Rugh, *Family in Contemporary Egypt* (Cairo: American University in Cairo Press, 1985), p. 45.

[31] Kevin Dwyer, *Arab Voices: The Human Rights Debate in the Middle East* (New York: Routledge, 1991), pp. 146–147.

ment in the area is notable by its absence. Cairo, for example, did not have its own municipal government until the mid-twentieth century. In most countries, administrative subdivisions are run by officials appointed from the capital. Where local elections do occur, they tend to be dominated by governmental organizations or by traditional social units, such as tribes, on which government relies when its power is insufficient to govern districts or towns directly. There are, in sum, few arenas in which those aspiring to play public political roles could engage in open, participatory politics.

It is important to note, however, that while democratic practices in formal political institutions are restricted, there is not a complete absence of pluralism in the political system, nor is the state able to interfere in all aspects of peoples' lives. The private sphere is populated by innumerable kin and communal groupings, and the public sphere—that which is dominated by the state—is, by Western standards, relatively constricted. As Suad Joseph observes:

> The organization of society is much more contested in the Middle East than in the West. Middle Eastern states and their rulers have not succeeded as have their Western counterparts in imposing their hegemony. Kinship and communal power flourish: rulers rely on them as a mainstay of their power, while citizens turn to them to protect themselves from state repression or to compensate for inefficient administration. The domestic sphere is a lively arena of social, political and economic action in the Middle East—far more so than in the West.[32]

The division between the private, domestic sphere and the public, governmental one means that even if democratic, egalitarian relations obtained within the former, which they certainly do in many instances, they are often peripheral to formal politics, which is the government's domain.

TRANSFORMATIONAL VERSUS ADAPTIVE MODERNIZATION

During the process of state formation, administrative and political institutions based on Western models have been superimposed on local structures and traditional practices. Results have been uneven.

---

[32] Suad Joseph, "Women and Politics in the Middle East," *Merip Middle East Report* 138 (January–February 1986): 4.

The tradition of military exploits may have facilitated the growth of newly created military organizations, but the long history of unified military and political leadership may also have impeded the professionalization of the officer corps and its subordination to civilian political leadership. Tribal and Islamic traditions of consultation have served as inspirations and justifications for the establishment of legislative and quasi-legislative bodies, but the consultative tradition has not yet been translated into truly representative parliaments.

Such uneven development is typical in the Third World. "The process of modernization in the developing countries is marked by the progressive creation of formally distinct social structures, adapted from Western models, to which differentiated political and administrative tasks are assigned. But in this process the older institutional base of a traditional society lingers on. Although eroded and embattled, it struggles to remain alive, to retain positions of influence."[33] Scholars of development disagree about the preferred outcome of this battle between Western-inspired, formal organizations on the one hand, and traditional institutions and practices on the other. The view held by many general theorists of development, such as Gabriel Almond and Bingham Powell, is that for stable governments capable of managing social and technical change to emerge, rational, secular organizations capable of harnessing the energies of large and expanding numbers of people must prevail. According to this position, traditional institutions are too small, too dependent on face-to-face interactions to cope adequately with the loads imposed by population growth, social mobilization, and technological advancements.[34] Modernization, in sum, requires the fundamental transformation of traditional political systems. One Middle East specialist who subscribes to this view is Manfred Halpern. He measures the political development of the Middle East in terms of the increasing coherence and efficacy of its militaries, bureaucracies, labor unions, parliaments, and other political institutions. With regard to political parties, for example, he writes:

> It has been customary to assume that political parties are not as important in the Middle East—or in other underdeveloped areas—as individual leaders and that few political parties matter at all. This view still had some

---

[33] Riggs, "Bureaucrats and Political Development," p. 411.

[34] See Gabriel A. Almond and G. Bingham Powell, Jr., *Comparative Politics: Systems, Process and Policy* (Boston: Little, Brown and Company, 1978).

validity during the 1940s. During the 1950s it became outdated. It is now quite apparent that individual leaders, however impressive their charismatic powers, will be unable to construct a single and enduring "political culture" unless they build effective political parties.[35]

An alternative interpretation, and one offered more frequently by Middle East specialists than by general theorists, is that traditional institutions and practices are sufficiently adaptable to cope with the increased loads imposed by modernization. By contrast, rational, secular, formal institutions, precisely because they are not rooted in Middle Eastern political cultures and traditions, will not attract nor integrate large numbers of people and will never, therefore, function as they have in the West. John Peterson, who has studied political participation in the traditional Arab polities of the Gulf, asserts,

> A prevalent assumption based on Western historical experience, holds that these political systems must be evolutionary. According to this view, changing expectations and increasing demands for fuller participation in all aspects of political life eventually will force the transformation of these polities, either through a voluntary dispersion of power on the part of ruling families or by dissidence and revolution. This assumption, however, may display a normative bias towards conceptions of Western-style democracy as a more just form of government and therefore a desirable consequence of political development.[36]

Samir Khalaf, a Lebanese sociologist and leading advocate of the adaptive modernization school, argues that "the fact that an agency is traditional in form or structure does not imply that it must espouse traditional values, or that it must devote itself exclusively to passing on sacred values or preserving traditional lore and skills. Conversely, a seemingly modern institution . . . is no guarantee that man will undergo a drastic transformation in his spirit and that he will, after all, acquire modern life styles."[37] Khalaf has conducted research for many years on such entities as family business firms, formally organized family associations, religious and communal voluntary associations, and patrimonial political leaders in order to demonstrate how they "have been effective in meeting some of the secular and rational demands of

---

[35] Manfred Halpern, *The Politics of Social Change,* 281.

[36] Peterson, *The Arab Gulf States,* 13.

[37] Samir Khalaf, *Lebanon's Predicament* (New York: Columbia University Press, 1987), pp. 17–18.

modernization (i.e., openness, receptivity to change, the ability to cope with problems and imbalances) without diluting primordial loyalties or dehumanizing the social fabric of society."[38]

The adaptive modernization school has been influenced by the poor performance of Western-inspired institutions in the Middle East as compared with many indigenous ones. When Manfred Halpern was writing his major work on the Middle East in the late 1950s and early 1960s, Nasserism, Ba'thism, and radical Arab nationalism more generally were in their heydays. Each version was accompanied with elaborate ideological and organizational formulations. It appeared as if it would be only a matter of time before the last vestiges of traditionalism, including the tribal rulers of the Gulf shaikhdoms, would be swept away. History, however, proved these tribally based polities to be more tenacious than even Gamal Abdel Nasser could have anticipated. "Although twenty-five years ago the conventional wisdom held that such systems were curious anachronisms ready to collapse of their own weight, yielding to Nasserism and other brave new Arab ideologies, these systems have survived, while it is the latter that are endangered species."[39]

Survival of traditional institutions and practices is due to the fact that they have been favored by many ruling elites over modern, potentially radical competitors and to the fact that they have adapted to perform the new functions required in these increasingly complex sociopolitical systems. While political parties have continued to be banned in the Arab Gulf states, loose networks of friendships formed among and within "school acquaintances, cultural and sport clubs, and the mosque and, among the Shia, the funeral homes," have served as vehicles through which political demands have been formulated and pressed on governments.[40] Tribes have been particularly adaptable sociopolitical institutions. In Kuwait, for example, during the 1985 parliamentary primary elections, they proved to be much more effec-

---

[38] *Ibid.*, p. 19.

[39] Malcolm C. Peck, *The United Arab Emirates: A Venture in Unity* (Boulder, Colo.: Westview Press, 1986), p. 125.

[40] Abdo I. Baaklini, "Legislatures in the Gulf Area: The Experience of Kuwait, 1961–1976," *International Journal of Middle East Studies* 14 (August 1982): 361. See also Fred H. Lawson, *Bahrain: The Modernization of Autocracy* (Boulder, Colo.: Westview Press, 1989), ch. 4.

tive organizations for selecting suitable candidates than ostensibly more modern groupings composed of merchants, Islamic fundamentalists, or the liberal/left nationalists.[41] Similarly, in the 1984 Jordanian parliamentary by-elections, tribes played a crucial role. "But there was no 'return to tribalism.' . . . New definitions are emerging about what it means to be a tribesman in Jordan today. . . . These new definitions of tribal identity are not contradictory with citizenship. . . ."[42]

The question does remain, however, as to whether such traditional institutions as tribes, *majlises* (councils), and informal networks can continue to cope with the increased loads imposed by modernization. If such institutions are utilized by regimes to protect their rule and to prevent the expansion of participation, they will not continue to adapt and will, therefore, ultimately be swept aside. As John Peterson states,

> The nostalgic and mythologized arguments that they [Arab Gulf states] possess a "tribal" or "social" democracy becomes increasingly specious as traditional ways disappear. . . . Such key democratic institutions as national councils are likely to be increasingly necessary as time goes on, particularly as growing populations and faster-paced lifestyles result in less personal contact between citizens, governments become more complex, access to rulers and ruling families decreases, and informal participation through traditional means, such as the *majlis,* or modern means, such as policy-influencing positions within the bureaucracy, loses relevance or possibility.[43]

Whatever ultimately occurs, for the foreseeable future the political systems of most Middle Eastern countries will continue to be heterogeneous, composed of traditional institutions—some stagnating, others adapting to changing conditions—and of modern organizations, some becoming increasingly coherent, rational, and effective, and others languishing—unassimilated transplants, serving only as arenas in which traditional, ascriptive behavior continues unmodified. But modern, ostensibly rational organizations have indisputedly been wholly or partially incorporated into Middle Eastern political systems as essen-

---

[41] Nicolas Gavrielides, "Tribal Democracy: The Anatomy of Parliamentary Elections in Kuwait," in *Elections in the Middle East: Implications of Recent Trends,* ed. by Linda L. Layne (Boulder, Colo.: Westview Press, 1987), pp. 153–214.

[42] Linda L. Layne, "Tribesmen as Citizens: Primordial Ties and Democracy in Rural Jordan," in Layne, *Elections in the Middle East,* p. 135.

[43] Peterson, *The Arab Gulf States,* pp. 22, 120–121.

tial elements of state building. It is, therefore, important to examine both militaries and bureaucracies, as well as the weaker institutions of politics, the most widespread and probably most important of which are legislatures.

THE MILITARY

The Middle East is the most militarized region in the world as measured by size of military establishments in relation to population, and by military expenditures in proportion to economic output and governmental expenditures. In absolute terms, the military in the Middle East is larger and more expensive than anywhere else in the Third World. Turkey's 850,000-man army is the world's fifth largest peacetime military establishment. The manpower of Iran's regular armed forces combined with the *pasdaran*—the Revolutionary Guard militia that was built up to some 350,000 men during the war with Iraq—is at least the size of Turkey's military. Iraq's army grew from 140,000 in 1977 to about 1 million in 1990. Israel's rate of conscription has progressively increased since 1967. Israel is now inducting into its military 90 percent of all males, who have to serve in the reserves until age 55, making Israel's conscript army of over one-half million (including reserves) the world's largest as a percentage of its population. The Egyptian military, which had declined to some 350,000 in 1977 from more than a half-million at the time of the 1973 October War, has since been built back up to some 450,000. Syria, with a population less than one-quarter that of Egypt's, has almost 400,000 men under arms plus 300,000 reserves.

Such massive military establishments are consuming a large and growing share of these countries' resources. In recent years Israel has devoted over 40 percent of the government's budget, as much as 30 percent of the GNP, and over 16 percent of total economic resources to military expenditures.[44] Of the ten developing countries identified by the International Monetary Fund (IMF) in 1991 as consistently spending more than 15 percent of their gross domestic product (GDP)

---

[44] Joel Beinin, "Challenge from Israel's Military," *Merip Reports* 92 (December 1980): 6; and Moshe Lissak, "Paradoxes of Israeli Civil-Military Relations: An Introduction," in *Israeli Society and Its Defense Establishment: The Social and Political Impact of a Protracted Violent Conflict,* ed. by Moshe Lissak (London: Frank Cass, 1984), p. 8.

on the military, nine are in the Middle East.[45] From 1976 to 1985, about 15 percent of all goods imported into the Arab world were arms and military supplies, in comparison with 1.8 percent for the world as a whole and 5.6 percent for all developing countries.[46] In Egypt, per capita military expenditure nearly doubled between 1980 and 1985.[47] During that same period the percentage of central governmental expenditure on the military at least doubled and may even have tripled. Arms imports as a percentage of total imports nearly quadrupled in that same period. While from 1976 to 1979 Egypt spent more on both social security/welfare and economic services than on the military, since 1980 the military's share has been outpacing that of all other categories of government expenditures.[48]

The trend of increasing financial allocations to the military is a general one in the region. In the United Arab Emirates, for example, oil revenues declined from $19 billion in 1980 to $13 billion in 1983. During this same period, defense expenditures increased from 50 percent to 60 percent of the total budget. Simultaneously, cutbacks were made in social services.[49] In the same year (1983), Saudi Arabia spent $539,442 on each soldier but only $869 per capita on education and $433 per capita on health. At the time, approximately 70 percent of the population was illiterate and infant mortality was over 10 percent of live births.[50] Since 1990, Saudi Arabia has been the world's largest arms importer. Despite having spent upwards of $50 billion in the war against Iraq, and having had to borrow money from Western financial institutions to cover budget commitments, it sought to purchase from the United States in 1991 arms worth $23 billion.

Weapons at the disposal of the region's militaries are increasingly

---

[45] Alex Brummer, "How Military Spending Causes Social Degradation," *Guardian Weekly* (July 14, 1991), p. 6.

[46] Mehran Tamadonfar, "American Arms Sales to Arabs: The Politics of Dissonance and Appeasement" (Paper delivered to the 1988 Annual Conference of the Western Political Science Association, San Francisco, March 10–12, 1988), 7.

[47] Arms Control and Disarmament Agency, *World Military Expenditures and Arms Transfers, 1987* (March 1988), cited in Robert B. Satloff, *Army and Politics in Mubarak's Egypt* (Washington: The Washington Institute for Near East Policy, Policy Paper no. 10, 1988), p. 3.

[48] *Ibid.*, pp. 4–9.

[49] Altaf Gauhar, "Arab Petro-dollars Dashed Hope for a New Economic Order," *World Policy Journal* (Summer 1987): 448.

[50] *Ibid.*, p. 451.

lethal. They now include the most advanced warplanes in the world, thermonuclear bombs, and short- and medium-range ballistic missiles capable of inflicting great destruction, as indicated by the devastation such missiles visited on Iranian cities during the final months of the Iran-Iraq war and on Israel and Saudi Arabia in the second Gulf war. Prior to 1991, Iraq possessed massive stockpiles of chemical weapons, which it used against Iranian troops and its own Kurdish population. Israel, one of the world's seven nuclear powers, has what is widely reputed to be the fifth most powerful military in the world and has joined the exclusive list of states that have sent satellites into orbit, indicating among other things that it possesses nuclear-capable inter-continental ballistic missiles.

Given the continuing increase in the size and costliness of virtually all Middle Eastern militaries, it seems logical that the political role of those militaries would likewise be expanding. Paradoxically, by the standard measures of military intervention into politics, which are coups d'état and presence of military officers within political elites, precisely the opposite occurred in the 1980s. There were fewer coups d'état in that decade than in any of the preceding three. The percentage of officers in top-level political positions also generally declined. In Egypt, for example, there was a progressive reduction of officers serving in cabinet positions after Nasser's death. Military presence in that body reached a peak in the wake of the 1967 June War, when it was 65.4 percent.[51] Over the entirety of the Nasser period, officers constituted about one-third of cabinet members. By comparison, those with military backgrounds constituted less than 13 percent of all Sadat's ministers, and two-thirds of these were officers who had further technical training.[52] In the final Sadat cabinet, only the portfolios of defense and foreign affairs were held by those of military background. Mubarak's cabinets have typically had three or four officers, who have constituted some 10 percent of all ministers. The downward trend of officer representation in the cabinet reflects the situation in

[51] Richard H. Dekmejian, "Egypt and Turkey: The Military in the Background," in *Soldiers, Peasants, and Bureaucrats*, p. 33.

[52] Mark N. Cooper, *The Transformation of Egypt* (Baltimore: Johns Hopkins University Press, 1982), p. 144. See also Mark N. Cooper, "The Demilitarization of the Egyptian Cabinet," *International Journal of Middle East Studies* 14:2 (May 1982): 203–225; and Raymond A. Hinnebusch, Jr., *Egyptian Politics Under Sadat: The Post-Populist Development of an Authoritarian-Modernizing State* (Cambridge: Cambridge University Press, 1985), pp. 100–105.

other organs of government. Sadat, for example, engineered a demilitarization of governorships; by 1980, less than 5 were held by military men, compared with 22 of 26 in 1964. Under Sadat and Mubarak, there has been a gradual but steady decline in the ratios of former officers in the bureaucracy, including the prestigious ministry of foreign affairs.[53] The last successful coup d'état in Egypt was that which brought Gamal Abdel Nasser, General Muhammad Naguib, and the Free Officers to power in July 1952.

In the Fertile Crescent region, Arab armies have also been further distanced from government. In Lebanon, the military sought a gradual takeover of power after its commanding officer, General Fuad Shihab, was elected president in 1958. From then until 1970, "The army, with the violent opposition of some legislatures [sic], came to play a major role in political decision making."[54] But in the 1970 election, the army failed to engineer the election of its candidate, Elias Sarkis. Civilian MPs immediately set about taking their revenge. In 1972 the Chamber of Deputies established a committee to investigate corruption in the army. "The thoroughness of its investigation and the candidness with which it reported its findings firmly reestablished the political authority of the Chamber over the army."[55] During the 1975–1976 civil war, General Ahdab sought to impose the military's will in what became known derisively as "the TV coup," for the hapless general appeared on television announcing a takeover while the troops with which that was to be accomplished dwindled to naught. General Michel Aoun, commander of the military at the time of the scheduled 1988 presidential election, coveted the presidency but could not mobilize sufficient support to obtain it. In late 1990, he was dispatched into exile by Syria. For the past 30 years the Lebanese political system has not managed to do much, but it has succeeded in keeping the military from coming to power.

In neighboring Syria, the military plays a key political role, but it has not imposed a military dictatorship. Civilians occupy important posts in the cabinet and the Ba'th Party. Perhaps the most accurate and recent test of strength between the incumbent, semimilitary

[53] Robert Springborg, "The President and the Field Marshal: Civil-Military Relations in Egypt Today," *Merip Middle East Report* 147 (July–August 1987): 5.

[54] Abdo I. Baaklini, *Legislative and Political Development: Lebanon, 1842–1972* (Durham: Duke University Press, 1976), p. 232.

[55] *Ibid.*, p. 233.

regime of Hafez al-Assad and challengers whose strength was based almost entirely on command of various military units occurred when President Assad became ill in the fall of 1983. When it appeared he might die, several hopeful successors, including al-Assad's brother Rif'at, made their bids by mobilizing troops they commanded in and around Damascus. The president recovered sufficiently to appear in public, organize a mass demonstration in his support, and then cut the ground from under his challengers. In so doing, he brought the military back under effective control.

Even more impressive testimony to the ability of civilians to subordinate the military to their control are the changes that have taken place in Iraq. The first military coup in the Arab world was conducted there in 1936. Several more occurred subsequently until the Ba'th Party, acting through sympathetic military officers, seized power in July 1968. The civilian wing of the party then gradually asserted itself over Ba'thist officers and the military more generally. The culmination of this process was symbolized by Vice President Saddam Hussein's replacement of the president, General Ahmad Hassan al-Bakr, in June 1979. Saddam, a party stalwart, was trained as a lawyer. As Iraq fought a war against Iran that required total mobilization and resulted in hundreds of thousands of casualties, the military was kept under strict control by the president and the party. U.S. attempts to induce the military to overthrow Saddam Hussein after Iraq's invasion of Kuwait had by mid-1993 come to nothing. The war against Iraq also failed to produce a military takeover in Iran. In fact, it provided an opportunity for the Islamic government to bring the military more directly under its control.

In the other two non-Arab countries in the region, Israel and Turkey, however, trends in civil-military relations appear to be running in favor of the latter. In the Jewish state, military officers occupy an increasing percentage of key government positions. Turkey witnessed a coup d'état in September 1980 that brought to an end a decade of uninterrupted parliamentary government. These developments are paradoxical, for Israel and Turkey have the longest, best-established traditions of participatory government in the region.

Israel, since its creation in 1948, has been characterized by widespread participation in politics by military officers. Service in the Haganah, the chief military organization of the Yishuv, which was the Jewish community in Palestine prior to the creation of the state of Israel, was a primary pathway into the cabinet. Since 1948, over one-third of senior cabinet posts, including prime minister, deputy prime minister, and defense and foreign affairs ministers, have been held by professional officers, and their percentage has been steadily increasing.[56] Whereas before 1967 there had never been more than two reserve officers in the cabinet, since then the range has been between three and five officers. In the Knesset, comparative figures are between 0 and 5 until 1967, and between 5 and 10 after that time. Before 1967 the office of defense minister had never been filled by a senior army officer, whereas that post has now become virtually monopolized by former officers. Between 1948 and 1977, one-third of all retired generals became involved in full-time political careers.[57] The heads of the Mossad (intelligence service), Border Police, Civil Guard, Civilian Administration, and Airports Administration are now invariably senior officers, as are the directors of businesses considered essential to security, such as the electric company, oil refineries, and the national airline, El Al. Even in municipal elections, officers have since the 1970s been playing much more active roles, both as candidates and as staff of party organizations.[58] The political system at all levels, as well as senior management positions in both the public and private sectors, have become areas in which Israeli military officers play increasingly important roles.

The Turkish military, which has never been as heavily represented in the political elite as its Israeli counterpart, intervened directly in politics in 1960, 1971, and 1980, in each case returning to the barracks after altering the constitution in accordance with its own preferences. The longest interregnum of military rule followed the coup of September 12, 1980, with the return to civilian government through elections coming in November 1983. But while the Turkish military has on these three occasions intervened and restructured the civilian political system, thereby underlining its permanent presence in the wings, it has by no means been able to dictate its specific political preferences to the voters or the politicians. In the most recent episode, the architect of the military intervention, General Kenan Evren, attempted to pave the way for a more permanent, supervisory role for the military.

---

[56] Peri, *Between Battles and Ballots,* pp. 102–104.

[57] Alex Mintz, "The Military-Industrial Complex: The Israeli Case," in *Israeli Society and Its Defense Establishments,* p. 108.

[58] Peri, *Between Battles and Bullets,* p. 105.

He ran successfully for president, while an officer-dominated National Security Council (NSC) was created to oversee the civilian political process, a function which included screening candidates for office. In the 1983 elections, the NSC refused permission to virtually all formerly prominent political leaders to offer their candidacies. Nevertheless, in those elections the military-backed candidate, former four-star general Turgut Sunalp, whose Nationalist Democracy Party ran on a slogan proclaiming that it would be guided by the philosophy of the "September 12 Movement," failed to win. His party received less than one-quarter of the votes and finished third, the victor being Turgut Ozal's Motherland Party. Although Ozal had served as the NSC's deputy prime minister and minister of state for economic planning until July 1982, he won not because of his association with the military but because he was the candidate most distant from it.[59] In October 1989, Ozal succeeded Evren as president. In October 1991, freely conducted parliamentary elections brought Suleyman Demirel, who more than a decade before had been ousted by the military, back to the prime ministry.

Coups d'état in Sudan in 1989 and in Algeria in 1992—the first bringing to power an Islamicist-influenced government and the second preventing that from happening—indicate that the growing challenge of Islamic revivalism may cause Arab militaries once again to assume direct control of government. If this were to occur, it would suggest that what had been an interregnum of mainly civilian rule was a period in which those civilians were a facade behind which the military had always lurked. But whether the military returns to a more direct, active role in politics or retreats further from them, there is a widespread belief in the region, and especially in the Arab world, that armed forces, and the governments they originally fostered, have impeded development, not enhanced it. The decreasing legitimacy of military rule, for example, probably underlay the decision by the Algerian military in the wake of its January 1992 takeover to form a High State Council and select Muhammad Boudiaf, one of the historic leaders of the war of independence, to head it. When Boudiaf was then assassinated on June 29, 1992, the military strongman, General Khalid Nezzar, immediately nominated a successor, lest there be no screen behind which he and the military could hide.

---

[59] John H. McFadden, "Civil-Military Relations in the Third Turkish Republic," *The Middle East Journal* 39 (Winter 1985):69–85.

THE FAILURES OF MILITARY RULERS

The coups d'état that brought military officers to power in many Arab countries in the 1950s and 1960s were generally greeted enthusiastically by their populations. Anciens régimes, dominated by royal families and by oligarchies of landowners, frequently with ethnic or religious minorities occupying key economic positions, had failed to appreciate the depth of nationalist sentiment. Nor had they rapidly expanded either their economies or political participation. They were, therefore, weak and unpopular. Young military officers, on the other hand, imbued with nationalist, populist ideologies and possessing a variety of modern skills, appeared to offer great hope for a better national future. Many Western analysts concurred in this view. Manfred Halpern, for example, interpreted Middle Eastern militaries as "the instrument of the new middle class."[60] Middle Easterners—and Halpern—expected the military and other elements of that progressive class to modernize the economy and the polity.

These expectations were frustrated in less than two decades of military rule. Military officers were committed to secular nationalisms and various interpretations of socialism. They sought to impose these Western-derived systems of political beliefs on populations that did not understand them and were prepared to accept them only as long as their governments performed adequately:

> The ideologies of Turkicization in Turkey carried out by Ataturk and his followers, Persianization in Iran adopted by Rida Shah Pahlavi and his successors, and Arab nationalism in Egypt adopted by Nasser and in Syria and Iraq by the Ba'th Party—these have not yet successfully superseded the religious folk base. In spite of many decades of elitist indoctrination in Turkey, Iran, Egypt, Syria, and Iraq, traditional religious organizations . . . plus a wide variety of community-based political alliances, still remain the basic instruments of collective action at the popular level. The gap between military elitist ideology at the top and the continuation of religious and community-based organisations at the graft is a source of tension to military regimes.[61]

As long as those military regimes were able to claim successes in domestic and foreign affairs, their ideological formulations went more

---

[60] Manfred Halpern, *The Politics of Social Change*, p. 253.

[61] Khuri, "The Study of Civil-Military Relations," pp. 20–21.

or less unchallenged. But when their performance lagged, they were immediately confronted by those religious and community-based organizations that had remained impervious to the protracted ideological onslaught. The Arab failure against Israel in the June 1967 War led to regime changes in both Syria and Iraq and paved the way for the de-Nasserization of Egypt. The avant-garde ideology of opposition in the Middle East, by the mid-1970s, had become that of Islamic fundamentalism.

The political failure of the military was matched by its inability to guide national economies toward development. Overspending on itself has been one of the causes, but there are others. Too many resources have been allocated by governments dominated by officers to large, showcase projects. While civilian regimes have also suffered from the "edifice complex," "a new political language focusing on the big, the magnificent, the visible socially and politically, seems to always mark the ascendancy of the military to power."[62] A desire to maintain control over all aspects of the economy, which led to massive nationalizations, also did tremendous damage. The military and its associates in the bureaucracy lacked the skills to manage the thousands of enterprises they came to own. Corruption inevitably accompanied such control. It gradually suffused the civilian and military sectors. Egyptian officers, for example, enriched themselves during the war in Yemen (1962–1967) by loading up on duty-free goods in Aden and shipping the loot home on military aircraft. They subsequently retired into bureaucratic sinecures in the public sector, where many of them supplemented their incomes with ill-gotten gains. A sizable proportion of the real estate and movable property confiscated from the Egyptian royal family, from assorted "feudalists," and from those whom the regime simply did not like ended up in the hands of officers.

The Syrian military has, if anything, exceeded the Egyptian in laying claim to the country's wealth. Officers control various aspects of the economy and demand bribes before authorizing the delivery of goods or services. The Syrian officer corps has, since the Lebanese civil war, managed a sprawling business in smuggled merchandise in Syria and Lebanon. The military economic corporations set up by President Ja'far Numairi in the Sudan in 1982 became satrapies into which Numairi could dump retiring officers and thereby buy the loyalty of his military, and where they, in turn, obtained illegal "commis-

[62] Khuri, "The Study of Civil-Military Relations," p. 17.

sions."[63] By arrogating to themselves rights and privileges denied other sectors of the population and by extorting goods and services from the public they were in theory protecting, Middle Eastern militaries undermined their very claim to rule.

The military also failed to achieve the principal goal it set for itself, which was to integrate the population into a national whole, with the military itself serving as the model for that integration. Middle Eastern societies are not substantially less divided along class, ethnic, and religious lines than they were before military officers seized power, although in some countries, such as Egypt, Iraq, and Syria, disparities in wealth are less now than they were under anciens régimes. Militaries themselves have not developed into meritocratic, classless, nonsectarian institutions. In some, such as the Syrian and Iraqi militaries, Alawis and Sunni Arabs, respectively, predominate in key command positions. Militaries there serve as instruments of control for minorities. In the Iraqi army, Shiʻi Arabs constitute 80 percent of the fighting ranks but only 20 percent of the officer corps.[64] The Sudanese military is controlled by northern Arabs, who are using it to subdue southerners, who are Christian and animist. The South Yemeni military was dominated by the tribe of its former president, killed in the January 1986 civil war. Under General Aoun, the Lebanese military split into Christian and Muslim factions.

In many militaries in the region, the officer corps has become increasingly elitist as it has enriched itself. The gap between officers and enlisted men in salaries and conditions is huge. While the former are supplied with apartments, automobiles, privileged access to health care, educational and other facilities, soldiers frequently have to depend on their families for supplements to their meager incomes if they are to maintain any sense of dignity. This division between officers and enlisted men has contributed to growing disaffection among the latter, one manifestation of which is their increasing tendency today to join radical underground Islamic movements.

In Egypt, for example, numerous such groups have been appre-

---

[63] Henry Bienen and Jonathan Moore, "The Sudan: Military Economic Corporations," *Armed Forces and Society* 13 (Summer 1987): 489–516.

[64] Faleh Abd al-Jabber, "Why the Uprisings Failed," *Middle East Report* 176 (May–June 1992): 2–14.

hended since the assassination of Sadat in October 1981. Virtually all of them have contained soldiers and some have had noncommissioned officers. A few—including the al-Jihad group that killed Sadat, a splinter from it that surfaced in 1987 known as "Those Salvaged from Hell," and the so-called Video group (because it burned shops dealing in "decadent" videos) rounded up in July 1986—have had commissioned officers as members. More than 30 officers and 100 enlisted men were dismissed from the military in the wake of Sadat's assassination because of their sympathy for Islamic fundamentalism.[65] This and other evidence suggests that the Egyptian military is divided between an officer corps that is increasingly indulged by a regime anxious to placate it and enlisted men who are treated as cannon fodder; between officers who benefit disproportionately from spoils and those who resent the greed of their colleagues; and between those who are attracted by Islamic activism and those who adhere to the canons of secular nationalism. The Egyptian military, like others in the region, is neither a model for nor a vehicle of national integration. It even could, in certain conditions, become an instrument of national disintegration.

The Middle Eastern military has succeeded in a comparatively short period in discrediting itself and its claim to integrate nations socially and politically, to develop them economically and, in the case of the Arab armies, even to discharge adequately the task of national defense. Consequently there is widespread hostility toward politicians in uniforms, a factor which has contributed to the decline of military intervention into politics. That decline also attests to the fact that most armies are much more complex organizationally, socially, and politically than they were in the 1950s and 1960s. Universal conscription has brought those from diverse religious, ethnic, and regional backgrounds into the military. While officer corps were stridently nationalistic prior to the 1970s, now they are ideologically much more heterogenous. The tremendous increase in size and the growing technical sophistication of military establishments impede the formation of similar worldviews among officers and make plotting more difficult. Neither the composition and structure of contemporary armed forces nor the political milieu in which they operate is now conducive to their playing the political role they once did.

---

[65] Satloff, *Army and Politics in Mubarak's Egypt,* p. 31.

Means of Regime Control

Regimes do not rely on abstract sociological phenomena when confronting matters as critical as subordinating the military. Each government develops a system of control by which it seeks to defend itself from politically ambitious officers. These methods, which differ according to level of political development, include dependence on tribes, sects, and/or mercenaries; reliance on manipulative strategies rooted in patrimonialism; and use of political institutions. Many governments employ more than one method, either simultaneously or sequentially.

Use of Tribes, Sects, and/or Mercenaries In the most traditional political systems in the region, control over the military is asserted by rulers through their families and the tribes with which they are allied, an arrangement that occasionally is buttressed by the use of mercenaries. In Saudi Arabia, for example, a large force of Pakistani mercenaries was maintained as the ultimate guarantor of the regime for much of the 1980s. In the United Arab Emirates, most enlisted men and noncommissioned officers are Omanis or Baluchis, while Jordanians, Pakistanis, and British, as well as a few Emirate citizens, make up the officer corps. In Oman, the Sultan's Armed Forces, which along with the Iranian military put down the uprising in the Dhofar Province in the early 1970s, consisted primarily of British, Australian, South African, Jordanian, and other mercenaries. The Omani military still relies heavily on foreign troops and officers. One of the most famous military officers in the Middle East since World War II was John Glubb, or Glubb Pasha as he was known, an Englishman who commanded Jordan's Arab Legion until dismissed by King Hussein in 1956.

As these states have modernized, however, they have relied less on foreigners and more on families and tribes to control the military. Saudi Arabia has developed this method of tribal control most fully. Hundreds of Saudi princes are in the Saudi army, navy, and air force. The ministry of defense and aviation is a stronghold of the powerful Sudairi clan, which includes King Fahd and his brothers through the Sudairi wife of Abdul Aziz Ibn Saud, the founder of the state. The minister of defense is Fahd's brother Sultan. Nearly all of Sultan's sons are senior air force officers, including Prince Khalid, who heads air defenses, the fourth command of the Saudi armed forces. Sultan's deputy is his brother Turki. The National Guard and ministry of interior are also headed by a half brother and brother of the king, respectively. "In short, no ministerial post related to national security is outside the hands of the sons of Ibn Saud, and it has always been this way."[66]

In Jordan, three-quarters of the officer corps is drawn from East Bank tribes closely attached to the royal family. In North Yemen, following the truce that ended the civil war of the 1960s and prior to the coup that brought the modernizing officer Ahmad Hamdi to power in 1974, the state itself was so weak that the army was controlled by the country's dominant tribes.[67] In South Yemen, the radical Marxist Yemeni Socialist Party (YSP), sought to control the military at least in part through tribal connections. This strategy backfired in January 1986, when Dhali and Awaliq tribesmen, loyal to the rebel, radical faction in the YSP, turned their guns on officers and soldiers of the Dathina tribe, which was loyal to President Ali Nasir Muhammad.

Another primordial allegiance employed in controlling Middle Eastern militaries is that of sect or ethnic group. President Hafez al-Assad of Syria, himself an Alawi, relies heavily on members of his family, clan, and the Alawi sect in staffing key units. The Iraqi officer corps, especially at the higher levels, is dominated by Sunni Arabs from the so-called triangle area of Baghdad-Anah-Mosul, where they are predominant, and at the very highest levels by President Hussein and his relatives from his hometown of Takrit. But in Syria and Iraq, sectarian recruitment into the officer corps is neither absolutely ubiquitous nor deemed a sufficient means of control. The governments of these countries also rely on other techniques.

Patrimonial Strategies A wide array of manipulative strategies is employed in those states where neither traditional nor modern institutions are sufficiently cohesive to insulate rulers from their organizations of coercion. One such strategy is to divide and thereby rule the officer corps. President Sadat of Egypt preferred this method. No

---

[66] Ghassan Salameh, "Political Power and the Saudi State," *Merip Reports* 91 (October 1980): 9–10.

[67] Robert Burrowes, "State-Building and Political Construction in the Yemen Arab Republic, 1962–1977," in *Ideology and Power in the Middle East: Studies in Honor of George Lenczowski,* ed. Peter J. Chelkowski and Robert J. Pranger (Durham, N. C.: Duke University Press, 1988), pp. 210–238.

sooner would he promote an officer into a command position or to the lofty heights of chief of staff or minister of defense, than he would begin to look about for a successor. In the decade of Sadat's rule, he rotated seven officers through the post of minister of defense. The shah of Iran was also a master of the divide-and-rule strategy, so much so that the military simply fell apart when subjected to intense pressure at the time of the revolution. The commanders of the army, navy, air force, and national police force and the directors of the various intelligence organizations were permitted to communicate with one another only through the shah or his personal staff.

The sensitive task of gathering intelligence on the military is typically divided between several agencies, lest one become too powerful. In the shah's Iran, there were a dozen different military-security organizations all bound in mutual competition to the person of the shah. Although the situation has become somewhat simplified in the Islamic Republic of Iran, that government for a time witnessed considerable competition and tension between the *pasdaran* (revolutionary guards) and the regular army. In Syria, "Three military intelligence bureaus spend as much or more energy supervising the behavior of the officer corps than they do on conventional espionage."[68]

The Saudis, not content to control the military only by monopolizing key positions, have created a National Guard as an entirely separate structure from the regular military. It is "an extension of loyalist tribal groups, while the army is an outgrowth of the Hijazi troops inherited from the Sherif of Mecca."[69] The Guard is under the control of Crown Prince Abdullah, who is a half brother and rival to Minister of Defense Sultan. While the military recruits throughout the country, the Guard draws on tribesmen in the region of its various garrisons. Its chain of command is based on tribal authority rather than on military rank order. It is, in every way, intended to be separate from and a counterbalance to the military. Similarly, in Syria, Hafez al-Assad in the 1970s carved the army into a handful of different units, each with its own commander, uniform, internal loyalties, and patronage networks. The largest of these, the Siraa al-Difaa, was under the command of Hafez's younger brother Rif'at until it was disbanded in

---

[68] Yahya M. Sadowski, "Ba'thist Ethics and the Spirit of State Capitalism," in *Ideology and Power*, pp. 179–180.

[69] Salameh, "Political Power and the Saudi State," p. 9.

1984–1985. Nasser created a counterweight to the Egyptian regular army in the wake of Field Marshal Abd al-Hakim Amer's unsuccessful coup attempt in August 1967. This was the Presidential Guard which Nasser placed under General al-Laithi Nassif, who, along with his troops, provided the means by which Sadat subsequently levered his chief opponents, including Minister of War Muhammad Fawzi, out of office in May 1971. Nasser also created the Central Security Force (CSF) under the minister of interior in 1968 to control domestic dissenters. Sadat expanded it after the 1977 riots to over 300,000 men, in part to serve as a check on the regular military.

Rulers have also tried to erect legal and geographical barriers between their military establishments and the political order. President Bourguiba disenfranchised the military and denied officers and enlisted men the right of political association, even in the ruling Destourian Socialist Party.[70] Sadat prohibited officers from running for elected office. Joining a political party other than the Ba'th is a capital offense for Iraqi officers. In Syria, "Fraternization between officers and civilian elites ... [is] carefully policed by the Ba'th's Political Bureau."[71] President Mubarak has sought to insulate the Egyptian military, especially conscripts and noncommissioned officers, from political trends, such as Islamic fundamentalism, by shifting army camps away from populated areas and into the desert.

Patrimonial control mechanisms include the carrot as well as the stick. The fantastic growth of expenditure on Middle Eastern militaries is due in part to the desire to maintain the loyalty and subservience of the officer corps. An increasing percentage of military expenditures appears to be dedicated to officers' well-being. Conditions that obtain in Syria are typical in the region: "Officers are pampered: army cooperatives provide them with cost-price articles and with duty-free foreign imports not obtainable elsewhere in the country; interest-free loans allow them to buy villas and speculate in very lucrative real estate; and they receive generous salaries, free medical care, liberal travel allowances, and miscellaneous other fringe benefits."[72]

---

[70] L. B. Ware, "The Role of the Tunisian Military in the Post-Bourguiba Era," *The Middle East Journal* 39 (Winter 1985):27–29.

[71] Sadowski, "Ba'thist Ethics and the Spirit of State Capitalism," p. 179.

[72] Drysdale, "The Syrian Armed Forces in National Politics," p. 70.

Political Institutions   In the former communist systems, the military was subordinated to political decision makers largely through the efforts of the party and other elements of the state apparatus. In democratic polities, a participatory political infrastructure insulates the civilian political system. In the Middle East, examples of both such arrangements exist. "The party commands the gun, and the gun must never command the party," is Mao's colorful statement of the Leninist approach to civil-military relations.[73] In the Arab world, the Iraqi Ba'th Party most closely resembles the communist prototype. Party supremacy over the military is sought through indoctrination of officers and men and by the dispersal throughout the armed forces of political commissars, whose job is to ensure strict adherence to the party's line. Officers are required to attend formal classes in Ba'thist doctrine. Party membership is a virtual prerequisite for promotion. Only members of the party gain entrance to the military academy. No other political party is allowed contact in any way with military personnel. This Iraqi version of the classic Soviet and Maoist technique of subordinating army to party, in combination with a variety of patrimonial manipulative techniques, ensured President Saddam Hussein's control of the military during the long war with Iran and in the wake of Iraq's catastrophic defeat in 1991.

After the revolution in 1979, the Iranian system of control over the military came to resemble that of Iraq. Immediately after Ayatollah Khomeini came to power, a purge of the military was instituted. By 1986 over 23,000 officers had been liquidated or retired, some 45 percent of the officer corps. This purge was partly intended to intimidate remaining officers so that they would obey orders.[74] Lest they be tempted to do otherwise, in October 1980 the government created the Supreme Defense Council (SDC), the secretariat of which provides civilian political and ideological oversight of the armed forces.

The other notable example of Leninist-style party control over the military occurred in the Yishuv and then in the early years of Israeli statehood. The highly politicized Zionist migrants to Palestine from Russia, especially those who came between 1904 and 1914 and who constituted the crucially important second *aliya,* or wave of migration,

---

[73] Mao Tse-tung, *Selected Military Writings* (Peking: Foreign Languages Press, 1963), p. 272.

[74] Schahgaldian, *The Iranian Military Under the Islamic Republic* (Santa Monica, Calif.: Rand, 1987), p. 27.

had formed their attitudes and approaches to politics in Russian revolutionary movements. They subscribed to the Leninist principle of "building an effective political organizational structure so as to ensure the party's hegemony in society."[75] When they set about constructing a military wing in the late 1920s, which they named Haganah (Defense), they placed it first under direct control of the Mapai Party, then under the Histadrut, an arm of Mapai responsible for labor organization; subsequently the Haganah was transferred to the representative institutions of the Zionist movement over which Mapai, which eventually became the Labor Party, had control.

The Leninist formula of party control of the military was inappropriate once the state of Israel was created as a parliamentary democracy. David Ben-Gurion, first prime minister and minister of defense, recognizing that fact, transferred control of the Hanagah to the state itself, renaming it Zahal (Israeli Defense Forces—IDF). But the strong links between the military and Mapai, which had been forged over a 20-year period, were not dissolved overnight. The nexus between the two had been mutually beneficial. Of 44 generals who served in the highest posts in the General Staff from 1949 to 1977 (when Labor was voted out of office), almost 70 percent were Mapai members and another 15 percent were nonactive Mapai supporters.[76] The Servicemen's Department of Mapai, which was established in 1949, served as the major link between army and party. Its primary tasks were to screen officers for promotion and to recruit them into the party, which it did in semiclandestine, quasi-legal fashion.[77] Shimon Peres, later to become prime minister, was a key figure in the organization from 1949 until 1965. Moshe Dayan, whose last major post was foreign minister in the first Begin government, likewise was active in it.

The continuing increase in the number of former officers in Israeli politics suggests that the party's control is inadequate. Israel between 1948 and 1977 was not a single-party but a one-party-dominant state. Mapai could not dominate the military in the same fashion as the Soviet Communist Party did or as the Ba'th in Iraq does. The

---

[75] Yoram Peri, "Party-Military Relations," in *Israeli Society and Its Defense Establishment*, p. 47.

[76] *Ibid.*, p. 52.

[77] *Ibid.*, p. 55.

balance between party and military, which favored the former in 1948, tilted gradually in the latter's favor as Mapai declined. Officers gradually became able to dictate terms to civilian party members, rather than vice versa. In 1977, when Likud won a plurality of seats in the Knesset and formed its first government, what was left of the Labor-military connection was rendered meaningless. Significantly, Likud itself seized advantage of its incumbency in government to tie itself more closely to the military. It promoted such officers as Raful Eytan, who became chief of staff and whom Likud leaders saw as sharing a similar conservative political outlook. But Likud has been no more capable of controlling officers than was Labor. Eitan himself subsequently commenced a political career, founding his own ultranationalist party. Similarly, Ariel Sharon, the retired general whom Menachem Begin made minister of defense following Likud's second election victory in 1981, has become a dominant figure in that party. The system of party control over the military has, in short, collapsed.

There are, however, two additional methods by which the Israeli military's influence is restrained. One is the systematic prevention of the creation a barrier between the military and the rest of society. Universal conscription, reliance on reserves who can be rapidly mobilized, and steps to prevent the emergence of an elitist, separatist officer corps, including the absence of a military college for officer training, and early retirement of officers all serve to ensure that the military is an integral part of Israeli society. A measure of the success of this method is that politically active former officers hold a wide array of opinions and are members of political parties ranging from the most dovish to the most hawkish. Widespread participation within interest groups, political parties, and parliament is the second barrier between the military and outright political control.

In Turkey there is a similar ongoing competition between the military and institutions of political participation for control over policymaking. This has resulted in a watchdog function for the military. In 1960 the military, displeased by the increasingly autocratic tendencies of the Menderes government and its assault on the socioeconomic bases of Kemalism, forced the introduction of various democratizing measures, such as an electoral system based on proportional representation and guarantees of freedoms to universities, interest groups, and the media. In 1971 the military intervened once again to thwart anti-Kemalist forces and to contain growing student unrest. In 1980, after almost a decade of political immobilism and a rising tide of political violence, the military again seized power, abrogated the constitution, and imposed harsh restrictions on political behavior. On each of these occasions two factors worked to ensure that the military ultimately restored a substantial measure of autonomy to civilian politicians. The first was that the officer corps was not unanimously agreed on a course of action. The second factor is that since the elections of 1950 Turkey has had a tradition of representative democracy. While there is much cynicism about politicians and political parties, Turks are relatively committed to political institutions, especially parliament. While certain elements in the military "argued in 1960 and again in 1971 for the indefinite dissolution of the National Assembly . . . the certainty of public resistance" to this repressive measure ultimately caused those in control of the military to reject this proposal[78] as it did again after the 1980 coup.

Elsewhere in the region, civilians have not been as successful in creating and sustaining political institutions that could serve as checks on the expansion of the military into general policy-making areas. There may, however, be some movement in this direction. In Sudan, for example, the widespread mobilization by political parties, universities, and political groupings opposed to military domination caused the army to retreat to the barracks in 1964 and again in 1985–1986. But in 1989, the military, in league with Islamicists, staged another coup. It then instituted a reign of terror against opposition political groups. Opposition political parties are becoming increasingly vociferous in Mubarak's Egypt. Eventually they might serve as a real obstacle to military intervention, although the pessimistic prognosis of Adil Hussain, a prominent figure in one of the main opposition parties, suggests at the very least that this will take time. "Frankly," he observes, "I do not think pluralism or a multiparty system is as operational as some people think. I am not optimistic about its future in Egypt."[79] In general, civilian political institutions remain too weak in the Middle East to restrain the military; it has to be checked through the traditional or patrimonial methods discussed above.

---

[78] Marvin G. Weinbaum, "Classification and Change in Legislative Systems: With Particular Application to Iran, Turkey and Afghanistan," in *Legislative Systems in Developing Countries,* ed. by G.R. Boynton and Chong Lim Kim (Durham, N.C.: Duke University Press, 1975), p. 62.

[79] Cited in Dwyer, *Arab Voices,* p. 73.

The Military-Industrial Complex

The paradox of increasing military expenditures and growth in the size of armed forces, while coups are relatively infrequent and the ratio of officers to civilians in political elites is decreasing, may be more apparent than real. The growth of military-industrial complexes in the region is changing the socioeconomic nature of military establishments and altering relations between them and the political order. Civilian and military economic enterprises are becoming more closely integrated. The military, to assert influence over policy, in the past had to seize power. With the development of military-industrial complexes, the military's influence over policy is becoming more diffuse, broadly based, and substantive. Officers do not have to be in cabinets or parliaments or stage coups d'état to have significant influence over important economic and political decisions.

The production of increasingly sophisticated weapons in factories under direct military control, the manufacture of civilian goods by those same factories, and the increasing dedication of civilian industry to military production result in officers assuming the roles of managers, engineers, and businessmen. This development, in combination with the officer corps' preferential access to goods and services and its recruitment of highly trained personnel, has led to the embourgeoisement of the military. Whereas in the 1950s and 1960s Middle Eastern military officers were drawn primarily from the lower middle classes, they are now being recruited from among the sons of officers who have capitalized on their fathers' positions by gaining entry to military academies. Or young officers are being recruited from the urban middle and upper middle classes, who can afford to educate their children to the level required by modern militaries. Political attitudes reflect changing class origins. Whereas the previous generation of officers tended to be radical nationalists who favored state control of the means of production, those of the present generation are much more conservative. Their nationalism is of a more moderate nature, and they are more inclined to favor the private sector than did the previous generation of officers. Even the Islamicist-influenced military government in Sudan, for example, has embarked on an ambitious privatization program.

The growth of military-industrial complexes is evident throughout the Middle East. Arms production in the region, which was minimal at the end of the World War II, amounted to some $4 billion in 1987 and is steadily rising. Of the 23 Third World countries that produce significant quantities of arms, 5 are in the Middle East. Israel is the largest arms exporter in the Third World and one of the world's leading producers of weapons. Egypt, Turkey, Iran, and Pakistan are also major arms producers, and Algeria, Iraq, Jordan, Morocco, Saudi Arabia, Syria, Sudan, and Tunisia all manufacture munitions and small arms.[80]

Although Jews living in Palestine in the 1930s and 1940s created small arms and ammunition workshops, large-scale arms manufacturing in Israel really began after the 1967 war. In the following decade there was a tenfold increase in arms production. The proportion of employees in the defense sector to all Israeli employees increased two and a half times between 1967 and 1980. During that period Israeli Aircraft Industries (IAI), a government-owned firm that is at the heart of the military-industrial complex, increased its work force by almost five times. One-quarter of all of Israel's exports are arms, and 75 percent of its electronic and metal exports are in the form of weapons. Israel's ratio of armaments exports to total exports is the world's highest. Approximately 46 percent of all Israeli government expenditures for research and development are for arms and ammunition, compared with 2 percent in Japan, 3 percent in Holland, and 8 percent in Canada.[81]

As military industries have grown in Israel, so has integration increased between the defense and civilian sectors of the economy, and in both sectors the role of officers and retired officers has grown. It has become common practice for retired officers and reserve officers to hold senior positions in all firms involved in weapons production. IAI, Beit Shemesh, which builds engines, the large metal firms Elbit and Koor, as well as specific weapons projects such as the Merkava tank and the Lavi fighter (until it was canceled) have been headed by senior reserve officers. Conversely, these officers, once they have served in defense industries, commonly assume crucial positions in the ministry of defense. Moshe Arens, for example, who served as minister of defense in the 1980s under the Likud government and who became foreign minister after the 1988 elections, previously was deputy director general of IAI. "It thus emerges that there is a network of senior military officers in key positions extending over

[80] Joe Stork, "Arms Industries of the Middle East," *Merip Middle East Report* 144 (January–February, 1987):12.

[81] Mintz, "The Military-Industrial Complex," pp. 110–112.

all branches of the complex," leading to "the increased influence of the complex . . . upon the formation of perceptions and policies."[82]

In Turkey, a military-industrial complex has also been emerging since the 1960s. The financial driving force behind the military's entry into the industrial and service economies has been military support funds. The first of these, Oyak, runs a chain of supermarkets, has large interests in Turkey's leading petrochemical, automotive, and food-processing businesses, and serves as the primary local partner in joint ventures with Renault, Goodyear, and various other multinational corporations. The other armed forces followed the lead of Oyak and the army. The air force, for example, created a support fund which in turn took up 45 percent of the shares of Tusas (Turkish Aircraft Industries), established in 1973. In a joint venture with General Dynamics and General Electric, it now produces the F-16 fighter plane.[83] Turkey's military industries in the mid-1980s employed over 40,000 people and exported in 1985 almost a half-billion dollars worth of weapons, compared with only $160 million in 1982. At present rates of growth, Turkey will become the world's 14th largest arms producer in the 1990s.[84]

The governments of Turgut Ozal and Suleyman Demirel have sought not only to encourage military production but also to integrate the activities of the military support funds, the public sector, and private firms. In 1986 the government established the Defense Industry Development and Support Administration in order to determine arms manufacturing priorities and to allocate $650 million annually in "defense funds."[85] Partly as a result of this encouragement, private firms are rapidly commencing defense-related manufacturing operations, particularly in the form of joint ventures with foreign companies. These developments have served further to interconnect military officers with the private sector of the economy. "It has now become almost a tradition to offer positions on the executive boards of corporations to high officers, especially generals."[86]

---

[82] *Ibid.*, p. 109.

[83] "The Private Sector Mounts an Attack," *South* (March 1988): 12.

[84] Omer Karasapan, "Turkey's Armaments Industries," *Merip Middle East Report* 144 (January–February 1987): 27–31.

[85] Omer Karasapan, "Turkey's Super Rich," *Merip Reports* 142 (September–October 1986): 31.

[86] Ahmed Kemal, "Military Rule and the Future of Democracy in Turkey," *Merip Reports* 122 (March–April 1984):13.

In many Arab countries the pattern of increased arms production by the military and by public and private sector and joint venture firms, accompanied by the expansion of military enterprises into the civilian economy and the deployment of military officers into technical and managerial positions, is also being followed. Egypt has gone furthest in this direction. By the early 1980s it was the Third World's ninth leading producer of weapons, manufacturing annually approximately $1.4 billion worth of arms. Two percent of the urban labor force (85,000 Egyptians) are employed in the arms industry, which makes Egypt the Third World's fourth-largest employer for weapons production. The military under President Mubarak has come to play an increasingly important economic role. It produces approximately one-fifth of all domestically produced and marketed foodstuffs; reclaims large tracts of desert land; builds more roads and installs more communication facilities than any other institution in the country; and runs hospitals, training academies, tourist resorts, shopping centers, and newly constructed desert cities. The military, in sum, operates a vast empire that extends far beyond weapons manufacturing. Thousands of officers and former officers are employed in these various operations. As a group they have become one of the very wealthiest categories of professionals in the country.[87]

In Syria, Iraq, and Sudan, as in Egypt, military officers now perform a wide variety of economic roles, many in association with local private sector firms or multinational corporations. Syria's military, although supporting a comparatively small arms industry, operates the largest construction business in the country, produces and processes large quantities of food, and manages a nationwide chain of retail outlets. The Iraqi military controls the Military Industries Commission, which produced, among other things, the modified Scud missiles used to bombard Iran and, subsequently, Israel and Saudi Arabia. Sudan's Military Economic Corporations, which operated in the final years of the Numairi era, became the largest business conglomerate in the country, concentrating particularly in importation and marketing. An estimated 80 percent of its trade was conducted with the private sector.[88] In these and other Arab countries, officers are rapidly developing into a visible and powerful economic elite.

---

[87] Robert Springborg, "The President and the Field Marshal," pp. 4–16.

[88] Bienen and Moore, "The Sudan: Military Economic Corporations," p. 503.

The emergence of military-industrial complexes is associated with the development of a new political role for the armed forces. In the two decades or so after World War II, Middle Eastern militaries, fired by nationalist ideology, played basically progressive roles, overthrowing oligarchies and establishing the state as the guiding force in economies. Since that time they have become much more conservative. Increasingly allied with urban middle and upper classes and tied to indigenous and foreign private businesses, officers no longer constitute a vanguard for radical change. Indeed, Middle Eastern militaries have come to play a role similar to that played for several decades by many of their Latin American counterparts. According to Samuel P. Huntington, this is because

> as society changes, so does the role of the military. In the world of oligarchy, the soldier is a radical; in the middle-class world he is a participant and arbiter; as the mass society looms on the horizon he becomes the conservative guardian of the existing order. Thus, paradoxically but understandably, the more backward a society is, the more progressive the role of its military; the more advanced a society becomes, the more conservative and reactionary becomes the role of its military.[89]

Armed forces in the Middle East, like those in Latin America, now desire not the expansion of political participation but the containment of it. Their preferred political role is a supervisory one, standing in the wings to ensure that the politicians do not undertake initiatives that run counter to the military's interests. L. B. Ware, commenting on the Tunisian military, sees this as a process of internal "colonization," where "senior military officers exercise a careful surveillance over important civilian posts—much in the same way the French organized a system of *contr[ô]le civil* parallel to the beylical government during the Protectorate period."[90] The Turkish military hesitated to seize power in the late 1970s despite the rising spiral of violence because

> the officers' class interests dictated a continuation of the status quo . . . rather than the assumption of direct military rule. Indeed, it was safer for the military to stay in the background and permit the civilian politicians to carry out its wishes and be blamed for the consequences. This conser-

---

[89] Samuel P. Huntington, *Political Order in Changing Societies* (New Haven, Conn.: Yale University Press, 1968), p. 225.

[90] Ware, "The Role of the Tunisian Military," p. 41.

vative orientation of the military elite was in sharp contrast to the reformist sentiments of the Turkish military in previous decades.[91]

In sum, the military in the Middle East may be no less powerful politically than it was when officers dominated cabinets and staged repeated coups d'état. What is new is that its influence is exerted subtly and through many channels. The outlook and political alliances of the military have also changed. Equally, Middle Eastern societies, economies, and polities have become more complex. Demands for political participation are increasing. So too are criticisms of the military, its embourgeoisement, and its "colonial" political role. The military and its critics are, therefore, set on a collision course that may, in some countries of the region, result in major conflicts during the 1990s, as it already has done in Algeria and Sudan.

THE BUREAUCRACY

Middle Eastern bureaucracies are in one of four possible stages of sequential development. The initial phase is characterized by the continuing supremacy of traditional political forces (rural notables, families, tribes) over bureaucracies as well as other governmental institutions. At this stage, bureaucracies, although they may be growing and staffed by increasingly well-trained personnel, lack political allies and administer only with sustained interference by powerful traditional forces. They are thoroughly penetrated by clientage networks that extend downward from traditional elites. The Saudi civil service, for example, expanded from a few hundred employees in the 1940s to about one-quarter of a million in 1980 and 624,000 in 1991.[92] Despite such rapid growth, the Saudi bureaucracy remains subordinate to royal authority. Until very recently this was exercised in a highly capricious fashion.

> Given the centralization of authority in the hands of the king and senior officials, initiative was rare and since promotion depended on ascriptive

---

[91] Dekmejian, "Egypt and Turkey," p. 46.

[92] Abdul Rahman Osama, *The Dilemma of Development in the Arabian Peninsula* (London: Croom Helm, 1987), p. 66; and John Presley and Tony Westaway, "Economic Liberalisation in Saudi Arabia," paper presented to the Symposium on Economic Liberalisation and Its Social and Political Effects in the Middle East, Exeter University, Exeter, England (September 26–28, 1991), p. 6.

factors rather than on ability or performance, there was hardly an incentive to perform well. Further, the importance of family ties dictated that senior bureaucrats promote family members and tribal relations regardless of their qualifications. Nepotism, far from being looked down upon, was a requisite and expected practice.[93]

The Jordanian civil service grew by 300 percent in 15 years—from 27,000 in 1970 to 74,000 in 1985. Despite various attempts to professionalize new recruits, "The Jordanian bureaucracy remains constrained by a particularistic style of decision making at all levels. Over the years, tribal loyalties have been a more powerful focal point of identification and action than loyalties to the state."[94] While the Jordanian and Gulf states' bureaucracies have become somewhat more insulated from interventions by tribes and ruling families in recent years, they are still far from playing the leading role in modernization that their counterparts have played elsewhere in the region.

The Lebanese bureaucracy, which along with the military was intended by President Fuad Shihab, who came to power in 1958, to serve as a principal tool of development, was not equal to the task. Traditional leaders of the various confessions mobilized against Shihabism, an alliance of the bureaucracy and the military, and defeated it in the 1970 election. The Lebanese bureaucracy, which for just over a decade had held out the promise of becoming a professional organization at least partially insulated from traditional notables, reverted to its previous role of being a source of patronage for these elites.

The second phase of bureaucratic development occurs when, usually in alliance with the military and typically led by a strong, modernizing figure, the bureaucracy takes charge of a wide range of development tasks and by so doing enhances its prestige and rewards. Joining the bureaucracy becomes the preferred career choice of bright, well-trained young men and women. This pattern obtained, for example, under Ataturk and into the 1950s in Turkey. In Egypt, Nasser relied heavily on the bureaucracy. Prominent bureaucrat-administrators became leading figures in the country. The bureaucracy came to overshadow not only policy-making institutions such as the parliament and

---

[93] Summer Scott Huyette, *Political Adaptation in Sa'udi Arabia: A Study of the Council of Ministers* (Boulder, Colo.: Westview Press, 1985), pp. 105–106.

[94] Jamil E. Jreisat, "Bureaucracy and Development in Jordan," *Journal of Asian and African Studies* 24 (1989): 99.

single party, but also the private sector of the economy. Similarly, Israel at independence in 1948 inherited a coherent, professional bureaucratic apparatus from the Yishuv. That bureaucracy continued to play important political and economic roles for the next 30 years, until a reaction against it began to gain momentum in the late 1970s.

The best current example of the second phase of bureaucratic development is to be found in Yemen, where the government, based on a coalition of party elites from the former South Yemen and military figures from what was the Yemen Arab Republic, has teamed up with the bureaucracy to modernize the country and undercut the power of the tribes. Resources for the rapidly expanding bureaucracy are being provided by steadily growing earnings from oil exports. Educated Yemenis, enthusiastic about their jobs and the prospects for having a positive impact on their country's future, are pouring into the bureaucracy. In a similar fashion, the ruling family of Bahrain established a modern central administration as part of its efforts to undermine the country's active labor movement during the 1950s and 1960s. The expansion of the Bahraini bureaucracy, while not initiated by the armed forces, has been accompanied by substantial increases in military spending.[95]

Erosion of professionalism, internal incoherence, weakening status, and decreasing rewards characterize the third phase through which bureaucracies pass. In Turkey, the transition from stage two to stage three began comparatively early. In the heyday of Kemalism, the bureaucracy "by itself jealously assumed the burden of the modernization function."[96] But as the Turkish polity modernized, new groups arose to challenge the hegemony of the bureaucracy. Politically, that challenge took the form of the Democrat Party, which recruited widely from among the emerging independent bourgeoisie. The Democrat Party won the 1950 election advocating laissez-faire policies. For the next three decades, Turkish politics centered on a struggle between the bureaucracy and new middle-class elements that supported it, most of which were loyal to the Republican People's Party (RPP), on the one hand, and a coalition of opposing forces, including small-town

---

[95] Lawson, *Bahrain,* ch. 4.

[96] Metin Heper, "Political Modernization as Reflected in Bureaucratic Change: The Turkish Bureaucracy and a Historical Bureaucratic Empire Tradition," *International Journal of Middle East Studies* 7 (October 1976): 510.

petit bourgeoisie and urban industrialists, merchants, and independent professionals on the other. Initially the military sided with the bureaucracy. The 1960 intervention was intended to support the civil administration and its call for state control of the economy at a time when such programs were losing their appeal. Those lower in the social order resented the prestige, power, and rewards of the bureaucrats. Entrepreneurs viewed bureaucrats as obstacles to their activities and a drain on the public treasury. Consequently, the RPP could not win parliamentary majorities and maintain control of government. Simultaneously, the growth of the military-industrial complex, which resulted in an embourgeoisement of the officer corps, placed increasing strain on the military-bureaucratic alliance. In 1980, when the military intervened once again, it associated itself not with the civil administration, but with its opponents and their preferred policy of supporting export-led economic growth under the auspices of the private sector.

Various manifestations of bureaucratic decay characterized this period of confrontation between the emerging bourgeoisie and the Turkish civil service, including loss of parliamentary seats by bureaucrats and their allies, growing strain in the alliance between the bureaucracy and the political party that formerly represented its interests, diminution of the status of bureaucrats, increasing conflict within the bureaucracy, and rising job dissatisfaction.[97] Civil servants, who constituted over half of the deputies in the 1927 Grand National Assembly and over a third in the 1946 Assembly, in the 1961, 1965, 1969, and 1973 Assemblies garnered about one-quarter of the seats. In 1977 civil servants won only 15 percent of the seats. Between 1950 and 1965 the purchasing power of the civil servants dropped by half.[98]

A further characteristic of the era of conflict between administrators and members of the bourgeoisie is that the latter, despite their growing influence, are still unable to establish autonomy and coherence as a collective pressure group. This is common in Third World settings, where "there develops a symbiotic relationship of 'antagonis-

---

[97] Leslie L. Roos, Jr., and Noralou P. Roos, *Managers of Modernization: Organizations and Elites in Turkey (1950–1969)* (Cambridge, Mass.: Harvard University Press, 1971), pp. 201–206.

[98] Metin Heper, "The Recalcitrance of the Turkish Public Bureaucracy to 'Bourgeois Politics': Multi-Factor Political Stratification Analysis," *The Middle East Journal* 39 (Autumn 1976): 492.

tic cooperation' between government official and private entrepreneur. The official supplements his inadequate official income. In exchange, the businessman is permitted to violate regulations."[99] In Turkey the parasitic character of indigenous capitalism is long-standing, where "dependence upon the state promoted an inclination to become grand manipulators of the bureaucratic mechanism. To have 'connections' and to develop close relations with the key figures in the bureaucracy have become most desirable."[100] Because businessmen seek connections to individuals in government rather than engaging in collective action to bring about structural changes, political organizations representing them remain weak and fragmented, as they did in Turkey through at least the mid-1970s.

Much of the Arab world is currently in this third stage of bureaucratic evolution. The military has from the late 1970s been deserting its former civil service allies, its officers instead seeking contacts with private entrepreneurs. The size of Arab bureaucracies has generally continued to expand, although there is much criticism of such growth and there have been numerous attempts to restrict it. In Iraq, for example, in the final stages of the war with Iran, the government abolished entire administrative departments, giving bureaucrats the choice of unemployment or volunteering for military service. In Egypt, the government has not yet dared to amend the Nasserist decree which provided every graduate the right to a government job, but it has expanded to several years the delay between graduation and appointment to a bureaucratic sinecure. Despite attempts to brake bureaucratic growth, the Egyptian civil service has swollen from 1.2 million employees in 1969–1970, when it constituted some 3.8 percent of the population, to over 5 million in 1992, or almost 10 percent of all Egyptians. One of every two Egyptians in the urban work force is employed by the government.[101]

The tremendous growth of the Egyptian and other Middle Eastern bureaucracies has been due in large measure to the desire by governments to buy the compliance of their citizens. That strategy is now being undermined because bureaucratic sinecures pay so little. Mid-

[99] Riggs, "Bureaucrats and Political Development," p. 422.

[100] Heper, "The Recalcitrance of the Turkish Public Bureaucracy," p. 496.

[101] Robert Springborg, *Mubarak's Egypt: Fragmentation of the Political Order* (Boulder, Colo.: Westview Press, 1989), pp. 137–138.

dle-ranking administrators in most Middle Eastern bureaucracies receive salaries that place them economically in the lower middle class, their incomes being well below those of skilled tradesmen. Moonlighting is a ubiquitous practice among Middle Eastern civil servants. The extortion of *bakhshish* (tips) from those wanting services has become a standard expectation.

The transition from stage two to stage three in the evolution of many Arab bureaucracies occurred in the wake of the October 1973 War and the associated oil embargo that ultimately resulted in vastly increased revenues for oil producers. President Sadat declared the policy of *infitah* (opening), which entailed, among other things, encouragement of the private sector and an attack on the institutional legacies of Nasserism, including the swollen bureaucracy. Other Arab countries followed suit, but in none of them has the bureaucracy's power been so reduced and that of representative institutions and voluntary associations so increased that the bureaucracy could be said to have become a servant of the popular will.

Bureaucratic tenacity is due principally to the fact that ruling elites, much of whose power rests on the bureaucracy, are wary of abandoning this support base for the unknown of democratic, participatory politics. Social forces desirous of increased freedoms and a reduction of the power of the bureaucracy, including entrepreneurial bourgeoisies, are insufficiently powerful to force this transformation. For their part, bureaucracies operate from entrenched bases of power and are not easy to dislodge. They either control or operate in conjunction with ruling political parties. The various rewards and punishments that the bureaucracy doles out, such as issuing of licenses, discriminatory application of regulations, and so on, underpin the dominant position of ruling parties and are at the heart of systems of political control. So while Arab bureaucracies generally are on the defensive, they have yet to be brought to heel by their challengers.

The transition from stage three to stage four, at which point the bureaucracy becomes thoroughly depoliticized, professionalized, and subordinate to popularly selected political leaders, is not an easy one. No Arab country has, in fact, made it. Israel and Turkey, however, are in the process of significantly reducing the power of their civil administrations and enhancing the autonomy of other economic and political actors. In Israel, this process was initiated when the Likud bloc won the 1977 elections. Much of the power of its chief rival, the Labor Party, had historically been based on its interconnections with first the

Zionist, and subsequently the Israeli, governmental bureaucracy. Likud adopted the strategy of seeking to undermine the bureaucracy while trying to seize control over as much of it as possible. Since the late 1970s, bureaucratic salaries and conditions have deteriorated, the private sector's share of economic output has increased, and the nexus between the bureaucracy and the Labor Party is neither as strong nor as efficacious as it was previously. Although these developments are not yet irreversible, Israel appears to have accomplished a reduction in the power of its civil administration, although it remains a much more prominent force in the political arena than its counterpart in the United States or in most European countries. The other components of the fourth stage of bureaucratic development, which are impartiality and competence, have yet to be achieved—but then they frequently are not yet achieved in the First World either.

Turkey's bureaucratic development in recent years has paralleled that of Israel. Those army officers who ran the country from September 1980 until November 1983 were strong supporters of private enterprise and trenchant critics of the bureaucracy and its connections to the remnants of the Republican People's Party. Turgut Ozal's Motherland Party, which is committed to encouraging private-sector growth, also kept the bureaucracy on the defensive from 1983 to 1991, as has its successor, the True Path Party of Soleyman Demirel. But as is the case in Israel, Turkey is still in the process of downgrading the bureaucracy and attempting to sever its long-standing connection with a particular political party. This has resulted in despondency and alienation among bureaucrats. The phase of professionalization and effective administration is yet to begin.

The level of bureaucratic development is a good measure of political development more generally. In the most traditional Arab countries, ruling oligarchies remain suspicious of bureaucrats and their political ambitions and continue to control them through personalistic means. Bureaucrats compete with oligarchs to establish clienteles and spheres of influence. At a second level, Yemen is currently at the stage of bureaucratic modernization that characterized Egypt, Syria, Iraq, Sudan, Algeria, and Lebanon in much of the 1950s and 1960s. Most of the latter have, in turn, passed on to a third stage, where the shortcomings of bureaucratic- and military-led development have resulted in economic and political crises that remain unresolved. Despite much lip service to democratization and reforms that would enhance the efficiency and integrity of their bureaucracies, political elites in most of these countries have come to power through the military-bureaucratic alliance. So far they have been unwilling to take the gamble, as has the Turkish political elite, of seeking to transform the system into a much more participatory one in which the bureaucracy's power would be reduced. Until this is attempted, the bourgeoisie and other social forces will continue to predicate both their economic and political strategies on assumptions of bureaucratic hegemony. Only in Israel and Turkey, which also have traditions of bureaucratic domination, but which also have comparatively well-developed countervailing institutions of political participation, has bureaucratic hegemony been severely challenged.

LEGISLATURES

Legislatures are typically the major governmental arena within which political forces legally contend for influence. Although in the Middle East most governments restrict access to legislatures and in various other ways prevent them from becoming representative bodies within which policies are made, legislatures are nevertheless worthy of analysis. They serve as a barometer, measuring degrees of institutionalized political participation. If legislatures are hampered by restrictions, so too will be political parties, interest groups, and other organs of the political infrastructure. Legislatures are also more widespread in the region than political parties, which are banned in all the Arab monarchies of the Gulf.

There is, both in Islam and in tribal traditions, respect for the practice of consultation, which in turn serves as cause and justification for the creation of consultative assemblies. Through the process of adaptive modernization described above, those assemblies may ultimately develop into full-blown legislatures. Indeed, it was precisely this path of development that parliaments followed in Europe. They began as assemblies of notables who advised the sovereign and served on his suffrance. Eventually they developed internal factions, which, in turn, ultimately looked outside the assembly to mobilize political support. In so doing they laid the foundations of political parties and parliamentary democracy.

Parallel developments have occurred in Middle Eastern legislatures. Khedive Isma'il of Egypt, for example, created an Assembly of Notables in 1866 in order to diffuse domestic criticism of his profligate expenditures and to enhance his standing with Western creditors. That Assembly, intended by Isma'il to be a docile gathering of traditional rural notables, grew increasingly vociferous in its criticism of the khedive, becoming a focal point for mobilization against him and the European powers. In 1878, a petition was presented to Isma'il demanding that he transfer some of his powers to the Assembly. He responded by dismissing it. The following year he was forced to abdicate in favor of his son Tawfiq.

The struggle between the Ottoman sultan Abd al-Hamid and liberal reformers also centered on parliament, which the sultan prorogued in 1878. The sultan was subsequently deposed by the Young Turks, who convened in 1908 a Majlis al-Mab'uthan (Chamber of Delegates), a federal parliament for the empire. Confrontation between Muhammad Ali Shah and the combined clerical and modernist opposition in Iran at the turn of the century crystallized on the demand by the latter for a parliament, a demand finally realized as a result of the 1905–06 constitutional revolution. In 1908 the shah repudiated the constitution and ordered his Cossack brigade to bombard the parliament. The following year he was forced to abdicate in favor of his son, and a new parliament was elected. Almost a half century later the challenge to Muhammad Reza Shah mounted by his prime minister, Muhammad Musaddiq, was channeled through parliament. In 1976 President Sadat permitted relatively free elections to the People's Assembly, in part to impress Washington, with which he was developing an alliance. Three years later he had to terminate the legislative session before it had completed half its legal term, for some of its members seized the opportunity to register their protest against his policy of peace with Israel. In Turkey the National Assembly is the principal focus of governmental legitimacy. By so being it has compelled the military to return to the barracks following its three interventions into politics since 1960.

Why Ruling Elites Establish Legislatures

Currently there are three different types of legislatures in the Middle East. The least well institutionalized, which generally are the newest, perform only consultative, not truly legislative functions. They serve at the behest of monarchs. A significant percentage if not all of their members are appointed by the ruler. Such bodies exist in Oman, the United Arab Emirates, Qatar, and, as of 1993, Saudi Arabia. The second type are legislatures that have some involvement in lawmaking; that enjoy, at least intermittently, the possibility of openly criticizing regime policies and personnel; that are constituted primarily through elections which are subject to manipulation; and that may incorporate formal or quasi-formal oppositions. These legislatures currently are to be found in Egypt, Iran, Iraq, Jordan, Tunisia, Morocco, Syria, and Yemen. They existed formerly in Kuwait (1963–1976 and 1981–1986), Bahrain (1973–1975), and Algeria prior to the coup of January 1992. Finally, legislatures that have major responsibilities for lawmaking; that are constituted as a result of elections which are contested by two or more parties and are more or less fair; that serve as the basis upon which government is formed; and in which active, formal oppositions have a well-established role, are to be found in Israel and Turkey. Such a legislature also existed between April 1986 and June 1989 in Sudan. The Lebanese parliament prior to 1975 was likewise within this third category, although it never established the autonomy and legislative powers characteristic of both the Israeli Knesset and the Turkish National Assembly.

All legislatures now functioning in the Middle East except those in Turkey and Israel have been created as a result of unilateral decisions by ruling elites. As there are numerous examples of parliaments challenging rulers, it must be asked why elites take the risk of bringing into existence bodies that could ultimately turn against them.

Legitimation   Eight monarchies remain in the Middle East, more than in any other region of the world. Their subjects today, in contrast with previous eras, "are profoundly aware of alternatives to dynastic rule." Such rule must, therefore, "be made to appear 'natural' and 'just.' . . . The late shah went so far as to assert that Persian kingship was based upon the will of the people. . . . Other Gulf rulers continue to make analogous claims."[102] In short, kingship no longer legitimates itself, if indeed it ever did. Royal authority now must be buttressed at a minimum by lip service being paid to popular participation in decision making. Parliaments perform this function better than other institutions.

> By its mere existence, the legislature creates the idea that the broad public is represented. Nothing is more likely to legitimate a political system

---

[102] Dale F. Eickelman, "Kings and People: Oman's State Consultative Council," *The Middle East Journal* 38 (Winter 1984): 51.

than the feeling that those who govern are representative of groups or interests in society. Because so many countries today are subdivided into political subcultures, the legislature is the critical means for creating the feeling that "one (or more) of ours is up there too!"[103]

Legitimation of regimes in the eyes of their neighbors and before the world is facilitated by the creation of legislatures or by enhancing the standing of preexisting ones. The al-Sabah rulers of Kuwait created a National Assembly immediately after attaining independence in 1961 in order to establish their country's claim to sovereignty against an Iraqi challenge. The al-Khalifa of Bahrain created an assembly shortly after announcing their islands' independence from Great Britain. President Sadat had his eye on Washington when he upgraded the Peoples' Assembly in the wake of the 1976 elections. Saddam Hussein, in announcing shortly after he became Iraq's president in June 1979 that elections to a newly created National Assembly would be held, was declaring before the Middle East and the world that the Ba'thist regime which had been established 11 years earlier by a coup was now legitimate, well established, and confident of its popularity. In Oman, Sultan Qabus, who was placed on the throne in 1970 by a British-supported coup against his tyrannical father, Sultan Said bin Taimur, had several years later still taken no steps to establish any form of permanent advisory council other than the cabinet. Western diplomats, mindful of the insurrection that had nearly succeeded in the Dhufar Province of Oman, urged Qabus to initiate steps to create some "form of consultative body such as had by then come into existence in neighboring states."[104] In 1981 the State Consultative Council was created, its 45 members were appointed by the sultan, and Oman entered the ranks of the more than 130 countries that have some form of legislature. A decade later the Council was reconstituted on the basis of elections to some of the seats and appointment to others. In Iran, the existence of a national legislative body (the Majlis) survived the shattering revolution of 1978–1979. The National Consultative Assembly has given way to the Islamic Consultative Assembly, an institution that is the scene of surprisingly lively debate and discussion.

---

[103] LaPalombara, *Politics Within Nations,* p. 159.

[104] Eickelman, "Kings and People," p. 54.

Communication   Creation of legislatures also facilitates communication among elite members as well as between the elite and the masses. In Oman, for example, the members of the State Consultative Council (SCC) were drawn principally from government and secondarily from the tribal and mercantile notabilities. Oman is highly diverse, both demographically and geographically. Governmental and so-called popular representatives, despite their elite status, had little if any previous contact. "A major achievement of the SCC has been to provide regional delegates with a structured forum through which they can develop working relationships with participating senior officials and delegates from other regions. Conversely, it provides officials participating in the SCC with regular access to the views from the periphery."[105] When the SCC was reorganized in 1991, representation of each of the country's provinces was mandated by the sultan.

The Lebanese parliament formerly provided an arena in which communication within the elite could occur. Those contacts were absolutely vital to the functioning of the country's "consociational democracy." This is a form of democracy in deeply divided societies in which lack of contact and mutual hostility between different ethnic and religious groups at the mass level is overcome by flexible, accommodating elites.[106] The Lebanese parliament provided an important arena in which Muslim and Christian elites could fraternize. Its virtual demise contributed to the polarization that characterized confessional relations at both the mass and elite levels during and after the civil war. Resuscitated in the wake of the Ta'if Accord of 1989, the Lebanese parliament remains hobbled by Syrian influence and is unable, as it once did, to facilitate extensive communication within the elite.

Communication between elites and masses may have been only marginally improved by many Middle Eastern legislatures. Since the majority of them are consultative assemblies of notables, or their membership is heavily dominated by government officials and those of the upper-middle and upper classes, the masses are generally not represented. There have been occasional efforts to rectify this deficiency. Nasser, for example, required after 1961 that 50 percent of members

---

[105] *Ibid.*, p. 60.

[106] Arend Lijphart, "Consociational Democracy," *World Politics* 21 (January 1969): 207–225.

of parliament be "workers or peasants." Each constituency in the country had to elect a worker or peasant along with a candidate in the "other" category. In the 1964 parliament, 60 percent of MPs were workers or peasants. While some of them were in reality government employees in administrative positions or were medium-sized landowners who managed to pass themselves off as peasants, during the Nasser era parliament did provide an important channel of access for these elements into national politics. Conversely, the presence there of relatively humble individuals provided a network through which the elite could communicate with rural and lower-middle-class urban Egypt. Under Sadat and Mubarak, the 50 percent requirement has been retained despite pressure to abolish it. Definitions of workers and peasants are now so elastic, however, that virtually anyone can qualify under either category. As a result, the Mubarak regime has lost an important channel of communication and is increasingly isolated from Egyptian mass society.

Co-optation/Appeasement   Functions closely related to communication also performed by legislatures include co-optation and appeasement of various social forces. Were those forces to gain permanent footholds within the elite through participation in legislatures, those bodies could be said to be recruiting and assimilating new members and the groups they represent. In fact, however, regimes tend to grant access only temporarily, ejecting representatives of threatening social forces when it suits them to do so. In Bahrain's first and only election to the National Assembly created following independence in 1971, 16 of the 30 elected seats were won by Shi'is. The popular bloc, consisting of leftists, nationalists, and reformers, won 8 seats, and the religious conservative bloc won 6 seats. It appeared as if the al-Khalifa ruling family was set on a course of utilizing the National Assembly to absorb these groups into the political order, rather than to exclude and repress them as it had done previously. Less than two years later, however, in August 1975, after labor riots and the Assembly's rejection of the amir's proposed legislation which would have given the ministry of the interior authority to arrest and detain for three years "anyone suspected of working against the state or even intending to act," the amir dissolved the Assembly and suspended the constitution.[107] The security law was declared to be in force and various political activists were

---

[107] Peterson, *The Arab Gulf States,* p. 76.

arrested, including three Assembly members. Since that time, no new elections have been held, nor has the Assembly been reconvened. Resentment against the ruling family persists, as indicated by an attempt by Islamicists to overthrow al-Khalifa rule in 1981.

The Kuwaiti National Assembly, from its creation in 1963 until it was suspended for the first time in 1976, also initially appeared to be functioning as an effective channel of political recruitment. "The old oligarchy of shaykhly families and the merchant elite, which had monopolized power in Kuwait in the past, found itself sharing power with sedentarized bedouin . . . and with the emerging middle class of businessmen, government officials, professionals, and intellectuals. Nearly a quarter of the first assembly's members were liberal nationalists."[108] But following the 1975 elections that resulted in many young, liberal reformers winning seats, and then a series of tense parliamentary sessions in the summer of 1976, the al-Sabah family became frightened of the Assembly they had created. In August 1976, Prime Minister Jabir al-Ahmad al-Sabah submitted his resignation to Amir Abdullah al-Salim al-Sabah, who immediately dissolved the Assembly, imposed press censorship, and suspended various articles of the constitution.

The al-Sabahs tried to create a pliant Assembly again in 1981, holding elections under a new electoral law that discriminated against their modernist opponents in favor of their traditional tribal allies. Encouraged by the relatively successful (i.e., quiescent) Assembly that resulted, the al-Sabahs permitted fresh elections in 1985. But this time more critics of the government were elected, and the 1986 session was one in which the government came under increasing criticism. The amir responded by suspending the Assembly on July 3, 1986, once again imposing press censorship and unilaterally amending the constitution. Some 3½ years later, Amir Jabir sought to deflect demands for the restoration of parliament by declaring the existence of a National Council of 75 members, 25 of whom were to be appointed by himself. The opposition's boycott of the June 1990 elections derailed this attempt to establish a pseudo-parliament and created a state of political crisis that prevailed when the country was invaded by Iraq in August. While in exile during the Iraqi occupation, the al-Sabah rulers led the opposition to believe that once the country was liberated, par-

---

[108] *Ibid.*, p. 38.

liament would be restored. In fact, however, on his return to Kuwait, Amir Jabir declared martial law. He subsequently consented under pressure to hold parliamentary elections in October 1992. Those elections resulted in a parliament which immediately resumed criticism of the government, but which by mid-1993 had failed to establish the principle that the royal family be accountable to parliament. Like the al-Khalifas, the al-Sabahs have used the legislature to co-opt and/or appease groups and individuals, while seeking to prevent parliament from becoming too powerful.

Jordan's King Hussein has pursued a similar strategy in his relations with popular assemblies. After permitting free elections in the 1950s to parliaments that became increasingly critical of governmental policies, Hussein finally struck back following an abortive coup attempt in 1957, expelling all radical members of parliament. In 1978, two years after dismissing an elected legislature, Hussein appointed members to a National Consultative Council in order to "co-opt intellectuals and businessmen, to appease traditional sectors of society, and to mobilize support for Royal policies."[109] As one of the measures taken to defuse tension in the wake of riots that shook the country in April 1989, King Hussein held elections to a new parliament in November of that year. This step proved to be prescient, for that parliament co-opted many potential dissenters, thereby helping to absorb much of the political pressure that resulted from the Gulf crisis and war of 1990–1991. King Hassan of Morocco, a veritable political maestro when it comes to playing off and with the opposition, responded to the 1984 food riots by holding parliamentary elections. These played a major role in defusing the crisis, because they brought into parliament some opposition elements. There they were easily dealt with by the king.

In every major crisis since 1962, the rulers of Saudi Arabia promised to create an assembly but reneged on that pledge once the threat to their rule had passed. In the wake of Operation Desert Storm, however, dissatisfaction among the Islamicist and modernist-nationalist oppositions with the manner in which the ruling family had dealt with the crisis forced King Fahd to commit himself in March 1992 to creating a 60-member appointive advisory council. Negative

---

[109] Nabeel Khoury, "The National Consultative Council of Jordan: A Study in Legislative Development," *International Journal of Middle East Studies* 13 (November 1981): 428.

reactions among the opposition, however, indicated that a council to which members are appointed may be an insufficient concession to demands for democracy.

It is not just monarchs who utilize legislatures to co-opt and appease critics. President Saddam Hussein of Iraq created an all-Kurdish parliament as part of his plan to reconcile Kurds to Iraqi sovereignty after the suppression of the Kurdish insurrection in 1975. That parliament had very limited powers over the country's predominantly Kurdish provinces, yet it did serve to co-opt various leadership elements and by so doing divided the Kurdish national movement. The Mubarak regime, in permitting a Muslim Brotherhood–dominated alliance of parties to emerge as the largest opposition force in parliament following the April 1987 elections, sought to soften the criticism of government by Islamicists, to attract some of their representatives into governmental sinecures, and to divide the Islamic movement between conservatives represented in the People's Assembly and radicals outside it.

Attempts to use legislatures to co-opt or appease demands for political participation can backfire if political mobilization is widespread. Algeria's President Chadli Benjedid responded to the violent riots of October 1988 by embarking on a rapid and dramatic political liberalization. A new constitution that authorized elections was ratified in February 1989. The Islamic Salvation Front (*al-Jabha al-Islamiyya li l-Inqadh*), known generally as the FIS, its French acronym, swept the June 1990 municipal and provincial elections. The government-backed party that had dominated the political system since independence in 1962, the FLN, could manage only 31 percent of the popular vote, compared to 55 percent for the FIS, which gave it control of 32 of the 48 provinces and over half of the municipalities. Frightened by the prospects of an FIS victory in parliamentary elections scheduled for June 1991, the government promulgated a new electoral law which replaced proportional representation with a two-round voting system that would enhance the prospects of the FLN. Islamicists associated with the FIS responded by taking to the streets, forcing the government to postpone elections for six months. When the first round of voting ultimately occurred in December, the FIS won 188 seats, compared to 16 for the FLN, thereby ensuring that in the decisive second round scheduled for January it would win a majority of seats and thus be in position to form a government. At this point the Algerian military intervened, deposed President Benjedid, canceled the forthcoming election, imposed martial law, outlawed the FIS, imprisoned thousands of its members in remote desert camps, and sentenced its leaders to long prison terms. The strategy to co-opt and appease Algerian Islamicists by granting what was intended to be a limited role in newly created democratic structures of local and national government thus failed utterly because the FIS was too strong and the FLN too weak. Whether these dramatic events in Algeria will cause other Arab governments to abandon attemps at co-optation/appeasement in favor of other policies remains unclear. Probably they will continue to seek to co-opt weak oppositions but will quickly employ more authoritarian methods if it appears that a real challenge to their authority may arise.

Containment/Supervision   Legislatures can play significant roles within rulers' strategies of supervising sprawling state apparatuses and containing opposition forces. Many Arab legislatures have come to play roles of ombudsmen, identifying irregularities that have taken place in bureaucracies and public sectors. While this serves to blow off steam, it is also a means by which rulers can supervise the performance of their administrators. Criticism by parliamentarians of programs and officials can also be used by rulers as justifications to jettison unwanted personnel, a tactic which is particularly useful to rulers seeking to deflect criticism from themselves or to undermine opposition elements that may be gathering strength. Nasser, for example, permitted parliament unusual latitude when debating the proposed annual budget of Prime Minister Zakariya Muhyi al-Din's government in 1965, in part because Nasser wanted to weaken the conservative trend that his prime minister represented. Sadat, by not signaling his displeasure, allowed parliament to criticize strongly and ultimately to reject Prime Minister Aziz Sidqi's proposed budget in 1972. Sadat had selected Sidqi to be prime minister, despite his strong personal dislike for him and his policies, because of domestic and foreign political calculations. Criticism in parliament thus served Sadat's purpose of destroying Sidqi's political career and discrediting the technocratic-socialist tendency he represented. The Syrian parliament also appears to be facilitating a rightward shift in President al-Assad's policies. In the May 1990 elections to that body, the regime ensured that private sector businessmen, selected intellectuals, and traditional leaders would win a larger proportion of seats than in any previous election under the Ba'th Party. According to Volker Perthes, this was to "be a warning to some of the regime's traditional centers of support—the party, the unions and the bureaucracy—that the regime might dispense with the critics in its own rows."[110] In Middle Eastern monarchies that have parliaments, rulers have ensured that traditional forces, especially tribes, are significantly overrepresented. This is to contain the more modern, urban-based critics of the regimes.

In sum, legislatures perform various useful services for political elites. They do, however, pose a threat to the monopoly of power enjoyed by rulers and are, therefore, closely monitored and carefully controlled. Such control focuses on the linkages between the legislature and the sociopolitical system as well as on the legislature itself.

Control over Linkages Between Legislatures and Sociopolitical Systems

Membership Selection   Control over entry into legislatures is the principal means by which the behavior of such bodies is regulated. Tightest control is maintained in Qatar, the United Arab Emirates, and Saudi Arabia, where all legislators are appointed by the rulers. A midpoint between appointment and election of all members is found in various countries where either the ruler appoints a set number of legislators in addition to those elected, which is the case, for example, in Egypt, or incumbents in various governmental posts have ex officio membership in the legislature. In the Bahrain National Assembly, for example, to which 30 members were elected in 1973, all cabinet ministers—and they were appointed by the ruler from outside the legislature—were entitled to ex officio membership. According to a Bahraini sociologist, "This voting bloc of 14 ministers proved to be impregnable."[111] Zine al-Abidine Ben Ali, who deposed Tunisian "President for Life" Habib Bourguiba in November 1987, announced at the "Salvation Congress" of the ruling party in July 1988, as part of a short-lived package of democratic reforms, that henceforth cabinet ministers would not sit in parliament. During the Gulf crisis in the fall of

---

[110] Volker Perthes, "Syria's Parliamentary Reform and Elections of 1990: Moving from Absolutist to Corporatist Authoritarianism?" Paper presented to the annual conference of the Middle East Studies Association of North America, Washington, D.C. (November 23–26, 1991), p. 10.

[111] Abd ul-Hadi Khalaf, "Labor Movement in Bahrain," *Merip Reports* 132 (May 1985): 25.

1990, Sultan Qabus, fearful of the destabilizing consequences of that crisis, made a concession to demands for democratic reforms when he announced that henceforth civil servants would not be permitted to hold seats in Oman's Consultative Council.

Except in Israel, which has had free elections since the creation of the state, and Turkey, in which the government seeks through various means to influence election outcomes but does not absolutely determine them, elections are not genuinely competitive contests. Election districts are commonly gerrymandered, arranged in such a way as to overrepresent those individuals or social forces loyal to government. In Kuwait, the government altered the number of districts and the boundaries between them for the 1981 elections to ensure that bedouins would win a large number of seats and modernist reformers and Islamic fundamentalists comparatively few. In 1984, the Egyptian prime minister decreed a new election law which abolished the electoral districts that, with various minor changes, had been extant since 1923. The purpose of this change was to centralize power over nominations in the hands of the prime minister and president and to ensure the defeat of candidates not backed by them.

Resources of bureaucracies and public-sector companies are mobilized to win votes for government-backed candidates. This may take the form of the carrot—granting pay raises or extra holidays to employees just prior to elections, or the stick—refusing to grant licenses, permits, or provide other services to supporters of opposition candidates. In addition, translation of the popular vote into parliamentary seats may be unfair. In the 1984 Egyptian elections, opposition parties won 27 percent of votes but obtained only 13 percent (58) of the 448 elected seats.[112] In October 1987, Turkish Prime Minister Turgut Ozal and his ruling Motherland Party rewrote the country's electoral laws. The following month the Motherland Party and its leader won the general election, securing 292 out of 450 seats in the National Assembly, or 65 percent. The party's share of the popular vote, however, was only 36.3 percent.[113] In the April 1989 Tunisian parliamentary elections, the ruling party of President Zine al-Abidine Ben Ali won all of the seats with only 57 percent of the popular votes.

[112] Abdel Monem Said Aly, "Democratization in Egypt," *American-Arab Affairs* 22 (Fall 1987): 18.

[113] Ken Mackenzie, "A Bizarre Affair," *Middle East International* 335 (October 7, 1988): 14.

The main Islamicist party, al-Nahda, despite capturing almost a quarter of the votes, did not gain a seat in parliament.[114]

A wide range of tactics designed to intimidate voters may also be employed. Ballots often are not secret; opposition candidates and their supporters may be turned away from polls or arrested on trumped-up charges; rallies and distribution of posters and handbills are restricted or completely illegal. What are widely considered to be the freest elections held in Tunisia in over 20 years, which were by-elections to vacant National Assembly seats in the early spring of 1988, were described as follows by a first-hand observer:

> The first thing I noticed when entering the building was that the entire entrance had been taken up by posters of the PSD (Constitutional Socialist Party) candidate—and no others. I immediately inquired but my guide—who turned out to be one of the local cell's leading members—simply said that the opposition candidates here were not very popular and had not bothered to put up posters. I entered one of the voting offices, filled to the ceiling with PSD posters in a soft pink color. I was a bit taken aback when a minute later the young woman behind the counter handed me a voting ballot: it was of the same soft pink! And later that day I was to find billboards, traffic indicators, even the cupola of a marabout shrine, swathed in pink. Inside the voting booths there were posters of the same color.[115]

If such comparatively subtle techniques fail of their objective, governments are not hesitant simply to forge results. In the Syrian parliamentary election of 1990, for example, a Damascene journalist with independent views initially was announced as being among the winners. A few days later the government overturned the result, claiming that all votes in Damascus had been recounted. In that same election Jamil al-Assad, the president's brother, won a seat in Lathaqiyyah. According to the official tally, he garnered more votes than were actually cast. Computerization of tabulation of returns has, according to a prominent Egyptian journalist noted for his satire, facilitated election fraud:

> The computer in charge of the law on election by party lists is well behaved. It speaks when we want it to speak and shuts up when we tell it

---

[114] Jamal Amiar, "In Five North African States, Talk of Democracy Outpaces Action," *The Washington Report on Middle East Affairs* (July 1991), p. 21.

[115] Dirk Vandewalle, "Returning to Tunisia, Part II," *Institute of Current World Affairs* DJV-26 (March 1988): 3.

to. At first it announced the election of Khaled Muhyi al-Din, leader of the NPUP, but an official glared at it, whereupon it announced the failure of Mr. Muhyi al-Din after he had won. The computer remembered that it is an official of the Ministry of Interior and announced that all candidates of the National Democratic Party had won and all opposition candidates had lost. Curses poured down on the head of the poor computer, which was only obeying orders. Then it announced that the Muslim Brotherhood and the Socialist Labor Party had won 40 seats but the Wafd was finished as it had not won a single seat. Some candidate dug the computer in the ribs, whereupon the computer said 40 Wafdists had been returned, then it brought down the figure to 35.[116]

In general, election returns are a better indicator of the desires of the ruling elite than of the preferences of voters. If no critics are permitted to win an election, it signals that the elite intends to rule with an iron fist. If some opposition elements are allowed into the legislature, it means the elite is seeking through co-optation and appeasement to contain the opposition's activities at a reasonably low level.

Control over the Political Infrastructure

Numerous observers of Middle Eastern legislatures have been surprised by the outspoken criticism of governmental personnel and policies that frequently occurs within them. One such observer, impressed by the level of debate in the Egyptian National Assembly from 1964, assessed it as a "pioneering experiment" and a sharp departure from previous Nasserist legislatures "which were little more than rubber stamps."[117] Another commented that a visitor to one of the sessions of the Kuwaiti National Assembly would find it "a constant and vociferous forum for criticizing the government."[118] Following the recall of parliament by King Hussein in 1984, an expert on Jordan stated that "debates in the newly constituted Chamber of Deputies have been lively, but decorous. Quite sensitive issues, such as the way in which the government handles security measures, have been the subject of thorough debate."[119]

---

[116] al-Akhbar, April 12, 1987 (in Arabic).

[117] R. Hrair Dekmejian, *Egypt Under Nasir: A Study in Political Dynamics* (Albany: State University of New York Press, 1971), p. 155.

[118] Hudson, *Arab Politics*, p. 186.

[119] Peter Gubser, "Jordan—Balancing Pluralism and Authoritarianism," *Ideology and Power*, pp. 103–104.

Ruling elites are willing to permit this surprising freedom of expression as a political safety valve to dissipate pressure building up in the system. But while criticism of government will frequently be tolerated, attempts to establish organizational linkages are usually impeded. Legislators in monarchies typically are allowed to form factions within their assemblies, but they usually are prohibited by law from joining political parties. When those legislators have appeared to be gaining popular followings, parliaments have been dissolved and the media censored. In Iraq, members of the National Assembly can in theory not be members of the ruling Ba'th Party, but in fact "candidates are screened, and only those who believe in the principles and aims of the Ba'th revolution may run for election."[120] In Egypt, where members of parliament can be active in opposition parties, the government works assiduously to exacerbate divisions between those parties and to frustrate relations between them and interest groups.

For parliamentarians to mobilize significant followings outside the legislature itself, they must be able to communicate through the media. In all countries in the region there is censorship with varying degrees of thoroughness. Even the relatively free Kuwaiti press was throttled on those two occasions prior to 1990 when opposition activism in the Assembly began to threaten al-Sabah domination of the state.

For parliamentary oppositions to become truly institutionalized and thereby restrict the powers and privileges of ruling elites, they need to be rooted in politics at lower levels, such as in villages and in quarters of major cities. In the Middle East, however, as in much of the Third World, local-level politics are not easily accessible to those in the national parliament who want to mobilize opposition to the regime. Such politics are frequently dominated by traditional elements cultivated by the regime itself. Elections at the local level are unusual. Such administrative units are typically governed by appointees. But even where elections are held, "they tend to be of limited significance. . . . Their function becomes primarily ceremonial. Electoral contests then determine relative prestige ratings, not program or policy issues."[121] Elections are not real choices between alternative policies because local units of government, unwilling to tax their

---

[120] Marr, "Iraq—Its Revolutionary Experience under the Ba'th," p. 188.

[121] Riggs, "Bureaucrats and Political Development," pp. 131–139.

constituents, depend on the central government for revenues. Local politicians who have access to central government patronage are the ones who dominate local government. Governments also interfere more blatantly in local elections because such interventions are less likely to invite scrutiny and condemnation. In Egypt, for example, opposition political parties have been active since 1976. They have won scores of parliamentary seats. They have yet, however, to win more than a handful of seats on local councils. As one informed observer put it, representation of the opposition "is not allowed at the level of local councils . . . where the ruling party occupies 100 percent of the seats."[122]

Without linkages to viable political parties, interest groups, or local-level politics, parliamentarians are left standing more or less alone if they choose to confront government. Since independence, no Arab government has been overthrown as a result of oppositional activity originating in legislatures. In almost every Arab country, the legislature has at one time or another been dissolved. Rulers can, in short, allow their legislatures to be active "talk shops," for they know that in the crunch, opposition legislators have insufficient resources to convert their words into actions.

Internal Controls

Constitutional/Legal Restrictions   The constitutional provisions under which Middle Eastern legislatures operate are generally restrictive. Those functioning in monarchical systems are in fact not true legislatures, for by law they have only consultative functions. Frequently there are explicit restrictions on the subjects that may be discussed in these legislatures. In Oman, for example, the Supreme Consultative Council is unable to "concern itself with mineral resources and the distribution of revenues derived from them."[123] Since oil accounts for more than 90 percent of government revenues and virtually 100 percent of exports, this is indeed a serious restriction. The Iraqi National

---

[122] Ahmed Abdalla, "Structure of Political Participation in Egypt," paper presented to the annual conference of the Middle East Studies Association of North America (November 23–26, 1991), p. 3. In the 1992 local council elections opposition parties won several seats.

[123] Eickelman, "Kings and People," p. 58.

Assembly may not deal with "military matters or with issues of internal security," restrictions which have rendered the Assembly virtually meaningless since 1980.[124]

In the Iraqi Assembly, as in most others, the primary legislative obligation is to review proposed legislation forwarded from a higher authority, in this case, the Revolutionary Command Council. The Iraqi Assembly, like most of those in other nonmonarchical systems, may in theory also initiate legislation. That step, however, typically requires a significant number of supporters. In Iraq's case it is 25 percent of the membership. By comparison, the Federal National Council in the United Arab Emirates may not initiate any legislation, "but only offers recommendations on draft laws issued by the Council of Ministers, which is not, in turn, obliged to accept any of the FNC's proposals."[125]

In Arab countries, governments are formed by executives who are not responsible to legislatures and who are not obliged to choose ministers from them. There are severe restrictions on votes of no confidence. In Kuwait, for example, the Assembly can vote no confidence in a particular minister but not in the cabinet as a whole. Legislative sessions are typically commenced and terminated on the initiative of the executive or the head of the legislature, who is in every case chosen by government. The speaker of the Egyptian parliament, for example, was from 1984 until 1987 not even an elected member of that body. In 1985 and again in 1986, he terminated the legislative session ahead of schedule in order to forestall opposition criticism. In 1987–1988, President Mubarak delayed the opening of parliament for several months, finally permitting the session to commence only after the opposition threatened a boycott. Constitutional provisions favorable to legislative development are frequently ignored with impunity. The Qatar constitution calls for elections to an assembly, but they have never been held. Similarly, the Iraqi constitution of 1970 called for a representative assembly, but for nine years none was created.

Internal Administration   To operate effectively, parliaments must provide their members with staff and appropriate physical facilities, there must be a committee system, and the sessions must be of suffi-

---

[124] Ahmad Yousef Ahmad, "The Dialectics of Domestic Environment and Role Performance: The Foreign Policy of Iraq," in Bahgat Korany and Ali E. Hillal Dessouki, *The Foreign Policies of Arab States* (Boulder, Colo.: Westview Press, 1984), p. 156.

[125] Peck, *The United Arab Emirates,* p. 123.

cient duration for reasonable deliberation to occur. These three conditions are nowhere completely satisfied. The consultative assemblies have no professional staffs. In the most highly developed Arab parliament now functioning, which is that of Egypt, the staff provided is entirely for administration, not research, and is available only to committee chairmen. In Oman, the council meets three times a year. The longest continual session in the region is that of Egypt's People's Assembly, which officially convenes in November and terminates in early summer. Even when in session, however, the Assembly rarely meets more than three times a week. Its committees typically convene only a few times throughout the year. Arab legislative committees do not draft legislation but approve (or occasionally reject or amend) proposed legislation handed down from the executive.

Guarantees of Members' Freedoms

If legislatures are to perform even the comparatively unimportant task of consultation, their members must be provided reasonable guarantees against retribution for their words and actions. Parliamentary immunity is generally recognized in Middle Eastern constitutions but is frequently not absolute, and legal guarantees are occasionally violated by governments. The underlying attitude of those in authority toward the idea of complete freedom of expression for legislators is conveyed by a comment of an advisor to King Hussein: "Parliamentary immunity does not mean you can say whatever you think."[126] The Kuwaiti and Egyptian constitutions stipulate that the government must request the legislature to waive the immunity of a member if the government wishes to prosecute him.

In the Kuwaiti Assembly's first 11 years, the government requested waivers of immunity on nine separate occasions, six of which were for statements made to the press by deputies. In all cases but one, the Assembly refused the request if the member chose to claim immunity.[127] Subsequently, however, when the Assembly was dissolved, large numbers of journalists, including former members of the Assembly, were arrested. On two occasions in Egypt under Sadat, the immunity of members of the People's Assembly was lifted when they criticized the president. Those members were also expelled from the Assembly. In Oman and Qatar, laws governing freedom of expression restrain not

---

[126] Day, *East Bank/West Bank*, p. 44.

[127] Baaklini, "Legislatures in the Gulf Area," pp. 368–369.

the government but members of the consultative assemblies. In Oman, delegates are prohibited from discussing Assembly delibera- tions with nonmembers, and in Qatar, the Advisory Council's sessions are not public and proceedings may not be published.

AUTHORITARIAN BUT NOT TOTALITARIAN

Most Middle Eastern governments can be classified as authoritarian. The autonomy of their political institutions is limited and there are serious constraints on personal political freedoms. These governments are, nevertheless, not totalitarian. The sharp distinction between the public and the private sphere, with strong traditions supporting the sanctity of the latter's freedom from governmental interference, com- bined with the weakness of Middle Eastern governments in compari- son with the totalitarian archetype, means that governments dominate the formal, public political arena but largely ignore the private sphere.

Patterns of political communication in the region illustrate the difference between authoritarian and totalitarian government and public as opposed to private domains. In the Arab world, according to William Rugh, restrictions on the media

> are by no means comprehensive. The media have not been forced, even under one-party regimes, into the single-minded agitation and propagan- da effort of the kind found in the Soviet or other totalitarian systems. The most restrictive Arab regimes have, in general, been satisfied with out- ward compliance by press, radio, and television, and they have not invad- ed the sphere of private, face-to-face communication which is still so important in the Arab societies.[128]

Governmental pressure, moreover, is typically applied not in a crude, official style but in more indirect, personal fashion. Implied threats are typically balanced with positive inducements. A Jordanian political scientist has described King Hussein's manner of containing the parliamentary opposition as follows:

> Often only a rumor among the "notables," the "personalities," is enough to make a prospective candidate decide not to run. It simply goes like this: "The Palace (meaning the King) or the government (meaning the

---

[128] William A. Rugh, *The Arab Press* (Syracuse N.Y.: Syracuse University Press, 1987), p. 28.

Ministry of Interior) is not happy with so-and-so" . . . the candidate is in a sense "refrigerated"; he is "put on ice" for a term, or maybe two. This makes him unhappy, but not so unhappy as to conspire. Well, there is always "next time"; furthermore, his relative or friend may be elected. . . . Elements of democracy do exist; people actually vote; on occasion a veto is overridden or a government is forced to resign. Antigovernment editorials appear in newspapers, and people make speeches and criticize. There are no large-scale concentration camps and no organized system of violence by the government. In other words, freedom of action extends only to the limits decided upon by the regime.[129]

The intense personalism of Middle Eastern sociopolitical systems is a strong deterrent to ideologies and forms of government that seek to impose total submission to the state. Formal governmental authority is comprehended, deflected, and, if possible, exploited through familial, local, small-group and other primordial ties. The gap between state and society, which is vigorously defended by informal social groupings, protects society from totalitarian rule, but it also prevents it from subordinating government to the popular will.

As social mobilization proceeds, the battleground between state and society may slowly shift to formal political organizations, which constitute the "level between the family and the state (which) . . . is of crucial importance for the power of citizens to affect public life. . . ." The critical issues increasingly will become, according to Kevin Dwyer, "How and to what extent do people with similar ideas come together to form groups and associations, to publish journals, hold meetings, lobby, create public pressure, attempt in any of various ways to put their ideas into the public arena in an organized manner?"[130]

One indicator of the emergence of stronger demands for formal political participation is the growth of human rights organizations throughout the Middle East. Such organizations could be precursors of more broadly based, policy-oriented interest groups and political parties. Although their membership is largely confined to the intelligentsia, they are perceived as irritants and sometimes as threats by governments in the region. The Arab Organization for Human Rights (AOHR), created in 1983, is the largest of its type in the region. It has branches or associated groups in Egypt, Jordan, Kuwait, Lebanon,

---

[129] Abu Jaber, "The Legislature of the Hashemite Kingdom," p. 111.

[130] Dwyer, *Arab Voices*, p. 146.

Yemen, and the states of the Maghrib other than Libya. It has been able to focus public attention on human rights abuses and possibly to prevent their occurrence at various times and places, but it has not been able to put an absolute stop to them or to evade harassment, intimidation and, in some cases, arrest and torture of its members. In addition, many of the successes of the AOHR have been quixotic. Egypt and Tunisia, for example, are the only two Arab countries that acceded to pressure from the AOHR and other human rights organizations to sign the Convention against Torture and Other Forms of Cruel, Inhuman or Degrading Treatment and Punishment. Yet, in June 1992, the Tunisian government dissolved the 15-year-old Human Rights League, the country's main human rights organization, while further intensifying its campaign of mass arrests and torture of Islamicists. In the late 1980s and early 1990s, Tunisia and Egypt have repeatedly been cited by Amnesty International, the U.S. State Department, and other authoritative sources, as indulging in systematic violations of human rights, including torture and other inhumane punishments. This suggests that the contraction of arbitrary state authority and concomitant expansion of civil society beyond the level of the family and small informal groups will not be brought about only by comparatively small numbers of intellectuals grouped in human rights organizations. At most they can provide openings through which larger, more broadly based movements may ultimately move to establish meaningful principles of political participation.

Evidence on the degree to which political participation has already been institutionalized is mixed. Since 1989 the Jordanian parliament has been as active and independent as at any time in the country's history. In the Arab Gulf states there are now four functioning legislatures, whereas there were none prior to the independence of those states. Yet Kuwait and Bahrain have dissolved their legislatures a total of four times and the Saudi Arabian consultative assembly is very new and constrained by a host of restrictions. The Tunisian legislature, which held out the promise of becoming a more vigorous body in the wake of the coup that brought President Ben Ali to power, has declined into irrelevance since the government decided in the wake of the 1989 elections to deal with the opposition by arrest and torture rather than through democratic means.

The Egyptian parliament under Mubarak, reinforced by comparatively outspoken opposition parties and newspapers, stands out as one of the more successful, sustained experiences of political institution-building in the 1980s and early 1990s. Yet the government maintains strict controls over parliament. The opposition political parties, which emerged with great hopes at the time of the 1984 election, are now languishing. The democratically elected government of Sadiq al-Mahdi in the Sudan, while presiding over the return of parliamentary life after an effective 17-year absence, proved unable to deal with the many threatening crises and fell in a coup in 1989. Since then a reign of Islamicist-endorsed terror has been imposed under the auspices of the military. The political liberalization that commenced in late 1988 in Iraq was stillborn.

In Turkey, the restrictions on political freedoms imposed by the military officers who seized power in 1980 are more severe than those decreed following the 1960 and 1971 military interventions. Although elections and freedom of the press have been restored, large numbers of Turkish political activists are still in jail, and restrictions on many political activities remain in place. Israel, which has extended nominal political freedoms to its Palestinian Arab minority, still has institutionalized discrimination against them. Palestinians living in territories occupied by Israel since 1967 have no political rights and are subject to harsh repression.

At the popular level, demands for political participation are intensifying and will continue to do so. Simultaneously, many of the prerequisites for democracy are being fulfilled. Literacy is growing, generation and dissemination of information is expanding, and economies are becoming increasingly diverse. Most Middle Easterners, having enjoyed a higher standard of living during the oil boom, are now experiencing an erosion of their economic well-being, a condition which typically stimulates political demands. Precisely how the contradiction between increasing demands for participation, on the one hand, and government instransigence, on the other, will be resolved is difficult to foretell. If repression is the only response, then political breakdown may occur. Informal participation in the private sphere and quasi-institutionalized formal political participation in the public sphere are unlikely to absorb enough citizens into politics to maintain the status quo indefinitely.

Chapter 7

The Arab–Israeli Connection

No other aspect of Middle Eastern politics has received the attention that has been devoted to the Arab-Israeli conflict. Paradoxically, even close observers have often failed to understand this important issue. For some, the conflict is so emotionally charged that they are unable to analyze it rationally and objectively. For all, it is extremely complex, involving actors and interactions at and between three different levels.

At the heart of the dispute is a clash between two peoples, Israeli Jews and Palestinian Arabs, for control of the same piece of land, known to the former as Israel and to the latter as Palestine. To Zionists—those who believe that Jews have a right to a national home in historic Palestine—the claim to this land is based on the existence of a Jewish nation there some two thousand years ago. It is further justified by perceptions of abiding anti-Semitism, by the trauma of the Holocaust, by claims that Jews have "made the desert bloom," by the relatively democratic nature of the state, and by the assertion that Palestinian claimants to the land are Arabs and thus should be accommodated by one or more of the many Arab states in the region.

Palestinian counterclaims rest on their ownership and occupation of the land for centuries, on the fact that they played no part in the

298

Holocaust and the denial by them that they harbor anti-Semitic beliefs (both Arabic and Hebrew are Semitic languages), on the argument that Western powers implanted Israel in the region without the permission of its residents, and on the basis that Palestinian national and civil rights are denied by the presence of a state that accords such rights exclusively or primarily to Jews. Since the beginning of Zionist settlement in Palestine in the late nineteenth century, each side has considered the other a mortal threat to its existence, an enemy with whom compromise may be more dangerous than resolute opposition.

The Arab states constitute a second level of participants in the conflict. That these 21 states—which possess about two-thirds of the world's proven oil reserves, now number nearly 200 million people, and have several million men under arms—have not been able to gain the upper hand diplomatically or militarily against Israel, to say nothing of regaining the West Bank and Gaza, an area about the size of metropolitan Los Angeles, attests to the fact that the Arab states have not really united behind the Palestinians. From the moment Jewish settlement began to pose a serious threat to Palestinians, Arab leaders sought to gain advantage for themselves and their states out of the confrontation between those two peoples.

Amir Faisal, who had cooperated with the British in leading the Arab revolt and who sought European consent to the establishment of his Arab Kingdom centered on Damascus, pledged in 1919 to the Zionist leader Chaim Weizmann his support for Jewish immigration to Palestine. In exchange, Weizmann promised that Zionists would use their influence in European capitals in support of Faisal's endeavor. In 1937, when the British Peel Commission proposed the creation of a Jewish state through the partition of Palestine, leaders of surrounding Arab states "saw the British predicament in Palestine as a unique opportunity to gain influence with His Majesty's Government, as well as to assert their rival claims to Arab leadership."[1] In 1938, Transjordan proposed incorporating that part of Palestine allotted to the Palestinians in the 1937 partition plan into a United Kingdom, a scheme which was to give King Abdullah control over the Palestinians, thereby elevating his leadership pretensions. The Egyptian, Lebanese, and Syrian military interventions in May 1948 into the civil war that had

---

[1] Aaron S. Klieman, "The Arab States and Palestine," in *Zionism and Arabism in Palestine and Israel*, ed. by Elie Kedourie and Sylvia G. Haim (London: Frank Cass, 1982), p. 118.

been raging since December 1947 between Jews and Palestinians "was not aimed at destroying the Jewish State. It was intended to prevent Abdullah from annexing the Arab part of Palestine as the first step in the implementation of his British-inspired Greater Syria plan. . . . Both [Abdullah and his Arab opponents] were ready to consider an alliance with Israel to further their aspirations."[2]

The Arab states have never fought a war against Israel to liberate Palestinians from Israeli control by military means. In 1956, Egypt defended itself against the Israeli, British, and French tripartite invasion. Egyptian-Syrian rivalry and attempts by each to outbid the other's radicalism, although neither had the intention of waging war, paved the way for the Israeli attack of June 1967. The War of Attrition along the Suez Canal in 1969–1970 was an attempt by Nasser to prevent Israel's occupation of Sinai from becoming a fait accompli. The October 1973 War was initiated by Egypt and Syria for the limited purpose of altering the context for diplomacy aimed at regaining the Sinai and Golan Heights and possibly the West Bank and Gaza.

Just as the Arab states have hesitated to dedicate themselves to the military objective of "liberating Palestine," so have they been unable to coordinate diplomatic strategies to that end. Since the 1930s, ruling elites in the Arab states have placed paramount emphasis on inter-Arab politics. They have subordinated their concerns for Palestinians and their conflicts with Israel to the desire of maintaining or enhancing their position within the never-ending Arab Cold War.[3] As Walid Kazziha states, "As far as the Arab regimes are concerned, the Palestinian cause is, and has been, a pawn in inter-Arab rivalry."[4]

Arab political leaders are also constrained by their obligations to seek to maximize their own states' interests—by *raison d'état*. They are aware that selfless national dedication to the Palestinian cause would lead immediately to a confrontation with Israel which no Arab state could win alone, nor even with support of several others. Nasser

---

[2] Simha Flapan, *The Birth of Israel: Myths and Realities* (New York: Pantheon Books, 1987), pp. 150, 151.

[3] The term *Arab Cold War* was coined by Malcolm Kerr to apply to the struggle for power between Nasser and his opponents in the 1950s and 1960s. It remains appropriate today. See Malcolm Kerr, *The Arab Cold War, Gamal'Abd al-Nasir and His Rivals, 1958–1970*, 3d ed. (Oxford: Oxford University Press, 1971).

[4] Walid Kazziha, *Palestine in the Arab Dilemma* (London: Croom Helm, 1979), p. 17.

urged his people to make considerable sacrifices for the Palestinians, resentment over which ultimately helped pave the way for Sadat's reaction, his "Egypt-first" policy. Statehood and resulting state interests inevitably erected a barrier between stateless Palestinians and other Arabs. Ruling elites could surmount this obstacle only by calling on their populations to risk a fight to the death, as the Palestinians have done. The alternative is partial commitment and diplomatic maneuvering involving the Arab states, Israel, the Palestinians, and various outside parties. Out of this diplomatic maneuvering, leaders of the Arab states hope a favorable resolution of the Arab-Israeli conflict will emerge, but they are reluctant to take great risks to achieve that end.

A plethora of extraregional actors who are involved in the Arab-Israeli conflict constitute the third dimension of analysis. No other conflict in the Third World has for so long attracted the interests of such a broad range of states and international organizations. Zionist aspirations in Palestine could never have been fulfilled had it not been for British support during and after World War I and American support since World War II. Even the fascist governments of Germany and Italy sought to further their own interests by supporting Zionism.[5] The Soviets first became heavily involved in the conflict after World War II. They supported the Zionists at that time out of the calculation that a Jewish state would reduce British influence in the Eastern Mediterranean region. The United Nations presided over the creation of the state of Israel by virtue of the General Assembly's endorsement of the Partition Resolution on November 29, 1947. Since then the United Nations and its various organizations have served as arenas in which much of the diplomacy surrounding the conflict has been conducted.

The Arab-Israeli conflict has received more attention than any other Third World issue in such disparate organizations as the European Community, the Organization of African States, the Non-Aligned Movement, and the International Socialist Organization. In much of the Third World, the Arab-Israeli conflict epitomizes and

---

[5] On relations between Zionism and European fascist movements and governments between 1920 and World War II, see Lenni Brenner, *Zionism in the Age of Dictators* (London: Croom Helm, 1983); and Brenner, *The Iron Wall: Zionist Revisionism from Jabotinsky to Shamir* (London: Zed Books, 1984). See also Francis R. Nicosia, *The Third Reich and the Palestine Question* (Austin, Tex.: University of Texas Press, 1985).

symbolizes the legacy of colonialism and continuing intervention by
the West into formerly colonized areas. The conflict served for over 40
years as a testing ground for the military equipment, ideological
appeal, international leverage, and diplomatic capacities of the superpowers. The inability of the world's other major powers, including the
Europeans, Chinese, and Japanese, to affect substantially the course
of the conflict stands as a stark reminder of their subordinate status in
global politics even after the collapse of the USSR. The world's states
and political organizations have, in sum, become entangled in the
Arab-Israeli conflict in differing and unique ways, thereby rendering it
all the more complex and difficult to resolve.

Precisely because of the intensity, durability, and intractability of
the Arab-Israeli conflict, observers and policy-makers commonly seek
to render it comprehensible by sharply reducing its complexity in their
own minds. This is understandable and occasionally desirable, for in
order to act decisively, decision makers may need to simplify reality.
President Jimmy Carter, for example, interpreted the conflict in religious terms, as the title of his book on the subject, *The Blood of Abraham,* suggests.[6] President Ronald Reagan, on the other hand, viewed
the conflict as one pitting pro-Soviet against pro-American forces in
the region. But there are dangers and costs in simplifying reality, as
both Presidents Carter and Reagan discovered when their attempts to
resolve the conflict met with failure. Their simplified perspectives
impeded understanding of the motives and behavior of key actors in
the dispute. For presidents and public alike, so many adages, myths,
and outright fallacies have grown up around the Arab-Israeli conflict
that its analysis is unusually problematical. Beliefs held by these two
former American presidents reflect the broader situation.

According to Jimmy Carter: "To understand the roots of the
hatred and bloodshed that still shape the relationships among the people of the region, it is useful to go back to the holy scriptures of ancient
times. To a remarkable degree, the will of God is the basis for both
esoteric debates and the most vicious terrorist attacks among Jews,
Muslims, and Christians."[7] This perspective—that the contemporary
Arab-Israeli conflict is a modern manifestation of a recurring religious
conflict of ancient origins—is inaccurate and misleading. There were

[6] Jimmy Carter, *The Blood of Abraham* (Boston: Houghton Mifflin, 1985).

[7] *Ibid.,* p. 4.

no "Arabs" (hence no Arab-Israeli conflict) in *Eretz Yisrael* (the bibli-cal term for the land of Israel). The Arab invasion of Syria-Palestine occurred in the seventh century, more than a half millennium after the Romans put down Jewish rebellions in Judea, sending some of the population into exile. A larger percentage of the Jewish population, in fact, remained in what in the later Roman Empire was called Pales-tine, a name the Greek historian Herodotus introduced into the writ-ten record in the fifth century B.C. The majority of Jews who remained converted to Christianity. Following the Arab invasion of Palestine, the majority of Christians converted to Islam. It is most probably the case, therefore, that a significant percentage of Muslim and Christian Palestinians are descended from Jews who converted over a thousand years ago.

The equation of ancient Hebrews with modern Jews is also ques-tionable, for "serious study of this matter has shown that the latter have no basis to claim genuine descent from the former to any mean-ingful extent."[8] According to Maxime Rodinson, "It is very probable, that the so-called Arab inhabitants of Palestine . . . have much more of the ancient Hebrews' 'blood' than most of the Jews of the Diaspora, whose religious exclusiveness in no way prevented them from absorb-ing converts of various religions."[9] For 1300 years Middle Eastern Jews have lived under Muslim rule. Until modern times, there were remarkably few incidents of religious conflict. Most clashes occurred after Zionism made its presence felt in the Middle East in the twenti-eth century. The contemporary Arab-Israeli conflict is not simply a rerun of ancient religious dramas, but a product of the creation of the state system in the area after the collapse of the Ottoman Empire in 1918.

---

[8] Ray L. Cleveland, "The Palestinians and the Diminution of Historical Legitimacy," in *Palestine: Continuing Dispossession,* ed. by Glenn E. Perry (Belmont, Mass.: Association of Arab-American University Graduates, 1986), p. 104. On this point see also Raphael Patai and Jennifer P. Wing, *The Myth of the Jewish Race* (New York: Scribner, 1975).

[9] Maxime Rodinson, *Israel: A Colonial Settler State?* (New York: Monad Press, 1973), p. 79. A group of ultra-Orthodox rabbis and scientists in Israel are of the opinion that there are specifically Jewish genes and therefore a Jewish race. This theory, however, is gen-erally discarded by other Israeli scientists and intellectuals as being religiously motivat-ed, unscientific speculation. See Hila Tov, "The Theory of the Jewish Race," *Hadashot* (March 13, 1992), reprinted in *From the Hebrew Press: Monthly Translations and Com-mentaries from Israel* 4 (May 1992): 10–16.

Interpretation of the conflict as nothing more than an extension of superpower rivalry was also inaccurate and misleading. Yet this was the predominant view of the Reagan administration and an outlook previously associated with President Eisenhower's secretary of state, John Foster Dulles. Communism had little popular support or organizational capacity in the region. Those states which had developed close relations with the Soviet Union did so out of *raison d'état* rather than ideological concerns. Arab states sought to draw the Soviet Union into the region to counterbalance U.S. support for Israel, but even this tactic was subject to reversal, as Sadat demonstrated by ordering Soviet military advisors out of Egypt in July 1972, and by subsequently forging an alliance with the United States. Middle Eastern decision makers are motivated by regional, not global, concerns, a fact that leaders of the United States, whose perspectives are precisely opposite, have been prone to overlook.

Those most intimately involved in the conflict reduce its complexity by creating caricaturized images that portray their enemies in unidimensionally evil terms. Many Israelis transpose images of the Nazis onto the Arabs. David Ben-Gurion, first prime minister and minister of defense and the "father" of Israel, described Arabs as "the pupils and even the teachers of Hitler, who claim that there is only one way to solve the Jewish question—one way only: total annihilation."[10] Menachem Begin, who served as Israeli prime minister from 1977 until 1983, referred to members of the Palestine Liberation Organization (PLO) as "two-legged animals" and justified Israeli attempts to kill Yasser Arafat in Beirut in the summer of 1982 by comparing the mission to the Allied bombings of Berlin in World War II intended to destroy Hitler in his bunker.[11] Prime Minister Yitzhak Shamir, condemning the UN General Assembly's move to Geneva in December 1988 to enable Yasser Arafat to address it, compared him to Nazi propaganda chief Goebbels.[12]

The perception of Arabs as bent on the destruction of Israel is accompanied by a heightened concern—bordering on a fixation—with security (*bitahon* in Hebrew). It is, according to Jean-Pierre Lan-

---

[10] David Ben-Gurion, *Memoirs* (Tel Aviv: United Kibbutz, 1974), vol. 4 (in Hebrew), p. 392, cited in Flapan, *The Birth of Israel*, p. 235.

[11] *Ibid.*, p. 235.

[12] World press services, December 13, 1988.

gellier, "the sledgehammer argument."[13] *Bitahon* is cited to justify a range of uncompromising policies, from refusal to withdraw from the occupied territories to making it a criminal offense for an Israeli to meet with a member of the PLO.

Arabs perceive Israelis as modern-day Crusaders, or colonial settlers, such as the Boers in South Africa, the French in Algeria, or the British or Spanish in various parts of the New World.[14] These images call for *sumud,* the Arabic term for persistence, steadfastness, perseverance. According to this perspective, *sumud* will ultimately reward the Arabs with the departure of the Israelis, just as the Crusaders and the French colonists were forced to depart. Thus, for each side, caricaturized images serve to justify uncompromising behavior and policies toward the other. Rooted so deeply in the political consciousnesses of the two peoples, policies of intransigence are extremely difficult to replace with those of accommodation.

Surrounding the adverse images of the enemy and the determined adherence to policies based on *bitahon* or *sumud* are partially or largely mythologized versions of the conflict itself. Over the years both sides have created their own interpretations, their own stories of the events that have made up this conflict during the course of the twentieth century. Each has sought to convince the rest of the world that its version is the correct one. Israel has enjoyed greater success in this effort for a variety of reasons, which are summed up in Rashid Khalidi's phrase, "History is written by the victors."[15] In this case the victors, largely of European origins, had the skills, contacts, and receptive audiences in the West that ensured the predominance of their arguments.

In recent years, first steps have been taken to restore balance in the struggle over the "truth" of the conflict. Palestinians, other Arabs, Western, and, most important, Israeli scholars, have undertaken to write histories that seek to revise accepted wisdoms by bringing to

---

[13] Jean-Pierre Langellier, "The New Palestinian Nationalism Changes Israeli Society," *The Guardian Weekly* 136 (June 14, 1987): 13.

[14] Rodinson, *Israel: A Colonial Settler State?* pp. 27–29; and Edward W. Said, *The Question of Palestine* (New York: Vintage Books, 1979), pp. 56–114.

[15] Rashid Khalidi, "Palestinian Peasant Resistance to Zionism Before World War I," in *Blaming the Victims: Spurious Scholarship and the Palestinian Question,* ed. by Edward Said and Christopher Hitchens (New York: Verso, 1988), p. 207.

light newly released information or by reinterpreting old facts. Of greatest importance in this regard has been the effort to disentangle myth from reality concerning the creation of Israel. The events of 1947–1949 are of special significance because interpretation of them served to legitimate Israel's claim to statehood and its refusal to accept the return of Palestinian refugees. Thus, contemporary efforts to negotiate a peace settlement inevitably turn back to this period, as, for instance, the PLO's proposal in November 1988 to resolve the conflict on the basis of UN Resolution 181 of 1947, known as the Partition Resolution. The Israeli victory in 1967 had an analogue in the creation of Israel in 1947–1949 because it entailed the occupation of Arab land and the dispossession of many of its inhabitants. It thereby, once again, raised questions about borders and relations with Arabs, issues that have yet to be resolved.

THE CREATION OF ISRAEL: OLD MYTHS AND NEW TRUTHS

Partition Plan

Leaders of the Yishuv (Jewish community in Palestine) accepted the November 29, 1947, Partition Resolution of the United Nations, but Palestinians rejected it. This has been commonly interpreted as indicating the moderateness of the former and the intransigence of the latter, despite the fact that by the conclusion of the armistice agreements with the Arab states in 1949 the new Jewish state occupied nearly 80 percent of the territory of Palestine, compared with some 55 percent that had been allotted it in the Partition Resolution. Palestinian rejection of partition helped deny them their state and facilitated the incorporation of their territory into Israel and Jordan.

That the Partition Resolution was unfavorable to Palestinians, both in its substance and in the procedure by which it was approved, has been part of the historical record since 1947, although it has not received wide attention. At the beginning of 1947 Palestinians numbered 1.3 million, compared with a Jewish population of 600,000. The latter owned only 6 to 7 percent of the total land area. Nevertheless, the Partition Plan awarded the Jewish state the larger portion and by so doing necessarily included within it an Arab minority of some 250,000, or about 40 percent of the population. That almost a third of

Palestinians were to be denied their hope for an independent Arab state and were to live under Jewish rule; that control over a large amount of property was, in effect, to be transferred from Arab to Jewish hands; and that the Arab state was to be relatively small, deprived of most of the fertile coastal area and cut off from Syria and the Red Sea, were the reasons that the Palestinians rejected the Partition Plan. Insult was added to Palestinian injury by the manner in which the resolution was passed in the United Nations, of which, at the time, few Third World nations were members. The United States, after an intense lobbying effort by American Zionists directed at the White House, brought leverage to bear on several recalcitrant but vulnerable member-states to induce them to vote for partition.[16]

An important addition to the historical record, made by Israeli revisionist and other scholars (most especially by Simha Flapan, an Israeli intellectual and political activist who died in 1987) is information that Jewish acceptance of partition was only a tactical move designed to pave the way for a military confrontation with the Palestinians. Jewish leaders knew them to be weak, neither desirous of nor prepared for war. David Ben-Gurion and others assumed that the Palestinians would lose further territories to the new Jewish state and that those Palestinians not under Jewish control would be denied statehood by King Abdullah of Jordan, with whom the Jewish leadership had made a secret arrangement.[17] Ben-Gurion is revealed by his diary and other sources to have accepted the principle of partition from 1937 on the grounds that it would legitimate the Jewish state, pave the way for the "transfer" of much if not all of the Arab population to surrounding Arab states, and leave open the question of borders, which he thought would ultimately be determined in a favorable manner by force of arms. In 1937, for example, he stated, "We shall accept a state in the boundaries fixed today—but the boundaries of Zionist aspirations are the concerns of the Jewish people and no external factor will be able to limit them."[18] In a letter written at this time

---

[16] For a judicious review of these lobbying activities, see John Snetsinger, *Truman, The Jewish Vote, and the Creation of Israel* (Stanford: Hoover Institution Press, 1974), pp. 58–72.

[17] Flapan, *The Birth of Israel*, pp. 13–80. See also Avi Shlaim, *The Politics of Partition: King Abdullah, the Zionist Movement, and the Partition of Palestine, 1921–1951* (New York: Columbia University Press, 1990).

[18] Ben-Gurion, *Memoirs*, vol. 4, p. 151, cited in Flapan, *The Birth of Israel*, p. 53.

he asserted, "We must expel Arabs and take their places."[19] In the following year, Ben-Gurion defended partition on the grounds that following the establishment of the state, "We will cancel the partition of the country (between Jews and Arabs) and we will expand throughout the land of Israel."[20] Three and a half months after fighting commenced between Palestinians and Jews in the wake of the UN's endorsement of the Partition Resolution, Ben-Gurion assessed the opponent as follows: "They, the decisive majority of them, do not want to fight us, and all of them together are unable to stand up to us."[21] For the Yishuv, partition was a golden opportunity to establish a Jewish state in almost all of Palestine, while at the same time opening the door for the expulsion of the Arabs.

Palestinian Exodus

Between December 1947 and September 1949 over 700,000 Palestinians, or more than half the total population, fled their homes, 130,000 to 160,000 remaining behind in the new state of Israel. The voluntary or compulsory "transfer" of the Arab population out of the Jewish state, which was a manifest Zionist desire to outside observers as early as 1919 and which had become an integral part of Zionist thinking no later than the 1930s, had been all but accomplished.[22] But how did this "miracle," as Ben-Gurion termed it, happen?

The claim "found in all official Zionist history and propaganda and all Israeli information publications" is that Israel was not responsible

---

[19] Letter from David Ben-Gurion to A. Ben-Gurion, October 5, 1937, cited in Shabtai Teveth, *Ben-Gurion and the Palestine Arabs* (Oxford: Oxford University Press, 1985), p. 89.

[20] Protocol of the meeting of the Jewish Agency Executive, June 7, 1938, Central Zionist Archives, 28, cited in Benny Morris, *The Birth of the Palestinian Refugee Problem, 1947–1949* (Cambridge: Cambridge University Press, 1987), p. 24.

[21] Document no. 274, p. 460, of the Central Zionist Archives, December 1947–May 1948), cited in *ibid.*, p. 73.

[22] For a review of the development of the notion of "transfer," see Morris, *The Birth of the Palestinian Refugee Problem,* pp. 23–28. The King-Crane Commission, sent to Palestine on a fact-finding mission in 1919, reported that "the Zionists look forward to a practically complete dispossession of the Palestinian people." Cited in Edward W. Said et al., "A profile of the Palestinian People," in *Blaming the Victims,* ed. by Said and Hitchens, p. 238.

for the Palestinian exodus. Indeed, it tried to stop it.[23] A key piece of evidence for this proposition is the allegation that Arab leaders broadcast radio messages urging Palestinians to flee, an assertion that continues to be found in pro-Israeli literature.[24] In 1961 Erskine Childers, an Irish journalist, later to become president of Ireland, proved beyond doubt that "there was not a single order, or appeal, or suggestion about evacuation from Palestine from any Arab radio station, inside or outside Palestine, in 1948. There is repeated monitored record of Arab appeals, even flat orders, to the civilians of Palestine to stay put." Childers did find evidence, however, that Zionist stations had been broadcasting in Arabic urging Palestinians to leave.[25]

The Palestinian claim is that the Zionists adopted a systematic campaign of terrorizing Arabs to induce them to flee and, when and if that failed, simply forced them from their homes and into exile at gunpoint. This interpretation may be closer to the truth, but it is not entirely correct. There were incidents of purposeful brutality. The massacre of more than 250 villagers at Deir Yassin, on April 9, 1948, by the Jewish underground groups known as the Irgun Zvai Leumi, led by Menachem Begin, and the Lohamei Herut Yisrael (LEHI, or Stern Gang), of which Yitzhak Shamir was a leader, was intended to strike terror into the Palestinian population and frighten the people into leaving. Following the massacre, Zionist forces drove into Arab villages with loudspeaker trucks instructing the inhabitants "to run for your lives unless you want another Deir Yassin."[26] Virtually the entire populations of two major Palestinian towns, Lydda and Ramle, which numbered some 50,000 to 70,000 inhabitants, were stampeded by the Yishuv's army, the Haganah, into a mass exodus as a result of a direct order given by Ben-Gurion to Generals Yigal Allon and Yitzhak Rabin.[27]

In mid-March 1948, Jewish military commanders put into effect

[23] Flapan, *The Birth of Israel*, p. 84.

[24] See for example Leonard J. Davis, *Myths and Facts 1985: A Concise Record of the Arab-Israeli Conflict* (Washington: Near East Report, 1984).

[25] Erskine Childers, "The Other Exodus," *The Spectator* (May 12, 1961), reprinted in *The Arab-Israeli Reader: A Documentary History of the Middle East Conflict*, ed. by Walter Laqueur and Barry Rubin (New York: Penguin, 1984), pp. 143–151.

[26] *Ibid.*, p. 148.

[27] Morris, *The Birth of the Palestinian Refugee Problem*, p. 207.

Plan D, which embodied a military strategy to secure territory. The doctrinal underpinning of Plan D was that the fewer Palestinians left behind, the better.[28] Nevertheless, "Plan D was not a political blueprint for the expulsion of Palestine's Arabs."[29] But the overall consequence of Israeli action was to contribute overwhelmingly to the Palestinians' desire to flee. According to Israeli military estimates of the time, "84 percent left in direct response to Israeli actions."[30] The government of Israel, however, has from the outset contended that because Palestinians fled of their own accord, as well as for other reasons, they have no right to return or to repatriation, as is specified in UN General Assembly Resolution 194 of December 1948.

Peace Negotiations

Another myth widely accepted as fact is that whereas Israel sought peace with the Arabs from the moment of its creation, the Arabs remained intransigent, consistently refusing to negotiate. Actually, before, during, and after the first Arab-Israeli war, leaders of the Arab states made numerous peace overtures that were rebuffed by an Israeli leadership "which maintained that time was on Israel's side and that Israel could manage perfectly well without peace with the Arab states and without a solution to the Palestinian refugee problem."[31] King Abdullah of Transjordan made a secret agreement with the Israelis prior to the outbreak of hostilities in 1947 to the effect that his troops would occupy the areas awarded to the Palestinians in the partition plan but would not attack Jewish positions. While Abdullah kept

---

[28] *Ibid.*, pp. 62–64, 113, 289.

[29] *Ibid.*, p. 62. Some revisionist historians do not accept this interpretation and argue instead that Plan D was part of an overall strategy to drive Palestinians out of areas occupied by Jewish forces. For a debate over this issue see Norman Finkelstein, Nur Masalha, and Benny Morris, "Debate on the 1948 Exodus," *Journal of Palestine Studies* 21 (Autumn 1991): 66–114; and Norman Finkelstein, "Debate on the 1948 Exodus: Rejoinder," *Journal of Palestine Studies* 21 (Winter 1992): 61–71. See also Laurence J. Silberstein, ed., *New Perspectives on Israeli History: The Early Years of the State* (New York: New York University Press, 1991).

[30] Flapan, *The Birth of Israel*, p. 89.

[31] Avi Shlaim, "Husni Za'im and the Plan to Resettle Palestinian Refugees in Syria," *Journal of Palestine Studies* 60 (Summer 1986): 79.

his side of the agreement, the Israelis did not keep theirs, seizing by force of arms portions of the Arab territory. In September 1948, Ben-Gurion even tried to persuade his provisional government to launch an all-out attack on the West Bank, including the Old City of Jerusalem, to incorporate it into the new state and deny Abdullah any land west of the Jordan River. That proposal was rejected for fear that it would jeopardize Israel's relations with Britain, the United States, and the UN.[32] Meanwhile, Abdullah continued to receive Israeli emissaries and make proposals for reducing the level of conflict right up until his assassination in February 1951.[33]

Other Arab leaders behaved quite like Abdullah, meeting with Israeli government officials and stating their conditions for terminating hostilities and recognizing Israel. Egyptian officials, including two prime ministers, had been in touch with leadership of the Yishuv prior to the outbreak of war for the purpose of trying to come to terms with the Jewish community. In September 1948, King Farouk offered to negotiate a separate peace with Israel. As these negotiations were proceeding, Ben-Gurion ordered military offensives against Egyptian positions in the Negev, thereby terminating the possibility of an Israeli-Egyptian settlement.[34] Several years later, President Nasser indicated a willingness to talk about peace with Israel, receiving an American mediator for that purpose. A massive raid on Egyptian positions in the Gaza ordered by Ben-Gurion in February 1955 caused those efforts to be stillborn.[35] In 1949, Husni Za'im, the Syrian leader, stated his desire to meet Ben-Gurion, sign a peace treaty with Israel, and settle at least 350,000 Palestinian refugees in eastern Syria. The U.S. State Department urged the Israeli prime minister to pursue the offer. His response was to set such impossible conditions that the "Americans could not believe their ears."[36]

Flapan's conclusion from the historical evidence is that "from the end of World War II to 1952, Israel turned down successive proposals made by Arab states and by neutral mediators that might have brought

---

[32] Tom Segev, *1949: The First Israelis* (New York: The Free Press, 1986), p. 14.

[33] *Ibid.*, pp. 15–21. See also Avi Shlaim, *The Politics of Partition.*

[34] Flapan, *The Birth of Israel*, pp. 133–134, 205–208.

[35] Elmore Jackson, *Middle East Mission* (New York: W.W. Norton, 1983).

[36] Segev, *1949: The First Israelis,* p. 16.

about an accommodation."[37] It did so because it did not want to make territorial concessions, to allow creation of a Palestinian state, or to repatriate even a token number of refugees. As a consequence, not only did it become more difficult for the Arab states in subsequent years to entertain the possibility of recognizing and negotiating a final peace with Israel, but the unresolved Palestinian issue ensured the perpetuation of hostility and violence that has as yet to abate.

Myths surrounding partition, the Palestinian exodus, and peace negotiations are only some of those that have grown up since 1947–1949, but they are those that careful historical scholarship has now most fully exposed. The prevalence of misconceptions detrimental to the Arab position is not, however, an indication that only the Israelis have taken liberties with the truth in presenting an interpretation favorable to themselves. The Arab states have sought to do the same, the difference being that they have been considerably less successful.

Nasser tried to justify the crushing defeat of his military in 1967 by claiming that planes from the U.S. Sixth Fleet had attacked Egypt. Although initially accepted as true by large numbers of Egyptians and Arabs, this claim was subsequently discarded as the fabrication it was. Sadat portrayed the October 1973 War as an outright Egyptian victory despite the encirclement of his Sixth Army in the Sinai and the presence of Israeli forces west of the Suez Canal. That attempt at myth making was also unsuccessful. Palestinians, more concerned with discrediting myths created at their expense than inventing new ones, have nevertheless occasionally succumbed to the temptation to lay the blame for everything at Israel's doorstep. Israel is not responsible for all the assassinations of Palestinian political activists that have occurred, despite ritualistic accusations to that effect by the PLO. Nor is it conceivable that Israeli agents provocateurs are behind attacks on Jewish institutions in Europe or elsewhere, as has sometimes been claimed by Palestinian political figures. Israel was alleged by Yasser Arafat and his supporters in the PLO to have distorted the record of Palestinian support for the Iraqi invasion of Kuwait in 1990. It was Arafat himself, however, who in the presence of a battery of television

---

[37] Flapan, *The Birth of Israel,* p. 10. For a refutation of the argument that Israel's intransigence was the key factor that impeded peace settlements with its Arab neighbors at this time, see Itamar Rabinovich, *The Road Not Taken: Early Arab-Israeli Negotiations* (New York: Oxford University Press, 1991).

THE ARAB–ISRAELI CONNECTION

cameras had embraced Saddam Hussein immediately after Iraqi troops had stormed into Kuwait. Finally, many Arabs have constructed an elaborate general myth in which Israel is blamed for all internal Arab bickering, their own clumsy public relations, their political instability, and other social and economic problems.

Israel's comparative success in convincing important audiences of the veracity of its claims and the justness of its position is due in part to the fact that in the critical period from the end of World War I until 1948, Zionists built far more effective political institutions than did the Palestinians. As Benny Morris observes, "The British Mandate of 1920–1948 can be seen as a nursery in which two societies competed and raced to achieve self-government. The Yishuv won the race outright. Its 'National Institutions' almost from the first were built with an eye to conversion into institutions of state."[38] By contrast, Palestinian political structures remained weak, riven with factionalism, and lacking support from the Arab states, which at the time were under the direct or indirect control of imperial powers. So while Jewish state formation is virtually a textbook case of the skillful combination of ideology, organization, and external support, Palestinian attempts to formulate mobilizational ideologies, construct large-scale organizations, and successfully enlist outside assistance only began to witness a modicum of success after the June 1967 war. But by that time, less than half the Palestinian population remained in the territory that had been Mandate Palestine.

ISRAELI STATE FORMATION

The leadership of the Yishuv declared the creation of the state of Israel on May 15, 1948. The two superpowers rushed to recognize the Jewish state, both hoping to establish preeminent influence within it. In a matter of weeks, the Israeli army had absorbed the initial advance by the armies of the Arab states and thrown them back, accumulating more territory in the process. Israel's war of independence was brought to successful conclusion in 1949 with the signing of armistice agreements with Egypt, Lebanon, Syria, and Transjordan. In that year the first Knesset elections were held, and the process of absorption of the additional 700,000 Jews who had arrived by 1952 began. Since

---

[38] Morris, *The Birth of the Palestinian Refugee Problem.* p. 16.

then, Israel has emerged not only as the militarily most powerful country in the region but also the one within which the participatory infrastructure of interest groups, political parties, and a parliament is best established. These successes owe much to the "state idea" of Israel—its legitimating ideology—which is Zionism.

Zionism is a product of the tumult of nineteenth-century Europe. The French revolution opened the door to the assimilation of French Jews, and that process rapidly spread throughout Western Europe. In Eastern Europe, on the other hand, and especially in Russia, Jews met with increasing persecution and enforced isolation from non-Jewish society. In this hostile environment, thoughts of establishing a Jewish state began to be expressed and to take organizational form. Y. L. Pinsker in 1881 published *Autoemancipation,* in which he argued that Jews must liberate themselves by becoming self-sufficient. This required their own territory somewhere, although not necessarily in Palestine. Pinsker subsequently became the leader of the Hibbat Zion (The Love of Zion) movement, which sent immigrants to Palestine, although at this stage most were inspired not by political Zionism and its commitment to a radical, agrarian-socialist nationalism but by religion.

Ultimately, Western Europe also provided critical ideological, organizational, and financial resources for the Zionist movement. The stimulus for Zionism there, as in Russia, was anti-Semitism. By the 1890s, commitment to assimilation into Western European society was being questioned by even prominent, well-established Jewish professionals, the most famous of whom was Theodor Herzl. A Viennese journalist born in Budapest, Herzl as a young man believed that discrimination against Jews was incompatible with the secular, liberal societies he saw emerging in Western Europe and would, therefore, disappear. That belief was shattered by the incidents of anti-Semitism he observed in France while a correspondent there in the early 1890s. The Dreyfus case, in which a French Jewish officer was wrongly convicted of treason, ultimately convinced Herzl that Jews could achieve true equality only if they created their own state, a position which he argued forcefully in *Der Judenstaat (The Jewish State),* published in 1896.

Like Pinsker, Herzl was less concerned with the location of that state than with the fact that sovereign control over territory would provide Jews guarantees against discrimination. Unlike Pinsker, Herzl was an established member of the bourgeoisie who sought to enlist the support of Europe's wealthiest Jews for his plan to colonize territory. At the first conference of the World Zionist Organization, convened in Basel by Herzl in 1897, it was agreed that Palestine should be the location for the proposed Jewish state, which was referred to officially as a "home" because it was thought unadvisable to offend the Ottomans by calling for the creation of a state on their territory.

European anti-Semitism stimulated Jewry's search for an answer to discrimination. The form that response took was an ideology that borrowed heavily from the predominant European belief systems of the day. These were strongly nationalist and colonialist as well as tinged with notions of racial supremacy. As Maxime Rodinson notes, "Colonization at the time was essentially taken to mean the spreading of progress, civilization and well-being."[39] Inhabitants of the Third World, referred to as "natives" and thought by most Europeans to be culturally if not physiologically inferior to themselves, were to be "civilized" through colonization. Resistance by "natives" or "savages" to European settlement was taken as an indication of their failure to understand and appreciate the benefits of an "advanced" civilization, another sign of the indigenes' own backwardness. Progress required subordination of the local population, by force if necessary. An alternative interpretation was to discount the very existence of such populations. Their failure to "develop" the lands they occupied virtually disqualified them as humans equal to Europeans, or at the very least disallowed their claims to that land.

Arabs, like other "natives," were described by European intellectuals of the day in terms that are today recognized as racist. R.A. Macalister intoned:

> It is no exaggeration to say that throughout these long centuries the native inhabitants of Palestine do not appear to have made a single contribution of any kind whatsoever to material civilization. It was perhaps the most unprogressive country on the face of the earth. Its entire culture was derivative.[40]

Sir Flinders Petrie, the renowned archaeologist, asserted that "the Arab has a vast balance of romance put to his credit very needlessly.

---

[39] Maxime Rodinson, *Israel: A Colonial-Settler State?* p. 42.

[40] Cited by Miriam Rosen, "The Last Crusade: British Archeology in Palestine, 1865–1920" (Unpublished M.A. thesis, Hunter College, 1976), pp. 18–21, cited by Edward W. Said, *The Question of Palestine* (New York: Vintage Books, 1979), p. 81.

He is as disgustingly incapable as most other savages, and not more worth romancing about than Red Indians or Maoris."[41]

Zionist ideology incorporated the prevailing European approach to Asia and Africa and applied it to Palestine. The Zionist slogan, "A land without a people for a people without a land," reflects the phenomenon of discounting to the point of nonexistence civilizations other than those of Europe or European origins. Herzl presented the Jewish state he advocated in his celebrated work as one which would form a defense for Europe's civilization against Asia's barbarism. Chaim Weizmann, who succeeded Herzl as the leader of the Zionist movement, argued that the land of Palestine, "one of the most neglected corners of the miserably neglected Turkish Empire," needed to be "redeemed" by Jewish labor and capital.[42] Weizmann's analogy for the comparison of Arab to Jew was "the desert against civilization."[43] It mattered little that in reality most of Palestine, other than the Negev, was no desert but an intensely and successfully cultivated fertile area. Max Nordau, a close friend of Herzl's from the time both were newspaper correspondents in Paris, stated that "we are going to Palestine to extend the moral boundaries of Europe as far as the Euphrates."[44] Such attitudes reflect the fact that the Zionist enterprise was part of the broader pattern of European colonization, requiring for its success cooperation with the imperial powers and subordination of the indigenous population.

There was no question in the minds of the early Zionists, such as Herzl and Weizmann, that their desire to create a Jewish state in Palestine could succeed only were it to appeal to powerful forces within Western nations, especially Britain. The organizational infrastructure created under Herzl's tutelage, including the Jewish National Fund founded in 1901, was modeled on the great "companies" that emerged in the seventeenth century, which effected colonial settle-

---

[41] *Ibid.,* p. 80.

[42] Chaim Weizmann, *Trial and Error: The Autobiography of Chaim Weizmann* (New York: Harper & Row, 1959) pp. 125, 128–129.

[43] Chaim Weizmann, "The Position in Palestine," *Palestine Papers* 2 (London: Jewish Agency for Palestine, 1929–1930), p. 24, cited by Richard P. Stevens, "Smuts and Weizmann," in Richard P. Stevens and Abdelwahab M. Elmessiri, *Israel and South Africa: The Progression of a Relationship* (New Jersey: North American, 1977), p. 36.

[44] Cited by Kenneth Brown, "Iron and a King: The Likud and Oriental Jews," *Merip Reports* 114 (May 1983): p. 7.

ment and imposition of imperial control, such as the British and Dutch East India Companies. Herzl sought to make the enterprise attractive to potential investors, stating that "the Jewish Company is conceived partly on the model of the great land-development companies . . . [and] will be set up as a joint-stock company, incorporated in England, under British laws and protection."[45] He successfully courted the support of the wealthy Rothschild family, to whom the first draft of *The Jewish State* was addressed. The famous Balfour Declaration of November 2, 1917, by which the British government pledged its support for "the establishment in Palestine of a national home for the Jewish people," took the form of a letter from the foreign secretary, Arthur J. Balfour, to Lord Lionel Rothschild, head of the most powerful branch of the House of Rothschild.

At the level of state interests, Zionists couched their appeal to European leaders in terms that stressed the potential utility of a Jewish state in Palestine to their imperial ambitions. Moses Hess, a nineteenth-century German socialist-Zionist, foresaw that the opening of the Suez Canal in 1869 would be accompanied by European settlement "along the road to India and China, settlements of such a character as will transform the neglected and anarchic states of the countries . . . into legal and cultivated States. This can occur only under the military protection of the European powers." Hess counseled Zionists to seize this opportunity to offer their services as middlemen between Europe and Asia.[46] Herzl originally sought to interest Bismarck and the Germans in fostering the establishment of a Jewish state to protect the proposed Berlin–Baghdad railroad.[47] When that failed, he turned to the British, to whom he pointed out that a "substantial colonization of our people at the strategic point where Egyptian and Indo-Persian interests converge" would strengthen British influence.[48]

By World War I, this logic had strong appeal to the British gov-

[45] Cited in *Theodore Herzl,* ed. by Ludwig Lewisohn (Cleveland World, 1955), p. 256.

[46] Moses Hess, *Rome and Jerusalem* (New York: Bloch, 1945), pp. 227–229, 139, cited in Stephen Halbrook, "The Philosophy of Zionism: A Materialist Interpretation," in Ibrahim Abu-Lughod and Baha Abu-Laban, *Settler Regimes in Africa and the Arab World: The Illusion of Endurance* (Wilmette, Ill.: The Medina University Press International, 1974), p. 22.

[47] Theodore Herzl, *The Diaries of Theodore Herzl,* ed. by Marvin Lowenthal (New York: Grosset & Dunlap, 1962), pp. 120–122.

[48] *Ibid.,* p. 371.

ernment, which saw multiple advantages in supporting the creation of a Jewish state in Palestine. It would serve to counter French interests in the Levant, while it would also gain the support for British war aims of influential Jewish communities in the United States and Russia. The Balfour Declaration was duly issued and almost five years later, on July 24, 1922, was incorporated into the terms of the Mandate for Palestine, awarded by the League of Nations to Britain. At that time the Arabs of Palestine, of whom there were in excess of 600,000, outnumbered the Jewish population ten to one.

The three principal requirements for successful state formation—a "state-idea" or ideology, political organizations, and international support—were accomplished by the Yishuv prior to the two great waves of Jewish migration. At the end of World War I, there were only 55,000 Jews in Palestine. Although Zionist organizations actively promoted immigration following the establishment of the Mandate in 1922, prior to 1933 the annual quota established by the Mandate was not filled. The coming to power of the Nazis, however, and the threatening climate of Europe stimulated immigration, so that by the outbreak of World War II the Jewish population had reached 450,000—about 30 percent of the total.

The second immigration wave began just after the declaration of independence in May 1948. In a year and a half, Israel's population had increased by 50 percent. These migrants, who by 1952 numbered almost three-quarters of a million, differed from their predecessors in that almost half were drawn from the Arab countries of the Middle East and North Africa, whereas about 80 percent of the Jewish population at the outbreak of hostilities in 1947 was of European origin. Absorption of this huge influx of diverse peoples, a large proportion of whom were utterly destitute and who, like almost all other new arrivals, spoke no Hebrew, is a testament to the capacities of the new state.

Zionism, which had in its early formulations included various and contradictory notions of agrarian socialism, Jewish capitalism, ardent secularism and Orthodox religious beliefs, was, however, in its essence a single idea—Jews should have a right to a state of their own, and that state was Israel. The Holocaust and the subsequent arrival of European Jewish refugees and over 200,000 Jews from Arab countries by 1951 overwhelmed any other considerations and rendered the core idea of Zionism sufficient basis upon which the new state could rest. Issues that previously had preoccupied the practitioners of Zionism—

including the role of religion in society, the organization of the economy, and relations with Palestinians and the Arab states—were of a second order of importance, to be dealt with subsequently by the new state rather than to impede its creation.

Two levels of organization facilitated the construction of the new state and assimilation of immigrants. The first was the infrastructure of international Zionist organizations that operated globally and within Israel, chief of which were the World Zionist Organization, the Jewish National Fund, and the Jewish Agency. They were responsible for raising funds, propagating Zionism, facilitating migration, lobbying governments, and purchasing and managing land in Palestine and then Israel. The second level of organization consisted of the various political movements within Palestine, most of which became political parties contesting elections after the creation of Israel. The Yishuv was an intensely political environment, characterized by tightly knit, highly ideological groupings, most of which had been influenced by their origins in Russia and Poland. While there were disagreements between these political movements, together they served as instruments for the articulation and aggregation of political demands, for recruitment of political leadership, for absorption of new participants into the political system, and for control of the geographically far-flung Zionist administration.

The dominant grouping, Mapai (Mifleget Poalei Eretz Yisrael, or the Land of Israel Workers Party), which was formed in 1930 and which ultimately became the Labor Party, was particularly closely linked to the international Zionist organizations. This close association was in part a result of the group's control of the Histadrut, the all-embracing Jewish labor organization. The World Zionist Organization distributed its funds through the Histadrut, thereby providing Mapai with the patronage necessary to expand its organization. By the mid-1930s, Mapai so dominated the World Zionist Organization that its chief rival, the Zionist Revisionists led by Vladimir Jabotinsky, left the organization and formed the New Zionist Organization. At the time of the creation of Israel, Mapai and its leader, David Ben-Gurion, had control over the nascent state structures and predominant influence in all the international Zionist organizations. The challenges from the right by the Revisionists and from the left, mounted principally by Mapam (Mifleget Poalim Meuhedet, or United Workers Party), were easily beaten back. The one-party-dominant political system, which came into being as a result of the first Knesset elections in 1949, lasted for almost three decades. It provided for close integration between the leading political party, Mapai, and state structures. This relationship initially facilitated the tasks of state building, but subsequently led to deterioration in the form of malaise, corruption, and lack of ideological clarity typical of one-party systems everywhere.

INCREASED POLITICAL TENSION WITHIN ISRAEL

Divisions between the major political movements in the Yishuv, which on at least one noted occasion led to Jew fighting Jew,[49] were not forgotten as a result of the creation of the Jewish state. They were put aside in the early years of statehood as the tasks of state building were all-consuming, and Mapai was in an overwhelmingly dominant position. The contentious issues, which involved disputes over the proper place of religion in society and in the legal system, the role of the state in the economy, relations with the United States, the USSR, and European countries, and, finally, the approach to be taken toward the Palestinians and the Arab states, remained unresolved. That they reemerged with such intensity and divisiveness in the 1970s and have continued since then is due in part to the gradual enervation of the Labor Party.

Ethnicity

Underlying Labor's decay was a basic demographic shift. While at independence Ashkenazim (European Jews) outnumbered Sephardim (Oriental Jews) four to one, by the late 1980s the latter had come to constitute at least 60 percent of the total population. While Sephardim are by no means a homogeneous group but come from enormously varied national, class, ethnic, and other backgrounds, a great many share in common the experience of having been discriminated against by Ashkenazim, who constituted the elite of virtually all political and state structures until recently. Not surprisingly Sephardim gave indications even as early as 1949 that their response

---

[49] The subordination of the Revisionists to Mainstream Zionists led by Mapai was ultimately accomplished when shortly after the declaration of independence in May 1948, Ben-Gurion ordered the military to shell the *Altalena*. This ship, carrying immigrants and weapons for the main underground terrorist organization associated with the Revisionists, the Irgun Zvai Leumi, caught fire and sank with many on board.

to discrimination by the party which controlled government, Mapai, would be to vote for the opposition, especially Herut, the party led by Vladimir Jabotinsky's disciple and inheritor of the leadership of Zionist Revisionism, Menachem Begin.[50] But it was not until the 1977 election that massive defection of Sephardim to Likud, the alliance of which Herut forms the core, occurred. In that election, 66 percent of all Sephardim voted for Likud, and 71 percent of those under 30 so voted. Sephardim support for Likud peaked in 1981, when their votes accounted for just under 70 percent of all those cast for this bloc. By contrast, almost two-thirds of Labor Party voters since 1977 have been Ashkenazim. During the spring 1992 election campaign, a pessimistic Labor Party activist observed that "each time an Ashkenazic Labor supporter and peace advocate is laid to rest in Tel Aviv, chances are that three Sephardim and potential Likud voters are born."[51]

Sephardim vote for Likud and other conservative parties not just out of resentment against Labor and its alleged role as a vehicle of Ashkenazi interests, but also because of their conservatism. It is true that there are marked differences between Sephardim of Moroccan and Yemeni backgrounds on the one hand and those from Egypt, Libya, Tunisia, Syria, and Iraq, on the other, the former generally being more traditional than the latter. It is also the case that polling data reveal little difference in political attitudes between Sephardim and Ashkenazim of equivalent incomes. But because Sephardim are generally poorer and because the Moroccan and Yemeni communities are comparatively large, as a whole, Sephardim are markedly more conservative than Ashkenazim. They are more religious, adhere to stricter personal codes of behavior, tend to favor private enterprise over government control and, most important, favor much harsher treatment of Arabs. A 1984 poll, for example, revealed that although 53 percent of Ashkenazim favored returning at least some of the occupied territories, 60 percent of Sephardim, and 64 percent of young Sephardim, favored outright annexation, despite the fact that Sephardim constitute only a very small percentage of Jewish settlers in

---

[50] Zalman Aran of the Mapai Central Committee observed in December 1949, "The Orientals are the mainstay of Herut. . . . In the poorer quarters of Tel Aviv they voted for Herut to revenge themselves on our party, for the sins of a whole generation." Cited in Segev, *1949: The First Israelis*, p. 174.

[51] Cited in Leon T. Hadar, "The Israeli Labor Party: Peacemaker or Likud II?" *Journal of Palestine Studies* 21 (Spring 1992): 83.

the occupied territories.[52] A previous poll found that 91 percent of Sephardim would refuse to rent a room to an Arab, as compared to 80 percent of Ashkenazim.[53] The rising percentage of Sephardim in the population, coupled with their increased political participation and the more conservative attitudes of younger Sephardim, thus contributed to the weakening of the Labor Party and the growing political polarization of the country.

The Electoral System

The growing division between secular and religious Israelis, however, is not just a consequence of the demographic shift. It is also an indirect result of Israel's electoral system based on proportional representation, which awards seats in the Knesset to parties in exact proportion to their share of the total vote. Such electoral systems invariably lead to the fragmentation of party systems, as it has done in Israel, where in 1992 ten parties won seats in the 120-member Knesset. Even Mapai in its heyday could not obtain a majority of parliamentary seats and thus form a government alone.

Because Mapai rejected parties associated with right-wing Revisionist Zionism as unsuitable coalition partners as well as those of the far left, it had no alternative but to form governments with the religious parties. The agreed trade-off was that Mapai would be given a free hand and key portfolios in the areas of foreign affairs, defense, internal security, economics, and finance in exchange for the religious parties' being awarded portfolios with direct relevance to religious practices, including those of education and religion. This led to the reinforcement of a separate religious education system and the introduction of religion into the public school system, the exemption of Yeshiva (religious seminary) students from military service, the banning of public transportation on the Sabbath and public holidays, and the awarding of jurisdiction over all personal status questions to religious courts. As a result, large numbers of Israeli youths have been educated in religious schools, and the curricula of public schools have

---

[52] Seker Dahaf (in Hebrew), May 1984, cited in Mordechai Bar-On, "Trends in the Political Psychology of Israeli Jews 1967–86," *Journal of Palestine Studies* 65 (Autumn 1987): 30–31.

[53] Yohanan Peres, "Ethnic Relations in Israel," *American Journal of Sociology* 76: 6 (1971): 1021–1047, cited by Maurice M. Roumani, "The Sephardi Factor in Israeli Politics," *The Middle East Journal* 42 (Summer 1988): 425.

incorporated religious material and values. All Israelis are subjected to religious law in their personal lives, which among other things means that there is no secular marriage or divorce; hence, women cannot initiate divorces. Possibly mindful of the consequences of having in the past awarded the education portfolio to religious parties, Labor Prime Minister Yitzhak Rabin, when forming his first government after the June 1992 elections, installed Shulamit Aloni, an outspoken secular leftist as minister of education. The United Torah Party, an ultra-Orthodox grouping, refused to join the coalition government in protest, alleging that Aloni "would lead a million children to 'apostasty' and 'assimilation.' "[54]

It should be noted, however, that some analysts of Israeli politics believe that even had there been a different electoral system that gave less leverage to the religious parties, religiosity would still have spread. Akiva Orr, for example, argues that growing religiosity is inherent in Zionism because the definition of who is a Jew ultimately has always to be decided on religious grounds. No other bond unites the highly diverse population of Israel.[55]

But whether its cause was inherent in the fact of Israel's being a multiethnic Jewish state or whether it was just a result of the electoral system, the outcome is the same; namely, Israel has become more religious, both in terms of personal beliefs and in the institutionalized power of religion. An indicator of both was the fact that in the November 1988 elections religious parties won more seats in the Knesset than in any previous election—18, compared with 12 in 1984. Despite the secular left's significant improvement in the 1992 election, when Labor won 45 and Meretz took 12 seats, the three successful religious parties contesting that election hung onto all but two of their parliamentary seats.

The Occupation of Arab Land

The factor of greatest importance in exacerbating tension between the major political trends, however, has not been the demographic shift or the rise of religiosity. It is the effect of the seizure of Arab territory in

---

[54] "Shas Finally Breaks Free of Rabbi Schach," *The Jerusalem Report* (July 30, 1992), p. 6.

[55] Akiva Orr, *The Unjewish State: The Politics of Jewish Identity in Israel* (London: Ithaca Press, 1983).

the 1967 war. By that act the issues that had divided the Mainstream, Revisionist, and religious trends in Zionism prior to 1948 were thrust back onto center stage, paradoxically because the 1967 victory differed from that of 1948 in two important respects. First, in 1948 territory beyond the partition lines conquered by Israel was taken primarily from what was to have comprised the Palestinian state. In 1967, however, land taken in the Golan, West Bank, Gaza, and Sinai Peninsula belonged to the Arab states of Syria, Jordan, and Egypt. This added a very important territorial issue to the conflict between Israel and those states.

Of even greater importance was that in 1947–1949 the majority of Palestinians left the area that was incorporated into Israel, not more than 160,000 remaining behind. In 1967 between 200,000 and 300,000 more Palestinians had to leave their homes, but over 1 million stayed put. Palestinians were a small minority in post-1948 Israel. They posed no real security threat to the state and were easily controlled. In territories occupied in 1967, however, there were some 1.3 million Arabs and virtually no Jews. The question arose immediately as to what should be done with this land—the question that stands as a central issue facing Israel today.

Except for East Jerusalem and the Old City, which along with 18,000 acres of adjoining land were, with virtually unanimous support by the Jewish population, formally annexed to Israel on June 28, 1967, the Israeli public has become increasingly divided over the disposition of the territories. Until well into 1968, a solid majority of Israelis expressed a desire to return the conquered lands in exchange for peace with and recognition by the Arab states.[56] From then until 1991, there was a declining willingness to make the "land for peace" swap. In March 1986, only 41 percent of those polled thought that should be done, while 50 percent opposed it.[57] In September 1986, 38 percent of respondents in a *Jerusalem Post* poll agreed with the statement "I support anyone who acts to get Arabs to leave Judea and Samiria."[58] By 1987, within the 18-to-22 age group, 73 percent were opposed to making any territorial concessions.[59] In August 1988, almost one-half of a

---

[56] Bar-On, "Trends in the Political Psychology of Israeli Jews," p. 24.

[57] *Ibid.*, pp. 24–25.

[58] *The Jerusalem Post*, October 11, 1986.

[59] Langellier, "The New Palestinian Nationalism," p. 13.

sample group polled by the Israel Institute of Applied Social Research endorsed "transfer" as a means to preserve "the democratic and Jewish nature of the state."[60] But in the wake of the second Gulf war, Israeli public opinion became markedly less intransigent. By 1992, about 60 percent of Israelis endorsed the land-for-peace trade, more than one-third were willing to accept an independent Palestinian state, and 90 percent supported peace negotiations with the Arabs, compared to 57 percent in 1986.[61]

Public opinion toward the occupied territories has closely paralleled government policy, which in turn is remarkably similar to that implemented by the Yishuv during the Mandate era (1922–1948) and by Israel in its own Galilee region after 1948. Land acquisition by the Jewish National Fund was designed prior to 1948 to pave the way for colonization and eventual creation of the Jewish state. The strategy was to create a security belt of Jewish settlements, then to populate that area as densely as possible. After 1948 the only region within Israel that had an Arab majority was the northern district of Galilee, which was 63 percent Arab. "In a concerted effort to break up this concentration and reduce the Arab population to minority status, the Israelis confiscated as much land as possible, destroyed villages and implanted Jewish settlements."[62] That was the essence of the Israeli approach to the occupied territories between 1967 and 1992, with the exception of the Sinai, where settlements were established but which was eventually traded back to Egypt for the peace that grew out of the Camp David Accords of 1978. One of the first steps taken by the Labor government formed by Yitzhak Rabin in July 1992 was to freeze further settlements in the occupied territories.

In the other two critical border areas seized in 1967, the Golan Heights and the Jordan Valley, settlement began almost as soon as the guns fell silent and was carried out under the auspices of the Labor Party. On July 15, 1967, Kibbutz Merom Hagolan, the first Jewish settlement in the occupied territories, was established adjacent to Qunaitra in the Golan. This area had essentially been cleared of its

---

[60] Glenn Frankel, "Expulsion of Arabs Favored," *The Guardian Weekly,* November 13, 1988, p. 18.

[61] Leon T. Hadar, "The Israeli Labor Party," pp. 80–94.

[62] Janet Abu-Lughod, "Israeli Settlements in Occupied Arab Lands: From Conquest to Colony," in *Palestinian Rights: Affirmation and Denial,* ed. by Ibrahim Abu-Lughod (Wilmette, Ill.: Medina Press, 1982), p. 122.

Arab inhabitants during the hostilities, when more than 90,000 of its some 100,000 residents were driven out. Similarly, in the major urban area of the Jordan Valley, which is the Jericho region, only 10,000 Palestinians of the 85,000 resident there on June 5, 1967, remained a week later. The Allon Plan, proposed in 1967 by General Yigal Allon, the mentor of Yitzhak Rabin, called for a string of over 20 settlements along the Syrian frontier in the Golan with 7,000 residents, a target which was in fact reached by the time the Golan was annexed by Israel in 1981. The Allon Plan also recommended "absorption into Israel of a security zone running the length of the Jordan rift," (i.e., the Jordan Valley), a zone which was initially described as being 10 to 15 kilometers wide but which was "thickened" over the years so that, by 1975, it stretched "to the very margins of Arab cultivation in the West Bank highlands."[63] By 1981 Israel controlled about half the cultivable land in the Jordan Valley. Jewish domination of Jerusalem was also a top priority. It was accomplished by destroying the Maghribi Arab quarter of the Old City and replacing it with new accommodation for Jews, and by establishing settlements on the surrounding hills. By 1979 over half the total population of the expanded Jerusalem district that had been annexed in 1967 was Jewish.

But the West Bank, other than the annexed Jerusalem area or the Jordan Valley, posed a much more intractable problem. Had it been annexed in the wake of the 1967 war, it would have added 600,000 Arabs to Israel's population, more than doubling the total number of Israeli Arabs. The Allon Plan, which subsequently informed Prime Minister Rabin's negotiating position in 1992, was designed to gain control of the land but not add the Arab population to that on the other side of the "Green Line" (the 1949 armistice line) in Israel proper. The imperative of demography in the calculations of Allon and subsequent Israeli policy-makers is indicated by the fact that Arabs in Israel itself and in the occupied territories made up 38.8 percent of the population in 1991 and were expanding at a rate of 5 percent a year, compared to a growth rate of 1 percent for the Jewish population. Even with an additional 400,000 Jewish immigrants from the former Soviet Union, the Arab population will constitute about 45 percent of those living under Israeli rule by the year 2000.[64] By the end of the

---

[63] William Wilson Harris, *Taking Root: Israeli Settlement in the West Bank, the Golan and Gaza-Sinai, 1967–1980* (New York: Research Studies Press, 1980), pp. 105–106.

[64] Andrew North, "Israel's Demographic Dilemma," *The Middle East* (May 1992), p. 12.

Labor era, 12 settlements had been established on the West Bank highlands and were connected to those in the Jordan Valley by the "Allon Plan Road." With the coming to power of Likud in 1977, the pace of settlement was accelerated dramatically. By 1988 the Israeli government had confiscated 52 percent of all land on the West Bank and established 135 settlements there with over 65,000 inhabitants. By 1992, in the occupied territories as a whole, there were 212 settlements with 112,000 inhabitants, who constituted 13 percent of the West Bank and Gaza population and nearly 6 percent of the entire population of Israel. But the issue of what to do with the Palestinian population, exacerbated by this Jewish settlement, remained unresolved.

The Gaza Strip, which had 400,000 Palestinians in 1967, presented even greater demographic and security problems than the West Bank. The original intention, as stated by the prime minister in the summer of 1967 and as reiterated in the Allon Plan, was to annex Gaza and resettle the 1948 refugees living there in the West Bank and Sinai. In 1973 Prime Minister Rabin called for the population to be dispatched to Jordan.[65] But the Labor Government, after breaking the back of Palestinian underground resistance in Gaza in 1971, did not put into effect the provisions of the Allon Plan for this area. It did not commit the required material resources or imbue the undertaking with sufficient ideological zeal to lure Jewish settlers to move into Gaza, where there were only 500 in four settlements when Likud took power. Over the next ten years, however, more government support for settlement was forthcoming. Fourteen new settlements were established and the Jewish population increased fivefold. Despite the fact that Gaza's Arab population in the early 1990s exceeded a half million (who were crammed into an area of 140 square miles, giving this artificial entity a population density equivalent to that of Hong Kong), the Israelis by 1992 had confiscated more than a third of the total area and awarded it to Jewish settlers who constituted one-half of 1 percent of the population. Settlers on average have 2.6 acres of land in Gaza, while Palestinians have 0.006 acre each.[66]

Just as land seizures and the implantation of settlements in the occupied territories have paralleled previous patterns established first

---

[65] *Ma'ariv,* February 16, 1973, cited in Joan Mandell, "Gaza: Israel's Soweto," *Merip Reports* 136–137 (October–December 1985):10.

[66] *Middle East Report* 152 (May–June 1988): 35.

in the Yishuv and then in Israel after 1948, so have other policies directed at the Palestinian population there resembled those used to contain the Arabs left in Israel at the end of hostilities in 1949. Because of the very different demographic balance that obtains in the occupied territories, however, and because of the much greater politicization of Palestinians since 1967 in comparison with 1948, Israeli policies intended to subordinate the Arab population of the occupied territories have had to be much more severe than those used in Israel. Whereas demolition of houses, wanton disregard for civil rights, imprisonment without trial, torture, deportation, and political killings have seldom occurred in Israel proper, they are commonplace in the territories. Between 1967 and the beginning of the Palestinian intifadah (uprising) in December 1987, there were more than a half-million detentions and arrests (an average of about one arrest/detention for every three Palestinians); there were also over 2,000 deportations and 1,500 house demolitions. From 1982 to 1987, more than 130 Palestinians lost their lives in political killings at the hands of Israeli soldiers or settlers.[67] By comparison, between 1968 and 1983 Israeli government statistics reveal that 14 Israeli civilians and 22 soldiers were killed by West Bank Palestinians. From April 1986 to May 1987 alone, Israeli forces killed 22 Palestinians, while armed attacks on Israelis took two lives.[68]

As early as 1977 the torture of Palestinians under detention was described as being "so widespread and systematic that it cannot be dismissed as 'rogue cops' exceeding orders. It appears to be sanctioned as deliberate policy."[69] Ten years later, a special Israeli judicial commission headed by former Supreme Court president Moshe Landau was formed to investigate allegations of torture against Shin Beth (the General Security Service). The commission reported that for the period covered by its review (1971–1987), Shin Beth officers had routinely extracted confessions by applying "physical and psychological pressure" and that they had regularly perjured themselves by denying in

---

[67] Meron Benvenisti, *1987 Report: Demographic, Economic, Legal, Social and Political Developments in the West Bank* (Jerusalem: West Bank Data Project, 1987).

[68] "Israel and the Palestinians, 1948–1988," *Middle East Report* 152 (May–June 1988): 35.

[69] *The Sunday Times,* June 17, 1977, cited in *Journal of Palestine Studies* 6 (Summer 1977): 190–219.

court that they had mistreated detainees.[70] Instead of condemning these practices and prohibiting their future use, the Landau Commission recommended that Shin Beth interrogators officially be permitted to use "psychological pressure and light violence when interrogating those suspected of terrorist acts."[71] There is an abundance of evidence, including that provided by the U.S. government, to suggest that torture has continued to be employed systematically by Israeli security forces against Palestinians.[72]

The legal system which even prior to the intifadah allowed for arrest and detention without charges or trial for up to six months (renewable on request to a military court), and which formally embodies the principle of appeal only on jurisdictional matters and then only against "administrative measures" (and not on "security charges"), is based on some 1,200 military regulations that strictly regulate every aspect of Palestinians' lives. Under these regulations tight censorship has been imposed (in 1985 over 1,600 books were banned); collective punishments, such as destruction of houses, imposition of curfews, and mass arrests meted out; all gatherings of ten people or more for "political purposes" prohibited; and any display of Palestinian nationalism, including possession of a Palestinian flag, rendered illegal. Use of the word *Palestine* can be unlawful. In 1980, for example, a court ruled that a business called Palestine Press Service could not be established because the term *Palestine* is "offensive to the Israeli public."[73] Israel has never permitted elections in occupied Gaza, although municipal elections were held in the West Bank in 1972 and 1976.

---

[70] For a review of this report and a more general account of human rights violations in the occupied territories, see "Israel and the Occupied Territories," *Country Report for Human Rights Practices for 1987,* submitted by the Department of State to the 100th Congress (February 1988), reprinted in the *Journal of Palestine Studies* 68 (Summer 1988): 105–115.

[71] O. Nir, "Justice Under Fire," *Ha'Aretz Weekend Supplement,* March 6, 1987 (in Hebrew), cited in Raija-Leena Punamäki, "Experiences of Torture, Means of Coping, and Level of Symptoms Among Palestinian Political Prisoners," in *Journal of Palestine Studies* 68 (Summer 1988): 82–83.

[72] See, for example, *Country Report on Human Rights Practices for 1991: Israel and the Occupied Territories* (Washington, D.C.: U.S. Government Printing Office, 1992), reprinted in *Journal of Palestine Studies* 21 (Spring 1992): 114–125.

[73] *The West Bank and the Rule of Law* (New York: The International Commission of Jurists, 1980), pp. 126–128, cited by John Quigley, "Human Rights and Palestine," in Abu-Lughod, *Palestinian Rights,* p. 147.

Since 1980, all except one of the mayors elected in 1976 have been deposed; two were deported and two others were maimed for life in bomb attacks perpetrated by settlers acting in collusion with security officials. Land confiscations, Jewish settlement, and the repressive legal measures employed to subordinate Palestinians in the occupied territories were deemed by a resolution of the United Nations Security Council of March 1, 1980, "to constitute a flagrant violation of the Fourth Geneva Convention relative to the protection of civilian persons in time of war."[74]

Associated with measures to facilitate Israeli control and restrict personal and collective political expression by Palestinians have been policies intended to deny them physical and economic resources. Access to water has been progressively limited by direct prohibition of its use by Palestinians and by diversion of it to Jewish settlements and to Israel. In 1990, the 1.1 million Palestinians in the West Bank received 119 cubic meters of water per person, compared to 354 cubic meters provided to each of the 110,000 Israeli settlers.[75] Economic resources have been systematically siphoned out of the occupied territories into Israel. More than 100,000 Palestinians work in Israel, mainly in menial and poorly paid jobs. In the first 20 years of occupation, $1 billion was deducted from the wages of Palestinians employed in Israel for employment benefits for which they are ineligible.[76] From 1967 to 1987, residents of the occupied territories paid $800 million in taxes, $2\frac{1}{2}$ times the total investments in the territories over that period.[77] Given this outward flow of resources, it is not surprising that Palestinian agriculture and industry have stagnated. Total industrial production by 1988 was a trifling $85 million, which constituted 8 percent of West Bank gross domestic product (GDP). In 1967, industry had accounted for 9 percent of the West Bank's GDP.[78] By the early 1990s, about half of the Palestinians in the occupied territories were

---

[74] UN Security Council Resolution 465 of March 1, 1980, cited in W. Thomas Mallison and Sally V. Mallison, *The Palestine Problem in International Law and World Order* (London: Longman, 1986), pp. 474–476.

[75] Jonathan C. Randal, "Water Becomes Increasing Bitter Issue in Mid-East," *Guardian Weekly* (May 24, 1992), p. 19.

[76] Raja Shehadeh, "Occupiers' Law and the Uprising," *Journal of Palestine Studies* 67 (Spring 1988): 33.

[77] "Israel and the Palestinians," p. 36.

[78] *Ibid.*, p. 36; and Benvenisti, *1987 Report*, p. 22.

unemployed. Of the 26,000 Palestinian high school students who graduated in 1990, some 20,000 joined the ranks of the unemployed. Only 1,000 found steady employment. The GNP per capita in the West Bank and Gaza Strip dropped from $1,562 and $1,081, respectively, in 1987, to $1,200 and $700, respectively, in 1989. Israel's per capita GNP in 1989 was more than five times that of the West Bank and almost ten times that of the Gaza Strip.[79] In a 1986 survey of the attitudes of Palestinians living under occupation, 2.1 percent said their living conditions had improved, 11.2 percent said their conditions had not changed since 1967, and 84.5 percent said that their conditions had deteriorated.[80]

Although repression of Palestinians in the occupied territories prior to December 1987, when the intifadah commenced, was harsh, it became truly draconian after that time. In the first two years of the intifadah, 159 children under 16, with an average age of 10, were killed by soldiers. More than half of those slain were not near a demonstration when they were killed and less than one-fifth were involved in stone throwing. As many as 63,000 children were gassed, beaten, or wounded.[81] In 1991, Israeli forces combating the intifadah deported 8 Palestinians, killed 99, wounded 13,500, and at any one time in that year had over 11,000 Palestinians in prison. Of the 99 killed, 27 were shot by "nonuniformed security personnel," otherwise known as death squads. Palestinian attacks on Israeli soldiers and civilians in 1991 resulted in 12 deaths.[82] By July 1992, the toll of human rights violations by Israeli forces during the intifadah included 1,045 deaths, 122,700 injuries, 66 expulsions, 2,100 house demolitions/sealings, and 15,200 administrative detentions.[83] The world community, including Israel's closest allies, has unanimously condemned Israel's repressive measures. Within Israel, the intifadah brought into even sharper focus the basic divisions that have characterized Zionism from the outset.

---

[79] Bernard Sabella, "The Demography of Conflict: A Palestinian Predicament," *New Outlook* 9 (April–May 1991): 9–11.

[80] Mohammed Shadid and Rick Seltzer, "Political Attitudes of Palestinians in the West Bank and Gaza Strip," *The Middle East Journal* 42 (Winter 1988): 21.

[81] These figures are provided in a study conducted by the Swedish Save the Children organization, cited in Colman McCarthy, "Exposing Israeli Violence," *Washington Post* (July 15, 1990), p. F2.

[82] *Country Report*, pp. 115–117.

[83] *The Washington Report on Middle East Affairs* (July 1992), p. 23.

DIVISIONS WITHIN ZIONISM

For over a half-century, there have been three major trends within Zionism. Mainstream Zionism, made up primarily of secular social democrats, represented first by Mapai and then by the Labor Party, is similar to European social democracy in its political agenda and strategies. Antagonistic to the radical left, especially to communists, mainstream Zionists have preferred to compromise with conservatives in order to exercise power. From 1949 to 1977, that compromise took the form of a coalition with the religious parties. Between 1984 and 1989, it was manifested in a coalition with Likud, the organizational legacy of Revisionism, historically the major competitor to Mainstream Zionism. Reflecting the shift in public attitudes, Mainstream Zionism moved progressively to the right from 1949 to the early 1990s, when disillusionment with the Likud government caused a leftward shift in public attitudes and Labor Party policies. The Labor Party's share of votes and Knesset seats declined from just more than one-half in 1949 to between one-third and two-fifths in the 1980s.[84] In the 1992 election, the Labor Party arrested its decline, capturing its largest share of votes since 1981.

Divided almost from the outset into those who favored territorial compromise and accommodation with the Arabs and those who preferred an activist military policy to attain maximum territory and subordination of Arabs, Mainstream Zionism has over the years become increasingly dominated by those of the activist persuasion. Labor's leadership reflects this trend. Former generals such as Shimon Peres and Yitzhak Rabin, who since the mid-1970s have alternated as leader and deputy leader of Labor, have come to exercise enormous influence within the party. Throughout the 1970s and 1980s, they perpetuated Mainstream Zionism's primary strategy concerning the Arabs, which evolved almost a half-century ago. The plan was to cooperate with Jordan in preventing the emergence of a Palestinian state. Thus, after 1967, the Labor Party was willing to return some part of the West Bank to King Hussein, but for various reasons such a deal was never struck. With the unilateral termination of the "Jordanian option" by King Hussein in July 1988, the Labor Party was left without a coher-

---

[84] Emmanuel Gutman, "Israel: The Politics of the Second Generation," in *Ideology and Power in the Middle East: Studies in Honor of George Lenczowski,* ed. by Peter J. Chelkowski and Robert J. Pranger (Durham, N.C.: Duke University Press, 1988).

ent foreign policy to present to Israeli voters in the November 1988 elections. Unwilling to countenance the creation of a Palestinian state, Labor resorted initially to seeking to repress Palestinian nationalism and to hang on to the territories.

This repressive strategy became increasingly counterproductive because it did not differentiate Labor from its chief rival, Likud; because it failed to stop the intifadah; and because it had catastrophic consequences for Israel internationally. Abandoning its junior-partner role in the coalition with Likud in the summer of 1989 in protest against Prime Minister Shamir's acceptance of his party's hardliners' conditions for proposed Palestinian elections, Labor began to distance itself from government policies, especially when it became evident in the fall of 1991 that they were seriously eroding support for Israel in the United States. In the 1992 election campaign, Labor promised that it would trade land for peace if it were elected. Paradoxically, its policy toward the Palestinians was to offer them not a state but "autonomy"—that is, some form of self-government under Israeli sovereignty. The possibility of a Palestinian state ultimately emerging from that self-governing enclave, however, was not precluded. The proposal of autonomy for the Palestinians had first been made by the Likud government of Menachem Begin in 1977 and was embodied in the Camp David Accords negotiated between Begin and President Sadat of Egypt in 1978. Prime Minister Shamir had also proposed limited autonomy in his plan announced in early 1989, but due to opposition from the right wing within the Likud Party and his own inflexibility, that plan had become a dead letter by the summer of 1990, when Iraq invaded Kuwait and altered fundamentally the diplomatic context surrounding the Arab-Israeli conflict. Likud's reaction to American preeminence in the region, to the further weakening of the Arabs in general and the Palestinians in particular, and to the prospect of much greater Jewish migration from the former Soviet Union was to delay negotiations and "create facts" (i.e., Jewish settlements) which would render Palestinian claims irrelevant. This strategy, however, became untenable in the face of opposition from the Bush administration. An opportunity was thus created for the Labor Party to offer a compromise and thereby win the tacit support of the U.S. government, which, among other things, signaled to the Israeli electorate that if Labor were to win the 1992 elections, Washington would look more favorably on Israel's request for $10 billion in loan guarantees to finance the resettlement of Jewish immigrants.

Likud's ambitions and diplomatic incompetence thus paved the way for Labor to co-opt Likud's policy of autonomy for the Palestinians, which helped to facilitate the Labor victory in the 1992 elections. In forming his government, Prime Minister Yitzhak Rabin sought initially to build a broad coalition that would include parties both to his left and to his right in order to gain support for the settlement he hoped to negotiate. Ultimately, however, he could not reconcile sharp differences between Raful Eytan's Tzomet Party and the leftist Meretz Party, so the former was left out of the government. The coalition he finally formed was in any case extremely heterogeneous, grouping as it did Labor, Meretz (a coalition of three secular leftist parties), and the ultra-Orthodox Shas. That Rabin sought to include Tzomet, which is stridently anti-Palestinian, and refused at all stages to countenance the inclusion of two small Arab parties in the governing coalition, indicates that there has been no major strategic change in Labor's approach to the Palestinian issue, although its tactics were altered after 1988–1989 as a result of the collapse of the Jordanian option and the progressive move to the right of Likud, which opened up political space to Labor in the center of the Israeli political arena.

Revisionism was more or less "beyond the pale" in the eyes of many Zionists until Likud formed its first government in 1977. So-named because its founder, Vladimir Jabotinsky, urged revision of the Palestine Mandate to include Transjordan and thereby make possible the creation of a Jewish state on both sides of the river Jordan, Revisionism sought to establish that state through violence directed against Arabs, the British, and even neutral mediators.[85] The balance of power between Mainstream and Revisionist Zionism began to shift in favor of the latter after 1967, partly because of the polarizing and conservatizing effects of the occupation. In 1977 Likud, the party most closely associated with Revisionism, won 43 seats, compared with Labor's 32. Likud formed a government with two religious parties and a breakaway faction from Labor. Some 51 percent of voters under age 25 in 1977 had chosen Likud, whereas only 20 percent of them voted Labor. From then until 1992, Likud was always in government, even though it ran only about neck and neck with Labor at the polls, capturing 48,

---

[85] Count Folke Bernadotte, a UN envoy, proposed during negotiations following the 1948 war that the UN take responsibility for Jerusalem and that Israel return areas conquered beyond the partition line to the Arab state called for in the 1947 Partition Plan. He was assassinated in 1949 by members of the Stern Gang.

41, 40, and 32 seats, compared with Labor's 47, 44, 39, and 45 seats in the 1981, 1984, 1988, and 1992 elections, respectively. Throughout this period, Likud has remained loyal to the basic tenets of Jabotinsky's Revisionism—that is, no withdrawal from the territory of Eretz Yisrael, no compromise with the Palestinians, little hesitation in using violence for political purposes, a commitment to self-reliance based on distrust of non-Jews, and support for private enterprise. While Jabotinsky was essentially a secularist, under Begin's leadership Revisionism became imbued with Jewish religious traditions and symbols.

The replacement of Labor by Likud as the dominant force in Israeli politics was not just due to the change in their respective electoral fortunes, but was also a result of the shift by Zionism's third major trend, the religious one, from an alliance with Mainstream to one with Revisionist Zionism. This realignment was signaled by the defection of two religious parties from Labor to Likud in 1977. Subsequently, the strength of the religious tendency was reinforced with the emergence of a group of ultra-Orthodox and ultranationalist parties even further to the right of the existing religious parties. The National Religious Party (NRP), also known by its Hebrew acronym Mafdal, which for 50 years prior to 1977 had been allied with Mainstream Zionism, joined the coalition with Likud as a result of growing nationalism among its younger members, many of whom had close links with the activist settler organization Gush Emunim (Bloc of the Faithful). Agudat Israel (Federation of Israel), made up principally of Hasidic (ultra-Orthodox) Jews—whose spiritual head, Rabbi Menachem Mendel Schneerson, lives in Brooklyn and has never visited Israel—is devoted to implementing the *halacha* (Orthodox Jewish law). Agudat Israel's leaders also perceived Likud to share their interests more fully and joined the coalition government.

Parties that subsequently have emerged to the right of the NRP and Agudat Israel are divided between those supported by the ultra-Orthodox and those backed by ultranationalists, and between those who appeal to Ashkenazim or to Sephardim. In 1984, 13 of the 26 parties that contested the election had been formed since the previous election in 1981. The most successful of these new parties was Shas (Sephardi Torah Guardians), comprised mainly of Sephardim who broke away from Agudat Israel. Shas won four seats in 1984, six in 1988, and seven in 1992. Its members are predominantly of Moroccan origin and of the lower middle class. Shas, along with Agudat Israel and another ultra-Orthodox party, Degel Hatorah (Torah Flag Party), demanded in the wake of the 1988 elections, as their price for joining a Likud-dominated government, the banning of abortion, closing of all forms of entertainment on the Sabbath, upgrading the importance of rabbinical courts, and, most critical to Israel's foreign relations, requiring all Jewish converts to gain Orthodox rabbinical approval before becoming Israeli citizens. Since the overwhelming majority of American Jews are of the Conservative or Reform branches of Judaism, this measure, had it been adopted, would immediately have strained relations between Israel and American Jewry. Despite its ultra-Orthodox religious nature, Shas has consistently been more willing to compromise with the Palestinians than have other ultra-Orthodox or ultranationalist parties. Partly for this reason, it was brought into the Labor government in 1992.

The ultranationalist parties share a generally anti-Arab perspective with the ultra-Orthodox, but the two tendencies are sharply divided over religious matters, with the ultranationalists being strong advocates of secularism. Raful Eytan's Tzomet Party has been the most successful of the ultranationalist parties, tripling its votes between 1988 and 1992 and becoming the fourth largest party in the Knesset. Eytan, who served as the army's chief of staff under Begin and entered politics with the Likud Party, has likened Palestinians to "stoned cockroaches" and divided them into good and bad: "The bad ones should be killed, the good ones deported."[86] But in the 1992 campaign, Eytan reserved his sharpest attacks for Jewish politicians whom he accused of corruption, especially the ultra-Orthodox. Moledet, an ultranationalist party to the right of Tzomet that openly endorses "transfer" of the Palestinian population, unlike Tzomet, did not improve on its 1988 performance in the 1992 elections. Strident ultranationalism had less of an appeal to Israeli voters in 1992 than it had four years earlier. Many voters were increasingly worried about various domestic political issues, including the state of the economy and the growing role of religion in all aspects of social life.

The coalition originally forged under Menachem Begin, which grouped Likud with various of the ultranationalist and ultra-Orthodox parties, did not survive the 1992 election. Internal bickering within Likud, especially between Prime Minister Shamir and longtime minister Ariel Sharon, contributed to that party's weakness. Divisions

---

[86] Peretz Kidron, "Rabin's Balancing Act Threatens His Commitment to Peace," *Middle East International* (July 10, 1992), pp. 3–4.

between secularists and the ultra-Orthodox further strained the coalition, as did growing resentments among Sephardim of Ashkenazim dominance of Likud and its government. As a result, the Israeli political system has become much more fluid, with the ultranationalist and ultra-Orthodox parties losing something of their appeal and simultaneously becoming more detached from Likud and willing to entertain prospects of joining with Labor. This new, more flexible atmosphere provided the government of Prime Minister Rabin with a reasonable amount of latitude in which to pursue a negotiated settlement of the conflict with the Palestinians and the Arab states. Despite their ardor and very considerable resources, Likud and its supporters among the ultranationalists and ultra-Orthodox appeared by 1992 to have failed to fulfill their dream of a "Greater Israel," in which no territory would be handed back to the Arabs. While this failure was due in part to international pressures and to political divisions within Israel, it resulted also from the fact that the Palestinians, like the Zionists before 1948, have systematically been creating institutions that give substance to their claims for recognition of their national rights.

PALESTINIAN STATE FORMATION

On November 15, 1988, in Algiers at the 19th session of the Palestine National Council (PNC), the 450-member parliament of the Palestinian national movement, the establishment of a Palestinian state was declared.[87] The acceptance of Security Council Resolutions 242 and 338, which implicitly recognize Israel, was announced for the first time. The PNC also renounced the use of terrorism, although in rather elliptical language. These measures were immediately denounced by Israeli Foreign Minister Shimon Peres as "tactical moves devoid of any importance" and by Prime Minister Yitzhak Shamir as "meaningless," as "gimmicks," and as "doubletalk." Shamir pledged not to negotiate with the PLO "because they're opposed to peace with Israel."[88] But the proceedings of the 19th session of the PNC and subsequent, unambiguous declarations by Yasser Arafat accepting the critical UN

---

[87] Two hundred fifty-two members voted for the resolution calling for the declaration, 46 voted against it, and 10 abstained. Israel had prevented members of the PNC from the occupied territories from attending.

[88] World wire services, November 15, 1988.

resolution and renouncing terrorism were a milestone for the Palestinians themselves. They also made possible United States-sponsored Israeli-Palestinian negotiations that commenced in October 1991.

Almost exactly a year before the PNC's 19th session, the Arab states at their Amman summit conference had relegated the Palestinian issue to the back burner and had snubbed PLO chairman Yasser Arafat. Now all those states, primarily as a result of the intifadah, were obliged to accept the Palestinian fait accompli and recognize the newly declared state, whatever their reservations and misgivings.[89] Just two weeks less than 40 years had elapsed since the UN had approved the Partition Plan that had paved the way for the creation of Israel. In the intervening two generations, the Palestinians articulated the ideology, created the organizations, and generated the level of international support required to approach the goal of establishing a state in some part of the territory of the Mandate. If this were to occur, Palestinians would be the last Arab peoples subjected to European control after World War I to gain their independence.

The process of Palestinian state formation, which is not yet completed, began at zero point in 1948. Having officially been labeled as "non-Jewish communities" in the Balfour Declaration and "Arabs" under the Mandate, Palestinians were from 1948 referred to as *refugees,* the term applied to them in UN Security Council Resolution 242, which was the principal reason why they rejected that resolution for so long. They wanted to be called neither Arabs nor refugees, but Palestinians or Palestinian Arabs. The use of that term implies recognition of their national existence and right to a state. It was not until the late 1960s, however, that Palestinian ideological and organizational resources were sufficient to make that demand with any forcefulness. Prior to that time Palestinian politics, organized along traditional lines, dominated by competing notables, fragmented between different geographical centers, and lacking any meaningful organization, simply were no match for the Israelis.

---

[89] Egypt, fearful of jeopardizing its relations with the United States and its role as mediator between Israel and the Arabs, and under intense pressure from U.S. and Israeli officials, at first sought to finesse the issue. It declared its support for the PNC resolution without actually recognizing the newly declared state. That evasive tactic proved untenable in the face of widespread criticism of Egypt's stance in the Arab press. Within a week of the declaration Egypt announced its recognition of the new state, simultaneously blasting "some media circles that continue to raise questions about Egypt's position" (Alan Cowell, "Palestine State Is Recognized by Egypt," *New York Times,* November 21, 1988).

PALESTINIAN NATIONALISM

Like other Arabs in the Levant, Palestinians participated in the "Arab Awakening" in the twilight of the Ottoman Empire, redefining their personal and political identities as Arab rather than Ottoman or exclusively as Muslim, Christian, tribal, or familial. After the collapse of Amir Faisal's Arab Kingdom in Damascus, Palestinians, again like other Levantine Arabs, began to formulate nationalist sentiments and identities centered on the sovereign territory into which the British and French had divided the region. For the Palestinians this was, of course, Palestine. But for them, as for the Syrians, Lebanese, Iraqis, and many other Arabs, Pan-Arabist ideas continued to coexist with state-based nationalism.

In the wake of the devastating defeat of 1947–1949, an Arab identity temporarily displaced the Palestinian one. It did so because Israel and the Arab states both sought to reinforce Arabism at the expense of Palestinian nationalism and because the Palestinians, too weak to challenge Israel alone, sought to enlist the Arab states in their cause. In particular, Gamal Abdel Nasser, by championing Arab rights, appeared to the Palestinians as a potential savior. Even before the catastrophic defeat of June 1967, however, Palestinians had become aware of the divergence of interests between their cause and Nasserism, so they sought once again to center their nationalism not on Arabism but on their Palestinian identities. This process was given added momentum by the 1967 war.

Israeli Response

That Palestinian nationalism has become so intense is due in part to the severity and thoroughness with which its opponents, including Israel, the Arab states, and the United States, have sought to subdue it. Israel in particular has tried to invalidate Palestinian claims to land occupied by Israel by obliterating references to Palestinians and manifestations of their separate culture. Since 1948, Israel has bulldozed 385 of the 475 Palestinian villages that were inside the "Green Line" (i.e., the border between Israel and the West Bank from 1949 to 1967) and wiped their names from maps, in many cases replacing them with Hebrew names.[90] Officially, Palestinians in Israel are known as Israeli Arabs. Prime Minister Golda Meir declared in 1969 that there was no

---

[90] "Israel and the Palestinians," p. 35.

such thing as the Palestinian people—"they did not exist."[91] In that same year Menachem Begin warned an Israeli audience of the consequences of allowing the term *Palestine* to be used. He said, "If this is Palestine and not the land of Israel, then you are conquerors and not tillers of the land. You are invaders. If this is Palestine, then it belongs to a people who lived here before you came."[92] Yitzhak Rabin, who as prime minister between 1974 and 1977 had refused to negotiate with "any Palestinian element" and who said "a third state between Israel and Jordan . . . will not be created," responded as minister of defense to the Palestinian intifadah by pledging to "break their bones" and by authorizing the use of a range of lethal weaponry.[93]

The invasion of Lebanon by Israel in the summer of 1982 was for the purpose of destroying the organizational infrastructure that gives political meaning to Palestinian nationalism. The Israeli response to the intifadah, a quintessential expression of nationalist commitment, has been to attempt to crush it. Intellectual efforts have also been made to impede the formation, legitimation, and global acceptance of Palestinian nationalism. In 1984, for example, a Zionist author, Joan Peters, published *From Time Immemorial*.[94] This book purported to document that the great majority of Palestinians are in fact not that at all, but are Arabs who illegally migrated to Palestine during the Mandate as a result of economic opportunities stimulated by Jewish settlement. The book was lauded by a great number of leading Israelis and supporters of Israel. It subsequently was convincingly argued that the author had flagrantly distorted, falsified, and concealed the true historical record.[95]

---

[91] *The Sunday Times,* June 15, 1969.

[92] *Yediot Aharanot* (October 17, 1969), cited in Ari Bober, *The Other Israel* (New York: Doubleday, 1972), p. 77.

[93] "Israel and the Palestinians," p. 40.

[94] Joan Peters, *From Time Immemorial* (New York: Harper & Row, 1984).

[95] For a discussion of the reaction to this book, see Edward W. Said, "Conspiracy of Praise", *Blaming The Victims*, pp. 23–31. The most informative reviews of the book are Norman G. Finkelstein, "Disinformation and the Palestine Question: The Not-so-strange Case of Joan Peters' *From Time Immemorial,*" in *Blaming the Victims,* pp. 33–69; Bill Farrell, "Joan Peters and the Perversion of History," *Journal of Palestine Studies* 53 (Fall 1984): 126–134; and Yehoshua Porath, "Mrs. Peters' Palestine," *New York Review of Books* 32 (January 16, 1986):36–39. For an authoritative account of Palestinian demography in this period, see Justin McCarthy, *The Population of Palestine: Population History and Statistics of the Late Ottoman Period and the Mandate* (New York: Columbia University Press, 1990).

The U.S. Response

The United States' approach to the Palestinians is similar to Israel's inasmuch as the United States has sought to prevent the emergence of a Palestinian state. In September 1970 the United States and Israel jointly reassured Jordan's King Hussein of their support for his military confrontation with Palestinian guerrilla organizations in that country. Five years later, Secretary of State Henry Kissinger, while mediating the second disengagement agreement in the Sinai between Israel and Egypt after the 1973 war, committed the United States not to recognize or negotiate with the PLO unless and until it specifically recognized Israel's right to exist under UN Resolution 242. A further precondition for contacts with the United States, that the PLO renounce the use of terrorism, was subsequently added.

The unambiguous acceptance of these conditions by Yasser Arafat in a press conference on December 14, 1988, paved the way for Secretary of State Shultz finally to open the door to a U.S.-PLO dialogue. This sudden departure from established U.S. policy was so surprising precisely because of the consistency of the anti-PLO position prior to that time. Secretary of State Alexander Haig had given tacit consent to the Israeli invasion of Lebanon in 1982, apparently out of the hope that the PLO would be eradicated. President Carter at Camp David in 1978 brokered a separate peace between Egypt and Israel. It spoke not of national or civil rights for Palestinians but of their "autonomy," which was interpreted by Begin and subsequently by Shamir (who initially rejected Camp David) to be perfectly compatible with their policies of settling Jews in the occupied territories and denying Palestinians both civil and national rights. Ronald Reagan endorsed the Israeli interpretation, when campaigning in 1980, by saying that he saw nothing illegal about Israel's settlements. After Camp David until December 1988, U.S. peace efforts concentrated on the "Jordanian option," which was an attempt to mediate a peace agreement between King Hussein and Israel, thereby excluding the Palestinian national movement from negotiations and precluding the possibility of the establishment of an independent Palestinian state. In 1988 the U.S. government closed the PLO information office in Washington and, in November, after the UN General Assembly had issued an invitation to PLO Chairman Yasser Arafat to address its annual debate on Palestine, refused him a visa to enter the United States on the grounds that the PLO is a terrorist organization.

In June 1990, the United States unilaterally suspended its dia-

logue with the PLO because of its failure to condemn an aborted
attack in the previous month on an Israeli beach by the Libyan-backed
Palestine Liberation Front. United States-sponsored Arab-Israeli
negotiations that commenced in the wake of the second Gulf war
included Palestinians resident in the occupied territories but specifically excluded the PLO. United States-endorsed proposals, which
served as the agenda for those negotiations, called for Palestinian
autonomy but not for a Palestinian state.

Even the language used by American officials in the 1970s and
1980s was carefully chosen either to avoid the terms *Palestine* or *Palestinian* or to sharply qualify their usage. Harold Saunders, then a
deputy assistant secretary of state, when testifying to Congress in
1975, referred to Palestinians as "the Arab people who consider themselves to be Palestinians." This was considered an extremely bold
statement at the time.[96] Phillip Habib, U.S. presidential envoy to the
Middle East, asked in July 1981 who had agreed to the cease-fire he
had negotiated in southern Lebanon between the Palestinians and the
Israelis, responded, "Israel." Then, after some hesitation, he added,
"Israel and the other parties involved."[97] The term *Palestinian* finally
entered the lexicon of U.S. administrations when President George
Bush and Secretary of State James Baker, anxious to redeem pledges
made to Arab leaders during the Gulf crisis of 1990–1991, embarked
upon a campaign to induce Israel to offer "autonomy" to the Palestinians in the occupied territories.

The Arab Response

Although the Arab states have not been as uniform or consistent as
Israel and the United States in seeking to repress and deny Palestinian
nationalism, the general thrust of Arab policy since 1947 has been in
that direction. During the cataclysmic events of 1947–1949, "both
Transjordan and Israel pursued a policy of 'politicide,' seeking to liquidate any Palestinian leadership striving for an independent state."[98]

---

[96] Kathleen Christison, "Blind Spots: Official U.S. Myths about the Middle East," *Journal of Palestine Studies* 66 (Winter 1988): 57.

[97] Bayan Nuwaihed Al Hout, "The Nature of the Palestine Liberation Organization," in
Palestinian Rights, p. 11.

[98] Flapan, *The Birth of Israel*, p. 150.

The other Arab states, despite their opposition to King Abdullah's schemes, rejected pleas by the Palestinians in late 1947 and early 1948 for money, arms, and reinforcements. In December 1948, the Transjordanian parliament ratified the annexation of the West Bank, and Abdullah worked assiduously to undermine the government of All-Palestine that had been set up by the Palestinian nationalist leader Haj Amin al-Husaini, the mufti of Jerusalem. That government in exile fell under Egyptian influence and, for all intents and purposes, had ceased to function by 1950. In that same year, a Jordanian government decree prohibited the use of the term *Palestine* to refer to the land west of the Jordan River under its jurisdiction, substituting for it the term *West Bank*.

Since then, all the front-line Arab states have repressed Palestinian political activity at one time or another. Within six weeks of the newly formed guerrilla group Fatah's first raid into Israel on December 31, 1964, the Egyptian government had arrested all Fatah leaders in Gaza, the territory under direct Egyptian administration.[99] In 1970 all the Arab states, with the exception of Syria, stood by as King Hussein undertook to liquidate the independent Palestinian national movement. In 1976 Syria intervened in the civil war in Lebanon to prevent a victory by the Palestinian-Lebanese Muslim alliance. Since 1983 Syria has used its own troops as well as militias under its influence in an attempt to destroy the Palestinian national movement in Lebanon. In the wake of the second Gulf war, most of the 400,000 Palestinians living in Kuwait were forced to flee as the Kuwaiti government meted out retribution for alleged Palestinian collaboration with the Iraqis.

Not surprisingly, Palestinians have come to believe that Israel, the United States, and even the Arab states all strongly oppose their aspirations for independence. In a January 1982 survey of the attitudes of 2,700 Palestinians, only 4 percent believed that the Arab states really support the Palestinian cause, and 42 percent said those states are indifferent to them or plotting against them.[100] According to Rashid Khalidi, "Most Palestinians consider individuals like ʿIsam Sartawi, Fahd al-Qawasmeh, and Saʿid Hamami (Palestinian political figures)

---

[99] Joan Mandell, "Gaza: Israel's Soweto," p. 10.

[100] Fouad Moughrabi, "The International Consensus on the Palestine Question," *Journal of Palestine Studies* 63 (Spring 1987): 126–131.

martyrs killed by Arab regimes."[101] The 1982 survey also found that only 2 percent of respondents believed the United States was serious about resolving the Palestine-Israel conflict. One percent accepted the idea of autonomy advocated by the United States and Israel, and 1 percent viewed King Hussein as the sole representative of the Palestinians.[102] A *Time* survey of that year revealed that 0.5 percent thought the United States was helpful to the Palestinians.[103] A poll conducted among Palestinian residents of the West Bank and Gaza Strip in the summer of 1986 revealed that 95 percent of the respondents wanted a Palestinian state for all or part of Palestine, 1 percent wanted a Palestinian entity linked to Jordan, and 3.7 percent preferred that the West Bank be returned to Jordan and the Gaza Strip to Egypt.[104]

The Reassertion of Identity

The impact of the suppression of Palestinian nationalism after 1948 was such that the creation of a Palestinian national movement from the mid-1960s required the rekindling of a national identity among the dispirited, dispersed, and disorganized Palestinians. Ali Salamah, a PLO member who was eventually assassinated, probably by Israeli agents, when asked in 1972 about his reasons for belonging to that organization, responded:

> Before 1967 a Palestinian was regarded as an unrespected, unprotected, dishonored fugitive who sold his land. I rejected being that man. . . . I can never forget one day when I was a teenager, I had to deny my identity. I was afraid of saying "I am a Palestinian" to a group of vagabonds, so I said that I was a Syrian. . . . Going back to Haifa is not the problem. The restoration of my identity is the problem.[105]

The process of restoring Palestinian identity took several forms, from writing nationalist poetry to adopting terrorist tactics on a global scale to prove to the world, and to the Palestinians themselves, that they still constituted a nation in need of a state. Thus the armed strug-

---

[101] Rashid Khalidi, "The Palestinian Dilemma: PLO Policy after Lebanon," *Journal of Palestine Studies* 57 (Autumn, 1985): 100.

[102] Moughrabi, "The International Consensus," pp. 126–127.

[103] Cited in *ibid.,* p. 128.

[104] Shadid and Seltzer, "Political Attitudes of Palestinians," pp. 20–21.

[105] Al Hout, "The Nature of the Palestine Liberation Organization," p. 19.

gle came to symbolize the assertion of Palestinian identity, as indicated by the slogan *hawiyyati bunduqiyyati* (My identity is my rifle), scrawled on the walls of refugee camps in the 1960s.[106]

Accompanying the use of violence as a tool to emphasize the reemergence of Palestinian national consciousness was the assertion of maximalist political claims, as embodied, for example, in the Palestinian National Covenant. That document, originally adopted by the first meeting of the Palestine National Council in May 1964 and subsequently amended at the fourth meeting of the council in July 1968, stated in Article 19 that "the partition of Palestine in 1947 and the establishment of the state of Israel are entirely illegal." Articles 5 and 6 designated those who have a right to live in Palestine, a definition which included all Palestinian Arabs and excluded all Jews who came there after 1917, and their children.[107] In the years after 1968, as Palestinian identity reformed and its organizational manifestations grew in size and capability, so did the maximalist position of armed struggle for the liberation of all Palestine give way to the more realistic position of negotiating a compromise settlement with Israel. In the wake of the second Gulf war, which divided and weakened the Palestinian national movement and stripped it of what support it had received from the oil-rich Gulf countries, the Palestinians began seriously to entertain the prospect of accepting "autonomy," or what they preferred to call self-government, as an interim step in the process of achieving an independent state.

But the radical acts and statements of the 1960s and early 1970s, which were integral features of the nationalist movement in its early phase, have not been entirely, unambiguously, and formally rejected by all elements of the Palestinian national movement. This is partly because several groups, especially those inspired by Islamicism, still adhere to those positions, and partly because extremist stances are deemed by some Palestinians to serve as bargaining chips in their continuing struggle against Israel—an implied threat to turn the clock back to the days of unbridled terrorist activity if Israel does not agree to negotiate with the PLO. For some Israelis, the failure to renounce the Covenant is indicative of real and continuing intentions of the PLO to liquidate Israel. Others, however, place the Covenant within

---

[106] *Ibid.*, pp. 20–21.

[107] See Yehoshofat Harkabi, *Palestinians and Israel* (Jerusalem: Keter Publishing, 1974), pp. 49–69.

the historical process in which Palestinian political consciousness was
reasserted. Yehoshafat Harkabi, formerly head of intelligence for the
Israeli Defense Forces and the person who first made the Covenant
available to many Israeli readers by providing a Hebrew translation,
has sought to reassure his countrymen that the Covenant and the maximalist statements of the past should not be taken as an indication of
the Palestinians' current or "real" intentions. In a 1987 interview he
stated:

> It used to be that every PNC resolution began with a reference to the
> Palestinian Covenant. However, in the last PNC, the seventeenth, it's not
> mentioned. . . . I understand that it is difficult to abrogate the Covenant,
> but you can consign it to oblivion, abolish it by no longer referring to it.
> So it's not that I give less weight to the Palestinian Covenant. It's *they*
> who give it less weight, except of course people like Abu Nidal.[108]

Palestinian nationalism has thus passed from the stage of identity
formation to a much more self-confident phase in which negotiations
can be entered into and compromises entertained because of the security of that national identification and because of the supremacy of the
main organizational embodiment of Palestinian nationalism, the PLO.

PALESTINIAN ORGANIZATIONS

During the Mandate, Palestinian political organization was no match
for the Zionists, the British, or the Arab states. An overwhelmingly
rural society, Palestine had no truly national political leadership. What
passed as such were the traditional notables of the largest cities, especially in Jerusalem, where political leadership was closely associated
with the religious traditions and institutions of the city. Two families in
particular, the Husainis and Nashashibis, competed throughout the
Mandate for preeminence—a struggle that reached down into villages
as clients of the two families struggled against one another.

Only during the revolt of 1936–1939 were the Palestinians able to
overcome factionalism and, largely through the mobilization of the
peasantry, mount sustained opposition to Zionist settlers and the

---

[108] Yehoshafat Harkabi, "Choosing Between Bad and Worse," *Journal of Palestine Studies* 63 (Spring 1987): 50. See also Harkabi, *Israel's Fateful Hour* (New York: Harper &
Row, 1988).

British. But the revolt was ultimately crushed by an overwhelming application of force by the British, who were desperate to secure their control of this strategic area as the Second World War approached. Less than a decade later, the Palestinians were confronted with another *force majeur,* this time the creation of Israel. In their state of weakness and disorganization, Palestinians were unable to act decisively. For at least a decade after 1948, there remained an organizational vacuum as the last surviving manifestations of traditional leadership, Haj Amin al-Husaini's Arab Higher Committee and the Government of All Palestine, withered in Beirut and Cairo, respectively. Security services of the Arab states and Israel frustrated efforts by other contenders.

The roots of most contemporary Palestinian political organizations are to be found in the 1960s. By then a new generation of educated, primarily middle-class Palestinians, strongly inspired by nationalism and intent on modernizing Palestinian politics, had emerged. In Cairo, leaders of the Palestine Students Union, including Salah Khalaf (Abu Iyad), Khalil al-Wazir (Abu Jihad), and Yasser Arafat (Abu Ammar) formed the nucleus of a group that in 1964 was to found the guerrilla organization Fatah. In Beirut the Arab National Movement, which after the 1967 war was to spawn the Popular Front for the Liberation of Palestine (PFLP) and then a breakaway faction from that guerrilla group, the Popular Democratic Front for the Liberation of Palestine (PDFLP), was formed by students, the best known of whom was Dr. George Habash, a Greek Orthodox Christian.

Young, well-educated Palestinians dispersed throughout the Arab world provided the leadership for these new groups, which recruited guerrillas from among the destitute youths of the refugee camps. These small organizations would not have prospered even with an abundance of recruits, however, had it not been for the Arab Cold War. The radicalization of the Arab world that gathered pace after 1958 and which saw various attempts to outbid Nasser from the left, created a climate in which Palestinian nationalist organizations could flourish. Syria, for example, supported Fatah in the early stages to demonstrate its leftist credentials and to undermine Nasser. He, in turn, seeking to contain independent Palestinian political activities and the general drift toward confrontation with Israel, engineered the creation of the Palestine Liberation Organization, which held its first meeting in Jerusalem in May 1964. Ahmad al-Shuqairi, a lawyer noted for his bombast who formerly had served as Saudi Arabia's representative at the United Nations, was selected by Nasser to head the PLO.

Most young Palestinian political activists assessed Shuqairi and the PLO as tools of the Arab regimes, rejecting them in favor of guerrilla organizations that embodied independent Palestinian interests.

The 1967 war, which discredited the Arab states, created as many as 300,000 new Palestinian refugees, mobilized much of the population of the Arab world, and made available new sanctuaries from which guerrilla war could be launched, provided the opportunity for the Palestinians to consolidate their hold over the Palestinian national movement. This they accomplished by finally taking over the PLO at the fifth session of the Palestine National Council (PNC) in February 1969. Yasser Arafat was elected chairman of its executive committee and Fatah took the majority of seats reserved for guerrilla organizations, an arrangement that has persisted until now. Although dominated by Arafat and Fatah, the PLO since 1969 has in fact been an umbrella organization into and out of which the competitors of Fatah have drifted as their relations have waxed and waned.

The PLO, however, rapidly became more than just a collection of guerrilla organizations. In order to serve as the principal vehicle of Palestinian nationalism, it expanded its membership to include representatives of as many sectors of the far-flung Palestinian population as possible. The PNC, which had 105 members at its fifth session in 1969, expanded to 180 in 1973 and then, in 1977, when 100 new members from the occupied territories were added (although their names were kept secret to avoid retaliation against them by Israel), to 293. By 1992, the PNC had 490 members. It is the supreme decision-making body in the PLO. The majority of its members are Palestinians who represent organizations, professional groups, or communities of Palestinians. In 1980, for example, the PNC was made up of 315 members, 94 of whom represented armed political groups (Fatah, PFLP, PDFLP, and five other groups essentially dominated by one Arab state or another), 51 representing mass organizations and trade unions, 62 representing communities in the diaspora, 75 independents, 20 deportees from Israel, and 13 intellectuals.[109] At least 10 members of the PNC are U.S. citizens.

Paralleling the expansion of the Palestinian parliament was the growth of the PLO's bureaucratic infrastructure, which employed some 8,000 Palestinians in noncombatant capacities by the 1980s. In

---

[109] Cheryl A. Rubenberg, "The Civilian Infrastructure of the Palestine Liberation Organization," *Journal of Palestine Studies* 47 (Spring 1983): 57.

1982 it included a health care service with 13 hospitals and 100 clinics; a vocational training unit for industry and agriculture; and a host of departments such as information and culture, mass organizations, social affairs and welfare, education, information, and politics, which functioned as ministries do in the states of the Middle East. Most of this organizational infrastructure was located in Lebanon and was destroyed during the Israeli invasion in 1982, but much of it has subsequently been reconstructed, principally in Tunis, the PLO's headquarters since that time.

The PLO, in short, built after 1969 the political, military, and bureaucratic organizations characteristic of statehood. This institutionalization of the chief organization of the national movement led to the usual pathologies of statism in the region, including corruption, abuse of power, favoritism, and the like. But precisely because the Palestinians do not have a state, they have clung to the PLO and excused its failings and inadequacies. It symbolizes their national aspirations; to abandon it is to abandon hope for an independent state.

The PLO has confronted both external and internal threats to its hegemony over the Palestinian national movement. Israel and the Arab states have mounted direct physical assaults against individuals and groups associated with it. King Hussein attempted to destroy it in 1970, Israel tried in 1982, and Syria has worked assiduously to that end in Lebanon since 1983. The two most important PLO leaders after Arafat, Salah Khalaf and Khalil al-Wazir, were both assassinated by the organization's enemies. In Wazir's case, Israel appears to have been responsible, while Khalaf was gunned down in Tunis on January 15, 1991, by agents of the Palestinian dissident Abu Nidal. The wealthy Arab oil-exporting states sought to bring the organization under their influence by subsidizing it. The manifest failure of that strategy, as evidenced by many Palestinians' favorable reaction to Iraq's invasion of Kuwait, caused those states, especially Kuwait and Saudi Arabia, to withdraw those subsidies and to seek in various ways to undermine the PLO. Egypt has used its diplomatic leverage with the United States and in the Middle East in an effort to bring the PLO into its orbit. The United States has backed various efforts to remove the PLO as a significant political actor, while the USSR attempted to induce it to toe a pro-Moscow line.

That none of these efforts has met with complete success is due to two principal factors. First, the very complexity of politics in the Middle East, where outside powers compete with one another and the

Arab states vie for influence and seek to gain the upper hand against Israel, means that while the PLO is never without enemies, it is also never without allies. When, in the mid-1980s, Syria sought to destroy the PLO, Syria's opponents, chief of whom were Iraq and Egypt, moved to counter that attempt. Israel's attacks on Palestinians engender sympathy for them among Arab populations, forcing the Arab states to at least give lip service to the Palestinian cause. The second factor underlying the PLO's ability to persist against external threats is the strength of Palestinian nationalism and the realization among the majority of Palestinians that if the PLO succumbs to any of these threats, their hopes will be dashed.

Internal threats to the PLO are, if anything, more difficult to counter. The social structure and geographical dispersion of Palestinians militate against organizational cohesion. Of the 5.6 million Palestinians, about a fifth are still registered as refugees, many of them living in camps in the Occupied Territories, Lebanon, Syria, and Jordan. Before 1990–1991, about a million Palestinians lived in the Arab oil states of Kuwait, Iraq, Saudi Arabia, Libya, and the lower Gulf principalities. About half of the Palestinians residing in those countries left them immediately before, during, or after the 1990–1991 Gulf crisis. Over 300,000 fled from Kuwait alone, with a quarter of a million of them going to Jordan. Over 700,000 Palestinians reside in Israel and another 1.7 million live in the Occupied Territories, so that slightly less than 45 percent of all Palestinians are under direct Israeli control. About 7 percent of Palestinians no longer live in the Middle East, having taken up residence in Europe, North America, or elsewhere.[110] The Palestinian population has the highest level of educational achievements of any Arab peoples, but it also has a high percentage of people living in squalor and destitution. The overwhelming majority of Palestinians are Sunni Muslims, yet the Christian minority is politically influential and comparatively well off. In the absence of a single state structure to impose order on such a diverse and far-flung population, maintaining unity of purpose and preventing underlying sociogeographical divisions from becoming politically unmanageable is a major and continuing task.

---

[110] Janet Abu-Lughod, "The Continuing Expulsions from Palestine: 1948–1985," in Glenn E. Perry, *Palestine: Continuing Dispossession* (Belmont, Mass.: Association of Arab-American University Graduates, 1986), pp. 17–45. See also Sabella, "The Demography of Conflict," pp. 9–11.

With the commencement of the intifadah in December 1987, it was clear that the center of Palestinian political activity had shifted to the Occupied Territories and that even Palestinians in Israel, long marginal to the nationalist movement, were closer geographically and politically to this new epicenter than Palestinians in Beirut, Amman, or elsewhere. This marked a fundamental change, for the PLO had arisen as a diaspora organization. The relatively conservative society of the West Bank, Israel's presence there, PLO infatuation with the armed struggle, and recruitment into guerrilla organizations from refugee camps, especially those in Lebanon, all caused the PLO before 1974 to concentrate its efforts outside historic Palestine. But in the wake of the 1973 war, as a negotiated settlement appeared to be possible and as the PLO began to moderate its stance, so did the Occupied Territories come to play an increasingly important role in overall strategy.

This tendency was reinforced by the competition the PLO faced from Jordan's King Hussein, who sought to regain control of the West Bank and preempt the creation of a Palestinian state. The other Arab states, however, not wanting Hussein to succeed in this effort, designated the PLO the "sole legitimate representative of the Palestinian people" at their Rabat summit conference in 1974. By so doing, the Arab states drew the PLO further into the diplomatic process, thereby adding momentum to its transformation from a collection of guerrilla organizations into a broadly based national movement with strong connections to the Occupied Territories.

Since that time, the ongoing problem for the PLO has been to reconcile its roots in the diaspora and its official exclusion from Israeli-controlled territory, on the one hand, with the aspirations and organizations of those in the Occupied Territories, on the other. The different conditions there, the need for local leadership to take initiatives, and the constant attempts by Israel to quash organizational activity connected to the PLO all contributed to organizational autonomy within the overall framework of the PLO. The Palestinian National Front (PNF), which operated from 1973 to 1978 in the West Bank and Gaza, was, like the PLO with which it was affiliated, an umbrella organization that coordinated political activities by various groups. It backed candidates in the April 1976 municipal elections, winning control of 18 of the 24 municipal councils. When the PNF was ultimately dissolved as a result of Israeli pressure in October 1978, its role was quickly filled by the National Guidance Committee, which was led by heads of unions, professional associations, and municipal officials. It succeeded in preventing the Village Leagues, which were another Israeli-backed effort to create an alternative to PLO-affiliated leadership, from becoming established. The National Guidance Committee was outlawed in May 1982. In its place a plethora of local-level groups, like Shabiba (Youth), which has ties to Fatah, sprang up.

Proliferation of Palestinian organizations in the 1980s, especially those of an Islamicist character, contributed to a rising spiral of violence. Minister of Defense Yitzhak Rabin, in an attempt to crush these activities, declared an "iron fist" policy on August 4, 1985. By October, 12 Palestinians had been deported, 5 killed, scores placed under administrative detention (imprisonment without charges), and strict censorship imposed. By the time the intifadah broke out two years later, hundreds of administrative detention orders had been issued, over one hundred homes demolished, more than twenty Palestinians killed, and Palestinian schools and universities repeatedly closed.[111]

The plethora of groups and organizations that had sprung up in refugee camps, villages, schools, universities, sports clubs, professional associations, and around mosques and churches, and which joined in the intifadah, along with the PLO's constituent organization, created the Unified Command of the uprising to coordinate their efforts. Its membership has never been made public, but it is thought to consist of representatives of the various groups and to be regularly changed so as to prevent detection. The Unified Command has proved to be successful in preventing various divisions from impeding efforts to challenge the occupation, even though the pressure applied by Israel has steadily been increased and internal dissension has mounted.

The greatest threat to continued coordination is hostility between secularists and Muslim activists. The latter, who are much stronger in Gaza than on the West Bank, are divided between various organizations ranging from the Muslim Brotherhood to the Islamic Jihad—an organization with no known links to other groups of that name elsewhere despite its perpetration of knife, grenade, and shooting attacks on Israeli troops and civilians since the early 1980s. While Islamic Jihad claims that it and other Islamicist organizations initiated the intifadah, it has cooperated with the Unified Command, Fatah, and

---

[111] Mouin Rabbani, "The Twenty Years Uprising," *Middle East Report* 152 (May–June 1988): 36–37.

the nationalists more generally. Three of its reputed leaders, including the prominent Shaikh Abd al-Aziz Odeh, have been deported.

The Muslim Brotherhood, on the other hand, although a force in Palestinian politics since the 1940s, rejects nationalism as antithetical to Islam. It refuses to cooperate with the PLO or the Unified Command. Shortly after the start of the intifadah, a new group, known as Hamas, which means "zeal" and is an acronym for the Islamic Resistance Movement, emerged from the Brotherhood and the Islamic movement more generally. It too refused to cooperate with nationalists on the grounds that it wants to create an Islamic, not a secular state, and because it rejects any compromise with Israel. By the fall of 1988 it was calling for general strikes on days other than those designated by the Unified Command. Following the PLO's declaration of the establishment of a Palestinian state, Hamas distributed a leaflet that declared: "This independence movement is imaginary. It is a quick move by some of the Palestinian ranks to steal the fruits of the intafada's victory."[112]

The crack between the largely secular PLO and its affiliates in the Occupied Territories, on the one hand, and Hamas and other Islamicists, on the other, was further widened by the decision reached in the fall of 1991 to participate in U.S.-sponsored peace negotiations with Israel. As the PLO was preparing to declare its willingness to sanction participation by Palestinians from the West Bank and Gaza in the U.S.-sponsored peace conference scheduled to be held in Madrid in October-November 1991, Hamas condemned the gathering as "a conference for selling land" and issued death threats to would-be participants.[113] It called for the total liberation of Palestine, an escalation of the intifadah, and armed struggle against Israel. As peace negotiations proceeded in 1991 and 1992, tensions between the two opposing sides boiled over, especially in Gaza, where pitched battles occurred. In one round of fighting between armed supporters of Hamas and those of the mainstream PLO organization Fatah in July 1992, 150 Palestinians were injured and one was shot dead.

The emergence of Islamic activism in the intifadah is not a sudden departure from previous political trends in the Occupied Territories.

---

[112] Rashid Khalidi, "The PLO and the Uprising," *Middle East Report* 154 (September–October 1988): 21–23.

[113] Daoud Kuttab, "Reaction in the Territories," *Middle East International* 406 (August 16, 1991): 9.

Following the Iranian revolution, there was an upsurge of recruitment into and activities by radical Islamicist organizations. By the late 1980s Islamic Jihad, for example, may have had several thousand followers. Mosques, which doubled in numbers in the Occupied Territories between 1967 and 1988, began to take on overt political roles even prior to the intifadah. Once it commenced, they became key command posts.[114] Public opinion surveys in the 1980s revealed that a quarter of the respondents wanted to live in a Palestinian state based on the sharia. Younger respondents evinced Islamicist attitudes and preferences more strongly.[115] By 1992 Hamas claimed to represent one-third of the Palestinians living in the Occupied Territories.[116] Students associated with Islamic groups have since the early 1980s vied with nationalists for control of student government bodies in the Islamic University in Gaza and in the West Bank universities, including even the Vatican-supported Bethlehem University. There have been numerous physical confrontations between nationalists and Islamic activists on campuses. Among Palestinian citizens of Israel, the Islamic Movement, a legal Islamicist political organization, has had increasing appeal. In local elections in 1989, it won 29 percent of the seats in the 12 Arab municipalities in which it ran. By 1992 it had control of seven town councils.

The growing rift in Israel and in the Occupied Territories between secular nationalists and Islamic activists has weakened but not completely undermined the intifadah. Despite the growing power of Islamicists, they have been unable to deflect the nationalists' move toward a negotiated settlement with Israel. Most Islamicists, moreover, do not contest the legitimacy of the PLO. Instead, they claim they are underrepresented in it, arguing that if there were UN sponsored elections in the Occupied Territories, they would win 40 percent of the votes.[117] The intifadah remains, as it was at the outset, prin-

---

[114] Robin Wright, "The New Dimension of Palestinian Politics," *Middle East Insight* 5: 6 (1988): 20–29.

[115] Shadid and Seltzer, "Political Attitudes of Palestinians," pp. 223–224; and Emile Sahliyeh, *In Search of Leadership: West Bank Politics Since 1967* (Washington, D.C.: The Brookings Institution, 1988), pp. 145–147.

[116] Muhammad Muslih, "The Shift in Palestinian Thinking," *Current History* (January 1992), p. 26.

[117] *Ibid.*, p. 27.

cipally a nationalist undertaking, although one with an increasingly powerful Islamic undercurrent.

Islamic activists are not the only critics of the leadership of the Palestinian national movement and especially the PLO. Dissatisfaction with the way in which Yasser Arafat responded to the Iraqi invasion of Kuwait caused many Palestinians to question his leadership and to call for greater democratization of the PLO. Khalid al-Hasan, for example, a founder of Fatah and the head of the PNC's Foreign Affairs Committee, condemned the "tyrannical line of Arafat" and called for new elections to the PNC under international supervision.[118] Even prior to the outbreak of the intifadah, secular, Westernized Palestinians living in the Occupied Territories had grown increasingly critical of the "old guard," whom they saw as old-fashioned, too much in the mold of traditional Arab politicians infatuated with manipulation rather than mobilization, and not well enough equipped linguistically or intellectually to appeal to Western audiences or negotiate with Western decision makers. These younger aspiring leaders are uninterested in the interminable struggles between the "historic" guerrilla organizations. They are far more interested in building a political base of support as wide as possible, which includes Israel, where they have extensive contacts with Jewish peace activists.

The peace negotiations that commenced in October 1991 provided the opportunity for this comparatively Westernized and young Palestinian leadership from the Occupied Territories to play a much more direct role in determining the fate of Palestinians living under Israeli control. The 14-member delegation was drawn from high-status families and from political organizations, with one-half coming from Fatah. Hanan Ashrawi, a Christian academic trained in the United States, assumed a particularly high profile as a spokesperson. But the delegation was firmly anchored within the PLO, even though that organization is illegal in the occupied territories and was prohibited from participating directly in the peace negotiations. The PLO Central Committee meeting of mid-October 1991 that approved Palestinian participation in the Madrid conference came up with a formula that provided the necessary latitude for the Palestinian delegation but ensured that it would operate with the PLO's support and within its policy guidelines. The formula included the creation of a steering committee to advise the delegation. Members of that committee were

[118] *Ibid.,* p. 25.

drawn from the Palestinian diaspora and from East Jerusalem. Thus, despite the intense pressure on the PLO from the outside and fissiparous tendencies within it, it nevertheless has managed to maintain reasonable coherence and to act as the representative of the Palestinian people. Most Palestinians are aware that the PLO is a much more participatory, democratic organization than are the governments of the Arab states. Their voice is heard and they do have possibilities of upward political mobility. As Akram Haniya, a Palestinian intellectual and member of the PNC stated, "The fact that people are able to differ while staying within the PLO means maturity."[119] Abilities to manage conflict, recruit new leadership, and develop an effective negotiating strategy are hallmarks of successful political institutions. They suggest that the Palestinians have succeeded in the past 40 years not only in rekindling a strong sense of nationalism but in constructing political organizations that could, in the proper circumstances, be converted into state structures, just as those of the Yishuv were in 1948.

INTERNATIONAL SUPPORT FOR THE PALESTINIANS

Although the nationalism of the Palestinians and their political organizations are now about as well developed as were those of the Zionists when they obtained their state in 1948, Palestinians still lack sufficient international support for their state to be formed. This is not to say, however, that international support for the Palestinians is lacking. Indeed, 110 countries grant some sort of official status to the PLO. Within two weeks of the declaration of Palestinian independence in November 1988, more than 60 countries had recognized the new state even though it could not claim to control any territory and had not even specified its borders. The level of support countries provide the Palestinians, however, is inversely proportional to their influence.[120]

Nations of the Arab and Muslim worlds, as well as the Third World more generally, overwhelmingly endorse the idea of a Palestinian state, but they lack the means to bring it into existence. At the other end of the spectrum, the United States has consistently opposed

---

[119] Timothy M. Phelps, "Unusually United PLO is Taking on a New Look of Moderation," *Minneapolis Tribune*, November 22, 1988.

[120] Godfrey Jansen, "Sixty in Ten Days," *Middle East International* 139 (December 2, 1988): 6.

statehood for Palestinians, and the United States, as President Sadat was fond of stating, "holds 90 percent of the cards in the Middle East." Between these two diametrically opposed positions are the rest of the OECD countries (Western Europe, Japan, Canada, Australia, and New Zealand) which, until recently, have generally acquiesced to U.S. policy despite their stronger support for the Palestinians. The East Bloc formerly provided important although not decisive support for the Palestinians, support which has all but evaporated as a result of the collapse of that bloc.

The Arab States

The Arab states, despite their discomfort with Palestinian nationalism and efforts to turn Palestinian organizations to their own purposes, have nevertheless come to provide solid diplomatic backing for the PLO's efforts to obtain concessions from Israel, although the Arab states are by no means uniformly supportive of the creation of a Palestinian state. The Arab states, like the Palestinians, have moderated their political positions toward Israel to the point that they are willing to coexist peacefully with it. At the Arab summit in Baghdad in November 1978, all participating members of the Arab League, including Syria and the PLO, agreed to pursue a negotiated settlement on the basis of Israel's withdrawing from all territories occupied in 1967 and the establishment of an independent Palestinian state. This Arab consensus was restated at the Fez summit in 1982, which declared support for "guarantees for peace for all the states of the region," meaning the acceptance of Israel. But it took another decade, the second Gulf war, and seven rounds of shuttle diplomacy by U.S. Secretary of State James Baker actually to bring the key Arab states, the Palestinians, and Israel to the first round of negotiations at Madrid in October–November 1991. During this period the Arab states accepted the Palestinians' prior claim to Jordan's over the West Bank and East Jerusalem and refused to countenance Damascus's attempts to subordinate the Palestinian cause to Syria's state interests. Egypt, the most powerful Arab country, played a leading role in this process.

Egypt alone has had the political strength both to support openly and to oppose the Palestinian cause, including signing a peace treaty with Israel. Other states, not as well established and more vulnerable to the Palestinian challenge, have had to finesse the issue, pledging verbal support but working surreptitiously to undermine the Palestinian position. Egypt in 1964 brought the PLO into existence. Ten years later at Rabat, Egyptian Foreign Minister Ismail Fahmy declared the PLO to be the "sole legitimate representative of the Palestinian people," thereby putting Egypt and the Arab states on record as rejecting King Hussein's bid to regain the West Bank and East Jerusalem. When Egypt left the Arab fold in 1978 as a result of negotiating a separate peace with Israel, Jordan made a comeback, which for almost the next decade placed it in constant competition with the PLO to be the rightful claimant to those territories. Egypt's return to the mainstream of Arab politics, however, which was officially recognized in November 1987, had the effect of creating a relatively coherent Arab consensus, which caused King Hussein to declare in July 1988 that Jordan was severing all legal and administrative ties to the West Bank. Jordan had neither sufficient Arab backing nor support among the Palestinians in the occupied territories to continue to press its claim.

The Arab consensus favoring negotiations with Israel, in which the Palestinians would be directly represented, was further solidified by the second Gulf war, which undermined, at least temporarily, more radical Arab positions. When those negotiations commenced in 1991, the Arab states, with Egypt playing an important role, signaled that their minimum conditions for agreeing to a permanent peace with Israel would be "autonomy" of the occupied territories from direct Israeli control, rather than an independent state. The Palestinians thus continue to receive substantial but not total support from the Arab states, whose own interests differ from those of the stateless Palestinians.

The Third World

Third World nations, which constitute a majority in the UN General Assembly, had by the early 1970s come overwhelmingly to support the creation of a Palestinian state in the occupied territories. Among African countries, for example, the UN General Assembly voting record underwent a dramatic shift from 1969 to 1973. In the former year, 34 percent of votes cast by these states were pro-Palestinian, and 28 percent were pro-Israeli. By 1973, 96 percent of votes were pro-Palestinian and none were pro-Israeli. The African voting record remains essentially unchanged since that time.[121]

Latin American states followed the African lead. In 1969, 5 per-

---

[121] Kemal Kirisci, *The PLO and World Politics: A Study of the Mobilization of Support for the Palestinian Cause* (New York: St. Martin's Press, 1986), p. 85.

cent of their votes were pro-Palestinian; 47 percent were pro-Israeli. By 1974, the voting record was virtually reversed, 43 percent of votes being pro-Palestinian and 19 percent pro-Israeli. In 1980, 87 percent of votes cast in the UN by Latin American states were pro-Palestinian; none was pro-Israeli.[122] Asian states voted in pro-Palestinian fashion at an 88 percent rate in 1974 and a 91 percent rate in 1980. They cast no votes that were in any way supportive of Israel.

But votes in the UN and other forms of support that were provided to the Palestinians by Third World nations had only a very marginal impact even in the 1970s and 1980s, when the Third World was most active in providing such assistance. Many African and Asian states that had broken diplomatic relations with Israel in the 1960s and 1970s, in order to demonstrate their solidarity with the Palestinians and Arabs more generally (and in some cases to receive substantial payments from the oil-rich Arab countries), restored those ties as part of the general move toward a negotiated settlement that began to gather momentum after the second Gulf war and the collapse of the Soviet Union. Palestinians and the Arabs more generally did not strenuously oppose these moves, partly because even their symbolic importance was not great, partly because the Palestinians and the Arab states had themselves entered negotiations with Israel that promised to result in mutual recognition, and partly because in the early 1990s the Arabs and much of the Third World had come to the conclusion that Washington had successfully established a *Pax Americana* in the Middle East that rendered irrelevant actions by other external actors, including those of the Third World.

The European States

In the 1970s and 1980s, European support for Israel eroded in favor of the Palestinians. Whereas in the General Assembly session in 1974 Western European nations had a voting record that was 43 percent pro-Palestinian and 33 percent pro-Israeli, by 1980 the comparative percentages were 39 and 8, respectively. Among Western European states, therefore, Palestinian support did not increase appreciably from 1974 to 1980, although it did after that time. Support for Israel, however, fell away markedly.[123]

European public opinion by the 1980s had come to endorse the

---

[122] *Ibid.*, p. 88.

[123] *Ibid.*, p. 145.

idea that the Palestinians should be represented in Middle East peace talks and that they should have a state of their own. A 1982 British poll revealed that 55 percent of respondents found acceptable the creation of a Palestinian state on the West Bank and Gaza, and in the same year 88 percent of Dutch citizens queried in a national poll agreed that the Palestinians are entitled to a state of their own. Sixty-one percent of the British sample thought the PLO should be included in peace talks.[124]

European diplomatic initiatives have reflected growing support for Palestinians. In 1974, only three of the nine members of the European Community (EC) voted in the UN General Assembly in favor of the motion urging participation of the PLO in UN deliberations. The others abstained. Two years later, however, the nine members announced jointly that there should be a territorial basis to the pursuit of Palestinian national identity. In the Venice Declaration of 1980, the European Community recognized the right of Palestinians to self-determination and specified that the PLO should be associated with peace negotiations. In the wake of the PNC meeting of November 15, 1988, the EC labeled the PNC's resolution as "positive" and stated that the declaration of independence reflects "the will of the Palestinian people to assert their national identity." The EC states did not, however, recognize the Palestinian state.[125] As the Palestinian intifadah continued in the early 1990s, the EC imposed various punitive measures on Israel and continued to urge it to respect Palestinian rights. At the peace conferences which commenced in 1991, the EC had observer status.

U.S. Public Opinion

Public opinion in the United States has generally followed the global trend of increasing support for the Palestinians. In a 1977 poll, 36 percent of respondents believed the Palestinians should have a separate nation.[126] By 1988, surveys of public opinion consistently revealed that more Americans support than oppose the establishment of an independent Palestinian state in the West Bank and Gaza. A majority of

---

[124] Moughrabi, "The International Consensus," pp. 122–123.

[125] "EEC Welcomes 'Positive Steps' by PLO Council," *Washington Post*, November 22, 1988.

[126] Moughrabi, "The International Consensus," p. 117.

Americans continue to perceive the PLO and Yasser Arafat negatively but believe nevertheless that the PLO should be included in the peace process and that the United States should negotiate with the PLO.[127] When Arab-Israeli negotiations did commence in the fall of 1991, American public opinion became more critical of Israel and more supportive of the Arabs in general and the Palestinians specifically. A poll conducted by the *Wall Street Journal* and NBC News revealed that Americans supported, by a margin of three to one, President Bush's decision to postpone loan guarantees to Israel and that 46 percent opposed economic aid to Israel, compared to 44 percent who supported it. The poll also revealed that for the first time since 1948, more Americans considered Israel to be the principal obstacle to peace than those who blamed the Arabs (37 percent to 35 percent). Of those polled, 49 percent believed that Israel should trade the occupied territories for peace, versus 31 percent who opposed that proposition.[128]

The American public, in short, has come to support the emerging international consensus on the Arab-Israeli conflict. This is that UN Resolution 242 should serve as the basis for its settlement, along with recognition of the Palestinians' right to self-government possibly within an independent state, and the acknowledgment of the PLO as the legitimate spokesman for that cause. The American public arrived at these positions before U.S. government policy began to embrace them in the wake of the second Gulf war. That it took so long for Washington to recognize the international consensus and begin to act to implement it is testament to the strength of the U.S.-Israeli relationship, which since 1948 has been of paramount importance to the Arab-Israeli conflict.

THE UNITED STATES AND ISRAEL

The "special relationship" between the United States and Israel results from the perception by key American officials that Israel is a

---

[127] Fouad Moughrabi, "American Public Opinion Far Ahead of U.S. Policy," *The Washington Report on Middle East Affairs* 7 (January 1989): 13; see also a "Nationwide Survey of U.S. Attitudes on the Middle East," *Arab Studies Quarterly* 8 (Winter 1986): 64–65; Michael W. Suleiman, "World Public Opinion and the Question of Palestine," in Perry, *Palestine*, p. 84; and Elia Zureik and Fouad Moughrabi, eds., *Public Opinion and the Palestine Question* (New York: St. Martin's Press, 1987).

[128] Cited in Leon T. Hadar, "High Noon in Washington: The Shootout Over the Loan Guarantees," *Journal of Palestine Studies* 82 (Winter 1992): 74.

strategic asset for the United States in the Middle East and from the impact of the pro-Israeli lobby on foreign policy decision making. Prior to the collapse of the Soviet Union, Israel was generally considered by U.S. administrations to be vital to U.S. security interests in the region because it provided military assets that could be used against both the USSR and radical Arab nationalism. Ronald Reagan, for example, stated that "Israel is the [American] military offset to the Soviet Union in the Middle East."[129] Secretary of State George Shultz told participants in the annual conference of the American Israel Public Affairs Committee (AIPAC), the main organization of the pro-Israeli lobby, in April 1985: "Every year we provide more security assistance to Israel than to any other nation. We consider that aid to be one of the best investments we can make—not only for Israel's security but for ours as well."[130]

The countervailing argument, prior to the demise of the USSR, was that support for Israel provided opportunities for the Soviets in the Arab world and led to destabilization of conservative Arab regimes. The "Israel first" policy, according to Michael Hudson, "places great strains on Arab regimes like Jordan, Egypt and Saudi Arabia. . . . One of the main consequences of 'Greater Israel' and United States support for 'Greater Israel' has been the growth of radical Islamic fundamentalist movements that threaten even the personal security of Americans in the Middle East."[131] Various secretaries of defense, including the first, James Forrestal, and Frank C. Carlucci and Caspar Weinberger, both of whom served under Reagan, considered the strategic relationship with Israel to be a mixed blessing. In particular they wanted to develop closer military relations with a variety of Arab states.

The second Gulf war and the almost simultaneous self-destruction of the Soviet Union fundamentally altered strategic realities in the region. United States interests were no longer threatened by either a communist or a radical Arab state, while the conservative Arab states of the Gulf lined up to sign military agreements with Washington and to purchase huge quantities of arms from American weapons manu-

---

[129] *The Middle East* (December 1980): 36.

[130] George Shultz, "The United States and Israel: Partner for Peace and Freedom," *Journal of Palestine Studies* 56 (Summer 1985): 123.

[131] Michael C. Hudson, "United States Policy in the Middle East: Opportunities and Dangers," *Current History* 85 (February 1986): 50–51.

facturers. The benefits to the United States of the strategic relationship with Israel were now very much less, while the costs had significantly increased. President Bush, therefore, could well afford to be much less responsive to Israeli requests than had his predecessors. But the "special relationship," resting as it does on the influence Israel is able to muster in the American political system, did not dissolve as a result of the changed security environment. Indeed, in the first months of his presidency, President Clinton reaffirmed that relationship in word and deed.

"The Lobby," as pro-Israeli forces spearheaded by the AIPAC have come to be known, is beyond question the most powerful nongovernmental participant in Middle East foreign policy decision making in Washington.[132] Based on the support of a large proportion of America's six million Jews, reinforced by the resources of the Israeli state, and further assisted by general sympathy for Israel in the United States, especially among fundamentalist Christians, the pro-Israeli lobby had established what was widely assumed to be an unassailable power base in Congress.

Such influence was built partially on this lobby's ability to raise campaign funds for candidates. Pro-Israeli political action committees, for example, have become the second largest source of funds for Democratic candidates for the Senate; only organized labor contributes more to their campaigns.[133] Several incumbent congressmen, including Paul Findley (Illinois), Roger Jepsen (Iowa), and Paul (Pete) McCloskey (California), as well as Senators Walter Huddelston (Kentucky) and Charles Percy (Illinois), have lost reelection campaigns primarily because the pro-Israeli lobby targeted them for defeat and contributed large sums to the campaigns of their opponents. As the pro-Israeli lobby's leverage in Congress increased, so did its influence within the executive branch grow. Each successive administration since that of Eisenhower has provided more economic and military assistance and diplomatic support to Israel than its predecessor.

But the Bush administration, operating in the new post-Cold War environment, having defended Israel against Iraqi Scud missile attacks, eager to demonstrate to the Arabs that the United States could

---

[132] Edward Tivnan, *The Lobby: Jewish Political Power and American Foreign Policy* (New York: Simon & Schuster, 1987).

[133] Rex B. Wintergerter, "The Pro-Israel PACs and the 1988 Elections," *Middle East International* 336 (October 21, 1988): 16.

resist Israeli pressure, and aware of the relative unpopularity in both Israel and the United States of the Likud government and its leader, Yitzhak Shamir, chose to confront the pro-Israeli lobby head-on. In September 1991 President Bush forced Congress to delay consideration of an Israeli request for a $10 billion loan guarantee in order to finance resettlement of Soviet Jews in Israel. Despite Prime Minister Shamir's efforts to induce the pro-Israeli lobby to pressure Congress to confront Bush on the issue, that lobby, aware that it would lose such a fight, gave way. Nine months later, Shamir's party lost the election, partly because it was widely perceived in Israel that the prime minister had gravely mishandled relations with Washington. In the wake of that election President Bush authorized the loan guarantee.

This episode suggests that while the pro-Israeli lobby remains strong, it is unlikely to be able to reestablish the enormous influence it wielded under the Reagan administration, even with a strong supporter of Israel, such as President Clinton, in the White House. The end of the Cold War, the moderation of most Arab states and the Palestinians, and American economic difficulties have created an environment in which the United States will apply pressure on Israel to resolve conflicts with the Palestinians and neighboring Arab states. The Clinton administration has tilted more toward Israel than its predecessor, as evidenced, for example, by its support in the United Nations for Israel's position on the issue of 417 Palestinians deported to the so-called "Security Zone" in South Lebanon in December 1992. Nevertheless, President Clinton and Secretary of State Warren Christopher sought actively to prevent that issue from jeopardizing peace negotiations. To encourage Palestinians to cease their opposition to attending the first "Clinton" round of peace talks until the deportee issue had been resolved, the new administration signaled to Palestinians its willingness to drop its objection to having the Palestinian delegation headed by a resident of East Jerusalem, a concession opposed by Israel. The American-Israeli relationship, however, underpinned by numerous ties and commitments, will withstand the considerable buffeting to which it will be exposed during the various phases of the peace process to which the United States is committed.

Economic Assistance

From 1952 to 1965 U.S. economic and military assistance to Israel averaged $60 million annually. For the next eight years, up to 1973, it rose to an average of $230 million. In the decade after the 1973 war, U.S. aid averaged $2.32 billion per year, and since that time it has not dropped below $3 billion annually. Whereas prior to 1985 most of this assistance was in the form of loans, after that time 100 percent of the funds were in grants that never have to be repaid. In 1984–1985, when Israel confronted a balance of payments and general economic crisis, the Reagan administration provided an emergency $1.5 billion supplementary grant over and above the $3 billion in economic and military assistance budgeted for the coming year. It also effectively wrote off Israel's $10 billion debt to the United States by pegging future economic assistance to the debt repayment schedule.

In 1990 the United States responded to increased Jewish immigration to Israel from the Soviet Union by providing $400 million in loan guarantees. During and immediately after the second Gulf war Washington topped up its "normal" $3.7 billion annual assistance package with an additional $650 million economic assistance grant, authorized transfer of $700 million in U.S. military equipment to Israel, earmarked $300 million for prepositioning in Israel U.S. weaponry, and provided *Patriot* missile batteries and various special military and civilian programs worth an additional $40 to $50 million.[134]

From 1978 to 1988, the U.S. government gave Israel $29 billion in economic and military assistance, more than double the cost of the Marshall Plan for all of Europe after World War II.[135] Between 1979 and 1991, the $40.1 billion provided to Israel by the United States amounted to 21.5 percent of all U.S. multilateral and bilateral aid.[136] Private U.S. contributions since 1948 have averaged $500 million per year. Most are tax deductible in the United States. Total U.S. aid to Israel from 1948 through 1991 amounted to $53 billion. Since the early 1970s, official public assistance to Israel has accounted annually for about 30 percent of U.S. aid to some 70 countries, with the percentage gradually rising, so that by the late 1980s it was over 37 per-

---

[134] Donald Neff, "Israelis Dependence on the US," *Middle East International* (May 1, 1992), p. 16.

[135] Tivnan, *The Lobby,* p. 217. See also Mohamed El-Khawas and Samir Abed Rabbo, *American Aid to Israel: Nature and Impact* (Brattleboro, Vt.: Amana Books, 1984); and George T. Abed, "Israel in the Orbit of America: The Political Economy of a Dependency Relationship," *Journal of Palestine Studies* 61 (Autumn 1986): 38–55.

[136] Neff, "Israelis Dependence on the US," p. 16.

cent. In 1978–1979, $4.81 billion of aid to Israel constituted 43 percent of all American foreign assistance. By the mid-1980s, Israel was receiving from the United States some $1,500 for each man, woman, and child in the country.[137] Unlike all other countries receiving U.S. assistance, Israel receives its funds at the beginning of each financial year, which provided it an additional $86 million in interest in 1991. What all this adds up to is "that Congress has transferred to Israel, one of the world's smallest nations, more of America's treasury than any country at any time in history has ever voluntarily donated to a foreign country."[138] In addition, as Democratic Senator Robert Byrd of West Virginia noted on the Senate floor on April 1, 1992, "We have poured foreign aid into Israel for decades at rates and terms given to no other nation. . . . Beyond the massive economic and military aid, however, is our so-called strategic relation with Israel. We have served as protector almost in the same sense as the government of the United States would protect one of our 50 states."[139]

Military and Security Assistance

Of the largesse bestowed by the U.S. government on Israel, about two-thirds since 1970 has been in the form of military assistance. Prior to 1962, Israel received virtually no such assistance from the United States. In the Kennedy and Johnson administrations, Israel received $250 million in military aid. This figure reached $6.7 billion during the eight years of the Nixon and Ford presidencies, further escalated to $7.4 billion under Carter, and doubled again under the Reagan administration. Since 1979, the baseline annual military assistance grant has been almost $1.9 billion.

Military assistance has also taken the form of the transfer of the United States' most sophisticated weapons technology, which has, in turn, been copied, manufactured, and then exported from Israel, providing further foreign currency. In 1986, the Reagan administration granted Israel non-NATO ally status, enabling it to bid on tenders

---

[137] Tivnan, *The Lobby,* pp. 217–218.

[138] Donald Neff, "The Backlash Against Israel's Washington Policy," *Middle East International* 338 (November 18, 1988): 15.

[139] Neff, "Israel's Dependence on the US," p. 17.

offered by the Department of Defense for a wide range of military equipment. In 1986, the U.S. Department of Defense purchased $205 million worth of Israeli armaments. Israel is the single largest foreign recipient of "Star Wars" research funds. Its Arrow antimissile missile program alone had received $126 million by 1991 and was scheduled to be given an additional $210 million over the next four years.[140] The intelligence organizations of the two countries have also established close working relationships, as indicated by cooperation between the CIA and Israel's equivalent, Mossad, in dispatching clandestine arms shipments to the Contra rebels in Nicaragua, to the Phalange and the Lebanese Forces in Lebanon, to the government of Ayatollah Khomeini in Iran, and to various other governments and guerrilla organizations.[141]

Besides their development of a policy to provide Israel with one of the most powerful militaries in the world, the United States has gradually provided increasingly explicit guarantees of Israel's security. The first quasi-official such pledge was made by President John F. Kennedy in a conversation with Golda Meir, then Israeli foreign minister, in December 1962. Kennedy's remarks were summarized as follows:

> The U.S. has a special relationship with Israel in the Middle East, really comparable only to that which it has with Britain over a wide range of world affairs. . . . We are in a position to make clear to the Arabs that we will maintain our friendship with Israel and our security guarantees. . . . I think it is quite clear that in the case of an invasion the United States would come to the support of Israel.[142]

By 1975, the United States had become willing to provide Israel with wide-ranging and direct security guarantees in writing. Two

---

[140] Dennis J. Wamsted, "Congressional Arms Control is Freeze for Arabs and Increase for Israel," *The Washington Report on Middle East Affairs* (July 1991), p. 15.

[141] Benjamin Beit-Hallahmi, *The Israeli Connection: Who Israel Arms and Why* (New York: Pantheon Books, 1987). See also Andrew and Leslie Cockburn, *Dangerous Liaison: The Inside Story of The U.S.-Israeli Covert Relationship* (New York: HarperCollins, 1991).

[142] Kennedy Library NSC Box 117–118, December 27, 1962, quoted in Mordechai Gazit, "Israeli Military Procurement from the United States," in *Dynamics of Dependence: U.S.-Israeli Relations,* ed. by Gabriel Sheffer (Boulder, Colo.: Westview Press, 1987), p. 98.

Memorandums of Agreement accompanying the Sinai II disengagement agreement of that year bound the United States to meet Israel's
long-term military and economic needs and guaranteed that the United States would provide Israel with oil from its own stocks if Israel was
confronted with a shortage. The agreements provided for contingency
plans to give Israel emergency military assistance and committed the
United States to uphold the "survival and security" of Israel.[143]
According to Nadav Safran, "But for the fact that it bore the label of
Executive Agreements, it exceeded in many ways a formal treaty
signed by the United States."[144] During the Reagan administration,
Secretary of State George Shultz constructed an elaborate network of
undertakings, commitments, agreements, and assurances to Israel
which, according to AIPAC's director, will "leave a legacy that will be
important to Israel's security for decades to come."[145] Shultz is reported to have pledged to Thomas Dine, head of AIPAC, to "build institutional arrangements so that eight years from now, if there is a secretary
of state who is not positive about Israel, he will not be able to overcome the bureaucratic relationship between Israel and the U.S. that
we have established."[146]

At the annual national convention of AIPAC in 1992, Director of
Foreign Policy Issues Steven Rosen noted his organization's continuing success in entwining the Israeli-U.S. defense relationship. According to him, Israeli military exports had jumped from $10 million to
$500 million annually in a decade, thanks to the provision of U.S. assis-
tance in various forms. He further observed that there are now 321
U.S.-Israeli joint programs in defense research, worth $2.9 billion.[147]
During the second Gulf war, the United States dispatched *Patriot* missiles and crews to defend Israel from Iraqi missile attacks—the first
time the United States had intervened directly on Israel's behalf in a
military conflict.

---

[143] Cited in Dilip Hiro, *Inside the Middle East* (London: Routledge and Kegan Paul,
1982), p. 225.

[144] Nadav Safran, *Israel: The Embattled Ally* (Cambridge: Harvard University Press,
1978), p. 557.

[145] Neff, "The Backlash," p. 14.

[146] *Ibid.*

[147] Ian Williams, "AIPAC 1992," *The Washington Report on Middle East Affairs* (June
1992), p. 16.

Diplomatic Support

Israel and the United States vote together more frequently in the United Nations General Assembly than does the United States with almost any other country. In 1986 they voted together 91.5 percent of the time. Egypt, Jordan, and Saudi Arabia, by contrast, voted with the United States on only 15.3 percent, 14.2 percent, and 13.6 percent of occasions, respectively.[148] This coincidence of votes is due largely to the fact that the United States has become one of Israel's few supporters (in some cases its sole supporter) in that body. Israel and the United States, for example, were outvoted 151 to 2 in November 1988 on a resolution deploring the U.S. decision to refuse Yasser Arafat a visa so that he could address the UN. Between 1981 and 1986, the Reagan administration used its veto in the Security Council against resolutions critical of Israel 13 times, almost twice the seven vetoes cast by the United States from 1948 to 1981. America's UN ambassador during the Carter administration voted in favor of a resolution condemning Israel's treatment of Palestinians in the occupied territories as being in violation of the Fourth Geneva Convention. The response by the pro-Israeli lobby was so intense that the president ordered the vote changed, explaining the original vote as the result of an error in communication. President Carter's previous UN ambassador had been forced to resign because he met with the PLO's UN representative, even though he did so in his capacity as chairman of the Security Council rather than as U.S. ambassador to the UN. By 1989, the United States had used its Security Council veto 23 times to block resolutions critical of Israel. In 1983, Congress passed a law that requires the United States to renounce its membership in the UN General Assembly if Israel were to be expelled from that body. In September 1991, President Bush, in an address to the UN General Assembly, called for repeal of the "Zionism is racism" resolution that the Assembly had adopted in November 1975. Before the end of the year, the U.S. delegation to the UN had successfully steered such a motion through the General Assembly. Following Israel's deportation of 417 Palestinians in December 1992, the United States blocked efforts in the Security Council to force Israel to allow them to return.

---

[148] "AIPAC Policy Statement, 1987," *Journal of Palestine Studies* 64 (Summer 1987), p. 113.

Tolerance for Israeli Unilateral Acts

Despite the massive economic, military, and diplomatic support provided to Israel by the United States, the former has undertaken various activities considered detrimental to the interests of the latter. But such actions have for the most part been tolerated or at least have not been allowed to strain the special relationship for more than a short period. A string of military/political actions in clear violation of international law that began while Menachem Begin was prime minister continues until now. In June 1981, Israel bombed an Iraqi nuclear reactor that was under construction. In December of that year, it annexed the Golan Heights. In June 1982, it invaded Lebanon, where its troops remain in occupation of some 20 percent of that country. In 1985, Israeli planes attacked PLO headquarters in Tunisia. In April 1988, Israeli Mossad operatives assassinated Khalil al-Wazir (Abu Jihad), number-two man in the PLO, in his home in suburban Tunis. Since late 1987, Israel has employed a host of measures against Palestinians in the occupied territories deemed by the UN to be gross violations of the Geneva Conventions on the treatment of civilians in times of war. During much of this period, Israel circumvented the UN-sponsored boycott against South Africa by trading in strategic commodities with it, including weapons. All of these measures rebounded unfavorably against the United States in the world arena.

Other actions undertaken by Israel have directly violated American interests. For some two decades, Israel has obtained vital components of nuclear weaponry by illegal means from U.S. manufacturers or from U.S. military stockpiles. The arrest in the United States in 1985 of Israeli spy Jonathan Pollard, who through his position in the U.S. Navy had obtained and then passed on to Israel top-secret information,[149] brought briefly to the surface the long-smouldering issue of Israeli espionage in the United States. In March 1992, it was revealed by the Bush administration that Israel was selling secret U.S. military technology to third countries, including South Africa and China, in Israeli versions of sophisticated U.S. weaponry, such as the AIM-9L

---

[149] According to Seymour Hersh, this information was then passed on to the Soviets as a result of a unilateral decision by Prime Minister Yitzhak Shamir, who was anxious to "end the long-standing enmity between Israel and the Soviet Union and initiate some kind of strategic cooperation." Seymour M. Hersh, *The Samson Option: Israel's Nuclear Arsenal and American Foreign Policy* (New York: Random House, 1991), p. 300.

Sidewinder airborne missile and TOW-2 antitank missile. Administration officials also leaked a report that Israel had even sold China secrets of the *Patriot* anti-missile missile. Referring to Israeli agents, Raymond W. Wannal, Jr., former assistant director of the FBI, observed, "They certainly have operated here before [Pollard]." He added that the FBI was aware of at least a dozen incidents in which American officials provided classified information to Israel.[150] But these and other incidents, which would have caused a major diplomatic crisis with virtually any other country, passed quickly into obscurity. Congress and the executive branch, either under pressure from "The Lobby," or anxious not to provoke a politically damaging confrontation with Israel, determined that the special relationship with Israel would be nurtured and protected, regardless of Israeli violations of U.S. law.

THE UNITED STATES, ISRAEL, AND NEGOTIATIONS WITH THE ARABS

Paradoxically, for Israel itself, virtually total U.S. support had become an increasingly mixed blessing by the early 1990s. As the key U.S. ally in the region, Israel had shouldered military burdens that militarized the economy and the polity and contributed to the ongoing crises within both spheres. Compromises necessary for peace with the Arabs were rendered politically difficult to support within Israel as a result of the American carte blanche given to the Israeli government. Israelis opposed to continued occupation of the territories conquered in 1967 and willing to negotiate with the PLO to establish a Palestinian state were unable to argue convincingly to their countrymen that suppression of Palestinians, attacks on Arab states, and other aggressive acts would necessarily result in a reduction of U.S. support.

That situation began to change rapidly as a result of U.S. diplomatic initiatives immediately following the second Gulf war. In an address to a joint session of Congress on March 6, 1991, President Bush announced that the United States would seek to facilitate a solution to the Arab-Israeli conflict on the basis of Arab recognition of Israel in exchange for the return of occupied land. Within a week, Secretary of State James Baker had begun his first round of negotiations

---

[150] David Shipler, "Close U.S.-Israeli Relationship Makes Keeping Secrets Hard," *New York Times,* December 22, 1985.

in the region. Seven months and seven visits later, he was able to announce that an Arab-Israeli peace conference would take place in Madrid on October 30, 1991. While that round proved to be largely ceremonial and included acrimonious exchanges, especially between the Israeli and Syrian delegations, at least, for the first time, Arabs and Israelis were together and seeking actively to negotiate a settlement to the conflict that has had such terrible consequences for both sides. The Madrid round was followed by a second in Washington in December, and then successive rounds in January–March 1992, which were also characterized by a lack of progress but a demonstrated willingness on the part of all participants to keep the process alive. Simultaneous with the latter rounds of bilateral talks, which included delegations representing Israel, Jordan and the Palestinians, Egypt, Syria, and Lebanon, were five separate sets of multilateral talks on key Middle Eastern issues, including water, refugees, the environment, the economy, and arms control. These talks were held in separate venues and included 12 of the 21 members of the Arab League, plus Israel and a range of interested outside parties, including the major arms suppliers to the region.

The change of government in Israel as a result of the June 1992 elections promised to lead to compromises by Israel which could bring about a successful outcome to the negotiations. Prime Minister Rabin immediately made several conciliatory gestures, including a promise to halt construction of new settlements. In July 1992, Secretary of State Baker once again traveled to the region and secured an agreement by the various parties to recommence negotiations in Washington. Just prior to the commencement of that new round of talks, President Bush announced, in the presence of visiting Prime Minister Rabin, that he would request Congress to approve the contentious U.S. guarantee for $10 billion of Israeli loans. Between March 1991 and the autumn of 1992 the Bush administration had succeeded in bringing the Arabs and Israelis to the peace table. By initially refusing to provide those loan guarantees until Israel promised to cease settlement activity in the occupied territories, the United States had contributed to bringing about a change of government in Israel that made the prospects for those talks very much brighter.

But peace is not yet at hand. The new Clinton administration immediately confronted Arab suspicion over its perceived lack of evenhandedness. Israeli settlers and their supporters in the Knesset put Prime Minister Rabin on notice that compromises he might make at their expense would be strenuously resisted. The intifadah by 1993 had evolved into a campaign of violence against Israelis which was met with massive retaliations. The steady growth of Islamic activism posed a threat to the coherence of the Palestinian national movement and to continuing Palestinian participation in the negotiations. Syria and Lebanon refused to join the multilateral talks because of Israel's unwillingness to commit itself to a withdrawal from occupied territory, especially the Golan Heights. The substantial financial resources which presumably would be required to lubricate a negotiated settlement are in short supply, both in the United States and even in the oil-rich Gulf states. There are, in sum, many obstacles still to be faced on the path to peace. But it can at least be said that the first serious steps down that path have at long last been taken.

Chapter 8

The Politics of War and Revolution in the Persian Gulf

*T*he Iranian revolution in the late 1970s, the eight-year Iran-Iraq war in the 1980s, and the internationally explosive Gulf war of the early 1990s demonstrate both the political significance and fragility of the Persian Gulf. Clustered around the Gulf are eight countries: Iraq, Iran, Oman, the United Arab Emirates, Qatar, Bahrain, Saudi Arabia, and Kuwait. Taken together, these countries account for over 60 percent of the world's proven reserves of petroleum.

It is this enormous oil wealth that magnifies the importance of every political conflict in the region, and it is this wealth also that tends to transform these conflicts into truly international issues. Therefore, when the Iraqi troops of Saddam Hussein invaded neighboring Kuwait on August 2, 1990, it was not long before a large international coalition force poured into the area to confront the aggressor.

Although the longtime U.S.-Soviet rivalry has ceased due to the dissolution of the Soviet Union, this very collapse has produced new problems and challenges for both the Persian Gulf region and the world. Inherently unstable and cut adrift from their political moorings, the Central Asian republics, from Azerbaijan on the west to Tajikistan on the east, threaten to transmit their uncertainties and difficulties down through the Persian Gulf states.

The Persian Gulf is, however, more than a "petroleum gulf" toward which international superpowers cast covetous eyes. It is a region of peoples, with all their varying hopes and aspirations, who seek to pursue what they perceive to be their political, economic, and religious interests. The drive to achieve these interests overlaps with the regional political issues of the day. Fundamental unresolved political problems exist in each of the Gulf countries. These states have yet to resolve such basic issues as national identity and political legitimacy. In a world in which the forces of democratization, participation, and liberalization gather momentum and meaning, all except one of the Arab states along the Persian Gulf remain monarchies. They continue to use their black gold to reinforce tradition, build military machines in the desert, and alternately crush and co-opt potential political opposition.

Of the eight political units that coexist around the Persian Gulf, only two have thus far experienced major political revolution, Iraq in 1958 and Iran in 1978–1979. The other six countries continue to be governed in the traditional patrimonial mode, with political power concentrated in the hands of ruling families. These traditional governments have large natural and financial resources at their disposal. The ruling elites of the Gulf states utilize these resources to enable them to confront the challenge of revolution that has emanated from the Iraqi and Iranian experiences. The Iranian revolution in particular intensified the challenge significantly. The fact that the traditional Gulf states have been able to survive in the face of such powerful challenges is worthy of analysis.

There are two main reasons why the traditional monarchies and minimonarchies of the Gulf have successfully protected their systems into the 1990s. First, petroleum reserves have been such that the ruling families have possessed the resources needed to placate their populations by meeting their growing economic demands. Since the actual size of the indigenous populations of these six countries is very small, it has been possible to upgrade the life-styles of citizens enormously as the result of policies of distribution and redistribution of wealth. Kuwait is an important case in point.

Even with the expulsion of 350,000 Palestinians following the Gulf war, Kuwait's citizen population of 600,000 was still less than 40 percent of the overall population of the country. The huge Kuwaiti oil wealth enabled the Amir's government to shower a restless population with economic and financial gifts. Every Kuwaiti citizen family was given a valuable plot of land and an interest-free loan of approximately $175,000 to build a new house on that land. After the war ended, the government forgave these loans and other consumer loans to the tune of billions of dollars. It increased by 50 percent grants and loans to all Kuwaiti males who marry Kuwaiti women and increased monthly child allowances from $100 to $175 per child per month. In March 1992, the government dramatically announced a 25 percent across-the-board salary increase for all Kuwaitis employed in the public sector. In accordance with the wishes of the Amir, the government decided to cancel all electric and water bills for its citizenry. Although such extravagant largesse made little economic sense, it did, in the minds of an elite seeking to placate a critical population, make eminently sound political sense. This process of "dinar politics" has until now been quite effective in enabling small family-centered elites to cling to power and privilege in the Persian Gulf.

A second factor that helps explain system preservation in the Persian Gulf concerns the element of political leadership. Over the years, the traditional Gulf states have generally been led by individuals of considerable political astuteness. The particular leaders have recognized the needs and demands of their people and have struggled to stay in touch with all strata in their societies. One of the greatest of these traditional leaders was King Faisal Ibn Abd al-Aziz, ruler of Saudi Arabia from 1964 to 1975. Faisal boasted over half a century of political experience; already at age 13 he led diplomatic delegations to London. In Abu Dhabi, Shaikh Zayid has been one of the most experienced and astute leaders in the Middle East. He has led Abu Dhabi since 1966 and has demonstrated great skill as a negotiator and mediator. It was primarily due to Zayid that the United Arab Emirates was formed as a political unit in December 1971. Other underrated traditional leaders in the Gulf include the late Shaikh Rashid of Dubai and the current Amir of Bahrain, Shaikh Isa.

These traditional leaders have relied very heavily on the informal institution of the *majlis* (informal assembly), where they have been regularly available to hear personally the requests and complaints of their people. Before his death in 1990, Shaikh Rashid held four majlises daily. Shaikh Isa of Bahrain holds his majlises regularly every Friday, Sunday, and Tuesday morning, as well as one on Saturday night. In Kuwait, the *diwaniyyah*, a variant of the majlis, is the most important decisional structure. All members of the ruling Al-Sabah family have their diwaniyyahs. Such open meetings, where petitions are heard and demands presented, have been encouraged by the rulers themselves, who set the style for other members of the political elites who convene their own majlises and diwaniyyahs.

Through the continued implementation of this direct, personalistic democracy of the desert, along with the resources available to enable them to meet the demands heard in such settings, the traditional Gulf leaders have been able to hang onto power in an age of democratization and revolution. In other words, they have been able to promote rapid modernization within the traditional social and political setting. Despite this impressive record, however, all traditional systems in the Persian Gulf possess significant weaknesses.

The traditional Gulf states face the following eight problems: (1) the shortage of indigenous manpower; (2) the existence of deep social, ethnic, and sectarian divisions; (3) the dramatic growth of a professional middle class; (4) the challenge of resurgent, populist Islam; (5) the existence of conspicuous corruption in many ruling circles; (6) the intimately close relationships between Gulf elites and Western governments; (7) the huge gap between economic modernization on the one hand and political development on the other hand; and (8) the critical issue of succession and political rulership for the future.

The manpower problem has become more serious with time as each country has elected to emphasize programs of modernization and economic growth. In Saudi Arabia and Kuwait, for example, the indigenous labor forces are far too small to carry effectively forward advanced industrialization and modernization. Yet, the labor force of expatriate workers is highly suspect socially and politically. As a result of the Gulf war of 1990–1991, for example, Saudi Arabia unceremoniously expelled nearly one million Yemeni workers; in Kuwait, the population of approximately 400,000 Palestinians was sharply reduced to 25,000. Besides the negative regional political fallout of such expulsions, the internal economic systems of both Saudi Arabia and Kuwait have undergone enormous stress and strain due to the absence of these skilled and unskilled workers.

The populations of the traditional Gulf states are deeply divided against themselves socially, ethnically, and religiously. Those of Persian origin (known in the region as *ajam*) compete quietly against those of Arab background. Shi'a are present in each and every Gulf country. In Bahrain, for example, the Shi'a represent nearly 70 percent of the population; in Kuwait and the United Arab Emirates, the figures are 30 and 25 percent respectively. Even in Saudi Arabia, there is a Shi'i population of half a million in the oil-rich eastern province. Each of the six traditional Gulf states is governed by a Sunni political elite, which discriminates against the Shi'a. Shi'i-Sunni tension in the Gulf increased significantly following the Iranian revolution.

The problems of manpower and social divisiveness intersect in the situation of women in the region. Since women are largely frozen out of professional and political positions, these states seek to enter the modern world with half of their populations inactive and subdued. The place of women is particularly unfavorable in countries like Saudi Arabia, Qatar, and Oman. Even in Kuwait, however, women are not allowed to vote and, with one notable exception, there are no female diwaniyyahs.

The dramatic growth of modern educational facilities also carries serious political implications as larger and larger numbers of young people from the Gulf acquire modern higher educations. They then enter the job market with high expectations and with a newly developed political consciousness. As they return from abroad in increasing numbers, they are no longer easily absorbed into the high-level political positions that they have come to expect. Lucrative private-sector positions are also increasingly scarce. Many of the professionals and technocrats who are not absorbed or absorbable into the traditional system become disgruntled and decry the personal favoritism, professional incompetence, and political repression that they allege is endemic to their countries.

Universities are the breeding grounds of this new class, and as the Gulf states build such institutions of higher learning, the ruling elites have come to understand the political risks involved. Saudi Arabia now has seven universities; the United Arab Emirates opened the new University of al-Ain in 1981; Oman also has its own national university, Sultan Qabus University. There is a national university in Qatar, and Bahrain boasts three major institutions of higher learning. Besides these schools, the six traditional countries of the Gulf have nearly 100,000 students in Western universities. These individuals will form the questioning, challenging, professional middle classes of the future in the Persian Gulf.

Cutting across the Gulf states and transcending even Shi'i-Sunni distinctions is the gathering force of populist Islam. Those who embrace this iteration of Islam from below criticize the rapid Westernization of their societies, the personal corruption of their leaders, and the political repression that they see accompanying this moral decay. Since 1979, dedicated Islamic activists have sporadically and violently challenged their governments in countries such as Saudi Arabia, Kuwait, and Bahrain. Today, Muslim opposition movements continue to take root and grow in soil fertilized by the twin granules of corruption and oppression, fostered by an increasingly insensitive Persian Gulf leadership.

The huge wealth derived from oil revenues has maximized opportunities for corruption in the Gulf. The sums involved have been enormous, as individuals have used their personal and familial positions to amass huge personal fortunes from the hundreds of billions of dollars that have accrued to the Persian Gulf governments. Since wealth begets wealth and wealth follows power, many of the leading political actors are among the most avid practitioners of corruption. The ruling families usually have a handful of members who are well known for their financial greed and insatiable appetites for material wealth. This behavior has caused increasing criticism among the populations of these countries and has provided effective cause for the growing alienation of both the professional middle classes and Islamic activists.

The tight linkages forged by traditional Persian Gulf elites with the West in general and the United States in particular have also eroded the credibility of these elites in the eyes of their populations. One result of the 1991 Gulf war, for example, was the view held by Arab populations in the Middle East generally and the Gulf specifically that the Saudi and Kuwaiti ruling families had sold their souls to American mercenaries who were called in to protect the few against the many.

Also, the consistently strong support of the United States for the state of Israel has damaged both America's image and the legitimacy of those Arab political leaders who work closely with the United States. This became eminently clear in the summer and fall of 1982 with the Israeli invasion and occupation of Lebanon. In this military mismatch—which saw Israel use American-made aircraft to bomb homes, hospitals, schools, and mosques—Arabs throughout the Gulf watched in horror as other Arabs suffered and died before their very eyes on television. One less-known effect of this kind of action was that the Israeli attacks helped widen the gap of confidence between the peoples of the Gulf countries and their political leaders, whose very association with the United States indirectly implicated them in the Israeli aggression.

A major problem area, and one that has been alluded to in the discussions above, is the tension between the extraordinary economic growth on the one hand and the absence of political development on the other. In no other area of the world is the division between economic growth and political development so pronounced as it is in the Persian Gulf. In a world in which issues of democratization and political participation have become core international preoccupations, the sluggish approach of the traditional Gulf elites to political development has only increased popular discontent and resentment. This political retardation is highlighted when contrasted with the impressive efforts in the fields of military modernization, technological advancement, and economic growth.

In the face of these deep-seated and interrelated challenges, the traditional countries of the Persian Gulf require especially sensitive and prescient leadership. As time passes, even the shrewd old desert shaikhs seem overwhelmed by the problems they confront. What does the future hold in this regard?

Unfortunately, the next generation of political leaders in the Gulf appears not to be of the same quality as the present generation. In the cases of Abu Dhabi and Dubai, the sons of Zayid and Rashid are clearly inferior to their fathers in terms of both personal charisma and political acumen. In Oman, succession to Sultan Qabus will prove to be a serious difficulty, as the sultan is without any sons. In Bahrain, Crown Prince Hamad carries considerable promise but will be unlikely to improve upon the underrated present Amir, Shaikh Isa. The future leadership pool in Saudi Arabia, Qatar, and Kuwait is also quite shallow. The members of the Al-Sabah family in Kuwait, for example, did not distinguish themselves either in anticipating the Iraqi invasion of 1990 or in developing policies to confront that invasion and its aftermath.

The social and political challenges to the traditional regimes in the Persian Gulf will surely magnify with time. The Iraqi invasion of 1990 blew the lid off the political Gulf kettle and opened the way for the massive influx of foreigners. As a result, the region will never again be the same. The ability of the Gulf political leadership to deal successfully with this new, transformed situation remains to be seen. If this ability should be lacking, there is every reason to believe that the coming years will see considerable political upheaval in the Persian Gulf.

The internal social and political problems that plague the traditional patrimonial Gulf countries do not, of course, exist in a political vacuum but fester in an explosive regional context marked by Iraqi military threats and Iranian ideological challenges. With the massive destruction of the Iraqi economic and military infrastructure by the U.S.-led coalition forces in 1991, the Iranian factor remains the most formidable regional reality. It is, therefore, essential to analyze the realities of the Iranian revolution and the circumstance of Iran today.

IRAN: SUPERPOWER OF THE PERSIAN GULF

The shah's regime in Iran collapsed in 1978–1979, when the Iranian people rose en masse to overthrow the Pahlavi government. Muhammad Reza Shah Pahlavi's style of patrimonial rule had been rotting from within for years as repression and corruption became two of the defining characteristics of the regime. Meanwhile, the shah cut himself off from his people, and the channels of access to the government withered and disappeared. In the 1970s, the gap between the rich and the poor increased, and the shah sought to concentrate all power into his own hands while turning his secret police (SAVAK) loose on the people.

In the end, the Iranian revolution is best described as a multiclass uprising in which the lower-class masses and the burgeoning middle classes joined hands against the Pahlavi political elite. During the revolution, the Shi'i religious leaders became the organizing nodes of the movement; after the overthrow, it was the ulema who took control of the government of revolutionary Iran.

In 1993, Iran is approaching the 15th anniversary of its revolution, which has now institutionalized itself. The first years of post-Pahlavi Iran were not pleasant ones for the Islamic Republic, as the new leaders found themselves entangled both with deep domestic problems and with a grim war imposed upon them by neighboring Iraq. In 1981–1982 and 1988 particularly, violence and internal war stalked the cities and countryside as an inexperienced regime of religious extremists remained locked in mortal combat with a series of committed terrorist groups dominated by the Mujahedin-i Khalq, the major opponent which still actively campaigns overseas against the Islamic Republic. The turbulence that occurred in Iran after the revolutionary overthrow should not have come as a complete surprise to students of Iran.

Any successor to the Pahlavi regime would inevitably have had to confront a number of formidable problems. These included the following twelve challenges: (1) the complete lack of any political institutions designed to provide effective political participation; (2) the absence of an experienced, committed cadre of political and administrative leaders; (3) a deep class conflict that had been intensifying through time; (4) a widespread atmosphere of personal distrust and cynicism; (5) a culture of corruption; (6) a multitude of serious tribal and ethnic cleavages; (7) a fragile economic system characterized by an extremely primitive infrastructure; (8) a demoralized military in disarray; (9) the unique role of Shi'i Islam, whose leaders lacked political experience; (10) the crushing violence and disruptive costs of the revolution itself; (11) a host of regional enemies both in the Persian Gulf and in the Middle East generally; and (12) the hostility of the United States, which opposed the Iranian revolution from the very beginning.

Despite the challenging nature of these problems, the Islamic Republic has made progress in many areas. In the process, it has finally begun to move away from a state of psychological paranoia and political extremism engendered by constant external attacks and has adopted policies of political pragmatism and normalcy. The turning point occurred in 1988–1989 with the end of the Iran-Iraq war and the death of Ayatollah Khomeini, the charismatic father of the revolution. Leading the return to normalcy are competent and realistic political leaders such as President Ali Akbar Hashemi-Rafsanjani and Foreign Minister Ali Akbar Velayati. In his speeches, Rafsanjani has repeatedly asked his countrymen to cool their ideological fervor and dedicate themselves to the positive reconstruction of their country. The leaders of the Islamic Republic continue to struggle to institutionalize their political system while at the same time attempting to solve a series of profound problems that plague their economic system.

Politically, there has been much tangible progress. There is a constitutional system in place that includes an elected president, an elected 270-person parliament (Majlis), a cabinet appointed by the president but approved by the Majlis, a predominant *faqih* or Islamic jurisprudent, and a series of intermediate councils whose members are both appointed and elected. With the death of Ayatollah Khomeini, the role of the powerful faqih has begun to wither and political participation and pluralism have begun to blossom as originally envisioned in the constitution.

By mid-1992, the struggle between the ideological extremists and the pragmatic reconstructionists had been won by the latter group, led by Rafsanjani. The spring 1992 Majlis elections witnessed a massive victory for the pragmatists as the system inexorably began to open up. The Islamic Majlis itself is the site of spirited and wide-ranging debate. The newspapers are often highly critical of the government and at times even of Rafsanjani. Meanwhile, blind polemicism and fanaticism are grudgingly giving way to technological competence and professional efficiency. Despite this, Iran is a long way from being "home free." Its economic system is in a state of severe crisis. This, in turn, does not bode well for continuing political stability, regardless of the political progress outlined above.

The Islamic Republic's major economic problems include an astronomical rate of population growth, a stagnant agricultural system, a vastly inadequate road and transportation system, a severe lack of foreign financial reserves, high inflation and unemployment, persistent corruption, and a bloated, inefficient bureaucracy.

Iran also confronts critical reconstruction responsibilities resulting from the war in the 1980s. The direct costs of the eight-year war were approximately $200 billion. Furthermore, Iran carries the burden of feeding, clothing, and sheltering nearly four million refugees (Kurds, Afghans, and Shi'ites from southern Iraq). In sum, Iran, with a population nearing 60 million, has an infrastructure that was barely able to sustain its population of 38 million at the time of the revolution in 1978–1979.

Partially because of these crushing economic problems and partly due to Iran's return to moderation and political pragmatism, the Islamic Republic has recently sought to establish friendly and cooperative relations with its Persian Gulf neighbors. This new policy was formally announced in November 1989 at a major international conference in Tehran entitled "The Persian Gulf." The themes of this conference were solidarity (*hambastegi*), cooperation (*hamkari*), and unity (*ettehad*). Since the 1989 conference, Iran has pursued a policy of rapprochement with its Persian Gulf neighbors, including Saudi Arabia. Despite enormous internal pressures condemning the American-led 1991 saturation bombing of neighboring Iraq, the Islamic Republic did not waver in its opposition to the Iraqi invasion of Kuwait and in its support of the international coalition.

At this point in history, one might argue that as goes Iran, so goes the Persian Gulf. Although Iran has repudiated its earlier aggressive policy of attempting to export its revolution to the other Gulf states and has successfully reknit relations with these neighbors, the Iranian revolution, by its very existence, looms as a persisting threat to the vulnerable traditional regimes in the region. The revolution carries three significant points of appeal to the lower and middle classes of the traditional Gulf countries.

First, in Iran the masses of people rose successfully and overthrew a venal and repressive traditional patrimonial regime dominated by one family, the Pahlavis. Second, the Iranian revolution resulted in a system of government whereby the new regime managed to cut its ties of dependence upon outside superpowers and to declare its national independence. The most quoted slogan of the revolution is "Neither East nor West." Third, the revolution in Iran represented a victory for Islam and a reaffirmation of the strength and relevance of that civilization in the modern world. To those who are dissatisfied and disaffected in the traditional countries of the Gulf, these three messages carry great potency. Their appeal transcends Sunni-Shi'i divisions, tribal and ethnic distinctions, and class cleavages.

The credibility of Iran and its revolution increased dramatically as a result of the two Persian Gulf wars in the 1980s and early 1990s. In these conflicts, the other revolutionary Gulf state and Iran's major nemesis in the region, Iraq, demonstrated its ambitious and aggressive drive for hegemony in the area. At the same time, Saddam Hussein's government overextended itself and as a result found much of its economic and military infrastructure destroyed. It is Iran that has risen from the ashes of Iraq's defeat, and it is the Islamic Republic that now stands as the preeminent power in the Persian Gulf.

The other factor, besides the Iranian revolution, that has profoundly affected the future of the Gulf is the occurence of major international warfare there. The generalized and destructive nature of this warfare has introduced psychological and political factors that promise to transform the region forever.

THE POLITICS OF WAR IN THE PERSIAN GULF

The 1980s and early 1990s represented an unpleasant and disruptive era of violence in the Persian Gulf as the region witnessed two international wars: the first Gulf war pitted Iraq against Iran (1980–1987); the second Gulf war saw Kuwait, supported by an international coalition dominated by the United States, in conflict with Iraq (1990–1991). In both wars, Iraq was the aggressor and Iraqi leader Saddam Hussein played a major decisional role. In the first war, the

United States played a central role in support of Saddam's Iraq. In the second conflict, the United States was the leading international actor opposing Saddam and his country.

On September 22, 1980, Iraqi troops invaded neighboring Iran along a 400-mile front. At the time of the Iraqi surprise attack, the Iranian revolutionary regime was besieged and faltering. Political leaders were engaged in intense power struggles; the economy was deteriorating rapidly; the Kurds and various tribal groupings were in a state of revolt; counterrevolutionary forces were committing punishing acts of terrorism; the hostage crisis was ongoing; and the United States and its Western allies were applying severe international pressure upon the Islamic Republic. Despite the fact that Iraq was clearly the aggressor state, the international community at the UN turned a blind eye to Iran's predicament and Saddam Hussein found himself holding a blank check for aggression.

Although much has been made of Iraq-Iran tensions over control of the Shatt al-Arab waterway, religious disagreements between Sunni and Shi'i regimes, and longtime Persian-Arab ethnic differences, the principal cause of the war centered on a struggle for hegemony of the Persian Gulf. Saddam Hussein, always the ambitious political opportunist, saw the disruptive revolutionary chaos in Iran as his opportunity to take political control of the region. In the process, Iraq hoped to suffocate and kill the Iranian revolution, an appealing goal at the time to such Western powers as the United States and Great Britain and to insecure regional states such as Saudi Arabia and the Gulf shaikhdoms.

Although the sudden Iraqi attack caught Iran by surprise, the Islamic Republic responded quickly and poured reinforcements into the southwest, where badly outnumbered Iranian soldiers, police, and citizens were engaged in a desperate war of defense. After a month of brutal hand-to-hand fighting, the city of Khurramshahr fell to the invaders. It was the only major Iranian city the Iraqis ever managed to capture. Khurramshahr was retaken by Iranian forces in May 1982. Having slowed the invasion, the Iranians counterattacked with some success in the fall of 1981 and the spring of 1982. Throughout 1983, Iran attempted to follow up its advantage and to drive into Iraqi soil, hoping for a breakthrough that would destroy Saddam's regime in Baghdad.

The decision by Ayatollah Khomeini and his advisors to continue the conflict—when Iran could have gone to the conference table and negotiated from a position of great strength—proved to be a profound strategic error. The war degenerated into a campaign of massive Iranian human-wave attacks on fixed Iraqi positions, where Saddam's forces enjoyed great technological and intelligence superiority. The casualties were horrendous. As the longest Middle East war in recent history, the Iran-Iraq conflict resulted in an estimated 400,000 deaths and 1 million wounded on the Iranian side and 300,000 deaths and 800,000 wounded on the Iraqi side. By 1987, Iran had suffered more battle deaths than the United States did in World War II, and Iran had but one-third the population that America had in 1945.

In July 1988, Iran grudgingly accepted a cease-fire, effectively ending the long, bloody Gulf war. In a rambling, poignant address to his people, Ayatollah Khomeini apologetically explained the decision to accept UN Resolution 598, which had been passed in July of 1987. Iran was simply unable to carry on any longer. In March and April of 1988, the Iraqis fired some 160 SCUD-B missiles outfitted with booster packs into Tehran, the capital city that Iranians had considered to be out of Iraqi missile range. These random attacks severely damaged the morale of the Iranian people. Even more destructive to Iran's morale was the Iraqi use of chemical gases, consisting of mustard, nerve, and cyanidic agents. Thousands of Iranians and Kurds died along Iran's western front as a result of Iraq's indiscriminate use of this deadly weapon. Saddam Hussein's terrifying threat to outfit his missiles with chemical warheads and to fire them into Iran's major cities was another factor that led Iran to accept a cease-fire.

Besides Iraqi pressure, the United States and the Soviet Union took pro-Saddam positions that ultimately led to Iran's decision to terminate the fighting. Beginning in the spring of 1986, the Soviet Union, for example, dramatically began increasing its aid to Iraq, at the time its only client state in the Persian Gulf. From 1986 until the end of the conflict in 1988, the Soviets poured money and machines into Iraq. They provided Saddam's regime with an estimated $7 billion of military aid and greatly increased the number of their military advisors in Iraq.

The administration of Ronald Reagan adopted a position of neutrality during the first two years of the war. However, beginning in 1982, and especially in 1983, American policy-makers began to tilt sharply to the Iraqi side. Leading State Department officials such as Secretary of State George Shultz and Assistant Secretary of State

Richard Murphy, along with Secretary of Defense Caspar Weinberger, deeply feared a perceived Iranian threat to Saudi Arabia.

In 1982, the United States removed Iraq from its list of countries considered supportive of international terrorism. High-level American officials began to visit Baghdad in late 1983, and the United States subsequently extended to Baghdad over $2 billion in commodity credits. In 1984, it became widely known that Iraq was benefiting from intelligence supplied through American sources. Saddam Hussein himself flatly stated in May 1984 that Iraq had the use of important intelligence provided by AWACS planes flown by American pilots based in Saudi Arabia. On November 26, 1984, the United States restored diplomatic relations with Iraq. When Iraqi-fired Exocet missiles struck the American frigate U.S.S. *Stark* on May 17, 1987, killing 37 U.S. sailors, the Reagan administration quickly accepted the official Iraqi claim that the attack was inadvertent. President Reagan then curiously stated that "Iran is the real villain in the piece," and his administration issued a series of sharp warnings to Iran.

Finally, in 1987 and 1988, as Saddam's Iraq intensified its military pressure on Iran, the United States increased its naval presence in the Persian Gulf and carried out a number of attacks against Iranian ships and oil platforms. On July 3, 1988, in a tragic and infamous incident, the sophisticated Aegis-class cruiser, the U.S.S. *Vincennes,* shot down an Iranian civilian Airbus on a routine passenger flight over the Persian Gulf, killing all 290 persons aboard—a purposeful act in the minds of many Iranians. Exactly two weeks later, badly battered and bloodied, Iran accepted a cease-fire.

The strong American (and Soviet) support for Saddam Hussein and Iraq during the first Gulf war set the stage for the second Gulf war. Although President George Bush adopted a relatively more conciliatory position toward the Islamic Republic of Iran, his administration actively supported Saddam's Iraq. The heavy pro-Iraqi tilt was evident from the very beginning.

In a document titled "Guidelines for U.S.-Iraq Policy," which was prepared in January 1989 by the Bush transition team, the new administration outlined its intention to develop close relations with Saddam's Iraq. "It is up to the new Administration to decide whether to treat Iraq as a distasteful dictatorship to be shunned where possible, or to recognize Iraq's present and potential power in the region and accord it relatively high priority. We strongly urge the latter view."

Bush's foreign policy analysts described Iraq's human rights record as "abysmal," but concluded that "in no way should we associate ourselves with the 60 year Kurdish rebellion in Iraq or oppose Iraq's legitimate attempts to suppress it." The "Guidelines" deemphasized the issue of human rights and emphasized the desire to strengthen and expand U.S. commercial relations with Iraq.[1]

The Bush administration approved an additional $1 billion in agricultural trade credits, expanded American exports of high-technology goods, and protected Saddam's regime from congressional queries into Iraq's human rights violations and its use of chemical weapons against its own population. On October 26, 1989, President Bush issued a secret National Security Directive (NSD) calling for the establishment of strengthened military ties with Iraq. Although the plan was never implemented, it is instructive to note that the Pentagon was considering this proposal only three months before Saddam invaded Kuwait in August 1990. By protecting and strengthening Saddam and by excusing and apologizing for the excesses of his regime, the United States puffed him up and inadvertently encouraged him to pursue further aggression in the region.

Iraq had long maintained that Kuwait had been artificially created in 1922, when Western colonial powers had arbitrarily drawn lines on a map that determined the boundaries of Iraq, Kuwait, and Saudi Arabia. To the overwhelming majority of Iraqis (including those in opposition to Saddam), Iraq has always had a legitimate claim to Kuwait. Furthermore, following the first Gulf war, Iraq saw its financial position move from $35 billion in the black to $75 billion in the red. Much of this debt was owed to countries such as Kuwait and Saudi Arabia. Having borne the brunt of the war against revolutionary Iran, the Iraqi government felt that these debts should be forgiven. Saddam became especially irate with the Kuwaitis, whose overproduction of oil helped depress the price of petroleum, seriously threatening Iraq's economic well-being. This policy by Kuwait was, in Iraq's view, nothing less than a direct threat to Iraqi national security.

In a controversial meeting on July 25, 1990, Saddam Hussein and

---

[1] This remarkable document was declassified by the State Department on June 1, 1992, at the urging of the House Foreign Affairs Committee. It was called to the attention of the authors by Thomas Blanton, Executive Director of The National Security Archive in Washington, D.C.

Tariq Aziz, his foreign minister, met with April Glaspie, U.S. ambassador to Iraq. During this meeting the two Iraqi leaders complained bitterly to Glaspie about Iraq's tenuous economic situation. In one exchange, Saddam Hussein complained that the drop in the price of oil had cost Iraq $6 to $7 billion, which was, in his words, a "disaster." In direct response, Ambassador Glaspie said: "I think I understand this. I have lived here for years. I admire your extraordinary efforts to rebuild your country. I know you need funds. We understand that and our opinion is that you should have the opportunity to rebuild your country. But we have no opinion on the Arab-Arab conflicts, like your border disagreement with Kuwait."[2] On August 2, 1990, the troops of Saddam Hussein's Iraq attacked Kuwait, effectively initiating the second Gulf war.

The Gulf crisis lasted from August 2, 1990, until February 28, 1991, when President George Bush declared a cease-fire. The seven-month conflict can be divided into two phases: (1) the diplomatic/economic sanction phase (August 2, 1990 to January 17, 1991); and the war/military campaign phase (January 17, 1991, to February 28, 1991). The diplomatic phase involved intensive political activities by the Bush administration as it sought to gather both domestic and international support to reverse the Iraqi occupation. Within the administration and within the country at large, there was strong support for a diplomatic and economic campaign against Saddam. There was considerably less support for military action. Internationally, the administration successfully cobbled together a large coalition of countries in opposition to the Iraqi action and skillfully used the UN to legitimize this position. Between August 2 and November 29, 1990, the UN Security Council passed a dozen resolutions directed against the Iraqi action.

During the diplomatic manuevering, the United States poured military troops into Saudi Arabia. President Bush first announced his intention to do so on August 6, 1990. On November 8, he stated that he was substantially reinforcing the 230,000 American troops already in Saudi Arabia. Ultimately, the United States moved over half a million military men and women into the region. As part of his strategy to

---

[2] As quoted from an Iraqi transcript and published in Congressional Quarterly, *The Middle East*, 7th ed. (Washington, D.C.: Congressional Quarterly Press, 1991), pp. 375–77. The transcript was translated by ABC News.

present an image of the world against Saddam Hussein, the Bush administration was able to point to 35,000 British troops, 17,000 French troops, and, most important, 30,000 Egyptian and 19,000 Syrian troops who also joined the coalition.

The Iraqi government resisted political pressures, economic sanctions, and military threats designed to force its withdrawal from Kuwait. At some early stage in the process, George Bush decided to resort to the military option. Although he had admittedly been influenced in his decision by Britain's Margaret Thatcher, the president had become embroiled in a highly personal feud with Iraq's Saddam Hussein. Bush made the military decision despite the misgivings of several members of his own administration, a significant block of opinion in the U.S. Congress, and the overwhelming majority of Middle East experts in the scholarly community. Those who represented this position argued that economic and political pressure be continued; that a military invasion would cause the Iraqi people to rally around Saddam Hussein, converting a hated despot into a lonely hero; that such a military mismatch would harm the American image in much of the Arab and Third World; that a heavy military defeat of Iraq would transform Iran into the Persian Gulf superpower; and that the long-term consequences of such dramatic action were dangerously unpredictable. Those who preferred the continuation of sanctions also stressed the human, economic, and environmental costs that war would entail.

Those who supported military action argued that Iraqi aggression must be defeated for both political and economic (oil) reasons. They believed that Iraq, with its large military establishment, its possession of chemical weapons, and its nuclear development program had to be brought under control. Finally, those in support of war stressed the fact that diplomatic measures and economic sanctions had clearly failed to change Iraqi behavior. Iraq had, in fact, announced its annexation of Kuwait. The longer the situation prevailed, the greater the chances that the Iraqi occupation would become a fait accompli. Meanwhile, every day that the Iraqis spent in Kuwait was one more day of suffering and terror for the Kuwaiti people. And, once in control of Kuwait, where would Saddam turn next? Neighboring oil-rich Saudi Arabia seemed a likely target.

On January 12, 1991, after three days of difficult debate, the U.S. Congress voted (52 to 47 in the Senate and 250 to 183 in the House) to give President Bush the authority to wage war against Iraq. The UN

Security Council had already, on November 29, 1990, authorized the use of force. Just before prime-time U.S. television news at 4:50 P.M. on January 16, 1991, allied warplanes took off from airfields in Saudi Arabia and attacked targets in Kuwait and Iraq. The second Gulf war was under way.

The military phase of the war against Iraq lasted only 42 days as the U.S.-led coalition forces obliterated Iraqi resistance through the most intensive bombing campaign since World War II. For 38 days, coalition aircraft pounded Iraq, flying an average of 2,000 sorties a day. An estimated 700,000 tons of bombs were dropped on Iraq as the world watched the onslaught on television, which, courtesy of the U.S. military, emphasized its high-tech component. On the very first day of the bombing, the allied forces knocked out the power and water supplies in Baghdad, causing enormous hardship and suffering for the civilian population of this capital city. Despite the ferocity of the offensive, Iraq refused to capitulate. As a result, the coalition forces were compelled to initiate a ground assault.

The ground offensive that resulted in the liberation of Kuwait began on February 23 and lasted exactly 100 hours. Utilizing a cleverly conceived battle plan that focused upon diversionary movements and end runs, the coalition forces easily overwhelmed the demoralized, undersupplied, war-weary Iraqi army, a force that lacked air cover and that had been softened up by coalition saturation bombing. On February 17, 1991, President Bush declared that "Kuwait is liberated. Iraq's army is defeated. Our military objectives are met." Despite the fact that Saddam Hussein and his regime survived, much of Iraq lay in smoldering ruins and the Iraqi military had been seriously crippled. Given the risks and costs associated with carrying the war on to Baghdad, including the possible dismemberment of Iraq, the Bush administration chose to cease the military phase of the war and not to support Kurdish and Shi'i insurrections that commenced at the time. From then on, the conflict between Iraq and the United States would continue in the political and economic arenas.

Although the Gulf war was widely hailed in America and in much of the West as a glorious victory against the forces of aggression in the Persian Gulf, with the perspective of time the results are not so clear-cut. On the positive side, the coalition action preserved Kuwait's existence as an independent nation-state, which ensured that its enormous oil reserves would remain accessible to the West at reasonable prices. The coalition campaign successfully dismantled much of Saddam Hussein's military and nuclear infrastructure.[3] The action also demonstrated a new pattern of international cooperation within the framework of the UN in the post-Cold War world, and it paved the way for a U.S.-led effort to negotiate a settlement of the Arab-Israeli conflict. Finally, the United States proved its ability to project force across the world through the mastery of technology.

On the other hand, Saddam Hussein and his regime survived the war and used the coalition retreat as an opportunity to search, identify, and destroy all pockets of potential opposition in the country. The brutal 1991–1992 Iraqi campaigns against the Kurds in the north and the Shi'a in the south are especially noteworthy in this respect. Other human costs of the war include an estimated 200,000 Iraqi deaths (both military and civilian),[4] several hundred casualties on the coalition side, subsequent suffering and death in Iraq caused by disease and malnutrition, and the creation of hundreds of thousands of refugees from the Gulf region. Environmental and economic costs were also very high. Politically, although Kuwait remains independent, the continuation of the patrimonial mode of governance by the Al-Sabah family defies world trends of democratization. The conflict also divided the Arab world against itself and seriously damaged the Palestinian cause when the PLO chose to side with Saddam.

---

[3] In May 1992, it became known that an extraordinary meeting of nuclear weapon designers from the United States, Britain, France, and Russia concluded on the eve of the Persian Gulf war that Iraq was far from producing a nuclear weapon. This conclusion directly contradicts statements made in November 1990 by President Bush that Iraq might be able to build a bomb within six months. The high-powered group of investigators reported that it would be at least five years before Iraq could produce such a weapon. See *New York Times,* May 20, 1992, p. A6.

[4] Although no one will ever know the number of Iraqi deaths caused by the Gulf war, the Pentagon has estimated that 100,000 Iraqi soldiers (with a 50 percent margin of error) were killed. Few informed estimates exist concerning civilian casualties. There is also the question of related and delayed deaths. One might argue that the slaughter of Kurds and Shi'a was directly related to the war. In may 1991, a Harvard University public health team projected that "at least 170,000 children under five years of age will die in the coming year from the delayed effects of the bombing." See the excellently researched article by Caryle Murphy in the *Washington Post* of June 23, 1991. Census Bureau demographer Beth Osborne Daponte estimated in January 1992 that 158,000 Iraqis died as a direct or indirect result of the war. Ms. Dapone was subsequently dismissed from her government job (*Washington Post,* March 6, 1992, p. A6). Both the regime of Saddam Hussein and the administration of George Bush were clearly reluctant to emphasize the issue of Iraqi casualties.

Finally, although the United States scored an impressive military/technological victory, it also demonstrated to the world its primitive understanding of the social and political realities in the Middle East. The very fact that the United States went to war against a country and a regime it had spent a decade supporting stands as an embarrassing reminder of this ignorance. This position was bluntly summarized by U.S. presidential aspirant Ross Perot:

> My position is if you don't like guys like Saddam Hussein—and obviously the president didn't at the end—don't spend 10 years and billions of dollars of American taxpayers' money creating him, which Vice President George Bush did. There's a long clear record. . . . putting 500,000 people's lives at risk against nuclear, chemical and bacteriological . . . did not make a lot of sense when you had the alternative of the embargo. You had a lot of options other than open warfare.[5]

Furthermore, the United States had been unable to convert military victory into a lasting peace in the region.

In 1993, over 20,000 American military men and women remained in the Gulf region, an area the Pentagon still termed a "combat zone." In September 1992, U.S. warplanes were once again in action over southern Iraq. And in January 1993, just before he left office, President George Bush ordered further attacks on Iraq. These included an intensive strike of 40 Tomahawk cruise missiles against a warehouse suspected of being a nuclear weapons-related facility. Such continuing attacks increasingly alienated Arabs and Muslims everywhere. Renowned novelist Jabra A. Jabra vividly describes the views of many educated Middle Easterners when he describes his reactions to the U.S. bombings. Sitting in his Baghdad study listening to a fugue by Bach, he was enjoying "complete faith in the kind of civilization that gave me such great joy. Suddenly everything began to shake. I thought, 'My God, the mongrels have taken over the West.' "[6]

The two Gulf wars represented a watershed in the political history of the region. The credibility of traditional rulers such as the lead-

---

[5] C-SPAN statement as reported in the *Washington Post,* May 24, 1992, p. C3. On another occasion, Perot made his point more graphically: "I believe we've had a pattern of covering up our past mistakes. We rescued the Emir of Kuwait. Now, if I go knock on your door and say I'd like to borrow your son to go to the Middle East so that this dude with 70 wives . . . can have his throne back, you'd probably hit me in the mouth." *Milwaukee Journal,* July 12, 1992, p. J3.

[6] *Wall Street Journal,* February 24, 1993, p. A11.

ers in Kuwait and Saudi Arabia suffered severely as a result of their need to call upon Western, Christian countries to preserve their power and privilege. The fact that many members of the political opposition in Kuwait, for example, chose to remain behind and fight the invaders while the ruling family fled to neighboring Saudi Arabia sharpened expectations that such loyalty presumed an enhanced future political role for all Kuwaitis. The presence of huge numbers of foreign military men and women in the region brought to the Gulf an unprecedented firsthand experience with outside manners and mores. In Saudi Arabia, for example, the mere presence of Western women performing numerous military functions led directly to a dramatic incident in November 1990 in which Saudi women conducted a "drive-in" as an attempt to break through restrictions denying them the right to drive automobiles.

Despite their profound differences, both Ayatollah Khomeini in Iran and Saddam Hussein in Iraq astutely recognized the fact that their most important political card was their appeal to the disaffected, the dispossessed, and the disenfranchised in their countries and in the region at large. It is not often realized that the majority of citizens in several Arab countries—including Jordan, Yemen, and those of Northwest Africa—identified with many of Saddam's arguments and criticized the international coalition that rushed to the aid of Kuwait. Saddam appealed quite effectively to the "poor Arabs," who lacked both financial resources and power, and to Moroccans, Algerians, and Tunisians, whose countries had experienced brutal treatment at the hands of French colonialism.

The six traditional Gulf states are today confronted by two inter-related crises: the crisis of identity and the crisis of legitimacy. The crisis of identity involves a fundamental problem of identification and authenticity. The Gulf states exist as mobile patchwork quilts whose individual patches and colors continually run into and through one another. Composed of Persians and Arabs and Shi'ites and Sunnis, deluged by waves of expatriate workers from dozens of different countries, torn by struggles between different social classes, confused by competing cultural models emanating from East and West, frustrated by the absence of an institutionalized democratic tradition, and ruled personalistically by shaikhly families, the "traditional Gulf six" have yet to determine who they are and where they are going. In 1992, a group of leading Kuwaiti intellectuals at the University of Kuwait argued forcefully that their country's major problem was one of an "identity crisis."[7]

Thorny problems of legitimacy often accompany confusions about identity. In the Persian Gulf, where certain tribal families possess a near monopoly over political power and national decision making, the issue of legitimacy is particularly crucial. The Iranian revolution and the second Gulf war have forced the traditional rulers of the region to seek genuine legitimacy in the eyes of their populations. Issues such as personal freedoms and human rights, the emphasis of rule by law, and genuine political participation must be addressed. The people must have a stake in the system; they must feel part of their government. Such participation will promote a kind of shared solidarity which will strengthen the state against internal disaffection and upheaval and against external threats such as those posed by Saddam Hussein. Increasingly, the ruling families must either share power or risk losing all power. They must open up their systems in order to gain the legitimacy necessary to political survival. Many of the traditional ruling families in the Gulf, who are oftentimes corrupt and arrogant, are severely lacking in legitimacy.

The crises of identity and legitimacy have been highlighted by events such as the Iranian revolution and then widened and deepened by the two Gulf wars. Political elites in the traditional Gulf states must develop prudent and effective policies in response. Furthermore, these regional challenges have taken place in the context of a world of increasing democratization and expanding calls for effective political participation. What are the various strategies available to the besieged Gulf regimes? What policies and programs have they in fact adopted? In brief, what are the chances that such political systems can survive as humankind approaches the year 2000?

POLITICAL STRATEGIES AND POLITICAL DEVELOPMENT IN THE GULF

The leaders of the traditional patrimonial countries of the Gulf can respond to their developmental challenges by pursuing one of three

---

[7] Interviews at Department of Political Science, University of Kuwait, March 13–16, 1992 (J. A. Bill).

political strategies: *repression, revision,* or *reform.* The reactive policy of *repression* involves battening down the political hatches and tightening the regime's control over the population. The opportunities for dissent and political participation are choked off, and the role of the police and security forces is enlarged considerably.

In a program of *revision,* the political leaders continue to tinker and revise their strategy of control. Sometimes, they take severely repressive measures; at other times, they loosen central control and allow more freedom of expression and temporarily open up new channels of political participation. The elite is constantly revising and modifying and shifting back and forth between policies of coercion and co-optation.

Response by *reform* is an enlightened attempt to address the challenges of identity and legitimacy by opening up the system and providing clear opportunities for individual expression, social mobility, and political participation. Reform strategies are based upon a recognition of the need to address directly the issue of political development. In particular, such strategies involve elite willingness to expand channels of participation beyond the traditional networks of majlises and to introduce effective institutions of local self-government and national consultative assemblies. In traditional Middle East patrimonial systems in particular, reform strategies include a special sensitivity to the need to spread major decision-making power beyond a small group of individuals in the ruling family.

From the perspective of ruling elites, all three strategies carry risks and consequences. Policy based on repression tends to bottle up grievances in the short run but often leads to explosive upheaval in the longer run. The violent revolutions in Iraq in 1958 and in Iran in 1978–1979 are excellent examples of this proposition.[8] Repression builds social and political pressure; it does not dissipate such pressure. Programs of revision help to buy time, but they tend to be reactive and inconsistent; therefore those who adopt them are often overwhelmed by new and unpredictable events. Also, revisionary tactics fail to address the root causes of problems. Finally, the strategy of reform requires that leaders be willing to make radical changes when necessary. Reform programs require prudent administration. Often political

---

[8] Saddam Hussein's long tenure in power in Iraq stands as an interesting exception to this principle. Saddam has, however, narrowly survived a number of assassination attempts.

elites decide to introduce reform as a last resort. By then it is too little, too late. Increasingly, the reform alternative in the Middle East in general and in the Gulf in particular must take the form of nothing less than revolution from above. Otherwise, it may very well be bloody revolution from below.

With the exception of Iraq (and Iran in the years immediately following the revolution), the leaders of the Gulf states have all adopted policies of revision which are actually blendings of repression and reform, coercion and co-optation. The mixture is quite different from one country to another. In Saudi Arabia in particular, but also in Oman and Qatar, the emphasis is away from reform and toward control. In Bahrain, the United Arab Emirates, and Kuwait, there has been relatively greater sensitivity to the need for some broader modes of political participation. This attention to opening the system became especially acute following the Gulf war of 1991, and the early 1990s have witnessed a noticeable tilt in the direction of reform. Examples abound.

After 30 years of promises, the Al-Saud ruling family in Saudi Arabia announced a plan to establish a national consultative assembly. In late February 1992, King Fahd publicly described plans to establish a 61-member appointive *Majlis al-Shura* with substantial advisory powers. The announcement also called for the establishment of provincial majlises and sharply changed the rules for determining succession to the throne. From now on, succession is to be decided by an electoral college of some 500 sons and grandsons of King Abd al-Aziz Ibn Saud. It is instructive to note that King Fahd admitted that this decision to broaden participation was a direct result of the second Gulf war. In his words, "Momentous events in the recent past . . . have made it necessary to develop the country's administrative structure."[9]

The Saudi initiative is only part of a more general drive to limited democratization in the Persian Gulf. In Kuwait, where the Amir had twice before dissolved the national assembly, new demands for meaningful elections followed the Iraqi occupation. After a clumsy delay, the Amir finally announced that elections were to be held in October 1992. In the months preceding the elections, political discussion and debate in Kuwait were vigorous and hard-hitting. When the election smoke cleared, the opposition had won a clear majority of the seats and a new era of serious parliamentary politics began in the country.

---

[9] *Washington Post*, March 2, 1991, p. 1.

In Qatar, 54 prominent Qatari citizens presented a petition to their amir demanding free parliamentary elections, a written constitution, and an expansion of personal freedoms. Although the Al-Thani ruling family, relatively unenlightened compared to its counterparts across the Gulf, rejected the initiative, the very existence of the petition was one more indication that the Gulf wars had shattered the political glass in the region.

Although these sporadic policies of reform are increasingly visible in the traditional countries of the Gulf, the underlying reality is one of strong central control. Policies of revision still dominate policies of reform. Police and security forces (often buttressed by powerful outside advisors) are heavily relied upon to protect the status quo. With the partial exception of Kuwait, censorship is severe. Control is tightest in Saudi Arabia, which, although not a police state in the style of Saddam's Iraq, nonetheless leans more heavily in the direction of repression than in the direction of reform. The financial and international power of Saudi Arabia gives it special influence in the region, and its counsel on these important developmental matters carries great weight in the decision-making processes of the other Gulf rulers. Because of Saudi pressures, Kuwait, Bahrain, and the United Arab Emirates have been less willing to pursue vigorously programs of reform.

The instrument through which Saudi Arabia exerts much of its political influence is the Gulf Cooperation Council (GCC), established in May 1981. Formed initially in response to the perceived threats emanating from the Iranian revolution, the GCC is composed of the six traditional Gulf states. In its first years of existence, the GCC emphasized issues of mutual defense and security. The 1990 Iraqi invasion of Kuwait demonstrated the actual weakness of this loosely knit alliance. It is questionable whether the GCC can ever succeed as long as it withholds membership from the two most populous and powerful countries in the Gulf, Iran and Iraq. Nonetheless, the GCC provides a forum where the besieged traditional Gulf countries can discuss political and developmental strategy.

Despite a growing sensitivity (often born out of necessity) to the need to respond creatively and fundamentally to the demands of their growing middle classes and deeply religious lower classes, the ruling elites of most Gulf countries have yet to implement the basic reform programs necessary to guarantee the survival of their systems in the long run. Economic inducements and announcements of promised consultative assemblies are not enough. The steady growth of an activist, political, populist Islam throughout the Gulf states provides an alternative movement whose members are not easily bought or co-opted. Only genuine reform programs that frontally address the deepening crises of identity and legitimacy can stave off political upheaval.

The internal contradictions present in the traditional countries of the Persian Gulf have not yet exploded into revolutionary violence because the benefits of the processes of modernization fueled by great wealth have been shared by the relatively small populations of citizens resident there. Beginning in 1979 with the Iranian revolution, however, and continuing a decade later with the second Gulf war, the tensions have increased profoundly. Internal developments and the introduction of external forces and ideas directly into the region have combined to place an unprecedented strain on the social and political systems of the Gulf countries. The response of the ruling families to these gathering and deepening challenges will determine the future of the region.

Chapter 9

Petroleum, Politics, and Development

*T*he historical precedent set by the West, wherein state formation was linked to economic development, suggests that the process of state-building in the Middle East should have been facilitated and hastened by the great oil boom that began in 1973. And what a boon it was. The price of a barrel of crude oil, which was $1.20 in 1900 and still only $1.69 in 1970, shot up from $2.90 in June 1973 to over $11 per barrel by the end of that year as a result of the oil embargo associated with the October 1973 Arab-Israeli War. The second oil shock, which accompanied the Iranian revolution, sent prices soaring from $13 in January 1979 to as high as $45 per barrel on the spot market later that year, the official posted price reaching an all-time high of $34 per barrel in March 1982. Middle Eastern oil revenues went from $6 billion in 1970 to over $270 billion a decade later. The revenues of Saudi Arabia alone in 1980 were over 15 times those received by all Middle Eastern countries in 1970.

While the major oil-producing states benefited directly from the price rise and growth of oil exports, countries that export little or no oil received substantial secondary benefits in the form of worker remittances, fees for the transport of oil across their territory, and public and private cash transfers and investments by the oil-rich states. The gross domestic products (GDP) of Jordan, Egypt, and what were then North and South Yemen grew during the seven "fat" years of 1974–1981 by an average annual rate of almost 20 percent. Per capita income in those countries more than tripled in the decade after 1972.[1] While much of the rest of the world's economy languished from the first oil shock until at least the early 1980s, during that period virtually all Middle Eastern countries recorded higher real annual economic growth rates than ever before in their histories.

The impact of petrodollars on living standards has been profound. In 1970, between 15 and 22 percent of Middle Easterners suffered from some form of malnutrition. A decade later, the incidence of malnutrition was reduced by half.[2] Between 1965 and 1989, daily per capita calorie intake in the low- and middle-income countries of the Middle East and North Africa (hereafter MENA) rose from 2,153 to 3,011, the fastest growth rate in the world.[3] In that same period, the ratio of doctors to population in those countries registered the world's greatest improvement, from 1:7,740 to 1:2,410.[4] Death rates have declined dramatically as a consequence of improved nutrition and health care, so the rate of population increase has soared. It rose from 2.6 percent in 1972, when the world's average was 1.9 percent, to 3.1 percent in 1990, then the world's highest.[5]

The oil boom also contributed to the rapid expansion of educational facilities. Illiteracy in the Arab world dropped from 70 to 40 percent in the ten years after 1972.[6] By 1990, only in Egypt, Sudan, Oman, and Yemen was more than half the population illiterate.[7] The percentage of the age group enrolled in primary and secondary schools in the low- and middle-income MENA countries rose in the

---

[1] George T. Abed, "The Lean Years: The Political Economy of Arab Oil in the Coming Decade," in Hisham Sharabi, *The Next Arab Decade: Alternative Futures* (Boulder, Colo.: Westview Press, 1988), p. 93.

[2] Joe Stork and Karen Pfeifer, "Bullets, Banks and Bushels: The Struggle for Food in the Middle East," *Middle East Report* 145 (March–April 1987): 6.

[3] The World Bank, *World Development Report, 1992* (Oxford: Oxford University Press, 1992), p. 273.

[4] *Ibid.,* p. 273.

[5] *Ibid.,* p. 269.

[6] Abed, "The Lean Years," p. 95.

[7] *World Development Report, 1992*, pp. 218–219.

quarter century after 1964 from 61 to 90 percent and from 17 to 53 percent, respectively. In that period there was a fourfold increase in the percentage of those in the relevant age group enrolled in higher education.[8]

Living conditions for most Middle Easterners improved significantly as a result of the oil boom. A panel study of poor families in Cairo, which began in 1969, revealed that by the mid-1980s, this sample of the urban poor believed "that matters have improved greatly over the last 15 years." Indeed, many in the sample resented still being referred to as poor and by most objective measures were no longer so.[9] Of the 43 countries classified as "low income" by the World Bank, only four—Egypt, Mauritania, Afghanistan, and Sudan—are in the MENA region.[10] All other countries in the region are categorized as middle- or high-income developing countries. The average per capita gross national product (GNP) of the low- and middle-income MENA countries in 1990 was $1,790, almost equivalent to that of the Latin America/Caribbean countries, almost three times higher than that of countries in East Asia, and some five times more than that of countries in South Asia or Sub-Saharan Africa.[11] Personal incomes, diets, access to health and educational facilities, and the living conditions in general of most Middle Easterners during the oil boom improved at a substantially faster pace than those of populations elsewhere in the Third World. Since the end of that boom, the rate of improvement as shown by these measures has slowed down considerably in the region, but progress has been real.

Providing better living conditions for important sectors of the population may be a necessary requisite, but it is not a sufficient condition for the creation of effective and legitimate states. Rapid economic growth carries with it dislocations that may destabilize governments. The pattern of growth may itself facilitate or impede the expansion of state power. Economic growth spurred principally by industrialization provided the basis for incorporating new recruits into both the economic and political systems of most Western countries. But in the Middle East, economic development, especially since the

---

[8] *Ibid.*, p. 275.

[9] Unni Wikan, "Living Conditions Among Cairo's Poor—A View from Below," *The Middle East Journal* 39 (Winter 1985): 7.

[10] *World Development Report*, 1992, p. 218.

[11] *Ibid.*, p. 219.

early 1970s, has been influenced disproportionately by one commodity—oil. The consequences of the region having become so heavily dependent on the extraction and exportation of that single natural resource are profound for both economies and polities. Uneven growth within and between the three major sectors of national economies—industry, agriculture, and services—is one generally negative result of the oil boom.

INDUSTRY

The industrial sector in most Middle Eastern countries exhibits sharp bimodalism, the oil-associated subsector performing well while virtually all other subsectors of industry are struggling to maintain adequate growth rates. Middle Eastern oil producers, whose deposits of that mineral are truly prodigious, have come to play an extremely powerful role in the world petroleum trade. The Middle East has over 60 percent of the world's petroleum reserves. The commanding position of the Middle East, and within it of the five countries with the largest revenues—Iran, Iraq, Kuwait, Saudi Arabia, and the UAE—is, if anything, increasing. Estimates of the proven reserves of these countries were in 1988 and 1989 vastly increased. In January 1989, Saudi Arabia—which possesses more oil than any other country—announced a rise of 51 percent in its recoverable oil reserves, from 167.4 to 252.4 billion barrels.[12] By 1992, Saudi Arabia claimed to have 300 billion barrels of oil, more than one-quarter of the world's proven reserves. In that year it was set to overtake the Commonwealth of Independent States (formerly USSR) as the world's largest producer. Although some Gulf countries may have purposely overestimated their reserves in order to obtain larger shares in OPEC production agreements, there is no question that the Persian Gulf is by far the world's largest repository of oil and will be so for the foreseeable future.

In addition to being plentiful, Middle Eastern oil is also cheap to produce. Depreciation, interest, and operating expenses together amount to less than $5 per barrel of oil produced in the Middle East. Elsewhere these expenses are very much higher. Additions to non-OPEC sources from 1973 to 1982 cost on average $60,000 per barrel/day, thus making oil from the three major new areas developed in

---

[12] *Middle East Economic Digest* (hereafter *MEED;* January 20, 1989):22–23.

the 1970s—the North Sea, North Slope, and Mexico—several times more expensive to extract and deliver to market than Middle East oil.[13] Whereas most Middle Eastern producers can still make profits if prices drop to even $10 per barrel, most others cannot. It is for this reason that in the mid- to late 1980s much of the world's productive capacity was shut down and little new exploration and development undertaken.

Since the oil price increases of the 1970s, the large oil producers in the Gulf have followed a systematic policy of "moving downstream." They have assumed greater roles in the refining, transport, and marketing of petroleum and constructed modern plants for adding value to crude oil and natural gas by converting them into other products, especially petrochemicals. By the late 1980s the move downstream had resulted in Gulf exporters becoming major marketers of refined petroleum products in Europe, North America, and the Far East and in their assuming a significant share of world petrochemical production. By 1989, 27 percent of oil exports from the Middle East OPEC countries were in the form of refined products.[14] In 1988, Saudi Arabia purchased half of the Texaco oil company's U.S. refining operations and formed a joint venture with it to supply petroleum products to some 12,000 service stations in 23 states. In the previous year, Kuwait had purchased over 20 percent of the shares of British Petroleum (BP), which, in addition to its string of 5,000 wholly-owned Q8 service stations in seven European countries, gave Kuwait a significant role in the world's retail petroleum market. By 1988, Kuwait was selling directly to consumers more than half of its total oil output.[15] In June 1988, Abu Dhabi, one of the seven emirates in the UAE, made a move downstream by purchasing 8.4 percent of the stock of the French oil company Total, making it the largest investor in that company after the French government.[16] The vast expansion of petrochemical plants has made the Gulf states, and Saudi Arabia in particular, major competitors in this market. By 1992, Saudi Arabia had captured some 10 percent of the world's market for petrochemicals. Sabic (Saudi Basic Industries Corporation), which employs almost 10,000

---

[13] Thomas Stauffer, "Income Measurement in Arab States," in *The Rentier State,* pp. 29–30; and Abed, "The Lean Years," pp. 98–99.

[14] *Middle East Times,* July 9–15, 1988, p. 9.

[15] *MEED* (July 8, 1988):2–3.

[16] "Penetrating the Market Place," *MEED* (July 8, 1988):2.

people, was in 1992 the world's sixth most profitable petrochemical company. Iran, which by 1990 was producing 14 percent of the Middle East's petrochemicals, plans to spend $18 billion in the 1990s in order to lift its share to 21 percent.[17]

There is a gray area between oil and nonoil industries in which considerable development has also occurred. The Gulf oil producers have established various industries that especially benefit from cheap energy, such as aluminium smelting and steel production. Qatar and Bahrain have added some 10 percent to their GDPs with such installations, and Saudi Arabia has undertaken an even more extensive industrialization program. But the success of these undertakings is directly proportional to the degree to which they are linked to hydrocarbon extraction, processing, and consumption and hence able to benefit from comparative advantage and outright subsidization. It remains an open question as to whether they would be competitive in the absence of access to oil and gas at less than world market prices.

In countries of the region that do not export large quantities of oil, industrial production remains concentrated in the usual areas of Third World manufacturing, which are food processing, textiles, and construction materials. Some progress has been made in establishing more sophisticated industries, such as vehicle production and electronics, but those activities generally remain limited to assembly of imported components. There is virtually no manufacturing of machine tools in the region, so almost all capital equipment involved in production must be imported.

Rates of growth in manufacturing in some key Middle Eastern countries, including Egypt, which is the most industrialized of the Arab states, were higher in the 1960s and 1970s than they have been subsequently. The average annual growth rate of industry in the low- and middle-income MENA countries was 6.3 percent from 1965 to 1980, but only 0.7 percent in the following decade, the lowest growth rate of any region in the world.[18] For the region as a whole, manufacturing still accounts for less than 10 percent of GDP.[19] It employs on average less than 20 percent of the labor force, compared to some 23 percent and 31 percent for middle-income and upper-middle-income

---

[17] *MEED* (May 22, 1992), p. 10.

[18] *World Development Report, 1992,* p. 221.

[19] Chatelus, "Policies for Development: Attitudes Toward Industry and Services," p. 127.

developing countries, respectively.[20] Between 1985 and 1990, employment in manufacturing industries in Saudi Arabia actually declined by 50,000 jobs.[21] Industrial goods constituted only between 1 and 2 percent of exports from the MENA countries through the early 1990s, which—along with Sub-Saharan Africa—is the lowest proportion in the world.[22] In various countries of the region, the share of manufactures in exports dropped between the mid-1960s and mid-1980s, as oil exports rose and nonoil industrial subsectors stagnated. In Egypt, for example, which is not a large exporter of oil, manufactured goods, including textiles, accounted for about one-third of exports in 1965, but only 18 percent by 1985. For middle-income developing countries as a whole, total manufactures constituted on average 24 percent of exports in 1965 and 50 percent in 1985.[23] Outside the oil sector and industries closely allied to it, industrial expansion in the region has failed to keep pace with rates of growth elsewhere in the developing world.

AGRICULTURE

The other major productive economic sector, agriculture, has, if anything, not even kept pace with the sluggish rate of growth in industry. In all MENA countries for which World Bank data are available except Morocco and Saudi Arabia, average annual growth rates of agricultural production were higher from 1965 to 1980 than they were from 1980 to 1990.[24] In Sudan, Algeria, Morocco, and Syria, growth rates fell by more than half between these two periods. Between 1980 and 1985, Sudanese agricultural production actually declined at an average annual rate of 5.5 percent and has continued to stagnate since

---

[20] Amara, "The State, Social Classes and Agricultural Policies in the Arab World," in *The Rentier State,* ed. by Hazem Beblau and Giacomo Luciani (London: Croom Helm, 1987), p. 155; *World Development Report, 1987,* pp. 264–265.

[21] John Presley and Tony Westaway, "Economic Liberalisation in Saudi Arabia," paper presented to the Symposium on Economic Liberalisation and Its Social and Political Effects in the Middle East, University of Exeter (September 26–28, 1991), p. 15.

[22] *World Development Report, 1992,* p. 249.

[23] *World Development Report 1987,* p. 222.

[24] *World Development Report, 1992,* pp. 220–221.

that time.[25] In the low- and middle-income MENA countries per capita food production grew between 1979 and 1990 more slowly than in any other region in the world except Sub-Saharan Africa.[26]

In all Middle Eastern countries for which World Bank data are available, the agricultural sector's contribution to GDP was considerably higher in 1965 than in 1990. Over that 25-year period it fell in Egypt from 29 percent to 17 percent, in Turkey from 34 percent to 18 percent, and in Oman from 61 percent to 3 percent.[27] Agriculture now contributes about 15 percent to GDP in the major MENA food producing countries.[28] The share of the labor force engaged in agriculture has declined at approximately the same rate in most of the Middle East as in other Third World middle-income countries, where it fell from 56 percent to 43 percent from 1965 to 1985.[29] Agriculture nevertheless still employs a larger percentage of the labor force than any other sector, and the absolute numbers of those engaged in agriculture have slightly increased in the Middle East in recent years.[30] The share of agricultural commodities in all Middle Eastern countries' exports has declined precipitously since the 1960s. It fell, for example, from 71 percent to 20 percent in Egypt and from 89 percent to 17 percent in Syria between 1965 and 1990.[31] In the 1970s several countries that had been net exporters of grain—including Egypt, Morocco, Iraq, and Syria—became net importers. Turkey is the only country in the region that went against the trend by becoming a net exporter not only of grains but also of agricultural commodities generally.[32]

As a result of growth rates of production falling behind rapidly increasing demand, the "food gap" in the Middle East has widened at an alarming rate. The Middle East is now the world's largest food-importing region. Whereas in 1972 the Middle East was nearly self-

---

[25] *World Development Report, 1987*, p. 205.

[26] *World Development Report, 1992*, p. 225.

[27] *World Development Report, 1992*, p. 225.

[28] Mushtak Parker, "The Food Gap Widens," *The Middle East* (June 1992), p. 29.

[29] *World Development Report, 1987*, pp. 264–265.

[30] Amara, "The State, Social Classes and Agricultural Policies," pp. 140–141.

[31] *World Development Report, 1992*, p. 225.

[32] Susannah Tarbush, "Food: Why Time Is Running Out," *The Middle East* 129 (July 1985):14.

sufficient in agricultural production, by 1986 farm output had fallen to
81 percent of needs and imports reached a staggering $25 billion, ten
times more than a decade earlier.[33] Agricultural imports by Arab
League states in 1990 accounted for almost one-third of all such
imports by Third World countries, despite the fact that Arabs do not
exceed 5 percent of the Third World's population. Idriss Jazairy, president of the International Fund for Agricultural Development, predicted in 1992 that before the end of the century the Arab food import
bill could reach $100 billion annually.[34] Seven out of every ten loaves
of bread eaten by Arabs are now baked from imported flour.[35]
Between 1974 and 1990, low- and middle-income MENA countries
increased their importation of cereals more rapidly than countries of
any other region, causing them to become the most cereal-dependent
region on earth.[36]

Food imports, as a percentage of export earnings and GDP, illustrate how dependent the Middle East has become on the rest of the
world for its "daily bread." Egypt, which was one of the Third World's
major agricultural exporting nations from the 1820s through the first
two-thirds of this century, and which was still self-sufficient in food
when Anwar al-Sadat came to power, had by 1990 become the world's
third largest importer of grain and produced only 40 percent of its own
food.[37] Other former major agricultural exporters in the Middle East
and North Africa, including Morocco, Tunisia, Sudan, and Syria, all
spend more than 25 percent of their export earnings to import foodstuffs.[38]

During the oil boom and even into the mid-1980s, many Middle
Eastern governments did little to try to reduce the food gap. A policy
of cheap food for urban populations was instituted in most countries to
reduce the possibilities of political unrest. Changes in the international terms of trade facilitated that policy. In 1970 a barrel of oil bought
about one bushel of wheat, but a decade later the same barrel could

---

[33] "Bridging the Food Gap," p. 2.

[34] Parker, "Food Gap Widens," p. 29.

[35] "Arab World Must Quickly Learn to Feed Itself," *Middle East Times,* January 7–13,
1989, p. 20.

[36] *World Development Report, 1992,* p. 225.

[37] Ray Bush, "Agriculture in Jeopardy," *The Middle East* (May 1992), p. 22.

[38] Stork and Pfeifer, "Bullets, Banks and Bushels," p. 5.

purchase six bushels.[39] It became easier to import food than to stimulate local production and establish market linkages between rural and urban areas.

The policy of cheap, plentiful food caused consumption to skyrocket, a trend further accelerated by population growth rates that have exceeded 2 percent in all countries in the region except Israel, and in some countries—including Iran, Iraq, and Algeria—have reached almost 4 percent.[40] As personal incomes rose faster than food prices during the oil boom, Middle Easterners vastly increased their per capita food consumption. In Saudi Arabia, for example, annual per capita consumption of food rose from 323 kilos in 1974 to 515 kilos in 1984.[41] Since 1966, the Middle East–North Africa region has had the most rapid growth of food consumption in the Third World—an annual average increase of 3.9 percent.[42] Food, which in the Middle East is used as an important measure of personal status, is typically the major expense in household budgets. Even in comparatively wealthy Saudi Arabia, 30 percent of personal expenditures are for food, compared with about 15 percent in Europe.[43] Among the urban poor in the region, food purchases consume well over half of disposable income.

During the oil boom, Middle Easterners also changed their diets. They moved up the "food chain," substituting red and white meat and animal products for vegetable proteins and eating a higher proportion of prepackaged, processed foodstuffs. Each Arab consumed annually an average of 4 kilograms of eggs in 1981–1983, about double the figure for 1970–1972. Consumption of poultry more than trebled, and red meat consumption doubled over that decade.[44] In the last two decades of this century, red meat consumption in the Arab world is expected to more than triple, with 40 percent of supplies having to be imported.[45] In sum, personal preferences, reinforced by local

---

[39] Alan Richards, "Arab Agriculture in 1995: Apocalypse Now or Muddling Through?" in *The Next Arab Decade*, p. 116.

[40] Tarbush, "Food," p. 13.

[41] "Bridging the Food Gap," p. 6.

[42] Stork and Pfeifer, "Bullets, Banks and Bushels," p. 5.

[43] "Bridging the Food Gap," p. 6.

[44] "Arab World Must Quickly Learn to Feed Itself," p. 20.

[45] Martha Wenger and Joe Stork, "The Food Gap in the Middle East," *Middle East Report*, 166 (September–October, 1990): 17.

government policies and global terms of trade, led to a vastly higher demand for increasingly expensive imported food after the 1973 oil price rise.

Caught between the downturn in oil prices after 1982 and the rising demand for food, governments have struggled to stimulate domestic agricultural production while trying to reduce consumption and importation. Cheap, plentiful food, however, became a vital component of the informal "social contracts" that emerged between governments and populations in the 1970s—"contracts" that require governments to make available consumer goods at relatively low prices in return for the population's acquiescence in their rule. Constriction of food supplies is a politically risky step. Since the late 1970s, food riots have occurred in Algeria, Egypt, Iran, Jordan, Lebanon, Morocco, Sudan, Tunisia, and Turkey.[46] For all governments other than those of the oil-exporting countries of the Gulf, however, there has been no alternative to raising prices of food and constricting its supply. Such measures, though, are imposed in tentative, incremental fashion and immediately rescinded in the face of serious opposition.

Even with these cutbacks, food import bills have continued to mount, in part because the terms of trade began to shift in favor of agricultural exporters after 1985. Oil prices since then have stagnated, while grain prices have more than doubled. Egypt, for example, spent $600 million importing wheat and flour in 1987 but had to spend $1 billion in 1988 to import virtually the same amount.[47] Ultimately, most Middle Eastern countries have no choice but to increase agricultural output and reduce their food dependency, for the availability of relatively inexpensive food on world markets is by no means guaranteed even for the decade of the 1990s. That the Arab world will confront a major food crisis is predicted by many experts, one of whom stated in early 1989 that in the year 2000 at least one-third of the Arab population "will definitely face starvation."[48]

---

[46] David Seddon, "Austerity Protest: Popular Responses to Economic Liberalisation in the Middle East and North Africa," in *Economic and Political Liberalization in the Middle East,* ed. by Tim Niblock and Emma Murphy (London: British Academic Press, 1993), pp. 88–89.

[47] David Butter, "Egypt," *MEED* (October 14, 1988):39.

[48] Hassan al-Nouman speaking to Arab Conference On Food and Agriculture, Sharjah, January 1989, as reported in "Arab World Must Quickly Learn to Feed Itself," p. 20.

SERVICES

Services include income-generating activities such as transportation, tourism, financial services, research-development, and engineering, as well as income-utilizing endeavors, such as the provision of health, educational, and social services.[49] Unlike industrial and agricultural sectors, service sectors of virtually all Middle Eastern countries have grown rapidly since the onset of the oil boom. Since 1970, expenditure on services has grown at a higher annual rate than GDP in almost all countries in the region. In states that export little or no oil, services typically account for about half of GDP; in the oil-exporting countries, the ratio of services to the nonoil GDP normally ranges between 70 and 80 percent.[50] In Saudi Arabia, for example, employment in productive sectors fell by 530,000 but increased in the service sector by 900,000 between 1985 and 1990.[51]

The bulk of services in Middle Eastern countries is performed by government; hence, as the service sector has expanded so the percentage of the labor force employed by government has grown. This is true regardless of the nominal categorization of a country's political economy as socialist or market-oriented. In Iran, for example, the trend of growing government employment that began under the shah has continued under the Islamic Republic. In 1966, public sector employees constituted less than 10 percent of Iran's employed population. A decade later they made up almost 20 percent of the labor force and about one-third of the urban work force. By 1986, 31 percent of the labor force was in the public sector, the ratio being 43 percent in urban areas. The average annual growth rate in public employment in Iran since 1976 has been 7 percent, although total employment has grown at only 2.5 percent per annum.[52] In Egypt, the public sector's share of employment actually increased at a faster pace under Sadat than under Nasser, despite the fact that the former advocated liberal

---

[49] This distinction is made by Michel Chatelus, "Policies for Development: Attitudes Toward Industry and Services," in *The Rentien State,* p. 133.

[50] *Ibid.,* p. 134.

[51] Presley and Westaway, "Economic Liberalisation in Saudi Arabia," p. 15.

[52] Paul Johnson, "The Impact of the Islamic Revolution on the State/Private Sector Symbiosis." Paper delivered to the Social Science Research Council's Conference on Expanding States and Retreating Societies, Aix-en-Provence (March 25–27, 1988), pp. 1, 9.

economic policies and the latter was a champion of Arab socialism. By 1992, the Egyptian state employed 5.3 million out of a total work force of 13.9 million people, some 38 percent.[53]

Such rapid growth of the service sector is a mixed blessing. While the development of the region's physical and human infrastructures, including roads, schools, and health care delivery systems, is critical to its economic growth and well-being, much of the expansion of the service sector reflects lack of opportunity elsewhere. Migrant workers returning from the Gulf to their homes in Egypt, Jordan, Syria, or Yemen, for example, typically invest their savings in real estate or service enterprises, such as retail trade and taxis, rather than in manufacturing or farming. Even as Middle Eastern economies stagnate, real estate booms continue.

Both governments and private sectors have failed to provide adequate investment opportunities in industry and agriculture. Until recently most governments of the region acted as employers of last resort, hiring those graduates who otherwise would be unemployed, then consigning them to unrewarding, unproductive labor in sprawling bureaucracies. But as governmental revenues have fallen and the number of such graduates has continued to expand at an ever accelerating pace, the inevitable result has been increasing unemployment. In the countries outside the Gulf, unemployment is typically estimated, officially, to be 10 to 15 percent, and in some of them, in reality, such as Tunisia, Morocco, and Sudan, it is at least double that rate. In Algeria, it was estimated in late 1988 to be about 40 percent.[54] Egyptian unemployment grew from less than 1 million in 1981 to 2.8 million at the end of 1988, at which time it constituted 20 percent of the work force.[55] Since the mid 1970s, some 70 to 90 percent of all new jobs for Egyptians have come through emigration or in government employment, two areas in which expansion has already slowed and will continue to stagnate.[56] The service sector, especially its governmental

[53] *MEED* (May 22, 1992), p. 20.

[54] John T. Haldane, "Algeria Moving Toward Major Economic Reform," *The Washington Report on Middle East Affairs* 7 (January 1989):39.

[55] Hassan al Qadi, "Already Critical Jobless Rate Getting Worse, Experts Say," *Middle East Times,* January 7–13, 1989, p. 4.

[56] Hans Lofgren, "Economic Policy in Egypt: A Breakdown in Reform Resistance," paper presented to the annual conference of the Middle East Studies Association of North America, Washington, D.C. (November 23–26, 1991), p. 10.

component, has heretofore acted as a sponge that has mopped up potential unemployment. It is now saturated or very close to it. Although ultimately this may be a good thing if productive employment opportunities can be generated in industry and agriculture, as many governments have begun to encourage, it is scant comfort for today's unemployed youths.

The oil boom and the partial oil "bust" have had major impacts on the region's political systems. In particular, the oil-price roller coaster since the early 1970s has led to two paradoxes that characterize the political economies of Middle Eastern countries. The first is that in the seven years of fat, between 1974 and 1981, most governments were stable, but the states themselves were not becoming stronger and more institutionalized. Sudden wealth did not facilitate the state-formation process. The second paradox is that over the lean years that began in 1982, many governments have faced greater threats to their stability and even their continued existence. However, they have begun to initiate political and economic changes that may ultimately lead to the establishment of much stronger states. These apparent anomalies require explanation.

PARADOX ONE: ECONOMIC GROWTH AND POLITICAL DECAY

Rentier States

European state formation occurred during a protracted period of broadly based economic growth, typically under the auspices of private sectors. In the Middle East, on the other hand, the oil boom was short lived, it was associated with rapid expansion of the service sector but not with adequate growth rates of manufacturing industry or agriculture, and the source of greatest wealth—the oil industry—was in all cases under direct governmental control. Revenues accrued to governments essentially as "rents." These included profits from the oil industry as well as other sources external to the productive economy itself and immediately available to government, such as foreign aid, borrowings, and fees imposed on the transport of oil. The "rentier state" is thus one in which the government does not have to extract much revenue from its own citizens through taxation.

Indeed, in the Middle East direct taxes on incomes, profits, and capital gains are among the lowest in the world. While in 1988 in the United States, Japan, and Canada, such taxes amounted to 50 percent, 68.8 percent, and 48.5 percent of total current revenues, respectively, in Egypt these taxes accounted for 15.2 percent, in Tunisia for 12.2 percent, and in Yemen for 13.3 percent of revenues. In Third World middle-income countries as a whole, such taxes provide on average about one-quarter of government revenues.[57] In most of the oil-exporting states in the Gulf, such taxes are nominal or entirely nonexistent. In Kuwait, for example, direct taxes amounted to a minuscule 0.9 percent of revenues in 1985.[58]

Egypt, which has one of the most highly developed systems of direct personal taxation in the Arab world, managed to collect from that source in 1983 only £E127.3 million (£E1 = approximately U.S. $1.25 in 1983), or about £E12 for each person in the labor force, for an overall taxation rate of about 1 percent of personal income.[59] The Egyptian-born director of the International Monetary Fund's (IMF) Middle East department, Abd al-Shakur Sha'lan, used the expression *mish ma'ul* (unbelievable, crazy) to describe Egypt's system of taxation, which applies essentially only to government employees.[60] But while Egypt's taxation policy may be "crazy," it is understandable. As a result of the oil boom, from which Egypt collected rents in various forms, the government had comparatively little need to raise revenues through taxes on individuals. In 1974, before the boom commenced, no more than 6 percent of all resources available to the government were from "exogenous" sources, such as foreign assistance, loans, and Suez Canal tolls. By 1983 the proportion had reached 45 percent and the gross amount was many times higher.[61]

Having access to rents provided directly or indirectly from the exportation of oil, Middle Eastern governments were in the 1970s and early 1980s in what seemed to be the enviable position of being able to

[57] Hazem Beblawi and Giacomo Luciani, "Introduction," *The Rentier State,* p. 9; and *World Development Report, 1987,* pp. 248–249.

[58] *Ibid.,* p. 249.

[59] Hesham Garaibeh, "Government Income Sources and the Development of the Taxation System—the Case of Jordan, Egypt and Kuwait," in *The Rentier State,* p. 206.

[60] "Shaalan Says No IMF Deal Before Six Months," *MEED* (November 1988):6.

[61] John Waterbury, "The 'Soft State' and the Open Door: Egypt's Experience with Economic Liberalization, 1974–1984," *Comparative Politics* (October 1985):68.

allocate resources to their populations rather than extract taxes from them. The emphasis on allocation, however, had negative economic and political consequences. In regard to the economy, it led to a consumption binge, facilitated by a package of economic measures known collectively as the policy of infitah, or opening. This policy included overvaluation of local currencies, which favored imports at the expense of exports; a general reduction of barriers to the movement of goods and services across national borders; and some preliminary, tentative steps to stimulate the private sector, which in the end worked more to the benefit of importers and others in the service sector than to those in industry or agriculture. Infitah policies, which stimulated consumption at the expense of production, were associated with high inflation rates, stagnating rates of investment in industry and agriculture, bias toward urban consumers rather than rural producers, and ultimately, with rapidly increasing rates of indebtedness.

The apparent inability of Middle Eastern governments to seize the opportunity provided by the oil boom to convert a high proportion of rents into permanently productive assets has as its root cause the political weakness of those states. In this regard, Arab economist George T. Abed has stated,

> Much of the reason why Arab development strategies have in part failed has been the prevailing illusion that economic and financial development can be accelerated in the absence of clear movement toward political modernization. Thus the absence of fully developed political institutions deprived broad sectors of the population of participation in (as distinct from benefit from) the development process and preempted the emergence of the minimal norms of public discourse and accountability essential to the prevention of waste and corruption.[62]

Middle Eastern states have not fully penetrated their respective societies, nor have those societies become permanently and actively engaged in the policy-making process. Low rates of taxation and the absence of effective formal institutions of political participation both testify to the wide gap between state and society. The social contract, by which governments dole out resources in exchange for submission to their rule, was substituted for closer integration of state and society, each of which wanted to be left alone by the other. "Rather than undertake painful and risky measures toward bridging the gap

---

[62] Abed, "The Lean Years," p. 102.

between state and society," according to Yahya Sadowski, the government of a rentier state "accepts the fact of divorce. . . . Like a veiled woman walking through the noise and dust of a *suq* [bazaar], these partioned spheres [e.g., rural life, the private sector, Islamicists, the family] are not totally isolated or invulnerable; but they are highly resistant to state control."[63] Governments remained in power, but their ability to raise taxes and compel general obedience to authority declined as oil revenues mounted.

The oil boom added further momentum to the "retreat" of the states of the Middle East and North Africa that had already begun as a result of the June 1967 War. This retreat includes both the loss of legitimacy and the diminution of capacity to regulate the economy.[64] Faced with the choice of imposing some austerity in exchange for greater political freedoms or buying off the public while continuing to restrict widespread political participation, political elites opted for the second alternative. By doing so they precluded a true economic liberalization. States had to continue to dominate economies in order to obtain the resources required to fulfill their obligations for allocations required by the social contact. The partial opening, insufficient to stimulate productive entrepreneurial activities as opposed to exploitative, parasitical ones, nevertheless further eroded governmental capability to manage the economy effectively.

Regional Integration

The oil boom tended to prolong the life of incumbent regimes while paradoxically undermining the power and effectiveness of the state. It also had contradictory consequences for the political economy of the region as a whole. Increasing regional integration "has been taking place simultaneously with the process of greater consolidation of indi-

---

[63] Yahya Sadowski, "Is This Society Civil? Rethinking the Logic of State Formation in Egypt," Paper delivered to the Social Science Research Council's Conference on Retreating States and Expanding Societies, Aix-en-Provence (March 25–27, 1988), pp. 44, 56.

[64] Clement Henry Moore, "Arab Financial Reforms: Bankers as Midwives of Civil Societies?" Paper delivered to the Social Science Research Council's Conference on Retreating States and Expanding Societies, Aix-en-Provence (March 25–27, 1988), p. 1.

vidual . . . *national* economies."[65] The Muslim states in the region, especially the Arab states, being drawn by economic forces into a regional oil economy, have steadfastly resisted encroachments on their economic autonomy and political sovereignty.

Economic logic demands coordination and unification within the region, if only because disproportions between the sizes and economic resources of the countries are so very marked. Qatar, for example, in 1991 had fewer than 200,000 native inhabitants, and Kuwait, Oman, and the UAE had less than 2 million citizens each. Egypt, on the other hand, had in 1991 a population of some 57 million. Qatar, Kuwait, and the UAE, as a result of their vast oil deposits, have GNPs per capita in excess of $16,000. Egypt, with comparatively little oil to export, had an annual GNP per capita of $750 in 1985, which slid to $600 in the following six years. Sudan's population and GNP per capita are about half of Egypt's. Yet Egypt and Sudan jointly dispose of significant industrial and agricultural resources, which are not fully developed because of a lack of capital. Economic integration of the oil-rich but otherwise resource-poor and sparsely populated oil-exporting states with the much larger but poorer states in the region appears eminently sensible. No country in the region has a sufficiently large market to support economies of scale in manufacturing, despite the fact that the region as a whole had a population of 314 million in 1989 and by the year 2000 will have increased 35 percent, to 423 million.[66] A semiprotected Arab market, equivalent to that of the European Common Market, is virtually a prerequisite for significant growth of manufacturing industry. Equally, "It is simply an exercise in self-delusion to pretend that individual Arab oil-producing countries can achieve self-sustained economic development either in isolation or in small exclusive 'rich man's clubs.'"[67]

The oil boom did stimulate very large movements of labor and capital between Arab countries. At any one time from the mid-1970s to the end of the 1980s, over 3 million Egyptians, Syrians, Jordanians, Palestinians, Yemenis, Sudanese, Lebanese, and North Africans were

---

[65] Samih K. Farsoun, "Class Structure and Social Change in the Arab World: 1995," in *The Next Arab Decade*, p. 222.

[66] Parker, "Food Gap Widens," p. 29.

[67] Abed, "The Lean Years, p. 103.

working in the oil-rich states of the Gulf and in Libya. They remitted at least $7 billion annually to their home economies.[68] As a result of the oil slump and the second Gulf war, the Arab migrant labor force has been reduced, but it is still sizable.

The exchange of labor for capital has been of profound proportions for both sides. Worker remittances as a percentage of total exports at the height of the boom were in Egypt almost 30 percent, in Morocco over 40 percent, just under 200 percent in Jordan, and almost 6,000 percent in North Yemen.[69] Between 1973 and 1989, net workers' remittances of $87 billion flowed into Arab countries.[70] In three of the labor-importing countries, immigrants make up over half the total population. In five others, they constituted between 40 percent and 75 percent of the labor force in the 1980s.[71]

A tremendous amount of capital other than worker remittances has also crossed Arab borders. Official bilateral and multilateral aid provided by the Arab oil-exporting states to other Arab countries totaled $55 billion between 1973 and 1989. But this financial assistance reached its peak in 1981 and has declined steadily since then. By 1989, in fact, there was a total net inflow into the wealthy Arab donor countries of $2.2 billion as a result of principal repayments and a reduction of new loans.[72] By far the largest transfers of funds have been for political reasons, such as supporting the Arab "front-line states" against Israel, or Iraq against Iran. In the 1970s Egypt alone received from the Gulf states over $20 billion; during Iraq's eight-year war with Iran, it obtained probably half again as much from those same sources.[73] For opposing Iraq during the second Gulf war, Egypt and Syria were paid some $7 billion and $2 billion, respectively, by Kuwait and Saudi Arabia. Much of this capital has been transferred in a manner that did little if anything to stimulate the growth of a network of financial institutions linking the various national economies;

---

[68] *Ibid.*, p. 93.

[69] Farsoun, "Class Structure and Social Change," p. 222.

[70] "IMF Plots Arab Aid Trends," *MEED* (March 6, 1992), p. 6.

[71] Fred Halliday, "Labor Migration in the Arab World," *Merip Reports* 123 (May 1984):4.

[72] *MEED* (March 6, 1992), p. 6.

[73] Roger Owen, "The Arab Oil Economy: Present Structure and Future Prospects," in *Arab Society: Continuity and Change,* ed. by Samih K. Farsoun (London: Croom Helm, 1985), pp. 17–18.

however, intra-Arab banks, development agencies, and private investment companies nevertheless have emerged.

According to Roger Owen, it is movement of labor and capital and the institutions underpinning such transfers "which allows one to speak, very generally, of an Arab 'oil economy' embracing all 21 of the Arab states."[74] Owen, however, is quick to add two qualifications. The first is that individual regimes have refused to surrender any measure of sovereignty or economic control. Instead, they have sought to bolster themselves against their own populations.

> Indeed, it could easily be argued that one of the major political effects of oil wealth has been to increase, not the power of Pan-Arabism, but that of the separate states, giving them new resources with which to buy off potential popular opposition with cheap food and other subsidies or, in some cases to finance much larger and more efficient security forces.[75]

Owen's second qualification is that individual economies were integrated more tightly into the world economy than into the regional one. Echoing these reservations, Michel Chatelus states flatly, "We do not believe in the existence of such an entity as 'the Arab economy'; for only political arguments can be called upon to support this concept."[76]

Economic evidence indicates that skepticism about the existence of a discrete Middle Eastern oil economy is justified. Inter-Arab capital movements are in fact minor compared to Arab capital flows to the Western industrialized countries. Between 1974 and 1981, only about 15 percent of the current account surpluses of the Arab oil exporters were officially transferred to other Arab countries. A far higher percentage of petrodollars was invested in the West.[77] The Gulf Cooperation Council (GCC), which links six oil-exporting states in the Gulf, and the Arab Cooperation Council, which grouped Egypt, Jordan, North Yemen, and Iraq, were created in the 1980s. The former functions primarily to coordinate internal security activities of member countries, while the latter was destroyed by the second Gulf war, which further weakened and divided the Arab League. The Arab

---

[74] *Ibid.,* p. 18.

[75] *Ibid.,* pp. 18–19.

[76] Chatelus, "Policies for Development," p. 108.

[77] Samir Makdisi, "Economic Interdependence and National Sovereignty," in *The Politics of Arab Integration,* ed. by Giacomo Luciani and Ghassan Salame (London: Croom Helm, 1987), p. 126.

Common Market exists in name only, as a comparison to the European Economic Community (EEC) suggests. The share of intra-Arab Common Market trade in 1978 between the four founding members of that organization—Egypt, Iraq, Jordan, Syria—was just over 2 percent of both imports and exports. By comparison, member states of the EEC increased their mutual trade from 35 percent to 50 percent in the first five years of that organization's existence.[78] Intra-Arab trade as a whole has yet to reach 10 percent of the Arab States' total trade.[79] Concessions on customs and tariffs within the Arab world have been negligible in amount and impact.

It is the case, however, that the intraregional transportation and communication infrastructure—including roads, maritime and airline services, telecommunication systems, and even radio and television programming—is far better developed and integrated than it was prior to the oil boom. It is now comparatively easy to ship goods, to fly or drive, or to make telephone calls between one Arab country and another. Regionwide distribution of electronic and print media is far greater and more timely than even a decade ago. The physical infrastructure that links together the region's states is developing much more rapidly than are intraregional political or economic institutions, in part at least because the latter pose a threat to national sovereignty.[80]

The comparatively slow growth of regionwide institutions is also a side effect of the stronger attraction of the center of the world's economic system, which is to be found in the advanced industrialized countries. The Middle East has the highest proportion of imports and exports to GDP of any region in the world.[81] The great bulk of that trade is conducted with the 20 countries of the Organization for Eco-

---

[78] R. Paul Shaw, "The Political Economy of Inequality in the Arab World," *Arab Studies Quarterly* 6 (Winter/Spring 1984):150.

[79] Owen, "The Arab Oil Economy," p. 19.

[80] The development and utilization of physical infrastructure can also be impeded by national economic, social, and political consideration. The causeway between Bahrain and Saudi Arabia, construction of which was delayed for several years for those reasons, after completion sat unused for months. Saudi decision makers fretted over the consequences of allowing citizens to drive over to comparatively freewheeling, fun-loving Bahrain.

[81] Michael J. Simpson, "The Prospects for Technological Growth in Arab Societies," in *The Next Arab Decade*, p. 131.

nomic Cooperation and Development (OECD). Between two-thirds and three-quarters of all imports and exports in the Arab world in the 1980s came from or went to such countries.[82] Increasing predominance of the West, including Japan, as a source of imports and a destination for exports characterizes the trade patterns of all types of Middle East regimes, "moderate" or "radical," "socialist" or "capitalist." More than four-fifths of all Algeria's imports, for example, come from the West.[83] Between 1965 and 1985 Iraq's exports to OECD countries rose from 24 percent to 83 percent.[84]

Types of imports, balance of trade, and growth of debt also suggest greater dependency on the West. By the early 1980s some two-thirds of imports were industrial goods, indicating that the Middle East is overwhelmingly a consumer rather than producer of new technologies.[85] This tendency was exacerbated by the oil boom. Whereas in 1970 the Arab countries spent 0.31 percent of their combined GNPs on research and development, in 1980 that ratio had dropped to 0.27 percent. By comparison, developing countries as a whole raised the percentage of their GNP spent for this purpose from 0.32 percent to 0.45 percent.[86] Growing economic dependence is also suggested by the changing balance of trade and the increase in external debt. In 1974 Arab oil-producing countries exported $68 billion and imported $14 billion worth of goods and services. In 1982, after eight years of the oil boom, their exports had reached $162 billion, but their imports had climbed, at a much faster rate, to $189 billion.[87] The total of Arab countries' external debt reached almost $100 billion in 1983, more than 20 times the level four years earlier. By 1988, three Arab countries alone, Iraq, Algeria, and Egypt, owed in total more than $120 billion.

The petrodollars that flowed into the Middle East between 1974 and 1981 did not facilitate the development of national or regional

---

[82] Makdisi, "Economic Interdependence and National Sovereignty," pp. 118–122.

[83] Korany, "Unwelcome Guests: The Political Economy of Arab Relations with the Superpowers," in *The Next Arab Decade*, p. 72.

[84] *World Development Report, 1987,* p. 229.

[85] Makdisi, "Economic Interdependence and National Sovereignty," pp. 118–122.

[86] *UN Statistical Yearbook, 1987,* pp. 5–19.

[87] Abbas Alnasrawi, "The Rise and Fall of Arab Oil Power," *Arab Studies Quarterly* 6 (Winter–Spring 1984):8.

political institutions capable of effectively managing the processes of political and economic development and integration. Governments simply opened the taps so that a deluge of consumer goods and services flowed out to their populations, that were for the most part excluded from playing any significant role in national decision making. The strategy of the "social contract" depended on a continual accumulation of rents in government accounts. This income began to drop rapidly from 1982 as oil prices sagged and the share of Middle Eastern oil in world trade also fell. The first response by most governments was to borrow more money in the hope that the petrodollar bonanza would somehow return before the debts fell due. By 1986–1987, however, not even the most optimistic of political elites still clung to that hope.

Just as the response to the oil boom had been more or less uniform in the countries of the region, so too was the response to the downturn similar. Political elites began virtually in unison in the late 1980s to tighten up on government spending, accompanying austerity measures in many instances with cautious political liberalization in the hope that new political freedoms would permit steam to escape from societies smoldering with the discontent caused by unaccustomed economic hardship. State and society, in short, were forced more closely together as a result of economic recession. Governments have had to augment rents with resources extracted from populations, which in turn are beginning to demand "no taxation without representation." Political development may, therefore, be facilitated more by conditions of scarcity than by those of plenty.

PARADOX TWO: ECONOMIC DECAY AND POLITICAL GROWTH

The Lean Years

As a result of declining oil prices and a decreasing share of a smaller world market for oil, Middle East oil exporters' revenues began to drop in 1982. By 1983, worldwide recession and increased energy savings had driven oil consumption down to the level it had been ten years earlier, just prior to the onset of the boom.[88] Between 1979 and

---

[88] Owen, "The Arab Oil Economy, p. 22.

1983, Arab oil output fell by more than one-half.[89] Arab states, which earned a total of $213.6 billion from oil exports in 1980, received only $147.4 billion two years later. OPEC sold half as much oil in 1985 as it had in 1980, at very much lower prices.[90]

By 1985 the current accounts of the three largest producers on the Arabian peninsula—Saudi Arabia, Kuwait, and the UAE—had moved into deficit in the amount of $10.6 billion, compared with a combined surplus of $78 billion in 1980. And 1986 was an even worse year for oil exporters, as prices dropped from an average of $26 per barrel in 1985 to $13 per barrel. Saudi Arabia's exports, which amounted to $27.4 billion in 1985, dropped to $20.2 billion in 1986. Although the average price of oil increased to $17 per barrel in 1987, weak demand for OPEC oil kept total earnings relatively low. In that year Saudi Arabia earned $17.6 billion from oil exports, whereas in 1974, the first year of the oil boom, it had earned $22.6 billion. Over that 13-year period, the purchasing power of the U.S. dollar had declined by more than one-half. In 1988 the six Gulf countries that are members of OPEC obtained $49.6 billion from oil exports, about $4 billion less than in 1987 and less than a third of export revenues in 1980. Oil prices and demand did begin to move up in early 1989 and were further accelerated by the Gulf crisis that commenced in August 1990. The earnings of member states of OPEC reached their highest level in a decade in 1990. Oil prices stabilized at about $21 per barrel in the wake of the second Gulf war, considerably higher than the average price levels of the late 1980s. Nevertheless, even Saudi Arabia, which increased its production after the Iraqi invasion of Kuwait from 5.4 to 8.5 million barrels per day, was still operating with a budget deficit in 1992, its tenth in a row. Saudi foreign assets, which had peaked in 1982 at $141 billion, slid well below $90 billion in 1990 and continued to fall, necessitating borrowings of $7 billion in early 1991 to pay expenses associated with the war.[91] While it is widely anticipated that by the mid-1990s Middle Eastern oil exporters will be benefiting from further increases in prices and market share, the boom con-

---

[89] Alnasrawi, "The Rise and Fall of Arab Oil Power," p. 7.

[90] Paul Jabber, "Forces of Change in the Middle East," *The Middle East Journal* 42: 1 (Winter 1988):9.

[91] Andrew Cunningham, "Why the Kingdom Has to Borrow," *The Middle East* (January 1992), p. 35.

ditions of 1974–1981 are not expected to be repeated in the foreseeable future.[92]

The plummeting of Middle Eastern countries' oil revenues from
1982 may be better gauged by data revealing the effect of the fall on
per capita income at constant prices. Iran's oil export earnings went
from $450 (in 1986 prices) per capita in 1972–1973 to $1,050 in
1977–1978. They then fell back to $110 in 1986–1987. While the oil
boom meant a 2.3-fold increase in real income per capita, the bust
resulted in a 9.5-fold fall. "As a result, Iran had real oil export earnings
in 1986–1987 that amounted to less than one-quarter the pre-1973
level, on a per capita basis."[93] By 1992 Iran, which during the 1980s
had almost no foreign debt, owed over $10 billion to international
creditors.

The leading oil-exporting states of the Gulf all experienced sharp
falls in export earnings and per capita incomes after 1982, a trend
which was reversed in the early 1990s for Saudi Arabia, Qatar, and the
UAE but not for Iran or the two countries devastated in the second
Gulf war, Kuwait and Iraq. The total foreign assets of Saudi Arabia,
Kuwait, and the UAE, which had been $270 billion as late as 1988, had
declined by more than one-third by 1992. They are unlikely to rise
rapidly again. Kuwait, Iraq, and Iran face massive expenses in recon-
structing their war-damaged economies. In sum, the collapse of the
great oil boom combined with the effects of the Gulf wars have substantially reduced financial surpluses of the richest Arab Gulf states
and left Iran and Iraq in parlous economic circumstances. But by the
standards of the region's poor states, the Gulf oil exporters are comparatively well off.

Virtually all other MENA countries, including even the significant
oil producer Algeria, which had increased its debt ten times between
1970 and 1980, borrowed more heavily as their direct or indirect earnings from oil began to fall.[94] Budget deficits, covered principally by
foreign loans, grew as governments hesitated to impose economic austerity in lockstep with the precipitous fall in national incomes. By
about 1986–1987, foreign indebtedness plateaued, in part because
governments finally began to cut back significantly on expenditures

[92] Abed, "The Lean Years," pp. 93–103.

[93] Patrick Clawson, "Islamic Iran's Economic Politics and Prospects," *The Middle East
Journal* 42:3 (Summer 1988): 372.

[94] Shaw, "The Political Economy of Inequality," p. 141.

and in part because foreign creditors, public and private, were no longer willing to lend large amounts to Middle Eastern or other Third World countries. That plateau, however, is at a disturbingly high level.

Although the debt of individual Middle Eastern countries is not large by the standards of Brazil or Mexico, debt service ratios are in several cases worse than those that obtain in the chronically indebted Latin American countries. Low- and middle-income MENA countries have a higher average total external debt as a percentage of GNP (52.6 percent in 1990) than any other region in the world with the exception of Sub-Saharan Africa.[95] Egypt's debt-to-GNP ratio in 1990 was three times that of Mexico and five times that of Brazil.[96] Sudan's external debt as a percentage of its exports of goods and services rose from 500 percent in 1980 to over 1,800 percent in 1990.[97] Algeria had the dubious distinction in 1990 of having to commit a higher percentage of its export earnings to debt service than any other lower- or middle-income developing country.[98] Israel's foreign debt of $29 billion in 1988 was the world's highest in per capita terms, five times that of Mexico and ten times that of Brazil.[99] Not surprisingly, a growing number of Middle Eastern countries have been unable to meet their debt service obligations and have had to enter into structural adjustment agreements with the IMF in order to renegotiate their loans.

Declining oil export revenues have accentuated the gap between rich and poor states in the region. In many of the poorer states, foreign currency reserves, eroded by, among other things, the downturn in worker remittances, are at precariously low levels, amounting in some instances to not more than a few weeks' worth of imports. Sudan, heralded at the outset of the oil boom as the "new Arab breadbasket," is now an international basket case, sustained only by international aid and relief. The oil roller coaster has converted the oil-rich states into prominent creditors on the world scene and the Arab labor-exporting states into chronic debtors. In 1982, the foreign assets of the former

---

[95] *World Development Report, 1992*, p. 265.

[96] *Ibid.*, pp. 264–265.

[97] *Ibid.*, pp. 264–265.

[98] *Ibid.*, pp. 264–265.

[99] Mohamed Rabie, "Foreign Aid and the Israeli Economy," *American-Arab Affairs* 25 (Summer, 1988): 71.

were some $6,100 per capita, compared with $42 for the latter.[100] "Inequalities in the access to liquid disposable assets are hardly a sleeping giant," observes Paul Shaw. "They are bulldozing a huge rift between oil-rich and oil-poor countries."[101]

During the oil boom, the rich states spent approximately ten times as much as the poor states per capita on physical and human infrastructural development. That ratio has since increased.[102] The results of these widely divergent investments in infrastructure are now becoming apparent in statistical indicators of human well-being. The death rate of children between 1 and 4 years of age fell between 1965 and 1985 in Saudi Arabia from 38 percent to 4 percent, in Kuwait from 5 percent to 1 percent, and in the UAE from 14 percent to 1 percent. In the labor-exporting states of Sudan and the then North and South Yemens, the rates fell much less rapidly, from 37 percent to 18 percent, 55 percent to 34 percent, and 52 percent to 30 percent, respectively.[103] The overall crude death rate in the wealthy Gulf states fell more than twice as fast between 1965 and 1985 as it did in the poorer states.[104] In Egypt, where funds have been insufficient to develop water and sewage systems in most rural and many urban areas, the water-borne parasitic disease known as bilharzia now affects at least 20 percent of the population, or some 10 million people, and its incidence is continuing to rise.[105] Government expenditure to treat the disease does not amount to more than a few dollars per person infected. By contrast, Saudi Arabia spends about $600 per bed per day in running its ultramodern hospital system.[106] As a result of the growing resource gap, "The process of convergence between labor exporters and oil producers discernible over the past decade will be reversed."[107]

Despite the fact that, with the exception of Iran, these labor- and

[100] Shaw, "The Political Economy of Inequality," p. 127.

[101] *Ibid.*, p. 127.

[102] *Ibid.*, pp. 127–128.

[103] *World Development Report, 1987,* pp. 258–259.

[104] *Ibid.*, pp. 256–257.

[105] "Egypt Battles Tradition in Fight Against Nile-borne Disease," *Middle East Times,* January 7–13, 1989, p. 5.

[106] "Cutting the Costs of Saudi Healthcare," *MEED* (July 1, 1988): 5.

[107] Rashid Khalidi, "The Shape of Inter-Arab Politics in 1995," in *The Next Arab Decade,* p. 58.

oil-exporting countries are all Arab states, the antagonistic relationship of debtor and creditor divides them. More than half of Egypt's foreign debt, for example, is owed to banks and suppliers, a significant percentage of the former being owned by Gulf Arabs.[108] Their attitude toward loan repayments may be even more stringent than that of their Western counterparts. In an international conference of bankers sponsored by the World Bank and IMF in the fall of 1988 to discuss the world debt problem, Arab bankers rejected European bankers' suggestions that loan forgiveness for highly indebted countries may be advisable. Ghazi Abd al-Jawad, general manager of Gulf International Bank, commented, "A debt is a debt is a debt. I get worried when I hear commercial bankers talking about debt forgiveness or debt reduction. Commercial banks are not development or charity organizations." His counterpart in the Arab Banking Corporation added, "It is unacceptable and unforgivable for commercial banks to forgive debt."[109] Even after politically motivated debt cancellation by oil-exporting states, indebted Arab countries are going to have to continue to service loans to Arab financial institutions. The lean years for those states appear likely to continue. The manner in which they have chosen to cope with their financial burdens is roughly the same throughout the region. These new economic policies may ultimately lead to significant political changes. If so, the economic gap between rich and poor Arab states will then be paralleled by a political one.

Infitah Intaji

The end of the oil boom was in Egypt conterminous with Husni Mubarak's consolidation of presidential power following Sadat's assassination in October 1981. Three factors coincided to bring pressure for change to the economic policy of infitah (opening) that Sadat had initiated in 1974. One was that it had not worked well, stimulating imports and consumption rather than exports and production. Another was that from 1983 there were insufficient resources to sustain a Sadat-style infitah. The third factor was that the infitah was unpopular, for it had exacerbated inequalities in the country, enabled numerous speculators to "get rich quick," and was associated in the public's mind

---

[108] "Facts and Figures of Egypt's Debts," *Middle East Times,* January 7–13, 1989, p. 3.

[109] Cited in "Arab Bankers Oppose Debt Forgiveness," *MEED* (October 7, 1988):4.

with increasing dependence on the West and the United States in particular. Mubarak, in an effort to disassociate his new regime from excesses of the infitah while retaining the essence of its message of economic liberalization, declared "war on profiteers and fat cats" and announced the end of the infitah *istihlaki* (infitah of consumption) and the commencement of an infitah *intaji* (infitah of production).[110]

At the core of the infitah intaji as it developed in the mid- to late 1980s in Egypt, and then throughout the region, was an attempt by government to impose austerity, stimulate investment and production by the private sector, lift the level of exports while keeping the lid on imports, and extract an increasing proportion of revenues directly from the population rather than from exogenous sources—or rents, as they have been called. Reforms associated with these objectives have varied from country to country. Generally included are some combination of currency devaluations to stimulate exports, provision of incentives for exporters, reduction of subsidies on consumer goods, increases in prices of agricultural commodities in order to stimulate production, lifting of restrictions on markets for goods and services, attempts to establish more efficient and regularized taxation systems, and moves to expand the role of capital markets in providing funds for investment. Not surprisingly, this policy package is virtually identical to the standard prescription handed out by the IMF, World Bank, and other development assistance agencies to those debtor countries coming to them cap in hand for loans. This new orthodoxy of development, with its emphasis on private enterprise and market mechanisms— instead of the previous theory of development's faith in the role of the state and structures of a command economy—has suffused the First and Third Worlds and even former communist countries. The infitah intaji was thus a product of the domestic constraints faced by Middle Eastern elites and a reflection of their new ideological orientations. It was also the result of the international climate and outright pressure on the region's decision makers by creditors.

Throughout the region, economic reform has been closely associated with political liberalization. Reforms implemented by the wealthy oil-exporting states have been less thoroughgoing, however, than those effected elsewhere. Since these governments have not had to ask their citizens to make many economic sacrifices, they have not been compelled to offer the trade-off of greater political participation.

---

[110] Waterbury, "The 'Soft State' and the Open Door," pp. 72–73.

But other states in the region have not had so much room to maneuver. They have had to reduce consumption more rapidly and to much lower levels, so they have in almost every case also sought to preempt political discontent (or to respond to it) by permitting political parties to function, by holding comparatively free elections to legislatures, by easing press censorship, and in general by extending greater political freedoms. Broadly speaking, the more severe the economic recession, the more ambitious are the steps toward political institutionalization.

GCC States   Economic policy changes made in Saudi Arabia, where oil revenues fell by about half between 1983 and 1988, illustrate the general approach to coping with the lean years among the oil-rich states of the Gulf Cooperation Council (GCC), which includes Saudi Arabia, Kuwait, Qatar, Bahrain, Oman, and the UAE. Saudi Arabia between 1983 reduced imports by more than 50 percent and lowered subsidies on petrol, electricity, water, some foodstuffs, and various other commodities. It did not, however, really squeeze the population through high levels of price inflation while holding salaries down. It instead attempted to make up for reductions in governmental revenues and expenditures by encouraging the private sector to invest more and become active across a broader front. Saudi Arabia and its wealthy neighbors enjoyed some success in this area, for within the GCC states the private sector's share in the GDP almost doubled from 1976 to 1986.[111] The bulk of private-sector activity, however, remains limited to commerce and construction, which together accounted for 54 percent of commercial bank loans in 1970, and 57 percent in 1985. Commercial bank loans to private clients for purposes of investment in manufacturing accounted for 15.3 percent of their portfolios of loans in 1975; by the mid-1980s that rate had dropped to 9 or 10 percent.[112] The associate secretary-general for economic affairs of the GCC, Abdullah Ibrahim El-Kuwaiz, commenting on the private sector, observed that "its role in the industrialization process is still below what it should be."[113]

In the wake of the second Gulf war, the government of Saudi Arabia suddenly abandoned its austerity policies, both because it had

---

[111] Abdullah Ibrahim El-Kuwaiz, "Economic Integration of the GCC: Challenges, Achievements and Future Outlook," *American-Arab Affairs* 19 (Winter 1986–1987): 32.

[112] Robert E. Looney, "Growth Prospects of the Saudi Arabia Private Sector," *American Arab Affairs* 23 (Winter 1987–1988): 67.

[113] El-Kuwaiz, "Economic Integration of the GCC," p. 32.

more revenue to dispense and because it hoped to divert new demands for political participation which had been stimulated by the events surrounding that war. In March 1992, the cabinet announced a surprise package of price reductions for gasoline; telephone, electricity, and water services; exit fees; port charges; and commercial registration fees. The price for gasoline was dropped 38 percent, from 64 to less than 40 cents a gallon. The government of Kuwait, also anxious to buy political support from elements disaffected by the al-Sabah's handling of the Iraqi invasion and its aftermath, commenced in the period leading up to the October 1992 elections to dole out funds. Government employees were paid in full for the period of the invasion, whether they were there or not. Families that had in fact stayed in Kuwait were given a bonus of $1,750. All consumer debts were forgiven and the bad debts of all Kuwaiti banks, which totaled more than $20 billion, were written off. These measures suggest that the rulers of the oil-rich Arab states adjudge as politically risky the austerity measures they introduced in the mid- to late 1980s. When and if resources become available or political pressure increases, ruling families can be expected to revert to profligate allocation strategies.

Agricultural policy in Saudi Arabia also demonstrates the subordination of rational economics to political calculations that typifies the political economies of the Gulf states. Since the mid-1970s the Saudis have directed an enormous amount of investment into agriculture. They have justified these expenditures on the grounds that they need to be agriculturally self-sufficient, in part to protect themselves against possible counteruse of the "food weapon" (i.e., embargo) in case they once again might be called upon to impose an oil boycott. More important, however, is their desire to demonstrate before the world and their own citizens that Saudi Arabia is not an artificial entity, a "tribe with a flag," but is a real nation-state capable of feeding and otherwise sustaining itself. Finally and most importantly, provision of massive subsidies to agriculture forms part of the general strategy of allocating financial resources in exchange for political loyalty. Princes, merchants, tribal leaders, and other influentials quickly "privatized"— became "farmers"—in the 1970s and 1980s in order to cash in on the largesse provided by government.

In 1975, when Saudi production of wheat yielded a meager 3,000 tons, the government announced that it would purchase that grain for $933 a ton, which was more than five times the prevailing world market price. Saudi entrepreneurs and public-sector companies responded by importing the agricultural expertise and technology required to produce wheat, principally on land irrigated from underground aquifers. Production surged to 740,000 tons in 1984, 2.8 million tons in 1988, and 4 million tons in 1991. This arid country, which was 22 percent self-sufficient in cereals in 1970 and only 7 percent self-suffi- cient in 1981, reached total self-sufficiency in 1984 despite its high population growth rate. Since then, it has become the world's sixth largest wheat exporter, selling abroad 1.4 million tons at $90 per ton in 1988. In that year, the government cut the support price back to $533 per ton, but this subsidy nevertheless still cost the government $1.4 billion. Because of the continuing gap between the support price and the world price, the massive wheat subsidy reduced the overall food import bill, which reached $5.5 billion in 1991, by only about $200 million. While Saudi Arabia has proven to the world that it can grow wheat, it has done so at tremendous monetary and ecological cost to itself. According to an informed observer, "What it boils down to is the Saudis are exporting their money and exporting their water."[114] He might have added that the massive subsidies further enriched Saudi private investors and the multinational agricultural companies employed by them.

Even at the height of its austerity phase, the Saudi government was reluctant to impose many sacrifices on the population, as taxation policy suggests. It announced an income tax on foreigners resident in the kingdom on January 3, 1988, as part of the annual budget, which also called for a 17 percent cut in government spending. The planned reimposition of the tax, which had been abolished in 1975, met with public outcry, and not just by foreigners. Saudis too objected vehe- mently, in part because they feared the ultimate extension of the tax to themselves, in part because many of them would suffer financially if their expatriate staff either left the country or demanded of their Saudi employers increased compensation. King Fahd himself rescinded the measure on January 5, less than 48 hours after it had been announced. The government did, however, retain a 5 percent tariff increase, which put Saudi Arabia out of step with the rest of the GCC, which had stan- dardized all tariffs at 7 percent several years previously. For most Saudis, customs duties, along with the *zakat* (Islamic tax) of some 2.4 percent of income, constitute the only taxes they pay. Company taxes,

[114] "Green Revolution in Trouble," *Middle East Times,* September 17–23, 1988, p. 9. See also "Squeezing Wheat Subsidies," *MEED* (September 3, 1988): 18.

which are nominally as high as 45 percent, are not assessed against Saudi concerns.[115] Such is the nature of austerity in a classic rentier state.

Belt tightening in Saudi Arabia and its wealthy neighboring states was undertaken reluctantly and halfheartedly in the wake of the oil bust that began in 1983. With the upturn in prices and demand following the second Gulf war, those states rushed to abandon policies of austerity and resume the previous pattern of generous allocations. They did so less out of economic calculations than from the desire for political survival. Even Saudi Arabia was forced to borrow funds abroad in 1991 and to sustain large budget deficits to support its allocations. Kuwait had to draw down its foreign assets, which once totaled in excess of $100 billion, by as much as half in the two years following the Iraqi invasion. These states are not awash in petrodollars, as they were in the 1970s and early 1980s. Having failed to establish viable institutions of political participation and governmental legitimacy, they are forced to spend what they have to buy the acquiescence of their populations. Rulers' fear of the consequences of liberalization is the principal obstacle impeding rational management of their economic resources, which further antagonizes domestic political oppositions and poorer Arabs generally.

Non-GCC Oil-Exporting States   Economically, there are two categories of Muslim Middle Eastern countries outside the GCC—those that export significant quantities of oil and those that do not. There is, however, remarkably little difference between the political economies of these oil and nonoil states in the wake of the oil downturn. All have sought with considerable dedication to privatize their economies and attract investments by multinational corporations, which for many constitute radical reversals of policies associated with Arab socialism in one of its many forms. They have also sought to direct investments away from the service sector and into industry and agriculture. Possibly of greatest political significance is the fact that many have also sought to lower real wages, impose greater discipline on the labor force, and reduce consumption by lowering or removing subsidies and raising prices. All have also sought to at least give the appearance of granting greater political freedoms.

The MENA countries that export significant quantities of oil but

---

[115] Carol Reader, "King Fahd Dilutes Budget's Strong Medicine," *Middle East Times*, January 10–16, 1988, p. 14.

are not in the GCC are Algeria, Iran, Libya, and—until the imposition of an international boycott as a result of its invasion of Kuwait—Iraq. All have accumulated significant foreign debts. By 1992, Algeria owed over $25 billion to foreign creditors. Servicing that debt, which absorbed $8.7 billion of Algeria's scarce foreign currency earnings and reserves in 1991, crippled the economy, rendering it incapable of generating jobs to alleviate massive unemployment. Iraq's debt, which exceeded $60 billion when it invaded Kuwait, was no doubt a key factor in Saddam Hussein's decision to embark on such a desperate course of action. When Iraq finally recommences oil exports, a very large share of its earnings will be consumed by debt service obligations, leaving little revenue for reconstruction and revitalization of the war-ravaged economy. Iran under Ayatollah Khomeini steadfastly refused to borrow abroad. With his death in June 1989 and consolidation of power by Ali Akbar Hashemi Rafsanjani, who was anxious to rebuild the economy, Iran rapidly amassed a foreign debt of $10 billion. These borrowings did not, however, alleviate chronic unemployment, nor slow runaway inflation and currency depreciation.

Until the mid to late 1980s, the economies of these four oil-exporting countries were heavily state-dominated. Since then, all have undertaken wide-ranging liberalization programs. The Iraqi infitah, which began in hesitant form shortly after Saddam Hussein assumed the presidency in 1979, moved into high gear toward the end of the first Gulf war and, although interrupted by the second, has continued. Among the economic reform measures announced in 1988 were the ending of the public-sector Rafidain Bank's 22-year monopoly on all banking in the country. A new bank, al-Rashid, was created, and it was announced that in 1989 six or seven mixed-sector joint-venture banks would be opened and GCC banks would be allowed to operate in Iraq. It was also announced that the government was preparing to establish a stock market to accommodate the growing number of share transactions.[116] In the previous year, the last of the country's remaining state farms had been sold to the private sector. In the summer of 1988, it was announced that 47 public-sector firms would be privatized and that the private sector would be able to buy or lease government-owned tourist hotels. In 1987, privatization of the national air carrier, Iraqi Airways, was decreed. In October 1988, it was announced that public-sector companies forming joint ventures with private ones would be exempted from the requirement to pay workers a quarter

---

[116] *MEED* (December 9, 1988): 21.

share of profits. It was also revealed at the end of 1988 that the government had been holding confidential talks with General Motors to establish an automobile industry in Iraq.[117] A few weeks previously, industrial projects were exempted from all tax for ten years and private companies were granted permission to compete in any sector with state monopolies.[118] The second Gulf war devastated the Iraqi economy but did not cause the government to backtrack on its professed commitment to economic liberalization. A shortage of resources and lack of investor confidence, however, have stalled the privatization drive.

Algeria's and Libya's infitahs are even more recent innovations, both being stimulated more obviously and directly by intense domestic dissatisfaction with economic austerity and political repression. In Algeria, the riots that swept through the country in October 1988 not only led to a host of political reforms but also stimulated the pace of economic change that had been under way for about a year. As the shops that had been virtually bare of goods for months were rapidly filled in the wake of the riots, hard liners in the ruling party, the FLN (National Liberation Front), who were known to oppose economic and political liberalizations, were forced out of their positions. Simultaneously it was announced that 70 state companies had been made financially autonomous and that all others would soon follow suit. Reforms that had been presaged in 1987, such as increased privatization of retail trade, improved conditions for foreign firms, introduction of credit cards, and greater managerial autonomy in the public sector, were implemented.[119] Still further reforms—including privatization of a portion of the import trade and granting citizens the right to purchase small amounts of foreign currency at the official rate—were enacted in the early 1990s. While Algeria's reforms so far are not so sweeping as those in Iraq, they indicate a sharp break with the pattern of stringent state control of the economy that had been in place since independence in 1962.

Even Libya's mercurial Mu'ammar Qaddafi has retreated from his previous commitment to a socialist economy. Grumbling about the lack of goods in Libya's shops paralleled the sharp drop in oil earnings

---

[117] "Local Car Production Plans," *MEED* (December 2, 1988): 8.

[118] *MEED* (October 14, 1988): 20.

[119] "Algeria's Struggle for the Future," *MEED* (November 4, 1988): 2–3.

from $22 billion in 1980 to $5.5 billion in 1987. By 1988, there were reports of demonstrations on university campuses in Tripoli and Benghazi by student Islamic activists.[120] The government—which had over the past 20 years nationalized all businesses, banned foreign ownership, and turned factories and most other installations over to people's committees—took fright. In mid-1988 it not only increased the flow of consumer goods that had been cut to a trickle since 1986, but also undertook numerous reforms that were dubbed by Western observers as the "green perestroika," the reference being to Qaddafi's *Green Book* and Gorbachev's initiatives in the Soviet Union. The black market was legalized by Qaddafi, who referred to it as the "people's market," and investors were invited to commence activities in virtually all sectors of the economy. Much rhetoric accompanied these initiatives. Qaddafi exhorted Libyans to "produce and become a bourgeois. Create a farm, breed sheep and be their shepherd. Set up a co-operative. Become rich. That is all right."[121] In January 1989, Qaddafi pledged to reduce the size of the bureaucracy by abolishing several ministries and agencies. In the early 1990s, most restrictions on the movement of goods in and out of the country were lifted. But the green perestroika, like its equivalent in Algeria and Iraq, did not bring about a full-blown liberal, neoclassical economic order. Without associated political changes, a transformation of the economy from state-dominated to capitalist proved impossible.

The revolution in Iran, combined with mobilization for the war with Iraq, resulted in the state's assuming a greater role in the economy than it had under the shah. The end of the war and the lessening of revolutionary ardor has led to a reassessment by the political elite of Iran's economic and political future. A consultative body—created at Ayatollah Khomeini's request in late 1988 to draw up a reconstruction policy and composed of the president, speaker of the majlis, and chief justice, who are the three heads of government, as well as the prime minister and some 20 additional members—gave its support to opening foreign trade to the private sector. It coupled this move with de facto legalization of the foreign currency black market.[122] Other lead-

---

[120] Anthony Walker, "Gaddafi: On the Road to Damascus?" *Sydney Morning Herald*, January 19, 1989, p. 11; and Charles Wallace, "Gaddafinomics Is Here," *Sydney Morning Herald*, December 3, 1988, p. 35.

[121] Wallace, "Gaddafinomics Is Here."

[122] "Iran Loosens the Reins," *MEED* (November 11, 1988): 2–3.

ing officials endorsed the principle that Iranians in exile, particularly those with needed skills and capital, should be induced to return to their country by being granted the appropriate freedoms, economic and political. The budget for 1989–1990 called for tax revenues to rise by 11 percent. On the tenth anniversary of the revolution in February 1989, the government announced that it would borrow from abroad to finance development projects.

After Ayatollah Khomeini's death in June 1989, the pace of economic reform quickened. Import and export regulations were further relaxed and the stock market, which was revived in late 1990, went through a boom in the following year. In May 1992, the government abandoned the state monopoly on banking it had established in the wake of the revolution and lifted all restrictions on foreign investors. Despite high rates of inflation, unemployment, and foreign borrowing and growing signs of economic hardship and popular resentment, the Iranian government in the early 1990s steadily accelerated the pace of economic liberalization.

The non-GCC oil-exporting states have been more reluctant to liberalize their polities than their economies, but numerous, generally tentative reforms have been undertaken. In Libya, for example, the revolutionary committees, which the government had used as agents of political control by vesting them with sweeping powers of arrest and trial, were curtailed in 1988. The government also abolished at that time the "blacklist" naming those denied the right to travel abroad. While there has been no attempt to overhaul the constitutional structure of government, which remains authoritarian, more tolerance of political expression has resulted in increasingly active political debate.

Political liberalization in Iran commenced in tentative, halting fashion prior to Ayatollah Khomeini's death in 1989. Since then it has gathered speed. Under President Rafsanjani, the government has tolerated violation of religious strictures, such as female dress codes; it has partially demobilized the revolutionary militias; it has granted greater freedom of political expression; and it has permitted an increased level of partisan political activity. But in the process of consolidating power, Rafsanjani and his supporters demonstrated a willingness to use antidemocratic tactics. In order to purge radicals from parliament, their last remaining stronghold, moderates grouped around Rafsanjani drafted a new electoral law nine months prior to the April 1992 elections. That law endowed the Council of Guardians, a group of conservative senior clergymen, with the power to determine which candidates would be eligible to contest the elections. That power was employed against radicals to good effect. More than 40 of their incumbent MPs were disqualified. Rafsanjani's supporters went on to win more than 200 of the 270 parliamentary seats.

But power and legitimacy are two different things. Shortly after the spring elections, serious rioting broke out in Arak, Mashhad, and other Iranian cities. The government responded with an overwhelming display of force and then meted out death sentences to those accused of fomenting the disturbances, which had been sparked by the eviction of squatters from private and religious properties. Given the magnitude of economic difficulties confronting the country and the likelihood that they will spark further unrest, the government is likely to proceed cautiously with further political reforms.

Iraqi President Saddam Hussein declared in late 1988 an end to Ba'thist hegemony over the political system. Henceforth, other political parties could operate and contest elections. But the April 1989 parliamentary elections were conducted in the absence of even semi-autonomous opposition parties. Subsequent promises to abolish the Revolutionary Command Council and to permit political parties to operate had not been fulfilled at the time Iraq invaded Kuwait. Following Iraq's humiliating defeat in 1991, Saddam Hussein jettisoned members of the elite known to favor political liberalization and replaced them with members of his family and clan. In the spring of 1992, he once again promised constitutional reforms but took no tangible steps to implement them.

Political reform in Algeria has followed a similar but more accentuated trajectory. In the wake of the October 1988 riots, the regime committed itself to free local elections, separation of the offices of president and head of the FLN, and a housecleaning of that ruling party. The political opposition, led by the FIS, quickly moved into the political space thus created and forced a reluctant government to continue the process of liberalization. When in January 1992 that process promised to culminate in the first significant change of government in the modern Arab world ever to be brought about by free elections, the military intervened and aborted the process. The Algerian and the Iraqi cases thus both suggest that political liberalization is a tactic employed by ruling elites to relieve political pressure rather than a goal in itself. Reforms will be adopted voluntarily only as long as they do not threaten the existence of the established order.

States That Export Little or No Oil

The negative correlation between oil wealth and rate and degree of liberalization is further evidenced by the economic and political reforms of such countries as Turkey, Egypt, Morocco, Tunisia, and Israel. Turkey has become virtually a textbook case of economic liberalization. Turgut Ozal, after becoming prime minister in 1983, accelerated the pace of reform that the military initiated when it seized power in 1980. Currency devaluation, removal of tariff and other barriers to trade, export subsidies, reduction of real wages and restrictions on labor union activities, incentives for investments by multinational corporations, and privatization of public-sector firms have all been undertaken. They have met with mixed results. Turkey's GDP and exports grew at a substantial rate in the 1980s, but so too did the foreign debt and inflation. The latter remained in excess of 70 percent from the late 1980s through the early 1990s. The factor share of wages in nonagricultural income fell from 44 percent in 1979 to below 18 percent in 1989. Real wages dropped by 38 percent in the same period. Not surprisingly, labor unrest increased dramatically. The numbers of workers involved in strikes rose from 21,000 in 1979 to 167,000 in 1990. The government of Suleyman Demirel, which came to power in late 1991, has not abandoned the economic liberalization policies of its predecessor, but, conscious of some of their negative consequences, has not pursued them with as much vigor.[123]

Other economic liberalization programs have been less extensive than Turkey's but significant within their own domestic contexts. Morocco, with a comparatively open political system since independence in 1956, has nevertheless followed the regional pattern of state domination of the economy. A myriad of state corporations, price controls and subsidies, coupled with reliance for foreign exchange principally on worker remittances and loans, has characterized the Moroccan economy since at least the onset of the oil boom. But since food riots in 1984 and the balance-of-payment and foreign exchange crises that intensified in 1986–1987, the government has sought to dismantle much of the public sector. The government submitted to parliament in October 1988 a draft law for the privatization of all but 6 pub-

---

[123] Canan Balkir, "The Economic Liberalisation Programme and Its Distributional Impact: The Turkish Case after 1980," unpublished paper delivered to the Symposium on Economic Liberalisation and its Social and Political Effects in the Middle East, University of Exeter, Exeter, England (September 26–28, 1991).

lic companies, meaning that over 400 firms would be affected. According to the proposed legislation, they would be sold through financial markets or tender calls. Speaking in favor of this privatization, Finance Minister Muhammad Berrada stated: "It is not a question of making the state disappear or to become impoverished, but it is a question of giving rise to outside initiatives capable of assuring developments. The government is committed to encouraging private enterprise and improving the state system."[124] Accompanying privatization have been offers of concessions for foreign investors, tax incentives for exporters, reductions in state spending, and attempts to broaden the tax base by reducing rates while improving collection methods.

The Tunisian case closely parallels that of Morocco. Since President Bourguiba finally rejected socialism in the early 1970s, the country's economy has nominally been based on free enterprise, but in fact has been characterized by significant government intervention. In the mid-1980s, widespread unemployment, a foreign exchange crisis, the requirements of "restructuring" imposed by the IMF, and, ultimately, the replacement of Bourguiba in 1987 paved the way for a host of liberalization steps by the new government of Zine al-Abidine Ben Ali. These have included privatization, freeing of financial markets, incentives for investment, and proposals to "give the labor market more flexibility."[125]

While Israel is not a part of the loosely integrated Middle East oil economy, its recent economic history traces a trajectory quite similar to that of most countries of the region. Despite massive inflation, its economy expanded in real terms during the oil boom, while in recent years it has confronted the problems of mounting budget deficits and foreign debt, unemployment, stagnating growth rates, and a crisis of confidence in the public sector. Its GDP grew at less than half the rate (3.2 percent) from 1980 to 1990 than it had from 1965 to 1980 (6.8 percent).[126] Under the Likud Party, nominally committed to private enterprise, the central government's expenditure as a percentage of GNP has continued to rise, reaching more than one-half in 1990, the highest rate for any country in the MENA region on which data are

---

[124] "Liberalisation Pushes Ahead," *MEED* (November 4, 1988): p. 49.

[125] "Privatization Faces Uphill Struggle in Tunisia," *Middle East Times,* September 24–30, 1988, p. 10.

[126] *World Development Report, 1992,* p. 221.

provided by the World Bank.[127] Unemployment in 1992 reached 12 percent. During the 1980s and into the 1990s, Israel's unenviable status as the world's largest debtor in relation to GNP remained unchanged. Israel's economy, according to Robert Loewenberg, president of the Institute for Advanced Strategic and Political Studies in Jerusalem, "suffers from price controls . . . and a national industrial policy that pours tax money into inefficient business. . . . Israel suffers from nothing that a strong dose of free-market capitalism couldn't cure."[128]

The Israeli coalition government formed by Likud and Labor after the 1988 elections was able to agree on little other than the need for economic reform. Paradoxically, it was Minister of Finance Shimon Peres, the Labor Party leader, who in early 1989 initiated a liberalization. It included devaluation, a major cut in food subsidies, reduction in welfare programs, deregulation of capital markets, and privatization of government companies. One of the finance minister's analysts commented: "It's what everyone else is doing—Prime Minister Thatcher in England, Mikhail Gorbachev in the Soviet Union. . . . The trend is reliance on markets for efficiency."[129] But Peres's liberalization enjoyed little success. Entrenched interests, chief of which are those employed directly or indirectly by government, resisted change. Moreover, the commencement of large-scale Jewish migration from the Soviet Union in late 1989 provided cause and justification for the government to continue, indeed to enhance, its already predominant role in the economy. Likud's seeming inability to provide solutions to Israeli economic problems contributed greatly to its defeat at the polls in the June 1992 election.

Egypt, whose original infitah provided the name for that process throughout the region and whose infitah intaji then served to some extent as a model for others, achieved some success in further liberalizing its economy in the 1980s. The pace of reform then quickened dramatically in the wake of the second Gulf war. As a result of its support for U.S.-led efforts to confront Iraq, Egypt was rewarded by hav-

---

[127] *Ibid.,* p. 239.

[128] Robert Loewenberg, "Israel Finally Fights a Major Financial Crisis," *Los Angeles Times,* January 8, 1989, p. V-2.

[129] Gershom Gorenbert and Myra Noveck, "Peres's Free Market Message Drives the Point Home," *Middle East Times,* January 7–13, 1989.

ing almost half of its total foreign debt of some $50 billion forgiven. This sudden windfall provided essential resources to facilitate liberalization measures, several of which were incorporated into a standby agreement signed with the IMF in May 1991. The foreign exchange system was rationalized and based firmly on a free market, as were interest rates. The government budget deficit was sharply reduced and its method of financing changed from increasing the money supply to the selling of treasury bills. Subsidies on basic commodities, which had already been cut in the 1980s, were further pared back. Most remaining restrictions on foreign trade were lifted and foreign investment procedures were simplified. Finally, privatization and public-sector reform, the areas in which there had been least change, were accelerated. Of the Arab countries Egypt—which originally had pioneered Arab socialism in the 1950s and 1960s and then economic liberalization in the 1970s and 1980s—had by the early 1990s demonstrated the greatest commitment to reshaping its economy according to free-market principles.

Virtually without exception, efforts to undo the economic legacy of governmental expansion into the economy over preceding decades and to renege on at least some part of the "social contract" have been accompanied, in at least their early stages, with concessions to demands for political freedoms. Tunisian President Zine al-Abidine Ben Ali's economic reforms were pushed through during the "springtime of freedom" that followed Bourguiba's removal from office. King Hassan of Morocco has indulged the parliamentary opposition while overseeing Morocco's economic liberalization. Yemeni President Ali Abdullah Salih, who permitted remarkably free elections to the then North Yemeni consultative council in February 1988, as attested by the fact that 25 percent of the 128 elected seats were won by Muslim Brothers, may have taken this step to forestall an anticipated negative political reaction to planned austerity measures. In Egypt, Sadat's infitah, initiated in the mid-1970s, originally proceeded in tandem with steps to liberalize politics—a linkage which his successor has maintained rather more successfully.

In all cases, however, when these political liberalizations have led to the emergence of opposition movements or parties that have challenged the government's authority, they have been vigorously suppressed, and the liberalizations themselves have been rolled back. In Tunisia, President Ben Ali, frightened of the growing power of al-Nahda (The Renaissance), an Islamicist political party, began from

1989 to restrict political freedoms. By 1992, the Tunisian government was involved in a draconian crackdown on all manifestations of political dissent. In Algeria, the military government that seized power in January 1992 suspended the political reforms that former President Chadli Benjedid had granted as part of his strategy to facilitate economic liberalization. As it moved to destroy the Islamicist Islamic Salvation Front (FIS), it was confronted with a violent backlash that included the assassination in June 1992 of Muhammad Boudiaf, the new president. Egypt's President Mubarak, like his predecessor, has permitted abuse of the human rights of political prisoners more or less in equal measure to the degree of political activity by the opposition, especially its Islamicist component. His purpose in so doing is to clearly demarcate the "acceptable" limits of political activity.

Political liberalization in the Muslim countries of the MENA region have been intended as shock absorbers to accompany economic austerity measures. Such reforms are quickly supplanted by other tactics when and if they fail of their objective. Most Middle Eastern countries are only in the early stages of a dialogue between state and society, between ruler and ruled. There remains a mutual lack of trust, an abiding suspicion among political elites that all political opposition is intent on subversion, and a belief by those critical of government that their rulers are just playing for time, waiting until they are once again able to impose their unquestioned domination of the polity. For the dialogue to develop into one based on trust and to lead eventually to firm guarantees of political and human rights for citizens—as well as to legitimacy and effectiveness for governments—compromise has to occur. Political elites have to surrender a part of their absolute control over decision making, while citizens have to be willing to adhere to public policies arrived at through some form of consultative process.

For these fundamental changes to occur, political systems must be insulated against the destabilizing effects of chronic economic malaise. Although some belt tightening is facilitating political liberalization, a continual increase in unemployment, unchecked deterioration of infrastructure, spreading impoverishment, and growing disparity between rich and poor individuals and states in the region—all of which have been occurring since the mid-1980s—would at some stage lead to political breakdown. Citizens must make some sacrifices for democracy but not starve to death. If economic reforms fail of their objectives, governments that have imposed austerity, invited in multinational companies on concessionary terms, sold off the state's assets, and encouraged the opening of stock markets and ritzy tourist hotels are going to be in deep trouble. For political reforms to work, economic reforms must work also. While oil incomes for Middle East exporters may continue to rise in the 1990s, they are unlikely to increase as they did in the 1970s. In the meantime, population growth is working inexorably to lower GDPs per capita in highly oil-dependent economies. Further economic development in the Middle East requires much higher growth rates in manufacturing and agriculture. Ruling elites have gambled big that economic liberalization will stimulate these sectors and other areas of their economies. Have they made the right bet?

THE FUTURE OF LIBERALIZATION

As the nonoil-productive sectors of the region's state-controlled economies stagnated even during the oil boom, a critique that focused on the inappropriateness of command economies for Middle Eastern conditions arose. It argued that while socialism and communism may work elsewhere, they are bound to fail in the Middle East, where personalism, a mercantile mentality, and bureaucratic ineptitude are firmly entrenched. The critique has been generalized as economic liberalizations have swept through the Second and Third Worlds. Now many Middle Easterners and those who study the region argue that state control inhibited economic growth, because that is what it does everywhere.

The problem, unfortunately, is that the converse is not true—that is, that free enterprise necessarily guarantees economic growth. While free enterprise may be more conducive to it than is smothering control by bureaucrats and military officers, the prerequisites for economic growth are many. A reasonably open economy based fairly firmly on market principles may be a necessary condition, but it is not sufficient for national economic success. Human and physical infrastructural development, proper macroeconomic policies, reasonable incentives for entrepreneurs and workers, political stability, and a host of other factors are involved. Regrettably, economic formulas, especially those for the Third World, tend to be reduced to their barest essence, so that they become ritualistic incantations. IMF and World Bank remedies, handed out to any and all Third World countries with balance-of-

payments problems, are a case in point. In the tradition of macroeco-
nomics, recommendations for "restructuring" do not take account of
noneconomic factors, such as local traditions and cultures. Frequently
it is only after such recommendations have been incorporated into
government policy, and negative or unanticipated consequences produced, that the contradiction between textbook development economics and entrenched local practice is recognized. There are many
examples of such contradictions in the Middle East.

At the most general level, conceptions of the proper role of government vary from country to country, culture to culture. An orientation widespread in the Middle East and observable over a long historical period is that government's principal obligation is to ensure the
necessities of life, especially people's daily bread. That was, in many
historical instances, virtually its only obligation and measure of success
and legitimacy. In periods of effective rule in Egypt dating back to the
pharaohs, government itself took responsibility for the distribution of
cereals and, in some instances, the production of them as well. This
was a common practice in the Mesopotamian empires. It also was a
feature of central governments in the great Islamic empires. In the
contemporary Middle East, populations expect government at a very
minimum to ensure the ready availability of food staples and, in many
instances, to provide them directly. Most Middle Eastern governments until very recently obliged by operating their own distribution
networks, subsidizing basic commodities, imposing price controls,
producing or importing commodities directly, or implementing some
combination of these measures.

The pressure applied by the IMF, World Bank, USAID, and
other foreign assistance agencies on recipients of aid to privatize food
production and marketing as well as to reduce subsidies on basic commodities thus has been directed at a critical element of governmental
claims to legitimacy. The most direct causes of domestic political violence in recent years in North Africa have been food price increases
and shortages. Reinforcing the centrality of food supply to governmental legitimacy is the fact that while the Middle East has enjoyed
rapid economic growth as a result of the oil boom, 16 to 25 million
people still suffer from some form of malnutrition. Food consumes a
much higher proportion of disposable incomes in the Middle East
than it does in the West. When and if economic liberalizations
adversely affect the supply of basic foodstuffs, governments in the
Middle East have no choice but to slow the pace of reforms or rescind
them.

Economics is a very secular faith, and the Middle East is predominantly Muslim. These belief systems may not necessarily clash, but they often do. One area of abiding difficulty is the charging of interest on borrowed money. *Riba* (usury) is prohibited in Islam, as it used to be in Christianity. The Muslim belief is that risk should be shared by debtor and creditor, rather than being borne entirely by the former while the latter is assured of a profit. Increasingly, Middle Easterners are turning to Islamic banks, which operate according to Islamic precepts, in order to comply with the dictates of their faith. But Middle Eastern countries are part of the world economic system, and that system is based not on Islamic but on secular capitalist principles. Muslim countries have to pay interest on their international loans, and they receive interest on their deposits.

One of the standard recommendations made by the IMF, World Bank, and development assistance agencies for reforming previously closed economies is that real interest rates be raised to approximate those obtaining in world markets. This usually means sizable increases in those rates, for governments have imposed low ceilings on them in part to facilitate their own borrowings. The problem is exacerbated by high inflation rates. In Iran in 1992, for example, if interest on bank deposits were to have been positive, it would have had to be over 300 percent, for inflation was almost that. As long as interest rates were kept at nominal levels, they did not stir much controversy. But if they are to rise to the high double digits, they will certainly arouse the ire of Islamicists, to say nothing of debtors. Thus most Middle Eastern governments have been reluctant to adopt real interest rates. Their failure to do so wreaks havoc with economic reform programs. For capital markets to function, for rational accounting procedures to prevail, and for savings to be generated within secular, liberal economic systems, the "real" cost of money must be taken into account. When it is not, those who are able to borrow are virtually guaranteed a profit by investing that money in developed countries, which is what countless thousands of those who through personal or other connections to sources of funds have done in recent years. The inability of weak, semisecular governments to reconcile their increasingly devout Muslim populations to Western financial procedures has worked to the benefit of parasitic rather than productive economic undertakings. While a 100 percent secular or a 100 percent Islamic economic system might work, one that is a compromise between the two may be doomed to failure.

Capital markets, including those for stocks and bonds and "paper" investments of all sorts, operate with difficulty in small economies because of problems with insider trading, an insufficient number of investment alternatives, lack of investment capital, vulnerability to rapid fluctuations, and so on. In the Middle East, these problems are compounded by virtue of the fact that there is no tradition of the joint stock, limited liability corporation owned by masses of shareholders, hence of "rational," impersonal investment. Gold, jewelry, carpets, and other precious objects, as well as real estate, are preferred sources for capital accumulation. Businesses in the Middle East are overwhelmingly family businesses. Business capital is generated within families and by borrowing, not by issuing shares that the general public might buy.

Turkey has the largest capital market in the Middle East, with total market capitalization exceeding $15 billion in 1991, about ten times that of either Egypt or Morocco, whose capital markets are among the largest in the Arab world.[130] The Turkish stock market, however, has encountered numerous difficulties as the government has attempted to upgrade it as part of its economic reform package and to use it as the arena within which shares in public-sector companies may be sold to private investors. Turks typically prefer gold to other savings and investment alternatives. In recent years they have been purchasing annually $400 million worth of it. Gold valued at $45 billion is estimated to be hoarded away. By comparison, bank deposits in the country in 1988 totaled $810 million, which was, in turn, several times the total value of shares traded on the Istanbul stock exchange that year. Ninety percent of private commerce and industry in Turkey is thought to be owned by 200 families. No company in Turkey has a sufficiently wide base of equity ownership to be quoted on a major exchange anywhere else in the world. In 1982, the bond market, which had been buoyed up by quasi-legal bank speculation, crashed, further eroding confidence in equities and capital markets.

Between 1987 and 1991, the ruling Motherland Party sought to implement its pledge to privatize more than 40 state enterprises that together accounted for 40 percent of the country's industrial output. Its preferred method of privatization was to sell $200 to $250 million a year in equities in those firms. Accordingly, 13 million dollars' worth of Teletas, a mixed-sector telecommunications company, was offered in February 1988, and the shares were sold out in three hours. By the

[130] *MEED* (June 5, 1992), p. 4.

end of the year, however, the value of Teletas shares had dropped by 40 percent, which caused analysts and potential investors to "interpret the experiment as a failure." As a result, the government postponed its plans to offer on the stock market shares in five additional companies. Instead, it attempted to interest Turkish private corporations in purchasing assets of public companies, but that approach also failed. The government then abrogated the law prohibiting foreign investment in Turkish company shares and in 1989 sold substantial parts of several public enterprises to foreign investors. Turkish business and labor organizations, however, opposed further sales. The Motherland Party, having suffered a major setback in local government elections in March 1989, was forced to abandon its privatization program.[131]

Privatization elsewhere in the region faces comparatively greater obstacles than in Turkey, where capital markets—despite their small size, the absence of legal prohibitions of insider trading, and other handicaps—function relatively well. The resounding crash of Suq al-Manakh, which was (until its demise in 1983) for all intents and purposes the Kuwaiti stock exchange although a wildly speculative and completely unregulated one, greatly diminished the enthusiasm of potential Gulf investors for dealing in local as opposed to more secure major Western markets. Despite a boom following the second Gulf war, the Saudi stock exchange in 1991 listed only some 50 companies, with a total of less than 86,000 shares having been traded in that year. The exchange has no formal trading floor.[132] The Iraqi stock exchange, which commenced trading in April 1992, lists only 38 companies. Throughout the region, there is not only a lack of interested investors to facilitate privatization but an absence of entrepreneurs with interests and skills in those fields which heretofore have been dominated by state enterprises. In Iraq, for example, "with the exception of the food-processing industry, the private sector in general has no real industrial experience."[133] The Saudi private sector "remains nervous and prefers to stick to traditional commercial or financial ventures."[134]

Despite pledges by governments from Morocco to Saudi Arabia

---

[131] Ziya Onis, "Privatization and the Logic of Coalition Building," *Comparative Political Studies,* 24 (July 1991): 231–253.

[132] "Special Report on Saudi Arabia," *MEED* (March 20, 1992), p. 17.

[133] Jonathan Crusoe, "Iraq: Still Living on Credit," *MEED* (November 25, 1988): 5.

[134] Riad Khouri, "Saudi Industry vs. Protectionism," *Middle East Times,* September 17–23, 1988, p. 8.

to privatize much of their public sectors, for that process to go forward, several economic preconditions, such as real interest rates and capital markets, must be established. Opposition by much of the labor force in public-sector companies and their political allies will also have to be overcome. Successful privatization, therefore, will need to be associated with more broadly based economic modernization and probably also with the development of political institutions within which issues of public policy can be debated, formulated, and made acceptable to those affected by them. Viewed as part of these general development processes, privatization may be a useful economic and political initiative. If, however, it is thought of as a panacea—a quick fix for ailing Middle Eastern economies—it will be a disappointing failure.

Other potential pitfalls in the path of economic liberalization are also suggested by Turkey's experience. It has adopted most of the recommendations consistent with the model of export-led economic growth, yet its balance of payments has deteriorated, its foreign debt mounted, and inflation rate soared. The latter may be an inherent aspect of liberalization, at least in its early stages. Withdrawal of long-established price controls, removal or reduction of subsidies, price incentives for producers, and a tendency by governments to increase the money supply, in part to cover budget deficits, all contribute to inflation which, if at a high enough rate, may alone erode public support for liberalization. Dilemmas caused by the transition from administered prices to those determined by markets are suggested by recent Iraqi experience. "Once you could not get eggs in the dairy shops," commented a diplomat in late 1988. "Enormous crowds would gather at the advent of eggs. Now there are no queues. . . . You can go and buy as many as you like, but at two or three times the price."[135] The Iraqi government's response to rapid inflation in food prices was to condemn "exploitative" and "parasitical" elements in production and marketing and to grant private import licenses for specific foodstuffs in an attempt to increase supply.[136]

Liberalization is also closely associated with increasing inequality, as the Turkish case so amply demonstrates. Civil servants experience an erosion of their standards of living, while many producers and sell-

---

[135] Jonathan Crusoe, "Iraq: Price Rises Hit Home," *MEED* (December 16, 1988): 19.

[136] *Ibid.*

ers of goods, as well as those with fixed capital assets, benefit. Urbanites, who consume a disproportionate share of government subsidies, generally are hurt by liberalizations, while rural producers are paid more for their output. Redistribution of resources inevitably is accompanied by political friction. As governments approach what they perceive to be the manageable limits to that friction, they are likely to slow the pace of economic change. Liberalization, therefore, will not be a linear process, proceeding forward at a steady pace. It will trace a zigzag pattern as governments seek to synchronize economic reforms with public opinion.

For at least the first part of the 1990s, however, despite encountering setbacks, governments throughout the region will probably continue to seek to implement various versions of the infitah intagi. They have no other attractive alternatives. Those countries with sizable debts have necessarily surrendered much of their autonomy in economic decision making. Pressure on them to reduce subsidies, rely on markets, sell off public-sector companies, and so on will be applied in proportion to their degree of indebtedness. Even in the absence of such pressure, many countries would voluntarily embark on liberalizations. The major alternative—state control of most economic activity—is widely discredited. Moreover, governmental revenues have stagnated since the oil bust. Tentative steps to enhance revenue collection through increased taxation remain insufficient to cover budget deficits in many countries, while the gap between what is really needed to maintain the current level of government services, to say nothing of implementing development projects, is growing. Governments hope to cover these shortfalls by attracting into domestic investment private resources accumulated by their citizens during the oil boom. But investors remain cautious, mindful of what governments have done in the past to private capital, not convinced that what is presently being offered is going to be profitable in any case, and, because their resources are generally held in internationally convertible assets, tempted by secure outlets for capital investment in the West.

Governments in the region have appealed to patriotism to guide private investment strategies, but that motive is unlikely to supplant profit as the dominant one. Governments must offer more than the intangible return of national pride to investors if they are to pry large amounts of capital out of the hands of their citizens. For the next few years, governments will probably follow the course of offering increasingly positive incentives for investors, rather than threatening them with negative sanctions. Ultimately, of course, governments may turn to the latter alternative if the offers they consider as reasonable are rejected or if disadvantaged sectors of the population are stimulated into forceful political activity by economic policies they believe to be unfair and unacceptable.

Political systems will be profoundly affected by the course of economic liberalizations. Authoritarian government in the Middle East, as elsewhere, must have control over the bulk of economic resources to sustain itself. Otherwise it will be challenged by those who do. If economic growth is rapid and private sectors of national economies prosper, resources beyond the control of the state will be available to reinforce political liberalization. The state's retreat from the economy would be paralleled by the expansion of civil society.

If, on the other hand, economies stagnate and reforms exacerbate inequalities without providing compensatory gains, the prospects for progressive, successful political liberalization will diminish. Governments in this circumstance would be confronted with the choice either of retreating to the stage of weak but authoritarian control of the economy and polity that they exercised until recently or of imposing greater economic sacrifices on the poorer sectors of the population while regimenting their political orders. In the latter case, most governments, which have been weakening since the onset of the oil boom, would have to turn to the military to provide the backbone for this stiffening process. Since Middle Eastern militaries have become more conservative, more reflective of the interests of the bourgeoisie than of the lower middle class, and in many cases linked to national and international business enterprises, an increased political role for the military would be associated with an expanded economic role for private business. As in Latin America, an alliance of the military and selected economic elites would control the political economy, but they would be locked into an ongoing struggle with politically excluded and economically deprived elements. This conflict would stand in the way of the further expansion of political participation and serve to exacerbate political instability.

Ultimately, however, it may not be governments that determine the direction taken. Governmental control over economies has been weakening as private sectors have expanded, one component of which is what may loosely be termed the Islamic private sector. This includes a range of business and other activities conducted according to Islamic principles and under the control of Muslims devoted to spreading the influence of Islam in the economy, society, and polity. The Islamic sector now includes service enterprises as well as those in industry and agriculture. Among the services offered are banking and financial management in Islamic banks and investment companies. In the closely related Islamic social sector, health care and education are made available in clinics and schools financed by devout Muslims, by voluntary payment of zakat to such institutions by thousands of individuals, or by the support of organizations of Islamic activists, including the Muslim Brotherhood and yet more radical groupings. Egyptians can now not only receive health care and education in Islamic institutions but can eat in restaurants, purchase and repair automobiles, rent or buy homes, and transact business in other areas with private firms that operate according to Islamic principles. While the Egyptian government moved in the early 1990s to restrict the activities of Islamic investment companies, partly in order to protect the market share of the state's financial institutions, a myriad of Islamic enterprises continue to do business. As Egypt tends to be the pacesetter for political and economic innovations in the Arab world, the spread of Islamic business enterprises can reasonably be anticipated to occur in other Arab countries.

The Islamic private sector, which has emerged since the onset of the oil boom, appears to be generally more successful than secular undertakings, public and private. This may result from the ability of its organizations to attract subsidies from Saudi Arabia and to mobilize capital from large numbers of investors, from the comparatively high levels of commitment by management and labor, and/or from widespread public acceptance of and support for Islamic enterprises. Public sectors are generally perceived as offering goods and services of inadequate and poor quality, while the secular private sector is thought of by many Middle Easterners as inherently exploitative. They prefer to do business in the Islamic sector if at all possible, just as a growing number of Muslims demand to live under Islamic law, the sharia. The slogan of the Muslim Brotherhood, "Islam is the solution," has in economics and law now taken on quite specific, tangible forms. The growth of an economic infrastructure run by Islamic activists parallel to but separate from that operated by the state or secular, national, or multinational businesses represents the emergence of a political economy over which the government has little control. Ultimately it may be that government in the Middle East, failing to reform the economy or polity quickly enough and otherwise respond to demands for change, will simply be shunted aside by an Islam that, partitioned off into its own sphere, will have developed viable social, economic, and political institutions.

That day, however, is not yet at hand. At present, governments in the Middle East are, with ever-increasing dedication, applying the semiofficial reform programs endorsed by the organizational representatives of the Western world's dominant economy. Whether those reforms, if finally enacted, will result in political systems being transformed into more open, participatory ones, will cause them to slip back into another era of military rule, or in the end will be deeply reshaped by virtue of the emergence of Islamic orders may well be determined in the 1990s. Whatever the case, the relative political stagnation of the 1970s and 1980s, principally a by-product of the oil boom, is already changing as governments are having to cope with austerity. While the boldest reforms thus far have been economic, political changes cannot be far behind.

Selected Bibliography

CHAPTER 1: POLITICAL DEVELOPMENT AND THE CHALLENGE OF MODERNIZATION

Ajami, Fouad. *The Arab Predicament.* New ed. Cambridge, England: Cambridge University Press, 1992.

Almond, Gabriel A., and G. Bingham Powell, Jr. *Comparative Politics: System, Process, and Policy.* Boston: Little, Brown, and Co., 1978.

Anderson, Lisa. *The State and Social Transformation in Tunisia and Libya.* Princeton, N.J.: Princeton University Press, 1986.

Antoun, Richard, and Iliya Harik, eds. *Rural Politics and Social Change in the Middle East.* Bloomington: Indiana University Press, 1972.

Bill, James A., and Robert Hardgrave, Jr. *Comparative Politics: The Quest for Theory.* Washington, D.C.: University Press of America, 1982 (ch. 2).

Damis, John. *Conflict in Northwest Africa: The Western Sahara Dispute.* Stanford, Calif.: Hoover Institution Press, 1983.

Goldschmidt, Arthur, Jr. *A Concise History of the Middle East.* 3d ed. Boulder, Colo.: Westview Press, 1988.

Goodell, Grace E. *The Elementary Structures of Political Life: Rural Development in Pahlevi Iran.* New York: Oxford University Press, 1986.

Halpern, Manfred. *The Politics of Social Change in the Middle East and North Africa.* Princeton, N.J.: Princeton University Press, 1963.

Hudson, Michael C. *Arab Politics: The Search for Legitimacy.* New Haven, Conn.: Yale University Press, 1978.

Long, David E., and Bernard Reich, eds. *The Government and Politics of the Middle East and North Africa.* 2d ed. Boulder, Colo.: Westview Press, 1986.

Moore, Clement Henry. *Politics in North Africa: Algeria, Morocco, and Tunisia.* Boston: Little, Brown and Co., 1970.

Muslih, Muhammad, and Augustus Richard Norton. *Political Tides in the Arab World.* New York: Foreign Policy Association, 1991.

Palmer, Monte. *Dilemmas of Political Development.* 4th ed. Itasca, Ill.: F. E. Peacock Publishers, 1988.

Peretz, Don. *The Middle East Today.* 5th ed. New York: Praeger Publishers, 1988.

Perry, Glenn E. *The Middle East.* 2d ed. Englewood Cliffs, N.J.: Prentice-Hall, 1992.

Richards, Alan, and John Waterbury. *A Political Economy of the Middle East.* Boulder, Colo.: Westview Press, 1990.

Sharabi, Hisham. *Neopatriarchy: A Theory of Distorted Change in Arab Society.* New York: Oxford University Press, 1988.

Tessler, Mark, Monte Palmer, Tawfic Farah, and Barbara Ibrahim. *The Evaluation and Application of Survey Research in the Arab World.* Boulder, Colo.: Westview Press, 1987.

CHAPTER 2: STATES, BELIEFS, AND IDEOLOGIES

Antonius, George. *The Arab Awakening: The Story of the Arab National Movement.* Beirut: Khayyat's, 1955.

Beblawi, Hazem, and Giacomo Luciani. *The Rentier State.* London: Croom Helm, 1987.

Ben-Dor, Gabriel. *State and Conflict in the Middle East: Emergence of the Postcolonial State.* New York: Praeger, 1983.

Boullata, Issa J. *Trends and Issues in Contemporary Arab Thought.* Albany: State University of New York Press, 1990.

Chelkowski, Peter J., and Robert J. Pranger. *Ideology and Power in the Middle East: Studies in Honor of George Lenczowski.* Durham, N.C.: Duke University Press, 1988.

Cole, Juan R. I., and Nikki R. Keddie, eds. *Shi'ism and Social Protest.* New Haven, Conn.: Yale University Press, 1986.

Davis, Eric, and Nicolas Gavrielides, eds. *Statecraft in the Middle East: Oil, Historical Memory, and Popular Culture.* Miami: Florida International University Press, 1991.

Dorraj, Manochehr. *From Zarathustra to Khomeini: Populism and Dissent in Iran.* Boulder; Colo.: Lynne Rienner Publishers, 1990.

Drysdale, Alasdair, and Gerald H. Blake. *The Middle East and North Africa: A Political Geography.* New York: Oxford University Press, 1985.

Enayat, Hamid. *Modern Islamic Political Thought.* Austin: University of Texas Press, 1982.

Esposito, John L. *Islam: The Straight Path.* 2d ed. New York: Oxford University Press, 1991.

Esposito, John L. *The Islamic Threat: Myth or Reality?* New York: Oxford University Press, 1992.

Farah, Tawfic E. *Pan-Arabism and Arab Nationalism: The Continuing Debate.* Boulder, Colo.: Westview Press, 1987.

Hourani, Albert. *Arabic Thought in the Liberal Age, 1798–1939.* London: Oxford University Press, 1962.

Hourani, Albert. *A History of Arab Peoples.* Cambridge, Mass.: The Belknap Press, 1991.

Kepel, Gilles. *Muslim Extremism in Egypt: The Prophet and the Pharaoh.* Berkeley and Los Angeles: University of California Press, 1986.

Khalidi, Rashid, et al., eds. *The Origins of Arab Nationalism.* New York: Columbia University Press, 1991.

Khoury, Philip S., and Joseph Kostiner. *Tribes and State Formation in the Middle East.* Berkeley: University of California Press, 1990.

Kramer, Martin. *Shi'ism, Resistance, and Revolution.* Boulder, Colo.: Westview Press, 1987.

Lapidus, Ira. *A History of Islamic Societies.* New York: Cambridge University Press, 1988.

Mansour, Fawzy. *The Arab World: Nation, State and Democracy.* London: Zed Books, 1992.

Munson, Henry, Jr. *Islam and Revolution in the Middle East.* New Haven, Conn.: Yale University Press, 1988.

Piscatori, James P., ed. *Islam in the Political Process.* Cambridge, England: Cambridge University Press, 1983.

Piscatori, James P. *Islam in a World of Nation-States.* Cambridge, England: Cambridge University Press, 1986.

Salamé, Ghassan, ed. *The Foundations of the Arab State.* London: Croom Helm, 1987.

Sivan, Emmanuel. *Radical Islam: Medieval Theology and Modern Politics.* New Haven, Conn.: Yale University Press, 1985.

Sonn, Tamara. *Between Qur'an and Crown: The Challenge of Political Legitimacy in the Arab World.* Boulder, Colo.: Westview Press, 1990.

Tibi, Bassam. *Arab Nationalism: A Critical Enquiry.* New York: St. Martin's Press, 1981.

Tibi, Bassam. *The Crisis of Modern Islam: A Preindustrial Culture in the Scientific-Technological Age.* Salt Lake City: University of Utah Press, 1988.

Vatikiotis, P. J. *Islam and the State.* London: Croom Helm, 1987.

Voll, John O. *Islam: Continuity and Change in the Modern World.* Boulder, Colo.: Westview Press, 1982.

Williams, John Alden, ed. *Themes of Islamic Civilization.* Berkeley: University of California Press, 1971.

CHAPTER 3: THE GENES OF POLITICS: GROUPS, CLASSES, AND FAMILIES

Ahmed, Leila. *Women and Gender in Islam: Historical Roots of a Modern Debate.* New Haven, Conn.: Yale University Press, 1992.

Barth, Fredrik. *Political Leadership Among Swat Pathans.* London: The Athlone Press, 1959.

Bill, James A. *The Politics of Iran: Groups, Classes, and Modernization.* Columbus, Ohio: Charles E. Merrill, 1972.

Binder, Leonard. *In a Moment of Enthusiasm: Political Power and the Second Stratum.* Chicago: University of Chicago Press, 1978.

Cantori, Louis J., and Iliya Harik. *Local Politics and Development in the Middle East.* Boulder, Colo.: Westview Press, 1983.

Eickelman, Dale F. *The Middle East: An Anthropological Approach.* 2d ed. Englewood Cliffs, N.J.: Prentice-Hall, 1989.

Fernea, Elizabeth Warnock. *Women and the Family in the Middle East: New Voices for Change.* Austin: University of Texas Press, 1985.

Gellner, Ernest, and John Waterbury, eds. *Patrons and Clients in Mediterranean Societies.* London: Duckworth, 1977.

Ghabra, Shafeeq N. *Palestinians in Kuwait: The Family and the Politics of Survival.* Boulder, Colo.: Westview Press, 1987.

Khalaf, Samir. *Lebanon's Predicament.* New York: Columbia University Press, 1987.

Levy, Reuben. *The Social Structure of Islam.* Cambridge, England: Cambridge University Press, 1957.

Sanasarian, Eliz. *The Women's Rights Movement in Iran.* New York: Praeger Publishers, 1982.

Springborg, Robert. *Family, Power, and Politics in Egypt.* Philadelphia: University of Pennsylvania Press, 1982.

Sullivan, Earl L. *Women in Egyptian Public Life.* Syracuse, N.Y.: Syracuse University Press, 1986.

Swearingen, Will D. *Moroccan Mirages: Agrarian Dreams and Deceptions, 1912–1986.* Princeton, N.J.: Princeton University Press, 1987.

SELECTED BIBLIOGRAPHY **457**

Tucker, Judith E. *Women in Nineteenth Century Egypt*. Cairo: American University in Cairo Press, 1986.

Waterbury, John. *The Commander of the Faithful: The Moroccan Political Elite: A Study in Segmented Politics*. New York: Columbia University Press, 1970.

Wikan, Unni. *Behind the Veil: Women in Oman*. Baltimore, Md.: Johns Hopkins University Press, 1982.

CHAPTER 4: THE POLITICS OF PATRIMONIAL LEADERSHIP

Andrae, Tor. *Mohammed: The Man and His Faith*. New York: Barnes and Noble, 1935.

Dekmejian, R. Hrair. *Patterns of Political Leadership: Lebanon, Israel, Egypt*. Albany: State University of New York Press, 1975.

Frey, Frederick W. *The Turkish Political Elite*. Cambridge: Massachusetts Institute of Technology Press, 1965.

Gellner, Ernest. *Saints of the Atlas*. Chicago: University of Chicago Press, 1969.

Guillaume, A. *The Life of Muhammad: A Translation of Ishaq's Sirat Rasul Allah*. London: Oxford University Press, 1955.

Hinnebusch, Raymond A. *Egyptian Politics Under Sadat: The Post-Populist Development of an Authoritarian-Modernizing State*. New York: Cambridge University Press, 1985.

Khuri, Fuad I., ed. *Leadership and Development in Arab Society*. Beirut: American University of Beirut, 1981.

Lenczowski, George, ed. *Political Elites in the Middle East*. Washington, D.C.: American Enterprise Institute, 1975.

Margoliouth, D. S. *Mohammed and the Rise of Islam*. 3d ed. New York: G. P. Putnam's Sons, 1905.

Rustow, Dankwart A. *Philosophers and Kings: Studies in Leadership*. New York: George Braziller, 1970.

Tachau, Frank, ed. *Political Elites and Political Development in the Middle East*. Cambridge, Mass.: Schenkman, 1975.

Vatikiotis, P. J. *The Fatimid Theory of State*. Lahore, Pakistan: Orientalia Publishers, 1957.

Watt, W. Montgomery. *Muhammad at Medina*. Oxford, England: The Clarendon Press, 1956.

Watt, W. Montgomery. *Islam and the Integration of Society*. London: Routledge and Kegan Paul, 1961.

Weber, Max. *The Theory of Social and Economic Organization.* New York: Oxford University Press, 1947.

Zartman, I. William, ed. *Political Elites in Arab North Africa.* New York: Longman, 1982.

Zonis, Marvin. *The Political Elite of Iran.* Princeton, N.J.: Princeton University Press, 1971.

Zonis, Marvin. *Majestic Failure: The Fall of the Shah.* Chicago: University of Chicago Press, 1991.

CHAPTER 5: THE POLITICS OF LEADERS AND CHANGE

Abrahamian, Ervand. *Iran Between Two Revolutions.* Princeton, N.J.: Princeton University Press, 1982.

Ansari, Hamied. *Egypt: The Stalled Society.* Albany: State University of New York Press, 1986.

Baker, Raymond William. *Sadat and After: Struggles for Egypt's Political Soul.* Cambridge, Mass.: Harvard University Press, 1990.

Bianchi, Robert. *Interest Groups and Political Development in Turkey.* Princeton, N.J.: Princeton University Press, 1984.

Bill, James A., and William Roger Louis, eds. *Musaddiq, Iranian Nationalism, and Oil.* Austin: University of Texas Press, 1988.

Goldschmidt, Arthur, Jr. *Modern Egypt: The Formation of a Nation-State.* Boulder, Colo.: Westview Press, 1988.

Green, Jerrold D. *Revolution in Iran: The Politics of Countermobilization.* New York: Praeger, 1982.

Heikal, Mohamed. *The Cairo Documents.* Garden City, N.Y.: Doubleday and Co., 1973.

Hooglund, Eric. *Reform and Revolution in Rural Iran.* Austin: University of Texas Press, 1982.

Kinross, Lord. *Ataturk: The Rebirth of a Nation.* London: Weidenfeld and Nicolson, 1964.

Limbert, John. *Iran: At War with History.* Boulder, Colo.: Westview Press, 1987.

Mottahedeh, Roy P. *The Mantle of the Prophet.* New York: Pantheon, 1986.

Özbudun, Ergun. *Social Change and Political Participation in Turkey.* Princeton, N.J.: Princeton University Press, 1976.

Sadat, Anwar El-. *In Search of an Identity: An Autobiography.* New York: Harper & Row, 1978.

Springborg, Robert. *Mubarak's Egypt: Fragmentation of the Political Order.* Boulder, Colo.: Westview Press, 1989.

Waterbury, John. *The Egypt of Nasser and Sadat: The Political Economy of Two Regimes.* Princeton, N.J.: Princeton University Press, 1983.

Weinbaum, Marvin G. *Egypt and the Politics of U.S. Economic Aid.* Boulder, Colo.: Westview Press, 1986.

CHAPTER 6: INSTITUTIONS OF GOVERNMENT: MILITARIES, BUREAUCRACIES, AND LEGISLATURES

al-Naqeeb, Khaldoun Hasan. *Society and State in the Gulf and Arab Peninsula.* New York: Routledge, 1991.

Baaklini, Abdo I. *Legislative and Political Development: Lebanon, 1842–1972.* Durham, N.C.: Duke University Press, 1976.

Be'eri, Eliezer. *Army Officers in Arab Politics and Society.* Jerusalem: Israel Universities Press, 1969.

Birand, Mehmet Ali. *Shirts of Steel: Anatomy of the Turkish Officer Corps.* London: I. B. Tauris, 1991.

"Bureaucracy and Development in the Arab World," special issue, *Journal of Asian and African Studies* 24 (1989).

"Democracy in the Arab World," special issue, *Middle East Report 174* (January–February 1992).

Dwyer, Kevin. *Arab Voices: The Human Rights Debate in the Middle East.* New York: Routledge, 1991.

Halpern, Manfred. *The Politics of Social Change in the Middle East and North Africa.* Princeton, N.J.: Princeton University Press, 1963.

Heper, Metin, and J. M. Landau. *Political Parties and Democracy in Turkey.* London: I. B. Tauris, 1991.

Hinnebusch, Raymond A. *Authoritarian Power and State Formation in Ba'thist Syria: Army, Party and Peasant.* Boulder, Colo.: Westview Press, 1989.

Hinnebusch, Raymond A. *Peasant and Bureaucracy in Baathist Syria: The Political Economy of Rural Development.* Boulder, Colo.: Westview Press, 1989.

Hurewitz, J. C. *Middle East Politics: The Military Dimension.* New York: Frederick A. Praeger, 1969.

Landau, Jacob M., Ergun Özbudun, and Frank Tachau. *Electoral Politics in the Middle East: Issues, Voters and Elites.* London: Croom Helm. 1980.

Lawson, Fred H. *Bahrain: The Modernization of Autocracy.* Boulder, Colo: Westview Press, 1989.

Layne, Linda L. *Elections in the Middle East: Implications of Recent Trends.* Boulder, Colo: Westview Press, 1987.

Middle East Watch. Syria *Unmasked: The Suppression of Human Rights by the Asad Regime.* New Haven, Conn.: Yale University Press, 1991.

Palmer, Monte, Leila Ali, and El Sayed Yassin. *The Egyptian Bureaucracy.* Syracuse, N.Y.: Syracuse University Press, 1988.

Peri, Yoram. *Between Battles and Ballots: Israeli Military in Politics.* Cambridge, England: Cambridge University Press, 1983.

Peterson J. E. *The Arab Gulf States: Steps Toward Political Participation.* New York: Frederick A. Praeger, 1988.

Picard, Elizabeth. "Arab Military in Politics: From Revolutionary Plot to Authoritarian State." *In Beyond Coercion: The Durability of the Arab State,* edited by Adeed Dawisha and I. William Zartman. London: Croom Helm. 1987 (pp. 116–146).

Reiser, Stewart. *The Israeli Arms Industry: Foreign Policy, Arms Transfers and Military Doctrine of a Small State.* New York: Holmes and Meier, 1989.

Roos, Leslie L., Jr., and Noralou P. Roos. *Managers of Modernization: Organizations and Elites in Turkey (1950–69).* Cambridge, Mass.: Harvard University Press, 1971.

Rugh, William A. *The Arab Press.* 2d ed. Syracuse, N.Y.: Syracuse University Press, 1987.

CHAPTER 7: THE ARAB–ISRAELI CONNECTION

Abu-Lughod, Ibrahim, ed. *The Transformation of Palestine.* Evanston, Ill.: Northwestern University Press, 1987.

Avineri, Shlomo. *The Making of Modern Zionism: The Intellectual Origins of the Jewish State.* New York: Basic Books, 1981.

Ball, George W., and Douglas Ball. *The Passionate Attachment.* New York: W. W. Norton, 1992.

Benvenisti, Meron. *The West Bank Handbook: A Political Lexicon.* Boulder, Colo.: Westview Press, 1986.

Brynen, Rex. *Sanctuary and Survival: The PLO in Lebanon.* Boulder, Colo.: Westview Press, 1990.

Chomsky, Noam. *The Fateful Triangle: The United States, Israel and the Palestinians.* London: Pluto Press, 1983.

Cockburn, Andrew, and Leslie Cockburn. *Dangerous Liaison: The Inside Story of the U.S.–Israeli Covert Relationship.* New York: HarperCollins, 1991.

Cohen, Mitchell. *Zion and State: Nation, Class and the Shaping of Modern Israel.* Oxford, England: Basil Blackwell, 1989.

Flapan, Simha. *The Birth of Israel: Myths and Realities.* New York: Pantheon Books, 1987.

Khouri, Fred J. *The Arab-Israeli Dilemma.* 3d ed. Syracuse, N.Y.: Syracuse University Press, 1985.

Lesch, Ann Mosley. *Transition to Palestinian Self-Government.* Bloomington: Indiana University Press, 1993.

Lesch, Ann Mosely, and Mark Tessler. *Israel, Egypt, and the Palestinians: From Camp David to Intifada.* Bloomington: Indiana University Press, 1989.

Lockman, Zachary, and Joel Beinin. *Intifada: The Palestinian Uprising Against Israeli Occupation.* Boston: South End Press, 1989.

Louis, William Roger, and Robert W. Stookey, eds. *The End of the Palestine Mandate.* London: I. B. Tauris and Company, 1986.

Lustick, Ian. *Arabs in the Jewish State: Israel's Control of a National Minority.* Austin: University of Texas Press, 1980.

Lustick, Ian. *For the Land and the Lord: Jewish Fundamentalism in Israel.* New York: Council on Foreign Relations, 1988.

Lustick, Ian S., and Barry Rubin, eds. *Critical Essays on Israeli Society, Politics, and Culture.* Albany: State University of New York Press, 1991.

Morris, Benny. *The Birth of the Palestinian Refugee Problem, 1947–1949.* Cambridge, England: Cambridge University Press, 1987.

Norton, Augustus R., and M. H. Greenberg, eds. *The International Relations of the PLO.* Carbondale: University of Southern Illinois Press, 1989.

Peretz, Don. *Intifada: The Palestinian Uprising.* Boulder, Colo.: Westview Press, 1990.

Quandt, William B. *Camp David: Peacemaking and Politics.* Washington D.C.: The Brookings Institution, 1986.

Quigley, John. *Palestine and Israel: A Challenge to Justice.* Durham, N.C.: Duke University Press, 1990.

Rabinovich, Itamar. *The Road Not Taken: Early Arab-Israeli Negotiations.* New York: Oxford University Press, 1991.

Romann, Michael, and Alex Weingrod. *Living Together Separately: Arabs and Jews in Contemporary Jerusalem.* Princeton, N.J.: Princeton University Press, 1991.

Sahliyeh, Emile. *In Search of Leadership: West Bank Politics Since 1967.* Washington, D.C.: The Brookings Institution, 1988.

Schiff, Ze'ev, and Ehud Ya'ari. *Intifada.* New York: Simon & Schuster, 1989.

Shlaim, Avi. *The Politics of Partition: King Abdullah, the Zionist Movement and the Partition of Palestine.* New York: Columbia University Press, 1990.

Silberstein, Laurence J., ed. *New Perspectives on Israeli History: The Early Years of the State.* New York: New York University Press, 1991.

Smith, Charles. *Palestine and the Arab-Israeli Conflict.* New York: St. Martin's Press, 1988.

Spiegel, Steven L. *The Other Arab-Israeli Conflict: Making America's Middle East Policy, from Truman to Reagan.* Chicago: University of Chicago Press, 1985.

Tivnan, Edward. *The Lobby: Jewish Political Power and American Foreign Policy.* New York: Simon & Schuster, 1987.

CHAPTER 8: THE POLITICS OF WAR AND REVOLUTION IN THE PERSIAN GULF

al-Khalil, Samir. *Republic of Fear: The Politics of Modern Iraq.* Berkeley: University of California Press, 1989.

Amirahmadi, Hooshang. *Revolution and Economic Transition: The Iranian Experience.* Albany: State University of New York Press, 1990.

Amirahmadi, Hooshang, and Manoucher Parvin, eds. *Post-Revolutionary Iran.* Boulder, Colo.: Westview Press, 1988.

Bill, James A. *The Eagle and the Lion: The Tragedy of American-Iranian Relations.* New Haven, Conn.: Yale University Press, 1988.

Cooley, John K. *Payback: America's Long War in the Middle East.* Washington, D.C.: Brassey's, 1991.

Crystal, Jill. *Oil and Politics in the Gulf: Rulers and Merchants in Kuwait and Qatar.* New York: Cambridge University Press, 1990.

Crystal, Jill. *Kuwait: The Transformation of an Oil State.* Boulder, Colo.: Westview Press, 1992.

Farouk-Sluggett, Marion, and Peter Sluggett. *Iraq Since 1958: From Revolution to Dictatorship.* London: I. B. Tauris, 1990.

Heard-Bey, Frauke. *From Trucial States to United Arab Emirates.* New York: Longman, 1982.

Helms, Christine. *Iraq: Eastern Flank of the Arab World.* Washington, D.C.: The Brookings Institution, 1984.

Holden, David, and Richard Johns. *The House of Saud.* New York: Holt and Rinehart, 1981.

Hunter, Shireen T. *Iran and the World.* Bloomington: Indiana University Press, 1990.

Keddie, Nikki R., and Mark J. Gasiorowski, eds. *Neither East nor West: Iran, the Soviet Union, and the United States.* New Haven, Conn.: Yale University Press, 1980.

Kelly, Michael. *Martyrs' Day: Chronicle of a Small War.* New York: Random House, 1993.

Khuri, Fuad. *Tribe and State in Bahrain.* Chicago: University of Chicago Press, 1981.

Lacey, Robert. *The Kingdom: Arabia and the House of Saud.* New York: Harcourt Brace Jovanovich, 1981.

Marr, Phebe. *The Modern History of Iraq.* Boulder, Colo.: Westview Press, 1983.

Milani, Mohsen M. *The Making of Iran's Islamic Revolution.* Boulder, Colo.: Westview Press, 1988.

Nakhleh, Emile A. *The Gulf Cooperation Council: Policies, Problems, and Prospects.* Westport, Conn.: Praeger, 1986.

Palmer, Michael A. *Guardians of the Gulf.* New York: The Free Press, 1992.

Peck, Malcolm C. *The United Arab Emirates: A Venture in Unity.* Boulder, Colo.: Westview Press, 1986.

Peterson, J. E. *The Arab Gulf States: Steps Toward Political Participation.* Washington, D.C.: Center for Strategic and International Studies, 1988.

Piscatori, James, ed. *Islamic Fundamentalism and the Gulf Crisis.* Chicago: University of Chicago Press, 1992.

Schraeder, Peter, ed. *Intervention into the 1990s.* Boulder, Colo.: Lynne Rienner, 1992.

Sifry, Mica L., and Christopher Cerf, eds. *The Gulf War Reader: History, Documents, Opinions.* New York: Random House, 1991.

U.S. Department of Defense. *Conduct of the Persian Gulf War: Final Report to Congress.* Washington, D.C.: Government Printing Office, 1992.

CHAPTER 9: PETROLEUM, POLITICS, AND DEVELOPMENT

Abdel-Khalek, Gouda, and Robert Tignor, eds. *The Political Economy of Income Distribution in Egypt.* New York: Holmes and Meier, 1982.

Alnasrawi, Abbas. *Arab Nationalism, Oil and the Political Economy of Dependency*. Westport, Conn.: Greenwood Press, 1991.

Barkey, Henri, ed. *The Politics of Economic Reform in the Middle East*. New York: St. Martin's Press, 1992.

Berberoglu, Berch, ed. *Power and Stability in the Middle East*. London: Zed Books, 1989.

Doran, Charles F., and Stephen W. Buck. *The Gulf, Energy, and Global Security*. Boulder, Colo.: Lynne Rienner, 1991.

El-Naggar, Said, ed. *Adjustment Policies and Development Strategies in the Arab World*. Washington, D.C.: International Monetary Fund, 1987.

El-Naggar, Said, ed. *Investment Policies in the Arab Countries*. Washington, D.C.: International Monetary Fund, 1990.

Farsoun, Samih K. *Arab Society: Continuity and Change*. London: Croom Helm, 1985.

Hansen, Bent. *Political Economy of Poverty, Equity and Growth: Egypt and Turkey*. New York: Oxford University Press, 1991.

Harik, Iliya, and Denis Sullivan. *Privatization and Liberalization in the Middle East*. Bloomington: Indiana University Press, 1992.

Ibrahim, Ibrahim. *Arab Resources: The Transformation of a Society*. London: Croom Helm, 1983.

Ibrahim, Saad Eddin. *The New Arab Social Order: A Study of the Social Impact of Oil Wealth*. Boulder, Colo.: Westview Press, 1982.

Issawi, Charles. *An Economic History of the Middle East and North Africa*. New York: Columbia University Press, 1982.

Kerr, Malcolm H., and El Sayed Yassin. *Rich and Poor States in the Middle East: Egypt and the New Arab Order*. Boulder, Colo.: Westview Press, 1982.

Kubursi, Atif A. Oil, *Industrialization and Development in the Arab Gulf States*. London: Croom Helm, 1988.

Levy, Victor, and Eliezer Sheffer. *Foreign Aid and Economic Development in the Middle East*: Egypt, Syria and Jordan. New York: Praeger, 1991.

Luciani, Giacomo, and Ghassan Salame. *The Politics of Arab Integration*. London: Croom Helm, 1988.

Moore, Clement Henry. *Images of Development: Egyptian Engineers in Search of Industry*. Cambridge: The Massachusetts Institute of Technology Press, 1980.

Niblock, Tim, and Emma Murphy, eds. *Economic and Political Liberalization in the Middle East*. London: British Academic Press, 1993.

Owen, Roger. *The Middle East in the World Economy.* London: Methuen, 1981.

Peterson, J. E. *The Politics of Middle Eastern Oil.* Washington D.C.: The Middle East Institute, 1983.

"Power, Poverty and Petrodollars." *Middle East Report* 170 (May–June 1991).

Richards, Alan. *Food, States and Peasants.* Boulder, Colo.: Westview Press, 1986.

Richards, Alan, and John Waterbury. *A Political Economy of the Middle East.* Boulder, Colo.: Westview Press, 1990.

Sadowski, Yahya M. *Political Vegetables: Businessman and Bureaucrat in the Development of Egyptian Agriculture.* Washington, D.C.: The Brookings Institution, 1991.

Sharabi, Hisham, ed. *The Next Arab Decade: Alternative Futures.* Boulder, Colo.: Westview Press, 1988.

Terzian, Pierre. *OPEC: The Inside Story.* London: Zed Books, 1985.

Tuma, Elias H. *Economic and Political Change in the Middle East.* Palo Alto, Calif.: Pacific Books, 1987.

Waterbury, John. *The Egypt of Nasser and Sadat: The Political Economy of Two Regimes.* Princeton, N.J.: Princeton University Press, 1983.

Weinbaum, Marvin G. *Food, Development and Politics in the Middle East.* Boulder, Colo.: Westview Press, 1982.

Wilson, Peter W. *A Question of Interest: The Paralysis of Saudi Banking.* Boulder, Colo.: Westview Press, 1991.

Wilson, Rodney, ed. *Politics and the Economy in Jordan.* London: Routledge, 1991.

Index